Lecture Notes in Computer Science   10015

Commenced Publication in 1973
Founding and Former Series Editors:
Gerhard Goos, Juris Hartmanis, and Jan van Leeuwen

More information about this series at http://www.springer.com/series/7410

Anderson C.A. Nascimento · Paulo Barreto (Eds.)

Information Theoretic Security

9th International Conference, ICITS 2016
Tacoma, WA, USA, August 9–12, 2016
Revised Selected Papers

 Springer

Editors
Anderson C.A. Nascimento
University of Washington Tacoma
Tacoma, WA
USA

Paulo Barreto
University of Washington
Tacoma, WA
USA

ISSN 0302-9743   ISSN 1611-3349 (electronic)
Lecture Notes in Computer Science
ISBN 978-3-319-49174-5   ISBN 978-3-319-49175-2 (eBook)
DOI 10.1007/978-3-319-49175-2

Library of Congress Control Number: 2016956491

LNCS Sublibrary: SL4 – Security and Cryptology

Printed on acid-free paper

This Springer imprint is published by Springer Nature
The registered company is Springer International Publishing AG
The registered company address is: Gewerbestrasse 11, 6330 Cham, Switzerland

Preface

ICITS 2016, the 9th International Conference on Information-Theoretic Security, was held in Tacoma, Washington, USA, during August 9–12, 2016. The conference took place on the campus of the University of Washington, Tacoma. The general and program co-chairs were Paulo Barreto (UW Tacoma and University of Sao Paulo) and Anderson C.A. Nascimento (UW Tacoma).

ICITS covers all aspects of information-theoretic security, from relevant mathematical tools to theoretical modeling to implementation. ICITS 2016 was an event in cooperation with The International Association for Cryptologic Research (IACR).

ICITS 2016 had two tracks, a conference and a workshop track. Conference-track articles appear in the proceedings, whereas workshop-track contributions were only presented on-site with a talk. This two-track format has the advantage of bringing together researchers from various areas with different publication cultures.

There were 40 submitted papers, 32 to the conference track and eight to the workshop track. In all, 14 submissions were accepted for the conference track and six for the workshop track. All submissions were reviewed by at least three members of the Program Committee, who sometimes were assisted by external reviewers. These proceedings contain the accepted papers for the conference track.

There were four invited talks:

- "Obfuscation Without the Vulnerabilities of Multilinear Maps," Sanjam Garg (UC Berkeley)
- "Tools for Quantum and Reversible Circuit Compilation and Applications to Quantum Cryptanalysis," Martin Roetteler (Microsoft Research)
- "Information Theoretic Techniques Underlying Secure Obfuscation," Amit Sahai (UCLA)
- "New Techniques for Information-Theoretic Indistinguishability," Stefano Tessaro (UC Santa Barbara)

We would like to thank the Steering Committee of ICITS, in particular Yvo Desmedt and Rei Safavi-Naini. We also thank the Program Committee members and external reviewers for their careful work. We are grateful to the wonderful local organizing team here at UW Tacoma: BrieAnna Bales, Zaide Chavez, Bob Landowski, Mike McMillan, Tyler Pederson, and Yana Wilson.

Finally, we would like to thank all the authors who submitted papers to ICITS 2016.

September 2016

Anderson C.A. Nascimento
Paulo Barreto

Organization

Program Committee

Divesh Aggarwal	EPFL, Switzerland
Paulo Barreto	University of Washington, USA
Anne Broadbent	University of Ottawa, Canada
Paolo D'Arco	University of Salerno, Italy
Frédéric Dupuis	Masaryk University, Hungary
Stefan Dziembowski	University of Warsaw, Poland
Nico Döttling	Aarhus University, Denmark
Ben Fuller	MIT, USA
Peter Gaži	IST, Austria
Divya Gupta	UCLA, USA
Goichiro Hanaoka	AIST
Carmit Hazay	Bar-Ilan University, Israel
Mitsugu Iwamoto	University of Electro-Communications, Japan
Iordanis Kerenidis	LIAFA
Robert Koenig	Technische Universität München, Germany
Ranjit Kumaresan	University of Maryland, USA
Tancrède Lepoint	CryptoExperts
Hemanta Maji	Purdue University, USA
Keith Martin	Information Security Group, Royal Holloway, University of London, UK
Anderson Nascimento	University of Washington, USA
Koji Nuida	National Institute of Advanced Industrial Science and Technology (AIST), Japan
Frederique Oggier	Research Center for Information Security
Arpita Patra	Indian Institute of Science, India
Krzysztof Pietrzak	IST, Austria
Samuel Ranellucci	Aarhus University, Denmark
Martin Roetteler	Microsoft Research
Rei Safavi-Naini	University of Calgary, Calgary
Rafael Schaefer	Princeton University, USA
Junji Shikata	Yokohama National University, Japan
Rainer Steinwandt	Florida Atlantic University, USA
Stefano Tessaro	UCSB
Marten van Dijk	University of Connecticut, USA
Stefan Wolf	USI
Mark Zhandry	Princeton University, USA

Contents

Entropy, Extractors and Privacy

Secret Sharing

Efficient Threshold Secret Sharing Schemes
Secure Against Rushing Cheaters

Avishek Adhikari[1], Kirill Morozov[2], Satoshi Obana[3], Partha Sarathi Roy[4(✉)],
Kouichi Sakurai[4], and Rui Xu[5]

[1] Department of Pure Mathematics, University of Calcutta, Kolkata, India
avishek.adh@gmail.com
[2] School of Computing, Tokyo Institute of Technology, Tokyo, Japan
morozov@c.titech.ac.jp
[3] Faculty of Computer and Information Sciences, Hosei University, Tokyo, Japan
obana@hosei.ac.jp
[4] Faculty of Information Science and Electrical Engineering, Kyushu University,
Fukuoka, Japan
royparthasarathi0@gmail.com, sakurai@csce.kyushu-u.ac.jp
[5] Information Security Group, KDDI Research, Inc., Fujimino, Japan
ru-xu@kddi-research.jp

Abstract. In this paper, we consider two very important issues namely
detection and identification of k-out-of-n secret sharing schemes against
rushing cheaters who are allowed to submit (possibly forged) shares *after*
observing shares of the honest users in the reconstruction phase. Towards
this, we present four different schemes. Among these, first we present two
k-out-of-n secret sharing schemes, the first one being capable of detecting
$(k-1)/3$ cheaters such that $|V_i| = |S|/\epsilon^3$ and the second one being
capable of detecting $n-1$ cheaters such that $|V_i| = |S|/\epsilon^{k+1}$, where S
denotes the set of all possible secrets, ϵ denotes the successful cheating
probability of cheaters and V_i denotes set all possible shares. Next we
present two k-out-of-n secret sharing schemes, the first one being capable
of identifying $(k-1)/3$ rushing cheaters with share size $|V_i|$ that satisfies
$|V_i| = |S|/\epsilon^k$. This is the first scheme, whose size of shares does not grow
linearly with n but only with k, where n is the number of participants. For
the second one, in the setting of public cheater identification, we present
an efficient optimal cheater resilient k-out-of-n secret sharing scheme
against rushing cheaters having the share size $|V_i| = (n-t)^{n+2t}|S|/\epsilon^{n+2t}$.

A. Adhikari—Research is partially supported by National Board for Higher
Mathematics, Department of Atomic Energy, Government of India, Grant No.
2/48(10)/2013/NBHM(R.P.)/R&D II/695. The author is also thankful to DST,
Govt. of India and JSPS, Govt. of Japan for providing partial support for this col-
laborative research work under India Japan Cooperative Science Programme (vide
Memo no. DST/INT/JSPS/P-191/2014 dated May 27, 2014.
K. Morozov—Research is partially supported by a Kakenhi Grant-in-Aid for Sci-
entific Research (C) 15K00186 from Japan Society for the Promotion of Science.
Research is partially supported by JST, CREST.
S. Obana—Research is partially supported by a Kakenhi Grant-in-Aid for Scientific
Research (C) 15K00193 from Japan Society for the Promotion of Science.

© Springer International Publishing AG 2016
A.C.A. Nascimento and P. Barreto (Eds.): ICITS 2016, LNCS 10015, pp. 3–23, 2016.
DOI: 10.1007/978-3-319-49175-2_1

The proposed scheme achieves *flexibility* in the sense that the security level (i.e., the cheater(s) success probability) is independent of the secret size. Each of the four proposed schemes has the smallest share size among the existing schemes having the mentioned properties in the respective models.

Keywords: Secret sharing · Cheating detection · Cheater identification · Rushing cheaters · Universal hash · Reed-Solomon code

1 Introduction

In the basic form of secret sharing scheme [3,19], it is assumed that everyone involved in the protocol is honest or semi-honest. However, in the real life scenario, this assumption may not hold. It may happen that some participants behave maliciously during the execution of the protocol. Malicious participants may submit incorrect shares resulting in reconstruction of an incorrect secret. This observation leads to some interesting protocols viz. *cheating detectable secret sharing scheme (CDSS), cheater identifiable secret sharing scheme (CISS), robust secret sharing scheme (RSS), verifiable secret sharing scheme (VSS)*.

However, most schemes known so far implicitly assume existence of *fully* simultaneous network, and they do not deal with cheating by rushing cheaters who submit their shares *after* observing shares of honest users. Constructing a secret sharing scheme secure against rushing cheaters is important in many real life applications. For example, consider the following scenario where there is no trusted party to reconstruct a secret and to detect/identify cheaters, and each user independently reconstructs the secret by receiving shares of the other users sent through the network which is not *fully* simultaneous. Since the network is not fully simultaneous, rushing cheaters can determine how to forge their shares after receiving shares of honest users. Rushing cheaters are so powerful that it is difficult to construct a scheme with small share size. In fact, most of efficient schemes whose bit lengths of shares do not grow linearly with n (i.e., the number of participants) (e.g., [1,2,5,10,12,13,16]) are vulnerable to cheating by rushing cheaters.

In this paper we study information-theoretically secure k-out-of-n secret sharing schemes secure against rushing cheaters with the following properties:

- secret reconstruction algorithm is allowed to perform multiple rounds of interaction with shareholders,
- t or less (computationally unlimited) rushing cheaters who submit their shares *after* observing shares of honest users are detected/identified with probability $1 - \epsilon$ even when k shares are submitted in secret reconstruction,
- probability distribution of a secret does not affect the successful cheating probability ϵ of rushing cheaters.

1.1 State of the Art and Our Results

Tompa and Woll [20] first presented a cheating detectable secret sharing scheme (CDSS). That work is followed by several other works (for example, [1,2,5,7,13, 16]). However, all these schemes can only detect cheating, without revealing the exact identity of the cheaters, who submitted incorrect shares.

McElice and Sarwate [11] pointed out cheater identification in secret sharing schemes by observing the connection between Shamir threshold scheme and Reed-Solomon error correcting codes. However, such approach requires more than k participants in the reconstruction phase of a (k,n) threshold secret sharing scheme to identify cheaters. The question is whether cheater identification is possible or not with the minimum number of shares (namely k), which are required to reconstruct the secret. *Cheater Identifiable Secret Sharing* (CISS) is the answer to this question. There are two types of cheater identification in secret sharing: *private* as e.g. in [4,15,17] and *public* as e.g. in [6,10,12,22]. A reconstruction algorithm of CISS with public cheater identification can be run by an external entity. This is an essential advantage of CISS with public cheater identification over those with private one. However, CISS with public cheater identification is only possible for the case of honest majority [10,12], while for the case of CISS with private cheater identification honest majority is not required [9]. Many CISS schemes with different features appear in the literature. The schemes differ on the number of tolerable cheaters, type of the adversary (rushing or not), reconstruction efficiency, and flexibility (security level is flexible or not). We call the scheme *flexible*, when the security level (i.e. success probability of the cheater(s)) can be set independently, i.e., independent of the secret size. Flexibility provides the power of partial customization of length of random strings, according to the requirement.

To have a comparison among the schemes present in the literature, let us first fix the notations. Here, we denote the number of malicious or cheating participants by t in a (k,n) CISS, where (k,n) are the parameters as in an ordinary threshold scheme, i.e., the number of participants is n, and any k of them will be able to reconstruct the secret, while any $k-1$ (or less) of them will have no information about the secret. It has been proved in [10] and [12] that a CISS scheme, with public cheater identification, capable of identifying up to t cheaters, is possible if and only if $t < k/2$. So any publicly cheater identifiable CISS scheme with $k = 2t+1$ is said to be an *optimal cheater resilient*. The lower bound [10] on the share size $|V_i|$ of such schemes is $|V_i| \geq \frac{|S|-1}{\epsilon} + 1$, where $|S|$ is the size of the secret and ϵ is cheater's success probability. In [12], two publicly cheater identifiable CISS schemes with optimal cheater resilience were proposed. However, both of them were inefficient. Choudhury [6] came up with an efficient solution, but the scheme in [6] deals with multiple secrets. In the case of a single secret, the scheme of [6] is not an optimal one. One improvement came from Xu et al. [22] but they did not achieve the optimal share size. Moreover, their scheme is not an optimal cheater resilient as it tolerates $t < k/3$ cheaters. In [18], Roy et al. provided a CISS scheme with better share size than [6] with optimal

Table 1. Comparison of proposed CDSS with existing CDSS.

Scheme	# Cheaters	Share size	Rushing
[5]	$t < k$	$|V_i| = |S|/\epsilon^2$	No
[14]	$t < n$	$|S|(\frac{k-1}{\epsilon})^2$	No
Proposed	$t < k/3$	$|V_i| = |S|/\epsilon^3$	Yes
Proposed	$t < n$	$|V_i| = |S|/\epsilon^{k+1}$	Yes

cheater resilience. Xu et al. [23] further proposed an optimal cheater resilient CISS with improved share size.

Our Contribution: The contributions of the paper are to present four efficient k-out-of-n secret sharing schemes.

1. We present two CDSS schemes, each of which is the first scheme in their respective model, such that the bit length of shares does not grow linearly with n. We compare the properties of the existing CDSS schemes in Table 1.
2. We also present two public CISS schemes against rushing cheaters. We compare the properties of existing CISS schemes with public cheater identification in Table 2.

From Table 2 we can see that our share size is smaller than all the other schemes within the same category except for that of Xu et al. [23]. However, for the cases $t = 1$ and $t = 2$, the proposed CISS has smaller share size as compared

Table 2. Comparison of proposed CISS with existing CISS.

Scheme	# Cheaters	Share size	Efficiency[a]	Rushing	Flexibility
[10]	$k/3$	$|S|/\epsilon^{t+2}$	Yes	No	Yes
[12]	$k/3$	$|S|/\epsilon$	Yes	No	Yes
[22]	$k/3$	$|S|/\epsilon^{n-t+1}$	Yes	Yes	No
Proposed	$k/3$	$|S|/\epsilon^k$	Yes	Yes	No
[12]	$k/2$	$(n \cdot (t+1) \cdot 2^{3t-1}|S|)/\epsilon$	No	No	No
[12]	$k/2$	$((n \cdot (t+1) \cdot 2^{3t})^2|S|)/\epsilon$	No	No	No
[6][b]	$k/2$	$(t+1)^{3n}|S|/\epsilon^{3n}$	Yes	Yes	No
[18]	$k/2$	$(t+1)^{2n+k-3}|S|/\epsilon^{2n+k-3}$	Yes	Yes	No
[23][c]	$k/2$	$(n-t)^{n+t+2}|S|/\epsilon^{n+t+2}$	Yes	Yes	No
Proposed	$k/2$	$(n-t)^{n+2t}|S|/\epsilon^{n+2t}$	Yes	Yes	Yes

[a]This column indicates, whether computational complexity of the reconstruction phase is polynomial in the number of participants n or not.
[b]Share size with respect to a single secret.
[c]With an additional assumption that the adversary can only corrupt k participants who take part in the reconstruction phase, Xu et al. get even smaller share size, however we list their share size in the general case for a fair comparison.

to [23]. Moreover, our scheme provides flexibility in the security level, which is not a feature of the scheme [23]. We achieve flexibility by adapting authentication technique from [21]. Recently, Xu et al. presented a scheme capable of identifying up to $(k-1)/3$ rushing cheaters [22]. The size of shares $|V_i|$ of the scheme is $|V_i| = |S|/\epsilon^{n-t+1}$ and the bit size of shares still grows linear in n. We proposed a scheme capable of identifying $(k-1)/3$ rushing cheaters which achieves the smallest size of shares when $k < \frac{3}{4}n+1$ and the bit size of shares does not grow linear in n. In Table 2, the column "Efficiency" indicates, whether computational complexity of the reconstruction phase is polynomial in the number of participants n or not.

2 Preliminaries

2.1 Secret Sharing Schemes

In the model of secret sharing schemes, there are n users $\mathcal{P} = \{P_1, \ldots, P_{\hat{n}}\}$ and a dealer D. The set of users who are allowed to reconstruct the secret is characterized by an *access structure* $\Gamma \subseteq 2^{\mathcal{P}}$; that is, users $P_{i_1}, \ldots, P_{i_k}$ are allowed to reconstruct the secret if and only if $\{P_{i_1}, \ldots, P_{i_k}\} \in \Gamma$. The model consists of two algorithms: a share generation algorithm ShareGen and a secret reconstruction algorithm Reconst. The share generation algorithm ShareGen takes a secret $s \in \mathcal{S}$ as input and outputs a list $(v_1, v_2, \ldots, v_n)$. Each $v_i \in \mathcal{V}_i$ is called a *share* and is given to a user P_i. In a usual setting, ShareGen is invoked by the dealer. The secret reconstruction algorithm Reconst takes a list of shares and outputs a secret $s \in \mathcal{S}$.

A secret sharing scheme **SS** = (ShareGen, Reconst) is called *perfect* if the following two conditions are satisfied for the output $(v_1, \ldots, v_n)$ of ShareGen$(\hat{s})$ where the probabilities are taken over the random tape of ShareGen.

1. if $\{P_{i_1}, \ldots, P_{i_k}\} \in \Gamma$ then $\Pr[\text{Reconst}(v_{i_1}, \ldots, v_{i_k}) = \hat{s}] = 1$,
2. if $\{P_{i_1}, \ldots, P_{i_k}\} \notin \Gamma$ then $\Pr[\mathcal{S} = s \mid \mathcal{V}_{i_1} = v_{i_1}, \ldots, \mathcal{V}_{i_k} = v_{i_k}] = \Pr[\mathcal{S} = s]$ for any $s \in \mathcal{S}$.

We note that only perfect secret sharing schemes are dealt with in this paper.

2.2 Cheating Detectable Secret Sharing Against Rushing Cheaters

Tompa and Woll [20] considered the scenario in which cheaters who do not belong to the access structure submit forged shares in the secret reconstruction phase. Such cheaters will succeed if the other users participating in the reconstruction accept an incorrect secret. In this paper, we consider very powerful cheaters called *rushing cheaters* who submit forged shares *after* observing shares of honest users.

As in the ordinary secret sharing schemes, the model of cheating detectable secret sharing scheme against rushing cheaters consists of two algorithms. A share generation algorithm ShareGen is the same as that in the ordinary secret sharing schemes. A secret reconstruction algorithm Reconst is slightly changed:

the reconstruction algorithm is modeled as an interactive Turing machine, which interacts with users multiple times, and users release a part of their shares to Reconst in each round. Therefore, Reconst takes round identifier rid, user identifier P_i, and part of share $v_{i(rid)}$ and state information state_R as input and outputs updated state information. When interactions with users are finished, Reconst outputs either the secret or the special symbol $\perp$ ($\perp \notin \mathcal{S}$.) Reconst outputs $\perp$ if and only if cheating has been detected.

Figure 1 below models the interaction between users and the reconstruction algorithm Reconst. Here, a pair of Turing machine $\mathcal{A} = (\mathcal{A}_1, \mathcal{A}_2)$ representing rushing cheaters $P_{i_1}, \ldots, P_{i_t}$ who try to cheat honest users $P_{i_{t+1}}, \ldots, P_{i_m}$. In the $\mathsf{Game}^{\mathsf{Rushing}}(\mathbf{SS}, \mathcal{A}), \mathcal{A}_1$ first chooses rushing cheater $P_{i_1}, \ldots, P_{i_t}$ to cheat users $P_{i_{t+1}}, \ldots, P_{i_m}$. Next, in each round, $\mathcal{A}_2$ determines the forged share, denoted by $(v_{i_1}'^{(rid)}, \ldots, v_{i_1}'^{(rid)})$, to be submitted by rushing cheaters. Note that $\mathcal{A}_2$ takes shares $(v_{i_{t+1}}^{(rid)}, \ldots, v_{i_m}^{(rid)})$ as input in determining forged shares, which captures the rushing capability of cheaters.

$\mathsf{Game}^{\mathsf{Rushing}}(\mathbf{SS}, \mathcal{A})$

$\quad s \leftarrow \mathcal{S} \qquad$ (according to the probability distribution over $\mathcal{S}$)
$\quad (v_1, \ldots, v_n) \leftarrow \mathsf{ShareGen}(s)$
$\quad ((i_1, \ldots, i_t), (i_{t+1}, \ldots, i_m), \mathsf{state}_C) \leftarrow \mathcal{A}_1()$
$\quad \mathsf{state}_R \leftarrow \emptyset$
$\quad \textbf{for } rid = 1 \textbf{ to } \mathtt{RidMax} \textbf{ do}$
$\quad\quad \textbf{for } \ell = t+1 \textbf{ to } m \textbf{ do}$
$\quad\quad\quad \mathsf{state}_R \leftarrow \mathsf{Reconst}(rid, P_{i_\ell}, v_{i_\ell}^{(rid)}, \mathsf{state}_R)$
$\quad\quad \textbf{done}$
$\quad\quad ((v_{i_1}'^{(rid)}, \ldots, v_{i_t}'^{(rid)}), \mathsf{state}_C) \leftarrow \mathcal{A}_2(rid, (v_{i_{t+1}}^{(rid)}, \ldots, v_{i_m}^{(rid)}), (v_{i_1}, \ldots, v_{i_t}), \mathsf{state}_C)$
$\quad\quad \textbf{for } \ell = 1 \textbf{ to } t \textbf{ do}$
$\quad\quad\quad \mathsf{state}_R \leftarrow \mathsf{Reconst}(rid, P_{i_\ell}, v_{i_\ell}'^{(rid)}, \mathsf{state}_R)$
$\quad\quad \textbf{done}$
$\quad \textbf{done}$
$\quad \mathsf{output} \leftarrow \mathsf{Reconst}(\cdot, \cdot, \mathsf{state}_R)$

Fig. 1. Game between Reconst and rushing cheaters for CDSS and CISS.

The successful cheating probability $\epsilon(\mathbf{SS}, \mathcal{A})$ of the cheaters $\mathcal{A}$ against $\mathbf{SS} = (\mathsf{ShareGen}, \mathsf{Reconst})$ is defined by

$$\epsilon(\mathbf{SS}, \mathcal{A}) = \Pr[s' \leftarrow \mathsf{Reconst}(\cdot, \cdot, \mathsf{state}_R) : s' \in \mathcal{S} \wedge s' \neq s],$$

where the probability is taken over the distribution of $\mathcal{S}$, and the random tapes of ShareGen and $\mathcal{A}$. The security of cheating detectable secret sharing schemes against t rushing cheaters are defined as follows:

Definition 1. *A k-out-of-n secret sharing* $\mathbf{SS} = (\mathsf{ShareGen}, \mathsf{Reconst})$ *is called* (t, ϵ) *cheating detectable against rushing cheaters if* $\epsilon(\mathbf{SS}, \mathcal{A}) \leq \epsilon$ *for any adversary* $\mathcal{A}$.

2.3   Cheater Identifiable Secret Sharing Against Rushing Cheaters

The model of cheater identifiable secret sharing also consists of a share generation algorithm ShareGen and a secret reconstruction algorithm Reconst. As in the model of (t, ϵ) cheating detectable secret sharing, ShareGen takes a secret as input and outputs a list of shares $(v_1, \ldots, v_n)$ and Reconst is also modeled as interactive Turing machine which interacts with users multiple times. The input of Reconst is the same as for cheating detectable secret sharing, but the final output is slightly different: Reconst in CISS outputs $(\hat{s}, \emptyset)$, if no cheating is detected. On the other hand, if Reconst detects cheating, it outputs $(\perp, L)$, where "$\perp$" is a special symbol indicating detection of cheating and L is a list of cheaters.

The security of cheater identifiable secret sharing is formalized through the same game as defined in Fig. 1. The cheater P_{i_j} submitting an invalid share succeeds, if Reconst fails to identify P_{i_j} as a cheater. The successful cheating probability of P_{i_j} against $\mathbf{SS} = (\mathsf{ShareGen}, \mathsf{Reconst})$ is denoted as $\epsilon(\mathbf{SS}, \mathcal{A}, P_{i_j})$ where the probability $\epsilon(\mathbf{SS}, \mathcal{A}, P_{i_j})$ is defined by

$$\epsilon(\mathbf{SS}, \mathcal{A}, P_{i_j}) = \Pr[(s', L) \leftarrow \mathsf{Reconst}(\cdot, \cdot, \mathsf{state}_R) : i_j \notin L].$$

Based on the above definition, we define the security of secret sharing schemes capable of identifying cheaters, who submit forged shares as follows:

Definition 2. *A k-out-of-n threshold secret sharing scheme, denoted as* $\mathbf{SS} = (\mathsf{ShareGen}, \mathsf{Reconst})$ *is called a* (t, ϵ) *cheater identifiable secret sharing scheme, if: (1)* $\epsilon(\mathbf{SS}, \mathcal{A}, P_j) \leq \epsilon$ *for any* $\mathcal{A}$ *representing set of t or less cheaters L, and for any cheater* $P_j \in L$ *who submits forged share* $v'_j \neq v_j$,
(2) $P_i \notin L$ *for any user* P_i *who does not forge its share.*

2.4   Building Blocks of Proposed Schemes

In this subsection, we briefly review building blocks of proposed schemes: Reed-Solomon codes, almost strongly universal family of hash functions, and k-wise independent random variables.

Strongly Universal Family of Hash Function: Here, we will review the definitions and constructions of strongly universal families of hash function.

Definition 3. *A family of hash function* $H : A \rightarrow B$ *is called* ϵ *almost strongly universal family of hash function* (ϵ-ASU_2 *for short) if it satisfies following two conditions:*

1. $|\{h \mid h \in H, h(a) = b\}| = |H|/|B|$ *holds for any* $a \in A$ *and for any* $b \in B$.
2. *For any distinct* $a, a' \in A$ *and for any* $b, b' \in B$, *the following equality holds:*

$$\frac{|\{h \mid h \in H, h(a) = b, h(a') = b'\}|}{|\{h \mid h \in H, h(a) = b\}|} \leq \epsilon.$$

H is called strongly universal family of hash function (SU_2 *for short) if* $\epsilon = 1/|B|$.

We define a key e of ASU_2 to specify an element of a hash family H and use a notation h_e to denote an element of the H specified by the key e. It is obvious that the size of keys of hash family is identical to the size of hash family $|H|$.

The subscript 2 of ASU_2 denotes the strength of hash families, and we can define the notion of strongly universal hash family SU_t of strength t for $t \geq 2$ as follows:

Definition 4. *A family of hash function $H : A \to B$ is called* strongly universal family of hash function of strength t *(SU_t for short) if $|\{h \mid h \in H, h(a_i) = b_i (i = 1, \ldots, j)\}| = |H|/|B|^j$ holds for any distinct $a_1, a_2, \ldots, a_j \in A$, for any (not necessarily distinct) $b_1, b_2, \ldots, b_j \in B$ and for any $j \leq t$.*

Here, we will review some known constructions of (almost) strongly hash families which we will use in the proposed schemes. In [8], the following efficient ASU_2 based on polynomials over a finite field is proposed.

Proposition 1. *Let $e_0, e_1 \in \mathbb{F}_p$ and $s = (s_1, \ldots, s_N) \in \mathbb{F}_{p^N}$, then the hash family $H_{1,N} : \mathbb{F}_{p^N} \to \mathbb{F}_p$ defined by $H_{1,N} = \{h_{1,N,(e_0,e_1)} \mid h_{e_0,e_1}(s) = e_0 + s_1 e_1 + s_2 e_1^2 + \cdots s_N e_1^N\}$ is N/p-ASU_2. Furthermore, the hash family $H_{1,1} : \mathbb{F}_p \to \mathbb{F}_p$ is SU_2.*

It is well known that strongly universal hash families with higher strength are also constructed based on polynomials over a finite field as follows:

Proposition 2. *Let $e_0, e_1, \ldots, e_{t-1} \in \mathbb{F}_p$ and $s \in \mathbb{F}_p$, then the hash family $H_{2,t} : \mathbb{F}_p \to \mathbb{F}_p$ defined by $H_{2,t} = \{h_{2,t,(e_0,e_1,\ldots,e_{t-1})} \mid h_{2,t,(e_0,e_1\ldots,e_{t-1})}(s) = e_0 + e_1 s + e_2 s^2 + \cdots e_{t-1} s^{t-1}\}$ is SU_t.*

Proposition 3. *Let $e_0, e_1 \in \mathbb{F}_p$ and $s_i = (s_{i,1}, \ldots, s_{i,N}) \in \mathbb{F}_{p^N}$, then the hash family $H_{3,N} : \mathbb{F}_{p^N} \to \mathbb{F}_p$ defined by $H_{3,N} = \{h_{3,N,(e_0,e_{1,1},e_{1,2},\ldots,e_{1,n})} \mid h_{e_0,e_{1,i}}(s_i) = \Sigma_{l=1}^{N} e_0^l . s_{i,l} + e_{1,i}\}$ is N/p-ASU_2. Furthermore, $h_{3,N,(e_0,e_{1,1},e_{1,2},\ldots,e_{1,n})}$ can be used to authenticate n messages.*

Proof. Let $a_i = h_{e_0,e_{1,i}}(s_i)$, we calculate the probability that the forged message and authentication tag are accepted by the authentication key. We assume the opponent tries her forging after seeing n pairs of message and tag $\{s_1, a_1, \ldots, s_n, a_n\}$ and substitutes all the n messages and tags by the following tuple $\{s'_1, a'_1, \ldots, s'_n, a'_n\}$. The substitution probability is

Pr[at least one forged message-tag pairs in $\{s'_1, a'_1, \ldots, s'_n, a'_n\}$ is accepted

$$| \{s_1, a_1, \ldots, s_n, a_n\} \text{ are accepted }]$$

Denote by E_1 the event that "at least one forged message-tag pair in $\{s'_1, a'_1, \ldots, s'_n, a'_n\}$ is accepted", and by E_2 the event that "$\{s_1, a_1, \ldots, s_n, a_n\}$ are accepted".

We first count how many keys satisfy event E_2. This is given by the following system of equations.

$$\Sigma_{l=1}^{N} e_0^l . s_{1,l} + e_{1,i} = a_1 \tag{1}$$
$$\Sigma_{l=1}^{N} e_0^l . s_{2,l} + e_{1,i} = a_2 \tag{2}$$
$$\cdots = \cdots \tag{3}$$
$$\Sigma_{l=1}^{N} e_0^l . s_{n,l} + e_{1,i} = a_n \tag{4}$$

Taking $e_0, e_{1,1}, e_{1,2}, \ldots, e_{1,n}$ as unknowns, for any fixed value of e_0, there exists one and only one solution for this system of equations. Thus, there are in total p solutions to the following equation system. More importantly, each possible key appears with equal probability.

Next, we count how many keys satisfy both events E_1 and E_2. The keys which satisfy both events must *in addition* satisfy *at least one* of the following n equations. In the following equations, we assume that $s'_{i,j} \neq s_{i,j}$ for all $j \in [N]$. This is quite a natural assumption: Since the opponent wants to forge the messages, she would choose a different message other than what is sent by the transmitter. The reason that we assume all the forged messages are different from the authentic ones is simply because this case maximizes the successful probability of a substitution attack by the opponent.

$$\Sigma_{l=1}^{N} e_0^l . s'_{1,l} + e_{1,i} = a'_1 \tag{5}$$
$$\Sigma_{l=1}^{N} e_0^l . s'_{2,l} + e_{1,i} = a'_2 \tag{6}$$
$$\cdots = \cdots \tag{7}$$
$$\Sigma_{l=1}^{N} e_0^l . s'_{n,l} + e_{1,i} = a'_n \tag{8}$$

If we subtract Eq. (1) by Eq. (5), we get $\Sigma_{l=1}^{N} e_0^k . (s_{1,l} - s'_{1,l}) = a_1 - a'_1$. We rephrase it as $f(e_0) = \Sigma_{l=1}^{N} e_0^k . (s_{1,l} - s'_{1,l}) - (a_1 - a'_1) = 0$. The function $f(e_0)$ represents a polynomial of degree at most N in the variable e_0. Since $s_1 \neq s'_1$, for any (s'_1, a'_1) of the opponent's choice, $f(e_0) \neq 0$. Thus there exist at most N values of e_0 satisfying Eqs. (9) and (13). We record these values as $e^*_{0,1,1}, \ldots, e^*_{0,1,N}$. This means that the forged message-tag pair s'_1, a'_1 would not be accepted as authentic, if and only if $e_0 \in \mathbb{F} \setminus \{e^*_{0,1,1}, \ldots, e^*_{0,1,N}\}$. The same arguments hold for the message-tag pairs s'_i, a'_i, that is s'_i, a'_i will not be accepted as authentic, if and only if $e_0 \in \mathbb{F} \setminus \{e^*_{0,i,1}, \ldots, e^*_{0,i,N}\}$, for any $i \in [n]$. Therefore, for any value of $\{s'_1, a'_1, \ldots, s'_n, a'_n\}$, there are at most $p - (p - N \cdot n) = N \cdot n$ keys satisfying the first equation system and at least one equation from the second equation system. In a nutshell, there are in total at most $N \cdot n$ keys satisfying both event E_2 and event E_1, and then $\Pr[E_1|E_2] \leq N \cdot n/p$. It is easy to show that for any particular (s'_i, a'_i) with $s'_i \neq s_i$, the probability that it is accepted as authentic is $N/p = N/|\mathbb{F}|$. Hence, the proposition follows. □

Remark 1. The above proposal is an adaption of the universal hash family by Wegman and Carter [21].

k-wise Independent Random Variables: k-wise independent random variables are used to construct schemes presented in Sects. 4 and 6.

Definition 5. *Random variables $X_1, \ldots, X_n$ over a finite set S are called k-wise independent if $\Pr[X_{i_1} = \alpha_{i_1}, \ldots, X_{i_k} = \alpha_{i_k}] = 1/p^k$ holds for any k indices $i_1, \ldots, i_k \in \{1, \ldots, n\}$ and for any $\alpha_{i_1}, \ldots, \alpha_{i_k} \in S$ where p is the cardinality of finite set S.*

It is well known that a polynomials of degree $k - 1$ over a finite field can be used to obtain k-wise independent random variables.

Proposition 4. *Let a polynomial $r(x) = r_0 + r_1 x + \cdots + r_{k-1} x^{k-1}$ be a randomly chosen polynomial over $\mathbb{F}_p$. Then $X_1 = r(1), X_2 = r(2), \ldots, X_n = r(n)$ are k-wise independent random variables over $\mathbb{F}_p$.*

We note that the size of memory to store the above k-wise independent variables $X_1, \ldots, X_n$ is p^k since it suffices to store all the coefficients of $r(x)$.

Reed-Solomon Error Correcting Code: Let $C(x) \in \mathbb{F}_p$ be a polynomial of degree at most t, and let $i_1, \ldots, i_k$ be distinct elements of $\mathbb{F}_p$, then it is well known that $(C(i_1), C(i_2), \ldots, C(i_k))$ constitutes a codeword of the Reed-Solomon code with minimum Hamming distance $k - t$. Therefore, when $k \leq 3t + 1$ (i.e., $t < k/3$) holds, the Reed-Solomon code corrects up to t errors with probability 1. Since the work by McEliece and Sarwate [11] pointing out the capability of Reed-Solomon codes to identify cheaters in secret sharing schemes, these codes have been playing the central role in secret sharing scheme capable of preventing cheating by $(k - 1)/3$ cheaters (see, e.g. [10,12,22]).

3   A Scheme Capable of Detecting $(k - 1)/3$ Rushing Cheaters

In this section, we present a scheme capable of detecting cheating by $(k - 1)/3$ rushing cheaters. The scheme is constructed based on the schemes presented in [5,13] which are capable of identifying $k - 1$ *non-rushing* cheater.

The basic idea of the proposed scheme is as follows. The share generation algorithm ShareGen generates shares $(v_{s,1}, \ldots, v_{s,n})$ of a secret s using Shamir's (k, n) threshold scheme. The share generation algorithm also generate shares $(v_{e,1}, \ldots, v_{e,n})$ for a key e of almost strongly universal hash family $H : \mathcal{S} \to \mathcal{H}$ using Shamir's $(t + 1, n)$ threshold scheme. Furthermore, ShareGen generates shares $(v_{a,1}, \ldots, v_{a,n})$ for hash value $a = h_e(s)$ using Shamir's (k, n) threshold scheme. The share v_i of user P_i is of the form $v_i = (v_{s,i}, v_{e,i}, v_{a,i})$.

Since $v_{s,i}$ and $v_{a,i}$ are shared using (k, n) threshold scheme, $k - 1$ users do not obtain any information about the secret even if they know the value of the key e. To guarantee security against t rushing cheaters, the secret reconstruction algorithm Reconst receives part of share $(v_{s,i}, v_{a,i})$ from P_i ($i = 1, 2, \ldots, k$) in the first round, and then receives v_e from P_i in the second round. Since the key e of hash family is shared using $(t + 1, n)$ threshold scheme, t rushing cheaters do not obtain any information about e even at the end of the first round. Therefore, the cheater cannot guess correct hash value a' for a forged secret s' in the first round. Further, from the error correcting capability of $(t+1, n)$ threshold scheme, rushing cheaters cannot alter the value of e no matter what shares they submit in the second round. The above discussion, together with the properties of ASU_2, directly derives the security of the scheme against rushing cheaters. The complete description of the scheme is given as follows.

Share Generation: On input a secret $s \in \mathbb{F}_{p^N}$, the share generation algorithm outputs a list of shares $(v_1, \ldots, v_n)$ as follows:

1. Generate a random polynomial $f_s(x) \in \mathbb{F}_{p^N}[X]$ of degree $k - 1$ such that $f_s(0) = s$.
2. Generate random polynomials $C_{e_0}(x), C_{e_1}(x) \in \mathbb{F}_p[X]$ of degree t. We will use $(e_0, e_1) = (C_{e_0}(0), C_{e_1}(0))$ as a key of $H_{1,N}$.
3. Generate a random polynomial $a(x) \in \mathbb{F}_p$ of degree $k - 1$ such that $a(0) = h_{1,N,(e_0,e_1)}(s)$.
4. Output a list of share $(v_1, \ldots, v_n)$ where $v_i = (f_s(i), C_{e_0}(i), C_{e_1}(i), a(i))$.

Secret Reconstruction: On input m shares $(v_{i_1}, \ldots, v_{i_m})$ (where $m \geq k$ and $v_i = (v_{s,i}, v_{e_0,i}, v_{e_1,i}, v_{a,i})$ for $1 \leq i \leq n$), the secret reconstruction algorithm outputs s or $\perp$ according to the following procedure:

1. [Round 1] Receive $(v_{s,i_1}, v_{a,i_1}), \ldots, (v_{s,i_m}, v_{a,i_m})$ from $P_{i_1}, \ldots, P_{i_m}$, respectively.
2. [Round 2] Receive $(v_{e_0,i_1}, v_{e_1,i_1}), \ldots, (v_{e_0,i_m}, v_{e_1,i_m})$ from $P_{i_1}, \ldots, P_{i_m}$, respectively.
3. Reconstruct $C_{e_0}(x)$ and C_{e_1} from $v_{e_0,i_1}, \ldots, v_{e_0,i_m}$ and $v_{e_1,i_1}, \ldots, v_{e_1,i_m}$, respectively, using a decoding algorithm of generalized Reed-Solomon Code (e.g., Berlekamp-Welch algorithm), and compute $e_0 = C_{e_0}(0)$ and $e_1 = C_{e_1}(0)$.
4. Output $\perp$ if error is detected.
5. Reconstruct $\hat{s} = f_{\hat{s}}(0)$ and $\hat{a} = f_{\hat{a}}(0)$ from $v_{s,i_1}, \ldots, v_{s,i_m}$ and $v_{a,i_1}, \ldots, v_{a,i_m}$, respectively.
6. Output $\hat{s}$ if $h_{1,N,(e_0,e_1)}(\hat{s}) = \hat{a}$ holds. Otherwise, output $\perp$.

Theorem 1. *If $t < k/3$ holds then the above scheme is (t, ϵ) cheating detectable k-out-of-n secret sharing scheme against rushing cheaters such that $|\mathcal{S}| = p^N, \epsilon = N/p$, and $|\mathcal{V}_i| = p^{N+3} \approx |\mathcal{S}|(\frac{\log |\mathcal{S}|}{\epsilon \log(1/\epsilon)})^3$. In particular, $|\mathcal{V}_i| = |\mathcal{S}|/\epsilon^3$ holds when $N = 1$.*

Proof. First, we will prove the scheme is *perfect*. Suppose that users $P_{i_1}, \ldots, P_{i_{k-1}}$ try to compute any partial information about the secret s. Since $v_{s,i_1}, \ldots, v_{s,i_{k-1}}$ is generated using Shamir's (k, n) threshold scheme, they do not obtain any information about the secret from $v_{s,i_1}, \ldots, v_{s,i_{k-1}}$. Therefore, the scheme is proven to be perfect if the equations $h_{1,N,(e_0,e_1)}(s) = a$ do not reveal any information about the secret. Since shares $v_{e_0,i}$ and $v_{e_1,i}$ are generated using Shamir's (t, n) threshold scheme, $P_{i_1}, \ldots, P_{i_{k-1}}$ obtain values of e_0 and e_1 from their shares. However, since a share $v_{a,i}$ is generated using Shamir's (k, n) threshold scheme, $P_{i_1}, \ldots, P_{i_{k-1}}$ obtain no information about the value $h_{1,N,(e_0,e_1)}(s)$. Therefore, they do not obtain any information about the secret s even if they know e_0 and e_1, which shows that the scheme is perfect.

Next, we prove that if $t < k/3$ the scheme is (t, ϵ) cheating detectable. Here, we consider the worst case where just k users $P_1, \ldots, P_k$ take part in secret reconstruction. Without loss of generality, we can assume $P_1, \ldots, P_t$ are cheater who try to fool $P_{t+1}, \ldots, P_k$ by submitting $(v'_1, \ldots, v'_t)$ to the secret reconstruction algorithm. Since cheaters are rushing, cheaters know all values of s (a value secret reconstructed from $(v_{s,1}, v_{s,2}, \ldots, v_{s,k})$), s' (a value reconstructed from $(v'_{s,1}, \ldots, v'_{s,t}, v_{s,t+1} \ldots, v_{s,k})$), a (a value reconstructed from $(v_{a,1}, v_{a,2}, \ldots, v_{a,k})$) and a' (a value reconstructed from $(v'_{a,1}, \ldots, v'_{a,t}, v_{a,t+1} \ldots, v_{a,k})$) after observing part of shares $(v_{s,i}, v_{a,i})$ submitted by honest users $P_{t+1}, \ldots, P_k$ in the first round. However, at this stage, cheaters do not obtain any information about the values of e_0 and e_1 since they are shared among users using Shamir's (t, n) threshold scheme. Moreover, even rushing cheaters cannot forge part of their shares $(v_{e_0,i}, v_{e_1,i})$ in order to alter the values of e_0 and e_1 reconstructed. In fact, if cheater P_i forges $(v_{e_0,i}, v_{e_1,i})$ into $(v'_{e_0,i}, v'_{e_1,i})$ in the second round, then P_i is identified as a cheater with probability 1 by t-error correction capability of Reed-Solomon codes. Therefore, the best strategy for cheater P_i is to submit $(v_{e_0,i}, v_{e_1,i})$ as is, which ensures that e_0 and e_1 are reconstructed without being forged. Now we compute the successful cheating probability ϵ of rushing cheaters. The cheaters succeed in cheating if $h_{1,N,(e_0,e_1)}(s') = a'$ holds. Since rushing cheater P_i must submit $(v'_{s,i}, v'_{a,i})$ in the first round without knowing the values of e_0 and e_1, The successful cheating probability of cheaters are computed by $\Pr[h_{1,N,(e_0,e_1)}(s') = a' \mid h_{1,N,(e_0,e_1)}(s) = a]$ where the probability is taken only over e_0 and e_1 since s, s', a and a' are known to cheaters when they submit $(v'_{s,i}, v'_{a,i})$. Since $H_{1,N}$ is N/p-ASU$_2$ and (e_0, e_1) are chosen uniformly and randomly from the set of keys satisfying $h_{1,N,(e_0,e_1)}(s) = a$, it is easy to see that $\Pr[h_{1,N,(e_0,e_1)}(s') = a' \mid h_{1,N,(e_0,e_1)}(s) = a] = N/p$ holds, which directly implies that the successful cheating probability of cheaters $P_1, \ldots, P_t$ is upper bounded by N/p. $\qquad\square$

4   A Scheme Capable of Detecting $n - 1$ Rushing Cheaters

In this section, we present a scheme capable of detecting cheating by $n - 1$ rushing cheaters. The idea of the scheme is similar to the scheme presented in the previous section in the sense that the share generation algorithm generates a key e of ASU$_2$ and $a = h_e(s)$ to check the correctness of a secret reconstructed. However, since $t = n - 1$ holds, we cannot use error correcting code to ensure correct reconstruction of e. In the proposed scheme, instead of sharing a single key e, the share generation algorithm generates a key e_i and a hash value a_i for each user P_i who verifies $h_{e_i}(s) = a_i$ to check the correctness of the secret s. However, unfortunately, the above naive scheme cannot be *perfect* since user P_i can compute (possibly partial) information about the secret from information held by P_i: $h_{e_i}(s) = a_i, e_i$ and a_i. For example, consider the case where we use $H_{1,1}$ defined in Proposition 1 for underlying hash family. In this case, any single user P_i can compute s from $e_{0,i}, e_{1,i}$ and $a_i = e_{0,i} + e_{1,i} \cdot s$ by $s = (a_i - e_{0,i}) \cdot e_{1,i}^{-1}$.

We introduce an additional trick to overcome this problem. Namely, we make the hash values a_i shared among users so that unauthorized set of users cannot obtain any information about the hash values and therefore any information about the secret. However, sharing completely independent and random hash values $a_1, \ldots, a_n$ causes the size of shares grow linearly with n. To reduce the size of share, we make hash values $a_1, \ldots, a_n$ derived from $(k-1)$-wise independent random variables, and share the seed a of the random values $a_1, \ldots, a_n$ instead of sharing $a_1, \ldots, a_n$ themselves. By replacing completely random $a_1, \ldots, a_n$ with $(k-1)$-wise independent random variables does not affect the perfectness of the resulting scheme since $k - 1$ users do not obtain any relation among hash values due to $(k-1)$-wise randomness of hash values. The complete description of the scheme is given as follows.

Share Generation: The share generation algorithm ShareGen takes a secret $s = (s_0, s_1, \ldots, s_{N-1}) \in \mathbb{F}_{p^N}$ as input and outputs a list of shares $(v_1, \ldots, v_n)$ according to the following procedure:

1. Generate a random polynomial $f_s(x) \in \mathbb{F}_{p^N}[X]$ of degree $k - 1$ such that $s = f_s(0)$.
2. Generate a random polynomial $f_a(x) \in \mathbb{F}_{p^{k-1}}[X]$ of degree $k - 1$. We will use $f_a(0) = (a_0, a_1, \ldots, a_{k-2})$ as coefficients of a polynomial $a(x)$ (i.e., $a(x) = a_0 + a_1 x + \cdots a_{k-2} x^{k-2}$) used to derive hash values in $(k-1)$-wise independent manner.
3. Compute keys $(e_{i,0}, e_{i,1})$ $(1 \leq i \leq n)$ of almost strongly universal family $H_{1,N}$ independently and randomly satisfying $h_{1,N,(e_{i,0}, e_{i,1})}(s) = a(i)$.
4. Output $(v_1, \ldots, v_n)$ where the share v_i of the user P_i is defined by $v_i = (f_s(i), f_a(i), e_{i,0}, e_{i,1})$.

Secret Reconstruction:

1. [Round 1] Receive $(v_{s,i_1}, v_{a,i_1}), \ldots, (v_{s,i_m}, v_{a,i_m})$ from $P_{i_1}, \ldots, P_{i_m}$, respectively.
2. [Round 2] Receive $(e_{i_1,0}, e_{i_1,1})$ from $(e_{i_m,0}, e_{i_m,1})$ from $P_{i_1}, \ldots, P_{i_m}$, respectively.
3. Reconstruct s and $a(x)$ from $(v_{s,i_1}, \ldots, v_{s,i_m})$ and $(v_{a,i_1}, \ldots, v_{a,i_m})$, respectively.
4. Check if $h_{1,N,(e_{i_j,0}, e_{i_j,1})}(s) = a(i_j)$ holds for all i_j $(1 \leq j \leq m)$.
5. Output s if the above equation holds for all i_j, otherwise output $\perp$.

The following theorem gives the security properties of the proposed scheme.

Theorem 2. *If $t \leq n-1$ holds then the above scheme is (t, ϵ) cheating detectable k-out-of-n secret sharing scheme against rushing cheaters such that $|\mathcal{S}| = p^N$, $\epsilon = \frac{N}{p}$, and $|\mathcal{V}_i| = p^{N+k+1} \approx |\mathcal{S}| \cdot (\frac{\log |\mathcal{S}|}{\epsilon \log(1/\epsilon)})^{k+1}$. In particular, $|\mathcal{V}_i| = |\mathcal{S}|/\epsilon^{k+1}$ holds when $N = 1$.*

Proof. First, we will prove the scheme is *perfect*. Suppose that users $P_{i_1}, \ldots, P_{i_{k-1}}$ try to compute any partial information about the secret s. Since $v_{s,i_1}, \ldots, v_{s,i_{k-1}}$ are generated using Shamir's (k,n) threshold scheme, they do not obtain any information about the secret from $v_{s,i_1}, \ldots, v_{s,i_{k-1}}$. Therefore, the scheme is proven to be perfect if the equations $h_{1,N,(e_{i_j,0},e_{i_j,1})}(s) = a(i_j)$ $(1 \leq j \leq k-1)$ does not reveal any information about the secret. Since shares $v_{a,i_1}, \ldots, v_{a,i_{k-1}}$ (i.e., shares for $a = (a_0, \ldots, a_{k-2})$) is also generated by Shamir's (k,n) threshold scheme $P_{i_1}, \ldots, P_{i_{k-1}}$ obtain no information about the hash value $a(i_j)$. Therefore, the participants cannot obtain any information from the knowledge $h_{1,N,(e_{i_j,0},e_{i_j,1})}(s) = a(i_j)$, which shows that the scheme is perfect.

Next, we prove that the scheme is $(n-1, \epsilon)$ cheating detectable. Without loss of generality, we can assume $P_2, \ldots, P_n$ are cheaters who try to fool P_1 by submitting $(v'_2, \ldots, v'_k)$ to the secret reconstruction algorithm. Since cheaters are rushing, cheaters know all values of s (a value secret reconstructed from $(v_{s,1}, v_{s,2}, \ldots, v_{s,k})$), s' (a value reconstructed from $(v_{s,1}, v'_{s,2}, \ldots, v'_{s,k})$), $a(x)$ (a polynomial reconstructed from $(v_{a,1}, v_{a,2}, \ldots, v_{a,k})$) and $a'(x)$ (a polynomial reconstructed from $(v_{a,1}, v'_{a,2}, \ldots, v'_{a,k})$) after observing $(v_{s,1}, v_{a,1})$ submitted by P_1 even when $k = n$. The cheaters succeed in cheating P_1 if $h_{1,N,(e_{1,0},e_{1,1})}(s') = a'(1)$ holds. We will show the success cheating probability is upper bounded by N/p. Since cheaters know $h_{e_1}(s) = a(1)$ the successful cheating probability can be computed by $\Pr[h_{1,N,(e_{1,0},e_{1,1})}(s') = a'(1) \mid h_{1,N,(e_{1,0},e_{1,1})}(s) = a(1)]$. From the second property of the almost strongly universal hash family and the fact e_1 is chosen uniformly and randomly from the set of keys such that $h_{1,N,(e_{1,0},e_{1,1})}(s) = a(1)$, the following equation holds:

$$\Pr[h_{1,N,(e_{1,0},e_{1,1})}(s') = a'(1) \mid h_{1,N,(e_{1,0},e_{1,1})}(s) = a(1)]$$
$$= \frac{|\{(e_{1,0},e_{1,1}) \mid h_{1,N,(e_{1,0},e_{1,1})}(s) = a(1), h_{1,N,(e_{1,0},e_{1,1})}(s') = a'(1)\}|}{|\{(e_{1,0},e_{1,1}) \mid h_{1,N,(e_{1,0},e_{1,1})}(s) = a(1)|} \leq \epsilon,$$

which directly implies that the successful cheating probability of cheaters $P_2, \ldots, P_n$ is upper bounded by N/p. □

5 A Scheme Capable of Identifying $(k-1)/3$ Rushing Cheaters

In this section, we present a scheme capable of identifying $(k-1)/3$ rushing cheaters. The scheme is constructed based on the scheme presented in [12] which is capable of identifying $(k-1)/3$ *non-rushing* cheater.

Roughly speaking, the share v_i of the scheme in [12] consists of (1) a share $v_{s,i}$ of Shamir's (k,n) threshold scheme for a secret s, and (2) a hash value $v_{C_i} = h_{2,t+1}(v_{s,i})$ where $h_{2,t+1} \in H_{2,t+1}$ is a strongly universal hash function of strength $t+1$ (see Proposition 2 for the complete description). Unfortunately, the scheme in [12] is vulnerable to cheating by a single rushing cheater no matter what order partial shares are sent to the reconstruction algorithm. This is because rushing cheaters obtain complete information about the hash function $h_{2,t+1}$ before they send v'_{C_i} to the reconstruction algorithm.

To make it impossible for rushing cheaters to obtain complete information about the hash function, we modify the scheme in a way that hash function h is chosen from $H_{2,k+t}$ instead of $H_{2,t+1}$. This modification makes rushing cheater difficult to cheat the scheme since at least $k+t$ shares are required to obtain complete information about the hash function h. Furthermore, to prevent rushing cheaters from modifying the hash function h, we introduce an additional share $v_{E,i}$ in the proposed scheme. Here, $v_{E,i}$ is a share of $(n, t+1)$ threshold scheme for a secret $(e_{t+1}, \ldots, e_{t+k-1}) \in \mathbb{F}_{p^{k-1}}$ where $e_{t+1}, \ldots, e_{t+k-1}$ represent higher-degree coefficients of $h \in H_{2,k+t}$. With the help of $v_{E,i}$, we can convert hash values $h(\psi_{i_1}), \ldots, h(\psi_{i_k})$ into hash values $\hat{h}(\psi_{i_1}), \ldots, \hat{h}(\psi_{i_k})$ in such a way that $\hat{h} \in H_{2,t+1}$ and that $\hat{h}(\psi)$ is a correct hash value of ψ if and only if $h(\psi)$ is a correct hash value of ψ. Since converted hash function $\hat{h}$ is a element of $H_{2,t+1}$, we can identify even rushing cheaters, as in the cheater identification procedure presented in [12]. The complete description of the proposed scheme is as follows:

Share Generation: On input a secret the share generation algorithm outputs a list of shares $(v_1, \ldots, v_n)$ as follows:

1. Generate a random polynomial $f_s(x) \in \mathbb{F}_p[X]$ of degree $k-1$ such that $f_s(0) = s$.
2. Generate a random polynomial $C(x) = \sum_{i=0}^{k+t-1} e_i x^i \in \mathbb{F}_q[X]$ of degree $k+t-1$ where q is a prime power satisfying $q \geq n \cdot p$.
3. Generate a random polynomial $C_E(x) \in \mathbb{F}_{q^{k-1}}[X]$ of degree t such that $C_E(0) = (e_{t+1}, e_{t+2}, \ldots, e_{t+k-2}, e_{t+k-1}) \in \mathbb{F}_{q^{k-1}}$ (i.e., $C_E(0)$ represents higher degree coefficients of $C(x)$.)
4. Output a list of share $(v_1, \ldots, v_n)$ where $v_i = (f_s(i), C(\psi(i, f_s(i))), C_E(i))$ and $\psi : [1, n] \times \mathbb{F}_p \to \mathbb{F}_q$ is an arbitrary 1-to-1 function.

Secret Reconstruction: On input m shares $(v_{j_1}, \ldots, v_{j_m})$ (where $m \geq k$ and $v_i = (v_{s,i}, v_{C,i}, v_{E,i})$ for $1 \leq i \leq n$), the secret reconstruction algorithm outputs $(s, \emptyset)$ or $(\bot, L)$ according to the following procedure:

1. Choose k users $i_1, \ldots, i_k$ arbitrarily.
2. [Round 1] Force $P_{i_1}, \ldots, P_{i_k}$ submit $(v_{s,i_1}, v_{C,i_1}), \ldots, (v_{s,i_k}, v_{C,i_k})$, respectively.
3. [Round 2] Force $P_{i_1}, \ldots, P_{i_k}$ submit $v_{E,i_1}, \ldots, v_{E,i_k}$, respectively.
4. Reconstruct $C_E(x)$ using a decoding algorithm of generalized Reed-Solomon Code.
5. Compute a list L' by $L' = \{i_j \mid v_{E,i_j} \neq C_E(i_j)\}$.
6. Compute $(e_{t+1}, \ldots, e_{t+k-1}) = C_E(0)$.
7. Compute $\hat{v}_{C,i_j} = v_{C,i_j} - \sum_{\ell=t+1}^{t+k-1} e_\ell \cdot \psi(i_j, v_{s,i_j})^\ell$.
8. Reconstruct $\hat{C}(x) = \sum_{\ell=0}^{t} e_\ell x^\ell$ from $\hat{v}_{C,i_1}, \ldots, \hat{v}_{C,i_k}$ using a decoding algorithm of generalized Reed-Solomon Code again.

9. Compute a list L by $L = L' \cup \{i_j \mid \hat{v}_{C,i_j} \neq \hat{C}(\psi(i_j, v_{s,i_j}))\}$.
10. Reconstruct $f_s(x)$ from $v_{s,i_1}, \ldots, v_{s,i_k}$ and output $(\bot, L)$ if $L \neq \emptyset$. Otherwise, output $(f_s(0), \emptyset)$.

Theorem 3. *If $t < k/3$ holds then the above scheme is a (t, ϵ) cheater identifiable k-out-of-n secret sharing scheme against rushing adversaries such that $|\mathcal{S}| = p$, $\epsilon = 1/q$, and $|\mathcal{V}_i| = p \cdot q^k = |\mathcal{S}|/\epsilon^k$.*

Proof. First, we show that the scheme is perfect. It is well known that the values $v_{s,i_1}, \ldots, v_{s,i_{k-1}}$ do not reveal any information about the secret since each $v_{s,i}$ is a share of Shamir's k-out-of-n secret sharing scheme. Further, it is easy to see that the knowledge about $v_{C,i}$ and $v_{E,i}$ do not reveal any information about the secret since the polynomials $C(x)$ and $C_E(x)$ are completely independent of the secret s.

Next we show that the scheme is (t, ϵ) cheater identifiable against rushing cheaters. The following two facts are important to prove (t, ϵ) cheater identifiability of the scheme:

1. A family of functions $\{C(x) \mid C(x) \in \mathbb{F}_q[X], \deg(C(x)) \leq t+k-1\}$ is a strong family of universal hash functions $\mathbb{F}_q \to \mathbb{F}_q$ with strength $t + k$. Therefore, even rushing cheaters who observed t shares of cheaters as well as $k-1$ honest users cannot send a correct value of $C(\psi')$ for unknown ψ' with probability better than $1/q$ in the first round.
2. $(C_E(x_1), C_E(x_2), \ldots, C_E(x_k))$ and $(\hat{C}(x_1), \hat{C}(x_2), \ldots, \hat{C}(x_k))$ are codewords of the Reed-Solomon Code with minimum distance $k-t$. Therefore, if $t < k/3$ holds, then $C_E(x)$ and $\hat{C}(x)$ can be reconstructed correctly even when t points are forged.

Without loss of generality, we can assume $P_k, \ldots, P_{t+k-1}$ are cheaters who cooperatively cheat users $P_1, \ldots, P_{k-1}$ by forging (part of) their shares. We consider the worst case where honest users $P_1, \ldots, P_{k-1}$ and the rushing cheater P_k are chosen to submit their shares to Reconst (this is the worst case since rushing cheater can observe the most number of shares in cheating).

Since only P_k is a cheater, P_k submits forged $v'_{s,k}$ in the first round. In this case, P_k is not identified as a cheater only if he submits correct $v'_{C,k}$ such that $v'_{C,k} = C(\psi(v'_{s,k}, k))$ since Reconst can recover correct $\hat{C}(x)$ whatever $v'_{E,k}$ he submits, and $\hat{v}_{C,k} = \hat{C}(\psi(v'_{s,k}, k))$ holds if and only if $v'_{C,k} = C(\psi(v'_{s,k}, k))$. It is easy to see that P_k cannot guess correct $v'_{C,k}$ with probability better than $1/q$ since $C(x)$ belongs to a strongly universal family of hash functions with strength $t + k$. where the probability is taken over the random choice of $C(x)$. $\square$

Note: Successful cheating probability ϵ can be chosen flexibly in the above scheme by using techniques introduced in [12].

6 A Scheme Capable of Identifying $(k - 1)/2$ Rushing Cheaters

In this section, we present a scheme capable of identifying $(k - 1)/2$ rushing cheaters. The scheme is based on a standard construction first presented in [17] such that the share v_i consists of (1) share $v_{s,i}$ of Shamir's (k,n) threshold scheme for a secret, (2) keys of ASU_2 (unconditionally secure MAC) to check the correctness of $v_{s,j}$ $(j \neq i)$, and (3) hash values to prove the correctness of $v_{s,i}$. Unfortunately, the bit length of the resulting scheme still grows linearly with n. Though, with the help of tag compression technique by Carpentieri [4], the proposed scheme reduces the number of keys of ASU_2, which results in smaller size of shares compared to the schemes by Roy et al. [18] and by Choudhury [6]. The complete description of the proposed scheme is as follows:

Share Generation: On input a secret $s \in \mathbb{F}_{p^N}$, the share generation algorithm ShareGen outputs a list of shares $(v_1, \ldots, v_n)$ as follows:

1. Generate a random polynomial $f_s(x)$ of degree at most $(k-1)$ in x from $\mathbb{F}_{p^N}[X]$ such that $f_s(0) = s$ and compute $f_s(i) = v_{s,i}$ in $\mathbb{F}_{p^N}$, where $i = 1, \ldots, n$.
2. Generate a random $e_{0,i} \in_R \mathbb{F}_p$ and a random polynomial of degree at most $k-1$ with free coefficient 0, $a_i(x) = a_{i,1}x + a_{i,2}x^2 + \cdots + a_{i,k-1}x^{k-1}$, from $\mathbb{F}_p[X]$.
3. Compute $a_{i,j} = a_i(j)$ and $e_{1,i,j} = a_j(i) - \Sigma_{l=1}^N e_{0,i}^l \cdot v_{s,j,l}$ for $i \in [n] \setminus j$.
4. Compute $v_i = (v_{s,i}, a_i(x), e_{0,i}, e_{1,i,1}, \ldots, e_{1,i,i-1}, e_{1,i,i+1}, \ldots, e_{1,i,n})$.

Secret Reconstruction: Denote the set of m $(\geq k)$ participants taking part in the reconstruction as *core*. On input a list of m shares, the secret reconstruction algorithm Reconst output a secret and a list of identities of cheaters or $\perp$ and a list of identities of cheaters as follows.

1. [Round 1] Receive $v'_{s,i}, a'_{i,1}, \ldots, a'_{i,k-1}$ from each $P_i \in core$.
2. [Round 1] Receive $e'_{0,i}, e'_{1,i,1}, \ldots, e'_{1,i,n}$ from each $P_i \in core$.
3. **Computation:** For each $P_i \in core$, computes $support_i = \{P_j : \Sigma_{l=1}^N e'^l_{0,j} \cdot v'_{s,i,l} + e'_{1,j,i} = a'_{i,1}j + a'_{i,2}j^2 + \cdots + a'_{i,k-1}j^{k-1}\} \cup \{P_i\}$.
   If $|support_i| < t+1$, then put P_i in L, where L is the list of the cheaters.
4. – If $m - |L| \geq k$: Using $v'_{s,i}$ for all $P_i \in core \setminus L$, interpolate a poly $f'_s(x)$. If degree of $f'_s(x)$ is less or equal to k, output $(f'_s(0), L)$ otherwise output $(\perp, L)$.
   – If $m - |L| < k$: Output $(\perp, L)$.

Lemma 1. *The above scheme provides perfect secrecy. That is, any adversary $\mathcal{A}$ controlling any $(k-1)$ parties during the sharing phase, will get no information about the secret s.*

Proof. Without loss of generality, we may assume that the first $(k-1)$ participants, i.e., $P_1, \ldots, P_{k-1}$, are under the control of the adversary $\mathcal{A}$. The listening adversary has the following information.

$$
\begin{pmatrix}
v_{s,1} & a_{1,1} & a_{1,2} & \cdots & a_{1,k-1} & e_{0,1} & \perp & e_{1,1,2} & \cdots & e_{1,1,n} \\
v_{s,2} & a_{2,1} & a_{2,2} & \cdots & a_{2,k-1} & e_{0,2} & e_{1,2,1} & \perp & \cdots & e_{1,2,n} \\
\cdots & \cdots & \cdots & \cdots & \cdots & \cdots & \cdots & \cdots & \cdots & \cdots \\
v_{s,k-1} & a_{k-1,1} & a_{k-1,2} & \cdots & a_{k-1,k-1} & e_{0,k-1} & e_{1,k-1,1} & e_{1,k-1,2} & \cdots & e_{1,k-1,n}
\end{pmatrix}
$$

Now, according to Lagrange's interpolation, k Shamir shares $v_{s,i}$ fully define a degree-$(k-1)$ polynomial. On the other hand, $k-1$ such values provide no information on s, according to the perfect privacy property of Shamir scheme. Thus, the adversary needs to choose one more $v_{s,i}$, where $i \in \{1, 2, \ldots, n\} \setminus I$ and $I = \{1, 2, \ldots, k-1\}$. Without loss of generality, we may assume that the adversary tries to learn $v_{s,k}$ with the information at hand. Note that each player P_i ($i \in I$) has the information $(e_{0,i}, e_{1,i,k})$ regarding $v_{s,i}$. Now,

$$\Sigma_{l=1}^{N} e_{0,1}^{l} v_{s,k,l} + e_{1,1,k} = a_{k,1}1 + a_{k,2}1^2 + \cdots + a_{k,k-1}1^{k-1}$$
$$\Sigma_{l=1}^{N} e_{0,2}^{l} v_{s,k,l} + e_{1,2,k} = a_{k,1}2 + a_{k,2}2^2 + \cdots + a_{k,k-1}2^{k-1}$$
$$\cdots = \cdots$$
$$\Sigma_{l=1}^{N} e_{0,k-1}^{l} s_{s,k,l} + e_{1,k-1,k} = a_{k,1}(k-1) + a_{k,2}(k-1)^2 + \cdots + a_{k,k-1}(k-1)^{k-1}$$

Suppose, the adversary $\mathcal{A}$ tries to find out $v_{s,k,1}$. Now, as the matrix

$$\begin{bmatrix} 1 & 1^2 & \cdots & 1^{k-1} \\ 2 & 2^2 & \cdots & 2^{k-1} \\ \cdots & \cdots & \cdots & \cdots \\ k-1 & (k-1)^2 & \cdots & (k-1)^{k-1} \end{bmatrix}$$

is non-singular, the above system of linear equations is consistent for all possible values of $v_{s,k,1}$. Similarly, for other $v_{s,k,l}$. So, the best probability for $\mathcal{A}$ to guess $v_{s,k}$ is $(1/p)^N = 1/p^N$.

Note also that the adversary can construct such system of linear equations for every P_j for $j \in \{k, \ldots, n\}$. However, all these systems of equations are consistent. In other words, for any fixed value of $v_{s,k}$, there exists one and only one solution satisfying all equations available to the adversary. This essentially means that all possible values of $v_{s,k}$ are consistent with the view of the adversary. So that the adversary has no information regarding the secret s. Hence, the theorem. □

Lemma 2. *The proposed scheme satisfies correctness condition. That is, during the reconstruction phase, if any $P_i \in core$ is under the control of rushing $\mathcal{A}$ and produces $v'_{s,i} \neq v_{s,i}$, then except with error probability $\epsilon = \frac{m-t}{|\mathbb{F}_p|}$, P_i will be identified as a cheater and will be included in the list L.*

Proof. Without loss of generality, let $core$ be formed by the first m parties, namely $P_1, \ldots, P_m$, where $m \geq k$. Moreover, let $P_1, \ldots, P_t$ be under the control of $\mathcal{A}$. Now suppose that P_1 submits $v'_{s,1} \neq v_{s,1}$ and P_1 is not identified as a cheater. This implies that $|support_1| \geq t + 1$. In the worst case, $P_1, \ldots, P_t$ may be present in $support_1$, as all of them are under the control of $\mathcal{A}$. But $|support_1| \geq t + 1$ implies that there exists at least one honest party in $core$, say P_j, such that $P_j \in support_1$. This is possible only if $\Sigma_{l=1}^{N} e_{0,j}^{l} v'_{s,1,l} + e_{1,j,1} = ja'_{1,1} + j^2 a'_{1,2} + \ldots + j^{k-1} a'_{1,k-1}$. Now in *Round 1* of reconstruction phase each player P_i broadcasts $v_{s,i}, a_{i,1}, \ldots, a_{i,k-1}$ and in *Round 2* of reconstruction phase P_i broadcasts $e_{0,i}, e_{1,i,1}, \ldots, e_{1,i,i-1}, e_{1,i,i+1}, \ldots, e_{1,i,n}$.

After round 1 of the reconstruction phase, the cheating adversary can see the Shamir share and authentication tags of each player. And $\mathcal{A}$ also knows the authentication keys of player $P_1, P_2, \ldots, P_t$. But he does not know the authentication keys of players $P_{t+1}, \ldots, P_m$.

Now we evaluate the probability that P_1 succeeds in deceiving at least one honest player to accept her fake share and fake tag. This probability is described by the following formula.

$$\Pr[\text{at least one player in } [P_{t+1}, \ldots P_m] \text{ accepts } (v'_{s,1}, a'_1(x))$$
$$| [P_{t+1}, \ldots P_m] \text{ accept } (v_{s,1}, a_1(x), \ldots, v_{s,n}, a_n(x))]$$

Denote by E_1 the event that
"at least one player in $[P_{t+1}, \ldots, P_n]$ accepts $(v'_{s,1}, a'_1(x))$", and by E_2 the event that "$[P_{t+1}, \ldots, P_n]$ accept $v_{s,1}, a_1(x), \ldots, v_{s,n}, a_n(x))$".

Now, using the same argument as in Proposition 3, we can conclude that $\Pr[E_1|E_2] < (m-t)/p$.

So we get ϵ-correctness for $\epsilon = (m-t)/p$. Hence, the theorem. □

Theorem 4. *If $t < k/2$ holds then the above scheme is a (t, ϵ) cheater identifiable k-out-of-n secret sharing scheme against rushing adversaries such that $|S| = p^N$, $\epsilon = \frac{m-t}{p}$, and $|V_i| = |S| \frac{(m-t)^{n+2t}}{\epsilon^{n+2t}}$.*

Remark 2. During the sharing phase, each party gets 1 element from the field $\mathbb{F}_{p^N}$ and $n + k - 1$ elements from the field $\mathbb{F}_p$. So, $|V_i| = p^N \cdot p^{n+k-1} = (m - t)^{n+2t}|S|/\epsilon^{n+2t}$. So, share size will be at most $(n - t)^{n+2t}|S|/\epsilon^{n+2t}$, when all the participants participate in the reconstruction phase and share size will be at least $(k - t)^{n+2t}|S|/\epsilon^{n+2t}$, when only k number of participants participate in the reconstruction phase. Moreover, if $t = 1, 2$, the proposed CISS scheme is the best one, with respect to the share size, among all the existing efficient CISS schemes secure against rushing adversary when we consider the worst case scenario.

Remark 3. In the proposed CISS, the error probability does not depend on the size of the secret space. We can independently choose the error probability according to the security parameter. Hence, our proposed scheme has *flexibility* property. So, within the natural restrictions, the parameters can be set flexibly.

7   Concluding Remarks

In this paper, we have presented four k-out-of-n secret sharing schemes secure against rushing adversaries with the following properties:

- capable of *detecting* up to $(k-1)/3$ rushing cheaters such that $|V_i| = |S|/\epsilon^3$,
- capable of *detecting* up to $n - 1$ rushing cheaters such that $|V_i| = |S|/\epsilon^{k+1}$,
- capable of *identifying* up to $(k-1)/3$ rushing cheaters such that $|V_i| = |S|/\epsilon^k$,
- capable of *identifying* up to $(k-1)/2$ rushing cheaters such that $|V_i| = |S|(\frac{(n-t)^{n+2t}}{\epsilon^{n+2t}})$.

Each of the first three schemes are the first scheme in the respective model, such that the bit length of shares does not grow linearly with n. The last scheme has the smallest share size among the schemes in that model.

One important future work is to derive lower bounds on share sizes for various models of secret sharing schemes secure against rushing cheaters.

References

1. Araki, T.: Efficient (k, n) threshold secret sharing schemes secure against cheating from $n - 1$ cheaters. In: Pieprzyk, J., Ghodosi, H., Dawson, E. (eds.) ACISP 2007. LNCS, vol. 4586, pp. 133–142. Springer, Heidelberg (2007). doi:10.1007/978-3-540-73458-1_11
2. Araki, T., Obana, S.: Flaws in some secret sharing schemes against cheating. In: Pieprzyk, J., Ghodosi, H., Dawson, E. (eds.) ACISP 2007. LNCS, vol. 4586, pp. 122–132. Springer, Heidelberg (2007). doi:10.1007/978-3-540-73458-1_10
3. Blakley, G.R.: Safeguarding cryptographic keys. In: Proceedings of AFIPS 1979, National Computer Conference, vol. 48, pp. 313–137 (1979)
4. Carpentieri, M.: A perfect threshold secret sharing scheme to identify cheaters. Des. Codes Cryptogr. **5**(3), 183–187 (1995)
5. Cabello, S., Padró, C., Sáez, G.: Secret sharing schemes with detection of cheaters for a general access structure. Des. Codes Cryptogr. **25**(2), 175–188 (2002)
6. Choudhury, A.: Brief announcement: optimal amortized secret sharing with cheater identification. In: Proceedings of PODC 2012, pp. 101–101. ACM (2012)
7. Cramer, R., Damgård, I., Fehr, S.: On the cost of reconstruction a secret, or VSS with optimal reconstruction phase. In: Kilian, J. (ed.) CRYPTO 2001. LNCS, vol. 2139, pp. 503–523. Springer, Heidelberg (2001). doi:10.1007/3-540-44647-8_30
8. den Boer, B.: A simple and key-economical unconditional authentication scheme. J. Comput. Secur. **2**, 65–71 (1993)
9. Ishai, Y., Ostrovsky, R., Seyalioglu, H.: Identifying cheaters without an honest majority. In: Cramer, R. (ed.) TCC 2012. LNCS, vol. 7194, pp. 21–38. Springer, Heidelberg (2012). doi:10.1007/978-3-642-28914-9_2
10. Kurosawa, K., Obana, S., Ogata, W.: t-cheater identifiable (k, n) threshold secret sharing schemes. In: Coppersmith, D. (ed.) CRYPTO 1995. LNCS, vol. 963, pp. 410–423. Springer, Heidelberg (1995). doi:10.1007/3-540-44750-4_33
11. McEliece, R.J., Sarwate, D.V.: On sharing secrets and Reed-Solomon codes. Commun. ACM **24**(9), 583–584 (1981)
12. Obana, S.: Almost optimum t-cheater identifiable secret sharing schemes. In: Paterson, K.G. (ed.) EUROCRYPT 2011. LNCS, vol. 6632, pp. 284–302. Springer, Heidelberg (2011). doi:10.1007/978-3-642-20465-4_17
13. Obana, S., Araki, T.: Almost optimum secret sharing schemes secure against cheating for arbitrary secret distribution. In: Lai, X., Chen, K. (eds.) ASIACRYPT 2006. LNCS, vol. 4284, pp. 364–379. Springer, Heidelberg (2006). doi:10.1007/11935230_24
14. Ogata, W., Eguchi, H.: Cheating detectable threshold scheme against most powerful cheaters for long secrets. Des. Codes Cryptogr., October 2012. (Published online 2012)
15. Ogata, W., Kurosawa, K.: Provably secure metering scheme. In: Okamoto, T. (ed.) ASIACRYPT 2000. LNCS, vol. 1976, pp. 388–398. Springer, Heidelberg (2000). doi:10.1007/3-540-44448-3_29

16. Ogata, W., Kurosawa, K., Stinson, D.R.: Optimum secret sharing scheme secure against cheating. SIAM J. Discrete Math. **20**(1), 79–95 (2006)
17. Rabin, T., Ben-Or, M.: Verifiable secret sharing and multiparty protocols with honest majority. In: Proc. STOC 1989, pp. 73–85 (1989)
18. Roy, P.S., Adhikari, A., Xu, R., Kirill, M., Sakurai, K.: An efficient t-cheater identifiable secret sharing scheme with optimal cheater resiliency. eprint.iacr.org/2014/628.pdf
19. Shamir, A.: How to share a secret. Commun. ACM **22**(11), 612–613 (1979)
20. Tompa, M., Woll, H.: How to share a secret with cheaters. J. Cryptol. **1**(3), 133–138 (1989)
21. Wegman, M.N., Lawrence Carter, J.: New hash functions and their use in authentication and set equality. J. Comput. Syst. Sci. **22**, 265–279 (1981)
22. Xu, R., Morozov, K., Takagi, T.: On cheater identifiable secret sharing schemes secure against rushing adversary. In: Sakiyama, K., Terada, M. (eds.) IWSEC 2013. LNCS, vol. 8231, pp. 258–271. Springer, Heidelberg (2013). doi:10.1007/978-3-642-41383-4_17
23. Xu, R., Morozov, K., Takagi, T.: Cheater identifiable secret sharing schemes via multi-receiver authentication. In: Yoshida, M., Mouri, K. (eds.) IWSEC 2014. LNCS, vol. 8639, pp. 72–87. Springer, Heidelberg (2014). doi:10.1007/978-3-319-09843-2_6

Dynamic and Verifiable Hierarchical Secret Sharing

Giulia Traverso$^{(\boxtimes)}$, Denise Demirel, and Johannes Buchmann

Technische Universität Darmstadt, Darmstadt, Germany
gtraverso@cdc.informatik.tu-darmstadt.de

Abstract. In this work we provide a framework for dynamic secret sharing and present the first dynamic and verifiable hierarchical secret sharing scheme based on Birkhoff interpolation. Since the scheme is dynamic it allows, without reconstructing the message distributed, to add and remove shareholders, to renew shares, and to modify the conditions for accessing the message. Furthermore, each shareholder can verify its share received during these algorithms protecting itself against malicious dealers and shareholders. While these algorithms were already available for classical Lagrange interpolation based secret sharing, corresponding techniques for Birkhoff interpolation based schemes were missing. Note that Birkhoff interpolation is currently the only technique available that allows to construct hierarchical secret sharing schemes that are efficient and allow to provide shares of equal size for all shareholder in the hierarchy. Thus, our scheme is an important contribution to hierarchical secret sharing.

Keywords: Hierarchical secret sharing · Distributed storage · Cloud computing · Long-term security · Birkhoff interpolation · Proactive secret sharing

1 Introduction

1.1 Motivation and Contribution

Secret sharing is an important primitive that allows to store sensitive data in distributed fashion. In classical secret sharing schemes any subset of a certain amount of shareholders can reconstruct the message distributed. This is different for *hierarchical secret sharing* [5,11,15,20–22]. Here the shares are generated, such that not only the amount of shareholders, but also the level in the hierarchy they are assigned to is crucial for message reconstruction. Assume, for instance, signature keys are distributed to employees of a company. Then, hierarchical secret sharing allows to introduce certain conditions to the signing process, e.g. that at least one department head or senior must attend for a valid signature.

This work was in part funded by the European Commission through grant agreement no. 644962 (PRISMACLOUD). Furthermore, it received funding from the DFG as part of project S6 within the CRC 1119 CROSSING.

A.C.A. Nascimento and P. Barreto (Eds.): ICITS 2016, LNCS 10015, pp. 24–43, 2016.
DOI: 10.1007/978-3-319-49175-2_2

However, compared to classical secret sharing schemes, the approaches concerning hierarchical secret sharing are less developed. For instance, *dynamic* schemes allowing, without reconstructing the shared massage, to add or remove shareholders (e.g. to reboot or reinstall servers holding shares), to renew the shares, and to modify the conditions for accessing the message are available for classical secret sharing only, while solutions for dynamic hierarchical secret sharing schemes have not been provided yet. Furthermore, classic schemes allow for verifiability, i.e. each shareholder can verify the correctness of its share received. For hierarchical secret sharing such algorithms are only available for the very inefficient early approaches.

Contribution. *In this work we provide the first dynamic and verifiable secret sharing scheme that is hierarchical, efficient, and ideal with respect to the size of the shares.* More precisely, like in [22] our solution uses Birkhoff interpolation to reconstruct the shared message. This allows to compute shares of equal size for all shareholders independent of their ability to reconstruct the message. We show how to enhance Birkhoff interpolation based schemes, i.e. *disjunctive secret sharing* and *conjunctive secret sharing*, by algorithms that allow, without message reconstruction, to add and remove shareholders, to modify the conditions for accessing the message, and to renew shares. Furthermore, our scheme is verifiable and therefore protects against malicious dealers and shareholders. Moreover, we provide the first definition of *dynamic secret sharing* and prove our scheme secure.

Organization. After providing preliminaries in Sect. 2, we introduce a framework for dynamic secret sharing in Sect. 3. Afterwards, we provide an introduction to hierarchical secret sharing in Sect. 4, present our verifiable and dynamic hierarchical secret sharing scheme in Sect. 5, and conclude with a summary and possible future work in Sect. 6.

1.2 Related Work

Hierarchical Secret Sharing. The first solutions for hierarchical secret sharing have been proposed by Shamir in [20] and Kothari in [15]. In Shamir's approach the higher a shareholder is in the hierarchy, the more shares it gets, overloading the most powerful shareholders. In Kothari's solution, shareholders are grouped in sets and for each set an independent secret sharing scheme is instantiated. This requires managing multiple secret sharing schemes and does not allow for cooperation among sets during the reconstruction. *Disjunctive secret sharing* as introduced by Simmons in [21], is the first approach using only one secret sharing scheme and supporting cooperations of shareholders assigned to different sets, or rather levels in a hierarchy. However, his approach is not ideal meaning that the higher a shareholder in the hierarchy the larger the share to be stored. Brickell in [5] improved this by providing a disjunctive secret sharing scheme that is ideal with respect to the size of the shares, but apart from that rather inefficient. Later, Ghodosi et al. showed in [11] how to achieve efficient schemes for specific access structures. Finally, in [22] Tassa further improved this line of research by providing an efficient disjunctive secret sharing scheme for general access structures. Furthermore, he introduced *conjunctive secret sharing* that does not only allow concurrency among levels, but strictly requires the presence of a minimum amount of shareholders from the highest levels. Both conjunctive and disjunctive secret sharing are good solutions for hierarchical secret sharing and our contribution builds on Tassa's work. None of these approaches provide verifiability, nor do they allow, without reconstructing the shared message, to add or remove shareholders, to modify the conditions for accessing the message, nor to renew shares.

Dynamical and Verifiable Hierarchical Secret Sharing. Notions of dynamic secret sharing have been already proposed, yet with different meanings and less functionalities with respect to our definition. More precisely, in the one hand, in [4] it is the dealer that decides which shareholders reconstruct which secret. On the other hand, in [3] it is not possible to add shareholders without changing all the shares already distributed. Moreover, none of these approaches are suitable for hierarchical secret sharing nor do they provide verifiability. The only step towards a dynamic Birkhoff interpolation-based secret sharing scheme has been made by Pakniat et al. in [17]. It is shown how to renew shares, but, again, this process does not allow to add or remove shareholders and to modify the conditions for accessing the message nor does it provide verifiability or addresses conjunctive secret sharing. At the same time, for classical secret sharing schemes dynamic and verifiable solutions have been developed. For instance, in [16] it is shown how to add shareholders, in [13] it is shown how shares can be renewed, and in [12] it is shown how even the entiré set of shareholders and the conditions for accessing the message can be changed. In addition, all these algorithms come with verifiability. Note that classical secret sharing is based on Lagrange interpolation and the protocols [13,16], and [12] allowing for dynamism are defined accordingly. However, these approaches cannot be used for secret sharing schemes based on Birkhoff interpolation and solutions introducing dynamism also for these schemes need to be found.

Thus, our work is the first to provide dynamic and verifiable secret sharing based on Birkhoff interpolation.

2   Preliminaries

Secret sharing is a cryptographic primitive enabling a *dealer* to distribute a message among a set of *shareholders*, each of whom is allocated a *share* of the message. More precisely, to distribute a message $m \in \mathcal{M}$ to a set of shareholders $S = \{s_1, \ldots, s_n\}$ the dealer computes shares $\sigma_1, \ldots, \sigma_n \in \Sigma$, where $\mathcal{M}$ is the message space and Σ the space of all possible shares. The message can be reconstructed only when an *authorized* subset $A \subset S$ of these shareholders combine their shares while *unauthorized* subsets $U \subset S$ are prevented from doing it. The *access structure* $\Gamma \in \mathcal{P}(S)^1$ determines both sets, i.e. $A \in \Gamma$ and $U \notin \Gamma$. From now on, the number of shareholders of a subset $R \subset S$ is denoted as $r := |R|$.

---

[1] $\mathcal{P}(S)$ denotes the partition of the set S.

Note that for security we assume that all data communicated by a dealer to a shareholder and between the shareholders is sent using private channels to prevent attackers from eavesdropping.

Definition 1. *For a message space $\mathcal{M}$, a space of shares Σ, a set of shareholders $S = \{s_1, \ldots, s_n\}$, where $i \in \mathcal{I}$ is the unique ID of shareholder $s_i \in S$, and an access structure $\Gamma \subset \mathcal{P}(S)$, a* secret sharing scheme *is a pair of PPT algorithms* Share *and* Reconstruct.

Share. *It takes as input a message $m \in \mathcal{M}$ and it outputs n shares $\sigma_1, \ldots, \sigma_n \in \Sigma$, where share σ_i is to be sent to shareholder s_i, for $i = 1, \ldots, n$.*
Reconstruct. *It takes as input a set of shares $\sigma_1, \ldots, \sigma_r$ held by a subset $R \subset S$ of shareholders. It outputs $m \in \mathcal{M}$ if $R \in \Gamma$, and $\perp$ otherwise.*

A secret sharing scheme is *perfectly secure* if any unauthorized subset of participants learns nothing about the message in an information-theoretic sense, while any authorized subset of participants is able to reconstruct the secret (*accessibility*). Since our improvements rely on the scheme proposed by Tassa in [22] we recall here his definition, which uses the *Shannon's entropy H*.

Definition 2. *Let us assume that $m \in \mathcal{M}$ is the message distributed by a secret sharing scheme among a set S of shareholders according to access structure Γ. For an authorized subset $A \in S$, i.e. $A \in \Gamma$, let us denote by σ_A the set of shares owned by the shareholders $s_i \in A$, i.e. $\sigma_A := \{\sigma_i \text{ such that } s_i \in A\}$. The accessibility of a secret sharing scheme is the property such that: $H(m|\sigma_A) = 0, \forall A \in \Gamma$. In contrast, any unauthorized subset $U \in S$, i.e. $U \notin \Gamma$, should not be able to reconstruct the secret. If in addition no information about $m \in \mathcal{M}$ is leaked to the shareholders in U, then the secret sharing scheme is* perfectly secure: $H(m|\sigma_U) = H(m), \forall U \notin \Gamma$.

Another interesting primitive is *verifiable secret sharing* (VSS) [6]: each algorithm within a secret sharing scheme outputs some audit data allowing to check whether the algorithms themselves were performed correctly.

Formally, a VSS scheme is a secret sharing scheme with the following additional requirements.

Definition 3 [18]. *The algorithms in which shares are computed are extended by an additional verification protocol executed between the dealer and the shareholders $S = \{s_1 \ldots s_n\}$, such that the following properties are fulfilled.*

Completeness. *If the parties computing the shares, e.g. dealers and shareholders, follow the algorithms correctly, then each shareholder accepts the new share with probability 1.*
Committing. *If for any two authorized subsets $A_1 \subset S$ and $A_2 \subset S$, i.e. $A_1, A_2 \in \Gamma$, the shareholders of A_1 and A_2 accept their shares, then the following holds except with negligible probability: if m_i is the message reconstructed by the shareholders in A_i (for $i = 1, 2$), then $m_1 = m_2$.*

Note that the committing property of Definition 3 holds except with negligible probability, because this definition covers solutions using Pedersen commitments that are unconditionally hiding, but only computationally binding. If Feldmann commitments are used the verification protocol provides completeness even with probability 1. However, these commitments are only computationally hiding and do not ensure confidentiality in the long-term.

3   Dynamic Secret Sharing

The standard secret sharing definition only covers the algorithms Share and Reconstruct. However, in practice it is desirable that secret sharing schemes provide algorithms allowing to Add new shareholders and to Reset the entire access structure (i.e. the conditions for accessing the message and the set of shareholders). Note that algorithm Reset can be run to refresh the shares only, without modifying the access structure nor the set of shareholders. The algorithm Add differs from Reset in the sense that the access structure remains unchanged and old shareholders keep their shares. This is of practical interest since renewing shares could be a quite demanding and expensive procedure, e.g. in case shares are distributed on smartcards. Note that the algorithm Reset allows to remove shareholders, since the set S of shareholders can be replaced by a subset $S' \subset S$. In the framework of dynamic secret sharing, we assume that all communication channels used guarantee reliable delivery of messages, any two shareholders can communicate via a private channel, all shareholders can receive messages sent over a broadcast channel, any shareholder can declare and no shareholder can spoof its identity, and a majority of the shareholders participating in each algorithm is trustworthy such that wrongly generated shares can be detected. Note that these are standard assumption for classical secret sharing schemes that provide verifiability and dynamism and that the latter assumption can be weakened using the complaint mechanism proposed in [12]. Furthermore, our algorithms assume a synchronous network, but can easily be adapted to asynchronous networks, for instance, by using the techniques proposed in [19]. In the following, we formally introduce *dynamic secret sharing schemes* as secret sharing schemes that in addition allow to perform Add and Reset in distributed fashion.

Definition 4. *For a message space $\mathcal{M}$, a space of shares Σ, a set of shareholders $S = \{s_1, \ldots, s_n\}$ where $i \in \mathcal{I}$ is the unique ID of shareholder $s_i \in S$, and an access structure $\Gamma \subset \mathcal{P}(S)$, a dynamic secret sharing scheme is a tuple of PPT algorithms* Share, Add, Reset, *and* Reconstruct.

Share. *It takes as input a message $m \in \mathcal{M}$. It outputs n shares $\sigma_1, \ldots, \sigma_n \in \Sigma$, where share σ_i is to be sent to shareholder $s_i \in S$, for $i = 1, \ldots, n$.*

Add. *It takes as input a set of shares $\sigma_1, \ldots, \sigma_r$ held by a subset $R \subset S$ of shareholders and the ID i, i.e. $i = n + 1$, of the new shareholder. If R is unauthorized, i.e. $R \notin \Gamma$, it outputs $\perp$. Otherwise, $R \in \Gamma$ and without message reconstruction, it outputs a corresponding share $\sigma_i \in \Sigma$ for the new shareholder s_i.*

Reset. *It takes as input a set of shares $\sigma_1, \ldots, \sigma_r$ held by a subset $R \subset S$ of shareholders, a new set of shareholders $S' = \{s'_1, \ldots, s'_{n'}\}$ (that need not be* *disjoint to S), and an access structure $\Gamma' \subset \mathcal{P}(S')$. If R is unauthorized, i.e. $R \notin \Gamma$, it outputs $\bot$. Otherwise, $R \in \Gamma$ and without message reconstruction, it outputs n' shares $\sigma'_1, \ldots, \sigma'_{n'}$, where share σ'_i is to be sent to each new shareholder $s'_i \in S'$, for $i = 1, \ldots, n'$. The shares $\sigma_1, \ldots, \sigma_n \in \Sigma$ held by the old shareholders are deleted.*[2]

Reconstruct. *It takes as input a set of shares $\sigma_1, \ldots, \sigma_r$ held by a subset $R \subset S$ of shareholders. It outputs $m \in \mathcal{M}$ if $R \in \Gamma$, and $\bot$ otherwise.*

In addition to the algorithms **Share**, **Add**, and **Reset**, a *Verifiable and Dynamic Secret Sharing Scheme* provides audit data for verification according to Definition 3.

4   Secret Sharing Based on Birkhoff Interpolation

Simmons introduced in [21] hierarchical secret sharing as a secret sharing scheme where shareholders are divided into disjoint levels $L_0, \ldots, L_\ell$ and the power of a shareholder to reconstruct the message depends on the level it is assigned to. The union of all shareholders from all levels constitutes the set of shareholders $S = \{s_1, \ldots, s_n\}$, i.e.

$$S = \bigcup_{h=0}^{\ell} L_h, \text{ such that } L_h \cap L_k = \emptyset \text{ for } h \neq k.$$

If n_h is the number of shareholders assigned to level L_h, then $n = |S| = \sum_{h=0}^{\ell} n_h$. Furthermore, assume that L_0 is the highest level and L_ℓ the lowest level. Clearly, it is expected that less shares are needed to reconstruct the message at the higher levels, i.e. shareholders assigned to the highest level have a larger ability to reconstruct the message. Therefore, denoted by t_h the threshold associated to level L_h, for $h = 0, \ldots, \ell$, it is plausible to assume that the lower a level the higher the threshold, i.e. $0 < t_0 < \cdots < t_\ell$.

For legibility, in the following we concentrate on conjunctive secret sharing as introduced by Tassa in [22]. The corresponding solution for disjunctive secret sharing can be found in brackets.

Definition 5. *Assume the existence of a message space $\mathcal{M}$, a space of shares Σ, and an access structure $\Gamma \subset \mathcal{P}(S)$ where t_h is the threshold for level L_h, for $h = 0, \ldots, \ell$ with $t := t_\ell$ and $t_{-1} := 0$. Furthermore, assume a set of n shareholders S where the pair $(i, j) \in \mathcal{I} \times \mathcal{I}$ is the unique ID of shareholder $s_{i,j} \in L_h$ and $j := t_{h-1}(j := t_\ell - t_h)$, for $i = 1, \ldots, n_h$ and $h = 0, \ldots, \ell$. Then a conjunctive (disjunctive) secret sharing scheme is a pair of PPT algorithms* **Share** *and* **Reconstruct**, *defined as follows.*

Share. *It takes as input a message $m \in \mathcal{M}$ and generates a polynomial $f(x) = a_0 + a_1 x + a_2 x^2 + \cdots + a_{t-1} x^{t-1}$ where $a_0 := m$ ($a_{t-1} := m$) and the coefficients*

---

[2] To renew the shares, the algorithm **Reset** is run with the old set of shareholder S and the old access structure Γ as input.

$a_1, \ldots, a_{t-1} \in \mathbb{F}_q$ ($a_0, \ldots, a_{t-2} \in \mathbb{F}_q$) *are chosen uniformly at random. It outputs n shares $\sigma_{i,j} \in \Sigma$, where share $\sigma_{i,j} := f^j(i)$ is to be sent to shareholder $s_{i,j} \in L_h$, for $i = 1, \ldots, n_h$ and $h = 0, \ldots, \ell$ and $f^j(x)$ is the j-th derivative of the polynomial $f(x)$.*

Reconstruct. *It takes as input a set of shares held by a subset $R \subset S$ of shareholders. It outputs $m \in \mathcal{M}$ if $R \in \Gamma$, where $m = a_0$ ($m = a_{t-1}$) is retrieved using Birkhoff interpolation. It outputs $\perp$ otherwise.*

In the following, it is described in details how Birkhoff interpolation is performed such that Reconstruct outputs the message $m \in \mathcal{M}$.

Let us assume a subset $R \subset S$ of $r := |R|$ shareholders participating in the reconstruction such that $R \in \Gamma$. The *interpolation matrix* associated to set R is a binary matrix E where entry $e_{i,j}$ is set to '1' if shareholder $s_{i,j}$ participates with share $\sigma_{i,j}$ (that is the j-th derivative of f on position i) and '0' otherwise. The *Birkhoff interpolation problem* is the problem of finding a polynomial $f(x) = a_0 + a_1 x + a_2 x^2 + \cdots + a_{t-1} x^{t-1} \in \mathbb{R}_{t-1}[x]$ satisfying the equalities $f^j(i) = \sigma_{i,j}$, where $\mathbb{R}_{t-1}[x]$ is the ring of the polynomials with degree at most $t - 1$.

In the following, $I(E) = \{(i,j) \text{ such that } e_{i,j} = 1\}$ is the set containing the entries of E in lexicographic order, i.e. the pair (i,j) precedes the pair (i',j') if and only if $i < i'$ or $i = i'$ and $j < j'$. The elements of $I(E)$ are denoted by $(i_1, j_1), (i_2, j_2), \ldots, (i_r, j_r)$. Furthermore, we set $\varphi := \{\phi_0, \phi_1, \phi_2, \ldots, \phi_{t-1}\} = \{1, x, x^2, \ldots, x^t\}$ and denote by ϕ_k^j the j-the derivative of ϕ_k, for $k = 0, \ldots, t-1$. Then the matrix $A(E, X, \varphi)$ is defined as follows:

$$
A(E, X, \varphi) = \begin{pmatrix}
\phi_0^{j_1}(i_1) & \phi_1^{j_1}(i_1) & \phi_2^{j_1}(i_1) & \cdots & \phi_{t-1}^{j_1}(i_1) \\
\phi_0^{j_2}(i_2) & \phi_1^{j_2}(i_2) & \phi_2^{j_2}(i_2) & \cdots & \phi_{t-1}^{j_2}(i_2) \\
\vdots & \vdots & \vdots & \cdots & \vdots \\
\phi_0^{j_r}(i_r) & \phi_1^{j_r}(i_r) & \phi_2^{j_r}(i_r) & \cdots & \phi_{t-1}^{j_r}(i_r)
\end{pmatrix}.
$$

Then polynomial $f(x) \in \mathbb{R}_{t-1}[x]$ can be reconstructed by computing

$$
f(x) = \sum_{k=0}^{t-1} \frac{\det(A(E, X, \varphi_k))}{\det(A(E, X, \varphi))} x^k,
$$

where $A(E, X, \varphi_k)$ is obtained from $A(E, X, \varphi)$ by replacing its $(k+1)$-th column with the shares $\sigma_{i,j}$ in lexicographic order.

Note that it depends on the interpolation matrix E whether the Birkhoff interpolation problem has a unique solution and, consequently, the secret sharing scheme is accessible (see Appendix A for the necessary and sufficient conditions). In the following, it is assumed that the access structure Γ is chosen such that the matrix E leads to a well posed Birkhoff interpolation problem, as already discussed by Tassa in [22].

5   Providing a Dynamic and Verifiable Hierarchical Secret Sharing Scheme

In this section, we show how Tassa's conjunctive and disjunctive hierarchical secret sharing schemes can be enhanced by introducing the algorithms Add and Reset to the existing algorithms Share and Reconstruct. This leads to dynamic secret sharing, as defined in Definition 4. Note that with respect to algorithm Reset that renews the shares our construction is more efficient compared to the protocol proposed in [17]. More precisely, they demand the shareholders to reconstruct the entire function in distributed fashion while in our scheme one coefficient of the function is sufficient Furthermore, we show how the algorithms can be enhanced such that verifiability is provided. In fact, this ensures that the distributed message cannot be changed by malicious shareholders when these algorithms are run.

From now on we simplify the notation referring to the shareholders within subset $R \subset S$ as s_l and no longer as $s_{(i,j)}$. However, we stress that shareholders in R are not equal from the hierarchical point of view.

5.1   Distributed Computation of Determinants

To fulfill Definition 4, the algorithms Add and Reset have to be performed without reconstructing the message $m \in \mathcal{M}$. This is possible since determinants $\det(A(E, X, \varphi_k))$, for $k = 0, \ldots, t-1$, can be computed in distributed fashion.

Theorem 1. *The polynomial $f(x) = a_0 + a_1 x + a_2 x^2 + \cdots + a_{t-1} x^{t-1} \in \mathbb{R}_{t-1}[x]$ can be computed by*

$$f(x) = \sum_{k=0}^{t-1} a_k x^k = \sum_{k=0}^{t-1} \sum_{l=1}^{r} a_{l,k} x^k,$$

where $a_{l,k}$ is computed by shareholder $s_l \in R$, for $l = 1, \ldots, r$ and $R \in \Gamma$ is an authorized subset of S, with $r =: |R|$.

Proof. Let us first recall that *Laplace's expansion formula* computes the determinant $\det(A)$ of an $n \times n$ matrix A as the weighted sum of the determinants of n sub-matrices of A, each of size $(n-1) \times (n-1)$. More precisely $\det(A) = \sum_{j'=1}^{n} a_{i,j'}(-1)^{i+j'} \det(A_{i,j'}) = \sum_{i'=1}^{n} a_{i',j}(-1)^{i'+j} \det(A_{i',j})$, where $A_{i,j}$ results from A by deleting the i-th row and j-th column.

The fact that $A(E, X, \varphi)$ can be computed by each shareholder from public information together with Laplace's expansion formula implies that each shareholder $s_l \in R$, for $l = 1, \ldots, r$, can compute the partial information $a_{l,k}$ for coefficient $a_k = \frac{\det(A(E,X,\varphi_k))}{\det(A(E,X,\varphi))}$, by $a_{l,k} := \sigma_{i,j}(-1)^{l-1+k} \frac{\det(A_{l-1,k}(E,X,\varphi))}{\det(A(E,X,\varphi))}$, where $\sigma_{i,j}$ is the share held by shareholder s_l, and $A_{l-1,k}(E, X, \varphi)$ is the matrix that results from $A(E, X, \varphi)$ by removing the l-th row and the $(k+1)$-th column. From Laplace's expansion formula it follows that:

$$\sum_{l=1}^{r} a_{l,k} = \sum_{l=1}^{r} \sigma_{i,j}(-1)^{l-1+k} \frac{\det(A_{l-1,k}(E,X,\varphi))}{\det(A(E,X,\varphi))} = \frac{\det(A(E,X,\varphi_k))}{\det(A(E,X,\varphi))} = a_k.$$

In conclusion, the coefficients a_k, for $k = 0, \ldots, t - 1$, of polynomial $f(x) = a_0 + a_1 x + a_2 x^2 + \cdots + a_{t-1} x^{t-1}$ are computed as the sum of the partial coefficients $a_{l,k}$, where $a_{l,k}$ is computed by shareholder $s_l \in R$ and $R \in \Gamma$ is an authorized set. Importantly, this also implies that $f(x) = \sum_{l=1}^{r} f_l(x)$, where $f(x) = \sum_{l=1}^{r} f_l(x) = \sum_{l=1}^{r} \sum_{k=0}^{t-1} a_{l,k} x^k$.

In the following, the notation defined above holds. That is, $a_{l,k}$ is the partial information held by shareholder s_l about the coefficient a_k of polynomial $f(x)$ and $f_l(x) = \sum_{k=0}^{t-1} a_{l,k} x^k$ is the partial Birkhoff interpolation polynomial of shareholder s_l. Note that Theorem 1 implies that also derivatives of polynomial $f(x)$ can be computed in a distributed fashion.

Theorem 2. *The j-th derivative $f^j(x)$ of polynomial $f(x) = a_0 + a_1 x + a_2 x^2 + \cdots + a_{t-1} x^{t-1}$ can be computed in distributed fashion as*

$$f^j(x) = \sum_{l=1}^{r} f_l^j(x),$$

where $f_l^j(x)$ is computed by shareholder $s_l \in R$, for $l = 1, \ldots, r$ and $R \in \Gamma$ is an authorized subset of S, with $r =: |R|$.

Proof. To compute the derivative of polynomial $f(x)$ each shareholder $s_l \in R$ first computes its partial Birhkoff interpolation polynomial $f_l(x) = \sum_{k=0}^{t-1} a_{l,k} x^k$. Then it computes the j-th derivative $f_l^j(x) = \sum_{k=j}^{t-1} \frac{k!}{(k-j)!} a_{l,k} x^{k-j}$. Note that due to the sum rule for derivatives, i.e. $(f(x) + g(x))' = f(x)' + g(x)'$, and $f(x) = \sum_{l=1}^{r} f_l(x)$ the j-th derivative $f^j(x)$ of polynomial $f(x)$ can be computed by adding all partial derivatives, i.e. $f^j(x) = \sum_{l=1}^{r} f_l^j(x)$. $\qquad \blacksquare$

5.2 Verifiable Algorithms for Dynamic Hierarchical Secret Sharing

In this section, we provide a verifiable dynamic conjunctive and a verifiable dynamic disjunctive secret sharing scheme using Birkhoff interpolation. The verification process is described using Feldman commitments [8]. However, it can easily be adapted to Pedersen commitments [18] to achieve information-theoretic confidentiality.[3] Like in Sect. 4, we focus on conjunctive secret sharing and show the differences to disjunctive secret sharing in brackets.

Let Γ be an access structure arranged in disjoint levels $L_0, \ldots, L_\ell$, where t_h is the threshold of level L_h for $h = 0, \ldots, \ell$. Let us assume a message space $\mathcal{M}$, a space of shares Σ, and a set of shareholders S where the pair $(i, j) \in \mathcal{I} \times \mathcal{I}$ is the unique ID of shareholder $s_{i,j} \in S$, such that $j = t_{h-1}$ ($j = t_\ell - t_h$) and $t_{-1} = 0$. Then the algorithms Share, Add, Reset, and Reconstruct for *verifiable dynamic conjunctive (disjunctive) secret sharing* are defined as follows.

---

[3] There exists solutions [2,9,10,14] for VSS providing both information-theoretic confidentiality and bindingness. However, they are not secure against a mobile adversary that is able to collect over time enough share to retrieve the message. The solution proposed in [2] is an interactive protocol while we only consider non-interactive protocol having less communication complexity.

Share. It takes as input a message $m \in \mathcal{M}$. This algorithm works like the one in Definition 5 except that some additional audit data is computed and distributed. More precisely, the algorithm randomly chooses two large primes p, q, such that $q|(p-1)$. Let g be a generator of the q-th order subgroup $\mathbb{F}_q$ of $\mathbb{F}_p^*$ and set $\mathcal{M} := \mathbb{F}_q$. After defining the polynomial $f(x) = a_0 + a_1 x + a_2 x^2 + \cdots + a_{t-1} x^{t-1}$, where $a_0 := m$ $(a_{t-1} := m)$ and $a_1, \ldots, a_{t-1} \in \mathbb{F}_q$ $(a_0, \ldots, a_{t-2} \in \mathbb{F}_q)$ are chosen uniformly at random, the dealer commits to each coefficient a_k by computing $c_k := g^{a_k} \bmod p$, for $k = 0, \ldots, t-1$. It broadcasts the commitments and sends each share $\sigma_{i,j}$ to shareholder $s_{i,j} \in L_h$, for $i = 1, \ldots, n_h$ and $h = 0, \ldots, \ell$ using a private channel. Shareholder $s_{i,j}$ accepts $\sigma_{i,j}$ as its valid share, if and only if

$$g^{\sigma_{i,j}} \equiv \prod_{k=j}^{t-1} c_k^{\frac{k!}{(k-j)!} i^{k-j}} = g^{f^j(i)}.$$

Add. It takes as input a set of shares $\sigma_1, \ldots, \sigma_r$ held by a subset $R \subset S$ of shareholders and the ID (i', j') of the new shareholder. If R is unauthorized, i.e. $R \notin \Gamma$, it outputs $\perp$. Otherwise, $R \in \Gamma$ and the shareholders compute $\sigma_{i',j'} := f^{j'}(i')$ in distributed fashion. More precisely, each shareholder $s_l \in R$ performs the following steps, for $l = 1, \ldots, r$.

1. It computes the j'-th derivative of its partial Birkhoff interpolation polynomial at $x = i'$, i.e.

$$\lambda_l := \sigma_l \sum_{k=j'}^{t-1} \frac{k!}{(k-j')!} (-1)^{l-1+k} \frac{\det(A_{l-1,k}(E, X, \varphi))}{\det(A(E, X, \varphi))} i'^{k-j'}.$$

2. It randomly splits the result into r values, i.e. $\lambda_l = \delta_{1,l} + \cdots + \delta_{r,l}$ and sends $\delta_{m,l}$ to shareholder $s_{m,j} \in R$, for $m = 1, \ldots, r$ and $m \neq l$ using a private channel.
3. It collects all values $\delta_{l,m}$ received and computes $\delta_l := \sum_{m=1}^{r} \delta_{l,m}$.
4. It sends δ_l to the new shareholder $s_{i',j'}$ using a private channel and broadcasts the audit data $c_0, \ldots, c_{t-1}$ received during the share algorithm.

The new shareholder $s_{i',j'}$ computes its share $\sigma_{i',j'}$ by adding all values δ_l received, i.e. $\sigma_{i',j'} := \sum_{l=1}^{r} \delta_l$. It can verify the correctness of its share by checking whether

$$g^{\sigma_{i',j'}} \equiv \prod_{k=j'}^{t-1} c_k^{\frac{k!}{(k-j')!} i'^{k-j'}} = g^{f^{(j')}(i')},$$

using the audit data received from the shareholders.

Reset. It takes as input a set of shares $\sigma_1, \ldots, \sigma_r$ held by a subset $R \subset S$ of shareholders a new set of shareholders $S' = \{s'_1, \ldots, s'_{n'}\}$, each accompanied with a unique ID (i', j'), and an access structure $\Gamma' \subset \mathcal{P}(S')$ with maximal threshold t'. If R is unauthorized, i.e. $R \notin \Gamma$, it outputs $\perp$. Otherwise, $R \in \Gamma$ and the subset of old shareholders jointly computes shares for the new shareholders in S'. More precisely, each old shareholder $s_l \in R$ performs the following steps, for $l = 1, \ldots, r$.

1. It computes its partial Birkhoff interpolation coefficient

$$a_{l,0} := \sigma_l (-1)^{l-1} \frac{\det(A_{l-1,0}(E, X, \varphi))}{\det(A(E, X, \varphi))}$$

$$\left(a_{l,t-1} = \sigma_l (-1)^{l+t-2} \frac{\det(A_{l-1,t-1}(E, X, \varphi))}{\det(A(E, X, \varphi))}\right).$$

2. It chooses a polynomial $f_l'(x) = a_{l,0}' + a_{l,1}'x + a_{l,2}'x^2 + \cdots + a_{l,t'-1}'x^{t'-1}$ of degree $t' - 1$, where $a_{l,0}' = a_{l,0}$ ($a_{l,t-1}' = a_{l,t-1}$) is the partial Birkhoff interpolation coefficient and coefficients $a_{l,1}', \ldots, a_{l,t'-1}' \in \mathbb{F}_q$ ($a_{l,0}', \ldots, a_{l,t'-2}' \in \mathbb{F}_q$) are chosen uniformly at random.
3. It computes subshare $\sigma_{l,i',j'}$ for shareholder $s_{i',j'}' \in S'$ as $\sigma_{l,i',j'} := f_l'^{j'}(i')$.
4. It sends subshare $\sigma_{l,i',j'}$ to shareholder $s_{i',j'}' \in S$ using a private channel and broadcasts the audit data, composed of commitments to each coefficient of polynomial $f_l'(x)$, i.e. $c_{l,k}' := g^{a_{l,k}'}$, for $k = 0, \ldots, t' - 1$, and commitment $c_0 = g^m$ ($c_{t-1} = g^m$) of the old polynomial $f(x)$.
5. It deletes its share.

Each new shareholder $s_{i',j'} \in S'$ computes its share $\sigma_{i',j'}'$ adding all subshares $\sigma_{l,i',j'}$ received, i.e. $\sigma_{i',j'}' := \sum_{l=1}^r \sigma_{l,i',j'}$. To verify the correctness of share $\sigma_{l,i',j'}$, each new shareholder $s_{i',j'} \in S'$ performs the following steps.

1. It checks the function value of each polynomial, i.e.

$$g^{\sigma_{l,i',j'}} \equiv \prod_{k=j'}^{t'-1} c_{l,k}'^{\frac{k!}{(k-j')!}i'^{k-j'}} = g^{f_l'^{(j')}(i')}, \text{ for } l = 1, \ldots, r.$$

2. It checks whether the free coefficient (last coefficient) of all polynomials $f_l'(i')$ leads to the original message $m \in \mathcal{M}$, i.e.

$$c_0 \equiv \sum_{l=1}^r c_{l,0}'$$

$$\left(c_{t-1} \equiv \sum_{l=1}^r c_{l,t'-1}'\right).$$

3. If both equations are satisfied, it accept $\sigma_{i',j'}'$ as its valid share.

Reconstruct. It takes as input shares held by a subset $R \subset S$ of shareholders. If $R \in \Gamma$, it outputs $m \in \mathcal{M}$ reconstructed using Birkhoff interpolation. It outputs $\perp$ otherwise. Having access to the original audit data $c_0 = g^{a_0}$ ($c_{t-1} = g^{a_{t-1}}$) it is possible to verify whether the reconstructed message $m \in \mathcal{M}$ is a correct opening value for commitment c_0 (c_{t-1}), i.e. $g^m \equiv c_0$ ($g^m \equiv c_{t-1}$).

5.3   Security and Efficiency

In this work, our achievement is enhancing Tassa's protocols by the algorithms Add and Reset. What we need to show is that even after performing these algorithms no information is leaked and the message can still be reconstructed, i.e.

perfect security and accessibility are provided. However, merging dynamic secret sharing with the verification protocol leads to an overall scheme that is either unconditionally binding or unconditionally hiding. A rigorous analysis can be found in Appendix B.

With respect to the algorithm Add, to compute a share for a new shareholder $s_{i',j'}$ each shareholder $s_l \in A$ of an authorized subset $A \in \Gamma$ computes $f_l^{j'}(i')$. Since this subshare leaks information about the own share, each shareholder randomly splits and distributes this value to the other shareholders. Then each shareholder only forwards the sum of all values received, hiding the individual subshares. Consequently, confidentiality is preserved. Accessibility is provided since the distributed subshares and the polynomials used for secret sharing are additively homomorphic. With respect to the algorithm Reset, each shareholder s_l of an authorized subset $A \in \Gamma$ use hierarchical secret sharing to distribute its share to a new (the same) set of shareholders. While security of this algorithm follows from the security of the used conjunctive or disjunctive secret sharing scheme, accessibility is provided by the homomorphic property of polynomials.

Verifiability is achieved with the help of homomorphic and computationally binding commitment schemes. They allow each shareholder $s_{i,j}$ to compute a commitment c^* to its share $\sigma_{i,j}$ using the commitments received, i.e. $c^* = \prod_{k=j}^{t-1} c_k^{\frac{k!}{(k-j)!} i^{k-j}} = g^{f^{(j)}(i)}$, where c_k is the commitment to coefficient a_k, for $k = 0, \ldots, t-1$. Thus, by verifying $c^* \equiv g^{\sigma_{i,j}}$ the correctness of its share can be checked.

Moreover, we argue that introducing dynamism and verifiability even increases the overall security of the secret sharing scheme when it is practically instantiated. If messages are distributed for a long period of time they are prone to *mobile adversaries* [13]. Given enough time a mobile adversary is able to collect enough shares to reconstruct the secret, e.g. by breaking into many servers storing shares or bribing a sufficient amount of former employees holding shares. Thus, to provide long-term security it is necessary to renew the shares from time to time and this is possible due to our Reset algorithm. In addition, the fact that our dynamic hierarchical secret sharing scheme is also verifiable ensures protection of shareholders from a malicious dealer and vice versa.

With respect to efficiency, the polynomial $f(x)$ is retrieved computing the value for each coefficient (see Sect. 4). However, in the secret sharing framework the only coefficient that matters is the free (last) coefficient for conjunctive (disjunctive) secret sharing. Therefore for message reconstruction only two determinants have to be computed. This leads to a complexity of $\mathcal{O}(t^3)$ for matrix A of dimension $t \times t$ in case the LU decomposition technique is used [1].

6 Conclusion and Future Work

In this work we introduced a framework for dynamic secret sharing and presented the first dynamic and verifiable secret sharing scheme based on Birkhoff interpolation. For future work, we would like to combine this technique with our solution to allow for distributed computations on secretly shared data.

Appendix

A Requirements for Birkhoff Interpolation Matrices Interpolation

In this section the necessary requirements and a sufficient condition for the interpolation matrix E are presented, such that the corresponding Birkhoff interpolation problem is well posed. For the corresponding proofs we refer to [22].

Lemma 1. *Let $A \subset S$ be an authorized subset of shareholders, i.e. $A \in \Gamma$, and E the corresponding interpolation matrix, where the entries $e_{i,j}$ of the matrix E satisfy the following condition:*

$$\sum_{j=0}^{k} \sum_{i=1}^{r} e_{i,j} \geq k+1, \quad 0 \leq k \leq d, \tag{1}$$

where d is the highest derivative order in the problem and $r := |A|$ is the number of interpolating points.

Before providing the sufficient condition (Theorem 3), the following definition is needed.

Definition 6 [22]. *In the interpolation matrix E a 1-sequence is a maximal run of consecutive 1s in a row of the matrix E itself. Namely, it is a triplet of the form (i, j_0, j_1) where $1 \leq i \leq r$ and $0 \leq j_0 \leq j_1 \leq d$, such that $e_{i,j} = 1$ for all $j_0 \leq j \leq j_1$, while $e_{i,j_0-1} = e_{i,j_1+1} = 0$. A 1-sequence (i, j_0, j_1) is called supported if E has 1s both to the northwest and southwest of the leading entry in the sequence, i.e. there exist indexes nw and sw, where $i_{nw} < i < i_{sw}$ and $j_{nw}, j_{sw} < j_0$ such that $e_{i_{nw},j_{nw}} = e_{i_{sw},j_{sw}} = 1$.*

Theorem 3. *The interpolation Birkhoff problem for an authorized subset A and the corresponding interpolation matrix E has a unique solution, if the interpolation matrix E satisfies (1) and contains no supported 1-sequence of odd length.*

In case the Birkhoff interpolation problem is instantiated over a finite field $\mathbb{F}_q$ with $q > 0$ a prime number, then also the following condition has to hold.

Theorem 4. *The Birkhoff interpolation problem for an interpolation matrix E has a unique solution over the finite field $\mathbb{F}_q$, if Theorem 3 holds and in addition also the following inequality is satisfied:*

$$q > 2^{-d+2} \cdot (d-1)^{\frac{(d-1)}{2}} \cdot (d-1)! \cdot x_r^{\frac{(d-1)(d-2)}{2}}, \tag{2}$$

where d is the highest derivative order of the problem.

B   Security Analysis

Conjunctive secret sharing has been introduced by Tassa in [22] and it has been proven ideal, perfect secure, and accessible. We argue that the algorithms Add and Reset we introduced enhance the protocol and do not affect the properties and the security of the original conjunctive secret sharing scheme. To prove that, we first provide a high level idea of the proof of perfect security and accessibility of Tassa's conjunctive secret sharing scheme. Then, we show that our dynamic hierarchical secret sharing scheme maintains perfect security and accessibility. Furthermore, it is possible to cope with malicious dealers and shareholders including a verification protocol to the algorithm Share, Add, Reset, and Reconstruct. If Pedersen commitments are used in the verification protocol unconditional hidingness is maintained while bindingness can only be achieved computationally. Feldmann commitments instead ensure unconditional bindingness, i.e. the correctness of the shares can be guaranteed, but at he expenses of providing only computational hidingness for the shares. Thus, the latter solution is not suitable if data is processed for which long-term or even everlasting confidentiality is required. Similarly, it can be proven that Add and Reset maintain also the same properties of disjunctive secret sharing. However, for readability in the following we focus on conjunctive secret sharing only.

Roughly speaking, reconstructing a distributed message is equal to finding a solution of the Birkhoff interpolation problem for a polynomial $f(x) = a_0 + a_1 x + a_2 x^2 + \cdots + a_{t-1} x^{t-1}$. Thus, Tassa proved the security of his approach by showing that authorized sets of shareholders $A \in \Gamma$ lead to interpolation matrices E for which the Birkhoff interpolation problem is well posed. Thus, accessibility is provided. Furthermore, any unauthorized set of shareholders $U \notin \Gamma$ leads to an unsolvable system and perfect security is therefore proven.

The introduction of the protocols Add and Reset making the Birkhoff interpolation based secret sharing scheme dynamic does not affect these properties. First, we show that accessibility and perfect security is provided if all shareholders act honestly. This corresponds to the setup of Tassa's security proof. Second, we prove that our scheme even provides verifiability, i.e. can cope with malicious dealers and shareholders.

Theorem 5. *The dynamic secret sharing scheme composed of the protocols* Share, Add, Reset, *and* Reconstruct *described in Sect. 5.2 is accessible and perfectly secure according to Definition 2.*

Proof. The proof for the algorithms Share and Reconstruct follows from Tassa's security proof. The algorithms Add and Reset are discussed individually in the following.

Add. If the shareholders follow the protocol correctly, then all shareholders, meaning the old set of shareholders together with the new shareholder, only hold shares of the polynomial $f(x) = a_0 + a_1 x + a_2 x^2 + \cdots + a_{t-1} x^{t-1}$ or of one of its derivatives. This prevents unauthorized subsets from reconstructing the message, meaning that perfect security is achieved. However, the share $\sigma_{i',j'}$

for the new shareholder $s_{i',j'}$ is generated by old shareholders in distributed fashion. More precisely, each old shareholder uses its share to generate a piece of information from which the new shareholder $s_{i',j'}$ can compute its own share $\sigma_{i',j'}$. Therefore, what is left to show is that no information about the other shares is leaked during the generation of the share $\sigma_{i',j'}$. To compute the share of a new shareholder $s_{i',j'}$ each shareholder $s_l \in A$ of an authorized subset $A \in \Gamma$ computes $f_l^{j'}(i')$, where $f_l^{j'}(x)$ is the j'-th derivative of the polynomial $f_l(x)$. Note that this value leaks information about the share of s_l, since $f_l^{j'}(i') = \sigma_l \sum_{k=j'}^{t-1} \frac{k!}{(k-j')!} \frac{(-1)^{l-1+k} \det(A_{l-1,k}(E,X,\varphi))}{\det(A(E,X,\varphi))} i'^{k-j'}$ and the latter part $\sum_{k=j'}^{t-1} \frac{k!}{(k-j')!} \frac{(-1)^{l-1+k} \det(A_{l-1,k}(E,X,\varphi))}{\det(A(E,X,\varphi))} i'^{k-j'}$ can be computed from public information. Thus, it generates shares to this value using an additive secret sharing scheme [7], i.e. computes $f_l^{j'}(i') = \sum_{k,s_k \in A} \delta_{k,l}$, and sends $\delta_{k,l}$ to shareholder $s_k \in A$. Each shareholder s_l then adds all subshares received by the other shareholders, i.e. $\delta_l = \sum_{k,s_k \in A} \delta_{l,k}$, and forwards only the result δ_l to the new shareholder. Due to the use of the additive secret sharing scheme perfect security of all shares remains preserved.

Since $\sum_{l,s_l \in A} \delta_l = \sum_{l,s_l \in A} \sum_{k,s_k \in A} \delta_{k,l} = \sum_{k,s_k \in A} f_l^{j'}(i') = f^{j'}(i')$ also accessibility is provided. This ensures that the new shareholder holds together with the other shareholders a point of polynomial $f(x)$ or of one of its derivatives and the shares of authorized subsets including the new shareholders can reconstruct the message.

Reset. In this algorithm each shareholder $s_l \in A$ of an authorized subset $A \in \Gamma$ uses hierarchical secret sharing to distribute its share to a new set of shareholders. More precisely, it computes its partial Birkhoff interpolation coefficient

$$a_{l,0} := \sigma_l (-1)^{l-1} \frac{\det(A_{l-1,0}(E,X,\varphi))}{\det(A(E,X,\varphi))}$$

of coefficient a_0 and then chooses a polynomial $f_l'(x) = a_{l,0}' + a_{l,1}' x + a_{l,2}' x^2 + \cdots + a_{l,t'-1}' x^{t'-1}$, where $a_{l,0}' = a_{l,0}$, containing this value in the free coefficient. In this way, shares of shares are sent to the new shareholders, since only one point of this polynomial or of one of its derivatives is sent. Therefore, perfect security follows from the perfect security of conjunctive secret sharing. Furthermore, it computes the value to be sent to a new shareholder in accordance to the new access structure and the IDs assigned to each new shareholder. Thus, any unauthorized subset $U \notin \Gamma$ cannot reconstruct the message and perfect security is provided.

Accessibility of this protocol is provided due to the homomorphic property of polynomials. More precisely each new shareholder $s_{i,j}$ receives from each old shareholder s_l share $f_l'^{j}(i)$ of polynomial $f_l'(x) = a_{l,0}' + a_{l,1}' x + a_{l,2}' x^2 + \cdots + a_{l,t'-1}' x^{t'-1}$, where $a_{l,0}' = a_{l,0}$ is the partial Birkhoff interpolation coefficient of a_0. Since the new shareholder adds all shares received to compute its new share it follows that it holds a point of polynomial $f'(x) = \sum_{l,s_l \in A} f_l'(x)$ $= \sum_{l,s_l \in A} (a_{l,0}' + a_{l,1}' x + \cdots + a_{l,t'-1}' x^{t'-1}) = \sum_{l,s_l \in A} a_{l,0}' + \sum_{l,s_l \in A} a_{l,1}' + \cdots +$

$\sum_{l,s_l \in A} a'_{l,t'-1} x^{t'-1} = a_0 + \sum_{l,s_l \in A} a'_{l,1} + \cdots + \sum_{l,s_l \in A} a'_{l,t'-1} x^{t'-1}$ or of one of its derivatives. So the free coefficient of $f'(x)$ is still a_0, meaning that any authorized subset of the new access structure is still able to retrieve message $a_0 = m$.

Next we show that our verifiable and dynamic hierarchical secret sharing scheme indeed provides verifiability. For this we assume a majority of trustworthy shareholders within an authorized subset. This assumption can be weakened by letting all shareholders participate during the Add and Reset algorithm and choose an authorized subset among the majority. This majority can be identified during Add by checking who reports the same set of commitments to function $f(x)$ and during Reset by checking who reported the same commitments c_0 to the free coefficient of $f(x)$. Note that the presence of a majority of trustworthy shareholders is a common assumption of classical secret sharing schemes that allow to reset access structures, e.g. [12].

Theorem 6. *In the presence of a majority of trustworthy shareholders within an authorized subset the verifiable and dynamic secret sharing scheme composed of the protocols Share, Add, Reset, and Reconstruct described in Sect. 5.2 is a verifiable secret sharing scheme according to Definition 3.*

Proof. To prove that each authorized subset of shareholders $A \in \Gamma$ reconstruct the same message $a_0 = m$ each shareholder must hold a point of the to-be-found polynomial $f(x) = a_0 + a_1 x + a_2 x^2 + \cdots + a_{t-1} x^{t-1}$ or of one of its derivatives. Furthermore, each shareholder must hold the point assigned to its ID $(i,j) \in \mathcal{I} \times \mathcal{I}$, i.e. must receive share $\sigma_{i,j} = f^j(i)$, where $f^j(x)$ is the j-th derivative of the polynomial $f(x)$. In the following we show for each algorithm that generates shares, i.e. Share, Add, and Reset, that the shareholders receiving these shares are able to verify these conditions.

Share. During this algorithm the dealer commits to each coefficient a_k of $f(x) = a_0 + a_1 x + a_2 x^2 + \cdots + a_{t-1} x^{t-1}$ by computing a commitment $c_k := g^{a_k}$ mod p, for $k = 0, \ldots, t-1$. It broadcasts the commitments and sends each share $\sigma_{i,j}$ to shareholder $s_{i,j} \in L_h$, for $i = 1, \ldots, n_h$ and $h = 0, \ldots, \ell$. If shareholder $s_{i,j}$ accepts $\sigma_{i,j}$ then the following equation holds

$$g^{\sigma_{i,j}} \equiv \prod_{k=j}^{t-1} c_k^{\frac{k!}{(k-j)!} i^{k-j}} = g^{f^j(i)}.$$

From this it follows directly that incorrect shares can be detected and rejected.
Add. During this algorithm the shareholders $s_l \in A$ of an authorized subset $A \in \Gamma$ compute share $\sigma_{i',j'}$ for a new shareholder $s_{i',j'} \in S$ in distributed fashion. Furthermore, each shareholder broadcasts the commitments to the coefficients $c_k := g^{a_k}$ mod p, for $k = 0, \ldots, t-1$ received from the dealer. Under the assumption that at least a majority of these shareholders is honest the new shareholder has access to a correct set of commitments and can verify whether

$$g^{\sigma_{i',j'}} \equiv \prod_{k=j'}^{t-1} c_k^{\frac{k!}{(k-j')!}i'^{k-j'}} = g^{f^{j'}(i')}.$$

From this it follows directly that incorrect shares can be detected and rejected.

Reset. During this algorithm the shareholders $s_l \in A$ of an authorized subset $A \in \Gamma$ compute shares for a set of new shareholders $S' = \{s_1', \ldots, s_{n'}'\}$, each accompanied with a unique ID $(i', j') \in \mathcal{I} \times \mathcal{I}$, and an access structure $\Gamma' \subset \mathcal{P}(S')$. Like for the other algorithms it has to be checked that share $\sigma_{i',j'}$ for the shareholder $s_{i',j'}' \in S'$ with ID $(i', j') \in \mathcal{I} \times \mathcal{I}$ are computed as $f'^{j'}(i')$. However, this algorithm has an additional requirement for correctness. The free coefficient of the to-be-found polynomial must be equal to the message m distributed by the dealer. To verify the first condition each shareholder $s_{i',j'}$ of the new access structure checks

$$g^{\sigma_{l,i',j'}} \equiv \prod_{k=j'}^{t'-1} c_{l,k}'^{\frac{k!}{(k-j')!}i'^{k-j'}} = g^{f_l'^{j'}(i')}, \text{ for } s_l \in A,$$

for each share $\sigma_{l,i',j'}$ received from shareholder l of the old set of shareholders. Finally, it checks that the sum of all shares is a point of a polynomial with free coefficient $a_0 = m$. This can be verified by multiplying all commitments to the individual free coefficients, i.e.

$$c_0 \equiv \prod_{l,s_l \in A} c_{l,0}' = \prod_{l,s_l \in A} g^{a_{l,0}} = g^{a_0} = g^m.$$

Under the assumption that a majority of the old shareholders sent the correct commitments incorrect shares can be detected.

Note that our scheme is also ideal. This clearly comes from the fact that each shareholder $s_i \in R$ receives a share $\sigma_{i,j} \in \mathbb{F}_q$ that is a field element of the same field as the message $m \in \mathbb{F}_q$.

C   Example of Tassa's Hierarchical Secret Sharing

In the following, an example explaining how Tassa's hierarchical secret sharing scheme [22] works is provided. More precisely, we show a numerical instantiation of the algorithms Share and Reconstruct described in Definition 5 for conjunctive secret sharing. Note that we shall perform all computations assuming a finite field $\mathbb{F}_q$ for a very large prime q. Thus, we do not perform the modulo operation assuming the values computed are always smaller than q.

Share. Let us assume a hierarchy composed of three levels L_0, L_1, L_2 (where L_0 is the highest level and L_2 is the lowest level) and thresholds $t_1 = 1, t_2 = 2, t_3 = 3$. Furthermore, let us assume the set S is composed of $n = 6$ shareholders. More precisely, one shareholder $s_{1,0}$ is assigned to level L_0, two shareholders $s_{1,1}, s_{2,1}$ are assigned to level L_1, and three shareholders $s_{1,2}, s_{2,2},$ and $s_{3,2}$ are assigned to level L_2. Finally, let us assume that a dealer wants to secretly share the message

$m := 2$. Denoted $t := t_3$, the dealer selects a polynomial $f(x) = a_0 + a_1 x + a_2 x^2$ of degree $t - 1$ setting $a_0 := 2$ and choosing the remaining two coefficients a_1, a_2 uniformly at random., e.g. $a_1 = 3, a_2 = 1$, and $f(x) = 2 + 3x + x^2$. The shares are computed as points over $f(x)$ or one of its derivatives $f'(x) = 3 + 2x$ or $f''(x) = 2$. With respect to level L_0 shareholder $s_{1,0}$ gets share $\sigma_{1,0} = f(1) = 6$. With respect to level L_1 shareholder $s_{1,1}$ gets share $\sigma_{1,1} = f'(1) = 5$ and shareholder $s_{2,1}$ gets share $\sigma_{2,1} = f'(2) = 7$. With respect to level L_2 shareholder $s_{1,2}$ gets share $\sigma_{1,2} = f''(1) = 2$, shareholder $s_{2,2}$ gets share $\sigma_{2,2} = f''(2) = 2$, and $s_{3,2}$ gets share $\sigma_{3,2} = f''(3) = 2$.

Reconstruct. For conjunctive secret sharing, the thresholds $0 < t_0 < t_1 < t_2$ have to be considered as a chain. More precisely, the access structure defined is such that the message can be retrieved if at least $t_2 = 3$ shareholders in total collaborate, at least $t_1 = 2$ of them belong to level L_1 or L_0, and at least $t_0 = 1$ of them belong to level L_0. Without loss of generality, let us assume that the shareholders collaborating are $s_{1,0}, s_{2,1}$, and $s_{3,2}$. The access structure is satisfied because the corresponding interpolation matrix

$$E = \begin{pmatrix} 1 & 0 & 0 \\ 0 & 1 & 0 \\ 0 & 0 & 1 \end{pmatrix}$$

leads to a Birkhoff interpolation problem with unique solution (see Appendix A). The message $m = 2$ can be retrieved as follows:

1. the set containing the coordinates of E in lexicographic order is $I(E) = \{(1,0),(2,1),(3,2)\}$ and the column containing the shares in lexicographic order is $(6,7,2)^t$;
2. the vector of the functions involved is $\varphi = \{1, x, x^2\}$;
3. the matrices involved in the Birkhoff's reconstruction formula are:

$$A(E, X, \varphi) = \begin{pmatrix} 1 & 1 & 1 \\ 0 & 1 & 4 \\ 0 & 0 & 2 \end{pmatrix}, \qquad A(E, X, \varphi_0) = \begin{pmatrix} 6 & 1 & 1 \\ 7 & 1 & 4 \\ 2 & 0 & 2 \end{pmatrix},$$

$$A(E, X, \varphi_1) = \begin{pmatrix} 1 & 6 & 1 \\ 0 & 7 & 4 \\ 0 & 2 & 2 \end{pmatrix}, \qquad A(E, X, \varphi_2) = \begin{pmatrix} 1 & 1 & 6 \\ 0 & 1 & 7 \\ 0 & 0 & 2 \end{pmatrix};$$

4. the determinants are $\det(A(E, X, \varphi)) = 2, \det(A(E, X, \varphi_0)) = 4$, $\det(A(E, X, \varphi_1)) = 6$ and $\det(A(E, X, \varphi_2)) = 2$, respectively;
5. applying Birkhoff's reconstruction formula the coefficients a_0, a_1, a_2 of polynomial $f(x)$ are computed as:

$$a_0 = \frac{\det(A(E, X, \varphi_0))}{\det(A(E, X, \varphi))} = \frac{4}{2} = 2, a_1 = \frac{\det(A(E, X, \varphi_1))}{\det(A(E, X, \varphi))} = \frac{6}{2} = 3,$$

$$a_2 = \frac{\det(A(E, X, \varphi_2))}{\det(A(E, X, \varphi))} = \frac{2}{2} = 1;$$

6. the polynomial reconstructed is exactly $f(x) = 2 + 3x + x^2$ and the secret is retrieved as $f(0) = a_0 = 2$.

References

1. Agarwal, M., Mehr, R.: Review of matrix decomposition techniques for signal processing applications. Int. J. Eng. Res. Appl. **4**(1), 90–93 (2014). www.ijera.com
2. Backes, M., Kate, A., Patra, A.: Computational verifiable secret sharing revisited. In: Lee, D.H., Wang, X. (eds.) ASIACRYPT 2011. LNCS, vol. 7073, pp. 590–609. Springer, Heidelberg (2011). http://dx.doi.org/10.1007/978-3-642-25385-0_32
3. Baron, J., Defrawy, K.E., Lampkins, J., Ostrovsky, R.: Communication-optimal proactive secret sharing for dynamic groups. In: Malkin, T., Kolesnikov, V., Lewko, A.B., Polychronakis, M. (eds.) ACNS 2015. LNCS, vol. 9092, pp. 23–41. Springer, Heidelberg (2015). http://dx.doi.org/10.1007/978-3-319-28166-7_2
4. Blundo, C., Cresti, A., Santis, A., Vaccaro, U.: Fully dynamic secret sharing schemes. In: Stinson, D.R. (ed.) CRYPTO 1993. LNCS, vol. 773, pp. 110–125. Springer, Heidelberg (1994). http://dx.doi.org/10.1007/3-540-48329-2_10
5. Brickell, E.F.: Some ideal secret sharing schemes. In: Quisquater, J.-J., Vandewalle, J. (eds.) EUROCRYPT 1989. LNCS, vol. 434, pp. 468–475. Springer, Heidelberg (1990). doi:10.1007/3-540-46885-4_45
6. Chor, B., Goldwasser, S., Micali, S., Awerbuch, B.: Verifiable secret sharing and achieving simultaneity in the presence of faults (extended abstract). In: 26th Annual Symposium on Foundations of Computer Science, Portland, Oregon, USA, 21–23 October 1985, pp. 383–395 (1985). http://dx.doi.org/10.1109/SFCS.1985.64
7. Doganay, M.C., Pedersen, T.B., Saygin, Y., Savaş, E., Levi, A.: Distributed privacy preserving k-means clustering with additive secret sharing. In: Proceedings of 2008 International Workshop on Privacy and Anonymity in Information Society, pp. 3–11. ACM (2008)
8. Feldman, P.: A practical scheme for non-interactive verifiable secret sharing. In: 28th Annual Symposium on Foundations of Computer Science, pp. 427–438. IEEE (1987)
9. Fitzi, M., Garay, J.A., Gollakota, S., Rangan, C.P., Srinathan, K.: Round-optimal and efficient verifiable secret sharing. In: Proceedings of 3rd Theory of Cryptography Conference Theory of Cryptography, TCC 2006, New York, NY, USA, 4–7 March 2006, pp. 329–342 (2006). http://dx.doi.org/10.1007/11681878_17
10. Gennaro, R., Ishai, Y., Kushilevitz, E., Rabin, T.: The round complexity of verifiable secret sharing and secure multicast. In: Proceedings on 33rd Annual ACM Symposium on Theory of Computing, 6–8 July 2001, Heraklion, Crete, Greece, pp. 580–589 (2001). http://doi.acm.org/10.1145/380752.380853
11. Ghodosi, H., Pieprzyk, J., Safavi-Naini, R.: Secret sharing in multilevel and compartmented groups. In: Boyd, C., Dawson, E. (eds.) ACISP 1998. LNCS, vol. 1438, pp. 367–378. Springer, Heidelberg (1998). doi:10.1007/BFb0053748
12. Gupta, V., Gopinath, K.: G_{its}^2 VSR: : an information theoretical secure verifiable secret redistribution protocol for long-term archival storage. In: 4th International IEEE Security in Storage Workshop, SISW 2007, pp. 22–33. IEEE (2007)
13. Herzberg, A., Jarecki, S., Krawczyk, H., Yung, M.: Proactive secret sharing or: how to cope with perpetual leakage. In: Coppersmith, D. (ed.) CRYPTO 1995. LNCS, vol. 963, pp. 339–352. Springer, Heidelberg (1995). doi:10.1007/3-540-44750-4_27
14. Katz, J., Koo, C., Kumaresan, R.: Improving the round complexity of VSS in point-to-point networks. Inf. Comput. **207**(8), 889–899 (2009). http://dx.doi.org/10.1016/j.ic.2009.03.007
15. Kothari, S.C.: Generalized linear threshold scheme. In: Blakley, G.R., Chaum, D. (eds.) CRYPTO 1984. LNCS, vol. 196, pp. 231–241. Springer, Heidelberg (1985). doi:10.1007/3-540-39568-7_19

16. Nojoumian, M., Stinson, D.R., Grainger, M.: Unconditionally secure social secret sharing scheme. Inf. Secur. IET **4**(4), 202–211 (2010)
17. Pakniat, N., Eslami, Z., Nojoumian, M.: Ideal social secret sharing using Birkhoff interpolation method. IACR Cryptology ePrint Archive 2014, 515 (2014). http://eprint.iacr.org/2014/515
18. Pedersen, T.P.: Non-interactive and information-theoretic secure verifiable secret sharing. In: Feigenbaum, J. (ed.) CRYPTO 1991. LNCS, vol. 576, pp. 129–140. Springer, Heidelberg (1992). doi:10.1007/3-540-46766-1_9
19. Schultz, D.A., Liskov, B., Liskov, M.: MPSS: mobile proactive secret sharing. ACM Trans. Inf. Syst. Secur. **13**(4), 34 (2010). http://doi.acm.org/10.1145/1880022.1880028
20. Shamir, A.: How to share a secret. Commun. ACM **22**(11), 612–613 (1979). http://doi.acm.org/10.1145/359168.359176
21. Simmons, G.J.: How to (really) share a secret. In: Goldwasser, S. (ed.) CRYPTO 1988. LNCS, vol. 403, pp. 390–448. Springer, Heidelberg (1990). doi:10.1007/0-387-34799-2_30
22. Tassa, T.: Hierarchical threshold secret sharing. J. Cryptol. **20**(2), 237–264 (2007)

Quantum Cryptography

Computational Security of Quantum Encryption

Gorjan Alagic[1], Anne Broadbent[2(✉)], Bill Fefferman[3], Tommaso Gagliardoni[4],
Christian Schaffner[5(✉)], and Michael St. Jules[2]

[1] Department of Mathematical Sciences,
University of Copenhagen, Copenhagen, Denmark
galagic@gmail.com
[2] Department of Mathematics and Statistics, University of Ottawa, Ottawa, Canada
{abroadbe, mstju032}@uottawa.ca
[3] Joint Center for Quantum Information and Computer Science (QuICS),
University of Maryland, College Park, USA
wjf@umd.edu
[4] Cryptoplexity, TU Darmstadt, Darmstadt, Germany
tommaso@gagliardoni.net
[5] QuSoft, University of Amsterdam and CWI, Amsterdam, The Netherlands
c.schaffner@uva.nl

Abstract. Quantum-mechanical devices have the potential to transform cryptography. Most research in this area has focused either on the information-theoretic advantages of quantum protocols or on the security of classical cryptographic schemes against quantum attacks. In this work, we initiate the study of another relevant topic: the encryption of quantum data in the computational setting. In this direction, we establish quantum versions of several fundamental classical results. First, we develop natural definitions for private-key and public-key encryption schemes for quantum data. We then define notions of semantic security and indistinguishability, and, in analogy with the classical work of Goldwasser and Micali, show that these notions are equivalent. Finally, we construct secure quantum encryption schemes from basic primitives. In particular, we show that quantum-secure one-way functions imply IND-CCA1-secure symmetric-key quantum encryption, and that quantum-secure trapdoor one-way permutations imply semantically-secure public-key quantum encryption.

1 Introduction

For the full paper, including some proofs and definitions omitted here, see the arXiv version [5].

Quantum mechanics changes our view of information processing: the ability to access, operate and transmit data according to the laws of quantum physics opens the doors to a vast realm of possible applications. Cryptography is one of the areas that is most seriously impacted by the potential of quantum information processing, since the security of most cryptographic primitives in use today relies on the hardness of computational problems that are easily broken by adversaries having access to a quantum computer [41].

© Springer International Publishing AG 2016
A.C.A. Nascimento and P. Barreto (Eds.): ICITS 2016, LNCS 10015, pp. 47–71, 2016.
DOI: 10.1007/978-3-319-49175-2_3

While the impact of quantum computers on cryptanalysis is tremendous, quantum mechanics itself predicts physical phenomena that can be exploited in order to achieve new levels of security. These advantages were already mentioned in the late 1970s in pioneering work of Wiesner [47], and have led to the very successful theory of quantum key distribution (QKD) [9], which has already seen real-world applications [6]. QKD achieves information-theoretically secure key expansion, and has the advantage of relatively simple hardware requirements (notwithstanding a long history of successful attacks to QKD at the implementation level [6]).

The cryptographic possibilities of quantum information go well beyond QKD. Indeed, quantum copy-protection [1], quantum money [2,37,47] and revocable time-release encryption [44] are just some examples where properties unique to quantum data enable new cryptographic constructions (see [18] for a survey). Thanks in part to these tremendous cryptographic opportunities, we envisage an increasing need for an information infrastructure that enables quantum information. Such an infrastructure will be required to support:

- **Quantum functionality:** honest parties can store, exchange, and compute on quantum data;
- **Quantum security:** quantum functionality is protected against quantum adversaries.

The current state-of-the-art is lacking even the most basic cryptographic concepts in the context of quantum functionality and quantum adversaries. In particular, the study of encryption of quantum data (which is arguably one of the most fundamental building blocks) has so far been almost exclusively limited to the quantum one-time pad [7] and other aspects of the information-theoretic setting [19,20] (one notable exception being [17]). The achievability of other basic primitives such as public-key encryption has not been thoroughly investigated for the case of fully quantum cryptography. This situation leaves many open questions about what can be achieved in the quantum world.

1.1   Summary of Contributions and Techniques

In this work, we establish quantum versions of several fundamental classical (*i.e.* "non-quantum") results in the setting of computational security. Following Broadbent and Jeffrey [17], we consider private-key and public-key encryption schemes for quantum data. In these schemes, the key is a classical bitstring,[1] but both the plaintext and the ciphertext are quantum states. Key generation, encryption, and decryption are implemented by polynomial-time quantum algorithms. Such schemes admit an appropriate definition of indistinguishability security, following the classical approach [17]: the quantum adversary is given access to an encryption oracle, and must output a challenge plaintext; given either the corresponding ciphertext or the encryption of $|0\rangle\langle 0|$ (each with probability 1/2), the adversary must decide which was the case.

---

[1] While quantum keys might be of interest, they are not necessary for constructing secure schemes [17].

Our main contributions are the following. First, we give several natural formulations of semantic security for quantum encryption schemes, and show that all of them are equivalent to indistinguishability. This cements the intuition that possession of the ciphertext should not help the adversary in computing anything about the plaintext. Second, we give two constructions of encryption schemes with semantic security: a private-key scheme, and a public-key scheme. The private-key scheme satisfies a stronger notion of security: indistinguishability against chosen ciphertext attacks (IND-CCA1). A more detailed summary of these contributions follows.

1.1.1 Semantic Security vs. Indistinguishability.

Semantic security formalizes the notion of security of an encryption scheme under computational assumptions. Originally introduced by Goldwasser and Micali [30], this definition posits a game: an adversary is given the encryption of a message x and some side information $h(x)$, and is challenged to output the value of an objective function f evaluated at x. An encryption scheme is deemed secure if every adversary can be closely approximated by a *simulator* who is given only $h(x)$; crucially, the simulator must work for every possible choice (h, f) of side information and objective function. This models the intuitive notion that having access to a ciphertext gives the adversary essentially no advantage in computing functions related to the plaintext.

While semantic security corresponds to a notion of security that is intuitively strong, it is cumbersome to use in terms of security proofs. In order to address this problem, Goldwasser and Micali [30] showed the equivalence of semantic security with another cryptographic notion, called *indistinguishability*. The intuitive description of indistinguishability is also in terms of a game, this time with a *single* adversary. The adversary prepares a pair of plaintexts x_0 and x_1 and submits them to a challenger, who chooses a uniformly random bit b and returns the encryption of x_b. The adversary then performs a computation and outputs a bit v; the adversary wins the game if $v = b$ and loses otherwise. An encryption scheme is deemed secure if no adversary wins the game with probability significantly larger than $1/2$. This definition models the intuitive notion that the ciphertexts are indistinguishable: whatever the adversary does with one ciphertext, the outcome is essentially the same if run on the other ciphertext.

In Sect. 4, we define semantic security for the encryption of *quantum* data—thus establishing a parallel with the notions and results of encryptions as laid out by Goldwasser and Micali. When attempting to transfer the definition of semantic security to the quantum world, the main question one encounters is to determine the quantum equivalents of $h(x)$ and $f(x)$ as described above (because of the no-cloning theorem [48], we cannot postulate a polynomial-time experiment that simultaneously involves some quantum plaintext *and* a function of the plaintext—see Sect. 4.2 for further discussions related to this issue). We propose a number of alternative definitions in order to deal with this situation (Definition 8, and SEM2 and SEM3 appearing in the arXiv version [5].) Perhaps the most surprising is our definition of SEM (Definition 8), which does away completely with the need to explicitly define analogues of the functions h and f, instead relying on a *message generator* that outputs three registers, consisting of the "plaintext", "side information" and "target output" (there is no further structure imposed on the contents of these registers). Intuitively, we think of the adversary's goal being to output the value contained in the "target output" register. Formally, however, Definition 8 shows that the role of the "target output" register is actually to help the distinguisher: semantic security corresponding to the situation where no distinguisher has a non-negligible advantage in telling apart the real scenario (involving the adversary) and the ideal scenario (involving the simulator), *even given access to the "target output" system*. Our main result in this direction (see Sect. 4.3) is the equivalence between semantic security and indistinguishability for quantum encryption schemes:

Theorem 1. *A quantum encryption scheme is semantically secure if and only if it has indistinguishable encryptions.*

What is more, because our definitions and proofs hold when restricted to the classical case (and in fact can be shown as generalizations of the standard classical definitions), our contribution sheds new light on semantic security: to the best of our knowledge, this is the first time that semantic security has been defined *without* the need to explicitly refer to functions h and f.

1.1.2 Quantum Encryption Schemes. In Sect. 5, we give two constructions of quantum encryption schemes that achieve semantic security (and thus also indistinguishability, by Theorem 1.) Our constructions make use of two basic primitives. The first is a *quantum-secure one-way function* (qOWF). This is a family of deterministic functions which are efficiently computable in classical polynomial time, but which are impossible to invert even in quantum polynomial time. It is believed that such functions can be constructed from certain algebraic problems [33,36]. The existence of qOWFs implies the existence of *quantum-secure pseudorandom functions* (qPRFs) [50]. We show that a qPRF can, in turn, be used to securely encrypt quantum data with classical private keys. More precisely, we have the following:

Theorem 2. *If quantum-secure one-way functions exist, then so do IND-CCA1-secure private-key quantum encryption schemes.*

The second basic primitive we consider is a *quantum-secure one-way permutation with trapdoors* (qTOWP). In analogy with the classical case, a qTOWP is a qOWF with an additional property: each function in the family is a permutation whose efficient inversion is possible if one possesses a secret string (the trapdoor). While our results appear to be the first to consider applications to quantum data, the notion of quantum security for trapdoor permutations is of obvious relevance in the security of classical cryptosystems against quantum attacks. Some promising candidate qTOWPs from lattice problems are known [26,39]. We show that such functions can be used to give secure public-key encryption schemes for quantum data, again using only classical keys.

Theorem 3. *If quantum-secure trapdoor one-way permutations exist, then so do semantically secure public-key quantum encryption schemes.*

We remark that Theorems 2 and 3 are analogues of standard results in the classical literature [28].

1.2 Related Work

Prior work has considered the computational security of quantum methods to encrypt classical data [34,38,49]. Information-theoretic security for the encryption of quantum states has been considered in the context of the one-time pad [7,13,32,35], as well as entropic security [19,20]. Computational indistinguishability notions for encryption in a quantum world were proposed in independent and concurrent work [17,25]. While [17] considers the encryption of quantum data (and proposes the first constructions based on hybrid classical-quantum encryption), [25] considers the security of *classical* schemes which can be accessed in a quantum way by the adversary.

The results of [25] are part of a line of research of *"post-quantum"* cryptography, which investigates the security of classical schemes against quantum adversaries, with the goal of finding "quantum-safe" schemes. This includes the study of encryption and signature schemes secure against attacks by quantum algorithms [10], and also the study of superposition attacks against quantum oracles [11,45,50]. Still in the model of superposition attacks, [12] studies quantum indistinguishability under chosen plaintext and chosen ciphertext attacks. This definition was improved in [25] to allow for a quantum challenge phase. The latter paper also initiates the study of quantum-secure security of classical schemes and gives the first classical construction of a quantum-secure encryption scheme from a family of quantum-secure pseudorandom permutations. Another quantum indistinguishability notion in the same spirit has been suggested (but not further analyzed) in [46, Definition 5.3].

Several previous works have considered how classical security proofs change in the setting of quantum attacks (see, e.g., [24,42,43].) Our results can be viewed as part of this line of work; one distinguishing feature is that we are able to extend classical security proofs to the setting of quantum functionality secure against quantum adversaries. This setting has seen increasing interest in the past decade, with progress being made on several topics: multi-party quantum computation [8], secure function evaluation [22,23], one-time programs [16], and delegated quantum computation [14,15].

Outline. The remainder of the paper is structured as follows. In Sect. 2, we set down basic notation and recall a few standard facts regarding classical and quantum computation. In Sect. 3, we define symmetric-key and public-key encryption for quantum states (henceforth "quantum encryption schemes"), as well as a notion of indistinguishability (including IND-CPA and IND-CCA1) for such schemes. Section 4 defines semantic security for quantum encryption schemes, and shows equivalence with indistinguishability. Section 5 gives our two constructions for quantum encryption schemes. Finally, we close with some discussion of future work in Sect. 6.

2   Preliminaries

We introduce some basic notation for classical (Sect. 2.1) and quantum (Sect. 2.2) information processing and information-theoretic encryption. Section 2.3 concerns basic issues in efficient algorithms and Sect. 2.4 discusses the use of oracles.

2.1   Classical States, Maps, and the One-Time Pad

Let $\mathbb{N}$ be the set of positive integers. For $n \in \mathbb{N}$, we set $[n] = \{1, \cdots, n\}$. Define $\{0,1\}^* := \cup_n \{0,1\}^n$. An element $x \in \{0,1\}^*$ is called a bitstring, and $|x|$ denotes its length, *i.e.*, its number of bits. We reserve the notation 0^n (resp., 1^n) to denote the n-bit string with all zeroes (resp., all ones).

For a finite set X, the notation $x \xleftarrow{\$} X$ indicates that x is selected uniformly at random from X. For a probability distribution S, the notation $x \leftarrow S$ indicates that x is sampled according to S. Given finite sets X and Y, the set of all functions from Y to X is denoted X^Y (or sometimes $\{X \rightarrow Y\}$). We will usually consider functions f acting on binary strings, that is, of the form $f : \{0,1\}^n \rightarrow \{0,1\}^m$, for some positive integers n and m. We will also consider function families $f : \{0,1\}^* \rightarrow \{0,1\}^*$ defined on bitstrings of arbitrary size. One can construct such a family simply by choosing one function with input size n, for each n. We will sometimes abuse notation by stating that $f : \{0,1\}^n \rightarrow \{0,1\}^m$ defines a function family; in that case, it is implicit that n is a parameter that indexes the input size and m is some function of n (usually a polynomial) that indexes the output size. Given a bitstring y and a function family f, the preimage of f under y is defined by $f^{-1}(y) := \{x \in \{0,1\}^* : f(x) = y\}$.

We will often write $\text{negl}(\cdot)$ to denote a function from $\mathbb{N}$ to $\mathbb{N}$ which is "negligible" in the sense that it grows at an inverse-superpolynomial rate. More precisely, $\text{negl}(n) < 1/p(n)$ for every polynomial $p : \mathbb{N} \rightarrow \mathbb{N}$ and all sufficiently large n. A typical use of negligible functions is to indicate that the probability of success of some algorithm is too small to be amplified to a constant by a feasible (*i.e.*, polynomial) number of repetitions.

Given two bitstrings x and y of equal length, we denote their bitwise XOR by $x \oplus y$. Recall that the *classical one-time pad* encrypts a plaintext $x \in \{0,1\}^n$ by XORing it with a uniformly random string (the key) $r \xleftarrow{\$} \{0,1\}^n$. Decryption is performed by repeating the operation, *i.e.*, by XORing the key with the ciphertext. Since the uniform distribution on $\{0,1\}^n$ is invariant under XOR by x, the ciphertext is uniformly random to parties having no knowledge about r [40]. A significant drawback of the one-time pad is the key length. In order to reduce the key length, one may generate r pseudorandomly; this key-length reduction requires making computational assumptions about the adversary.

2.2   Quantum States, Maps, and the One-Time Pad

Given an n-bit string x, the corresponding quantum-computational n-qubit basis state is denoted $|x\rangle$. The 2^n-dimensional Hilbert space spanned by n-qubit basis states will be denoted $\mathcal{H}_n := \text{span}\{|x\rangle : x \in \{0,1\}^n\}$. We denote by $\mathfrak{D}(\mathcal{H}_n)$

the set of density operators (i.e., valid quantum states) on $\mathcal{H}_n$. These are linear operators on $\mathfrak{D}(\mathcal{H}_n)$ which are positive-semidefinite and have trace equal to 1. When considering different physical subsystems, we will denote them with uppercase Latin letters; when a Hilbert space corresponds to a subsystem, we will place the subsystem label in the subscript. For instance, if $F \cup G \cup H = [n]$ then $\mathcal{H}_n = \mathcal{H}_F \otimes \mathcal{H}_G \otimes \mathcal{H}_H$. Sometimes we will write explicitly the subsystems a state belongs to as subscripts; this will be useful when considering, $e.g.$, the reduced state on some of the subspaces. For example, we will sometimes express the statement $\rho \in \mathfrak{D}(\mathcal{H}_F \otimes \mathcal{H}_G \otimes \mathcal{H}_H)$ simply by calling the state ρ_{FGH}; in that case, the state obtained by tracing out the subsystem H will be denoted ρ_{FG}.

Given $\rho, \sigma \in \mathfrak{D}(\mathcal{H})$, the trace distance between ρ and σ is given by half the trace norm $\|\rho - \sigma\|_1$ of their difference. When ρ and σ are classical probability distributions, the trace distance reduces to the total variation distance. Physically realizable maps from a state space $\mathfrak{D}(\mathcal{H})$ to another state space $\mathfrak{D}(\mathcal{H}')$ are called $admissible$—these are the completely positive trace-preserving (CPTP) maps. For the purpose of distinguishability via input/output operations, the appropriate norm for CPTP maps is the diamond norm, denoted $\| \cdot \|_\diamond$. The set of admissible maps coincides with the set of all maps realizable by composing (i.) addition of ancillas, (ii.) unitary evolutions, (iii.) measurements in the computational basis, and (iv.) tracing out subspaces. We remark that unitaries $U \in U(\mathcal{H}_n)$ act on $\mathfrak{D}(\mathcal{H}_n)$ by conjugation: $\rho \mapsto U\rho U^\dagger$. The identity operator $\mathbb{1}_n \in U(\mathcal{H}_n)$ is thus both a valid map, and (when normalized by 2^{-n}) a valid state in $\mathfrak{D}(\mathcal{H}_n)$—corresponding to the classical uniform distribution.

Recall the single-qubit Pauli operators defined as:

$$I = \begin{pmatrix} 1 & 0 \\ 0 & 1 \end{pmatrix}, \qquad X = \begin{pmatrix} 0 & 1 \\ 1 & 0 \end{pmatrix}, \qquad Y = \begin{pmatrix} 0 & -i \\ i & 0 \end{pmatrix}, \qquad Z = \begin{pmatrix} 1 & 0 \\ 0 & -1 \end{pmatrix}.$$

The Pauli operators are Hermitian and unitary quantum gates, i.e. $P^\dagger = P$ and $P^\dagger P = PP^\dagger = P^2 = I$ for all $P \in \{I, X, Y, Z\}$. It is easy to check that applying a uniformly random Pauli operator to any single-qubit density operator results in the maximally mixed state for all $\rho \in \mathfrak{D}(\mathcal{H}_1)$:

$$\frac{1}{4}\left(\rho + X\rho X + Y\rho Y + Z\rho Z\right) = \frac{\mathbb{1}_1}{2} \qquad \text{for all } \rho \in \mathfrak{D}(\mathcal{H}_1). \tag{1}$$

Since the Pauli operators are self-adjoint, we may implement the above map by choosing two bits s and t uniformly at random and then applying $\rho \mapsto X^s Z^t \rho Z^t X^s$. To observers with no knowledge of s and t, the resulting state is information-theoretically indistinguishable from $\mathbb{1}_1/2$. Of course, if we know s and t, we can invert the above map and recover ρ completely.

The above map can be straightforwardly extended to the n-qubit case in order to obtain an elementary $quantum\ encryption\ scheme$ called the $quantum\ one\text{-}time\ pad$. We first set $X_j = \mathbb{1}^{\otimes j-1} \otimes X \otimes \mathbb{1}^{\otimes n-j}$ and likewise for Y_j and Z_j. We define the n-qubit Pauli group $\mathcal{P}_n$ to be the subgroup of $\mathrm{SU}(\mathcal{H}_n)$ generated by $\{X_j, Y_j, Z_j : j = 1, \ldots, n\}$. Note that Hermiticity is inherited from the single-qubit case, i.e. $P^\dagger = P$ for every $P \in \mathcal{P}_n$.

Definition 4 (quantum one-time pad). *For* $r \in \{0,1\}^{2n}$, *we define the* quantum one-time pad (QOTP) *on* n *qubits with classical key* r *to be the map* $P_r := \prod_{j=1}^{n} X_j^{r_{2j-1}} Z_j^{r_{2j}} \in \mathcal{P}_n$.

The effect of P_r on any quantum state $\rho \in \mathfrak{D}(\mathcal{H}_n)$ is simply

$$\frac{1}{2^{2n}} \sum_{r \in \{0,1\}^{2n}} P_r \rho P_r = \frac{\mathbb{1}_n}{2^n}. \tag{2}$$

As before, the map $\rho \mapsto P_r \rho P_r$ (for uniformly random key r) is an information-theoretically secure symmetric-key encryption scheme for quantum states.

Just as in the classical case [40], any reduction in key length is not possible without compromising information-theoretic security [7,13]. Of course, in practice the key length of the one-time pad (quantumly or classically) is highly impractical. This is a crucial reason to consider—as we do in this work—encryption schemes which are secure only against computationally bounded adversaries.

2.3 Efficient Classical and Quantum Computations

We will refer to several different notions of efficient algorithms. The most basic of these is a deterministic polynomial-time algorithm (or PT). A PT $\mathcal{A}$ is defined by a polynomial-time uniform[2] family $\mathcal{A} := \{\mathcal{A}_n\}_{n \in \mathbb{N}}$ of classical Boolean circuits over some gate set, with one circuit for each possible input size. For a bitstring x, we define $\mathcal{A}(x) := \mathcal{A}_{|x|}(x)$. We say that a function family $f : \{0,1\}^n \to \{0,1\}^m$ is PT-computable if there exists a PT $\mathcal{A}$ such that $\mathcal{A}(x) = f(x)$ for all x; it is implicit that m is a function of n which is bounded by some polynomial, e.g., the same one that bounds the running time of $\mathcal{A}$.

A probabilistic polynomial-time algorithm (or PPT) is again a polynomial-time uniform family of classical Boolean circuits, one for each possible input size n. The nth circuit still accepts n bits of input, but now also has an additional "coins" register of $p(n)$ input wires. Note that uniformity enforces that the function p is bounded by some polynomial. For a PPT $\mathcal{A}$, n-bit input x and $p(n)$-bit coin string r, we set $\mathcal{A}(x; r) := \mathcal{A}_n(x; r)$. In contrast with the PT case, the notation $\mathcal{A}(x)$ will now refer to the random variable $\mathcal{A}(x; r)$ where $r \xleftarrow{\$} \{0,1\}^{p(n)}$. Overloading notation slightly, $\mathcal{A}(x)$ can also mean the corresponding probability distribution; for example, the set of all possible outputs of $\mathcal{A}$ on the input 1^n is denoted **supp** $\mathcal{A}(1^n)$.

We define a quantum polynomial-time algorithm (or QPT) to be a polynomial-time uniform family of quantum circuits, each composed of gates that may perform general admissible operations, chosen from some finite, universal set. A commonly used alternative is to specify that the elements of the gate

---

[2] Recall that polynomial-time uniformity means that there exists a polynomial-time Turing machine which, on input n in unary, prints a description of the nth circuit in the family.

set are unitary. In terms of computational power, the models are the same [4], however using admissible operations (versus unitary ones only) allows us to formalize a wider range of oracle-enabled QPT machines (see Sect. 2.4). In general, a QPT $\mathcal{A}$ defines a family of admissible maps from input registers to output registers: $\mathcal{A} : \mathfrak{D}(\mathcal{H}_n) \rightarrow \mathfrak{D}(\mathcal{H}_u)$. As before, the nth circuit in the family will be denoted by $\mathcal{A}_n$. When ρ is an n-qubit state, $\mathcal{A}(\rho)$ denotes the corresponding $u(n)$-qubit output state (by uniformity, u is bounded by some polynomial). Overloading the notation even further, for n-bit strings x we set $\mathcal{A}(x) := \mathcal{A}(|x\rangle\langle x|)$. The expression $\mathcal{A}(x) = y$ for classical y is taken to evaluate to true if the output register of the circuit contains the state $|y\rangle\langle y|$ exactly. Unless explicitly stated, any statements about the probability of an event involving a QPT are taken over the measurements of the QPT, in addition to any indicated random variables. For instance, the expression $\Pr_{x \in_R \{0,1\}^n}[\mathcal{A}(x) = y]$ means the probability that, given a uniformly random input string x, the output register of the nth circuit of the QPT $\mathcal{A}$ executed on $|x\rangle\langle x|$, after all gates and measurements have been applied, is in the state $|y\rangle\langle y|$.

At times, we will define QPTs with many input and output quantum registers. In these cases, some straightforward bookkeeping (e.g., via an additional classical register) may be required; for the sake of clarity, we will simply assume that this has been handled.

Throughout this work, we are concerned only with polynomial-time *uniform* computation. That is to say, the circuit families that describe any PT, PPT, or QPT will always be both of polynomial length *and* generatable by some fixed (classical) polynomial-time Turing machine. In particular, we consider uniform adversaries only—although all of our results carry over appropriately to the non-uniform setting as well.

2.4   Oracles

We denote by $\mathcal{A}^f$ an algorithm which has oracle access to some function family f. Such an algorithm (whether PT, PPT, or QPT) is defined as above, except each circuit in the algorithm can make use of additional "oracle gates" (one for each possible input size) which evaluate f. In the case of PTs and PPTs, oracles can implement any function from bitstrings to bitstrings. In the case of QPTs, we consider two different oracle types.

First, we allow purely classical oracles. Just as in the case of PTs and PPTs, a classical oracle implements a function f from bitstrings to bitstrings. In the case of a QPT with a classical oracle, *queries can be made on classical inputs only* (this is sometimes referred to as "standard-security" [50]). We emphasize that we do not require that the oracle is made reversible, nor do we allow the QPT to input superpositions. Note that any such oracle can be implemented by an admissible map, such that classical inputs x are deterministically mapped to $f(x)$ (to see this, start with a Boolean circuit for f, make it reversible, and then recall that adding ancillas and discarding output bits are admissible operations). While it might seem that disallowing superposition inputs is an artificial and unrealistic restriction, in our case it actually strengthens results. For instance, we will show that secure quantum encryption can be achieved using pseudorandom functions which are secure only against quantum adversaries possessing just classical oracle access. One can of course also ask for *more powerful* functions (which are secure against superposition access, or "quantum-secure" [50]) but this turns out to be unnecessary in our case. Second, we also allow oracles that are admissible maps. More precisely, for an admissible map family $\mathcal{C}$, we write $\mathcal{A}^{\mathcal{C}}$ to denote a QPT whose circuits can make use of special "oracle gates" which implement admissible maps from the family $\mathcal{C}$. Each such gate accepts a quantum register as input, to which it applies the appropriate admissible map from the family, and returns an output register. It is not necessary for the input and output registers to have the same number of qubits.

In any case, each use of an oracle gate counts towards the circuit length, and hence also towards the total computation time of the algorithm. In particular, no PT, PPT or QPT algorithm may make more than a polynomial number of oracle calls.

3   Quantum Encryption and Indistinguishability

In this section, we give general definitions of encryption schemes for quantum data (Sect. 3.1) and a corresponding notion of indistinguishability, including IND-CPA and IND-CCA1 (Sect. 3.2.)

3.1   Quantum Encryption Schemes

We start by defining *secret-key encryption for quantum data*. In the following we assume that the secret key is a classical bitstring, while the plaintext and the ciphertext can be arbitrary quantum states. We refer to $\mathcal{K}$, $\mathcal{H}_M$ and $\mathcal{H}_C$ as the key space, the message (or plaintext) space, and the ciphertext space, respectively. We remark that these are actually infinite families of spaces, each with a number of (qu)bits which scales polynomially with n. We assume that $\mathcal{K} := \{0,1\}^n$, so that the key-length is n bits, and the plaintext and the ciphertext lengths are $m \leq \text{poly}(n)$ and $c \leq \text{poly}(n)$ qubits, respectively. The key-generation algorithm accepts a description of the security parameter n in unary and outputs a classical key of length n. Later, we will define an additional Hilbert space $\mathcal{H}_E$ in order to model auxiliary information used by some adversary. Encryption accepts a classical key and a plaintext, and outputs a ciphertext; decryption accepts a classical key and a ciphertext, and outputs a plaintext. The correctness guarantee is that plaintexts are preserved (up to negligible error) under encryption followed by decryption under the same key.

Definition 5. *A* quantum symmetric-key encryption scheme (or qSKE) *is a triple of QPTs:*

1. *(key generation)* $\mathsf{KeyGen} : 1^n \mapsto k \in \mathcal{K}$
2. *(encryption)* $\mathsf{Enc} : \mathcal{K} \times \mathfrak{D}(\mathcal{H}_M) \to \mathfrak{D}(\mathcal{H}_C)$
3. *(decryption)* $\mathsf{Dec} : \mathcal{K} \times \mathfrak{D}(\mathcal{H}_C) \to \mathfrak{D}(\mathcal{H}_M)$

such that $\|\mathsf{Dec}_k \circ \mathsf{Enc}_k - \mathbb{1}_M\|_\diamond \leq \text{negl}(n)$ *for all* $k \in \mathbf{supp}\, \mathsf{KeyGen}(1^n)$.

In the above, we used a convenient shorthand notation for encryption and decryption maps with a fixed key k (which is classical), formally defined by $\mathsf{Enc}_k : \rho \mapsto \mathsf{Enc}(k, \rho)$ and $\mathsf{Dec}_k : \sigma \mapsto \mathsf{Dec}(k, \sigma)$.

Next, we define a notion of *public-key encryption for quantum data*. In addition to the usual spaces from the symmetric-key setting above, we now also have a public key of length $p(n) \leq \mathrm{poly}(n)$ bits. We define the related public-key space as $\mathcal{K}_{pub} \subset \{0, 1\}^p$ and reuse $\mathcal{K}$ for the corresponding private-key space.

Definition 6. *A* quantum public-key encryption scheme (or qPKE) *is a triple of QPTs:*

1. *(key-pair generation)* $\mathsf{KeyGen} : 1^n \mapsto (pk, sk) \in \mathcal{K}_{pub} \times \mathcal{K}$
2. *(encryption with public key)* $\mathsf{Enc} : \mathcal{K}_{pub} \times \mathfrak{D}(\mathcal{H}_M) \to \mathfrak{D}(\mathcal{H}_C)$
3. *(decryption with private key)* $\mathsf{Dec} : \mathcal{K} \times \mathfrak{D}(\mathcal{H}_C) \to \mathfrak{D}(\mathcal{H}_M)$

such that $\|\mathsf{Dec}_{sk} \circ \mathsf{Enc}_{pk} - \mathbb{1}_m\|_\diamond \leq \mathrm{negl}(n)$ *for all* $(pk, sk) \in \mathbf{supp}\,\mathsf{KeyGen}(1^n)$.

In this case, we again placed the relevant keys in the subscript.

3.2 Indistinguishability of Encryptions

Following the classical definition, the security notion of *quantum indistinguishability under chosen plaintext attacks* has been considered previously for the case of quantum encryption schemes in [17] and for classical encryption schemes in [25]. Here, we present the definition from [17], which we slightly extend to the CCA1 (chosen ciphertext attack) setting. The security definitions are formulated with the public-key (or asymmetric-key) setting in mind, and we clarify when meaningful differences in the symmetric-key setting arise.

Our definition models a situation in which an honest user encrypts messages of the adversary's choice; the adversary then attempts to match the ciphertexts to the plaintexts. In our formulation, an IND adversary consists of two QPTs: the *message generator* and the *distinguisher*. The message generator takes as input the security parameter and a public key, and outputs a challenge state consisting of a plaintext and some auxiliary information. The auxiliary information models, for instance, the fact that the output state might be entangled with some internal state of the adversary itself. Then the distinguisher receives this auxiliary information, and a state which might be either the encryption of the original challenge state or the encryption of the zero state. The distinguisher's goal is to decide which of the two is the case.

Security in this model requires that the adversary does not succeed with probability significantly better than guessing. We also define two standard variants: indistinguishability under chosen plaintext attack (IND-CPA) and indistinguishability under chosen-ciphertext-attack (IND-CCA1). We leave the definition of CCA2 (adaptive chosen ciphertext attack) security as an interesting open problem. As before, all circuits are indexed by the security parameter.

Definition 7 (IND). *A qPKE scheme* (KeyGen, Enc, Dec) *has* indistinguishable encryptions *(or is* IND secure*) if for every QPT adversary* $\mathcal{A} = (\mathcal{M}, \mathcal{D})$ *we have:*

$$\left| \Pr\left[\mathcal{D}\{(\mathsf{Enc}_{pk} \otimes \mathbb{1}_E)\rho_{ME}\} = 1 \right] - \Pr\left[\mathcal{D}\{(\mathsf{Enc}_{pk} \otimes \mathbb{1}_E)(|0\rangle\langle 0|_M \otimes \rho_E)\} = 1 \right] \right|$$

$\leq \mathsf{negl}(n)$, *where* $\rho_{ME} \leftarrow \mathcal{M}(pk)$, $\rho_E = \mathrm{Tr}_M(\rho_{ME})$, *and the probabilities are taken over* $(pk, sk) \leftarrow \mathsf{KeyGen}(1^n)$ *and the internal randomness of* Enc, $\mathcal{M}$, *and* $\mathcal{D}$.

- **IND-CPA:** *In addition to the above,* $\mathcal{M}$ *and* $\mathcal{D}$ *are given oracle access to* Enc_{pk}.
- **IND-CCA1:** *In addition to IND-CPA,* $\mathcal{M}$ *is given oracle access to* Dec_{sk}.

Here we use $|0\rangle\langle 0|_M$ to denote $|0^m\rangle\langle 0^m|$, where m is the number of qubits in the M register.

The definition is illustrated in Fig. 1. The symmetric-key scenario is the same, except $pk = sk$, and $\mathcal{M}$ receives only a blank input. We remark that in the public-key setting, IND implies IND-CPA: an adversary with knowledge of pk can easily simulate the Enc_{pk} oracle. Note that, under CPA, the IND definition is known to be equivalent to IND in the *multiple-message* scenario [17].

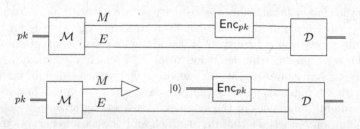

Fig. 1. IND posits that a QPT $(\mathcal{M}, \mathcal{D})$ cannot distinguish between these two scenarios

4 Quantum Semantic Security

This section is devoted to defining quantum semantic security (Sect. 4.2), and showing its equivalence with quantum indistinguishability (Sect. 4.3).

Following the classical definition, the security notion of *quantum semantic security under chosen plaintext attacks* has been given previously in [25] for the case of a special class of quantum states arising when considering quantum access to classical encryption schemes. Here, we give a more general definition for arbitrary quantum plaintexts. As we outlined the classical situation with semantic security in Sect. 1.1, we start with a discussion of some difficulties in transitioning to the quantum setting. A similar discussion can be found in [25] and we explain below where and why we make different choices.

4.1 Difficulties in the Quantum Setting

When attempting to transfer the definition of semantic security to the quantum world, the main question one encounters is to determine the quantum equivalents of $h(x)$ and $f(x)$ (as it is relatively clear that the plaintext x would have as quantum equivalent a quantum state ρ_M, in a *message register*, M).

For the case of the side-information, $h(x)$, one might attempt to postulate that this side information is available via the output of a quantum map Φ_h, evaluated on ρ_M. There are, however, two obvious problems with this approach: firstly, it is unclear how to *simultaneously* generate both ρ_M and $\Phi_h(\rho_M)$ (the main obstacle stemming from the quantum *no-cloning* Theorem [48], according to which it is not possible to perfectly copy an unknown quantum state).[3] Secondly, it is well-established that the most general type of quantum side-information includes entanglement (contrary to the scenario studied in [25]). We therefore conclude that side information should be modelled simply as an extra register (called E) such that ρ_{ME} are in an arbitrary quantum state (as generated by some process—for a formal description, see Definition 8).

For the case of the target function f, one might also postulate a quantum map Φ_f, the goal then (for both the adversary and simulator), being to output $\Phi_f(\rho_M)$. However, given that quantum states and maps form a continuum, one must exercise care in quantifying when a simulator has successfully simulated the adversary. We propose three possible tests for quantifying "success" in the semantic security game, each leading to its own definition. Since we show that all three definitions are equivalent, we conclude that it is a matter of taste (or context) which definition to label as *the* definition of quantum semantic security. We focus in this section on the first one, which we called SEM, because we find that it the most natural. We give formal definitions and proofs of equivalence for all three definitions in the arXiv version [5]. Here is an overview of the three different notions:

– **SEM.** In Definition 8, a state ρ_{MEF} is generated; intuitively, the contents of register F can be seen as a "target" output that the adversary tries to achieve (however, this is not quite the case as we point out shortly). We then postulate a quantum polynomial time *distinguisher* who is given the F register and charged with distinguishing the output of the adversary from the output of the simulator, with security being associated with the inability of the distinguisher in telling the two situations apart. We thus see that the role of register F is actually to assist the distinguisher: semantic security corresponds to the situation where the distinguisher essentially cannot tell the real from ideal apart, *even with access to the F system.*
– **SEM2.** We specify instead that the state ρ_{MEF} be a *classical-quantum state.* That is, ρ_{ME} is quantum, but the register F contains a classical state. Thus,

---

[3] [25] solves the issue by requiring a quantum circuit that takes classical randomness as input and outputs plaintext states. Hence, multiple plaintext states can be generated by using the same randomness.

correlations shared between the two systems are classical only. The requirement for security is that the simulator should provide a classical output that equals the contents of F, essentially just as well as the adversary can.

- **SEM3.** We introduce a classical function f, thus closely mimicking the classical definition. Namely, we specify as in SEM2 that F contains a classical state y, which we furthermore assume to be precisely the results of any measurements used to generate ρ_{ME} (thus, y is, in a sense, a full "classical description" of ρ_{ME}). The requirement for security is that the simulator is able to output $f(y)$ (for any f) with essentially the same probability as the adversary.

4.2   Definition of Semantic Security

As before, we work primarily in the public-key setting; adaptation to the symmetric-key setting is again straightforward. In our concrete formulation of SEM (Definition 8), we define the following QPT machines: the *message generator* $\mathcal{M}$ (which generates ρ_{MEF}), the *adversary* $\mathcal{A}$, the *simulator* $\mathcal{S}$ and the *distinguisher* $\mathcal{D}$.

Definition 8 *[SEM]. A qPKE scheme* (KeyGen, Enc, Dec) *is semantically secure if for any QPT adversary $\mathcal{A}$, there exists a QPT simulator $\mathcal{S}$ such that for all QPTs $\mathcal{M}$ and $\mathcal{D}$,*

$$\left| \Pr\left[\mathcal{D}\{(\mathcal{A} \otimes \mathbb{1}_F)(\mathsf{Enc}_{pk} \otimes \mathbb{1}_{EF})\rho_{MEF}\} = 1 \right] - \Pr\left[\mathcal{D}\{(\mathcal{S} \otimes \mathbb{1}_F)\rho_{EF}\} = 1 \right] \right|$$

$\leq \mathrm{negl}(n)$, *where* $\rho_{MEF} \leftarrow \mathcal{M}(pk)$, $\rho_{EF} = \mathrm{Tr}_M(\rho_{MEF})$, *and the probability is taken over* $(pk, sk) \leftarrow \mathsf{KeyGen}(1^n)$ *and the internal randomness of* Enc, $\mathcal{A}$, $\mathcal{S}$ *and* $\mathcal{D}$.

- **SEM-CPA:** *In addition to the above, all QPTs are given oracle access to* Enc_{pk}.
- **SEM-CCA1:** *In addition to IND-CPA, $\mathcal{M}$ is given oracle access to* Dec_{sk}.

The interactions among the QPTs are illustrated in Fig. 2. A few remarks are in order. First, all the registers above are uniformly of size polynomial in n. Second, the input and output registers of the relevant QPTs are understood from context, e.g., the expression $(\mathcal{S} \otimes \mathbb{1}_F)\rho_{EF}$ makes clear that the input register of $\mathcal{S}$ is E. Third, we note that SEM implies SEM-CPA in the public-key setting, since access to the public key implies simulatability of Enc_{pk}. Finally, just as in the case of IND, adapting to the symmetric-key setting is simply a matter of setting $pk = sk$ and positing that $\mathcal{M}$ receives only a blank input.

The classical (uniform) definition of semantic security is recovered as a special case, as follows. All of the QPTs are PPTs, and the message generator $\mathcal{M}$ outputs classical plaintext m, side information $h(m)$ and target function $f(m)$. The distinguisher $\mathcal{D}$ simply checks whether the adversary's (or simulator's) output is equal to the contents of the F register.

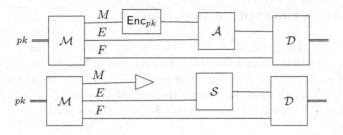

Fig. 2. SEM: for all adversaries $\mathcal{A}$ there exists a simulator $\mathcal{S}$ such that these two scenarios are indistinguishable

4.3   Semantic Security Is Equivalent to Indistinguishability

While semantic security gives a strong and intuitively meaningful definition of security, indistinguishability is typically easier to prove and work with. In this section we show that—just as in the classical setting—the two notions are equivalent. This proves Theorem 1. The equivalence holds for all of the variants of Definitions 7 and 8: under either public or private-key, we have equivalence of IND with SEM, IND-CPA with SEM-CPA, and IND-CCA1 with SEM-CCA1. Here, we focus on the SEM definition; see the Appendix in the arXiv version [5] for the equivalence with the SEM2 and SEM3 definitions.

Theorem 9 (IND $\implies$ SEM). *If a quantum encryption scheme* (KeyGen, Enc, Dec) *has indistinguishable encryptions (IND), then it is semantically secure (SEM).*

Proof. Suppose that an encryption scheme (KeyGen, Enc, Dec) has indistinguishable encryptions. Let $\mathcal{A}$ be QPT SEM attacker against semantic security as in Definition 8. We define the QPT SEM simulator $\mathcal{S}$ as follows: $\mathcal{S}$ does not receive $\mathsf{Enc}_{pk}(\rho_M)$, but instead runs $\mathcal{A}$ on input $(\mathsf{Enc}_{pk} \otimes \mathbb{1}_E)(|0\rangle\langle 0| \otimes \rho_E)$ and outputs whatever $\mathcal{A}$ outputs. Let $\mathcal{M}$ be a QPT SEM message generator that outputs ρ_{MEF}.

Assume for a contradiction the existence of a QPT SEM distinguisher $\mathcal{D}$ which successfully distinguishes the output of $\mathcal{A}$ from the output of $\mathcal{S}$ (with the help of register F), then the combination of $\mathcal{A}$ and $\mathcal{D}$ successfully distinguishes $(\mathsf{Enc}_{pk} \otimes I_{EF})\rho_{MEF}$ from $(\mathsf{Enc}_{pk} \otimes I_{EF})(|0\rangle\langle 0| \otimes \rho_{EF})$, hence contradicting the indistinguishability. $\square$

The proof is easily modified for the private-key setting, as well as CPA and CCA1; see the arXiv version for details [5].

Theorem 10 (SEM $\implies$ IND). *If a quantum encryption scheme* (KeyGen, Enc, Dec) *is semantically secure (SEM), then it has indistinguishable encryptions (IND).*

For the proof, see the arXiv version [5].

5   Quantum Encryption Schemes

We now turn to the question of existence for encryption schemes for quantum data. We present two schemes based on the existence of classical functions which are difficult to invert for quantum computers. The first scheme (Sect. 5.1) is symmetric-key and IND-CCA1-secure; the second scheme (Sect. 5.2) is public-key and IND-CPA-secure. By the results of Sect. 4, these schemes are also semantically secure.

5.1   Quantum Symmetric-Key Encryption from One-Way Functions

In this section, we prove Theorem 2: *If quantum-secure one-way functions exist, then so do IND-CCA1-secure private-key quantum encryption schemes.*

The proof proceeds in two steps. First, we define quantum-secure one-way functions (qOWFs) and quantum-secure pseudo-random functions (qPRFs); we can argue as in the classical world that qPRFs exist if qOWFs do (Theorem 13.) Second, we show that any qPRF can be used to construct an explicit IND-CCA1-secure symmetric-key scheme for quantum data.

We begin with the formal definitions of qOWFs and qPRFs, and a statement of the result connecting the two.

Definition 11. *A PT-computable function* $f : \{0,1\}^* \to \{0,1\}^*$ *is a* quantum-secure one-way function (qOWF) *if for every QPT* $\mathcal{A}$,

$$\Pr_{x \xleftarrow{\$} \{0,1\}^n} [\mathcal{A}(f(x), 1^n) \in f^{-1}(f(x))] \leq \mathrm{negl}(n).$$

Definition 12. *A PT-computable function family* $f : \{0,1\}^n \times \{0,1\}^m \to \{0,1\}^\ell$ *is a* quantum-secure pseudorandom function (qPRF) *if for every QPT* $\mathcal{D}$ *equipped with a classical oracle,*

$$\left| \Pr_{k \xleftarrow{\$} \{0,1\}^n} [\mathcal{D}^{f_k}(1^n) = 1] - \Pr_{g \xleftarrow{\$} \{\{0,1\}^m \to \{0,1\}^\ell\}} [\mathcal{D}^g(1^n) = 1] \right| \leq \mathrm{negl}(n).$$

We remark that, to some readers, the restriction to classical oracles might seem artificial. While one can certainly consider functions with the *stronger* guarantee of resistance to quantum adversaries with quantum oracle access, stronger functions are not necessary to establish our results. We thus opt for the weaker primitive. In either case, the following holds.

Theorem 13. *If qOWFs exist, then qPRFs exist.*

Since our definitions are in terms of *classical* oracles, the classical proof that shows that qOWFs imply qPRFs carries through [29, 31]. We remark that Zhandry [50] extended this result to the case of functions secure against quantum superposition queries, what he calls "quantum-secure PRFs." It should be noted that the proof of the Theorem 13 actually implies the existence of a qPRF for any (polynomial) choice of the parameters m and ℓ in Definition 12.

We are now ready to proceed with the second part of the proof of Theorem 2, namely the construction of an encryption scheme from a given qPRF. Essentially, this scheme encrypts a quantum state ρ by first selecting a random string r, then inputing r into a qPRF; the output $f_{k(r)}$ is then used as an encryption key for the quantum one-time pad, $P_{f_{k(r)}}$.

Scheme 1. *Let $f : \{0,1\}^n \times \{0,1\}^{2n} \to \{0,1\}^{2n}$ be a qPRF. Let qPRF-SKE be the following triple of QPT algorithms:*

1. *(key generation)* $\mathsf{KeyGen}(1^n)$: *output $k \xleftarrow{\$} \{0,1\}^n$;*
2. *(encryption)* $\mathsf{Enc}_k(\rho)$: *choose $r \xleftarrow{\$} \{0,1\}^{2n}$ and output $|r\rangle \langle r| \otimes P_{f_k(r)} \rho P_{f_k(r)}$.*
3. *(decryption)* $\mathsf{Dec}_k(\sigma)$: *measure the first $2n$ qubits in the computational basis to obtain $r' \in \{0,1\}^{2n}$; apply $P_{f_k(r')}$ to remaining $2n$ qubits and output the result.*

For simplicity, we chose $\mathfrak{D}(\mathcal{H}_n)$ for the key space and the plaintext space, and $\mathfrak{D}(\mathcal{H}_{2n})$ for the ciphertext space; we can easily adapt the above to other polynomially-related cases by selecting a qPRF with different parameters. Correctness of Scheme 1 is easily verified.

We show that the scheme is secure against non-adaptive chosen ciphertext attacks. The classical version of this result is standard, and we use essentially the same proof; see, e.g., Proposition 5.4.18 in Goldreich's textbook [28].

Lemma 14. *If f is a qPRF, then Scheme 1 is an IND-CCA1-secure symmetric-key quantum encryption scheme as defined in Definition 7.*

Proof. First, we analyse the security of the scheme in an idealized scenario where f is a truly random function. We claim that in this case, $\mathcal{A}$ correctly guesses the challenge with probability at most $1/2 + \mathrm{negl}(n)$ (see IND' as defined in the arXiv version [5]). In fact, this bound holds for a stronger adversary $\mathcal{A}'$, who has access to a classical oracle for f prior to the challenge, and access to polynomially many pairs $(r_i, f(r_i))$ for random $r_i, 1 \le i \le q$, after the challenge. This adversary is stronger than $\mathcal{A}$ since it can simulate $\mathcal{A}$ by implementing Enc_f and Dec_f oracles using its f oracles. Since the input r into f in the challenge ciphertext is uniformly random, the probability that any of the polynomially many oracle calls of $\mathcal{A}'$ uses the same r is negligible. In the case that no oracle calls use r, the mixtures of the inputs to $\mathcal{A}'$ (including the pairs $(r_i, f(r_i))$) are the same for the original challenge and the zero challenge. This fact can be verified by first averaging over the values of $f(r)$: since f is uniformly random, $f(r)$ is also uniformly random as well as independent of the other values of f. In both cases, applying the quantum one-time pad results in the state:

$$|r\rangle \langle r| \otimes \frac{1}{2^n} \mathbb{1} \otimes \rho_E \otimes |r_1\rangle \langle r_1| \otimes |f(r_1)\rangle \langle f(r_1)| \otimes \cdots \otimes |r_q\rangle \langle r_q| \otimes |f(r_q)\rangle \langle f(r_q)|,$$

and indistinguishability follows.

Next, we consider the case that f is a pseudorandom function. We show that a successful IND-CCA1 adversary $\mathcal{A}$ (i.e., one that distinguishes challenges with better than negligible probability) can be used to construct a successful f-adversary $\mathcal{A}_0$ (i.e., one that distinguishes f from random with non-negligible probability.) The adversary $\mathcal{A}_0$ is a QPT with classical oracle access to a function $\varphi : \{0,1\}^{2n} \to \{0,1\}^{2n}$, and aims to output 0 if φ is perfectly random and 1 if $\varphi = f_k$ for some k. Define the simulated oracles

$$\mathsf{Enc}_\varphi : \rho \mapsto \left(r, P_{\varphi(r)} \rho P_{\varphi(r)} \right), \ r \xleftarrow{\$} \{0,1\}^{2n}, \text{ and } \mathsf{Dec}_\varphi : |r'\rangle \langle r'| \otimes \rho \mapsto P_{\varphi(r')} \rho P_{\varphi(r')},$$

where, as before, we assume that Dec_φ measures the first register before decrypting the second. Note that if $\varphi = f_k$ then these are exactly the encryption and decryption oracles (with key k) of the qPRF-SKE scheme.

The QPT $\mathcal{A}_0^\varphi$ proceeds as follows. First, it simulates $\mathcal{A}$, and replies to its queries to the encryption oracle with Enc_φ and its queries to the decryption oracle with Dec_φ. When it transmits the challenge, $\mathcal{A}_0^\varphi$ replies with either the encryption of the challenge, or the encryption of $|0^n\rangle \langle 0^n|$, each with probability $1/2$. If $\mathcal{A}$ responds correctly, $\mathcal{A}_0^\varphi$ outputs 1; otherwise it outputs 0. If $\varphi = f_k$ then we have exactly simulated the IND-CCA1 game with adversary $\mathcal{A}$; in that case, since $\mathcal{A}$ is IND-CCA1-breaking, $\mathcal{A}_0^\varphi$ outputs 1 with probability at least $1/2 + 1/p(n)$ for some polynomial p, for infinitely many n.

We conclude that

$$\left| \Pr_{k \xleftarrow{\$} \{0,1\}^n} [\mathcal{A}_0^{f_k}(1^n) = 1] - \Pr_{\varphi \xleftarrow{\$} \{\{0,1\}^{2n} \to \{0,1\}^{2n}\}} [\mathcal{A}_0^\varphi(1^n) = 1] \right| \geq 1/p(n) - \mathrm{negl}(n),$$

$$(3)$$

for infinitely many n, i.e., f is not a qPRF. $\square$

Putting together Theorem 13 and Lemma 14, we arrive at a proof of Theorem 2.

5.2 Quantum Public-Key Encryption from Trapdoor Permutations

For the construction of public-key schemes, we will need qOWFs with an additional property: the existence of *trapdoors* which enable efficient inversion. Following the classical approach of Diffie and Hellman [21], we set down the notion of a quantum-secure trapdoor one-way permutation (or qTOWP), and then show how to use any qTOWP to construct IND-CPA secure public-key encryption schemes for quantum data. This will establish Theorem 3: *If quantum-secure trapdoor one-way permutations exist, then so do semantically secure public-key quantum encryption schemes.*.

We begin with a definition of qTOWPs. We require a slight (but standard) variation of Definition 11, namely the notion of a quantum-secure one-way permutation (or qOWP). A qOWP is a qOWF whose input domains are sets D_i; moreover, the function restricted to any such domain must be a permutation (from the domain to the corresponding range.) When we augment such a qOWP with trapdoors, we arrive at the following definition.

Definition 15. *A quantum-secure trapdoor one-way permutation (qTOWP) is a qOWF*

$$\{f_i : D_i \to \{0,1\}^*\}_{i \in I}$$

(where each f_i is a bijection), together with a triple of PPTs $(\mathcal{G}, \mathcal{S}, \mathcal{I})$ which

1. *(generate (index, trapdoor) pair)* $\mathbf{supp}\,\mathcal{G}(1^n) \subseteq (I \cap \{0,1\}^n) \times \{0,1\}^n$;
2. *(sample from domain) for all $i \in I$,* $\mathbf{supp}\,\mathcal{S}(i) = D_i$;
3. *(invert using trapdoor) for all $(i,t) \in \mathbf{supp}\,\mathcal{G}(1^n)$ and all $x \in D_i$, $\mathcal{I}(f_i(x),t) = x$.*

Before we can describe the public-key scheme and prove its security, we need two additional (well-known) primitives which can be constructed from any qOWP, with or without trapdoors. The first is a quantum-secure "hard-core" predicate, which is a "yes" or "no" question about inputs x which is difficult to answer if one only knows $f(x)$.

Definition 16. *A PT-computable $b : \{0,1\}^* \to \{0,1\}$ is a* hard-core *of a qOWP f if for every QPT $\mathcal{A}$,*

$$\Pr_{x \xleftarrow{\$} \{0,1\}^n} [\mathcal{A}(f(x), 1^n) = b(x)] \le \frac{1}{2} + \mathrm{negl}(n).$$

Theorem 17. *([3], quantum analogue of [27]) If qOWPs exist, then qOWPs with hard-cores exist.*

The other primitive we need is a quantum-secure pseudorandom generator, which is defined below. The classical proof that hard-cores imply pseudorandom generators carries over with little modification (see Lemma 19).

Definition 18. *A PT-computable deterministic function $G : \{0,1\}^n \to \{0,1\}^m$ is a* quantum-secure pseudorandom generator (qPRG) *if for every QPT $\mathcal{D}$,*

$$\left| \Pr_{s \xleftarrow{\$} \{0,1\}^n} [\mathcal{D}(G(s)) = 1] \; - \; \Pr_{y \xleftarrow{\$} \{0,1\}^m} [\mathcal{D}(y) = 1] \right| \le \mathrm{negl}(n).$$

Lemma 19. *Suppose f is a qOWP, b its hard-core predicate, and let t be polynomial in n. Then $G : s \mapsto b(f^{t-1}(s))b(f^{t-2}(s))\ldots b(s)$ is a qPRG.*

Proof (Sketch). The proof proceeds almost identically as in the classical case (see, e.g., [28].) Let $\mathcal{D}$ be a quantum adversary that distinguishes $G(U_n)$ from uniform. Note that, as stated in Definition 18, $\mathcal{D}$ gets only classical bitstring outputs from the pseudorandom generator. In the classical proof, one constructs an adversary $\mathcal{A}$ which uses $\mathcal{D}$ as a black-box subroutine, and breaks the hard-core of f. We use the exact same $\mathcal{A}$ now; in particular, we only need to invoke $\mathcal{D}$ on classical inputs and read out its (post-measurement) classical outputs (0 or 1). Of course, by virtue of needing to invoke $\mathcal{D}$, $\mathcal{A}$ itself will now be a QPT.

In slightly greater detail, we use a standard hybrid argument to give a "predictor" algorithm $\mathcal{A}$ that, for some index $i \leq t$, can predict the $i + 1^{\text{st}}$ bit of $G(U_n)$, given as input the first i bits of the output of G. $\mathcal{A}$ succeeds with non-negligible advantage over random, i.e., the probability over s that $\mathcal{A}(b(f^{t-1}(s))\ldots b(f^{t-i}(s)))$ outputs $b(f^{t-(i+1)}(s)$ is at least $1/2 + 1/p(n)$ where $p(n)$ is some polynomial. Crucially, since f implements a permutation over $\{0,1\}^n$, we have that $b(f^{i-1}(U_n))\ldots b(U_n)$ is distributed identically to $b(f^{t-1}(U_n))\ldots b(f^{t-i}(U_n))$. Therefore, given uniform x, and $y = f(x)$, we can use the output of the predictor, $\mathcal{A}(b(f^{i-1}(y))\ldots b(y)) = \mathcal{A}(b(f^i(x))\ldots b(f(x)))$ to predict $b(x)$ with non-negligible advantage, in violation of the security guarantee of the hard-core predicate. □

We now have all of the ingredients needed to describe a public-key scheme for encrypting quantum data.

Scheme 2 *Let f be a qTOWP, and let b and $G : \{0,1\}^n \to \{0,1\}^{2n}$ be a corresponding hard-core and qPRG, respectively. Let qTOWP-PKE be the following triple of algorithms:*

1. *((public, private) key-pair generation)* $\mathsf{KeyGen}(1^n)$: *output* $\mathcal{G}(1^n) = (i,t) \in \{0,1\}^n \times \{0,1\}^n$;
2. *(encryption with public key)* $\mathsf{Enc}_i(\rho)$:
   - *apply $\mathcal{S}(i)$ to select $d \in D_i$, and compute $r := G(d)$;*
   - *output $|f_i^{2n}(d)\rangle \langle f_i^{2n}(d)| \otimes P_r \rho P_r$*
3. *(decryption with private key)* $\mathsf{Dec}_t(|s\rangle \langle s| \otimes \sigma)$:
   - *for $j = 1, \ldots, 2n$, apply $b \circ (\mathcal{I})^j$ to (s,t); concatenate the resulting bits to get $u \in \{0,1\}^{2n}$;*
   - *output $P_u \sigma P_u$.*

It remains to show that this scheme is secure against chosen-plaintext attacks. We first set the following notation. Recall from Sect. 2.2 that a string r of $2n$ bits determines a Pauli group element $P_r \in U(2^n)$. Given an n-qubit register A, an arbitrary register B, and $\rho \in \mathfrak{D}(\mathcal{H}_A \otimes H_B)$, define $\mathbb{P}_{r;A}(\rho) := (P_r \otimes \mathbb{1}_B)\rho(P_r \otimes \mathbb{1}_B)$. Furthermore, $\mathsf{Enc}_i(\rho) = |f_i^{2n}(d)\rangle\langle f_i^{2n}(d)| \otimes P_r \rho P_r$ where $r = G(d)$. We can prove indistinguishability by extending the hybrid argument in the proof of Lemma 19 in a standard way. To sketch the argument, first recall that the "predictor" algorithm succeeds at predicting the $j + 1^{\text{st}}$ bit of $G(U_n)$ given as input the first j bits of the output of G. Now we also allow the predictor to read the bits of $f_i^{2n}(d)$. Success implies breaking the hard-core of f (which is used to define and ensure the security of the qPRG G). We conclude that the strings

$$i \; f_i^{2n}(d) \; G(s) \quad \text{and} \quad i \; f_i^{2n}(d) \; r'$$

are computationally indistinguishable for uniformly random s, r', and $(i,t) \leftarrow \mathcal{G}(1^n)$. Hence the states

$$|i\rangle \langle i| \otimes |f_i^{2n}(d)\rangle\langle f_i^{2n}(d)| \otimes \mathbb{P}_{G(s);M}(\rho_{ME}) \quad \text{and} \quad |i\rangle \langle i| \otimes |f_i^{2n}(d)\rangle\langle f_i^{2n}(d)| \otimes \mathbb{P}_{r';M}(\rho_{ME})$$

must also be computationally indistinguishable, since they are obtained by the application of a quantum algorithm to the previous pairs of strings, respectively, where $\rho_{ME} \leftarrow \mathcal{M}(i)$ (i is copied and $\mathcal{M}$ is applied to one of the copies, and then the quantum one-time pad is applied to the result with $G(s)$ or r', respectively). The right-hand side encryption above obviously satisfies IND-CPA, so we also have the computational indistinguishability of

$$|i\rangle\langle i| \otimes |f_i^{2n}(d)\rangle\langle f_i^{2n}(d)| \otimes \mathbb{P}_{r';M}(\rho_{ME}) \qquad \text{and}$$
$$|i\rangle\langle i| \otimes |f_i^{2n}(d)\rangle\langle f_i^{2n}(d)| \otimes \mathbb{P}_{r';M}(|0\rangle\langle 0|_M \otimes \rho_E).$$

By transitivity of computational indistinguishability, we conclude that

$$|i\rangle\langle i| \otimes |f_i^{2n}(d)\rangle\langle f_i^{2n}(d)| \otimes \mathbb{P}_{G(s);M}(\rho_{ME}) \qquad \text{and}$$
$$|i\rangle\langle i| \otimes |f_i^{2n}(d)\rangle\langle f_i^{2n}(d)| \otimes \mathbb{P}_{G(s);M}(|0\rangle\langle 0|_M \otimes \rho_E)$$

are indistinguishable, which completes the proof of Theorem 3.   □

6   Conclusion

We have defined semantic security for the encryption of quantum data and shown its equivalence with indistinguishability; these results are given in the uniform model for quantum computations, but as is standard classically (see Chap. 5 of Goldreich's text [28]), these definitions can be adjusted to the case of "non-uniform" (but still polynomial-time) adversaries, whose messages need not be generated efficiently. While the proof is somewhat different, the equivalence of IND and SEM still hold in this case. The constructions of encryption schemes (IND-CCA1 symmetric-key and IND-CPA public-key) presented above carry over as well, except that we now require primitives (qPRFs and qTOWPs, respectively) which are secure against non-uniform adversaries.

6.1   Extensions and Future Work

We now briefly discuss some possible extensions of the above results. In most cases, these extensions are a matter of modifying our definitions and proofs in a fairly straightforward way. We leave the other cases as interesting open problems.

– Our definitions of IND-CPA, IND-CCA1 and SEM assume that all of the relevant messages are generated in polynomial time. In other words, our results assume "uniform" adversaries. As is standard classically (see Chap. 5 of Goldreich's text [28]), these definitions can be adjusted to the case of "non-uniform" (but still polynomial-time) adversaries, whose messages need not be generated efficiently. While the proof is of course somewhat different, the equivalence of IND and SEM still hold in this case. The encryption schemes (IND-CCA1 symmetric-key and IND-CPA public-key) presented above carry over as well, except that we now require primitives (qPRFs and qTOWPs, respectively) which are secure against non-uniform adversarics.

- Our symmetric-key encryption scheme assumes that the decryption algorithm measures a portion of the input in order to recover a classical randomness string, prior to decrypting. One might find this requirement suspicious, e.g., if a perfect measurement device is too much to assume. This requirement can be removed, but we then need to assume that the relevant primitives (OWFs and qPRFs) are secure against superposition queries. This can also be achieved (see [50]).

- One outstanding open problem is to define and construct schemes for CCA2 (adaptive chosen ciphertext attack) security in the case of the encryption of quantum states. Classically, CCA2 security is defined as CCA1, with the further property that the adversary is allowed to query the decryption oracle even *after* the challenge query, *provided* he does not query about the challenge ciphertext itself (otherwise the challenger aborts the game.) The obvious way to define this in the quantum world is to require that every decryption query performed by the adversary after the challenge query is 'very different' from the challenge query itself (e.g., it is orthogonal to the challenge ciphertext.) But the problem here is that this condition might be impossible for the challenger to check: for example, the adversary might embed in a decryption query a component non-orthogonal to the challenge query, but with such a small amplitude that the challenger cannot detect it with high probability. Even if it is unclear whether this issue could raise problems in any actual reduction, it would be anyway a striking asymmetry to the classical case, because there would be no way for the challenger to check that the adversary actually fulfilled the required condition. Hence, giving a satisfactory definition for CCA2 security in the quantum world remains an interesting open problem.

Acknowledgements. G. A. was supported by a Sapere Aude grant of the Danish Council for Independent Research, the ERC Starting Grant "QMULT" and the CHIST-ERA project "CQC". A. B. was supported by Canada's NSERC. B. F. was supported by the Department of Defense. T. G. was supported by the German Federal Ministry of Education and Research (BMBF) within CRISP and CROSSING. C. S. was supported by a 7th framework EU SIQS and a NWO VIDI grant. M. S. was supported by the Ontario Graduate Scholarship Program. T. G. and C. S. would like to thank COST Action IC1306 for networking support. A. B., G. A., T. G., and C. S. would like to thank the organizers of the Dagstuhl Seminar 15371 "Quantum Cryptanalysis" for providing networking and useful interactions and support during the writing of this paper.

References

1. Aaronson, S.: Quantum copy-protection and quantum money. In: 24th Annual IEEE Conference on Computational Complexity, CCC 2009, pp. 229–242. IEEE (2009)
2. Aaronson, S., Christiano, P.: Quantum money from hidden subspaces. In: Proceedings of the Forty-Fourth Annual ACM Symposium on Theory of Computing, pp. 41–60. ACM (2012)

3. Adcock, M., Cleve, R.: A quantum Goldreich-Levin theorem with cryptographic applications. In: Alt, H., Ferreira, A. (eds.) STACS 2002. LNCS, vol. 2285, pp. 323–334. Springer, Heidelberg (2002). doi:10.1007/3-540-45841-7_26

4. Aharonov, D., Kitaev, A., Nisan, N.: Quantum circuits with mixed states. In: Proceedings of the Thirtieth Annual ACM Symposium on Theory of computing, pp. 20–30. ACM (1998)

5. Alagic, G., Broadbent, A., Fefferman, B., Gagliardoni, T., Schaffner, C., Jules, M.S.: Computational security of quantum encryption (2016). http://arxiv.org/abs/1602.01441

6. Alléaume, R., Branciard, C., Bouda, J., Debuisschert, T., Dianati, M., Gisin, N., Godfrey, M., Grangier, P., Länger, T., Lütkenhaus, N., Monyk, C., Painchault, P., Peev, M., Poppe, A., Pornin, T., Rarity, J., Renner, R., Ribordy, G., Riguidel, M., Salvail, L., Shields, A., Weinfurter, H., Zeilinger, A.: Using quantum key distribution for cryptographic purposes: a survey. Theoret. Comput. Sci. **560**, 62–81 (2014)

7. Ambainis, A., Mosca, M., Tapp, A., de Wolf, R.: Private quantum channels. In: 41st Annual Symposium on Foundations of Computer Science, Proceedings, pp. 547–553 (2000)

8. Ben-Or, M., Crépeau, C., Gottesman, D., Hassidim, A., Smith, A.: Secure multiparty quantum computation with (only) a strict honest majority. In: 47th Annual IEEE Symposium on Foundations of Computer Science, FOCS 2006, pp. 249–260. IEEE (2006)

9. Bennett, C., Brassard, G.: Quantum cryptography: public key distribution and coin tossing. In: Proceedings of the International Conference on Computers, Systems, and Signal Processing, pp. 175–179 (1984)

10. Bernstein, D.J., Buchmann, J., Dahmen, E. (eds.): Post-Quantum Cryptography. Springer, Berlin (2009)

11. Boneh, D., Dagdelen, Ö., Fischlin, M., Lehmann, A., Schaffner, C., Zhandry, M.: Random oracles in a quantum world. In: Lee, D.H., Wang, X. (eds.) ASIACRYPT 2011. LNCS, vol. 7073, pp. 41–69. Springer, Heidelberg (2011). doi:10.1007/978-3-642-25385-0_3

12. Boneh, D., Zhandry, M.: Secure signatures and chosen ciphertext security in a quantum computing world. In: Canetti, R., Garay, J.A. (eds.) CRYPTO 2013. LNCS, vol. 8043, pp. 361–379. Springer, Heidelberg (2013). doi:10.1007/978-3-642-40084-1_21

13. Oscar Boykin, P., Roychowdhury, V.: Optimal encryption of quantum bits. Phys. Rev. A **67**(4), 042317 (2003)

14. Broadbent, A.: Delegating private quantum computations. Can. J. Phys. **93**(9), 941–946 (2015)

15. Broadbent, A., Fitzsimons, J., Kashefi, E.: Universal blind quantum computation. In: 50th Annual IEEE Symposium on Foundations of Computer Science, FOCS 2009, pp. 517–526. IEEE (2009)

16. Broadbent, A., Gutoski, G., Stebila, D.: Quantum one-time programs. In: Canetti, R., Garay, J.A. (eds.) CRYPTO 2013. LNCS, vol. 8043, pp. 344–360. Springer, Heidelberg (2013). doi:10.1007/978-3-642-40084-1_20

17. Broadbent, A., Jeffery, S.: Quantum homomorphic encryption for circuits of low T-gate complexity. In: CRYPTO 2015, pp. 609–629 (2015). doi:10.1007/978-3-662-48000-7_30

18. Broadbent, A., Schaffner, C.: Quantum cryptography beyond quantum key distribution. Des. Codes Crypt. **78**, 351–382 (2016)

19. Desrosiers, S.P.: Entropic security in quantum cryptography. Quantum Inf. Process. **8**(4), 331–345 (2009)
20. Diffie, W., Hellman, M.: Quantum entropic security and approximate quantum encryption. IEEE Trans. Inf. Theory **56**(7), 3455–3464 (2010)
21. Diffie, W., Hellman, M.E.: New directions in cryptography. IEEE Trans. Inf. Theory **22**(6), 644–654 (1976)
22. Dupuis, F., Nielsen, J.B., Salvail, L.: Secure two-party quantum evaluation of unitaries against specious adversaries. In: Rabin, T. (ed.) CRYPTO 2010. LNCS, vol. 6223, pp. 685–706. Springer, Heidelberg (2010). doi:10.1007/978-3-642-14623-7_37
23. Dupuis, F., Nielsen, J.B., Salvail, L.: Actively secure two-party evaluation of any quantum operation. In: Safavi-Naini, R., Canetti, R. (eds.) CRYPTO 2012. LNCS, vol. 7417, pp. 794–811. Springer, Heidelberg (2012). doi:10.1007/978-3-642-32009-5_46
24. Fehr, S., Katz, J., Song, F., Zhou, H.-S., Zikas, V.: Feasibility and completeness of cryptographic tasks in the quantum world. In: Kushilevitz, E., Malkin, T. (eds.) TCC 2016. LNCS, vol. 9563, pp. 281–296. Springer, Heidelberg (2013). doi:10.1007/978-3-642-36594-2_16
25. Gagliardoni, T., Hülsing, A., Schaffner, C.: Semantic security and indistinguishability in the quantum world. In: Advances in Cryptology - CRYPTO 2016 - 36th Annual International Cryptology Conference, Santa Barbara, CA, USA, August 14–18, 2016, Proceedings, Part III, pp. 60–89 (2016). http://dblp.uni-trier.de/rec/bibtex/conf/crypto/GagliardoniHS16
26. Gentry, C., Peikert, C., Vaikuntanathan, V.: Trapdoors for hard lattices and new cryptographic constructions. In: Proceedings of the Fortieth Annual ACM Symposium on Theory of Computing, STOC 2008, New York, NY, USA, pp. 197–206. ACM (2008)
27. Goldreich, O., Levin, L.A.: A hard-core predicate for all one-way functions. In: Proceedings of the Twenty-First Annual ACM Symposium on Theory of Computing, STOC 1989, New York, NY, USA, pp. 25–32. ACM (1989)
28. Goldreich, O.: Foundations of Cryptography. Basic Applications, vol. 2. Cambridge University Press, Cambridge (2004)
29. Goldreich, O., Goldwasser, S., Micali, S.: How to construct random functions. J. ACM **33**(4), 792–807 (1986)
30. Goldwasser, S., Micali, S.: Probabilistic encryption. J. Comput. Syst. Sci. **28**(2), 270–299 (1984)
31. Håstad, J., Impagliazzo, R., Levin, L.A., Luby, M.: A pseudorandom generator from any one-way function. SIAM J. Comput. **28**, 1364–1396 (1999)
32. Hayden, P., Leung, D., Shor, P.W., Winter, A.: Randomizing quantum states: constructions and applications. Commun. Math. Phys. **250**(2), 371–391 (2004)
33. Kashefi, E., Kerenidis, I.: Statistical zero knowledge and quantum one-way functions. Theoret. Comput. Sci. **378**(1), 101–116 (2007)
34. Koshiba, T.: Security notions for quantum public-key cryptography. IEICE Trans. Fundam. Electron. Commun. Comput. Sci. **J90–A**(5), 367–375 (2007)
35. Leung, D.W.: Quantum Vernam cipher. Quantum Inf. Comput. **2**(1), 14–34 (2002)
36. Moore, C., Russell, A., Vazirani, U.: A classical one-way function to confound quantum adversaries. eprint arXiv:quant-ph/0701115, January 2007
37. Mosca, M., Stebila, D.: Quantum coins. Error-Correcting Codes Finite Geometries Crypt. **523**, 35–47 (2010)
38. Okamoto, T., Tanaka, K., Uchiyama, S.: Quantum public-key cryptosystems. In: Bellare, M. (ed.) CRYPTO 2000. LNCS, vol. 1880, pp. 147–165. Springer, Heidelberg (2000). doi:10.1007/3-540-44598-6_9

39. Peikert, C., Waters, B.: Lossy trapdoor functions and their applications. In: Proceedings of the Fortieth Annual ACM Symposium on Theory of Computing, STOC 2008, New York, NY, USA, pp. 187–196. ACM (2008)
40. Shannon, C.E.: Communication theory of secrecy systems. Bell Syst. Tech. J. **28**(4), 656–715 (1949)
41. Shor, P.W.: Algorithms for quantum computation: discrete logarithms and factoring. In: FOCS 1994, pp. 124–134. IEEE Computer Society Press (1994)
42. Song, F.: A note on quantum security for post-quantum cryptography. In: Mosca, M. (ed.) PQCrypto 2014. LNCS, vol. 8772, pp. 246–265. Springer, Heidelberg (2014). doi:10.1007/978-3-319-11659-4_15
43. Unruh, D.: Universally composable quantum multi-party computation. In: Gilbert, H. (ed.) EUROCRYPT 2010. LNCS, vol. 6110, pp. 486–505. Springer, Heidelberg (2010). doi:10.1007/978-3-642-13190-5_25
44. Unruh, D.: Revocable quantum timed-release encryption. In: Nguyen, P.Q., Oswald, E. (eds.) EUROCRYPT 2014. LNCS, vol. 8441, pp. 129–146. Springer, Heidelberg (2014). doi:10.1007/978-3-642-55220-5_8
45. Unruh, D.: Non-interactive zero-knowledge proofs in the quantum random oracle model. In: Oswald, E., Fischlin, M. (eds.) EUROCRYPT 2015. LNCS, vol. 9057, pp. 755–784. Springer, Heidelberg (2015). doi:10.1007/978-3-662-46803-6_25
46. Velema, M.: Classical encryption and authentication under quantum attacks. Master's thesis, Master of Logic, University of Amsterdam (2013). http://arxiv.org/abs/1307.3753
47. Wiesner, S.: Conjugate coding. ACM Sigact News **15**(1), 78–88 (1983)
48. Wootters, W.K., Zurek, W.H.: A single quantum cannot be cloned. Nature **299**(5886), 802–803 (1982)
49. Xiang, C., Yang, L.: Indistinguishability, semantic security for quantum encryption scheme. In: Proceedings of SPIE, vol. 8554, p. 85540G–8 (2012)
50. Zhandry, M.: How to construct quantum random functions. In: FOCS 2012, pp. 679–687. IEEE (2012)

Efficient Simulation for Quantum Message Authentication

Anne Broadbent$^{(\boxtimes)}$ and Evelyn Wainewright

Department of Mathematics and Statistics, University of Ottawa, Ottawa, Canada
{abroadbe,ewain031}@uottawa.ca

Abstract. Quantum message authentication codes are families of keyed encoding and decoding maps that enable the detection of tampering on encoded quantum data. Here, we study a new class of simulators for quantum message authentication schemes, and show how they are applied in the context of two codes: the *Clifford* and the *trap* code. Our results show for the first time that these codes admit an *efficient simulation* (assuming that the adversary is efficient). Such efficient simulation is typically crucial in order to establish a composable notion of security.

1 Introduction

Quantum cryptography is the study of the security of information processing in a quantum world. While quantum key distribution [4] is today the most widely successful quantum cryptographic technology [7,12], quantum information effectively re-defines many cryptographic paradigms [6]. Among these is the need for new definitions and protocols for cryptographic tasks that operate on quantum data, such as quantum secret sharing [9] and quantum multi-party computation [3]. Another fundamental task is quantum message authentication.

Quantum message authentication schemes, introduced in [2], are families of keyed encoding and decoding maps which allow for the detection of tampering on encoded quantum data. These codes were originally given in a very efficient form, based on *purity testing* [2], and were shown to also satisfy a composable security notion [14].

Further quantum message authentication schemes have been proposed, including the *signed polynomial code*[1,3], the trap code [5] and the *Clifford* code [1,11]. These schemes have a nice algebraic form, which makes them particularly easy to study. Perhaps the main reason for interest in these schemes is that they have a sufficient amount of "structure" to enable evaluation of quantum gates over the encoded data (this technique is called *quantum computing on authenticated data (QCAD)*). This has lead to protocols for multi-party quantum computation [3], quantum one-time programs [5] and the verification of quantum computations [1].

The security of quantum message authentication schemes is typically defined in terms of the existence of a *simulator* that, given access only to the ideal functionality for quantum message authentication (which is a virtual device that

© Springer International Publishing AG 2016
A.C.A. Nascimento and P. Barreto (Eds.): ICITS 2016, LNCS 10015, pp. 72–91, 2016.
DOI: 10.1007/978-3-319-49175-2_4

either transmits the quantum data directly and outputs "accept", or replaces it with a dummy state and outputs "reject"), is able to emulate the behaviour of the adversary so that the real-world protocol (involving the adversary) is statistically indistinguishable from the ideal-world protocol (involving the simulator). This type of definition fits in the quantum Universal Composability (UC)[8,16] framework, as long as we add a further condition: if the adversary runs in polynomial time, so must the simulator (an *efficient* simulation). Until now, direct efficient simulations were known only for the purity-testing based codes [2].

In this work, we show a new family of efficient simulators for quantum message authentication schemes. The main idea is that the simulator replaces the entire codeword by half-EPR pairs (keeping the remaining half to itself), and runs the adversary on these entangled states (as well as the reference system for the original input). After the attack is applied, the simulator performs Bell basis measurements in order to verify the integrity of the EPR pairs. So long as enough EPR pairs are found to be intact, the simulator makes the ideal functionality "accept"; otherwise, it makes it "reject". It is well-known that this Bell basis measurement will detect any non-identity Pauli attack—given the structure of the codes that we analyze, we show that this is sufficient.

We apply this type of simulator to the Clifford and trap quantum message authentication codes. We note that the Clifford code was previously proven secure according to an algebraic definition, without an efficient simulation [1,11], and that the trap scheme was proven secure according to a simulator for a more elaborate ideal functionality for *quantum one-time programs* [5]. We thus establish for the first time efficient simulators for these codes (note, however, that we make extensive use of the algebraic tools developed in these prior works, and that we achieve the same security bounds). We also note that the idea of using EPR-pair testing as a proof technique for quantum message authentication has appeared in [2], where a more elaborate type of testing (called *purity testing*) is used.

Roadmap. The remainder of the paper is structured as follows. In Sect. 2, we give some details on the standard notation and well-known facts that are used throughout. In Sect. 3, we formally define quantum message authentication in terms of correctness and security. Section 4 gives the Clifford and trap schemes, while in Sect. 5 we show security of the schemes.

2 Preliminaries

Here, we present basic notation (Sect. 2.1) and well-known facts about the Pauli (Sect. 2.2) and Clifford (Sect. 2.3) groups.

2.1 Basic Notation

We assume the reader is familiar with the basics of quantum information [15], but nevertheless give a quick review of the most relevant notation in this section. We will use the density operator formalism to represent quantum states. Density matrices are represented with a greek letter, typically ρ. The subscripts of the quantum states indicate which spaces (registers) the states reside in. We therefore represent the density operator for the state in the M register as ρ_M.

The *trace norm* of a state, ρ, denoted $\|\rho\|_1$, is defined as $\|\rho\|_1 = tr[\sqrt{\rho^\dagger \rho}]$. The *trace distance* between two states ρ and σ, denoted $D(\rho, \sigma)$, is defined as $D(\rho, \sigma) = \frac{1}{2}\|\rho - \sigma\|_1$. The trace distance is a measure of distinguishability between the two states ρ and σ. The trace distance is equal to 0 if and only if ρ and σ are the same state (and therefore indistinguishable) and the trace distance is equal to 1 if and only if ρ and σ are orthogonal (and therefore perfectly distinguishable). The trace norm, and therefore the trace distance, satisfies the triangle inequality: $\|\rho + \sigma\|_1 \leq \|\rho\|_1 + \|\sigma\|_1$.

Let $\mathcal{B}(\mathcal{H})$ be the space of bounded linear operators acting on a Hilbert space, $\mathcal{H}$. Given $\mathcal{A} \subseteq \mathcal{B}(\mathcal{H}_1)$ and $\mathcal{B} \subseteq \mathcal{B}(\mathcal{H}_2)$ then given a linear map T from $\mathcal{A} \rightarrow \mathcal{B}$, T is called *positive* if $T(A) \geq 0$ for all positive $A \in \mathcal{A}$. T is a *completely positive* map, (*CP* map), if $T \otimes Id : \mathcal{A} \otimes \mathcal{B} \rightarrow \mathcal{B}(\mathcal{H}_1) \otimes \mathcal{B}(\mathbb{C}^n)$ is positive for all $n \in \mathbb{N}$. In this case, Id is the identity map on $\mathcal{B}(\mathbb{C}^n)$ and $\mathbb{C}^n$ is isomorphic to a complex Hilbert space of dimension n. A map, T, is *trace preserving* if $tr(T(\rho)) = tr(\rho)$. T is a *quantum channel* if it is a *completely positive* and *trace preserving* map (*CPTP* map). A family of quantum maps is *polynomial-time* if they can be written as a polynomial-time uniform family of quantum circuits. A quantum state is *polynomial-time generated* if it given as the output of a polynomial-time quantum map (which takes as input the all-zeros state) [17].

A permutation map, denoted throughout by π, is a unitary operation that acts on n qubits and permutes the order of the n qubits. This can equivalently be seen as a permutation, σ, of the indices of the qubits, where π would take the ith qubit to the $\sigma(i)^{th}$ position. Permutation maps are orthogonal, real valued matrices so $\pi^{-1} = \pi^\dagger$. We use Π_n to denote the set of all permutation maps on n qubits.

We denote a two-qubit maximally entangled pure state as $|\Phi^+\rangle = \frac{1}{\sqrt{2}}(|00\rangle + |11\rangle)$. This is one of four Bell states. The other three Bell states are also maximally entangled pure states, $|\Phi^-\rangle = \frac{1}{\sqrt{2}}(|00\rangle - |11\rangle)$, $|\Psi^+\rangle = \frac{1}{\sqrt{2}}(|01\rangle + |10\rangle)$, and $|\Psi^-\rangle = \frac{1}{\sqrt{2}}(|01\rangle - |10\rangle)$. The four Bell states are orthogonal and form a basis for two-qubit states. The four Bell states are therefore perfectly distinguishable and so we can perform a projective measurement into the Bell basis and determine which of the four Bell states we have. This is called a *Bell basis measurement*.

An $[[n, 1, d]]$-code is a quantum error correcting code that encodes one logical qubit into n qubits and has distance d; if $d = 2t + 1$, the code can correct up to t bit or phase flips. We assume that the decoding map can always be applied, but if more than t errors are present, it is not guaranteed to decode to the original input.

2.2 Pauli Matrices

The single-qubit *Pauli matrices* are given by:

$$I = \begin{bmatrix} 1 & 0 \\ 0 & 1 \end{bmatrix}, X = \begin{bmatrix} 0 & 1 \\ 1 & 0 \end{bmatrix}, Z = \begin{bmatrix} 1 & 0 \\ 0 & -1 \end{bmatrix}, \text{ and } Y = iXZ = \begin{bmatrix} 0 & -i \\ i & 0 \end{bmatrix}. \tag{1}$$

Recall that if we allow complex coefficients, the any single-qubit gate can be written as a linear combination of the four single-qubit Pauli matrices.

An n-qubit Pauli matrix is given by the n-fold tensor product of single-qubit Paulis. We denote the set of all n-qubit Pauli matrices by $\mathbb{P}_n$, where $|\mathbb{P}_n| = 4^n$. Any n-qubit unitary operator, U, can also be written as a linear combination of n-qubit Paulis, again allowing for complex coefficients. This gives $U = \sum_{P \in \mathbb{P}_n} \alpha_P P$, with $\sum_{P \in \mathbb{P}_n} |\alpha_P|^2 = 1$, since U is unitary. This is called the *Pauli decomposition* of a unitary quantum operation.

The *Pauli weight* of an n-qubit Pauli, denoted $\omega(P)$, is the number of non-identity Paulis in the n-fold tensor product. We will also define sets of Paulis composed only of specific Pauli matrices, such as $\{I, X\}^{\otimes n}$ which is the set of all n-qubit Paulis composed of only I and X Paulis, or $\{I, Z\}^{\otimes n}$ which is the set of all n-qubit Paulis composed of only I and Z Paulis. Finally, Paulis are self-inverses, so $P = P^{-1} = P^\dagger$.

The following lemma, called the *Pauli Twirl* [10], shows how we can greatly simplify expressions that involve the twirling of an operation by the Pauli matrices:

Lemma 2.1 (Pauli Twirl). *Let P, P' be Pauli operators. Then for any ρ it holds that:*

$$\frac{1}{|\mathbb{P}_n|} \sum_{Q \in \mathbb{P}_n} Q^\dagger P Q \rho Q^\dagger P'^\dagger Q = \begin{cases} 0, & P \neq P' \\ P \rho P^\dagger, & otherwise. \end{cases}$$

2.3   Clifford Group

The *Clifford group*, $\mathcal{C}_n$, on n qubits are unitaries that map Pauli matrices to Pauli matrices (up to a phase of ± 1 or $\pm i$). Specifically, if $P \in \mathbb{P}_n$, then for all $C \in \mathcal{C}_n$, $\alpha C P C^\dagger \in \mathbb{P}_n$, for some $\alpha \in \{\pm 1, \pm i\}$. Not only do Cliffords map Paulis to Paulis, but they do so with a uniform distribution [1]:

Lemma 2.2 (Clifford Randomization). *Let P be a non-identity Pauli operator. Applying a random Clifford operator (by conjugation) maps it to a Pauli operator chosen uniformly over all non-identity Pauli operators. More formally, for every $P, Q \in \mathbb{P}_n \setminus \{\mathbb{I}\}$, it holds that:*

$$\left| \{ C \in \mathcal{C}_n | C^\dagger P C = Q \} \right| = \frac{|\mathcal{C}_n|}{|\mathbb{P}_n| - 1}.$$

We also state a lemma that is analogous to the Pauli twirl, the *Clifford Twirl* [10].

Lemma 2.3 (Clifford Twirl). *Let $P \neq P'$ be Pauli operators. For any ρ it holds that:*

$$\sum_{C \in \mathcal{C}_n} C^\dagger P C \rho C^\dagger P' C = 0.$$

Finally, we note that sampling a uniformly random Clifford can be done efficiently [13].

3 Quantum Message Authentication

Following [11], we define a *quantum message authentication scheme* as a pair of encoding and decoding maps that satisfy the following:

Definition 1 (Quantum Message Authentication Scheme). A *quantum message authentication scheme* is a polynomial-time set of encoding and decoding channels $\{(\mathcal{E}_k^{M \to C}, \mathcal{D}_k^{C \to MF}) \mid k \in \mathcal{K}\}$, where $\mathcal{K}$ is the set of possible keys, M is the input system, C is the encoded system, and F is a flag system that is spanned by two orthogonal states: $|\mathrm{acc}\rangle$ and $|\mathrm{rej}\rangle$, such that for all ρ_M, $(\mathcal{D}_k \circ \mathcal{E}_k)(\rho_M) = \rho_M \otimes |\mathrm{acc}\rangle \langle \mathrm{acc}|$.

In order to define security for a quantum message authentication scheme, we first consider a reference system R, so that the input can be described as ρ_{MR} and we can furthermore assume that the system consisting of the encoded message, together with the reference system, undergoes a unitary adversarial attack U_{CR}. For a fixed key, k, we thus define the *real-world* channel as:

$$\mathcal{E}_k^{MR \to MRF} : \rho_{MR} \mapsto (\mathcal{D}_k \otimes \mathbb{I}_R)(U_{CR}(\mathcal{E}_k \otimes \mathbb{I}_R)(\rho_{MR})U_{CR}^\dagger), \tag{2}$$

where $\mathbb{I}_R$ is the identity map on the reference system, R. From now on, we will not include the identity maps, since it will be clear from context which system undergoes a linear map and which one does not.

Security is given in terms of the existence of a *simulator*, which has access only to the ideal functionality. This ideal functionality either accepts (and leaves the message register M intact), or rejects (and outputs a fixed state Ω_M); the simulator can interact with the ideal functionality by selecting *accept* or *reject*. In both cases, the simulator can also alter the reference system R. This ideal-world process is modeled by the quantum channel $\mathscr{F}$, called the *ideal* channel, where for each attack, U_{CR}, there exists two CP maps $\mathscr{U}^{acc}$ and $\mathscr{U}^{rej}$ acting only on the reference system R such that $\mathscr{U}^{acc} + \mathscr{U}^{rej} = \mathbb{1}$:

$$\mathscr{F}^{MR \to MRF} : \rho_{MR} \to (\mathbb{1}_M \otimes \mathscr{U}_R^{acc})\rho_{MR} \otimes |\mathrm{acc}\rangle \langle \mathrm{acc}|$$
$$+ tr_M((\mathbb{1}_M \otimes \mathscr{U}_R^{rej})\rho_{MR})\Omega_M \otimes |\mathrm{rej}\rangle \langle \mathrm{rej}| . \tag{3}$$

Definition 2 (Security of Quantum Message Authentication). Let $\{(\mathcal{E}_k^{M \to C}, \mathcal{D}_k^{C \to MF}) \mid k \in \mathcal{K}\}$ be a quantum message authentication scheme, with keys k chosen from $\mathcal{K}$. Then the scheme is ϵ-secure if for all attacks, there exists a simulator such that:

$$D\left(\frac{1}{|\mathcal{K}|} \sum_{k \in \mathcal{K}} \mathcal{E}_k(\rho_{MR}), \mathscr{F}(\rho_{MR})\right) \leq \epsilon, \forall \rho_{MR}. \tag{4}$$

Furthermore, we require that if $\mathcal{E}_k$ is polynomial-time in the size of the input register M, then $\mathscr{F}$ is also polynomial-time in the size of the input register, M.

We note that this definition is similar to the definition in [11]; however we require a *polynomial-time simulation* whenever the attack is polynomial-time.

This does not limit the proof to polynomial-time attacks, but merely restricts the simulator to have at most the complexity of the attack. This condition being satisfied is typically a crucial ingredient in order for the composability to carry through [16].

4 Quantum Message Authentication Schemes

Here, we present two quantum message authentication schemes, the *Clifford* code (Sect. 4.1) and the *trap* code (Sect. 4.2). The two encoding procedures both proceed by appending trap qubits (in a fixed state) to the message register, and then *twirling* by a Clifford (for the Clifford code) or a Pauli (for the trap code). The trap code also has a permutation in addition to the Pauli twirl acting on the message register. Decoding simply consists of undoing the permutation in the trap code and then in both cases measuring the traps to check for any sign of tampering. In the case of the Clifford code, only one set of traps (all in the same state) is needed because the Clifford twirl breaks any Pauli attack into a uniform mixture of Paulis which is detected on the traps with high probability. The trap code, however, relies on two sets of traps (in two different states) with both a Pauli twirl and a permutation of the message and trap qubits. Furthermore, the trap scheme requires that we first *encode* the input message into an error correcting code (essentially, this is because the Pauli twirl is not as powerful as the Clifford twirl and will catch only high-weight Pauli attacks with the error correcting code taking care of the low-weight ones).

4.1 The Clifford Code

We define a message authentication scheme using a Clifford encryption as follows:

1. The encoding, $\mathcal{E}_k^{M \to C}$, takes as input an n-qubit message in the M system; it appends an additional d-qubit trap register in the state $|0\rangle \langle 0|^{\otimes d}$. A uniformly random Clifford is then applied to the resulting $n+d$-qubit register, according to the key, k. The output register is called C.
   Mathematically, the encoding, $\mathcal{E}_k^{M \to C}$, indexed by a secret key, k, on input ρ_M (where C_k the kth Clifford) is given by:

$$\mathcal{E}_k : \rho_M \mapsto C_k(\rho_M \otimes |0\rangle \langle 0|^{\otimes d})C_k^{\dagger}. \tag{5}$$

2. The decoding, $\mathcal{D}_k^{C \to MF}$, takes the C register and applies the inverse Clifford, according to the key, k. The last d qubits are then measured in the computational basis. If this measurement returns $|0\rangle \langle 0|^{\otimes d}$ then an additional qubit $|\text{acc}\rangle \langle \text{acc}|$ is appended in the flag system, F. If the measurements return anything else, then the remaining system, M, is traced out and replaced with a fixed n-qubit state, Ω_M, and an additional qubit, $|\text{rej}\rangle \langle \text{rej}|$, is appended in the flag system.
   Mathematically, the decoding, $\mathcal{D}_k^{C \to MF}$, also indexed by the secret key, k, is given by:

$$\mathcal{D}_k : \rho_C \mapsto tr_0(\mathcal{P}_{acc}C_k^\dagger(\rho_C)C_k\mathcal{P}_{acc}^\dagger) \otimes |acc\rangle \langle acc|$$
$$+tr_{M,0}(\mathcal{P}_{rej}C_k^\dagger(\rho_C)C_k\mathcal{P}_{rej}^\dagger)\Omega_M \otimes |rej\rangle \langle rej|, \tag{6}$$

where $\mathcal{P}_{acc} = \mathbb{1}^{\otimes n} \otimes |0\rangle \langle 0|^{\otimes d}$ and $\mathcal{P}_{rej} = \mathbb{1}^{\otimes(n+d)} - \mathcal{P}_{acc}$ are measurement projectors representing the trap qubits being in their initial states or altered, respectively. Finally, tr_0 refers to the trace over the d trap qubits.

4.2 The Trap Code

We define a trap code message authentication scheme as follows:

1. The encoding, $\mathcal{E}_k^{M \to C}$, takes as input ρ_M and applies an $[[n, 1, d]]$-error correcting code to the single-qubit M register, which will correct up to t errors (where $d = 2t + 1$). It then appends two additional n-qubit trap registers, the first in the state $|0\rangle \langle 0|^{\otimes n}$ and the second in the state $|+\rangle \langle +|^{\otimes n}$. The resulting $3n$-qubit register is then permuted and a Pauli encryption is applied, according to the key, k. The resulting register is called C.
   Mathematically the encoding, $\mathcal{E}_k^{M \to C}$, indexed by a two-part secret key $k = (k_1, k_2)$ is given by:

$$\mathcal{E}_k : \rho_M \mapsto P_{k_2}\pi_{k_1}(Enc_M(\rho_M) \otimes |0\rangle \langle 0|^{\otimes n} \otimes |+\rangle \langle +|^{\otimes n})\pi_{k_1}^\dagger P_{k_2}, \tag{7}$$

   where $Enc_M(\rho_M)$ represents the input state after the error correcting code has been applied to the M system, π_{k_1} is the k_1^{th} permutation and P_{k_2} is the k_2^{th} Pauli matrix.
   We note that we use the error-correcting properties of the code only (it is sufficient in our context to simply correct low-weight Paulis on the message, as opposed detecting them and rejecting).
2. The decoding, $\mathcal{D}_k^{C \to MF}$, takes the C register and applies the inverse Pauli and then the inverse permutation according to the key, k. The last n qubits are then measured in the Hadamard basis and the second last n qubits are measured in the computational basis. If these two measurements return $|+\rangle \langle +|^{\otimes n}$ and $|0\rangle \langle 0|^{\otimes n}$ respectively, then an additional qubit $|acc\rangle \langle acc|$ is appended in the flag system F and the resulting M register is decoded (according to the error correcting code applied in the encoding). If the measurements return anything else, then the remaining system M is traced out and replaced with a fixed single-qubit state Ω_M and an additional qubit, $|rej\rangle \langle rej|$, is appended in the flag system.
   Define $\mathbb{P}_\mathcal{E} = \{P \otimes R \otimes Q | P \in \mathbb{P}_n, R \in \{I, Z\}^{\otimes n}, Q \in \{I, X\}^{\otimes n}\}$. Then define the measurement projector corresponding to the protocol accepting as $\mathcal{P}_{acc} = \mathbb{1}^{\otimes n} \otimes |0\rangle \langle 0|^{\otimes n} \otimes |+\rangle \langle +|^{\otimes n}$. The accepted states are then the states that can be achieved by applying any $P \in \mathbb{P}_\mathcal{E}$ to $\rho_M \otimes |0\rangle \langle 0|^{\otimes n} \otimes |+\rangle \langle +|^{\otimes n}$. We define $\mathcal{P}_{rej} = \mathbb{1}^{\otimes 3n} - \mathcal{P}_{acc}$, the measurement projector corresponding to the protocol rejecting, where the states achieved by applying any $P \in \mathbb{P}_{3n} \backslash \mathbb{P}_\mathcal{E}$ to $Enc_M(\rho_M) \otimes |0\rangle \langle 0|^{\otimes n} \otimes |+\rangle \langle +|^{\otimes n}$ are rejected.
   Mathematically, the decoding, $\mathcal{D}_k^{C \to MF}$, also indexed by the two-part secret key, k, is given by:

$$\mathcal{D}_k : \rho_C \mapsto Dec_M tr_{0,+}(\mathcal{P}_{acc}\pi_{k_1}^\dagger P_{k_2}(\rho_C)P_{k_2}\pi_{k_1}\mathcal{P}_{acc}^\dagger) \otimes |\text{acc}\rangle\langle\text{acc}|$$

$$+tr_{M,0,+}(\mathcal{P}_{rej}\pi_{k_1}^\dagger P_{k_2}(\rho_C)P_{k_2}\pi_{k_1}\mathcal{P}_{acc}^\dagger)\Omega_M \otimes |\text{rej}\rangle\langle\text{rej}|, \tag{8}$$

where Dec_M is the decoding of the error correcting code applied in the encryption and $tr_{0,+}$ refers to the trace over the last two sets of n trap qubits.

5 Security of Quantum Message Authentication Schemes

In this section, we present simulation-based proofs for the Clifford (Sect. 5.1) and the trap (Sect. 5.2) codes. At a high level, the security of the two codes is analyzed in very similar ways (see the discussion in Sect. 1). The main idea (in both cases) is to use a simulator that replaces the encoded message in C with half EPR pairs, without encryption in the Clifford code, and with only a permutation in the trap code; the attack is then applied to these half EPR pairs, as well as any reference system R. From there we are able to compare the accepted and rejected states between the real world and ideal protocols in order to find the upper bound for the trace distance between them. We will notice that these differences are the cases where the real world protocol accepts something that the simulator rejects. Specifically, this is where an attack gets through and changes a logical qubit but is not detected in the traps. Of course, these same states are not rejected by the real world protocol but they are rejected by the simulator. Because the Clifford twirl maps any non-identity Pauli attack to a uniform mixture of non-identity Paulis, the bound for this distance is simple to compute in the case of the Clifford code. In the case of the trap code, a more complicated argument is needed based on permuting the attack and a combinatorial argument that bounds the undetected attacks that can alter the logical data.

5.1 Security of the Clifford Code

Simulator. Recall (Sect. 3) that the simulator interacts with the ideal functionality by only altering the reference system and selecting either *accept* or *reject*. Given the attack, U_{CR}, to which the simulator has access, the simulator will apply the attack to half EPR pairs in place of the C system and then perform a Bell basis measurement on the EPR pairs. It will select *accept* if the EPR pairs are still in their original state, and *reject* otherwise. Let $\mathcal{P}_{acc}^{\mathcal{U}} = \mathbb{1}_{MR} \otimes |\Phi^+\rangle\langle\Phi^+|_{C_1C_2}^{\otimes(n+d)}$ and $\mathcal{P}_{rej}^{\mathcal{U}} = \mathbb{1} - \mathcal{P}_{acc}^{\mathcal{U}}$. The ideal channel is then:

$$\mathscr{F}^{MR \to MRF} : \rho_{MR} \to$$
$$tr_{C_1C_2}(\mathcal{P}_{acc}^{\mathcal{U}}U_{C_1R}(\rho_{MR} \otimes |\Phi^+\rangle\langle\Phi^+|_{C_1C_2}^{\otimes(n+d)})U_{C_1R}^\dagger \mathcal{P}_{acc}^{\mathcal{U}\dagger}) \otimes |\text{acc}\rangle\langle\text{acc}|$$
$$+tr_M(tr_{C_1C_2}(\mathcal{P}_{rej}^{\mathcal{U}}U_{C_1R}(\rho_{MR} \otimes |\Phi^+\rangle\langle\Phi^+|_{C_1C_2}^{\otimes(n+d)})$$
$$U_{C_1R}^\dagger \mathcal{P}_{rej}^{\mathcal{U}\dagger}))\Omega_M \otimes |\text{rej}\rangle\langle\text{rej}|. \tag{9}$$

According to the above, we define $\mathscr{U}^{acc}$ and $\mathscr{U}^{rej}$ that satisfy Eq. (3) as:

$$\mathscr{U}^{acc} : \rho_R \to tr_{C_1 C_2}(\mathcal{P}_{acc}^{\mathscr{U}} U_{C_1 R}(\rho_R \otimes |\Phi^+\rangle \langle \Phi^+|_{C_1 C_2}^{\otimes(n+d)}) U_{C_1 R}^{\dagger} \mathcal{P}_{acc}^{\mathscr{U}\dagger}), \qquad (10)$$

and

$$\mathscr{U}^{rej} : \rho_R \to tr_{C_1 C_2}(\mathcal{P}_{rej}^{\mathscr{U}} U_{C_1 R}(\rho_R \otimes |\Phi^+\rangle \langle \Phi^+|_{C_1 C_2}^{\otimes(n+d)}) U_{C_1 R}^{\dagger} \mathcal{P}_{rej}^{\mathscr{U}\dagger}). \qquad (11)$$

For a fixed attack $U_{CR} = \sum_{P \in \mathbb{P}_{n+d}} \alpha_P P_C \otimes U_R^P$, with $\sum_{P \in \mathbb{P}_{n+d}} |\alpha_P|^2 = 1$, we note the effects of $\mathscr{U}^{acc}$ and $\mathscr{U}^{rej}$, recalling, of course, that $\mathscr{U}^{acc}(\rho_{MR})$ is understood to be $(\mathbb{1}_M \otimes \mathscr{U}^{acc})(\rho_{MR})$, with the same understanding for $\mathscr{U}^{rej}$:

$$\mathscr{U}^{acc}(\rho_{MR}) = tr_{C_1 C_2}(\mathcal{P}_{acc}^{\mathscr{U}} U_{C_1 R}(\rho_{MR} \otimes |\Phi^+\rangle \langle \Phi^+|_{C_1 C_2}^{\otimes(n+d)}) U_{C_1 R}^{\dagger} \mathcal{P}_{acc}^{\mathscr{U}\dagger})$$

$$= |\alpha_{\mathbb{1}}|^2 (\mathbb{1}_M \otimes U_R^{\mathbb{1}}) \rho_{MR} (\mathbb{1}_M \otimes U_R^{\mathbb{1}\dagger}) \qquad (12)$$

$$\mathscr{U}^{rej}(\rho_{MR}) = tr_{C_1 C_2}\Big(\mathcal{P}_{rej}^{\mathscr{U}} \Big(\sum_{P \neq \mathbb{1}} |\alpha_P|^2 P_{C_1} \otimes U_R^P\Big)$$

$$(\rho_{MR} \otimes |\Phi^+\rangle \langle \Phi^+|_{C_1 C_2}^{\otimes(n+d)})\Big(\sum_{P \neq \mathbb{1}} |\alpha_P|^2 P_{C_1} \otimes U_R^{P\dagger}\Big) \mathcal{P}_{rej}^{\mathscr{U}\dagger}\Big)$$

$$= \sum_{P \neq \mathbb{1}} |\alpha_P|^2 (\mathbb{1}_M \otimes U_R^P)(\rho_{MR})(\mathbb{1}_M \otimes U_R^{P\dagger}). \qquad (13)$$

We are now ready to state and prove our main theorem on the security of the Clifford message authentication scheme.

Theorem 5.1. *Let* $\{(\mathcal{E}_k^{S \to C}, \mathcal{D}_k^{C \to SF}) \mid k \in \mathcal{K}\}$ *be the Clifford quantum message authentication scheme, with parameter* d. *Then the Clifford code is an* ϵ-*secure quantum authentication scheme, for* $\epsilon \leq \frac{3}{2^d}$.

Proof. We will follow the proof structure used in [1,11].

Using the simulator described above, we wish to show that:

$$D\Big(\frac{1}{|\mathcal{K}|} \sum_{k \in \mathcal{K}} \mathcal{E}_k(\rho_{MR}), \mathscr{F}(\rho_{MR})\Big) \leq \epsilon, \forall \rho_{MR}. \qquad (14)$$

Consider a general attack U_{CR}, written as $U_{CR} = \sum_{P \in \mathbb{P}_{n+d}} \alpha_P P_C \otimes U_R^P$ where $\sum_{P \in \mathbb{P}_{n+d}} |\alpha_P|^2 = 1$. The real-world channel is then represented as:

$$\mathcal{E}_k^{MR \to MRF} : \rho_{MR} \mapsto \mathcal{D}_k\Big(\Big(\sum_{P \in \mathbb{P}_{n+d}} \alpha_P P_C \otimes U_R^P\Big) \mathcal{E}_k(\rho_{MR})$$

$$\Big(\sum_{P \in \mathbb{P}_{n+d}} \overline{\alpha_P} P_C \otimes U_R^{P\dagger}\Big)\Big). \qquad (15)$$

We will use $\psi = \rho_{MR} \otimes |0\rangle \langle 0|^{\otimes d}$ to simplify the following expressions. Consider the effect of the real protocol on input ρ_{MR} with attack $\sum_{P \in \mathbb{P}_{n+d}} \alpha_P P_C \otimes U_R^P$,

conditioned on acceptance:

$$\frac{1}{|\mathcal{K}|} \sum_{k \in \mathcal{K}} tr_0 \Big(\mathcal{P}_{acc} C_k^\dagger \Big(\sum_{P \in \mathbb{P}_{n+d}} \alpha_P P_C \otimes U_R^P \Big) (C_k \psi C_k^\dagger)$$

$$\Big(\sum_{P \in \mathbb{P}_{n+d}} \overline{\alpha_P} P_C^\dagger \otimes U_R^{P\dagger} \Big) C_k \mathcal{P}_{acc}^\dagger \Big) \otimes |acc\rangle \langle acc|. \tag{16}$$

Now we can apply the Clifford Twirl (Lemma 2.3), since the sum over all keys is, of course, the sum over all Cliffords (since the keys index all $n + d$-qubit Cliffords) and then simply split the sum over all Paulis into the case with the identity Pauli from the attack, and all other Paulis. What we are left with is:

$$\frac{1}{|\mathcal{K}|} \sum_{k \in \mathcal{K}} tr_0 \Big(\sum_{P \in \mathbb{P}_{n+d}} |\alpha_P|^2 \mathcal{P}_{acc} C_k^\dagger (P_C \otimes U_R^P)(C_k \psi C_k^\dagger)$$

$$(P_C^\dagger \otimes U_R^{P\dagger}) C_k \mathcal{P}_{acc}^\dagger \Big) \otimes |acc\rangle \langle acc|$$

$$= \frac{1}{|\mathcal{K}|} \sum_{k \in \mathcal{K}} tr_0 \Big(|\alpha_{\mathbb{1}}|^2 \mathcal{P}_{acc} C_k^\dagger (\mathbb{1}_C \otimes U_R^{\mathbb{1}})(C_k \psi C_k^\dagger)$$

$$(\mathbb{1}_C \otimes U_R^{\mathbb{1}\dagger}) C_k \mathcal{P}_{acc}^\dagger \Big) \otimes |acc\rangle \langle acc|$$

$$+ \frac{1}{|\mathcal{K}|} \sum_{k \in \mathcal{K}} tr_0 \Big(\sum_{P \neq \mathbb{1}} |\alpha_P|^2 \mathcal{P}_{acc} C_k^\dagger (P_C \otimes U_R^P)(C_k \psi C_k^\dagger)$$

$$(P_C^\dagger \otimes U_R^{P\dagger}) C_k \mathcal{P}_{acc}^\dagger \Big) \otimes |acc\rangle \langle acc|. \tag{17}$$

Clearly the first term is exactly what the simulator will accept, and the second term is in exactly the right form to use a Clifford Randomization (Lemma 2.2), resulting in:

$$= \mathscr{U}^{acc}(\rho_{MR}) \otimes |acc\rangle \langle acc|$$

$$+ \frac{1}{|\mathcal{C}_n|} tr_0 \Big(\sum_{\tilde{P} \neq \mathbb{1}} \sum_{P \neq \mathbb{1}} |\alpha_P|^2 \frac{|\mathcal{C}_n|}{|\mathbb{P}_n| - 1} \mathcal{P}_{acc} (\tilde{P}_C \otimes U_R^P) \psi$$

$$(\tilde{P}_C^\dagger \otimes U_R^{P\dagger}) \mathcal{P}_{acc}^\dagger \Big) \otimes |acc\rangle \langle acc|. \tag{18}$$

The $\tilde{P}$s are the results of the Clifford Randomization applied to a Pauli, P. The randomization is not applied to the reference system, so the U_R^P terms are not changed by the randomization. We can use the properties of the trace to move the trace inside the first sum, and we can move the $\frac{|\mathcal{C}_n|}{|\mathbb{P}_n| - 1}$ coefficient out of both of the sums:

$$= \mathscr{U}^{acc}(\rho_{MR}) \otimes |acc\rangle \langle acc|$$

$$+ \frac{1}{|\mathcal{C}_n|} \frac{|\mathcal{C}_n|}{|\mathbb{P}_n| - 1} \Big(\sum_{\tilde{P} \neq \mathbb{1}} tr_0 \sum_{P \neq \mathbb{1}} |\alpha_P|^2 \, \mathcal{P}_{acc}(\tilde{P}_C \otimes U_R^P) \psi$$

$$(\tilde{P}_C^\dagger \otimes U_R^{P\dagger}) \mathcal{P}_{acc}^\dagger \Big) \otimes |acc\rangle \langle acc| . \tag{19}$$

We recognize the R register in the second sum as the states that the simulator will reject. Recall that the simulator is in terms of the sum over all non-identity Paulis and includes the α_P coefficients. We can therefore write the previous line in terms of the simulator as:

$$= \mathscr{U}^{acc}(\rho_{MR}) \otimes |acc\rangle \langle acc|$$

$$+ \frac{1}{|\mathbb{P}_{n+d}| - 1} \Big(\sum_{\tilde{P} \neq \mathbb{1}} tr_0 \mathcal{P}_{acc}(\tilde{P}_C(\mathscr{U}^{rej}(\rho_{MR})$$

$$\otimes |0\rangle \langle 0|^{\otimes d}) \tilde{P}_C^\dagger) \mathcal{P}_{acc}^\dagger \Big) \otimes |acc\rangle \langle acc| . \tag{20}$$

If we let $\mathbb{P}_t$ be the set of all Paulis that do not alter the trap qubits, then when we apply $\mathcal{P}_{acc}$ to the above, we end up with the sum over the $\tilde{P} \in \mathbb{P}_t \setminus \{\mathbb{1}\}$. Therefore the previous line can be simplified to:

$$= \mathscr{U}^{acc}(\rho_{MR}) \otimes |acc\rangle \langle acc|$$

$$+ \frac{1}{|\mathbb{P}_{n+d}| - 1} \sum_{\tilde{P} \in \mathbb{P}_t \setminus \mathbb{1}} tr_0(\tilde{P}_C(\mathscr{U}^{rej}(\rho_{MR}) \otimes |0\rangle \langle 0|^{\otimes d}) \tilde{P}_C^\dagger) \otimes |acc\rangle \langle acc| .$$

$$\tag{21}$$

The effect of the real protocol on input ρ_{MR} with attack $\sum_{P \in \mathbb{P}_{n+d}} \alpha_P P_C \otimes U_R^P$, conditioned on rejection, can be manipulated in the same way:

$$\frac{1}{|\mathcal{K}|} \sum_{k \in \mathcal{K}} \Big(tr_{M,0} \Big(\mathcal{P}_{rej} C_k^\dagger \Big(\sum_{P \in \mathbb{P}_{n+d}} \alpha_P P_C \otimes U_R^P \Big) (C_k(\psi) C_k^\dagger)$$

$$\Big(\sum_{P \in \mathbb{P}_{n+d}} \overline{\alpha_P} P_C^\dagger \otimes U_R^{P\dagger} \Big) C_k \mathcal{P}_{rej}^\dagger \Big) \Big) \Omega_M \otimes |rej\rangle \langle rej|$$

$$= \frac{1}{|\mathcal{K}|} \sum_{k \in \mathcal{K}} \Big(tr_{M,0}(|\alpha_{\mathbb{1}}|^2 \, \mathcal{P}_{rej} C_k^\dagger (\mathbb{1}_C \otimes U_R^{\mathbb{1}}) (C_k(\psi) C_k^\dagger)$$

$$(\mathbb{1}_C \otimes U_R^{\mathbb{1}\dagger}) C_k \mathcal{P}_{rej}^\dagger \Big) \Big) \Omega_M \otimes |rej\rangle \langle rej|$$

$$+ \frac{1}{|\mathcal{K}|} \sum_{k \in \mathcal{K}} \Big(tr_{M,0} \Big(\sum_{P \neq \mathbb{1}} |\alpha_P|^2 \, \mathcal{P}_{rej} C_k^\dagger (P_C \otimes U_R^P) (C_k(\psi) C_k^\dagger)$$

$$(P_C^\dagger \otimes U_R^{P\dagger}) C_k \mathcal{P}_{rej}^\dagger \Big) \Big) \Omega_M \otimes |rej\rangle \langle rej|$$

$$= \frac{1}{|\mathbb{P}_{n+d}| - 1} \sum_{\tilde{P} \neq \mathbb{1}} \sum_{P \neq \mathbb{1}} |\alpha|^2 \Big(tr_{M,0}(\mathcal{P}_{acc}(\tilde{P}_C \otimes U_R^P)(\psi)$$

$$(\tilde{P}_C^\dagger \otimes U_R^{P\dagger})\mathcal{P}_{acc}^\dagger) \Big) \Omega_M \otimes |rej\rangle \langle rej|$$

$$= tr_M(\mathcal{U}^{rej}(\rho_{MR})) \Omega_M \otimes |rej\rangle \langle rej|$$

$$- \frac{1}{|\mathbb{P}_{n+d}| - 1} tr_M \Big(\sum_{P \in \mathbb{P}_t \backslash \mathbb{1}} \mathcal{U}^{rej}(\rho_{MR}) \Big) \Omega_M |rej\rangle \langle rej|$$

$$= tr_M(\mathcal{U}^{rej}(\rho_{MR})) \Omega_M \otimes |rej\rangle \langle rej|$$

$$- \frac{4^n 2^d - 1}{|\mathbb{P}_{n+d}| - 1} tr_M(\mathcal{U}^{rej}(\rho_{MR})) \Omega_M \otimes |rej\rangle \langle rej|. \tag{22}$$

When we combine the accepted states and the rejected states into the real world protocol given by Eq. (15), we can write it in terms of the simulator as:

$$\mathcal{D}_k(U_{CR}\mathcal{E}_k(\rho_{MR})U_{CR}^\dagger)$$
$$= \mathcal{U}^{acc}(\rho_{MR}) \otimes |acc\rangle \langle acc|$$
$$+ \frac{1}{|\mathbb{P}_{n+d}| - 1} \sum_{\tilde{P} \in \mathbb{P}_t \backslash \mathbb{1}} tr_0(\tilde{P}_C(\mathcal{U}^{rej}(\rho_{MR}) \otimes |0\rangle \langle 0|^{\otimes d})\tilde{P}_C^\dagger) \otimes |acc\rangle \langle acc|$$
$$+ tr_M(\mathcal{U}^{rej}(\rho_{MR})) \Omega_M \otimes |rej\rangle \langle rej|$$
$$- \frac{4^n 2^d - 1}{|\mathbb{P}_{n+d}| - 1} tr_M(\mathcal{U}^{rej}(\rho_{MR})) \Omega_M \otimes |rej\rangle \langle rej|. \tag{23}$$

We can therefore write Eq. (14) as:

$$\frac{1}{2} \Big\| \mathcal{U}^{acc}(\rho_{MR}) \otimes |acc\rangle \langle acc|$$
$$+ \frac{1}{|\mathbb{P}_{n+d}| - 1} \sum_{\tilde{P} \in \mathbb{P}_t \backslash \mathbb{1}} tr_0(\tilde{P}_C(\mathcal{U}^{rej}(\rho_{MR}) \otimes |0\rangle \langle 0|^{\otimes d})\tilde{P}_C^\dagger) \otimes |acc\rangle \langle acc|$$
$$+ tr_M(\mathcal{U}^{rej}(\rho_{MR})) \Omega_M \otimes |rej\rangle \langle rej|$$
$$- \frac{4^n 2^d - 1}{|\mathbb{P}_{n+d}| - 1} tr_M(\mathcal{U}^{rej}(\rho_{MR})) \Omega_M \otimes |rej\rangle \langle rej|$$
$$- (\mathcal{U}^{acc}(\rho_{MR}) \otimes |acc\rangle \langle acc| + tr_M(\mathcal{U}^{rej}(\rho_{MR})) \Omega_M \otimes |rej\rangle \langle rej|) \Big\|_1$$

$$= \frac{1}{2} \Big\| \frac{1}{|\mathbb{P}_{n+d}| - 1} \sum_{\tilde{P} \in \mathbb{P}_t \backslash \mathbb{1}} tr_0(\tilde{P}_C(\mathcal{U}^{rej}(\rho_{MR}) \otimes |0\rangle \langle 0|^{\otimes d})\tilde{P}_C^\dagger) \otimes |acc\rangle \langle acc|$$
$$- \frac{4^n 2^d - 1}{|\mathbb{P}_{n+d}| - 1} tr_M(\mathcal{U}^{rej}(\rho_{MR})) \Omega_M \otimes |rej\rangle \langle rej| \Big\|_1 \tag{24}$$

Since $|\mathbb{P}_t \setminus \mathbb{1}| = 4^n 2^d - 1$, and the maximum trace distance between two states is 1, we can see that by the triangle inequality, the above is bounded by:

$$\leq \frac{4^n 2^d - 1}{|\mathbb{P}_{n+d}| - 1}$$

$$= \frac{4^n 2^d - 1}{4^{n+d} - 1} = \frac{1 - \frac{1}{4^n 2^d}}{2^d - \frac{1}{4^n 2^d}}$$

$$\leq 3 \times \frac{1}{2^d}. \tag{25}$$

This concludes the proof, showing that the Clifford code is $\frac{3}{2^d}$-secure.   □

This is identical to the bound of $\frac{6}{2^d}$ achieved in [11] when we consider that we use the trace distance in our definition of security, and [11] uses the trace norm, which differs from the trace distance by a factor of 2.

5.2 Security of the Trap Code

Simulator. Recall (Sect. 3) that the simulator interacts with the ideal functionality by only altering the reference system and selecting either *accept* or *reject*. Given the attack, U_{CR}, to which the simulator has access, the simulator will apply the attack to randomly permuted half EPR pairs in place of the C system and then de-permute the EPR pairs and perform a Bell basis measurement. It will select *accept* if the first n of the EPR pairs have $\leq t$ errors, the next n of the EPR pairs are either unchanged or have phase flip errors, and the last n of the EPR pairs are either unchanged or have bit flip errors. It will select *reject* otherwise. Let $\mathbb{P}_{\mathcal{F}} = \{P \otimes R \otimes Q | P \in \mathbb{P}_n, \omega(P) \leq t, R \in \{I, Z\}^{\otimes n}, Q \in \{I, X\}^{\otimes n}\}$. Specifically, $\mathbb{P}_{\mathcal{F}}$ is the set of all Paulis that the ideal protocol will accept being applied to the half EPR pair—Paulis that would apply at most t non-identity Paulis on the message space and would not alter the $|0\rangle\langle 0|^{\otimes n}$ or the $|+\rangle\langle +|^{\otimes n}$ traps in the real world protocol. Finally, define the measurement projector corresponding to the simulator selecting *accept* as:

$$\mathcal{P}_{acc}^{\mathcal{U}} = \sum_{Q \in \{I,X\}^{\otimes n}} \sum_{R \in \{I,Z\}^{\otimes n}} \sum_{P \in \mathbb{P}_n | \omega(P) \leq t} \mathbb{1}_{MR} \otimes (P \otimes R \otimes Q)_{C_1}$$

$$|\Phi^+\rangle\langle\Phi^+|_{C_1 C_2}^{\otimes 3n} (P \otimes R \otimes Q)_{C_1}$$

$$= \sum_{P \in \mathbb{P}_{\mathcal{F}}} \mathbb{1}_{MR} \otimes (P_{C_1} |\Phi^+\rangle\langle\Phi^+|_{C_1 C_2}^{\otimes 3n} P_{C_1}^{\dagger}), \tag{26}$$

and the measurement projector corresponding to the simulator selecting *reject* as:

$$\mathcal{P}_{rej}^{\mathcal{U}} = \mathbb{1} - \mathcal{P}_{acc}^{\mathcal{U}}. \tag{27}$$

The ideal channel with attack $U_{C_1 R}$ is therefore:

$$
\mathscr{F}^{MR \to MRF} : \rho_{MR} \to tr_{C_1 C_2} \frac{1}{|\Pi_{3n}|} \sum_{\pi \in \Pi_{3n}} \left(\mathcal{P}_{acc}^{\mathscr{U}} \pi_{C_1}^\dagger U_{C_1 R} \pi_{C_1} \right.
$$

$$
(\rho_{MR} \otimes |\Phi^+\rangle \langle \Phi^+|_{C_1 C_2}^{\otimes 3n}) \pi_{C_1}^\dagger U_{C_1 R}^\dagger \pi_{C_1} \mathcal{P}_{acc}^{\mathscr{U} \dagger} \Big) \otimes |\text{acc}\rangle \langle \text{acc}|
$$

$$
+ tr_M \left(tr_{C_1 C_2} \frac{1}{|\Pi_{3n}|} \sum_{\pi \in \Pi_{3n}} \left(\mathcal{P}_{rej}^{\mathscr{U}} \pi_{C_1}^\dagger U_{C_1 R} \pi_{C_1} (\rho_{MR} \otimes |\Phi^+\rangle \langle \Phi^+|_{C_1 C_2}^{\otimes 3n}) \right. \right.
$$

$$
\left. \left. \pi_{C_1}^\dagger U_{C_1 R}^\dagger \pi_{C_1} \mathcal{P}_{rej}^{\mathscr{U} \dagger} \right) \right) \Omega_M \otimes |\text{rej}\rangle \langle \text{rej}| . \tag{28}
$$

For a fixed attack $U_{CR} = \sum_{P \in \mathbb{P}_{3n}} \alpha_P P_C \otimes U_R^P$, with $\sum_{P \in \mathbb{P}_{3n}} |\alpha_P|^2 = 1$ and where for the sake of brevity we will represent $\rho_{MR} \otimes |\Phi^+\rangle \langle \Phi^+|_{C_1 C_2}^{\otimes 3n}$ with $\phi_{MRC_1 C_2}$, the ideal channel becomes:

$$
\mathscr{F}^{MR \to MRF} : \rho_{MR} \to
$$

$$
tr_{C_1 C_2} \frac{1}{|\Pi_{3n}|} \sum_{\pi \in \Pi_{3n}} \left(\mathcal{P}_{acc}^{\mathscr{U}} \pi_{C_1}^\dagger \left(\sum_{P \in \mathbb{P}_{3n}} \alpha_P P_{C_1} \otimes U_R^P \right) \pi_{C_1} \phi_{MRC_1 C_2} \right.
$$

$$
\left. \pi_{C_1}^\dagger \left(\sum_{P \in \mathbb{P}_{3n}} \overline{\alpha_P} P_{C_1} \otimes U_R^{P \dagger} \right) \pi_{C_1} \mathcal{P}_{acc}^{\mathscr{U} \dagger} \otimes |\text{acc}\rangle \langle \text{acc}| \right.
$$

$$
+ tr_M \left(\mathcal{P}_{rej}^{\mathscr{U}} \pi_{C_1}^\dagger \left(\sum_{P \in \mathbb{P}_{3n}} \alpha_P P_{C_1} \otimes U_R^P \right) \pi_{C_1} \phi_{MRC_1 C_2} \right.
$$

$$
\left. \left. \pi_{C_1}^\dagger \left(\sum_{P \in \mathbb{P}_{3n}} \overline{\alpha_P} P_{C_1} \otimes U_R^{P \dagger} \right) \pi_{C_1} \mathcal{P}_{rej}^{\mathscr{U} \dagger} \right) \Omega_M \otimes |\text{rej}\rangle \langle \text{rej}| \right). \tag{29}
$$

From here we will move the permutations to act on the attack Paulis, since they're all applied to the same register, C_1:

$$
= tr_{C_1 C_2} \frac{1}{|\Pi_{3n}|} \sum_{\pi \in \Pi_{3n}} \left(\left(\mathcal{P}_{acc}^{\mathscr{U}} \left(\sum_{P \in \mathbb{P}_{3n}} \alpha_P \pi_{C_1}^\dagger P_{C_1} \pi_{C_1} \otimes U_R^P \right) \phi_{MRC_1 C_2} \right. \right.
$$

$$
\left. \left(\sum_{P \in \mathbb{P}_{3n}} \overline{\alpha_P} \pi_{C_1}^\dagger P_{C_1} \pi_{C_1} \otimes U_R^{P \dagger} \right) \mathcal{P}_{acc}^{\mathscr{U} \dagger} \right) \otimes |\text{acc}\rangle \langle \text{acc}|
$$

$$
+ tr_M \left(\mathcal{P}_{rej}^{\mathscr{U}} \left(\sum_{P \in \mathbb{P}_{3n}} \alpha_P \pi_{C_1}^\dagger P_{C_1} \pi_{C_1} \otimes U_R^P \right) \phi_{MRC_1 C_2} \right.
$$

$$
\left. \left. \left(\sum_{P \in \mathbb{P}_{3n}} \overline{\alpha_P} \pi_{C_1}^\dagger P_{C_1} \pi_{C_1} \otimes U_R^{P \dagger} \right) \mathcal{P}_{rej}^{\mathscr{U} \dagger} \right) \Omega_M \otimes |\text{rej}\rangle \langle \text{rej}| \right). \tag{30}
$$

Finally we apply the projectors:

$$= tr_{C_1 C_2} \frac{1}{|\Pi_{3n}|} \sum_{\pi \in \Pi_{3n}} \Bigg(\Big(\sum_{P | \pi^\dagger P \pi \in \mathbb{P}_{\mathscr{F}}} |\alpha_P|^2 \, (\pi_{C_1}^\dagger P_{C_1} \pi_{C_1} \otimes U_R^P)(\phi_{MRC_1 C_2})$$

$$(\pi_{C_1}^\dagger P_{C_1} \pi_{C_1} \otimes U_R^{P\dagger}) \Big) \otimes |\text{acc}\rangle \langle \text{acc}|$$

$$+ tr_M \Big(\sum_{P | \pi^\dagger P \pi \notin \mathbb{P}_{\mathscr{F}}} |\alpha_P|^2 \, (\pi_{C_1}^\dagger P_{C_1} \pi_{C_1} \otimes U_R^P)(\phi_{MRC_1 C_2})$$

$$(\pi_{C_1}^\dagger P_{C_1} \pi_{C_1} \otimes U_R^{P\dagger}) \Big) \Omega_M \otimes |\text{rej}\rangle \langle \text{rej}| \Bigg). \tag{31}$$

We are now ready to present our main theorem on the security of the trap code:

Theorem 5.2. Let $\{(\mathcal{E}_k^{S \to C}, \mathcal{D}_k^{C \to SF}) \mid k \in \mathcal{K}\}$ be the trap quantum message authentication scheme with parameter t, the number of bit or phase flip errors that the error correcting code applied to the input message qubit can correct. Then the trap code is an ϵ-secure quantum message authentication scheme, for $\epsilon \leq (\frac{1}{3})^{t+1}$.

Proof. Using the simulator described above, we wish to show that:

$$D\Big(\frac{1}{|\mathcal{K}|} \sum_{k \in \mathcal{K}} \mathcal{E}_k(\rho_{MR}), \mathcal{F}(\rho_{MR}) \Big) \leq \epsilon, \forall \rho_{MR}. \tag{32}$$

Consider a general attack U_{CR}, written as $U_{CR} = \sum_{P \in \mathbb{P}_{3n}} \alpha_P P_C \otimes U_R^P$ with $\sum_{P \in \mathbb{P}_{3n}} |\alpha_P|^2 = 1$. Let $\psi = Enc_M(\rho_{MR}) \otimes |0\rangle \langle 0|^{\otimes n} \otimes |+\rangle \langle +|^{\otimes n}$. The real-world channel is then represented as:

$$\mathcal{E}_k^{MR \to MRF} : \rho_{MR} \mapsto \mathcal{D}_k \Big(\Big(\sum_{P \in \mathbb{P}_{3n}} \alpha_P P_C \otimes U_R^P \Big) \mathcal{E}_k(\rho_{MR})$$

$$\Big(\sum_{P \in \mathbb{P}_{3n}} \overline{\alpha_P} P_C \otimes U_R^{P\dagger} \Big) \Big) \tag{33}$$

$$= \frac{1}{|\mathcal{K}|} tr_{0,+} \sum_{k \in \mathcal{K}} \Big(Dec_M \Big(\mathcal{P}_{acc} \pi_{k_1}^\dagger P_{k_2} \Big(\sum_{P \in \mathbb{P}_{3n}} \alpha_P P_C \otimes U_R^P \Big) P_{k_2} \pi_{k_1} \psi$$

$$\pi_{k_1}^\dagger P_{k_2} \Big(\sum_{P \in \mathbb{P}_{3n}} \overline{\alpha_P} P_C \otimes U_R^{P\dagger} \Big) P_{k_2} \pi_{k_1} \mathcal{P}_{acc}^\dagger \Big) \otimes |\text{acc}\rangle \langle \text{acc}|$$

$$+ tr_M \Big(\mathcal{P}_{rej} \pi_{k_1}^\dagger P_{k_2} \Big(\sum_{P \in \mathbb{P}_{3n}} \alpha_P P_C \otimes U_R^P \Big) (P_{k_2} \pi_{k_1} \psi \pi_{k_1}^\dagger P_{k_2})$$

$$\Big(\sum_{P \in \mathbb{P}_{3n}} \overline{\alpha_P} P_C \otimes U_R^{P\dagger} \Big) P_{k_2} \pi_{k_1} \mathcal{P}_{rej}^\dagger \Big) \Omega_M \otimes |\text{rej}\rangle \langle \text{rej}| \Big). \tag{34}$$

From here we apply the Pauli Twirl (Lemma 2.1):

$$
= \frac{1}{|\mathcal{K}_1|} tr_{0,+} \sum_{k_1 \in \mathcal{K}_1} \Bigg(Dec_M \Big(\mathcal{P}_{acc} \pi_{k_1}^\dagger \Big(\sum_{P \in \mathbb{P}_{3n}} |\alpha_P|^2 \, (P_C \otimes U_R^P) \pi_{k_1} \psi
$$
$$
\pi_{k_1}^\dagger (P_C \otimes U_R^{P\dagger}) \Big) \pi_{k_1} \mathcal{P}_{acc}^\dagger \Big) \otimes |acc\rangle \langle acc|
$$
$$
+ tr_M \Big(\mathcal{P}_{rej} \pi_{k_1}^\dagger \Big(\sum_{P \in \mathbb{P}_{3n}} |\alpha_P|^2 \, (P_C \otimes U_R^P) \pi_{k_1} \psi
$$
$$
\pi_{k_1}^\dagger (P_C \otimes U_R^{P\dagger}) \Big) \pi_{k_1} \mathcal{P}_{rej}^\dagger \Big) \Omega_M \otimes |rej\rangle \langle rej| \Bigg). \tag{35}
$$

Since the permutations act on the same register as the attack Paulis, we can move the permutations to be considered to be acting on the Paulis instead of the message and traps:

$$
= \frac{1}{|\mathcal{K}_1|} tr_{0,+} \sum_{k_1 \in \mathcal{K}_1} \Bigg(Dec_M \Big(\mathcal{P}_{acc} \Big(\sum_{P \in \mathbb{P}_{3n}} |\alpha_P|^2 \, (\pi_{k_1}^\dagger P_C \pi_{k_1} \otimes U_R^P) \psi
$$
$$
(\pi_{k_1}^\dagger P_C \pi_{k_1} \otimes U_R^{P\dagger}) \Big) \mathcal{P}_{acc}^\dagger \Big) \otimes |acc\rangle \langle acc|
$$
$$
+ tr_M \Big(\mathcal{P}_{rej} \Big(\sum_{P \in \mathbb{P}_{3n}} |\alpha_P|^2 \, (\pi_{k_1}^\dagger P_C \pi_{k_1} \otimes U_R^P) \psi
$$
$$
(\pi_{k_1}^\dagger P_C \pi_{k_1} \otimes U_R^{P\dagger}) \Big) \mathcal{P}_{rej}^\dagger \Big) \Omega_M \otimes |rej\rangle \langle rej| \Bigg). \tag{36}
$$

Finally we apply the projectors and notice that $\mathcal{K}_1 = \Pi_{3n}$:

$$
= \frac{1}{|\Pi_{3n}|} tr_{0,+} \sum_{\pi \in \Pi_{3n}} \Bigg(Dec_M \Big(\sum_{P | \pi^\dagger P \pi \in \mathbb{P}_{\mathcal{E}}} |\alpha_P|^2 \, (\pi^\dagger P_C \pi \otimes U_R^P) \psi
$$
$$
(\pi^\dagger P_C \pi \otimes U_R^{P\dagger}) \Big) \otimes |acc\rangle \langle acc|
$$
$$
+ tr_M \Big(\sum_{P | \pi^\dagger P \pi \in \mathbb{P}_{3n} \backslash \mathbb{P}_{\mathcal{E}}} |\alpha_P|^2 \, (\pi^\dagger P_C \pi \otimes U_R^P) \psi
$$
$$
(\pi^\dagger P_C \pi \otimes U_R^{P\dagger}) \Big) \Omega_M \otimes |rej\rangle \langle rej| \Bigg). \tag{37}
$$

Then:

$$
\frac{1}{2} \Big\| \frac{1}{|\mathcal{K}|} \sum_{k \in \mathcal{K}} \mathcal{E}_k(\rho_{MR}) - \mathcal{F}(\rho_{MR}) \Big\|_1
$$
$$
= \frac{1}{2} \Big\| \frac{1}{|\Pi_{3n}|} \sum_{\pi \in \Pi_{3n}} \Big(tr_{0,+} \Big(Dec_M \Big(\sum_{P | \pi^\dagger P \pi \subset \mathbb{P}_{\mathcal{E}}} |\alpha_P|^2 \, (\pi^\dagger P_C \pi \otimes U_R^P) \psi
$$

$$(\pi^\dagger P_C \pi \otimes U_R^{P\dagger})) \otimes |\mathrm{acc}\rangle\langle\mathrm{acc}|$$

$$+ tr_M \Big(\sum_{P|\pi^\dagger P\pi \in \mathbb{P}_{3n}\setminus\mathbb{P}_{\mathscr{E}}} |\alpha_P|^2 (\pi^\dagger P_C \pi \otimes U_R^P)\psi$$

$$(\pi^\dagger P_C \pi \otimes U_R^{P\dagger})) \Omega_M \otimes |\mathrm{rej}\rangle\langle\mathrm{rej}| \Big)$$

$$- tr_{C_1 C_2} \Big(\sum_{P|\pi^\dagger P\pi \in \mathbb{P}_{\mathscr{F}}} |\alpha_P|^2 (\pi_{C_1}^\dagger P_{C_1}\pi_{C_1} \otimes U_R^P)(\phi_{MRC_1C_2})$$

$$(\pi_{C_1}^\dagger P_{C_1}\pi_{C_1} \otimes U_R^{P\dagger})) \otimes |\mathrm{acc}\rangle\langle\mathrm{acc}|$$

$$- tr_{MC_1 C_2} \Big(\sum_{P|\pi^\dagger P\pi \notin \mathbb{P}_{\mathscr{F}}} |\alpha_P|^2 (\pi_{C_1}^\dagger P_{C_1}\pi_{C_1} \otimes U_R^P)(\phi_{MRC_1C_2})$$

$$(\pi_{C_1}^\dagger P_{C_1}\pi_{C_1} \otimes U_R^{P\dagger})) \Omega_M \otimes |\mathrm{rej}\rangle\langle\mathrm{rej}| \Big) \Big\|_1. \tag{38}$$

We will subtract the accepted states in the ideal protocol from those accepted in the real protocol and we will subtract the rejected states in the real protocol from the rejected states in the ideal protocol. Note that $\mathbb{P}_{\mathscr{E}} \setminus \mathbb{P}_{\mathscr{F}} = \{P \otimes R \otimes Q | P \in \mathbb{P}_n, \omega(P) > t, R \in \{I, Z\}^{\otimes n}, Q \in \{I, X\}^{\otimes n}\}$.

$$= \frac{1}{2}\Big\| \frac{1}{|\Pi_{3n}|} \sum_{\pi \in \Pi_{3n}} \sum_{P|\pi^\dagger P\pi \in \mathbb{P}_{\mathscr{E}}\setminus\mathbb{P}_{\mathscr{F}}} \Big(tr_{0,+}\Big(Dec_M(|\alpha_P|^2 (\pi^\dagger P_C \pi \otimes U_R^P)\psi$$

$$(\pi^\dagger P_C \pi \otimes U_R^{P\dagger}))\Big) \otimes |\mathrm{acc}\rangle\langle\mathrm{acc}|$$

$$- tr_{MC_1 C_2}\Big(|\alpha_P|^2 (\pi_{C_1}^\dagger P_{C_1}\pi_{C_1} \otimes U_R^P)(\phi_{MRC_1C_2})$$

$$(\pi_{C_1}^\dagger P_{C_1}\pi_{C_1} \otimes U_R^{P\dagger})) \Omega_M \otimes |\mathrm{rej}\rangle\langle\mathrm{rej}| \Big) \Big\|_1. \tag{39}$$

Here we will use the triangle inequality to remove the sums from the trace distance:

$$\leq \frac{1}{2}\frac{1}{|\Pi_{3n}|} \sum_{\pi \in \Pi_{3n}} \sum_{P|\pi^\dagger P\pi \in \mathbb{P}_{\mathscr{E}}\setminus\mathbb{P}_{\mathscr{F}}} \Big\| tr_{0,+}\Big(Dec_M(|\alpha_P|^2 (\pi^\dagger P_C \pi \otimes U_R^P)\psi$$

$$(\pi^\dagger P_C \pi \otimes U_R^{P\dagger}))\Big) \otimes |\mathrm{acc}\rangle\langle\mathrm{acc}|$$

$$- tr_{MC_1 C_2}\Big(|\alpha_P|^2 (\pi_{C_1}^\dagger P_{C_1}\pi_{C_1} \otimes U_R^P)(\phi_{MRC_1C_2})$$

$$(\pi_{C_1}^\dagger P_{C_1}\pi_{C_1} \otimes U_R^{P\dagger})) \Omega_M \otimes |\mathrm{rej}\rangle\langle\mathrm{rej}| \Big\|_1. \tag{40}$$

Since the maximum trace distance between two states is 1 we have:

$$\leq \frac{1}{|\Pi_{3n}|} \sum_{k_1 \in \mathcal{K}_1} \sum_{P|\pi^\dagger P\pi \in \mathbb{P}_{\mathscr{E}}\setminus\mathbb{P}_{\mathscr{F}}} |\alpha_P|^2. \tag{41}$$

Now if we let η_P be the number of permutations, π of P such that $\pi^\dagger P \pi \in \mathbb{P}_{\mathscr{E}} \setminus \mathbb{P}_{\mathscr{F}}$, then the above can be written as:

$$= \frac{1}{|\Pi_{3n}|} \sum_{P \in \mathbb{P}_{3n}} \eta_P \times |\alpha_P|^2. \tag{42}$$

In Appendix A, we give Lemma A.1, which gives us $\eta_P \leq \binom{n}{t+1}(t+1)!$ $(3n - (t+1))!$. Thus, since $\sum_{P \in \mathbb{P}_{3n}} |\alpha_P|^2 = 1$, the above expression can be bounded by:

$$\leq \frac{1}{(3n)!} \times \binom{n}{t+1}(t+1)!(3n - (t+1))!$$

$$= \frac{\prod\limits_{i=1}^{n} i \ \prod\limits_{i=1}^{3n-t-1} i}{\prod\limits_{i=1}^{n-t-1} i \prod\limits_{i=1}^{3n} i} = \frac{\prod\limits_{i=n-t}^{n} i}{\prod\limits_{i=3n-t}^{3n} i} = \prod_{i=0}^{t} \frac{n-t+i}{3n-t+i}$$

$$\leq \prod_{i=0}^{t} \frac{1}{3} = \left(\frac{1}{3}\right)^{t+1} \tag{43}$$

Therefore, $D\left(\frac{1}{|\mathcal{K}|} \sum_{k \in \mathcal{K}} \mathscr{E}_k(\rho_{MR}), \mathscr{F}(\rho_{MR})\right) \leq (\frac{1}{3})^{t+1}, \forall \rho_{MR}.$ □

We note that this is very similar to the bound in [5] of $(\frac{2}{3})^{d/2}$: note that the trap code in [5] uses the error *detection* property of the code. Since a code of distance d can detect up to $d/2$ errors, this bound is consistent with our bound of $(\frac{1}{3})^{t+1}$.

Acknowledgements. We would like to thank Florian Speelman for feedback on a prior version of this work, as well as the anonymous reviewers for useful corrections.

A   Appendix

Lemma A.1. *For a fixed $P \in \mathbb{P}_{3n}$, let η_P denote the number of permutations π of P such that $\pi^\dagger P \pi \in \mathbb{P}_{\mathscr{E}} \setminus \mathbb{P}_{\mathscr{F}}$ Then for all P:*

$$\eta_P \leq \binom{n}{t+1}(t+1)!(3n - (t+1))!. \tag{44}$$

An intuitive argument for the above lemma is that η_P can be upper-bounded by fixing a Pauli $P \in \{I, X\}^{3n}$ of weight $t+1$. We show that a Pauli with greater weight will have $\leq \eta_P$ possible allowed permutations. To find the number of possible allowed permutations, we will consider the first n positions, where we require at least $t+1$ non-identity Paulis (for a total of $\binom{n}{t+1}(t+1)!$ permutations). The remaining positions are then simply permuted, since we have used all of the non-identity Paulis already, contributing a multiplicative factor of $(3n-(t+1))!$ permutations. This is formalized below (where we also consider general attack Paulis consisting of combinations of X, Y and Z).

Proof. In order to find an upper bound for η_P, we look to find the Pauli, P, that has the largest number of permutations, π, such that $\pi^\dagger P\pi \in \mathbb{P}_\mathscr{E} \setminus \mathbb{P}_\mathscr{F}$.

For a Pauli P with $\omega(P) = d$, we write $d = d_x + d_y + d_z + x_1 + y + z_1 + x_2 + z_2$ for values $d_x, d_y, d_z, x_1, y, z_1, x_2, z_2$ as follows:

1. d_x, d_y, d_z where $d_x + d_y + d_z = t + 1$. These are the $t+1$ X, Y, and Z Paulis that must be applied to the first n qubits for the Pauli to be in $\mathbb{P}_\mathscr{E} \setminus \mathbb{P}_\mathscr{F}$.
2. y where $y + d_y$ is the total number of Y Paulis in P and y are the additional Y Paulis applied to the first n qubits. Note that Y Paulis cannot be applied to either set of traps without altering them.
3. x_1, x_2 where $x_1 + x_2 + d_x$ is the total number of X Paulis in P and x_1 are the additional X Paulis applied to the first n qubits and x_2 are the X Paulis applied to the $|+\rangle\langle+|^{\otimes n}$ traps.
4. z_1, z_2 where $z_1 + z_2 + d_z$ is the total number of Z Paulis in P and z_1 are the additional Z Paulis applied to the first n qubits and z_2 are the Z Paulis applied to the $|0\rangle\langle0|^{\otimes n}$ traps.

Then the possible permutations on P are found by multiplying the following terms:

1. $\binom{n}{d_x, d_y, d_z, n-t-1} d_x! d_y! d_z!$ Which is the number of ways to choose the required $t + 1$ spots for the minimum number of Paulis applied to the first n qubits, multiplied by the number of ways of permuting each of the sets of X, Y, and Z Paulis. Note that this term simplifies to $\frac{n!}{(n-t-1)!}$,
2. $\binom{n-t-1}{x_1} x_1!$, the number of ways to apply x_1 additional X Paulis to the first n qubits,
3. $\binom{n-t-1-x_1}{y} y!$, the number of ways to apply y additional Y Paulis to the first n qubits,
4. $\binom{n-t-1-x_1-y}{z_1} z_1!$, the number of ways to apply z_1 additional Z Paulis to the first n qubits,
5. $\binom{n}{x_2} x_2!$, the number of ways to apply x_2 X Paulis to the n traps that will not be changed by them,
6. $\binom{n}{z_2} z_2!$, the number of ways to apply z_2 Z Paulis to the n traps that will not be changed by them, and
7. $(3n - (d_x + d_y + d_z + x_1 + y + z_1 + x_2 + z_2))!$ the number of ways to permute the remaining identity qubits, which simplifies to $(3n - d)!$.

The product, once simplified, is then:

$$\eta_P = \frac{n! n! n! (3n - d)!}{(n - t - 1 - x_1 - y - z_1)!(n - x_2)!(n - z_2)!}$$

$$= \prod_{n-t-x_1-y-z_1}^{n} i \prod_{n-x_2+1}^{n} i \prod_{n-z_2+1}^{n} i \prod_{i=1}^{3n-t-1-x_1-y-z_1-x_2-z_2} i \qquad (45)$$

Since t is fixed, in order to maximize the above expression, we need to minimize x_1, y, z_1, x_2, z_2. This is achieved by setting $x_1 = y = z_1 = x_2 = z_2 = 0$, and therefore $d = t + 1$: we thus find that $\eta_P \leq \prod_{n-t}^{n} i \prod_{i=1}^{3n-t-1} i = \binom{n}{t+1}(t + 1)!$ $(3n - (t + 1))!$. □

References

1. Aharonov, D., Ben-Or, M., Eban, E.: Interactive proofs for quantum computations. In: Innovations in Computer Science–ICS 2010, pp. 453–469 (2010). arXiv:0810.5375
2. Barnum, H., Crépeau, C., Gottesman, D., Smith, A., Tapp, A.: Authentication of quantum messages. In: 43rd Annual Symposium on Foundations of Computer Science–FOCS 2002, pp. 449–458 (2002). doi:10.1109/SFCS.2002.1181969
3. Ben-Or, M., Crépeau, C., Gottesman, D., Hassidim, A., Smith, A.: Secure multiparty quantum computation with (only) a strict honest majority. In: 47th Annual Symposium on Foundations of Computer Science–FOCS 2006, pp. 249–260, (2006). doi:10.1109/FOCS.2006.68
4. Bennett, C.H., Brassard, G.: Quantum cryptography: public key distribution and coin tossing. In: International Conference on Computers, Systems and Signal Processing, pp. 175–179 (1984)
5. Broadbent, A., Gutoski, G., Stebila, D.: Quantum one-time programs. In: Canetti, R., Garay, J.A. (eds.) CRYPTO 2013. LNCS, vol. 8043, pp. 344–360. Springer, Heidelberg (2013). doi:10.1007/978-3-642-40084-1_20
6. Broadbent, A., Schaffner, C.: Quantum cryptography beyond quantum key distribution. Des. Codes Crypt. **78**, 351–382 (2016). doi:10.1007/s10623-015-0157-4
7. Bruß, D., Erdélyi, G., Meyer, T., Riege, T., Rothe, J.: Quantum cryptography: a survey. ACM Comput. Surv. (CSUR) **39**(2) (2007). doi:10.1145/1242471.1242474
8. Canetti, R.: Universally composable security: a new paradigm for cryptographic protocols. In: 42nd Annual Symposium on Foundations of Computer Science FOCS 2001, pp. 136–145 (2001). doi:10.1109/SFCS.2001.959888
9. Cleve, R., Gottesman, D., Lo, H.-K.: How to share a quantum secret. Phys. Rev. Lett. **83**(3), 648–651 (1999). doi:10.1103/PhysRevLett.83.648
10. Dankert, C., Cleve, R., Emerson, J., Livine, E.: Exact and approximate unitary 2-designs and their application to fidelity estimation. Phys. Rev. A **80**, 012304 (2009). doi:10.1103/PhysRevA.80.012304
11. Dupuis, F., Nielsen, J.B., Salvail, L.: Actively secure two-party evaluation of any quantum operation. In: Safavi-Naini, R., Canetti, R. (eds.) CRYPTO 2012. LNCS, vol. 7417, pp. 794–811. Springer, Heidelberg (2012). doi:10.1007/978-3-642-32009-5_46
12. Fehr, S.: Quantum cryptography. Found. Phys. **40**(5), 494–531 (2010). doi:10.1007/s10701-010-9408-4
13. Gottesman, D.: Stabilizer codes and quantum error correction. Ph.D. thesis, California Institute of Technology (1997). arXiv:quant-ph/9705052
14. Hayden, P., Leung, D., Mayers, D.: Universal composable security of quantum message authentication with key recycling. In: QCRYPT 2011 (2011)
15. Nielsen, M.A., Chuang, I.L.: Quantum Computation and Quantum Information. Cambridge University Press, Cambridge (2000)
16. Unruh, D.: Universally composable quantum multi-party computation. In: Gilbert, H. (ed.) EUROCRYPT 2010. LNCS, vol. 6110, pp. 486–505. Springer, Heidelberg (2010). doi:10.1007/978-3-642-13190-5_25
17. Watrous, J.: Guest column: an introduction to quantum information and quantum circuits. ACM SIGACT News **42**(2), 52–67 (2011). doi:10.1145/1998037.1998053

Visual Cryptography

Private Visual Share-Homomorphic Computation and Randomness Reduction in Visual Cryptography

Paolo D'Arco[1], Roberto De Prisco[1(✉)], and Yvo Desmedt[2]

[1] Dipartimento di Informatica, University of Salerno,
Via Giovanni Paolo II, 132, 84084 Fisciano, SA, Italy
{pdarco,robdep}@unisa.it
[2] Department of Computer Science, The University of Texas at Dallas,
800 W. Campbell Road, Richardson, Texas 75080-3021, USA
Yvo.Desmedt@utdallas.edu

Abstract. Secure computation through non standard methods, suitable for users who have to perform the computation without the aid of a computer, or for settings in which the degree of trustworthiness of the hardware and software equipments is very low, are an interesting, very challenging and quite unexplored research topic. In this paper we put forward a collection of ideas and some techniques which could be useful in order to make some progress in designing protocols with such properties. Our contribution is twofold: we explore the power of *visual cryptography as a computing tool*, exploiting alternative uses and share manipulations, and we address the central issue of *randomness reduction* in visual schemes, by showing a strict relation with existing results in secure multiparty computation. More specifically, we prove that:

- by properly defining *operations* on the shares, we show that visual shares are homomorphic with respect to some functions f. More precisely, in the two-party case, each user, by applying to his two shares a_i, b_i of the secrets a, b the operation, gets a share $g_i(a_i, b_i)$, $i = 1, 2$, such that the superposition of $g_1(a_1, b_1)$ and $g_2(a_2, b_2)$ visually provides, applying the standard Naor and Shamir superposition reconstruction strategy, the value of the function f;
- we link our analysis to a general known result on private two-party computation, and we classify all the boolean functions of two input bits which admit homomorphic visual share computation;
- we prove that by encoding pixels in groups, instead of encoding each pixel independently, and exploiting dependencies, some randomness can be saved if and only if the pixel dependencies can be expressed through some specific boolean functions. For example, given three pixels, if the third one is the **and** or the **or** of the first two, randomness reduction is impossible, while if it is the **xor** of the first two, randomness reduction can be achieved.

Keywords: Information theory · Visual cryptography · Secure computation · Unconditional privacy

© Springer International Publishing AG 2016
A.C.A. Nascimento and P. Barreto (Eds.): ICITS 2016, LNCS 10015, pp. 95–113, 2016.
DOI: 10.1007/978-3-319-49175-2_5

1 Introduction

Need for Trust. The unquestionable advantages that offer the diffusion of the digital technologies come along with new challenges against user privacy and freedom. One of these challenges is the *implicit or explicit need for trust in the hardware and software equipment*, which provides access and processing capability to the user for each service of the infrastructure. The average user buys the hardware from a vendor, and usually his choice is among the products offered by few big competitors on the market, the basic software is pre-installed, applications for specific computing needs can be bought or downloaded from Internet stores, and in all this process the user has *to trust* that the hardware and software do *all and only what they are supposed to*.

Unfortunately, it does not work always this way. A significant example helps to get the point: participants of a recent international meeting among national delegates were offered pen-drives equipped with a hidden software for stealing sensitive data and spying computer activities [2]. Moreover, a lot of research, e.g., funded by Departments of Defence, is focusing on how to introduce malware both in hardware and in software.

After the Snowden leaks, many non-Western countries have realized that the hardware might not be trustworthy. For example, Cisco sale in China has plunged [1]; India has decided to switch to typewriters for its top security documents [3].

It is clear that countermeasures are needed. Secure computation through non standard methods, which remove the need for trust, suitable for users who have to perform the computation without the aid of a computer, or for situations where the degree of trustworthiness of the hardware and software equipments is very low (as could have been in the above cited meeting), is an interesting, very challenging and not really explored research topic.

Visual Cryptography. Visual Cryptography can be a tool to build systems where the degree of trustworthiness that the user needs to have in the system is reduced. It is a method through which a secret image is encrypted in random-looking images printed on transparencies. Its captivating peculiarity is that the reconstruction of the secret is performed *without any* computational machinery: it is enough to superpose the transparencies in order to reconstruct the secret. Such an operation does not require *trust* in the hardware! It is then not surprising that hundreds of papers have been published on visual cryptography. Indeed, the work by Naor-Shamir has more than 2200 citations (Google Scholar).

Motivations. Our research has two motivations. The first motivation is to *further explore the power of visual cryptography as a computing tool*. Let us explain why and summarize the previous work. Several projects are underway for implementing secure multiparty computation. The topic is receiving a lot of attention to deal with insider attacks, e.g., untrusted software or untrusted hardware. The idea is that if one cannot trust a single platform, then we can use n of them. If at most t are not trustworthy, then it seems that secure multiparty computation will solve the problem. Unfortunately, this argument is false. It is not enough.

Indeed, the model of secure multiparty computation assumes that t *parties are untrustworthy* and that the *remaining parties' computers are trusted*!

In many settings such an assumption is unrealistic. Hence, alternative solutions are needed. To this aim, we study *private visual share homomorphic computation*. Indeed, hybrid systems where visual cryptography is used as an intermediate step within a certain process, in order to mitigate the trust in the digital equipment providing the service or to cope with specific attacks, have already been proposed. Chaum's voting system [7] or the transaction authentication scheme of [16], are valuable examples of such an approach. Our efforts are therefore directed towards identifying strategies for hybrid systems for secure multiparty computation, where inputs and outputs are provided to/received from the weakly trusted computer/cluster/cloud through user-friendly low-cost nondigital technology, e.g., transparencies, and where as much as possible of the computation is performed through untrusted cheap devices (e.g., a system of light projectors, if visual cryptography is employed), while the rest of the computation is performed digitally.

The second motivation is to *reduce randomness in visual schemes*. This motivation finds its origin in the problem of source coding in information theory. In source coding the problem is to exploit the redundancy in the source, e.g., text, to shorten its representation. Obviously, in visual cryptography that seems impossible, since pixels are transmitted. Indeed, in the large body of literature on visual cryptography schemes, the encoding process has always been considered as a *pixel-by-pixel* operation: in other words, each pixel is shared among the parties *independently and uniformly at random*. Such an approach requires a huge amount of random bits. However, there are cases where the pixels in some areas of the image are function of pixels in other areas. We would like to explore such dependencies to reduce randomness.

Secure Visual Computing. Visual Cryptography can be used to perform secure visual computation. Specifically, in [11], it has been shown that two parties can privately evaluate a function $f(\cdot, \cdot)$ of their inputs, x and y, through a *pure physical visual* process. One of the parties prepares a set of transparencies and the other, after receiving a subset of them which represent the inputs of both parties, performs the visual computation and communicates the result to the other party. More precisely, the steps of the computation are defined by a circuit which computes $f(\cdot, \cdot)$, and gate evaluation visual secret sharing schemes are used to implement the functionalities of each gate. In the set-up phase, starting from the output wire, transparencies for all the circuit wires are generated. Later on, the evaluation consists in superposing *properly chosen parts* of the transparencies which represent the inputs held by the parties, until the representation of the value of the function is visually reconstructed.

Roughly speaking, we could say that visual cryptography is used in [11] *as it is*, in a sort of black-box manner: two multi-secret visual secret sharing schemes are employed in order to implement the functionality of each gate and produce the transparencies for the input wires of the gate. Such an approach ends up in an unavoidable doubling of the size at each level of the circuit of the transparencies associated to the right wire of each gate, compared to the size of the transparencies associated to the left wire (see details in [11]). Moreover the protocol in [11] involves a physical oblivious transfer.

In this paper we would like to understand whether we could do visual private computation in a different, and perhaps more efficient, way compared to [11] (e.g. without share expansion and without the need for a physical oblivious transfer).

The key idea we pursue is the following: in digital general solutions for unconditionally secure multiparty computation (e.g., [4,6,10]) parties process their shares non-interactively or interactively (e.g., think about the *add* and *multiply* operations of shares defined over a finite field) in order to compute new shares for the subsequent steps of the computation. The first question we would like to answer is:

Can we efficiently manipulate the shares so that when superposing the newly obtained shares (i.e., reconstructing the secret) the result of the computation is revealed while maintaining privacy of the inputs?

In other words, as shown in Fig. 1, we would like to manipulate the transparencies in order to introduce suitable changes on the pixels, in such a way that the new transparencies, when superposed, visually reconstruct the output value of a function of the input values, represented through the input transparencies.

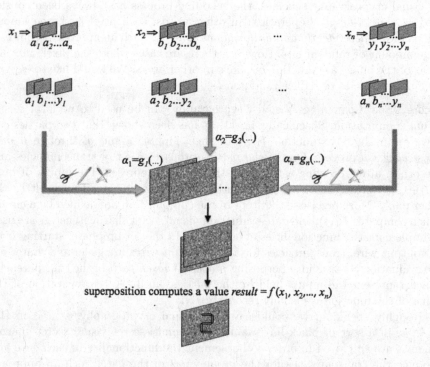

Fig. 1. Visual computation model

Leds labeling

Fig. 2. Leds digits encoding

Randomness Reduction in Visual Schemes. The construction of the shares in visual cryptography requires some amount of *randomness*: for every pixel of the secret image we need to choose uniformly at random a (distribution) matrix from a given collection of (distribution) matrices. Some papers have addressed the issue but in the model in which image is shared through a *pixel-by-pixel* approach (e.g., [12]). Pixel dependencies have not been considered yet. A concrete example of pixel dependencies in an image is the following. Imagine that the secret information in an image is represented as digits drawn in a led display with a total of 7 leds (see Fig. 2). In this case we have that led g is a function of leds a, b, c and d. Indeed we have that $g = \overline{abcd}$. A more complicated function ties led f to leds a, b, c, d, e, namely $f = \overline{eabgd}(e + g) = \overline{eab\overline{abcd}d}(e + \overline{abcd})$.

Therefore, the second question we would like to answer is:

Can pixel dependencies be exploited in order to get randomness reduction in visual cryptography?

Summary of the contribution. We provide the following results.

- *Visual Computation.* For some boolean functions, we show that it is possible to provide pixel transformations for producing new shares from received ones, such that the superposition of the new shares corresponds to a visual computation of a function defined on the input bits (pixels of the original image). We provide a full characterization for two-bit input boolean functions.
- *Randomness Reduction.* We show that there are pixel dependencies for which it is possible to save randomness during the share construction process and, surprisingly, others for which saving randomness is not possible.

2   Visual Cryptography

Visual cryptography is a special type of secret sharing in which the secret is an image and the shares are random-looking images printed on transparencies. The idea was introduced independently by Kafri and Keren [14], in a *random grid* model, and by Naor and Shamir [17], in a *deterministic* model. Later on, Yang [18] introduced a *probabilistic* model, which was shown to be a re-discovery of the random grid model in [13]. The probabilistic model was generalized in [9], which provided a connection between the random grid model and the deterministic model.

In a visual cryptography scheme a secret image has to be shared among a set of participants. A trusted party, the dealer, knows the secret and generates shares, one for each participant, in the form of a printed transparency. Among the participants there are some subsets that are allowed to reconstruct the secret by using collectively their shares. These are called *qualified* subsets and are denoted with $\mathcal{Q}$. On the other hand, there are other subsets of participants, called *forbidden*, denoted with $\mathcal{F}$, that are not able to get *any* information from the shares. Often $\mathcal{Q}$ and $\mathcal{F}$ are a partition of the power-set defined on the set of participants. When this is not the case, for the subsets not included neither in $\mathcal{Q}$ nor in $\mathcal{F}$, we just don't care (about their ability to reconstruct the secret or their ability to acquire information about the secret).

The captivating peculiarity of visual cryptography is that the reconstruction of the secret is performed *without any* computational machinery: a set of qualified participants has to simply superpose the shares (transparencies) in order to reconstruct the secret. Forbidden participants do not get any information from the shares, neither by superposing them, nor by any other computation.

A visual cryptography scheme can be described by means of *distribution matrices*. Precisely, let n and m be two integers, where n represents the number of parties and m the pixel expansion (each secret pixel is expanded into m pixels). A scheme is defined by two collections $\mathcal{C}_\circ$ and $\mathcal{C}_\bullet$ of $n \times m$ matrices with elements in $\{\circ, \bullet\}$. To construct the shares, for each secret pixel, the dealer needs to randomly choose a distribution matrix M from $\mathcal{C}_\circ$, if the secret pixel is white, or from $\mathcal{C}_\bullet$, if the secret pixel is black, and to use row i of M to assign the pixels on the i-th share.

The participants that wish to reconstruct the secret need only to superpose their shares. The superposition operation will be denoted with the symbol $\oplus$.

Example 1 (Scheme-(2,2)-NS). The following collections of distribution matrices can be used to realize a deterministic visual cryptography scheme for $\mathcal{Q} = \{\{1, 2\}\}$ and $\mathcal{F} = \{\{1\}, \{2\}\}$. This scheme is the instantiation for $n = 2$ of the (n, n)-threshold [1] scheme of Naor and Shamir [17]. We call such a scheme Scheme-(2,2)-NS:

$$\mathcal{C}_\circ = \left\{ \begin{bmatrix} \circ\bullet \\ \circ\bullet \end{bmatrix}, \begin{bmatrix} \bullet\circ \\ \bullet\circ \end{bmatrix} \right\} \qquad \mathcal{C}_\bullet = \left\{ \begin{bmatrix} \circ\bullet \\ \bullet\circ \end{bmatrix}, \begin{bmatrix} \bullet\circ \\ \circ\bullet \end{bmatrix} \right\}.$$

In order to share a black-and-white image, *for each pixel* of the image, the dealer repeats the following steps: randomly chooses a matrix from $\mathcal{C}_\sigma$ where σ is the color of the pixel that has to be shared. Then, row 1 of the chosen matrix is

---

[1] (k, n)-threshold schemes are schemes in which the collection $\mathcal{Q}$ of qualified subsets of participants consists of all the subsets containing at least k out of n participants, while the collection $\mathcal{F}$ of forbidden subsets consists of all the subsets with at most $k - 1$ participants.

the share for participant 1, and row 2 is the share of participant 2. With this particular scheme each secret pixel gets expanded into $m = 2$ pixels.

It should not be hard to see that it is guaranteed that a white secret pixel is always reconstructed as one white and one black pixel, while a black secret pixel is always reconstructed as two black pixels. Indeed we have that when the shares are taken from $\mathcal{C}_\circ$, the superposition operation performed for the reconstruction is either $[\circ\bullet] \oplus [\circ\bullet] = [\circ\bullet]$ or $[\bullet\circ] \oplus [\bullet\circ] = [\bullet\circ]$ while, when the shares are taken from $\mathcal{C}_\bullet$, the superposition is either $[\circ\bullet] \oplus [\bullet\circ] = [\bullet\bullet]$ or $[\bullet\circ] \oplus [\circ\bullet] = [\bullet\bullet]$.

Moreover, a single share does not provide any information about whether the secret pixel is white or black because each share appears in either one of the distribution collections.

An example of application of the scheme is given in Fig. 3.

Fig. 3. Example of shares and superposition for the $(2, 2)$-scheme.

For the purpose of this paper this scheme is all we need. Thus, we do not provide further details about visual cryptography. We only recall that Scheme-(2,2)-NS satisfies correctness (qualified subsets reconstruct the secret) and privacy (forbidden subsets do not get any information). The interested reader can find more information in the papers cited at the beginning of the section or in [8], where a collection of surveys on several aspects of visual cryptography is provided.

3   Privately Computable Functions

We restrict our attention to two-bit boolean functions and we use the definitions and the results provided in [15] restricted to the case of two-bit boolean functions. Parties P_1 and P_2 need to compute a function f of their private inputs x and y. In order to do so they use a protocol A to exchange messages and might locally use random choices.

Informally a function is privately computable if P_1 and P_2 can compute the correct value of the function without learning anything (in the information theoretic sense) about the other party's input value. More formally we have the following definition.

Definition 1 [15]. *A boolean function $f : \{0,1\} \times \{0,1\} \rightarrow \{0,1\}$ is privately computable with respect to P_1 if there exists a protocol A that always computes the correct value, that is $A(x,y) = f(x,y)$, and such that for every pair of inputs (x, y_1) and (x, y_2) such that $f(x, y_1) = f(x, y_2)$, every communication pattern c, and every string of random bits r_1 held by P_1, it holds that*

$$Pr(c|r_1, (x, y_1)) = Pr(c|r_1, (x, y_2)),$$

where the probability is taken over all possible random strings of P_2. A similar definition can be stated for P_2.

A complete (combinatorial) characterization of privately computable functions was given by Kushilevitz in [15]. In a nutshell, the characterization is obtained as follows: any function $f : \{0,1\}^n \times \{0,1\}^n \rightarrow \{0, 1, \ldots, m-1\}$ can be visualised as a $2^n \times 2^n$ matrix with entries in $\{0, 1, \ldots, m-1\}$. Let M_f be such a matrix. A submatrix of M_f is called *monochromatic* if f is constant over it.

Definition 2. *Let $M = C \times D$ be a matrix. The relation $\sim$ on the rows of the matrix M is defined as follows: $x_1, x_2 \in C$ satisfy $x_1 \sim x_2$ if there exists $y \in D$ such that $M_{x_1,y} = M_{x_2,y}$. The equivalence relation $\equiv$ on the rows of the matrix M is defined as the transitive closure of the relation $\sim$. That is, $x_1, x_2 \in C$ satisfy $x_1 \equiv x_2$ if there exist $z_1, \ldots, z_\ell \in C$ such that $x_1 \sim z_1 \sim \ldots \sim z_\ell \sim x_2$. Similarly the relations $\sim$ and $\equiv$ are defined on the columns of the matrix.*

Definition 3. *A matrix M is called forbidden if it is not monochromatic, all its rows are equivalent, and all its columns are equivalent. That is, every $x_1, x_2 \in C$ satisfy $x_1 \equiv x_2$ and every $y_1, y_2 \in D$ satisfy $y_1 \equiv y_2$.*

Examples of a forbidden submatrices are:

	y_1	y_2
x_1	0	0
x_2	0	1

	y_1	y_2	y_3
x_1	0	0	1
x_2	2	4	1
x_3	2	3	3

If a function is represented by a matrix M_f which contains a forbidden submatrix, then f is not privately computable.

Theorem 1 [15]. *Let f be a function. If M_f contains a forbidden submatrix $M = C \times D$, then f is not privately computable.*

The special case of Theorem 1, where M is a 2×2 submatrix, is useful for proving that particular functions are not privately computable. It says that if there exists $x_1, x_2, y_1, y_2 \in \{0,1\}$ such that $f(x_1, y_1) = f(x_1, y_2) = f(x_2, y_1) = a$ and $f(x_2, y_2) = b$, then f is not privately computable.

Notice that in [15] it was shown that the condition of Theorem 1 is not only necessary but also *sufficient*. Namely, if the matrix M_f does not contain a forbidden submatrix then f is privately computable.

It immediately follows that the **and** and **or** functions are not privately computable, which, as we will see later, in our problem means that pixel transformations on transparencies for **and** and **or** functions cannot be found.

Kushilevitz's characterization allows to classify all two-bit boolean functions by looking at the corresponding matrix M_f.

0	$y=0$	$y=1$
$x=0$	0	0
$x=1$	0	0

and	$y=0$	$y=1$
$x=0$	0	0
$x=1$	0	1

$x\overline{y}$	$y=0$	$y=1$
$x=0$	0	0
$x=1$	1	0

x	$y=0$	$y=1$
$x=0$	0	0
$x=1$	1	1

$\overline{x}y$	$y=0$	$y=1$
$x=0$	0	1
$x=1$	0	0

y	$y=0$	$y=1$
$x=0$	0	1
$x=1$	0	1

xor	$y=0$	$y=1$
$x=0$	0	1
$x=1$	1	0

or	$y=0$	$y=1$
$x=0$	0	1
$x=1$	1	1

$\overline{or}$	$y=0$	$y=1$
$x=0$	1	0
$x=1$	0	0

$\overline{xor}$	$y=0$	$y=1$
$x=0$	1	0
$x=1$	0	1

$\overline{y}$	$y=0$	$y=1$
$x=0$	1	0
$x=1$	1	0

$x+\overline{y}$	$y=0$	$y=1$
$x=0$	1	0
$x=1$	1	1

$\overline{x}$	$y=0$	$y=1$
$x=0$	1	1
$x=1$	0	0

$\overline{x}+y$	$y=0$	$y=1$
$x=0$	1	1
$x=1$	0	1

$\overline{\text{and}}$	$y=0$	$y=1$
$x=0$	1	1
$x=1$	1	0

1	$y=0$	$y=1$
$x=0$	1	1
$x=1$	1	1

Thus, we can partition the 16 2-bit boolean functions in two groups:

- GROUP 1: $0, x, y, xor, \overline{xor}, \overline{y}, \overline{x},$ and 1
- GROUP 2: $and, x\overline{y}, \overline{x}y, or, \overline{or}, x+\overline{y}, \overline{x}+y,$ and $\overline{and}$

and state the following corollaries.

Corollary 1. *The two-bit boolean functions in Group 1 are privately computable.*

Corollary 2. *The two-bit boolean functions in Group 2 are not privately computable.*

4   Secret Sharing Homomorphism

Benaloh [5] introduced the notion of secret sharing homomorphism. Roughly speaking a secret sharing scheme is homomorphic if, when sharing two secrets, the sum of the two shares received by each participant is a share of the sum of the secrets. For the purpose of this paper we focus our attention on boolean functions and provide the following definition of a function that is computable through a secret sharing homomorphism.

Definition 4. *Let* $f : \{0,1\} \times \{0,1\} \rightarrow \{0,1\}$ *be a function, and let* a *and* b *be two secret bits. Moreover, for* $i = 1, 2$, *let* a_i *and* b_i *be the shares of* a *and* b. *Function* f *is computable through a secret sharing homomorphism (for short,* f *is share-homomorphic) if there exist efficient computable functions* $g_1 :$ $\{0,1\}^+ \times \{0,1\}^+ \rightarrow \{0,1\}^+$ *and* $g_2 : \{0,1\}^+ \times \{0,1\}^+ \rightarrow \{0,1\}^+$ *such that, given* $c_i = g_i(a_i, b_i)$ *for* $i = 1, 2$, *it holds that* $Rec(c_1, c_2) = f(a, b)$, *where* Rec *is the secret sharing reconstruction function.*

If f is share-homomorphic, then two parties, P_1 and P_2, holding shares of two secret bits a and b, can compute by themselves, using g_1 and g_2, new shares such that, reconstructing the secret from them, they get the same result they would obtain by applying f to the secret bits a and b.

The share-homomorphic functions are also *privately computable*. Indeed, intuitively, we might look at a and b as to the two secret inputs held by the parties: then, the shares a_i and b_i, due to the security property of secret sharing schemes, do not provide any information about a and b, the computation of $c_i = g(a_i, b_i)$ is a non-interactive private computation and, hence, does not leak any information about a and b. It follows that the computation of $f(c_1, c_2)$ does not leak any information about the inputs, apart what can be inferred by each party from the resulting function value and his own input.

More formally, we prove the following result:

Theorem 2. *If* f *is a share-homomorphic function, then* f *can be computed privately in a two-party computation.*

Proof. Assume that f is a share-homomorphic function. Let a and b be the input bits of the two parties and let a_1, a_2 be shares of a computed by P_1 and b_1, b_2 be shares of b computed by P_2. By definition of share-homomorphic function, there exists two efficiently computable functions g_1 and g_2 such that $Rec(c_1, c_2) = f(x, y)$, where $c_1 = g_1(a_1, b_1)$ and $c_2 = g_2(a_2, b_2)$. Given this, we can easily provide a two-party protocol that privately computes $f(a, b)$. Party P_1 sends a_2 to party P_2 and party P_2 sends b_1 to party P_1. Each party i applies function g_i to compute c_i. Then party P_1 sends c_1 to P_2 and P_2 sends c_2 to P_1. Finally each party computes $Rec(c_1, c_2)$. By the share-homomorphic function property we have that $Rec(c_1, c_2) = f(a, b)$.

The privacy of the input is guaranteed by the sharing scheme: each party receives only one share from the other party and thus it receives no information about the other party's input bit. Notice that also c_i cannot contain information about the input bit since it is computed from one share of a and from one share of b and each share reveals no information about the input bit.

The converse might not be true.

5   Visual Homomorphic Functions

In this section we explore the use of visual cryptography as the sharing technique and we consider homomorphic functions that can be computed visually.

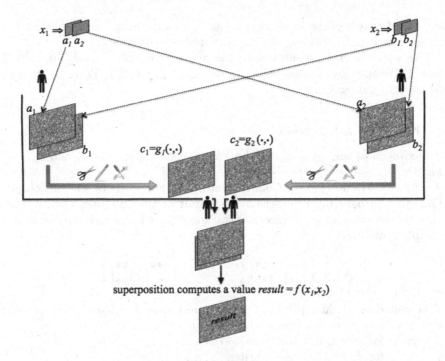

$$c_1 = g_1(\cdot,\cdot) \qquad c_2 = g_2(\cdot,\cdot)$$

superposition computes a value *result* $= f(x_1,x_2)$

Fig. 4. Model

By Theorem 2 and Corollary 2 we know that all the functions in Group 2 cannot be share-homomorphic (and thus they cannot be visually share-homomorphic). So the question we want to ask concerns the functions in Group 1, which we know are privately computable. Which of these functions is also visually share-homomorphic? It turns out that they are all visually share-homomorphic.

In order to prove the above assertion we define the following framework, which is an instantiation of the general model shown in Fig. 1. Two parties need to securely compute a function $f(x,y)$ of two input bits, x belonging to party 1, and y belonging to party 2. In order to achieve this goal each party, using a Scheme-(2,2)-NS, splits its own input bit into two visual shares. Then the party passes one of the shares to the other party (see Fig. 4). At this point both parties can manipulate the shares in their possession to produce new ones: party P_1 uses g_1 to produce c_1 and party P_2 uses g_2 to produce c_2. Finally, the two parties meet and superpose their transparencies c_1 and c_2 to obtain the result $c_1 \oplus c_2$. The result of the superposition is a visual representation of $f(x,y)$. More precisely, the value of the function f is computed visually according to the Scheme-(2,2)-NSreconstruction rule, i.e., by interpreting [••] as "1" and either one of $\{[\bullet\circ], [\circ\bullet]\}$ as "0".

We remark that, as we will see shortly, functions $g_1(\cdot,\cdot)$ and $g_2(\cdot,\cdot)$ *are not* visual superpositions of shares. However they can be easily (and physically) implemented since the result is equal to either one of the input shares or to the complement of one of the input shares and the complement can be obtained in several ways, e.g., by rotating the input share by 180 degrees.

Next we show how to instantiate the above protocol for each function in Group 1. We start by considering the functions $x, \bar{x}, y, \bar{y}, 0, 1$. Then we consider the functions xor and $\overline{\text{xor}}$.

5.1   Functions $X, \bar{x}, y, \bar{y}, 0, 1$

- $f = x$: $g_1 = a_1$ and $g_2 = a_2$. In this case we have that $c_1 = a_1$ and $c_2 = a_2$ and thus $c_1 \oplus c_2 = a_1 \oplus a_2 = x$.
- $f = \bar{x}$: $g_1 = \bar{a}_1$ and $g_2 = a_2$. Complementing the first share of scheme Scheme-(2,2)-NS, we basically complement the result of the reconstruction, as it is clear by the following explicit representation of the scheme with the first shares complemented:

$$\mathcal{C}_\circ = \left\{ \begin{bmatrix} \bullet\circ \\ \circ\bullet \end{bmatrix}, \begin{bmatrix} \circ\bullet \\ \bullet\circ \end{bmatrix} \right\} \qquad \mathcal{C}_\bullet = \left\{ \begin{bmatrix} \bullet\circ \\ \bullet\circ \end{bmatrix}, \begin{bmatrix} \circ\bullet \\ \circ\bullet \end{bmatrix} \right\}$$

When sharing a white pixel (0) we now reconstruct a black pixel (1) and viceversa. Hence, in this case we have that $c_1 \oplus c_2 = \bar{x}$.
- $f = y$: As for $f = x$, just use b_i instead of a_i.
- $f = \bar{y}$: As for $f = \bar{x}$, just use b_i instead of a_i.
- $f = 0$: $g_1 = a_2$ and $g_2 = a_2$. In this case we have $c_1 \oplus c_2 = a_2 \oplus a_2 = a_2$. Share a_2 can be either $[\circ\bullet]$ or $[\bullet\circ]$. In both cases it represents 0.
- $f = 1$: $g_1 = \bar{a}_2$ and $g_2 = a_2$. In this case we have $c_1 \oplus c_2 = \bar{a}_2 \oplus a_2 = [\bullet\bullet]$ which represents 1.

5.2   Function Xor

For $f = \text{xor}$ functions g_1 and g_2 are a little bit more complicated since they cannot be expressed as formulas. The following table specifies the functions (the two functions are equal).

	$\circ\bullet$	$\circ\bullet$	$\bullet\circ$	$\bullet\circ$
	$\circ\bullet$	$\bullet\circ$	$\circ\bullet$	$\bullet\circ$
$g_1(\cdot,\cdot) = g_2(\cdot,\cdot)$	$\circ\bullet$	$\bullet\circ$	$\bullet\circ$	$\circ\bullet$

To prove that the above choice of g_1, g_2 allows to visually compute the xor function we proceed with a case-by-case analysis, reported in the following tables. Notice that r denotes the possible random bits chosen by the parties to create the shares of their inputs.

Case 1: $x = 0,\ y = 0$

	a_1	a_2	b_1	b_2	c_1	c_2	$c_1 \oplus c_2$
$r = 00$	[○●]	[○●]	[○●]	[○●]	[○●]	[○●]	[○●] (0)
$r = 01$	[○●]	[○●]	[●○]	[●○]	[●○]	[●○]	[●○] (0)
$r = 10$	[●○]	[●○]	[○●]	[○●]	[●○]	[●○]	[●○] (0)
$r = 11$	[●○]	[●○]	[●○]	[●○]	[○●]	[○●]	[○●] (0)

Case 2: $x = 0,\ y = 1$

	a_1	a_2	b_1	b_2	c_1	c_2	$c_1 \oplus c_2$
$r = 00$	[○●]	[○●]	[○●]	[●○]	[○●]	[●○]	[●●] (1)
$r = 01$	[○●]	[○●]	[●○]	[○●]	[●○]	[○●]	[●●] (1)
$r = 10$	[●○]	[●○]	[○●]	[●○]	[●○]	[○●]	[●●] (1)
$r = 11$	[●○]	[●○]	[●○]	[○●]	[○●]	[●○]	[●●] (1)

Case 3: $x = 1,\ y = 0$

	a_1	a_2	b_1	b_2	c_1	c_2	$c_1 \oplus c_2$
$r = 00$	[○●]	[●○]	[○●]	[○●]	[○●]	[●○]	[●●] (1)
$r = 01$	[○●]	[●○]	[●○]	[●○]	[●○]	[○●]	[●●] (1)
$r = 10$	[●○]	[○●]	[○●]	[○●]	[●○]	[○●]	[●●] (1)
$r = 11$	[●○]	[○●]	[●○]	[●○]	[○●]	[●○]	[●●] (1)

Case 4: $x = 1,\ y = 1$

	a_1	a_2	b_1	b_2	c_1	c_2	$c_1 \oplus c_2$
$r = 00$	[○●]	[●○]	[○●]	[●○]	[○●]	[○●]	[○●] (0)
$r = 01$	[○●]	[●○]	[●○]	[○●]	[●○]	[●○]	[●○] (0)
$r = 10$	[●○]	[○●]	[○●]	[●○]	[●○]	[●○]	[●○] (0)
$r = 11$	[●○]	[○●]	[●○]	[○●]	[○●]	[○●]	[○●] (0)

In all cases we have that $f(x,y) = \mathtt{xor}(x,y)$.

5.3 Function $\overline{\mathtt{xor}}$

The $\overline{\mathtt{xor}}$ function is as the $\mathtt{xor}$ with function g_2 complemented pixel-wise ($\circ \leftrightarrow \bullet$) with respect to g_1. That is:

$g_1(\cdot,\cdot)$	○●	○●	●○	●○
	○●	●○	○●	●○
	○●	●○	●○	○●

$g_2(\cdot,\cdot)$	○●	○●	●○	●○
	○●	●○	○●	●○
	●○	○●	○●	●○

A case by case inspection is very similar to the one already seen for the $\mathtt{xor}$ function with the difference that c_2 is complemented ($\circ \leftrightarrow \bullet$). It should be not difficult to see that complementing c_2, the result $c_1 \oplus c_2$ gets also complemented ($1 \leftrightarrow 0$).

6 On Randomness Saving: Strategies and Impossibility Results

The classical approach to visual cryptography is to make shares for each pixel, regardless whether the pixels are correlated, or not. For an example of correlated pixels see Fig. 2 in the Introduction section. In this section we discuss an *approach to make visual shares of multiple pixels grouped together, exploiting the fact they might be correlated*. We start with an high level discussion and then proceed to give formal statements.

Obviously, since images superposition is used, we cannot compress the shares. Indeed, it would require some computer to decompress the shares. However, we will show that in some circumstances we can reduce *the dealer's randomness*.

The first question we pose is what security requirement we impose on such a new approach. We address this in Sect. 6.1. We then show the unexpected result that links randomness reduction to secure multiparty computation. We show impossibility and possibility results.

6.1   Security Definition

We first motivate the need for a definition. If shares are made for each pixel independently, then obviously, shares of one pixel are of no help to gain any information about another pixel. However, if the construction of shares is based on multiple pixels, then this observation may no longer be true. To better understand this take the following scenario.

Imagine a cabinet document is stored using visual cryptography. Now, when Prime Minister Tatcher came to power, ministers she inherited from the Heath Government, leaked parts of such documents to the press. Obviously, we want that a *leak of a part of document* stored using visual cryptography, does not leak anything extra *besides* what logically follows from the leak. Indeed, if a pixel in the unleaked part follows logically from the leaked pixels (as g in Fig. 2), then nothing can be done to prevent this extra leak. In our definition we will indicate tuples (or vectors) by $\underline{s}$. We call $x \in X$ the document in question.

Definition 5. *We consider two settings. In the first, a traitor leaks x_L, some part of the original document x to an unauthorized subset of participants B'; for simplicity we can think of x_L as some pixels of x and we let L be a set of indices of the leaked pixels. In the second setting this traitor leaks* additionally *all visual secret shares, i.e., $\underline{s}_L$, corresponding with the leaked pixels. We say that the secret sharing scheme maintains* pixel independence *if for any probability distribution of $x \in X$, for all unauthorized subset B' of participants,*

$$prob\left(x \mid x_L, \underline{s}_{B'}\right) = prob\left(x \mid \underline{s}_L, x_L, \underline{s}_{B'}\right), \tag{1}$$

where $\underline{s}_{B'}$ are shares of all or of some pixels of an unauthorized set B'.

6.2   Impossibility Results

We now show that if a pixel is a (deterministic) function of other pixels (as g in Fig. 2), the reduction of randomness for certain functions is impossible.

For the moment we restrict ourselves to the case that Pixel 3 is $f(\text{Pixel 1}, \text{Pixel 2})$ and that we have two parties and none alone should learn the secret. We let $X = GF(2^2)$, i.e., the set of all possible values for the first two pixels.

We let $s_{i,j}$ be the share of Party i of Pixel j. Moreover, when $B' = \{1\}$ or $B' = \{2\}$, we let $\underline{s}_{B'}$ be the shares of B' of the first 2 pixels. Also, we let $x_L = f(x)$, correspond to the 3rd pixel, (i.e., when $x \in X$), and $\underline{s}_L = (s_{1,3}, s_{2,3})$.

Lemma 1. *Suppose that the shares of the three pixels are pixel independent, as defined in Definition 5. Then, $\forall x, x' \in X$, for all probability distributions over X, $\forall \underline{s}_L$*

$$f(x) = f(x') \implies prob(\underline{s}_L \mid \underline{s}_{B'}, x) = prob(\underline{s}_L \mid \underline{s}_{B'}, x').$$

Proof. We have

$$prob(x \mid f(x), \underline{s}_{B'}, \underline{s}_L) \; = \; \frac{prob(\underline{s}_{B'}, x, \underline{s}_L)}{prob(\underline{s}_{B'}, f(x), \underline{s}_L)} \; = \; \frac{prob(\underline{s}_{B'}, x \mid \underline{s}_L)}{prob(\underline{s}_{B'}, f(x) \mid \underline{s}_L)} \, , \quad (2)$$

and similarly,

$$prob(x \mid f(x), \underline{s}_{B'}) \; = \; \frac{prob(\underline{s}_{B'}, x)}{prob(\underline{s}_{B'}, f(x))} \; = \; prob(x \mid f(x)) \cdot F \quad (3)$$

where $F = prob(\underline{s}_{B'} \mid x)/prob(\underline{s}_{B'} \mid f(x))$. Since the sharing guarantees pixel independence, the formula on the left-hand-side in (2) and on the left-hand-side in (3) are equal, giving

$$\frac{prob(\underline{s}_{B'}, x \mid \underline{s}_L)}{prob(\underline{s}_{B'}, f(x) \mid \underline{s}_L)} \; = \; prob(x \mid f(x)) \cdot F \, . \quad (4)$$

Then using (4),

$$\begin{aligned}
prob(\underline{s}_L \mid \underline{s}_{B'}, x) &= \frac{prob(\underline{s}_{B'}, x \mid \underline{s}_L) \cdot prob(\underline{s}_L)}{prob(\underline{s}_{B'}, x)} \\
&= \frac{prob(x \mid f(x)) \cdot F \cdot prob(\underline{s}_{B'}, f(x) \mid \underline{s}_L) \cdot prob(\underline{s}_L)}{prob(\underline{s}_{B'}, x)} \\
&= \frac{prob(x) \cdot F \cdot prob(\underline{s}_{B'}, f(x), \underline{s}_L)}{prob(f(x)) \cdot prob(\underline{s}_{B'} \mid x) \cdot prob(x)} \; = \; \frac{prob(\underline{s}_{B'}, f(x), \underline{s}_L)}{prob(\underline{s}_{B'}, f(x))} \, .
\end{aligned}$$

The result follows by observing that the last expression is identical for x and x' such that $f(x) = f(x')$.

We now prove our main theorem. We say that a two-out-of-two visual secret sharing scheme is *share revealing* when given pixel j and $s_{1,j}$, we can uniquely compute $s_{2,j}$ and similarly, when given pixel j and $s_{2,j}$, we can uniquely compute $s_{1,j}$. Note that Naor-Shamir's scheme satisfies this condition.

Theorem 3. *Let us assume that Pixel 3 = f (Pixel 1, Pixel 2) and that function f, cannot be privately computed. A dealer trying to reduce the randomness, i.e., reuse the randomness used for the shares of Pixel 1 and Pixel 2, when generating shares of Pixel 3, will breach the pixel independence requirement when using a visual secret sharing scheme which is share revealing.*

Proof. Since $B' = \{1\}$ or $B' = \{2\}$, for simplicity, let $B' = \{1\}$. Then Lemma 1 becomes that if $f(x) = f(x')$ then $prob(\underline{s}_L \mid \underline{s}_{\{1\}}, x) = prob(\underline{s}_L \mid \underline{s}_{\{1\}}, x')$, where $\underline{s}_{\{1\}}$ are Party 1's shares of the first two pixels, which we write from now on as $\underline{s}_1$. Since the secret sharing scheme we use is share revealing, the implication of Lemma 1 is equivalent to

$$f(x) = f(x') \implies prob(\underline{s}_L \mid \underline{s}_1, \underline{s}_2) = prob(\underline{s}_L \mid \underline{s}_1, \underline{s}_2'), \quad (5)$$

where $\underline{s}_2$ are the shares of Party 2 of the first two pixels. Condition (5) is exactly the privacy condition given in Definition 1. So, if f cannot be computed privately by a two-party protocol, then the pixel independence condition will be violated when trying to make a share revealing visual secret sharing scheme. (Note that if we would have taken $B' = \{2\}$, we would have come to a similar formula but we would had $\underline{s}_1'$ instead of $\underline{s}_2'$.)

As an application, we show that the dealer cannot reduce randomness when making shares of LED g in Fig. 2. Indeed, as pointed out earlier, $g = \overline{a}bcd$. As before, we let the four pixels (LEDs) correspond to four parties. The reduction to show that 4 parties cannot privately compute $g = \overline{a}bcd$ from $\overline{a}$, b, c, and d to the impossibility of two parties privately computing $\overline{xy}$ is well known and straightforward. Moreover, we have seen that $\overline{xy}$ is not privately computable.

We remark that if f cannot be computed in a two-party protocol 1-private, then pixel independence can (obviously) still be achieved choosing $s_{1,3}$ independently of $s_{1,1}$ and $s_{1,2}$.

7   Randomness Reduction

On the positive side, we have that all the functions that are visually share-homomorphic computable, that is, the functions in Group 1, allow for a randomness reduction in the share distribution phase.

More precisely, if the pixels of the secret image can be grouped in triples, where the third pixel is a function of the first two, and the function belongs to Group 1, we can construct a scheme that uses random bits only for encoding the first two pixels. As an example, let us assume that we have groups of three pixels, each appearing only in one of the following patterns:

$$[\circ\circ\circ] \quad [\circ\bullet\bullet] \quad [\bullet\circ\bullet] \quad [\bullet\bullet\circ].$$

that is, the third pixel is the xor of the first two.

We can construct a generalized Scheme-(2,2)-NSby using the standard Scheme-(2,2)-NSfor encoding the first two pixels and encoding the third one using the functions g_i that are needed to implement the visual share-homomorphic computation of the function.

For the xor function, a generalized Scheme-(2,2)-NSfor encoding the patterns is provided through the following collections $\mathcal{C}_{\circ\circ\circ}, \mathcal{C}_{\circ\bullet\bullet}, \mathcal{C}_{\bullet\circ\bullet}$ and $\mathcal{C}_{\bullet\bullet\circ}$ of matrices:

$$\mathcal{C}_{\circ\circ\circ} = \left\{ \begin{bmatrix} \circ\bullet\bullet\circ\circ\bullet \\ \circ\bullet\bullet\circ\circ\bullet \end{bmatrix}, \begin{bmatrix} \circ\bullet\circ\bullet\circ\bullet \\ \circ\bullet\circ\bullet\circ\bullet \end{bmatrix}, \begin{bmatrix} \bullet\circ\bullet\circ\circ\bullet \\ \bullet\circ\bullet\circ\circ\bullet \end{bmatrix}, \begin{bmatrix} \bullet\circ\circ\bullet\bullet\circ \\ \bullet\circ\circ\bullet\bullet\circ \end{bmatrix} \right\}$$

Consider the first distribution matrix and let us look at the first row, that is $[\circ\bullet\bullet\circ\circ\bullet]$. The first two pixels $\circ\bullet$ come from the first distribution matrix of $\mathcal{C}_\circ$ of Scheme-(2,2)-NS, because the first pixel of the triple is $\circ$; the subsequent two pixels $\bullet\circ$ come from the second distribution matrix of $\mathcal{C}_\circ$ of Scheme-(2,2)-NS, because the second pixel of the triple is also $\circ$; finally the last two pixels of $[\circ\bullet\bullet\circ\circ\bullet]$ do not come from any distribution matrix but instead they are obtained by applying function $g = g_1 = g_2$ from Sect. 5.2 to ○● and ●○. The other distribution matrices are constructed considering all possible combinations of the shares from $\mathcal{C}_\circ$ and $\mathcal{C}_\bullet$ of Scheme-(2,2)-NS.

In a similar way we construct the other distribution collections:

$$\mathcal{C}_{\circ\bullet\bullet} = \left\{ \begin{bmatrix} \circ\bullet\bullet\circ\bullet\circ \\ \circ\bullet\circ\bullet\circ\bullet \end{bmatrix}, \begin{bmatrix} \bullet\circ\bullet\circ\circ\bullet \\ \bullet\circ\circ\bullet\bullet\circ \end{bmatrix}, \begin{bmatrix} \circ\bullet\circ\bullet\circ\bullet \\ \circ\bullet\bullet\circ\bullet\circ \end{bmatrix}, \begin{bmatrix} \bullet\circ\circ\bullet\bullet\circ \\ \bullet\circ\bullet\circ\circ\bullet \end{bmatrix} \right\}$$

$$\mathcal{C}_{\bullet\circ\bullet} = \left\{ \begin{bmatrix} \bullet\circ\bullet\circ\circ\bullet \\ \circ\bullet\bullet\circ\bullet\circ \end{bmatrix}, \begin{bmatrix} \bullet\circ\circ\bullet\bullet\circ \\ \circ\bullet\circ\bullet\circ\bullet \end{bmatrix}, \begin{bmatrix} \circ\bullet\bullet\circ\bullet\circ \\ \bullet\circ\bullet\circ\circ\bullet \end{bmatrix}, \begin{bmatrix} \circ\bullet\circ\bullet\circ\bullet \\ \bullet\circ\circ\bullet\bullet\circ \end{bmatrix} \right\}$$

$$\mathcal{C}_{\bullet\bullet\circ} = \left\{ \begin{bmatrix} \bullet\circ\bullet\circ\circ\bullet \\ \circ\bullet\circ\bullet\circ\bullet \end{bmatrix}, \begin{bmatrix} \bullet\circ\circ\bullet\bullet\circ \\ \circ\bullet\bullet\circ\bullet\circ \end{bmatrix}, \begin{bmatrix} \circ\bullet\bullet\circ\bullet\circ \\ \bullet\circ\circ\bullet\bullet\circ \end{bmatrix}, \begin{bmatrix} \circ\bullet\circ\bullet\circ\bullet \\ \bullet\circ\bullet\circ\circ\bullet \end{bmatrix} \right\}$$

Notice that, the above scheme needs only two random bits for choosing a distribution matrix in each collection. A standard visual crypto scheme needs to use 3 random bits. Moreover, it is immediate to check that:

- each row of each matrix does not provide any information on the group of pixel it encodes
- superposing the two rows of each matrix of $\mathcal{C}_{\circ\circ\circ}$ we get a row with 3 black subpixels out of 6
- superposing the two rows of each matrix of $\mathcal{C}_{\circ\bullet\bullet}$ we get a row with 5 black subpixels out of 6
- superposing the two rows of each matrix of $\mathcal{C}_{\bullet\circ\bullet}$ we get a row with 5 black subpixels out of 6
- superposing the two rows of each matrix of $\mathcal{C}_{\bullet\bullet\circ}$ we get a row with 5 black subpixels out of 6

As another example, let us assume that the third pixel is the $\overline{xor}$ of the first two:

$$[\bullet\bullet\bullet] \quad [\bullet\circ\circ] \quad [\circ\bullet\circ] \quad [\circ\circ\bullet].$$

As done before, we can construct a generalized Scheme-(2,2)-NS. In this case the first rows are exactly as the ones that we have constructed for the xor function, because function g_1 in Sect. 5.3 is equal to function g of Sect. 5.2, while in the second rows the third 2-pixel pair is obtained applying function g_2 in Sect. 5.3, which is equal to $\bar{g}$. The collections are:

$$\mathcal{C}_{\bullet\bullet\bullet} = \left\{ \begin{bmatrix} \circ\bullet\circ\bullet\bullet\circ \\ \bullet\circ\bullet\circ\bullet\circ \end{bmatrix}, \begin{bmatrix} \bullet\circ\circ\bullet\bullet\circ \\ \circ\bullet\bullet\circ\circ\bullet \end{bmatrix}, \begin{bmatrix} \circ\bullet\bullet\circ\bullet\circ \\ \bullet\circ\circ\bullet\circ\bullet \end{bmatrix}, \begin{bmatrix} \bullet\circ\bullet\circ\circ\bullet \\ \circ\bullet\circ\bullet\bullet\circ \end{bmatrix} \right\}$$

$$\mathcal{C}_{\bullet\circ\circ} = \left\{ \begin{bmatrix} \circ\bullet\bullet\circ\bullet\circ \\ \bullet\circ\circ\bullet\circ\bullet \end{bmatrix}, \begin{bmatrix} \bullet\circ\circ\bullet\bullet\circ \\ \circ\bullet\circ\bullet\circ\bullet \end{bmatrix}, \begin{bmatrix} \circ\bullet\bullet\circ\bullet\circ \\ \bullet\circ\circ\bullet\circ\bullet \end{bmatrix}, \begin{bmatrix} \bullet\circ\bullet\circ\circ\bullet \\ \circ\bullet\bullet\circ\bullet\circ \end{bmatrix} \right\}$$

$$\mathcal{C}_{\circ\bullet\circ} = \left\{ \begin{bmatrix} \circ\bullet\circ\bullet\bullet\circ \\ \circ\bullet\bullet\circ\circ\bullet \end{bmatrix}, \begin{bmatrix} \bullet\circ\circ\bullet\bullet\circ \\ \bullet\circ\circ\bullet\circ\bullet \end{bmatrix}, \begin{bmatrix} \circ\bullet\bullet\circ\bullet\circ \\ \circ\bullet\circ\bullet\bullet\circ \end{bmatrix}, \begin{bmatrix} \bullet\circ\bullet\circ\circ\bullet \\ \bullet\circ\circ\bullet\circ\bullet \end{bmatrix} \right\}$$

$$\mathcal{C}_{\circ\circ\bullet} = \left\{ \begin{bmatrix} \circ\bullet\circ\bullet\bullet\circ \\ \circ\bullet\bullet\circ\bullet\circ \end{bmatrix}, \begin{bmatrix} \bullet\circ\circ\bullet\bullet\circ \\ \bullet\circ\circ\bullet\circ\bullet \end{bmatrix}, \begin{bmatrix} \circ\bullet\bullet\circ\bullet\circ \\ \circ\bullet\bullet\circ\circ\bullet \end{bmatrix}, \begin{bmatrix} \bullet\circ\bullet\circ\circ\bullet \\ \bullet\circ\bullet\circ\bullet\circ \end{bmatrix} \right\}$$

As before, the above scheme needs only two random bits. Again, it is immediate to check that:

- each row of each matrix does not provide any information on the group of pixel it encodes
- superposing the two rows of each matrix of $C_{\bullet\bullet\bullet}$ we get a row with 6 black subpixels out of 6
- superposing the two rows of each matrix of $C_{\bullet\circ\circ}$ we get a row with 4 black subpixels out of 6
- superposing the two rows of each matrix of $C_{\circ\bullet\circ}$ we get a row with 4 black subpixels out of 6
- superposing the two rows of each matrix of $C_{\circ\circ\bullet}$ we get a row with 4 black subpixels out of 6.

8   Conclusions and Open Problems

In this paper we have shown that:

- by properly defining *operations* on the shares, visual shares are homomorphic with respect to some functions f. In the two-party case, each user, by applying the operation to his two shares a_i, b_i of the secrets a, b, gets a share $g_i(a_i, b_i)$, $i = 1, 2$, such that the superposition of $g_1(a_1, b_1)$ and $g_2(a_2, b_2)$ visually provides, applying the standard Naor and Shamir superposition reconstruction strategy, the value of the function f;
- by linking our analysis to a general known result on private two-party computation, we have classified all the boolean functions of two input bits which admit homomorphic visual share computation;
- by encoding group of pixels together, instead of encoding each pixel independently as visual cryptography usually does, and exploiting pixel dependencies, some randomness can be saved. For the case of three pixels, where the third is a function of the first two, randomness can be saved if and only if the pixel dependencies can be expressed through functions 0, x, y, xor, $\overline{\text{xor}}$, $\bar{\text{y}}$, $\bar{\text{x}}$, and 1.
- by using reduction arguments, we have provided concrete examples of pixel dependencies in images which cannot be exploited: in a led display with a total of 7 leds, which could be used for input-output purposes in secure multiparty computation hybrid systems, led g is a function of leds a, b, c and d, i.e., $g = \overline{a}bcd$. Due to the impossibility of exploiting and dependencies there is no way to save randomness in an implementation based on visual cryptography. The same result holds for other leds.

Directions for future research include: (i) a formal model for *generalized* Scheme-(2,2)-NS(multi-collections of matrices) which encode groups of pixels together, providing bounds on the randomness and other parameters in terms of standard Scheme-(2,2)-NS; (ii) Characterization of dependencies among n-tuple of bits in terms of $(n-1)$-bit boolean functions; (iii) Look at the power of other visual crypto models.

References

1. International Business Times: Cisco Faces Challenges as Chinese Media Urge Switching to Domestic Products for National Security Reasons in Wake of NSA Surveillance Leaks. http://www.ibtimes.com/cisco-faces-challenges-chinese-media-urge-switching-domestic-products-national-security-reasons-wake. Accessed 25 June 2013

2. The Telegraph: Russia spied on G20 leaders with USB sticks. http://www.telegraph.co.uk/news/worldnews/europe/russia/10411473/Russia-spied-on-G20-leaders-with-USB-sticks.html. Accessed 29 October 2013

3. The Telegraph: Indian High Commission returns to typewriters. http://www.telegraph.co.uk/news/worldnews/asia/india/10339111/Indian-High-Commission-returns-to-typewriters.html. Accessed 27 September 2013

4. Asharov, G., Lindell, Y.: A Full Proof of the BGW Protocol for Perfectly-Secure Multiparty Computation, September 2014. https://eprint.iacr.org/2011/136.pdf

5. Benaloh, J.C.: Secret sharing homomorphisms: keeping shares of a secret secret (extended abstract). In: Odlyzko, A.M. (ed.) Crypto 1986. LNCS, vol. 263, pp. 251–260. Springer, Heidelberg (1987). doi:10.1007/3-540-47721-7_19

6. Ben-Or, M., Goldwasser, S., Wigderson, A.: Completeness theorems for non-cryptographic fault-tolerant distributed computation. In: Proceedings of STOC (1988)

7. Chaum, D.: Secret-Ballot Receipts and Transparent Integrity. http://www.vreceipt.com/article.pdf

8. Cimato, S., Yang, C.-N.: Visual Cryptography and Secret Image Sharing. CRC Press, Boca Raton (2012)

9. Cimato, S., De Prisco, R., De Santis, A.: Probabilistic visual cryptography schemes. Comput. J. **49**(1), 97–107 (2006)

10. Chaum, D. , Crépeau, C., Damgaard, I.: Multiparty unconditionally secure protocols. In: Proceedings of STOC (1988)

11. D'Arco, P., Prisco, R.: Secure Two-Party Computation: A Visual Way. In: Padró, C. (ed.) ICITS 2013. LNCS, vol. 8317, pp. 18–38. Springer, Heidelberg (2014). doi:10.1007/978-3-319-04268-8_2

12. De Bonis, A., De Santis, A.: Randomness in secret sharing and visual cryptography schemes. Theor. Comput. Sci. **314**(3), 351–374 (2004)

13. De Prisco, R., De Santis, A.: On the relation of random grid and deterministic visual cryptography. IEEE Trans. Inf. Forensics Secur. **9**(4), 653–665 (2014)

14. Kafri, O., Keren, E.: Encryption of pictures and shapes by random grids. Opt. Lett. **12**(6), 377–379 (1987)

15. Kushilevitz, E.: Privacy and communication complexity. In: Proceedings of IEEE Symposium on Foundations of Computer Science (FOCS), pp. 416–421 (1989)

16. Maeng, Y.-J., Mohaisen, A., Lee, M.-K., Nyang, D.: Transaction authentication using complementary colors. Comput. Secur. **48**, 167–181 (2015)

17. Naor, M., Shamir, A.: Visual cryptography. In: Santis, A. (ed.) EUROCRYPT 1994. LNCS, vol. 950, pp. 1–12. Springer, Heidelberg (1995). doi:10.1007/BFb0053419

18. Yang, C.-N.: New visual secret sharing schemes using probabilistic method. Pattern Recogn. Lett. **25**, 481–494 (2004)

19. Zhang, Y., Steele, A., Blanton, M.: PICCO: a general-purpose compiler for private distributed computation. In: Proceedings of the Conference on Computer and Communications Security, CCS13, Berlin, Germany, November 4–8, pp. 813–826 (2013)

Revisiting the False Acceptance Rate Attack on Biometric Visual Cryptographic Schemes

Koray Karabina[✉] and Angela Robinson

Florida Atlantic University, Boca Raton, USA
kkarabina@fau.edu, arobin65@my.fau.edu

Abstract. Visual cryptography is an increasingly popular cryptographic technique which allows for secret sharing and encryption of sensitive data. This method has been extended and applied to secure biometric data in various protocols. In this paper, we propose a general framework to help assess the security of these extended biometric visual cryptographic schemes (e-BVC). First, we formalize the notion of "perfect resistance against false authentication" under our framework and show that our formalization captures the traditional false acceptance attack under plausible assumptions. Second, we modify the traditional false acceptance attack and propose a new and generic strategy for attacking e-BVC schemes. As an application, we present a case analysis for a recent implementation of a face recognition protocol and verify the practical impact of our proposed framework and attack in detail.

1 Introduction

Biometric authentication systems are employed worldwide, in both public and private sectors. For example, facial and fingerprint recognition systems are valuable border control tools, and are currently deployed by the United States via the Global Entry program[1] as well as at automated border patrols in the Frankfurt Rhein-Main international airport[2]. Biometric authentication systems are convenient for users, requiring no generation and memorization of passwords. However, there is a greater risk in the event that the database storing biometric information is compromised or hacked. One may always create a new password, but one cannot easily create a new face or fingerprint. Thus confidentiality and privacy of biometric data is of supreme importance. The sensitive nature of enrolled biometric information requires heightened security and privacy measures of cryptographic protocols in biometrics. There are several techniques to design secure biometric schemes. Some examples are biometric cryptosystems [12], cancelable biometrics [18], secure multiparty computation, encryption, private information retrieval [4,5,7,8,24], and hybrid biometrics [9,11].

Biometric visual cryptography (BVC) [13,20] is another approach to design secure and privacy-preserving biometric systems. Visual cryptography (VC)

---

[1] http://www.cbp.gov/travel/trusted-traveler-programs/global-entry.
[2] http://www.easypass.de/EasyPass/EN/Service/FAQ/captured-data.html.

© Springer International Publishing AG 2016
A.C.A. Nascimento and P. Barreto (Eds.): ICITS 2016, LNCS 10015, pp. 114–125, 2016.
DOI: 10.1007/978-3-319-49175-2_6

allows for concealing of a secret image such that the recovery procedure does not require any computation. The main ingredient of a classical visual crypto-graphic construction is a (t, n)-threshold secret sharing scheme [6,21], where a secret is divided into n shares and the secret can be recovered if t or more shares are available. Otherwise, a collection of less than t shares is not supposed to reveal any information about the secret. For example, when $t = n = 2$, a secret image is divided into two secret shares such that none of the shares reveal any information about the original image. The original image can be reconstructed only when both shares are combined together. Therefore, VC enjoys the fact that sensitive information can securely be distributed over several databases rather than storing it in a central database. Naor and Shamir [15] are credited with the first visual cryptographic scheme using a (t, n)-threshold secret sharing scheme. In the case $t = 2$, reconstruction of an image in [15] is achieved by overlaying any of the 2 out of n secret shares, where the shares are in the form of trans-parencies. Semantic security is achieved in [15] because secret transparencies are indistinguishable from random transparencies, whence they do not reveal any information about the original image. Ateniese et al. [3] extend the work in [15] and establish a framework for visual cryptography for general access structures while preserving semantic security. In [15], the authors discuss how to extend their scheme (from VC to Extended VC (e-VC)) so that the shares of a secret image looks like meaningful images rather than random transparencies. This approach is further extended [2,13] to work with natural images and to improve the quality of output images. The extension of VC to e-VC in biometrics is motivated in [20] as follows:

> Since these sheets (shared secrets) appear as a random set of pixels, they may pique the curiosity of an interceptor by suggesting the existence of a secret image. To mitigate this concern, the sheets could be reformulated as natural images as stated by Naor and Shamir.

It is noted in [13] that there is a trade-off between the image quality and the security, and that their e-VC scheme is not perfectly secure. It is also noted that security assessments should take the human perception into account. Similarly, [20] reports on an implementation of an e-VC scheme for securing face images. In particular, equal error rates are presented with respect to a various set of parameters and databases, and the security of their scheme is discussed based on experiments. Based on experimental results in [20], several security claims are made. For example, based on Experiment 7 in [20], it is stated that exposing the identity of a secret face image by using the sheets alone is difficult. On the contrary, the picture taken from [20] (see Fig. 1) suggests that a single sheet of a secret image reveals significant information about the image itself. Similarly, based on Experiment 8 in [20], it is stated that performing cross-matching across different applications is difficult. However, we are not aware of a concrete formal security analysis of the protocols proposed and implemented in [13,20]. Several other visual biometric authentication schemes exist such as [14,17,19,20], but there is no formal framework for analyzing biometric visual cryptographic schemes and quantifying their security claims.

Original Image   Generated sheets   Reconstructed Image

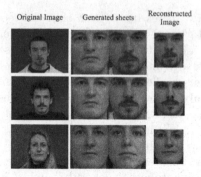

Fig. 1. The picture is taken from [20].

In this paper, we initiate the study of formal security analysis of biometric e-VC schemes (e-BVC). To our knowledge, this is the first comprehensive attempt that outlines a theoretical analysis and its practical impact on some recent implementations of biometric authentication schemes. In summary, our contributions are as follows:

1. In Sect. 2, we develop a framework and describe BVC schemes generically under our framework. In particular, we show how the face recognition protocol, recently proposed by Ross and Othman [20], fits our framework. In our analysis and examples, we choose [20] because, to our knowledge, it stands as the state-of-the-art e-BVC implementation with the most reasonable false accept and false reject rates. Moreover, [20] includes detailed security discussions with very strong security claims. However, none of the claims were proven due to the lack of a formal framework. Therefore, [20] is a natural choice to emphasize the practical impact of our framework.
2. In Sect. 3, we formalize the notion of "perfect resistance against false authentication" under our framework and show that our formalization captures the traditional false acceptance attack under plausible assumptions; see Definition 1 and Remark 2.
3. In Sect. 4, we propose a new and generic strategy for attacking e-BVC schemes. As an application, we present a case analysis for a recent implementation of a face recognition protocol in [20]. We disprove some of the security claims in [20] and verify that [20] does not achieve perfect resistance against false authentication. More concretely, we show that an adversary can utilize our new attack and authenticate with probability of success greater than 0.45.
4. As a result of our framework and analysis, we are able to derive a new and quantifiable upper bound on the security of e-BVC schemes; see Remark 4.

Remark 1. As is common in provable security works [1,22], our framework contains definitions of security games and reductions. The purpose is to provide more rigor in the security assessment of e-BVC schemes as well as creating proofs which are easy to verify.

2   Framework

Visual biometric authentication protocols require an enrollment and an authentication phase. During enrollment, a biometric image is captured and decomposed into, say n, obfuscated images. These decomposed components of the image are then distributed into n databases. During the authentication phase, some biometric image is captured and systematically compared against reconstructed images. Here, input to the reconstruction procedure is a subset of images held in the databases. This "comparison" is performed through a matching algorithm that computes a matching score. The matching score must exceed a certain value, so called a *matching threshold*, for a successful authentication.

To illustrate this idea, we elaborate on one of the biometric authentication protocols proposed in [20]. During the enrollment phase proposed in the face recognition scheme in [20], a biometric image is decomposed into two other face images, called sheets. The sheets are stored in separate databases, and according to security claim in [20] the individual sheets do not reveal the identity of the private face image. In fact, the private image is supposed to be recovered only when both sheets are present. The reconstruction is performed by superimposing the two sheet images to recover the original biometric image. This process of overlaying images is equivalent to the OR operator at the bit level [20]. Finally, the authentication of an image α requires the ORing of all pairs of sheet images until one ORed pair is a match with α with respect to a given matching threshold. We formalize this concept as follows.

Let Ω be a space of biometric images and S a space of images (not necessarily biometric). Note that Ω is a subset of S. In the following, M is a well-ordered set with "$\geq$" the comparison operator. Our framework requires the following oracles.

Decomposition is defined by the function

$$\mathcal{D}_n : \Omega \to \underbrace{S \times S \times \cdots \times S}_{n \text{ copies}},$$

which decomposes one biometric image into n images (a.k.a. *sheets*), not necessarily biometric.

Reconstruction is defined by the function

$$\mathcal{R}_t : \underbrace{S \times S \times \cdots \times S}_{t \text{ copies}} \to \Omega,$$

which takes t sheets as input, and constructs a biometric image.

Matching is defined by the function

$$\mathcal{M} : \Omega \times \Omega \to M,$$

which outputs some matching score $m_0 \in M$ given a pair of biometric images as input.

Authentication is defined by the function

$$\mathcal{A}_m : \Omega \times \underbrace{S \times S \times \cdots \times S}_{t \text{ copies}} \to \{0,1\},$$

where $m \in M$ is the matching threshold of the authentication protocol. $\mathcal{A}_m$ takes a tuple $(\alpha, s_1, s_2, \ldots s_t), \alpha \in \Omega, s_i \in S$ as input. Suppose $\beta = \mathcal{R}_t(s_1, s_2, \ldots, s_t)$ and $m_0 = \mathcal{M}(\alpha, \beta)$. Then the output of $\mathcal{A}_m$ is 1 if $m_0 \geq m$, indicating a successful authentication. Otherwise, $\mathcal{A}_m$ outputs 0.

Suppose now that $\mathcal{D}_n(\alpha) = (s_1, s_2, \ldots s_n)$ and $\beta = \mathcal{R}_t(s_{i_1}, s_{i_2}, \ldots, s_{i_t})$, where $i_j \in \{1, \ldots, n\}$ are pairwise distinct. For the robustness of a system, it is expected that $\mathcal{M}(\alpha, \beta) = m_0 \geq m$. That is, $\mathcal{A}_m(\alpha, s_{i_1}, s_{i_2}, \ldots, s_{i_t}) = 1$.

In our framework, we may denote a BVC scheme by the tuple $(\Omega, S, M, \mathcal{D}_n, \mathcal{R}_t, \mathcal{M}, \mathcal{A}_m)$.

Ross and Othman Scheme in our Framework: The face recognition protocol presented by Ross and Othman in [20] fits our framework with $t = n = 2$ as follows. The protocol employs a preselected collection of face images, called *host images*. Once a face image α is presented for enrollment, an *Active Appearance Model* (AAM) is created, as outlined in [10,23], based on facial landmarks and textures. Once the AAM has been created, the image undergoes annotation and has an associated registration cost. These factors determine which two host images h_1, h_2 are selected for the given image. These three images (α, h_1, h_2) are then sent through a digital halftoning and pixel expansion process before α is decomposed into two sheets. We may denote this decomposition in our framework as:

$$\mathcal{D}_2(\alpha) = (s_1(\alpha), s_2(\alpha)). \tag{2.1}$$

The reconstruction algorithm is performed by stacking the two sheet images atop each other. This is computed as the binary OR operation on each pair of bits in the sheets. We may denote this process in our framework as:

$$\mathcal{R}_2(s_1, s_2) = s_1 \oplus s_2, \tag{2.2}$$

where $\oplus$ denotes the binary OR operator.

Due to the nature of the digital halftoning and pixel expansion process, the stacking of sheets will not fully reconstruct the original image α. However, the face image will be recognizable to the human visual system as well as by the matching software. These claims are supported by experimental results in [20]. The matching and authentication oracles $\mathcal{M}$ and $\mathcal{A}_m$ are implemented by the Verilook SDK [16]. We denote Ross and Othman's extended biometric authentication scheme (for face recognition) by RO-e-BVC throughout the rest of this paper.

As mentioned earlier in Sect. 1, RO-e-BVC is based on a further extension of e-VC, which improves on the quality of output images. The main motivation is to improve on the performance (e.g. equal error rates) of the biometric scheme.

The trade-off between image quality and security is already noted in [13] even though we are not aware of a concrete analysis of this trade-off. On the contrary, some strong security properties about RO-e-BVC are claimed in [20]. In Sect. 3, we attempt to quantify the security of BVC schemes with respect to the *false authentication* notion. In particular, we show that RO-e-BVC in [20] does not achieve perfect resistance against false authentication.

3   Revisiting the False Acceptance Attack

First, we recall some common definitions in biometrics. A *genuine pair* is a pair of biometric images or some cryptographic transformation of images derived from the same person or entity. An *imposter pair* is a pair of biometric images which do not correspond to the same person. Given some matching oracle $\mathcal{M}$ and authentication oracle $\mathcal{A}_m$, we define a *Genuine Accept* as the event that the matching oracle $\mathcal{M}$ computes a matching score $m_0 \geq m$, given a genuine pair of biometric images. That is, $\mathcal{A}_m(\alpha, \beta) = 1$ for a genuine pair (α, β). A *False Reject* is the event that $\mathcal{A}_m(\alpha, \beta) = 0$ for a genuine pair (α, β). A *Genuine Reject* is the event that $\mathcal{M}$ computes $m_0 < m$, given an imposter pair. That is, $\mathcal{A}_m(\alpha, \beta) = 0$ for an imposter pair (α, β). A *False Accept* is the event that $\mathcal{A}_m(\alpha, \beta) = 1$ for an imposter pair (α, β). The *False Reject Rate* $\mathrm{FRR}(m)$ with respect to a matching threshold m is computed by counting the number of false rejects found from a list of genuine pairs, and diving this number by the size of the list. Similarly, the *False Accept Rate* $\mathrm{FAR}(m)$ with respect to a matching threshold m is computed by counting the number of false accepts found from a list of imposter pairs, and dividing this number by the size of the list.

In a traditional false acceptance attack, an adversary inserts a biometric image and hopes for a successful authentication. It is known that the success probability of an adversary in this attack is correlated with the false acceptance rate of the system. First, we capture this false acceptance rate attack idea and formalize it under the authentication game $\mathsf{G_{AUTH}}$. In particular, the guessing strategy in $\mathsf{G_{AUTH}}$ corresponds to an adversary who inserts random biometric images for authentication and whose success probability is asymptotically the same as the false acceptance rate of the underlying scheme.

Before describing $\mathsf{G_{AUTH}}$, we recall some common definitions in biometrics and induce some natural structure to the space of biometric images Ω. We assume that Ω is a universal finite set of biometric images so that $\Omega = \{\omega_1, \omega_2, \ldots, \omega_\ell\}$. Let N denote the number of unique individuals with at least one biometric image contained in Ω. We consider a partitioning of Ω as a disjoint union of W_i subsets, where W_i denotes the set of all genuine images that correspond to the ith individual for $i = 1, ..., N$. In summary, we have

1. For $x, y \in \Omega$, if $x \in W_i$ and $y \in W_j$ for some $i \neq j$, then (x, y) is an imposter pair.
2. For $x, y \in \Omega$, if $x, y \in W_i$ for some i, then (x, y) is a genuine pair.
3. $W_1 \cup W_2 \cup \ldots \cup W_N = \Omega$, $W_i \cap W_j = \emptyset$ for all $i \neq j$, and $\sum_{i=1}^{N} |W_i| = |\Omega|$.

Now, we are ready to describe G_{AUTH}. Let $(\Omega, S, M, \mathcal{D}_n, \mathcal{R}_t, \mathcal{M}, \mathcal{A}_m)$ represent an e-BVC scheme. For simplicity, we assume $t = n = 2$. In G_{AUTH}, $\mathcal{A}$ is a computationally bounded adversary and $\mathcal{C}$ represents a challenger. It is assumed that $\mathcal{A}$ knows the parameter set of the e-BVC scheme except the private images (denoted by Ω' below). It is also assumed that $\mathcal{A}$ has access to the first sheets of the decomposed biometric images in a database. This is a valid attack scenario because in an ideal BVC, the first sheet of a decomposed biometric image is not supposed to reveal any information about the original image.

Authentication Game. G_{AUTH}

1. The challenger $\mathcal{C}$ chooses k indices $i_1, ..., i_k$ uniformly at random, where $1 \leq k \leq N$. $\mathcal{C}$ generates a secret subcollection $\Omega' = \{w_{i_1}, ..., w_{i_k}\} \subseteq \Omega$ of private biometric images, where $w_{i_j} \in W_{i_j}$ for all $j = 1, ..., k$.
2. $\mathcal{C}$ computes $\mathcal{D}_2(w') = (s_1(w'), s_2(w'))$ and sends $s_1(w')$ for all $w' \in \Omega'$.
3. $\mathcal{A}$ outputs an image $w \in \Omega$ and wins if $\mathcal{A}_m(w, w') = 1$ for some $w' \in \Omega'$.

We define the success probability of $\mathcal{A}$ in G_{AUTH} as $\Pr[\mathcal{A}_m(w, w') = 1]$, and the advantage of $\mathcal{A}$ attacking an e-BVC scheme in G_{AUTH} as

$$\mathsf{Adv}_{\mathcal{A}}^{\mathsf{AUTH}} = | \Pr[\mathcal{A}_m(w, w') = 1] - \frac{\sum_{j=1}^{k} |W_{i_j}|}{|\Omega|} \cdot \mathrm{GAR}$$

$$- \frac{k|\Omega| - (\sum_{j=1}^{k} |W_{i_j}|)}{|\Omega|} \cdot \mathrm{FAR}|, \tag{3.1}$$

where FAR and GAR are the false acceptance and genuine acceptance rates of the underlying system. The definition of $\mathsf{Adv}_{\mathcal{A}}^{\mathsf{AUTH}}$ makes sense because we show in Theorem 1 that the adversarial advantage in the guessing attack is zero as expected.

We are now ready to formalize the notion of *perfect resistance against false authentication* based on G_{AUTH} and $\mathsf{Adv}_{\mathcal{A}}^{\mathsf{AUTH}}$.

Definition 1. *We say that an e-BVC scheme resists false authentication if* $\mathsf{Adv}_{\mathcal{A}}^{\mathsf{AUTH}}$ *is negligible for all possible $\mathcal{A}$. In particular, we say an e-BVC achieves perfect resistance against false authentication if* $\mathsf{Adv}_{\mathcal{A}}^{\mathsf{AUTH}} = 0$ *for all possible $\mathcal{A}$.*

Note that, in an authentication attack, $\mathcal{A}$ can always choose $w \in \Omega$ at random and hope that $\mathcal{A}_m(w, w') = 1$ for some $w' \in \Omega'$. This concept is formalized in the following guessing attack.

Guessing Attack. Suppose the adversary $\mathcal{A}$ plays the authentication game G_{AUTH}. Then $\mathcal{A}$ receives $s_1(w')$ for all $w' \in \Omega'$. In the guessing attack, $\mathcal{A}$ chooses $w \in \Omega$ uniformly at random and outputs w.

In the following, we compute the success probability of $\mathcal{A}$ in the guessing attack and conclude that it is practically the same as the false acceptance rate of the underlying scheme.

Theorem 1. *The success probability of $\mathcal{A}$ in the guessing attack is*

$$\Pr[\mathcal{A}_m(w, w') = 1] = \min(M, 1),$$

where

$$M = \frac{\sum_{j=1}^{k} |W_{i_j}|}{|\Omega|} \cdot \mathrm{GAR} + \frac{k|\Omega| - (\sum_{j=1}^{k} |W_{i_j}|)}{|\Omega|} \cdot \mathrm{FAR}.$$

The advantage of $\mathcal{A}$ is $\mathsf{Adv}_{\mathcal{A}}^{\mathsf{AUTH}} = 0.$

Proof. The success probability of $\mathcal{A}$ in the guessing attack can be computed as $\Pr[\mathcal{A}_m(w, w') = 1] = \min(M, 1)$, where M is the expected number of matches when w is compared against all w' in the database. We can write

$$
\begin{aligned}
M &= \sum_{j=1}^{k} [\Pr(w \in W_{i_j}) \Pr(\mathcal{M}(w, w_{i_j}) \geq m | w \in W_{i_j}) \\
&\quad + \Pr(w \notin W_{i_j}) \Pr(\mathcal{M}(w, w_{i_j}) \geq m | w \notin W_{i_j})] \\
&= \sum_{j=1}^{k} \left[\frac{|W_{i_j}|}{|\Omega|} \cdot \mathrm{GAR} + \frac{|\Omega| - |W_{i_j}|}{|\Omega|} \cdot \mathrm{FAR} \right] \\
&= \frac{\sum_{j=1}^{k} |W_{i_j}|}{|\Omega|} \cdot \mathrm{GAR} + \frac{k|\Omega| - (\sum_{j=1}^{k} |W_{i_j}|)}{|\Omega|} \cdot \mathrm{FAR},
\end{aligned}
$$

as required. Finally, $\mathsf{Adv}_{\mathcal{A}}^{\mathsf{AUTH}} = 0$ follows from (3.1).

Remark 2. In a robust authentication system, it is expected that $\mathrm{GAR} > \mathrm{FAR}$, whence,

$$\Pr[\mathcal{A}_m(w, w') = 1] \geq \min(k \cdot \mathrm{FAR}, 1). \tag{3.2}$$

On the other hand, in a practical authentication system, $\Pr[\mathcal{A}_m(w, w') = 1]$ cannot be much higher than $\min(k \cdot \mathrm{FAR}, 1)$ because it is also expected that k (the number of enrolled users in a database) is much smaller than N (the total number of users) and so $k/N \approx 0$. Consequently, under the plausible assumption that $|W_i| \approx |W_j|$ for all i, j, we can write

$$M = \frac{k}{N} \cdot (\mathrm{GAR} - \mathrm{FAR}) + k \cdot \mathrm{FAR} \approx k \cdot \mathrm{FAR}$$

and

$$\Pr[\mathcal{A}_m(w, w') = 1] \approx \min(k \cdot \mathrm{FAR}, 1).$$

Therefore, we see that the guessing attack in $\mathsf{G}_{\mathsf{AUTH}}$ is a way of formalizing the so-called false acceptance attack.

Based on Remark 2, we may state the adversarial advantage in $\mathsf{G}_{\mathsf{AUTH}}$ in a rather simplified form as follows:

$$\mathsf{Adv}_{\mathcal{A}}^{\mathsf{AUTH}^*} = |\Pr[\mathcal{A}_m(w, w') = 1] - \min(k \cdot \mathrm{FAR}, 1)|. \tag{3.3}$$

4   A New Strategy for Attacking E-BVC

Note that, in an ideal scheme, one would expect that $\mathcal{A}$'s success probability is no better than the success probability of a random guess and that $\mathcal{A}$ has zero advantage $\mathsf{Adv}_{\mathcal{A}}^{\mathsf{AUTH}} = 0$ (or $\mathsf{Adv}_{\mathcal{A}}^{\mathsf{AUTH}^*} \approx 0$). In this section, we modify the traditional false acceptance attack and introduce a new strategy for attacking e-BVC schemes. We compute the success probability and advantage of an adversary in this modified false acceptance attack. Finally, we compare the advantage of adversaries in the guessing attack and the new false acceptance rate attack. As an example, our analysis yields that the success probability of an adversary attacking RO-e-BVC [20] under the new false acceptance rate attack increases from 0.005 to 0.45.

First, we define new genuine accept (reject) and false accept (reject) notions.

Definition 2. Let $(\Omega, S, M, \mathcal{D}_n, \mathcal{R}_t, \mathcal{M}, \mathcal{A}_m)$ represent an e-BVC scheme. $\mathrm{GAR}'(m)$ (or, simply GAR') is defined to be a function of the matching threshold m and denotes the rate at which $\mathcal{M}(s_1(\alpha), \beta) \geq m$ given that (α, β) is a genuine pair. Similarly, $\mathrm{FAR}'(m)$ (or, simply FAR') is a function of m and denotes the rate at which $\mathcal{M}(s_1(\alpha), \beta) \geq m$ given that (α, β) is an imposter pair.

Note that in an ideal e-BVC scheme one would intuitively expect that $\mathrm{GAR}' \approx 0$ and $\mathrm{FAR}' \approx 0$ because a sheet of a biometric image is not supposed to reveal any information about the image itself. Our new authentication attack and its analysis in Theorem 2 confirms this intuition by showing that the success probability and the advantage of an adversary increases as GAR' and FAR' increase.

A New Authentication Attack (N-AUTH). Suppose $\mathcal{A}$ plays $\mathsf{G}_{\mathsf{AUTH}}$ and so she receives a set of sheets $\{s_{1,j} : s_{1,j} = s_1(w_{i_j}), w_{i_j} \in \Omega', j = 1, ..., k\}$. $\mathcal{A}$ chooses an index $j \in [1, k]$ uniformly at random and outputs $s_{1,j}$ as an attempt for authentication.

Theorem 2. The success probability of $\mathcal{A}$ in N-AUTH is

$$\Pr[\mathcal{A}_m(w, w') = 1] = \min(\mathrm{GAR}' + (k-1)\mathrm{FAR}', 1), \tag{4.1}$$

and the simplified advantage of $\mathcal{A}$ is

$$\mathsf{Adv}_{\mathcal{A}}^{\mathsf{AUTH}^*} = \left| \min(\mathrm{GAR}' + (k-1)\mathrm{FAR}', 1) - \min(k \cdot \mathrm{FAR}, 1) \right|. \tag{4.2}$$

Proof. Note that $\mathcal{A}$ in N-AUTH outputs $s_{1,j} = s_1(w_{i_j})$, where (w_{i_j}, w') is an imposter pair for all $w' \in \Omega'$ except when $w' = w_{i_j}$. Therefore, $s_{1,j}$ and the set Ω' form $(k-1)$ imposter pairs and 1 genuine pair in total, and we can compute the success probability of $\mathcal{A}$ in N-AUTH

$$\Pr[\mathcal{A}_m(w, w') = 1] = \min(\mathrm{GAR}' + (k-1)\mathrm{FAR}', 1). \tag{4.3}$$

It follows from (3.3) that

$$\mathsf{Adv}_{\mathcal{A}}^{\mathsf{AUTH}^*} = \left| \min(\mathrm{GAR}' + (k-1)\mathrm{FAR}', 1) - \min(k \cdot \mathrm{FAR}, 1) \right|.$$

Remark 3. In an ideal e-BVC, $s_1(\alpha)$ is not supposed to reveal any information about the original image α. Therefore, it is expected that the three distributions $\{(s_1(\alpha), \beta) : (\alpha, \beta) \text{ is genuine}\}$, $\{(s_1(\alpha), \beta) : (\alpha, \beta) \text{ is imposter}\}$, and $\{(\alpha, \beta) : (\alpha, \beta) \text{ is imposter}\}$ are indistinguishable, and hence $\text{GAR}' \approx \text{FAR}' \approx \text{FAR}$. This implies that, an ideal e-BVC satisfies

$$\text{Adv}_{\mathcal{A}}^{\text{AUTH}^*} = \left| \min(\text{GAR}' + (k-1)\text{FAR}', 1) - \min(k \cdot \text{FAR}, 1) \right|$$
$$\approx \left| \min(k \cdot \text{FAR}', 1) - \min(k \cdot \text{FAR}, 1) \right| \approx 0.$$

In other words, N-AUTH does not yield any adversarial advantage over the guessing attack for ideal e-BVC, as expected.

Remark 4. Based on our analysis of the guessing attack and the new authentication attack, we can conclude that the success probability of an adversary in an authentication game G_{AUTH} is

$$\Pr[\mathcal{A}_m(w, w') = 1] \geq \max \left[\min(\text{GAR}' + (k-1)\text{FAR}', 1), \min(k \cdot \text{FAR}, 1) \right].$$

This gives a quantifiable upper bound on the security of e-BVC schemes, where the quantification is performed based on the size k of the system database, and measurable rates GAR', FAR', and FAR. On the other hand, one should be careful assessing the security of the system as this is only an upper bound on the security based on just two attack methods. There may exist other and better attacks in general.

4.1   A Case Analysis for RO-e-BVC

As described earlier in Sect. 2, a visual face recognition protocol (RO-e-BVC) was proposed and implemented in [20]. More concretely, the scheme in [20] is implemented for 2 different databases (IMM and XM2VTS) and each database is considered with respect to 3 different datasets (A, F, and G) with a various number of host images. Several experiments were conducted in [20] to analyze the security and privacy-preserving properties of RO-e-BVC. In particular, Experiment 3 in [20] considers the possibility of matching one of the secret sheets of an image against the image itself, and does not consider this as a security threat.

On the contrary, we observe based on the illustration in Fig. 15 in [20] that at least one of the sheets of the decomposed images looks similar to the original image. Therefore, an adversary is expected to have significant advantage in attacking RO-e-BVC by mounting the N-AUTH attack as described in Sect. 3. In fact, in Experiment 3 in [20] it is reported that the equal error rate of a particular implementation of the RO-e-BVC scheme is very small: FAR = FRR $\approx$ 0 when the IMM database is used with the dataset A and FAR = FRR $\approx$ 0.005 when the XM2VTS database is used with the dataset A. It is also reported under the same setting that if single sheets are compared against original images then the resultant equal error rates are greater than 0.45. In other words, $\text{FAR}' = 1 - \text{GAR}' > 0.45$. It follows from Theorem 2 that the success probability of an adversary in attacking RO-e-BVC under

N-AUTH is $\Pr[\mathcal{A}_m(w, w') = 1] > 0.45$, which is significantly greater than the success probability of an adversary in attacking RO-e-BVC under the traditional false acceptance attack, or equivalently the guessing attack. We conclude that RO-e-BVC in [20] does not achieve perfect resistance against false authentication and adversaries can gain significant advantage in attacking RO-e-BVC under N-AUTH.

5 Conclusion

We formalized the notion of "perfect resistance against false authentication" for biometric visual cryptographic schemes and showed that our formalization captures the traditional false acceptance attack under plausible assumptions. We also introduced a new and effective attack strategy for e-BVC schemes. Our quantitative analysis verifies the practical impact of our framework and offers a concrete upper bound on the security of e-BVC.

References

1. Affeldt, R., Tanaka, M., Marti, N.: Formal proof of provable security by game-playing in a proof assistant. In: Susilo, W., Liu, J.K., Mu, Y. (eds.) ProvSec 2007. LNCS, vol. 4784, pp. 151–168. Springer, Heidelberg (2007). doi:10.1007/978-3-540-75670-5_10
2. Ateniese, G., Blundo, C., Santis, A.D., Stinson, D.: Extended capabilities for visual cryptography. Theoret. Comput. Sci. **250**, 143–161 (2001)
3. Ateniese, G., Blundo, C., Santis, A.D., Stinson, D.R.: Visual cryptography for general access structures. Inf. Comput. **129**(2), 86–106 (1996)
4. Barbosa, M., Brouard, T., Cauchie, S., Sousa, S.M.: Secure biometric authentication with improved accuracy. In: Mu, Y., Susilo, W., Seberry, J. (eds.) ACISP 2008. LNCS, vol. 5107, pp. 21–36. Springer, Heidelberg (2008). doi:10.1007/978-3-540-70500-0_3
5. Barni, M., Bianchi, T., Catalano, D., Raimondo, M., Labati, R., Failla, P., Fiore, D., Lazzeretti, R., Piuri, V., Scotti, F., Piva, A.: Privacy-preserving fingercode authentication. In: ACM Workshop on Multimedia and Security, pp. 231–240 (2010)
6. Blakley, G.: Safeguarding cryptographic keys. Proc. Natl. Comput. Conf. **48**, 313–317 (1979)
7. Blanton, M., Gasti, P.: Secure and efficient protocols for Iris and fingerprint identification. In: Atluri, V., Diaz, C. (eds.) ESORICS 2011. LNCS, vol. 6879, pp. 190–209. Springer, Heidelberg (2011). doi:10.1007/978-3-642-23822-2_11
8. Bringer, J., Chabanne, H., Izabachène, M., Pointcheval, D., Tang, Q., Zimmer, S.: An application of the goldwasser-micali cryptosystem to biometric authentication. In: Pieprzyk, J., Ghodosi, H., Dawson, E. (eds.) ACISP 2007. LNCS, vol. 4586, pp. 96–106. Springer, Heidelberg (2007). doi:10.1007/978-3-540-73458-1_8
9. Bringer, J., Chabanne, H., Kindarji, B.: The best of both worlds: applying secure sketches to cancelable biometrics. Sci. Comput. Program. **74**, 43–51 (2008)
10. Cootes, T.F., Edwards, G.J., Taylor, C.J.: Active appearance models. In: Burkhardt, H., Neumann, B. (eds.) ECCV 1998. LNCS, vol. 1407, pp. 484–498. Springer, Heidelberg (1998). doi:10.1007/BFb0054760

11. Hao, F.: Combining crypto with biometrics effectively. IEEE Trans. Comput. **55**, 1081–1088 (2006)
12. Jain, A., Nanadakumar, K.: Biometric authentication: system security and user privacy. IEEE Comput. Soc. **45**, 87–92 (2012)
13. Nakajima, M., Yamaguchi, Y.: Extended visual cryptography for natural images. J. WSCG **10**(2), 303–310 (2002)
14. Naor, M., Pinkas, B.: Visual authentication and identification. In: Kaliski, B.S. (ed.) CRYPTO 1997. LNCS, vol. 1294, pp. 322–336. Springer, Heidelberg (1997). doi:10.1007/BFb0052245
15. Naor, M., Shamir, A.: Visual cryptography. In: Santis, A. (ed.) EUROCRYPT 1994. LNCS, vol. 950, pp. 1–12. Springer, Heidelberg (1995). doi:10.1007/BFb0053419
16. Neurotechnology. Verilook SDK (1998). http://www.neurotechnology.com
17. Rao, Y.S., Sukonkina, Y., Bhagwati, C., Singh, U.K.: Fingerprint based authentication application using visual cryptography methods (improved id card). In: TENCON 2008–2008 IEEE Region 10 Conference, pp. 1–5. IEEE (2008)
18. Rathgeb, C., Uhl, A.: A survey on biometric cryptosystems and cancelable biometircs. EURASIP J. Inf. Secur. **1**, 1–25 (2011)
19. Revenkar, P., Anjum, A., Gandhare, W.: Secure iris authentication using visual cryptography. arXiv preprint arXiv:1004.1748 (2010)
20. Ross, A., Othman, A.: Visual cryptography for biometric privacy. IEEE Trans. Inf. Forensics Secur. **6**(1), 70–81 (2011)
21. Shamir, A.: How to share a secret. Commun. ACM **22**, 612–613 (1979)
22. Shoup, V.: Sequences of games: a tool for taming complexity in security proofs (2004). http://eprint.iacr.org/2004/332
23. Stegmann, M.B.: Active appearance models, theory, extensions and cases. Master's thesis, Informatics and Mathematical Modelling, Technical University of Denmark, DTU, Richard Petersens Plads, Building 321, DK-2800 Kgs. Lyngby, August 2000
24. Stoianov, A.: Cryptographically secure biometric. SPIE, Biometric Technology for Human Identification VII, vol. 7667, pp. 1–12 (2010)

Cryptographic Protocols

Detecting Algebraic Manipulation in Leaky Storage Systems

Fuchun Lin$^{(\boxtimes)}$, Reihaneh Safavi-Naini, and Pengwei Wang

Department of Computer Science, University of Calgary, Calgary, Canada
`fuchun.lin@ucalgary.ca`

Abstract. Algebraic Manipulation Detection (AMD) Codes detect adversarial noise that is added to a coded message which is stored in a storage that is opaque to the adversary. We study AMD codes when the storage can leak up to $\rho \log |\mathcal{G}|$ bits of information about the stored codeword, where $\mathcal{G}$ is the group that contains the codeword and ρ is a constant. We propose ρ-AMD codes that provide protection in this new setting. We define weak and strong ρ-AMD codes that provide security for a random and an arbitrary message, respectively. We derive concrete and asymptotic bounds for the efficiency of these codes featuring a rate upper bound of $1 - \rho$ for the strong codes. We also define the class of ρ^{LV}-AMD codes that provide protection when leakage is in the form of a number of codeword components, and give constructions featuring a family of strong ρ^{LV}-AMD codes that asymptotically achieve the rate $1 - \rho$. We describe applications of ρ-AMD codes to, (i) robust ramp secret sharing scheme and, (ii) wiretap II channel when the adversary can eavesdrop a ρ fraction of codeword components and tamper with all components of the codeword.

1 Introduction

Algebraic Manipulation Detection (AMD) Codes [1] protect messages against additive adversarial tampering, assuming the codeword cannot be "seen" by the adversary. In AMD codes, a message is encoded to a codeword that is an element of a publicly known group $\mathcal{G}$. The codeword is stored in a private storage which is perfectly opaque to the adversary. The adversary however can add an *arbitrary* element of $\mathcal{G}$ to the storage to make the decoder output a different message. A δ-secure AMD code guarantees that any such manipulation succeeds with probability at most δ. Security of AMD codes has been defined for "weak" and "strong" codes: weak codes provide security assuming message distribution is uniform, while strong codes guarantee security for any message distribution. Weak AMD codes are primarily deterministic codes and security relies on the randomness of the message space. Strong AMD codes are randomized codes and provide security for any message. AMD codes have wide applications as a building block of cryptographic primitives such as robust information dispersal [1], and anonymous message transmission [1], and have been used to provide a generic construction for robust secret sharing schemes from linear secret sharing schemes [1].

© Springer International Publishing AG 2016
A.C.A. Nascimento and P. Barreto (Eds.): ICITS 2016, LNCS 10015, pp. 129–150, 2016.
DOI: 10.1007/978-3-319-49175-2_7

AMD codes with leakage were first considered in [2] where the leakage was defined for specific parts of the encoding process. An α-*weak AMD code with linear leakage*, also called α-weak LLR-AMD code, is a deterministic code that guarantees security when part of the message is leaked but the min-entropy of the message space is at least $1 - \alpha$ fraction of the message length (in bits). An α-*strong LLR-AMD* is a randomized code that guarantees security when the randomness of encoding, although partially leaked, has at least min-entropy $(1 - \alpha) \log |\mathcal{R}|$ where $\mathcal{R}$ is the randomness set of encoding.

In this paper we consider leakage from the storage that holds the codeword. This effectively relaxes the original model of AMD codes that required the codeword to be perfectly private. As we will show this model turns out to be more challenging compared to LLR-AMD models where the leakage is in a more restricted part in the encoding process.

A more detailed relation between our model and LLR-AMD models is given in Sect. 3.1.

Our work

We define ρ-Algebraic Manipulation Detection (ρ-AMD) codes as an extension of AMD codes when the storage that holds the codeword (an element of $\mathcal{G}$), leaks up to $\rho \log |\mathcal{G}|$ bits of information about the codeword. We assume the adversary can apply an arbitrary function to the storage and receive up to $\rho \log |\mathcal{G}|$ bits of information about the codeword. Similar to the original AMD codes, we define weak and strong ρ-AMD codes as deterministic and randomized codes that guarantee security for a uniformly distributed message and any message, respectively.

Efficiency of ρ-AMD codes is defined concretely (similar to [1]) and asymptotically (using the *rate of the code family*, which is the asymptotic ratio of the message length to the codeword length, as the message length approaches infinity). We prove concrete bounds for both strong and weak ρ-AMD codes and a non-trivial upper bound $1 - \rho$ on the rate of the strong ρ-AMD codes. Comparison of bounds for different models of AMD codes is summarized in Table 1.

Table 1. G denotes the size of the group $\mathcal{G}$ that codewords live in and M denotes the size of the message set $\mathcal{M}$. δ is the security parameter.

Codes	Concrete bound	Rate bound
Strong AMD	$G \geq \frac{M-1}{\delta^2} + 1$	1
Strong ρ-AMD	$\mathbf{G^{1-\rho} \geq \frac{M-1}{\delta^2} + 1}$	$\mathbf{1 - \rho}$
α-strong LLR-AMD	$G \geq \frac{(M-1)(1-e^{-1})}{\delta^{\frac{2}{1-\alpha}}} + 1$	1
Weak AMD	$G \geq \frac{M-1}{\delta} + 1$	1
Weak ρ-AMD	$\mathbf{G \geq \frac{M-1}{\delta} + 1}$ **and** $\mathbf{M \geq \frac{G^\rho}{\delta}}$	1
α-weak LLR-AMD	$G \geq \frac{(M-1)(1-e^{-1})}{\delta^{\frac{1}{1-\alpha}}} + 1$ and $G \geq \frac{M^\alpha(M-1)(1-e^{-1})}{\delta} + 1$	$\frac{1}{1+\alpha}$

For construction, we use the relationship between ρ-AMD codes and LLR-AMD codes, to construct (non-optimal) ρ-AMD codes, and leave the construction of rate optimal ρ-AMD codes as an interesting open problem. We however define a special type of leakage in which leakage is specified by the number of codeword components that the adversary can select for eavesdropping. The model is called *limited-view* ρ-AMD (ρ^{LV}-AMD). The ρ^{LV}-AMD adversary is allowed to select a fraction ρ of the *codeword components*, and select their tampering (offset) vector after seeing the values of the chosen components. This definition of limited-view adversary was first used in [3] where the writing power of the adversary was also parametrized. We give an explicit construction of strong ρ^{LV}-AMD codes that achieve rate $1 - \rho$, using an AMD code and a wiretap II code as building blocks. We note that this rate is achievable for large constant size alphabets, if we allow a seeded encoder involving a universal hash family (see [15]). That is the alphabet size depends on the closeness to the actual capacity value. Also we do not know if $1 - \rho$ is the capacity of strong ρ^{LV}-AMD codes. Finding the capacity of strong ρ^{LV}-AMD codes however is an open question as the type of leakage (component wise) is more restricted than strong ρ-AMD codes. We also construct a family of weak ρ^{LV}-AMD codes that achieve rate 1 for any leakage parameter ρ.

We consider two applications. The first application can be seen as parallel to the application of the original AMD codes to robust secret sharing scheme. The second application is a new variation of active adversary wiretap channel II.

Robust Ramp Secret Sharing Scheme. A (t, r, N)-ramp secret sharing scheme [7,13] is a secret sharing scheme with two thresholds, t and r, such that any t or less shares do not leak any information about the secret while any r or more shares reconstruct the secret and if the number a of shares is in between t and r, an $\frac{a-t}{r-t}$ fraction of information of the secret will be leaked. We define a *robust ramp secret sharing scheme* as a ramp secret sharing scheme with an additional (ρ, δ)-robustness property which requires that the probability of reconstructing a wrong secret, if up to $t + \lfloor \rho(r - t) \rfloor$ shares are controlled by an active adversary, is bounded by δ. Here ρ is a constant. We will show that a (t, r, N, ρ, δ)-robust secret sharing scheme can be constructed from a linear (t, r, N)-ramp secret sharing scheme, by first encoding the message using a ρ-AMD code with security parameter δ, and then using the linear ramp secret sharing scheme to generate shares.

Wiretap II with an Algebraic Manipulation Adversary. Wiretap model of communication was proposed by Wyner [4]. In wiretap II setting [5], the goal is to provide secrecy against a passive adversary who can adaptively select a fraction ρ of transmitted codeword components to eavesdrop. We consider active wiretap II adversaries that in addition to eavesdropping the channel, algebraically manipulate the communication by adding a noise (offset) vector to the sent codeword. The code must protect against eavesdropping and also detect tampering. An algebraic manipulation wiretap II code is a wiretap II code with security against an eavesdropping adversary and so the rate upper bound for wiretap II codes is applicable. Our construction of ρ^{LV}-AMD codes gives a family of algebraic manipulation wiretap II codes which achieve this rate upper bound and so the construction is capacity-achieving. The result effectively shows that algebraic manipulation detection in this case can be achieved for "free" (without rate loss), asymptotically

Table 2 summarizes the code constructions and applications.

Table 2. Summary of codes constructed in this paper and their applications.

Codes constructed	Asymptotic rate	Applications
strong ρ-AMD	**N.A.**	(ρ, δ)-**robust ramp secret sharing**
strong ρ^{LV}-AMD	$1 - \rho$	$(\rho, 0, \delta)$-**algebraic adversary wiretap II**
weak ρ-AMD	**N.A.**	**N.A.**
weak ρ^{LV}-AMD	1	**N.A.**

Related works

Related Works. AMD codes were proposed in [1] and have found numerous applications. A work directly comparable to ours is [2] where LLR-AMD code with different leakage models for weak and strong codes are introduced. Our leakage model uses a single leakage model for both weak and strong codes and is a natural generalization of the original AMD codes. The relation between our model and LLR-AMD codes is given in Sect. 3.1. More generally, there is a large body of work on modelling leakage and designing leakage resilient systems. A survey can be found in [6].

Ramp secret sharing schemes (ramp SSS) are introduced in [7]. Robust secret sharing schemes (robust SSS) are well studied (see for example [1]). To our knowledge robust ramp secret sharing schemes (robust ramp SSS) have not been considered before. In a robust SSS, robustness is defined only when the number of the compromised players is below the privacy threshold of the underling SSS. Our definition of robust ramp SSS has robustness guarantee even when the number of compromised players is bigger than the privacy threshold.

Wiretap II model with active adversary was first studied in [14], where the eavesdropped components and tampered components are restricted to be the same set. A general model of wiretap II adversaries with additive manipulation was defined in [8]. In this model (called adversarial wiretap or AWTP) the adversary can read a fraction ρ_r, and add noise to a fraction ρ_w, of the codeword components. The goal of the encoding scheme is to provide secrecy and guarantee reliability (message recovery) against this adversary. A variation of AWTP called eAWTP is studied in [15], where erasure of codeword components instead of additive tampering is considered. Interestingly, both AWTP and eAWTP have the same capacity $1 - \rho_r - \rho_w$. The alphabet of known capacity-achieving codes are, $\mathcal{O}(\frac{1}{\xi^4}^{\frac{1}{\xi^2}})$ for AWTP codes and $\mathcal{O}(2^{\frac{1}{\xi^2}})$ for eAWTP codes, respectively, where ξ is the difference of the actual rate and capacity [15]. The adversary of algebraic manipulation wiretap II codes defined in this paper can be seen as the AWTP adversary with $\rho_r = \rho$ and $\rho_w = 1$, yielding $1 - \rho_r - \rho_w < 0$. In this case recovering the message is impossible. Our results on algebraic manipulation wiretap II show that a weaker goal against active attack, that is *to detect* manipulation of the message, is achievable and can be achieved with capacity $1 - \rho$, which is the same as the capacity of wiretap II codes with no security against active attacks.

Organization: In Sect. 2, we give notations and introduce AMD codes (with/ without leakage) and wiretap II codes. In Sect. 3, we define ρ-AMD codes and derive efficiency bounds. In Sect. 4, we study ρ^{LV}-AMD codes and give concrete constructions. In Sect. 5, we give two applications.

2   Preliminaries

Calligraphy letters $\mathcal{X}$ denote sets and their corresponding capital letters denote the cardinality, $|\mathcal{X}| = X$. Boldface letters $\mathbf{x}$ denote vectors. $\mathbf{x}_{|S}$ denotes the sub-vector of $\mathbf{x}$ consisting of the components specified by the index set S. $[n]$ denotes $\{1, 2, \cdots, n\}$. Capital boldface letters $\mathbf{X}$ denote random variables, and $\mathbf{X} \leftarrow \mathcal{X}$ denotes sampling of the random variable $\mathbf{X}$ from the set $\mathcal{X}$, with $\mathbf{X} \xleftarrow{\$} \mathcal{X}$ denoting a uniform distribution in sampling. The statistical distance between $\mathbf{X}$ and $\mathbf{Y}$ that are both defined over the set $\mathcal{W}$, is defined as,

$$\mathsf{SD}(\mathbf{X}, \mathbf{Y}) \triangleq \frac{1}{2} \sum_{w \in \mathcal{W}} |\Pr[\mathbf{X} = \mathbf{w}] - \Pr[\mathbf{Y} = \mathbf{w}]|.$$

We say $\mathbf{X}$ and $\mathbf{Y}$ are δ-close if $\mathsf{SD}(\mathbf{X}, \mathbf{Y}) \leq \delta$. The *min-entropy* $\mathsf{H}_\infty(\mathbf{X})$ of a random variable $\mathbf{X} \leftarrow \mathcal{X}$ is

$$\mathsf{H}_\infty(\mathbf{X}) = -\log \max_{\mathbf{x} \in \mathcal{X}} \Pr[\mathbf{X} = \mathbf{x}].$$

The *(average) conditional min-entropy* $\tilde{\mathsf{H}}_\infty(\mathbf{X}|\mathbf{Z})$ of $\mathbf{X}$ conditioned on $\mathbf{Z}$ is defined [9] as,

$$\tilde{\mathsf{H}}_\infty(\mathbf{X}|\mathbf{Z}) = -\log \left(\mathbb{E}_{\mathbf{Z}=\mathbf{z}} \max_{\mathbf{x}} \Pr[\mathbf{X} = \mathbf{x}|\mathbf{Z} = \mathbf{z}] \right).$$

The following bound on the amount of information about one variable that can leak through a correlated variable is proved in [9].

Lemma 1 [9]. *Let* $\mathbf{X} \leftarrow \mathcal{X}$ *and* $\mathbf{Z} \leftarrow \mathcal{Z}$ *with* $\ell = \log |\mathcal{Z}|$. *Then*

$$\tilde{\mathsf{H}}_\infty(\mathbf{X}|\mathbf{Z}) \geq \mathsf{H}_\infty(\mathbf{X}) - \ell.$$

Definition 1. *An* (M, G, δ)-*algebraic manipulation detection code, or* (M, G, δ)-*AMD code for short, is a probabilistic encoding map* $Enc : \mathcal{M} \rightarrow \mathcal{G}$ *from a set* $\mathcal{M}$ *of size* M *to an (additive) group* $\mathcal{G}$ *of order* G, *together with a deterministic decoding function* $Dec : \mathcal{G} \rightarrow \mathcal{M} \bigcup \{\perp\}$ *such that* $Dec(Enc(\mathbf{m})) = \mathbf{m}$ *with probability 1 for any* $\mathbf{m} \in \mathcal{M}$. *The security of an AMD code requires that for any* $\mathbf{m} \in \mathcal{M}$, $\Delta \in \mathcal{G}$, $\Pr[Dec(Enc(\mathbf{m}) + \Delta) \notin \{\mathbf{m}, \perp\}] \leq \delta$.

The AMD code above is said to provide *strong security*. *Weak AMD* codes provide security for randomly chosen messages. Efficiency of (M, G, δ)-AMD codes is measured by the *effective tag size* which is defined as the minimum tag length $\min\{\log_2 G\} - u$, where the minimum is over all (M, G, δ)-AMD codes with $M \geq 2^u$. Concrete lengths are important in practice, and additionally, the asymptotic rate (defined as the limit of the ratio of message length to codeword length as the length grows to infinity) of both weak and strong AMD codes has been shown [1] to be 1.

Lemma 2 [1]. *Any weak, respectively strong, (M, G, δ)-AMD code satisfies*

$$G \geq \frac{M-1}{\delta} + 1, \ \text{respectively,} \ G \geq \frac{M-1}{\delta^2} + 1.$$

The following construction is optimal with respect to effective tag size.

Construction 1 [1]. *Let $\mathbb{F}_q$ be a field of size q and characteristic p, and let d be any integer such that $d + 2$ is not divisible by p. Define the encoding function,*

$$Enc : \mathbb{F}_q^d \to \mathbb{F}_q^d \times \mathbb{F}_q \times \mathbb{F}_q, \mathbf{m} \mapsto (\mathbf{m}, \mathbf{r}, f(\mathbf{r}, \mathbf{m})), \ \text{where} \ f(\mathbf{r}, \mathbf{m}) = \mathbf{r}^{d+2} + \sum_{i=1}^{d} m_i \mathbf{r}^i.$$

The decoder Dec verifies a tagged message $(\mathbf{m}, \mathbf{r}, t)$ by comparing $t = f(\mathbf{r}, \mathbf{m})$ and outputs $\mathbf{m}$ if agree; $\perp$ otherwise. (Enc, Dec) gives a $(q^d, q^{d+2}, \frac{d+1}{q})$-AMD code.

Definition 2 (strong LLR-AMD) [2]. *A randomized code with encoding function $Enc : \mathcal{M} \times \mathcal{R} \to \mathcal{X}$ and decoding function $Dec : \mathcal{X} \to \mathcal{M} \bigcup\{\perp\}$ is a $(M, X, |\mathcal{R}|, \alpha, \delta)$-strong LLR-AMD code if for any $\mathbf{m} \in \mathcal{M}$ and any $\mathbf{r} \in \mathcal{R}$, $Dec(Enc(\mathbf{m}, \mathbf{r})) = \mathbf{m}$, and for any adversary $\mathbb{A}$ and variables $\mathbf{R} \xleftarrow{\$} \mathcal{R}$ and $\mathbf{Z}$ such that $\tilde{H}_\infty(\mathbf{R}|\mathbf{Z}) \geq (1 - \alpha) \log |\mathcal{R}|$, it holds for any $\mathbf{m} \in \mathcal{M}$:*

$$\Pr[Dec(Enc(\mathbf{m}, \mathbf{R}) + \mathbb{A}(\mathbf{Z})) \notin \{\mathbf{m}, \perp\}] \leq \delta, \tag{1}$$

where the probability is over the randomness of encoding.

Definition 3 (weak LLR-AMD) [2]. *A deterministic code with encoding function $Enc : \mathcal{M} \to \mathcal{X}$ and decoding function $Dec : \mathcal{X} \to \mathcal{M} \bigcup\{\perp\}$ is a (M, X, α, δ)-weak LLR-AMD code if for any $\mathbf{m} \in \mathcal{M}$, $Dec(Enc(\mathbf{m})) = \mathbf{m}$, and for any adversary $\mathbb{A}$ and variables $\mathbf{M} \leftarrow \mathcal{M}$ and $\mathbf{Z}$ such that $\tilde{H}_\infty(\mathbf{M}|\mathbf{Z}) \geq (1 - \alpha) \log |\mathcal{M}|$, it holds:*

$$\Pr[Dec(Enc(\mathbf{M}) + \mathbb{A}(\mathbf{Z})) \notin \{\mathbf{M}, \perp\}] \leq \delta, \tag{2}$$

where the probability is over the randomness of the message.

In the above two definitions, leakages are from randomness (bounded by $\tilde{H}_\infty(\mathbf{R}|\mathbf{Z}) \geq (1 - \alpha) \log |\mathcal{R}|$) and message space (bounded by $\tilde{H}_\infty(\mathbf{M}|\mathbf{Z}) \geq (1 - \alpha) \log |\mathcal{M}|$), respectively.

Wiretap II Codes. Wiretap II model [5] of secure communication considers a scenario where Alice wants to send messages to Bob over a reliable channel that is eavesdropped by an adversary, Eve. The adversary can read a fraction ρ of the transmitted codeword components, and is allowed to choose any subset (the right size) of their choice. A wiretap II code provides information-theoretic secrecy for message transmission against this adversary.

Definition 4. *A (ρ, ε) wiretap II code, or (ρ, ε)-WtII code for short, is a probabilistic encoding function $Enc : \mathbb{F}_q^k \to \mathbb{F}_q^n$, together with a deterministic decoding function $Dec : \mathbb{F}_q^n \to \mathbb{F}_q^k$ such that $Dec(Enc(\mathbf{m})) = \mathbf{m}$ for any $\mathbf{m} \in \mathbb{F}_q^k$. The security of a (ρ, ε)-WtII code requires that for any $\mathbf{m}_0, \mathbf{m}_1 \in \mathbb{F}_q^k$, any $S \subset [n]$ of size $|S| \leq n\rho$,*

$$\mathsf{SD}(Enc(\mathbf{m}_0)_{|S}; Enc(\mathbf{m}_1)_{|S}) \leq \varepsilon \tag{3}$$

A rate R is achievable if there exists a family of (ρ, ε)-WtII codes with encoding and decoding functions $\{Enc_n, Dec_n\}$ such that $\lim_{n \to \infty} \frac{k}{n} = R$.

The above definition of security is in line with [8] and is stronger than the original definition [5], and also the definition in [10].

Lemma 3 [8]. *The achievable rate of $(\rho, 0)$-WtII codes is upper bounded by $1 - \rho$.*

When $\varepsilon = 0$ is achieved in (3), the distribution of any ρ fraction of the codeword components is independent of the message. This is achieved, for example, by the following construction of wiretap II codes.

Construction 2 [5]. *Let $G_{(n-k) \times n}$ be a generator matrix of a $[n, n-k]$ MDS code over $\mathbb{F}_q$. Append k rows to G such that the obtained matrix $\begin{bmatrix} G \\ \tilde{G} \end{bmatrix}$ is nonsingular. Define the encoder WtIIenc as follows.*

$$WtIIenc(\mathbf{m}) = [\mathbf{r}, \mathbf{m}] \begin{bmatrix} G \\ \tilde{G} \end{bmatrix}, \text{ where } \mathbf{r} \xleftarrow{\$} \mathbb{F}_q^{n-k}.$$

WtIIdec uses a parity-check matrix $H_{k \times n}$ of the MDS code to first compute the syndrome, $H\mathbf{x}^T$, and then map the syndrome back to the message using the one-to-one correspondence between syndromes and messages. The above construction gives a family of $(\rho, 0)$-WtII codes for $\rho = \frac{n-k}{n}$.

3   AMD Codes for Leaky Storage

We consider codes over a finite field $\mathbb{F}_q$, where q is a prime power, and assume message set $\mathcal{M} = \mathbb{F}_q^k$ and the storage stores an element of the group $\mathcal{G} = \mathbb{F}_q^n$.

3.1 Definition of ρ-AMD

Definition 5. *An (n, k)-coding scheme consists of two functions: a randomized encoding function* $Enc : \mathbb{F}_q^k \to \mathbb{F}_q^n$, *and deterministic decoding function* $Dec : \mathbb{F}_q^n \to \mathbb{F}_q^k \cup \{\perp\}$, *satisfying* $\Pr[Dec(Enc(\mathbf{m})) = \mathbf{m}] = 1$, *for any* $\mathbf{m} \in \mathbb{F}_q^k$. *Here probability is taken over the randomness of the encoding algorithm.*

The information rate *of an (n, k)-coding scheme is $\frac{k}{n}$.*

We now define our leakage model and codes that detect manipulation in presence of this leakage. Let $\mathbf{X} = Enc(\mathbf{m})$ for a message $\mathbf{m} \in \mathcal{M}$, and $\mathbb{A}_{\mathbf{Z}}$ denote an adversary with access to a variable $\mathbf{Z}$, representing the leakage of information about the codeword.

Definition 6 *(ρ-**AMD**).* *An (n, k)-coding scheme is called a* strong ρ-AMD code *with security parameter δ if* $\Pr[Dec(\mathbb{A}_{\mathbf{Z}}(Enc(\mathbf{m}))) \notin \{\mathbf{m}, \perp\}] \leq \delta$ *for any message $\mathbf{m} \in \mathbb{F}_q^k$ and adversary $\mathbb{A}_{\mathbf{Z}}$ whose leakage variable $\mathbf{Z}$ satisfies* $\tilde{\mathsf{H}}_\infty(\mathbf{X}|\mathbf{Z}) \geq \mathsf{H}_\infty(\mathbf{X}) - \rho n \log q$, *and is allowed to choose any offset vector in $\mathbb{F}_q^n$ to add to the codeword.*

The code is called a weak ρ-AMD code *if security holds for $\mathbf{M} \xleftarrow{\$} \mathbb{F}_q^k$ (rather than an arbitrary message distribution). The encoder in this case is deterministic and the probability of outputing a different message is over the randomness of the message.*

A family $\{(Enc_n, Dec_n)\}$ of ρ-AMD codes is a set of $(n, k(n))$-coding schemes indexed by the codeword length n, where for any value of δ, there is an $N \in \mathbb{N}$ such that for all $n \geq N$, (Enc_n, Dec_n) is a ρ-AMD code with security parameter δ.

A rate R is achievable *if there exists a family $\{(Enc_n, Dec_n)\}$ of ρ-AMD codes such that $\lim_{n\to\infty} \frac{k(n)}{n} = R$ as δ approaches 0*

Our definition bounds the amount of leakage in comparison with an adversary who observes up to ρn components of the stored codeword. We call this latter adversary a *Limited-View (LV) adversary* [3]. According to Lemma 1, the min-entropy of the stored codeword given an LV-adversary will be $\tilde{\mathsf{H}}_\infty(\mathbf{X}|\mathbf{Z}) \geq \mathsf{H}_\infty(\mathbf{X}) - \rho n \log q$. We require the same min-entropy be left in the codeword, for an arbitrary leakage variable $\mathbf{Z}$ accessible to the adversary.

Figure 1 shows places of leakage in AMD encoding in our model, and the models in Definitions 2 and 3.

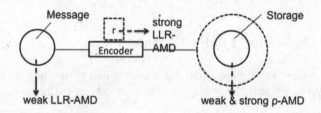

Fig. 1. The arrow shows the part of the system that leaks.

Proposition 1. *Let* $\mathbf{X}$ *denote a random variable representing the codeword of a message* $\mathbf{m}$ *(*$\mathbf{M}$ *for weak codes), and* $\mathbf{Z}$ *denote the leakage variable of the adversary* $\mathbb{A}_{\mathbf{Z}}$ *who uses the leakage information to construct the best offset vector to make the decoder output a different message. For a* ρ-*AMD code with security parameter* δ, *we have* $\tilde{H}(\mathbf{X}|\mathbf{Z}) \geq \log \frac{1}{\delta}$.

Proof. We write the proof for strong ρ-AMD codes. (The proof for weak ρ-AMD codes follows similarly.) According to the security definition of ρ-AMD codes, we have

$$\Pr[\mathrm{Dec}(\mathbb{A}_{\mathbf{Z}}(\mathbf{X})) \notin \{\mathbf{m}, \perp\}] \leq \delta,$$

where the probability is over the randomness of $\mathbf{X}$, and is the expectation over $\mathbf{z} \in \mathcal{Z}$. If the adversary with the leakage variable $\mathbf{Z} = \mathbf{z}$ can correctly guess the value $\mathbf{x}$ of $\mathbf{X}$, then a codeword $\mathbf{x}'$ corresponding to another message $\mathbf{m}'$ can be constructed to cause the decoder to output $\mathbf{m}'$, by using $\mathbb{A}_{\mathbf{z}}(\mathbf{X}) = \mathbf{X} + (\mathbf{x}' - \mathbf{x})$. We then have

$$\Pr[\mathrm{Dec}(\mathbb{A}_{\mathbf{Z}}(\mathbf{X})) \notin \{\mathbf{m}, \perp\}|\mathbf{Z} = \mathbf{z}] \geq \max_{\mathbf{x}} \Pr[\mathbf{X} = \mathbf{x}|\mathbf{Z} = \mathbf{z}],$$

which by taking expectation over $\mathbf{z} \in \mathcal{Z}$ yields

$$\mathbb{E}_{\mathbf{z}}\left(\Pr[\mathrm{Dec}(\mathbb{A}_{\mathbf{Z}}(\mathbf{X})) \notin \{\mathbf{m}, \perp\}|\mathbf{Z} = \mathbf{z}]\right) \geq \mathbb{E}_{\mathbf{z}}\left(\max_{\mathbf{x}} \Pr[\mathbf{X} = \mathbf{x}|\mathbf{Z} = \mathbf{z}]\right) = 2^{-\tilde{H}(\mathbf{X}|\mathbf{Z})},$$

The last equality follows from the definition of conditional min-entropy. The desired inequality then follows directly from the security definition of ρ-AMD codes as follows.

$$2^{-\tilde{H}(\mathbf{X}|\mathbf{Z})} \leq \Pr[\mathrm{Dec}(\mathbb{A}_{\mathbf{Z}}(\mathbf{X})) \notin \{\mathbf{m}, \perp\}|\mathbf{Z} = \mathbf{z}] \leq \delta \iff \tilde{H}(\mathbf{X}|\mathbf{Z}) \geq \log \frac{1}{\delta}.$$

$\square$

Definition 7. *Let* $\mathcal{C}$ *denote the set of codewords of a code, and* $\mathcal{C}_{\mathbf{m}}$ *denote the set of codewords corresponding to the message* $\mathbf{m}$, *i.e.* $\mathcal{C}_{\mathbf{m}} = \{Enc(\mathbf{m}, \mathbf{r})|\mathbf{r} \in \mathcal{R}\}$. *A randomised encoder is called regular if* $|\mathcal{C}_{\mathbf{m}}| = |\mathcal{R}|$ *for all* $\mathbf{m}$.

We note that because the code has zero decoding error when there is no adversary corruption, we have

$$\mathcal{C}_{\mathbf{m}} \cap \mathcal{C}_{\mathbf{m}'} = \emptyset, \ \forall \mathbf{m}, \mathbf{m}' \in \mathcal{M}. \tag{4}$$

This means that for regular randomised encoders, a codeword uniquely determines a pair $(\mathbf{m}, \mathbf{r})$. Assuming that the randomized encoder uses r uniformly distributed bits, the random variable $\mathbf{X} = \mathrm{Enc}(\mathbf{m}, \mathbf{R})$ is flat over $\mathcal{C}_{\mathbf{m}}$.

Lemma 4. *The relations between Strong LLR-AMD codes and strong* ρ-*AMD codes are as follows.*

1. *If there exists a regular randomized encoder for a $(q^k, q^n, 2^r, \alpha, \delta)$-strong LLR-AMD code, then there is an encoder for strong ρ-AMD code with security parameter δ and leakage parameter ρ where $\rho \le \frac{\alpha r}{n \log q}$.*
2. *If there exists a regular randomized encoder for a strong ρ-AMD code with security parameter δ and leakage parameter ρ, then there is an encoder for a $(q^k, q^n, 2^r, \alpha, \delta)$-strong LLR-AMD code with α and r where $\alpha \le \frac{n\rho \log q}{r}$ and $r \ge \log \frac{1}{\delta} + n\rho \log q$.*

Proof of Lemma 4 is given in Appendix A.

In [2], it is shown that the optimal AMD code in Construction 1 gives a $(q^d, q^{d+2}, q, \alpha, \frac{d+1}{q^{1-\alpha}})$-strong LLR-AMD code. The parameters of this LLR-AMD code are $k = d$, $n = d + 2$, $r = \log q$ and $\delta = \frac{d+1}{q^{1-\alpha}}$. A simple mathematical manipulation of these equations gives $\alpha = 1 - \log_q \frac{n-1}{\delta}$, and substituting them into Lemma 4, item 1, we obtain

$$\rho \le \frac{(1 - \log_q \frac{n-1}{\delta}) \log q}{n \log q} = \frac{1 - \log_q \frac{n-1}{\delta}}{n}.$$

This results in the following.

Corollary 1. *The code in Construction 1 is a strong ρ-AMD code with $k = d$, $n = d + 2$, security parameter δ and leakage parameter $\rho \le \frac{1 - \log_q \frac{n-1}{\delta}}{n}$.*

It is easy to see that $\rho < \frac{1}{n}$. Thus the resulting construction of strong ρ-AMD codes can only tolerate a very small leakage. Moreover the upper bound on ρ vanishes as n goes to infinity and so this construction cannot give a non-trivial family of strong ρ-AMD code. We note that the same construction resulted in a family of strong LLR-AMD codes with asymptotic rate 1.

Lemma 5. *The relations between weak LLR-AMD codes and weak ρ-AMD codes are as follows.*

1. *A $(q^k, q^n, \alpha, \delta)$-weak LLR-AMD code is a weak ρ-AMD code with security parameter δ and leakage parameter ρ satisfying $\rho \le \frac{\alpha k}{n}$.*
2. *A weak ρ-AMD code with security parameter δ and leakage parameter ρ is a $(q^k, q^n, \alpha, \delta)$-weak LLR-AMD code satisfying $\alpha \le \frac{\rho n}{k}$.*

Proof of Lemma 5 is given in Appendix B.

A construction of $(q^d, q^{d+1}, \alpha, \frac{2}{q^{1-\alpha d}})$ weak LLR-AMD codes is given in [2, Theorem 2]. The code has parameters $k = d$, $n = d + 1$ and $\delta = \frac{2}{q^{1-\alpha d}}$. A simple mathematical manipulation of these equations gives $\alpha = \frac{1 - \log_q \frac{2}{\delta}}{n-1}$, and so from Lemma 5, item 1, we obtain

$$\rho \le \frac{(\frac{1 - \log_q \frac{2}{\delta}}{n-1})(n-1)}{n} = \frac{1 - \log_q \frac{2}{\delta}}{n}.$$

Corollary 2. *The code in [[2], Theorem 2] is a weak ρ-AMD code with $k = d$, $n = d + 1$, security parameter δ and leakage parameter $\rho \leq \frac{1 - \log_q \frac{2}{\delta}}{n}$.*

This construction gives ρ-AMD codes with small ρ, and cannot be used to construct a family of ρ-AMD codes for $\rho > 0$.

3.2 Efficiency Bounds for ρ-AMD Codes

Theorem 1. *If an (n, k)-coding scheme is a strong ρ-AMD code with security parameter δ, then,*

$$k \leq n(1 - \rho) + \frac{2 \log \delta - 1}{\log q}. \tag{5}$$

The achievable rate of strong ρ-AMD codes is upper bounded by $1 - \rho$.

Proof. Consider a strong ρ-AMD code with security parameter δ. By Proposition 1, $\tilde{H}_\infty(\mathbf{X}|\mathbf{Z}) \geq \log \frac{1}{\delta}$ should hold for any $\mathbf{Z}$ satisfying $\tilde{H}_\infty(\mathbf{X}|\mathbf{Z}) \geq H_\infty(\mathbf{X}) - \rho n \log q$. In particular, the inequality should hold for $\mathbf{Z}$ such that $\tilde{H}_\infty(\mathbf{X}|\mathbf{Z}) = H_\infty(\mathbf{X}) - \rho n \log q$. We then have $H_\infty(\mathbf{X}) - \rho n \log q \geq \log \frac{1}{\delta}$. On the other hand, we always have $\log |\mathcal{C}_{\mathbf{m}}| \geq H_\infty(\mathbf{X})$, where $\mathcal{C}_{\mathbf{m}}$ denotes the set of codewords corresponding to message $\mathbf{m}$, which is the support of $\mathbf{X}$. This gives the following lower bound on $|\mathcal{C}_{\mathbf{m}}|$.

$$|\mathcal{C}_{\mathbf{m}}| \geq \frac{2^{\rho n \log q}}{\delta} = \frac{q^{\rho n}}{\delta}. \tag{6}$$

Now consider the adversary randomly choose an offset $\Delta \neq 0^n$, we have

$$\begin{aligned} \delta &\geq \Pr[\mathrm{Enc}(\mathbf{m}) + \Delta \in \cup_{\mathbf{m}' \neq \mathbf{m}} E_{\mathbf{m}'}] \\ &\geq \frac{|\cup_{\mathbf{m}' \neq \mathbf{m}} E_{\mathbf{m}'}|}{|\mathbb{F}_q^n| - 1} \\ &\overset{(4),(6)}{\geq} \frac{(q^k - 1) \cdot \frac{q^{\rho n}}{\delta}}{q^n - 1}. \end{aligned} \tag{7}$$

Therefore,

$$k \leq n(1 - \rho) + \frac{2 \log \delta - 1}{\log q}.$$

$\square$

Proposition 2. *If an (n, k)-coding scheme is a weak ρ-AMD code with security parameter δ, then $q^{\rho n - k} \leq \delta$ and $\frac{q^k - 1}{q^n - 1} \leq \delta$.*

Proof of Proposition 2 is given in Appendix C.

4 Limited-View ρ-AMD Codes

We consider a special type of leakage where the adversary chooses a subset $S, |S| = \rho n$ (n is the codeword length), and the codeword components associated with this set will be revealed to them. The adversary will then use this information to construct their offset vector. A tampering strategy is a function from $\mathbb{F}_q^n$ to $\mathbb{F}_q^n$ which can be described by the notation $f_{S,g}$, where $S \subset [n]$ and a function $g : \mathbb{F}_q^{n\rho} \to \mathbb{F}_q^n$, with the following interpretation. The set S specifies a subset of ρn indexes of the codeword that the adversary choose. The function g determines an offset for each read value on the subset S. A ρ^{LV}-AMD code provides protection against all adversary strategies. (This approach to defining tampering functions is inspired by Non-Malleable Codes (NMC) [11].)

Let $\mathcal{S}^{[n\rho]}$ be the set of all subsets of $[n]$ of size $n\rho$. Let $\mathcal{M}(\mathbb{F}_q^n, \mathbb{F}_q^n)$ denote the set of all functions from $\mathbb{F}_q^{n\rho}$ to $\mathbb{F}_q^n$, namely, $\mathcal{M}(\mathbb{F}_q^{n\rho}, \mathbb{F}_q^n) := \{g : \mathbb{F}_q^{n\rho} \to \mathbb{F}_q^n\}$.

Definition 8 *($\mathcal{F}_\rho^{add}$). The class of tampering function $\mathcal{F}_\rho^{add}$, consists of the set of functions $\mathbb{F}_q^n \to \mathbb{F}_q^n$, that can be described by two parameters, $S \in \mathcal{S}^{[n\rho]}$ and $g \in \mathcal{M}(\mathbb{F}_q^{n\rho}, \mathbb{F}_q^n)$. The set $\mathcal{F}_\rho^{add}$ of limited view algebraic tampering functions are defined as follows.*

$$\mathcal{F}_\rho^{add} = \left\{ f_{S,g}(\mathbf{x}) \mid S \in \mathcal{S}^{[n\rho]}, g \in \mathcal{M}(\mathbb{F}_q^{n\rho}, \mathbb{F}_q^n) \right\}, \tag{8}$$

where $f_{S,g}(\mathbf{x}) = \mathbf{x} + g(\mathbf{x}_{|S})$ for $\mathbf{x} \in \mathbb{F}_q^n$.

Definition 9 *(ρ^{LV}-**AMD**). An (n, k)-coding scheme is called a strong ρ^{LV}-AMD code with security parameter δ if $Pr[Dec(f(Enc(\mathbf{m}))) \notin \{\mathbf{m}, \bot\}] \le \delta$ for any message $\mathbf{m} \in \mathbb{F}_q^k$ and any $f_{S,g} \in \mathcal{F}_\rho^{add}$. It is called a weak ρ^{LV}-AMD code if it only requires the security to hold for a random message $\mathbf{M} \leftarrow \mathbb{F}_q^k$ rather than an arbitrary message $\mathbf{m}$.*

We first give a generic construction of strong ρ^{LV}-AMD codes from WtII codes and AMD codes.

Construction 3. *Let (AMDenc, AMDdec) be a $(q^k, q^{n'}, \delta)$-AMD code and let (WtIIenc, WtIIdec) be a linear $(\rho, 0)$-wiretap II code with encoder WtIIenc : $\mathbb{F}_q^{n'} \to \mathbb{F}_q^n$. Then (Enc, Dec) defined as follows is a strong ρ^{LV}-AMD codes with security parameter δ.*

$$\begin{cases} Enc(\mathbf{m}) = WtIIenc(AMDenc(\mathbf{m})); \\ Dec(\mathbf{x}) = AMDdec(WtIIdec(\mathbf{x})). \end{cases}$$

When instantiated with the $(q^k, q^{k+2}, \frac{k+1}{q})$-AMD code in Construction 1 and the linear $(\rho, 0)$-wiretap II code in Construction 2, we obtain a family of strong ρ^{LV}-AMD codes with security parameter $\frac{k+1}{q}$ that achieves rate $1 - \rho$.

Proof. Since both AMDenc and WtIIenc are randomised encoders, in this proof we write the randomness of a randomized encoder explicitly. Let I denote the randomness of AMDenc and let J denote the randomness of WtIIenc. As illustrated in Fig. 2, a message $\mathbf{m}$ is first encoded into an AMD codeword $A_\mathbf{m}^I = $ AMDenc$(\mathbf{m}, I)$. The AMD codeword $A_\mathbf{m}^I$ is then further encoded into a WtII codeword, which is the final ρ^{LV}-AMD codeword: Enc$(\mathbf{m}) = $ WtIIenc$(A_\mathbf{m}^I, J)$. According to (3), SD $\left(\text{WtIIenc}(A_\mathbf{m}^{i_1}, J)_{|S}; \text{WtIIenc}(A_\mathbf{m}^{i_2}, J)_{|S} \right) = 0$. This says

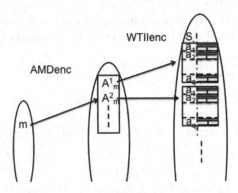

Fig. 2. WtII∘AMD construction with A_m^i denoting the values of AMDenc(**m**)

that A_m^I and $Enc(\mathbf{m})_{|S}$ are independent random variables, in particular, **I** and $Enc(\mathbf{m})_{|S}$ are independent. According to Definition 9, to show that (Enc, Dec) is a strong ρ^{LV}-AMD code with security parameter δ, we need to show that for any message **m**, and any $f_{S,g} \in \mathcal{F}_\rho^{add}$, $Pr[Dec(f_{S,g}(Enc(\mathbf{m}))) \notin \{\mathbf{m}, \bot\}] \leq \delta$, where the probability is over the randomness $(\mathbf{I}, \mathbf{J})$ of the encoder Enc. We show this in two steps.

Step 1. In this step, we assume that $Enc(\mathbf{m})_{|S} = \mathbf{a}$ has occurred and bound the error probability of (Enc,Dec) under this condition. We compute

$$Pr[Dec(f_{S,g}(Enc(\mathbf{m}))) \notin \{\mathbf{m}, \bot\}|(Enc(\mathbf{m})_{|S} = \mathbf{a})]$$
$$= Pr[Dec(Enc(\mathbf{m}) + g(\mathbf{a})) \notin \{\mathbf{m}, \bot\}|(Enc(\mathbf{m})_{|S} = \mathbf{a})]$$
$$= Pr[AMDdec(WtIIdec(WtIIenc(AMDenc(\mathbf{m}, \mathbf{I}), \mathbf{J}) + g(\mathbf{a}))) \notin \{\mathbf{m}, \bot\}$$
$$|(Enc(\mathbf{m})_{|S} = \mathbf{a})]$$
$$= Pr[AMDdec(AMDenc(\mathbf{m}, \mathbf{I}) + WtIIdec(g(\mathbf{a}))) \notin \{\mathbf{m}, \bot\}|(Enc(\mathbf{m})_{|S} = \mathbf{a})]$$
$$= Pr[AMDdec(AMDenc(\mathbf{m}, \mathbf{I}) + WtIIdec(g(\mathbf{a}))) \notin \{\mathbf{m}, \bot\}],$$
$$\leq \delta,$$

where the third equality follows from the linearity of (WtIIenc,WtIIdec), the last equality follows from the fact that **I** and $Enc(\mathbf{m})_{|S}$ are independent discussed in the beginning of the proof, and the inequality follows trivially from the security of (AMDenc, AMDdec).

Step 2. In this step, we conclude the first part of the proof by showing

$$Pr[Dec(f_{S,g}(Enc(\mathbf{m}))) \notin \{\mathbf{m}, \bot\}]$$
$$= \sum_{\mathbf{a}} Pr[Enc(\mathbf{m})_{|S} = \mathbf{a}] \cdot Pr[Dec(f_{S,g}(Enc(\mathbf{m}))) \notin \{\mathbf{m}, \bot\}|(Enc(\mathbf{m})_{|S} = \mathbf{a})]$$
$$\leq \sum_{\mathbf{a}} Pr[Enc(\mathbf{m})_{|S} = \mathbf{a}] \cdot \delta$$
$$= \delta,$$

where the inequality follows from **Step 1.**

Finally, the rate of the $(\rho, 0)$-wiretap II code in Construction 2 is $\frac{k+2}{n} = 1 - \rho$. So the asymptotic rate of the strong ρ^{LV}-AMD code family is

$$\lim_{n \to \infty} \frac{k}{n} = \lim_{n \to \infty} \frac{(1 - \rho)n - 2}{n} = 1 - \rho.$$

$\square$

We next show a construction of weak ρ^{LV}-AMD codes that achieves asymptotic rate 1.

Construction 4. *Let $\mathbb{F}_q$ be a finite field of q elements. Let G be a $k \times k$ nonsingular matrix over $\mathbb{Z}_{q-1}$ such that each column of G consists of distinct entries, i.e., $g_{i,j} \neq g_{i',j}$ for any j and $i \neq i'$. Assume the entries of G (viewed as integers) is upper-bounded by ψk for constant ψ, i.e., $g_{i,j} \leq \psi k$. Then the following construction gives a family of weak LV-AMD codes of asymptotic rate 1 with any leakage parameter $\rho < 1$.*

$$Enc : (\mathbb{F}_q^*)^k \to (\mathbb{F}_q^*)^k \times \mathbb{F}_q : \mathbf{m} \mapsto (\mathbf{m} || f(\mathbf{m}, G)),$$

where $\mathbb{F}_q^*$ denotes the set of non-zero elements of $\mathbb{F}_q$ and the tag $f(\mathbf{m}, G)$ is generated as follows.[1]

$$f(\mathbf{m}, G) = \sum_{j=1}^{k} \prod_{i=1}^{k} m_i^{g_{i,j}}. \tag{9}$$

The decoder dec checks if the first k-tuple of the input vector, when used in 9, match the last component.

The proof of Construction 4 is given in Appendix D.

Concrete constructions of the matrix G can be found in [[2], Remark 2].

5   Applications

5.1   Robust Ramp SSS

A *Secret Sharing Scheme (SSS)* consists of two algorithms (Share,Recover). The algorithm Share maps a secret $s \in \mathcal{S}$ to a vector $\mathbf{S} = (S_1, \ldots, S_N)$ where the shares S_i are in some set $\mathcal{S}_i$ and will be given to participant P_i. The algorithm Recover takes as input a vector of shares $\tilde{\mathbf{S}} = (\tilde{S}_1, \ldots, \tilde{S}_N)$ where $\tilde{S}_i \in \mathcal{S}_i \bigcup \{\bot\}$, where $\bot$ denotes an absent share. For a (t, N)-threshold SSS, t shares reveal no information about the secret $\mathbf{s}$ and $t + 1$ shares uniquely recover the secret $\mathbf{s}$. For a (t, r, N)-*ramp* SSS [7] with (Share$_{\text{rsss}}$, Recover$_{\text{rsss}}$) as sharing and recovering algorithms, the access structure is specified by two thresholds. The privacy

---

[1] The message distribution in this construction is not exactly uniform over $\mathbb{F}_q^k$ but $(\mathbb{F}_q^*)^k$. So this construction can achieve security even when the message distribution is not uniform.

threshold is t, and the reconstruction threshold is r. In a (t, r, N)-ramp SSS, subsets of t or less shares do not reveal any information about the secret, and subsets of r or more shares can uniquely recover the secret $\mathbf{s}$. A set of shares of size $t < a < r$ may leak some information about the secret. In particular, we consider ramp schemes in which a set of $t + \alpha(r - t)$ shares leak α fraction of secret information.

Definition 10 *((t, r, N))-(Ramp Secret Sharing Scheme).* *A (t, r, N)-ramp secret sharing scheme is consist of a pair of algorithms* (Share$_{\text{rsss}}$, Recover$_{\text{rsss}}$), *where* Share$_{\text{rsss}}$ *randomly maps a secret $\mathbf{s} \in \mathcal{S}$ to a share vector $\mathbf{S} = (S_1, \cdots, S_N)$ and* Recover$_{\text{rsss}}$ *deterministically reconstruct a $\tilde{\mathbf{s}} \in \mathcal{S}$ or output $\perp$, satisfy the following.*

- *Privacy: The adversary can access up to $r - 1$ shares. If the number of shares accessed by the adversary is $a \leq t$, no information will be leaked about the secret. If the number of leaked share is $a = t + \alpha(r - t)$, where $0 < \alpha < 1$, then $\tilde{H}_\infty(S | S_{i_1} \cdots S_{i_a}) \geq H_\infty(S) - \alpha \log |\mathcal{S}|^2$, for $S \leftarrow \mathcal{S}$ and any $\{i_1, \cdots, i_a\} \subset [N]$.*
- *Reconstruction: Any r correct shares can reconstruct the secret $\mathbf{s}$.*

A *linear ramp SSS* has the additional property that the Recover function is linear, namely, for any $\mathbf{s} \in \mathcal{G}$, any share vector $\mathbf{S}$ of $\mathbf{s}$, and any vector $\mathbf{S}'$ (possibly containing some $\perp$ symbols), we have Recover$_{\text{rsss}}(\mathbf{S} + \mathbf{S}') = \mathbf{s} + $ Recover$_{\text{rsss}}(\mathbf{S}')$, where vector addition is defined element-wise and addition with $\perp$ is defined by $\perp + \mathbf{x} = \mathbf{x} + \perp = \perp$ for all $\mathbf{x}$. In a linear SSS, the adversary can modify the shares $\tilde{S}_i = S_i + \Delta_i$, such that the difference $\Delta = \tilde{\mathbf{s}} - \mathbf{s}$ between the reconstructed secret and the shared secret, is known.

In a (t, N, δ)-robust SSS, for any $t + 1$ shares with at most t shares modified by the adversary, the reconstruction algorithm can recover the secret $\mathbf{s}$, or detect the adversarial modification and output $\perp$, with probability at least $1 - \delta$ [1]. That is with probability at most δ the secret is either not recoverable, or a wrong secret is accepted. A modular construction of the robust SSS using an AMD code and a linear SSS is given by Cramer *et al.* [1].

We define robust ramp secret sharing scheme when the adversary can adaptively corrupt up to $t + \rho(r - t)$ shares, where $0 < \rho < 1$ is a constant (level of robustness against active adversaries).

Definition 11 *((t, r, N, ρ, δ)-Robust Ramp Secret Sharing Scheme).* *A (t, r, N, ρ, δ)-robust ramp secret sharing scheme is consist of a pair of algorithms* (Share$_{\text{rrsss}}$, Recover$_{\text{rrsss}}$), *where* Share$_{\text{rrsss}}$ *randomly maps a secret $\mathbf{s} \in \mathcal{S}$ to a share vector $\mathbf{S} = (S_1, \cdots, S_N)$ and* Recover$_{\text{rrsss}}$ *deterministically reconstruct a $\tilde{\mathbf{s}} \in \mathcal{S}$ or output $\perp$, satisfy the following.*

- *Privacy: The adversary can access up to $r - 1$ shares. If the number of shares accessed by the adversary is $a \leq t$, no information will be leaked*

---

[2] This definition of leakage is seemingly different from [13], where uniform distribution of secret S is assumed and Shannon entropy is used instead of min-entropy.

about the secret. If the number of leaked share is $a = t + \alpha(r - t)$, where $0 < \alpha < 1$, then $\tilde{H}_\infty(S|S_{i_1} \cdots S_{i_a}) \geq H_\infty(S) - \alpha \log |S|$, for $S \leftarrow S$ and any $\{i_1, \cdots, i_a\} \subset [N]$.

- Reconstruction: Any r correct shares can reconstruct the secret s.
- Robustness: For any r shares with at most $t + \rho(r - t)$ corrupted shares, the probability that either the secret is correctly reconstructed, or the adversary's modifications being detected, is at least $1 - \delta$.

We propose a general construction of robust ramp secret sharing scheme using a ρ_{amd}-AMD and (t, r, N)-ramp secret sharing scheme.

Theorem 2. *Consider a linear (t, r, N)-ramp secret sharing scheme with the algorithm pair $(\text{Share}_{\text{rsss}}, \text{Recover}_{\text{rsss}})$ and shares $S_i \in \mathbb{F}_q^m$, $i = 1, \cdots, N$, and let (Enc, Dec) be a ρ_{amd}-AMD code $\mathbb{F}_q^k \rightarrow \mathbb{F}_q^n$, with failure probability δ_{amd} and $n = (r - t)m$. Then there is a robust ramp secret sharing scheme with algorithm pair $(\text{Share}_{\text{rrsss}}, \text{Recover}_{\text{rrsss}})$ given by $\text{Share}_{\text{rrsss}}(\mathbf{s}) = \text{Share}_{\text{rsss}}(Enc(\mathbf{s}))$ and $\text{Recover}_{\text{rrsss}}(\tilde{\mathbf{S}}) = Dec(\text{Recover}_{\text{rsss}}(\tilde{\mathbf{S}}))$ is a (t, r, N, ρ, δ)-Robust Ramp Secret Sharing Scheme with $\rho \leq \rho_{\text{amd}}$ and $\delta \leq \delta_{\text{amd}}$.*

Proof. First, we show that if the adversary reads at most $t + \rho(r - t)$ shares, the ρ_{amd}-AMD codeword c leaks at most $\rho n \log q$ informations. Since the ρ_{amd}-AMD codeword is encoded by a (t, r, N) ramp secret sharing scheme, t shares will not leak any information about the ρ_{amd}-AMD codeword c. Given that the share size $|S_i| \leq q^m$ and $n = (r - t)m$, the leakage of the extra $\rho(r - t)$ shares will leak at most $\rho n \log q$ bit of information about the ρ_{amd}-AMD codeword c.

Second, we show that the resulting secret sharing scheme is δ-robust. For a secret $\mathbf{s}$, let $\mathbf{S} \leftarrow \text{Share}_{\text{rrsss}}(\mathbf{s})$ be the original share vector and $\tilde{\mathbf{S}}$ be the corrupted one, and let $\mathbf{S}' = \tilde{\mathbf{S}} - \mathbf{S}$. For any r shares, the failure probability of the reconstruction is given by,

$$\Pr[\text{Recover}_{\text{rrsss}}(\tilde{\mathbf{S}}) \notin \{\mathbf{s}, \bot\}] \overset{(1)}{=} \Pr[Dec(\text{Recover}_{\text{rsss}}(\mathbf{S}) + \text{Recover}_{\text{rsss}}(\mathbf{S}')) \notin \{\mathbf{s}, \bot\}]$$
$$= \Pr[Dec(Enc(\mathbf{s}) + \Delta) \notin \{\mathbf{s}, \bot\}],$$

where $\Delta = \text{Recover}_{\text{rsss}}(\mathbf{S}')$ is chosen by the adversary $\mathbb{A}$, and (1) uses the linearity of the ramp scheme. In choosing Δ, the adversary $\mathbb{A}$ can use at most ρ fraction of information in the ρ_{amd}-AMD codeword $c = Enc(\mathbf{s})$. Since at most $\rho n \log q$ information bit is leaked to the adversary, that is $\tilde{H}_\infty(C|\mathbf{Z}) \geq H_\infty(C) - \rho n \log q$, from the definition of ρ_{amd}-AMD code with $\rho \leq \rho_{\text{amd}}$, the decoding algorithm Dec outputs correct secret $\mathbf{s}$, or detects the error $\bot$, with probability at least $1 - \delta_{\text{amd}}$. This means that the ramp secret sharing scheme is robust and outputs either the correct secret, or detects the adversarial tampering, with probability at most $1 - \delta \geq 1 - \delta_{\text{amd}}$. Thus a (t, r, N)-ramp secret sharing scheme and a ρ_{amd}-AMD with security parameter δ_{amd}, give a (t, r, N, ρ, δ)-robust ramp secret sharing scheme with $\delta \leq \delta_{\text{amd}}$ and $\rho \leq \rho_{\text{amd}}$. □

5.2   Wiretap II with Algebraic Adversary

The Wiretap II [5] problem considers a passive adversary that can read a ρ fraction of the codeword components and the goal is to prevent the adversary from learning information about the sent message. Wiretap II with an active adversary has been considered in [14] and later generalized in [8,15]. In this latter general model, called Adversarial Wiretap (AWTP) mode, the adversary is characterized by two parameters ρ_r and ρ_w, denoting the fraction of the codeword components the adversary can "read" and "modify additively", respectively. The goal is two-fold: to prevent the adversary from obtaining any information (secrecy) and, to recover the message despite the changes made by the adversary (reliability). It was proved [8] that in AWTP model, where the adversary can write to a ρ_w fraction of the codeword components additively, secure and reliable communication is possible if, $\rho_r + \rho_w < 1$. This says that when $\rho_r + \rho_w > 1$, one can only hope for weaker type of security, for example, secrecy and error detection. We consider wiretap II with an algebraic adversary, who can read a ρ fraction of the codeword components and tamper with the whole codeword algebraically, namely, adding a non-zero group element to the codeword (codewords are assumed to live in a group). The adversary in this model is equivalent to the AWTP adversary with $\rho_r = \rho$ and $\rho_w = 1$. But the coding goal of wiretap II with an algebraic adversary is different from AWTP.

Definition 12. *An algebraic tampering wiretap II channel is a communication channel between Alice and Bob that is (partially) controlled by an adversary Eve with two following two capabilities.*

- *Read: Eve adaptively selects a fraction ρ of the components of the transmitted codeword $\mathbf{c} = c_1, \cdots, c_n$ to read, namely, Eve's knowledge of the transmitted codeword is given by $\mathbf{Z} = \{c_{i_1}, \cdots, c_{i_{\rho n}}\}$, where $S = \{i_1, \cdots, i_{\rho n}\} \subset [n]$ is chosen by Eve.*
- *Write: Assume $\mathbf{c} \in \mathcal{G}$ for some additive group $\mathcal{G}$. Eve chooses an "off-set" $\Delta \in \mathcal{G}$ according to $\mathbf{Z}$ and add it to the codeword $\mathbf{c}$, namely, the channel outputs $\mathbf{c} + \Delta$.*

Definition 13 ((ρ, ϵ, δ)-algebraic tampering wiretap II). *(ρ, ϵ, δ)-(AWtII))] A (ρ, ϵ, δ)-AWtII code is a coding scheme (Enc,Dec) that guarantees the following two properties.*

- Secrecy: *For any pair of messages $\mathbf{m}_0$ and $\mathbf{m}_1$, any $S \subset [n]$ of size $|S| \leq n\rho$, (3) should hold, namely,*

$$\mathsf{SD}(Enc(\mathbf{m}_0)_{|S}; Enc(\mathbf{m}_1)_{|S}) \leq \varepsilon.$$

- Robustness: *If the adversary is passive, Dec always outputs the correct message. If the adversary is active, the probability that the decoder outputs a wrong message is bounded by δ. That is, for any message $\mathbf{m}$ and any ρ-algebraic tampering wiretap II adversary $\mathbb{A}$,*

$$\Pr[\mathsf{Dec}(\mathbb{A}(\mathsf{Enc}(\mathbf{m}))) \notin \{\mathbf{m}, \bot\}] \leq \delta.$$

The secrecy of (ρ, ϵ, δ)-AWtII code implies that a (ρ, ϵ, δ)-AWtII code is a (ρ, ϵ)-WtII code. The following rate upper bound follows directly from Lemma 3.

Corollary 3. *The rate of* $(\rho, 0, \delta)$-*AWtII codes is bounded by* $R \leq 1 - \rho$.

The robustness property of (ρ, ϵ, δ)-AWtII code is the same as the security of a strong ρ^{LV}-AMD code (see Definition 9). Furthermore, the construction of ρ^{LV}-AMD codes in Construction 3 uses a $(\rho, 0)$-WtII code to encode $\mathbf{c} = \text{AMDenc}(\mathbf{m})$, which guarantees secrecy with respect to any pair of $(\mathbf{c}_0, \mathbf{c}_1)$, and hence secrecy with respect to any pair of $(\mathbf{m}_0, \mathbf{m}_1)$. These assert that Construction 3 yields a family of $(\rho, 0, \delta)$-AWtII codes.

Corollary 4. *There exists a family of* $(\rho, 0, \delta)$-*AWtII codes that achieves rate* $R = 1 - \rho$.

6   Conclusion

We considered an extension of AMD codes when the storage leaks information and the amount of leaked information is bounded by $\rho \log |\mathcal{G}|$. We defined ρ-AMD codes that provide protection in this scenario, both with weak and strong security, and derived concrete and asymptotic bounds on the efficiency of codes in these settings. Table 1 compares our results with original AMD codes and an earlier work (called LLR-AMD) that allow leakage in specific parts of the encoding process. Unlike LLR-AMD that uses different leakage requirements for the weak and strong case, we use a single model to express the leakage and require that the left-over entropy of the codeword be lower bounded. This makes our analysis and constructions more challenging. In particular, optimal constructions of LLR-AMD codes follow directly from the optimal constructions of original AMD codes. However constructing optimal ρ-AMD code, in both weak and strong model, remain open. We gave an explicit construction of a family of codes with respect to a weaker notion of leakage (ρ^{LV}-AMD) whose rate achieves the upper bounds of the ρ-AMD codes. We finally gave two applications of the codes to robust ramp secret sharing schemes and algebraic manipulation wiretap II channel.

Appendices

A   Proof of Lemma 4

Proof. Assume a regular encoder and consider a message $\mathbf{m}$.

The codeword $\mathbf{X} = \text{Enc}(\mathbf{m}, \mathbf{R})$ where the randomness of encoding $\mathbf{R}$ is a uniformly distributed r-bit string. Now consider an adversary with leakage variable $\mathbf{Z}$. Because of the one-to-one property of the regular encoder, we have

$$H_\infty(\mathbf{X}) = H_\infty(\mathbf{R}) = r, \tag{10}$$

and

$$\begin{aligned}
\tilde{H}_\infty(\mathbf{X}|\mathbf{Z}) &= -\log \mathbb{E}_\mathbf{z} \left(\max_\mathbf{x} \Pr[\mathbf{X} = \mathbf{x}|\mathbf{Z} = \mathbf{z}]\right) \\
&= -\log \mathbb{E}_\mathbf{z} \left(\max_\mathbf{r} \Pr[\mathbf{R} = \mathbf{r}|\mathbf{Z} = \mathbf{z}]\right) \\
&= \tilde{H}_\infty(\mathbf{R}|\mathbf{Z}).
\end{aligned} \tag{11}$$

For a leakage variable $\mathbf{Z}$, we consider two classes of adversaries denoted by $\mathbb{A}_Z$ and $\mathbb{B}_Z$, depending on the conditions that they must satisfy, as follows: $\mathbb{A}_Z()$ is an adversary whose leakage variable must satisfy a lower bound on $\tilde{H}_\infty(\mathbf{R}|\mathbf{Z})$ and, $\mathbb{B}_Z()$ is an adversary whose leakage variable must satisfy a lower bound on $\tilde{H}_\infty(\mathbf{X}|\mathbf{Z})$. Both adversaries, when applied to a vector x, use their leakage variables to select an offset vector to be added to a codeword. That is $\mathbb{A}_Z(x) = x + \Delta_z$ where $\Delta_z \in F_q^n$ is chosen dependent on the leakage $\mathbf{Z} = z$. We have the same definition for $\mathbb{B}_Z(x) = x + \Delta_z$.

i. strong LLR-AMD code $\Rightarrow$ strong ρ-AMD

Now consider a $(q^k, q^n, 2^r, \alpha, \delta)$-strong LLR-AMD code $\mathbf{C}$ with encoder and decoder pair, (Enc,Dec). For an adversary $\mathbb{A}_Z$ whose leakage variable satisfies $\tilde{H}_\infty(\mathbf{R}|\mathbf{Z}) \geq (1 - \alpha)r$, we have

$$\Pr[\text{Dec}(\mathbb{A}_Z(\text{Enc}(\mathbf{m}, \mathbf{R}))) \notin \{\mathbf{m}, \perp\}] \leq \delta,$$

where the probability is over the randomness of encoding, and is an expectation over $\mathbf{z} \in \mathcal{Z}$.

Note that using (10) and (11), the $\mathbb{A}_Z$ adversary is also a $\mathbb{B}_Z$ adversary satisfying,

$$\tilde{H}_\infty(\mathbf{X}|\mathbf{Z}) \geq \tilde{H}_\infty(\mathbf{X}) - \alpha r \tag{12}$$

Both these adversaries have the same leakage variable $\mathbf{Z}$ and so any algorithm Offset(z) used by one, taking the value $\mathbf{Z} = z$ as input and finding the offset Δ_z, can be used by the other also (the two adversaries have the same information). This means that the success probabilities of the two adversaries are the same,

$$\Pr[\text{Dec}(\mathbb{A}_Z(\text{Enc}(\mathbf{m}, \mathbf{R}))) \notin \{\mathbf{m}, \perp\}] = \Pr[\text{Dec}(\mathbb{B}_Z(\text{Enc}(\mathbf{m}, \mathbf{R}))) \notin \{\mathbf{m}, \perp\}] \leq \delta.$$

For ρ-AMD codes, security is defined against a $\mathbb{B}_Z$ adversary whose leakage variable $\mathbf{Z}$ satisfies,

$$\tilde{H}_\infty(\mathbf{X}|\mathbf{Z}) \geq H_\infty(\mathbf{X}) - \rho n \log q \tag{13}$$

Comparing (13) and (12), we conclude that $\mathbf{C}$ is a ρ-AMD code for ρ values that satisfy $\alpha r \geq \rho n \log q$, namely $\rho \leq \frac{\alpha r}{n \log q}$.

ii. strong ρ-AMD $\Rightarrow$ strong LLR-AMD code

An argument similar to **i.** immediately gives that the $(q^k, q^n, 2^r, \alpha, \delta)$-strong LLR-AMD code obtain from ρ-AMD code should satisfy $\alpha \leq \frac{\rho n \log q}{r}$. Next we show the bound on r follows from Proposition 1 together with (10). Indeed, by Proposition 1, $\tilde{H}_\infty(\mathbf{X}|\mathbf{Z}) \geq \log \frac{1}{\delta}$ should hold for any $\mathbf{Z}$ satisfying $\tilde{H}_\infty(\mathbf{X}|\mathbf{Z}) \geq H_\infty(\mathbf{X}) - \rho n \log q$. In particular, we must have $H_\infty(\mathbf{X}) - \rho n \log q \geq \log \frac{1}{\delta}$. Now we can use (10) to conclude that $r \geq \log \frac{1}{\delta} + \rho n \log q$. $\qquad\square$

B   Proof of Lemma 5

Proof. The encoder Enc is a one-to-one correspondence between messages and codewords. Consider a message variable $\mathbf{M} \leftarrow \mathcal{M}$ (in particular, the uniform distribution is emphasized by $\mathbf{M}_u \overset{\$}{\leftarrow} \mathcal{M}$). The codeword is a variable $\mathbf{X} = \mathrm{Enc}(\mathbf{M})$. Now consider an adversary with leakage variable $\mathbf{Z}$. Because of the one-to-one property of the encoder, we have

$$H_\infty(\mathbf{X}) = H_\infty(\mathbf{M}), \tag{14}$$

and

$$\begin{aligned}\tilde{H}_\infty(\mathbf{X}|\mathbf{Z}) &= -\log \mathbb{E}_{\mathbf{z}}\left(\max_{\mathbf{x}} \Pr[\mathbf{X} = \mathbf{x}|\mathbf{Z} = \mathbf{z}]\right)\\ &= -\log \mathbb{E}_{\mathbf{z}}\left(\max_{\mathbf{m}} \Pr[\mathbf{M} = \mathbf{m}|\mathbf{Z} = \mathbf{z}]\right)\\ &= \tilde{H}_\infty(\mathbf{M}|\mathbf{Z}).\end{aligned} \tag{15}$$

For a leakage variable $\mathbf{Z}$, we consider two classes of adversaries denoted by $\mathbb{A}_Z$ and $\mathbb{B}_Z$, depending on the conditions that they must satisfy, as follows: $\mathbb{A}_Z()$ is an adversary whose leakage variable must satisfy a lower bound on $\tilde{H}_\infty(\mathbf{M}|\mathbf{Z})$ and, $\mathbb{B}_Z()$ is an adversary whose leakage variable must satisfy a lower bound on $\tilde{H}_\infty(\mathbf{X}|\mathbf{Z})$. Both adversaries, when applied to a vector x, use their leakage variables to select an offset vector to be added to a codeword. That is $\mathbb{A}_Z(x) = x + \Delta_z$ where $\Delta_z \in F_q^n$ is chosen dependent on the leakage $\mathbf{Z} = z$. We have the same definition for $\mathbb{B}_Z(x) = x + \Delta_z$.

i. weak LLR-AMD code $\Rightarrow$ weak ρ-AMD
Now consider a $(q^k, q^n, \alpha, \delta)$-weak LLR-AMD code $\mathbf{C}$ with encoder and decoder pair, (Enc,Dec). For an adversary $\mathbb{A}_Z$ whose leakage variable satisfies $\tilde{H}_\infty(\mathbf{M}|\mathbf{Z}) \geq (1 - \alpha)k \log q$, we have

$$\Pr[\mathrm{Dec}(\mathbb{A}_Z(\mathrm{Enc}(\mathbf{M}))) \notin \{\mathbf{M}, \bot\}] \leq \delta,$$

where the probability is over the randomness of encoding, and is an expectation over $\mathbf{z} \in \mathcal{Z}$.

Note that using (14) and (15), the $\mathbb{A}_Z$ adversary is also a $\mathbb{B}_Z$ adversary satisfying,

$$\tilde{H}_\infty(\mathbf{X}|\mathbf{Z}) \geq (1 - \alpha)k \log q \tag{16}$$

Both these adversaries have the same leakage variable $\mathbf{Z}$ and so any algorithm $\mathrm{Offset}(z)$ used by one, taking the value $\mathbf{Z} = z$ as input and finding the offset Δ_z, can be used by the other also (the two adversaries have the same information). This means that the success probabilities of the two adversaries are the same,

$$\Pr[\mathrm{Dec}(\mathbb{A}_Z(\mathrm{Enc}(\mathbf{M}))) \notin \{\mathbf{M}, \bot\}] = \Pr[\mathrm{Dec}(\mathbb{B}_Z(\mathrm{Enc}(\mathbf{M}_u))) \notin \{\mathbf{M}_u, \bot\}] \leq \delta.$$

For ρ-AMD codes, security is defined against a $\mathbb{B}_Z$ adversary whose leakage variable $\mathbf{Z}$ satisfies,

$$\tilde{H}_\infty(\mathbf{X}|\mathbf{Z}) \geq H_\infty(\mathbf{X}) - \rho n \log q, \text{ where } \mathbf{X} = \mathrm{Enc}(\mathbf{M}_u). \tag{17}$$

Comparing (17) and (16), we conclude that $\mathbf{C}$ is a ρ-AMD code for ρ values that satisfy $\alpha k \geq \rho n$, namely $\rho \leq \frac{\alpha k}{n}$.

ii. weak ρ-AMD $\Rightarrow$ weak LLR-AMD code
An argument similar to **i.** immediately gives that the $(q^k, q^n, \alpha, \delta)$-weak LLR-AMD code obtain from ρ-AMD code should satisfy $\alpha \leq \frac{\rho n}{k}$. $\qquad\square$

C   Proof of Proposition 2

Proof. By Proposition 1, $\tilde{H}_\infty(\mathbf{X}|\mathbf{Z}) \geq \log \frac{1}{\delta}$ should hold for any $\mathbf{Z}$ satisfying $\tilde{H}_\infty(\mathbf{X}|\mathbf{Z}) \geq H_\infty(\mathbf{X}) - \rho n \log q$. In particular, we must have $H_\infty(\mathbf{X}) - \rho n \log q \geq \log \frac{1}{\delta}$. Since the message $\mathbf{M}$ of weak ρ-AMD is uniform and the encoder is one-to-one correspondence, $H_\infty(\mathbf{X}) = H_\infty(\mathbf{M}) = k \log q$. We conclude that $k \log q - \rho n \log q \geq \log \frac{1}{\delta}$, namely,

$$q^{\rho n - k} \leq \delta. \tag{18}$$

Similar to the proof of Theorem 1, we also consider a random attack strategy. Then the total number of valid codewords that do not decode to $\mathbf{M}$ is at least $(q^k - 1)$, which is the number of offsets that lead to undetected manipulations. A randomly chosen offset $(\Delta \neq 0^n)$ leads to undetected manipulation with probability at most

$$\frac{q^k - 1}{q^n - 1}$$

and we must have

$$\frac{q^k - 1}{q^n - 1} \leq \delta. \tag{19}$$

$\qquad\square$

D   Proof of Construction 4

Proof. Let β be a primitive element of $\mathbb{F}_q$. Then every element $m_i \in \mathbb{F}_q^*$ can be written as a power of β: $m_i = \beta^{m_i'}$. (9) is rewritten as follows.

$$f(\mathbf{m}, G) = \sum_{j=1}^{k} \beta^{\sum_{i=1}^{k} m_i' g_{i,j}} \bmod (q-1).$$

According to [[2], Theorem 4] and the proof therein, (Enc, Dec) satisfies $\Pr[\mathrm{Dec}(\mathrm{Enc}(\mathbf{m}) + \Delta(\mathbf{Z}_\rho)) \notin \{\mathbf{m}, \bot\}] \leq \frac{\psi k}{q-1}$ as long as the leakage parameter ρ satisfies $k - (k+1)\rho \geq 1$. What is left to show is for any $\rho < 1$ and $\delta > 0$, there exists an N such that for all $k + 1 \geq N$, $k - (k+1)\rho > 0$ and $\frac{\psi k}{q-1} \leq \delta$ are both satisfied. Indeed, $k - (k+1)\rho = k(1-\rho) - \rho$, which is bigger than 1 if $k > \frac{1+\rho}{1-\rho}$. So we can simply let $N = \lceil \frac{1+\rho}{1-\rho} \rceil + 1$. And $\frac{\psi k}{q-1} \leq \delta$ can be achieved by choosing a big enough q, for example, $q = \omega(\psi k)$ and choose a big enough k. $\qquad\square$

References

1. Cramer, R., Dodis, Y., Fehr, S., Padró, C., Wichs, D.: Detection of algebraic manipulation with applications to robust secret sharing and fuzzy extractors. In: Smart, N. (ed.) EUROCRYPT 2008. LNCS, vol. 4965, pp. 471–488. Springer, Heidelberg (2008). doi:10.1007/978-3-540-78967-3_27
2. Ahmadi, H., Safavi-Naini, R.: Detection of algebraic manipulation in the presence of leakage. In: Lehmann, A., Wolf, S. (eds.) ICITS 2015. LNCS, vol. 9063, pp. 238–258. Springer, Heidelberg (2014). doi:10.1007/978-3-319-04268-8_14
3. Safavi-Naini, R., Wang, P.: Codes for limited view adversarial channels. In: IEEE International Symposium on Information Theory (ISIT), pp. 266–270 (2013)
4. Wyner, A.D.: The wire-tap channel. Bell Syst. Tech. J. **54**, 1355–1367 (1975)
5. Ozarow, L.H., Wyner, A.D.: Wire-tap channel II. AT & T Bell Lab. Tech. J. **63**(10), 2135–2157 (1984)
6. Standaert, F.-X., Pereira, O., Yu, Y., Quisquater, J.-J., Yung, M., Oswald, E.: Leakage Resilient Cryptography in Practice. https://eprint.iacr.org/2009/341.pdf
7. Blakley, G.R., Meadows, C.: Security of ramp schemes. In: Beth, T., Cot, N., Ingemarsson, I. (eds.) EUROCRYPT 1984. LNCS, vol. 209, pp. 242–268. Springer, Heidelberg (1985). doi:10.1007/3-540-39568-7_20
8. Wang, P., Safavi-Naini, R.: A model for adversarial wiretap channels. IEEE Trans. Inf. Theor. **62**(2), 970–983 (2016)
9. Dodis, Y., Reyzin, L., Smith, A.: Fuzzy extractors: how to generate strong keys from biometrics and other noisy data. In: Cachin, C., Camenisch, J.L. (eds.) EUROCRYPT 2004. LNCS, vol. 3027, pp. 523–540. Springer, Heidelberg (2004). doi:10.1007/978-3-540-24676-3_31
10. Cheraghchi, M., Didier, F., Shokrollahi, A.: Invertible extractors and wiretap protocols. IEEE Trans. Inf. Theor. **58**(2), 1254–1274 (2012)
11. Dziembowski, S., Pietrzak, K., Wichs, D.: Non-malleable codes. In: ICS, pp. 434–452 (2010)
12. Shamir, A.: How to share a secret. Commun. Assoc. comput. Mach. **22**(11), 612–613 (1979)
13. Strongly secure ramp secret sharing schemes for general access structures
14. Aggarwal, V., Lai, L., Calderbanand, A.R., Poor, H.V.: Wiretap channel type II with an active eavesdropper. In: IEEE International Symposium on Information Theory (ISIT) 2009, pp. 1944–1948 (2009)
15. Wang, P., Safavi-Naini, R., Lin, F.: Erasure adversarial wiretap channels. In: 53rd Annual Allerton Conference on Communication, Control and Computing (2015)

Cheater Detection in SPDZ Multiparty Computation

Gabriele Spini[1,2,3(✉)] and Serge Fehr[1]

[1] CWI Amsterdam, Amsterdam, Netherlands
spini@cwi.nl
[2] Mathematical Institute, Leiden University, Leiden, Netherlands
[3] Institut de Mathématiques de Bordeaux, UMR 5251, Université de Bordeaux, Bordeaux, France

Abstract. In this work we revisit the SPDZ multiparty computation protocol by Damgård et al. for securely computing a function in the presence of an unbounded number of dishonest parties. The SPDZ protocol is distinguished by its fast performance. A downside of the SPDZ protocol is that *one single dishonest party* can enforce the computation to fail, meaning that the honest parties have to *abort* the computation without learning the outcome, whereas the cheating party may actually learn it. Furthermore, the dishonest party can launch such an attack without being identified to be the cheater. This is a serious obstacle for practical deployment: there are various reasons for why a party may want the computation to fail, and without cheater detection there is little incentive for such a party not to cheat. As such, in many cases, the protocol will actually fail to do its job.

In this work, we enhance the SPDZ protocol to allow for cheater detection: a dishonest party that enforces the protocol to fail will be identified as being the cheater. As a consequence, in typical real-life scenarios, parties will actually have little incentive to cheat, and if cheating still takes place, the cheater can be identified and discarded and the computation can possibly be re-done, until it succeeds.

The challenge lies in adding this cheater detection feature to the original protocol without increasing its complexity significantly. In case no cheating takes place, our new protocol is as efficient as the original SPDZ protocol which has no cheater detection. In case cheating does take place, there may be some additional overhead, which is still reasonable in size though, and since the cheater knows he will be caught, this is actually unlikely to occur in typical real-life scenarios.

1 Introduction

The SPDZ MPC Protocol. Since the initial theoretical possibility results for multiparty computation (MPC) in the late eighties [2,5,8,10], much effort has been put into reducing the (communication and computation) complexity of MPC,

G. Spini—Supported by the Algant-Doc doctoral program, www.algant.eu.

A.C.A. Nascimento and P. Barreto (Eds.): ICITS 2016, LNCS 10015, pp. 151–176, 2016.
DOI: 10.1007/978-3-319-49175-2_8

and we are now at a stage where MPC is at the verge of being practical. One of the currently known protocols that is (close to) efficient enough for practical deployment is the so-called SPDZ protocol by Damgård et al. [7], and its variations from [6]. The efficiency of the SPDZ protocol is due to a clever mix of cryptographic operations, which can mostly be pushed into a preprocessing phase, and very efficient information-theoretic techniques.

The SPDZ MPC protocol offers security against a dishonest majority, i.e., there is no bound on the number of corrupt parties the protocol can tolerate: even if all but one of the parties are corrupt, that one single party is still protected. A downside of such protocols with security against a dishonest majority is that they are inherently susceptible to a "denial-of-service" attack: even *one single dishonest party* can enforce the protocol to fail, meaning that the honest parties have to *abort* the computation without learning the outcome, whereas the cheating party may actually learn it. Furthermore, the SPDZ MPC protocol is such that the cheating party who launches the attack remains *covert*: the (honest) parties know that there is a cheater among them that caused the protocol to fail, but they have no way to identify the culprit. As such, with little effort and with nothing to fear, a single party can prevent the SPDZ protocol from doing its job.

Identifiable vs Non-identifiable Abort. We feel that such an non-identifiable abort, where the honest parties *cannot* identify the cheating party that caused the abort, is a serious drawback for practical deployment. In real-life scenarios, there are many reasons for why a party may be tempted to enforce the protocol to fail: he may know or suspect that he is not going to like the outcome, he may gain an advantage by learning the outcome but preventing the others from learning it, he may want to sabotage the computation out of malevolence, etc. And of course, if that party does not have to fear any consequence because he knows that he will not be caught, there is little incentive for him not to cheat. As such, in real-life scenarios, it is not unlikely that such an abort will actually take place. Furthermore, once such an abort does take place, the affected honest parties are stuck — there is nothing they can do: they cannot call anyone to account, and re-trying the computation is (almost) useless, because the cheating party can just re-do the attack.

In contrast to this is the concept of *identifiable abort*, where we require that, as a consequence of launching a denial-of-service attack, the cheating party will be identified as being the culprit. Obviously, for a protocol that offers identifiable abort, there is much less incentive for a party to cheat and enforce the protocol to fail, because he knows that he will be caught and have to deal with the consequences. Thus, if there is some severe enough punishment, an abort is unlikely to occur. Furthermore, even if an abort does occur, the affected honest parties have room for further actions: not only can they call the cheating party to account, they can also re-do the computation with the culprit excluded, and this way they can still obtain the outcome of the computation eventually.[1]

We point out that non-identifiable abort is no issue in case of *two*-party computation: if the protocol fails then it is clear to the honest party that *the other party* must be cheating.

Our Results. We propose a new version of the SPDZ protocol that supports *identifiable* abort: if the protocol aborts then at least one dishonest party will be identified as having cheated. We emphasize that the challenge lies in adding identifiability to SPDZ without increasing its complexity too much; in particular, we want the protocol to run (almost) as fast as the original version in case parties do not misbehave (too much). This is what our protocol achieves.

– In case no cheating takes place, i.e., all the players behave honesty, our protocol is essentially as efficient as the original SPDZ protocol: namely, it has an asymptotic communication complexity of $O(n)$ point-to-point communications per gate and an asymptotical computational cost of $O(n)$ field operations per gate.
  We perform extra broadcasts compared to the original SPDZ protocol, but since their number is independent of the circuit size, this can be neglected for large enough circuits.
– In case cheating does take place, but to an extent that the protocol can handle it and does not abort, our protocol is slower by a factor at most 2, hence still with an asymptotic complexity of $O(n)$ per gate for both communication and computation.
  Again, the extra broadcasts can be neglected.
– In case cheating takes place and the protocol does abort (with identification), we distinguish between the following two cases (which case occurs depends on the kind of cheating):
  • *Identification with no agreement:* Every honest player has identified at least one player as a cheater, but there may not be agreement among the honest players about the list of cheaters.[2] In this case, our protocol is slower still by a factor 2 only.
  • *Identification with agreement:* There is common agreement among the honest players about at least one player being a cheater. In this case, our protocol may take substantially longer to identify the cheater, namely in this case the number of cryptographic operations to be performed grows with the size of the circuit.

Thus, the only case when our version is significantly slower than the original SPDZ protocol is when a dishonest player cheats so bluntly that he is *publicly*

---

[1] One has to be careful with this "solution" though: collaborating dishonest parties that remained passive during the first run may now adjust their inputs, given that *they* have learned the output from the first (failed) run.

[2] But every player that is identified by an honest player to be a cheater *is* a cheater; thus, this case can only occur if there is more than one cheater.

recongnized as being a cheater. However, in many practical scenarios, there seems to be little gain for a dishonest player in slowing down the protocol at the cost of being publicly caught as a cheater, and thus having to face the consequences. Therefore, in typical scenarios, our protocol is similarly efficient as the original SPDZ protocol but, in contrast to the original version, it discourages dishonest players from enforcing the protocol to abort.

Related Work. Cheater detection is achieved by early MPC protocols such as [8], and by other protocols that are based on the paradigm that players prove in zero-knowledge that they followed the protocol instructions honestly. However, the high communication complexity of these protocols make them unsuitable for practical deployment.

On the other hand, recent MPC protocols (in a so-called offline/online model) are designed to have very high efficiency, like the protocols from the SPDZ family [6,7], which feature a very attractive asymptotic communication and computational complexity of $O(n)$ per multiplication gate (for the online phase). However, these protocols do not offer cheater detection. An earlier protocol by Bendlin et al. [3] offers a very weak form of cheater detection: namely, at least one honest player will identify a dishonest one, but other honest players may have no clue on the identity of cheating parties; the protocol has a computational complexity of $O(n^2)$ per multiplication gate.

The work by Ishai et al. [9] is the first to rigorously define and discuss the notion of cheater detection (in the universal-composability model of Canetti [4]); the article presents a general compiler that adds cheater detection to any semi-honest MPC protocol in the preprocessing model.

A very recent protocol, due to Baum et al. [1], builds up on the Bendlin et al. approach and achieves full cheater detection with a communication and computational complexity of $O(n^2)$ per multiplication gate; this also improves on the best protocol obtained by means of the techniques by Ishai et al.

The goal of our work is to develop a MPC protocol that is "strictly stronger" than SPDZ, in that when not under attack it has the same running time than SPDZ, and when under attack it either gives away cheaters or the protocol can handle the attack and still has the same (asymptotic) running time than SPDZ. This is achieved by our protocol, but is not achieved by any of the above. Indeed, in case no severe cheating takes place, our protocol is at most a factor 2 slower than SPDZ, hence achieving a communication and computation complexity of $O(n)$ per multiplication gate. If cheating does take place to the extent that the protocol aborts, than either we obtain a weaker notion of cheater detection ("identification with no agreement") at the same cost, or we obtain the same notion ("identification with agreement"), but with a overhead in local computations.

2 The Original SPDZ Protocol

2.1 The Setting

SPDZ allows n players $P_1, \cdots, P_n$ holding private inputs over a finite field $\mathbb{F}_q$ to securely evaluate an arithmetic circuit C on their inputs. We assume a *synchronous point-to-point communication network* that allows for perfectly private and reliable communication between any two players. We also consider a *broadcast channel*, though this one may have to be implemented using the point-to-point channels (and cryptographic techniques).

2.2 Ingredients

SPDZ follows the standard paradigm and computes the circuit C on shared values. At the core are additive sharings, for which the following notation/terminology is used.

- A $[\cdot]$-*sharing* of a value $z \in \mathbb{F}_q$ is an additive sharing of z, meaning that each player P_i holds a random *share* $z_i \in \mathbb{F}_q$ subject to $\sum_i z_i = z$. This is denoted by $[z] = (z_1, \cdots, z_n)$.

Furthermore, to ensure correctness, every shared value is accompanied by a sharing of an authentication tag for the shared value. This is formalized as follows.

- For an arbitrary but fixed $\alpha \in \mathbb{F}_q$, a $\langle \cdot \rangle_\alpha$-*sharing* of z consists of $[\cdot]$-sharings of z and of $\alpha \cdot z$, i.e., $\langle z \rangle_\alpha = ([z], [\alpha \cdot z])$. The element α is called the *global key*, and αz is called the *tag* of z and usually denoted by $\gamma(z)$. If α is clear from the context, we may write $\langle \cdot \rangle$ instead of $\langle \cdot \rangle_\alpha$.

We say that a sharing $[z]$ or a sharing $\langle z \rangle_\alpha = ([z], [\gamma(z)])$ is *privately opened* to a player P_i if each player P_j sends his share z_j to P_i via a point-to-point and P_i computes $z := \sum_j z_j$. We say that a sharing is *publicly* opened if it is privately opened to a designated "king player" P_k, and then P_k sends the reconstructed value z to all the players via point-to-point channels.[3]

Note that (for a fixed global key α) a $\langle \cdot \rangle_\alpha$-sharing is linear, in the sense that linear combinations can be computed *on the shares*:

$$\langle z + w \rangle = \langle z \rangle + \langle w \rangle := ([z_i + w_i]_{i=1, \cdots, n}, [\gamma(z)_i + \gamma(w)_i]_{i=1, \cdots, n})$$
$$\langle \lambda z \rangle = \lambda \cdot \langle z \rangle := ([\lambda z_i]_{i=1, \cdots, n}, [\lambda \gamma(z)_i]_{i=1, \cdots, n}) .$$

Furthermore, if α is $[\cdot]$-shared then the same holds for addition with a constant:

$$\langle \lambda + z \rangle = \lambda + \langle z \rangle := ([\lambda + z_1, z_2, \cdots, z_n], [\lambda \alpha_1 + \gamma(z)_1, \cdots, \lambda \alpha_n + \gamma(z)_n]) .$$

Finally, a triple $(\langle a \rangle_\alpha, \langle b \rangle_\alpha, \langle c \rangle_\alpha)$ is called a *multiplication triplet* if it consists of three $\langle \cdot \rangle_\alpha$-shared random values a, b, c subject to $ab = c$.

---

[3] We emphasize that, by definition, these private and public openings do *not* involve any checking of the correctness of z by means of its tag; this will have to be done on top.

2.3   Outline of the SPDZ Protocol

SPDZ is divided into a *offline* (or *pre-processing*) phase, and an *online* phase. The idea is to push most of the (somewhat) expensive cryptographic techniques into the offline phase (which can be executed *before* the inputs to the computation — or even the actual computation — are known), and rely mainly on very efficient information-theoretic techniques in the online phase.

More concretely, in the offline phase the players make use of an *additive-homomorphic* and *somehwhat multiplicative-homomorphic* encryption scheme Enc to produce

- a $[\cdot]$-sharing $[\alpha]$ of a random and unknown global key α,
- a list of $\langle \cdot \rangle_\alpha$-sharings $\langle r \rangle_\alpha$ of random and unknown values r, and
- a list of multiplication triplets $(\langle a \rangle_\alpha, \langle b \rangle_\alpha, \langle c \rangle_\alpha)$ with random and unknown $a, b, c = ab$.

Additionally, sort of as a "side product" of the generation of all these sharings with the help of the encryption scheme Enc, the following is given at the end of the offline phase for every $[\cdot]$-sharing $[z] = (z_1, \ldots, z_n)$ that occurs as (first or second) component of a $\langle \cdot \rangle_\alpha$-sharing (as well as for the $[\cdot]$-sharing $[\alpha]$). Every player P_i is *committed* to his share z_i by means of an encryption $e_{z_i} := \text{Enc}(z_i, \rho_{z_i})$ of z_i that is publicly known, and player P_i knows the corresponding randomness ρ_{z_i}. Recall that Enc is additively-homomorphic, so that linear combinations (and addition with constants) can be computed on the commitments.

The actual computation takes place in the online phase. By using the sharings produced in the offline phase as a resource, the online phase can be executed to a large extent by means of very efficient information-theoretic techniques — the number of cryptographic operations needed is independent of the circit size. Concretely, the online phase is composed of the following gadgets.

- *Input sharing:* For each input x held by a player P_i, a fresh (meaning: yet unused) sharing $\langle r \rangle_\alpha$ from the offline phase is selected and privately opened to P_i. P_i then sends $\varepsilon := x - r$ to all the players, and altogether the players can then compute a sharing of x as $\langle x \rangle_\alpha = \varepsilon + \langle r \rangle_\alpha$.
- *Distributed addition (and multiplication/addition with constants):* For each addition gate in the circuit with shared inputs $\langle z \rangle_\alpha$ and $\langle y \rangle_\alpha$, a sharing of $z + y$ is computed (non-interactively) as $\langle z + y \rangle_\alpha = \langle z \rangle_\alpha + \langle y \rangle_\alpha$. Correspondingly for multiplication/addition with a constant.
- *Distributed multiplication:* For each multiplication gate in the circuit with shared inputs $\langle z \rangle_\alpha$ and $\langle y \rangle_\alpha$, a sharing of $z \cdot y$ is computed (interactively) by means of the multiplication subprotocol below, which consumes one fresh multiplication triple from the offline phase.
- *Output reconstruction:* For each shared output value $\langle z \rangle_\alpha$, the players publicly reconstruct z.

– *Tag checking:* For a shared value $\langle z \rangle_\alpha = ([z], [\gamma(z)])$ that has been publicly opened, the players can check the correcntess of z as follows. Every player P_i computes $y_i := \gamma(z)_i - z \cdot \alpha_i$ and broadcasts a commitment of y_i, and then every player opens the commitment and the players compute $y := \sum_i y_i = \gamma(z) - z \cdot \alpha$. If $y = 0$ then z is declared to be correct; otherwise, it is declared incorrect and the protocol is immediately *aborted*.

We do not detail how these gadgets are put together, in particular how/when exactly the *tag checking* is used, as this is not very relevant to us. However, let us emphasize that a single dishonest player can easily enforce the protocol to abort, e.g., by submitting an incorrect share for a sharing $\langle z \rangle_\alpha$ that is publicly opened and then checked; the check will recognize (with high probability) that the reconstructed value z is incorrect, and so the protocol will abort, but there is no way for the honest players to find out *who* submitted an incorrect shares. Hence, any such dishonest player gets away with it, and hence there is no incentive for a dishonest player *not* to cheat, should it give him any advantage or satisfaction whatsoever.

Multiplication subprotocol

A fresh multiplication triplet $(\langle a \rangle, \langle b \rangle, \langle c \rangle)$ is selected, and the following is performed.

1. The players compute $\langle \varepsilon \rangle := \langle z - a \rangle$ and $\langle \delta \rangle := \langle y - b \rangle$.
2. The sharings $\langle \varepsilon \rangle$ and $\langle \delta \rangle$ are publicly opened:
   – $\langle \varepsilon \rangle$ and $\langle \delta \rangle$ are privately opened to a designated king player P_k, and
   – P_k sends ε and δ to the others player via the point-to-point channels.
3. The players compute $\langle z \cdot y \rangle := \langle c \rangle + \varepsilon \langle b \rangle + \delta \langle a \rangle + \varepsilon \delta$.

---

3   Our Protocol

3.1   An Overview of Our Protocol

We explain on a high level how our protocol works. First, notice that there are three distinct ways for dishonest players to disrupt the protocol execution (and enforce an abort in the original SPDZ protocol):

– During the input sharing phase, dishonest players could send incorrect shares of r to P_i, or P_i could send inconsistent values ε to the players.[4]
– During the multiplication step, dishonest players could send incorrect shares of ε and δ to the king player.

---

[4] Note that there is no issue of ε being *incorrect* since any ε corresponds to a possible input for P_i.

- During the multiplication step, a dishonest king player could send false and/or inconsistent values for ε and δ.
- In the output reconstruction phase, dishonest players could announce false shares of the output.

We will focus on the two possible attacks in the multiplication step, since our techniques to deal with those can easily be used to also deal with the attacks in the input sharing and output reconstruction phases.

As pointed out above, the players have two "checking mechanisms" available in order to verify the correctness of a reconstructed value z:

- they can use the *tag* $\gamma(z)$ of z to check the correctness of z, and
- they can use the *commitments* to check the correctness of the shares z_i.

The former technique is very efficient but cannot be used to identify *who* submitted a false share in case of an incorrect z; this can be done by the latter, but that one is computationally more expensive, and so we want to avoid it as much as possible and use it only as a "last resort".

Now, a first and straightforward approach to achieve cheater detection but use the computationally expensive techniques only as a last resort, seems as follows: first, use the "cheap" tag checks to verify the correctness of every reconstructed value (as in the original SPDZ protocol), and then resort to the commitments if and only if an error is detected, in order to find out who claimed an incorrect value.

Unfortunately, this does not work. The reason is that only the king player knows the shares of, say, ε. As such, if ε claimed by the king player turns out to be incorrect, there is no way for an honest player to distinguish the case of a dishonest player P_i who has sent an incorrect share ε_i to the king player, from the case of a dishonest king player who pretends that he has received an incorrect share ε_i from P_i. There is no way such a dispute can be resolved, even with the help of the commitments — except if these shares are broadcast from the start, but that would greatly increase the complexity of the protocol.

To deal with such a situation, we use an idea from *dispute control*: we re-do (part of) the computation in such a way that this particular dispute cannot occur anymore (essentially by choosing a fresh king player). Since the number of disputes is bounded, this means that there is a limit on how often something needs to be re-done, and setting the parameters right ensures that this merely gives a factor-2 blowup.

On the other hand, if a dishonest player P_i keeps on claiming an incorrect share for, say, ε, even when the players are asked to *broadcast* their shares because a fault was detected, then the players can use the (computationally expensive) commitments to find the incorrect share, and the honest players will unanimously identify P_i as cheater.

The overall structure of (the computation phase of) our protocol is thus as follows.

Set-up: The circuit C is divided into consecutive blocks, each comprising ca. $|C|/n$ gates (where "consecutive" here means that C can be evaluated in a block-by-block manner). Furthermore, a list $\mathcal{L}_{\texttt{suspects}}$ of *suspect* players is initialized as the empty set.

Computation: Sequentially, for each block the following is done:

I. A king player $P_k \notin \mathcal{L}_{\texttt{suspects}}$ is selected, and the computation is done as in the normal SPDZ protocol by repeatedly invoking the multiplication sub-protocol and doing local computations.

II. Once the block has been processed, a checking protocol `BlockCheck` is invoked that verifies the correctness of the computation. `BlockCheck` has three possible outcomes:

- *Success:* The block has been correctly processed. In this case, the players simply move to the next block.
- *Fail with Conflict:* The block has *not* been correctly processed, and P_k accuses some player(s) of faulty behaviour. In this case, P_k and all accused players are added to $\mathcal{L}_{\texttt{suspects}}$, and the players go back to step I. and re-do the computation with a "fresh" $P_k \notin \mathcal{L}_{\texttt{suspects}}$. Should $\mathcal{L}_{\texttt{suspects}}$ now consist of *all* players then the protocol stops; in this case, every honest player has identified at least one dishonest player.
- *Fail with Agreement:* The block has *not* been correctly processed, and it is guaranteed that some player has *broadcast* an incorrect share during the run of `BlockCheck`. In this case, the players make use of the commitments to unanimously identify the cheating player.

3.2   The Checking Protocol `BlockCheck`

We will now provide a more precise discussion of the check-phase mentioned in the previous section. What it will do is check the correctness and consistency of all the ε's and δ's that were announced by the king player during the multiplication subprotocols in the block to be checked. Let us write $\langle z^{(1)} \rangle, \cdots, \langle z^{(t)} \rangle$ for the sharings of these ε's and δ's. This means that each player P_i has communicated his share $z_i^{(j)}$ to P_k, who in turn has computed $z^{(j)} = \sum_i z_i^{(j)}$ and communicated it to all other players. In the following discussion, we will denote by $\tilde{z}_i^{(j)}$ the *actual* share communicated by P_i to P_k (so that if P_i is dishonest, it may be the case that $\tilde{z}_i^{(j)} \neq z_i^{(j)}$), and by $\tilde{z}^{(j)}$ the value that P_k has communicated to the other players. However, we emphasize that that P_k is dishonest then he may be inconsistent with the value of $\tilde{z}^{(j)}$, different players may receive different values for $\tilde{z}^{(j)}$.

The subprotocol `Block Check` now works as follows. As a first step, as checking each value individually is too expensive, a quasi-random linear combination of the $\langle z^{(j)} \rangle$'s is computed:

> *Step 1:* The players run a subroutine `Rand` to produce a random element e, and they compute the linear combination $\langle z \rangle := \sum_h e^h \langle z^{(h)} \rangle$.

Let $\tilde{z}_i$ and $\tilde{z}$ be the respective linear combinations of $\tilde{z}_i^{(1)}, \cdots, \tilde{z}_i^{(t)}$ and of $\tilde{z}^{(1)}, \cdots, \tilde{z}^{(t)}$. The correctness of $\tilde{z}$ is then verified as follows.

> *Step 2: Public Reconstruction.* Each player broadcasts his share of $\langle z \rangle$, upon which the king player P_k broadcasts a list of players that he accuses of inconsistent behaviour; if he does so, `BlockCheck` outputs the message "Fail with Conflict" and the list of accused players.
>
> If P_k has not accused anybody, then each player can broadcast an accusation against P_k, stating that the value $\tilde{z}$ that he received is different from z (which is now public, since its shares have been broadcast). If that is the case, then once again we are in the "Fail-with-Conflict" case: `BlockCheck` outputs the corresponding error message and the list of players accusing P_k.

Now if no accusations have been produced, the next step consists in checking the tag of the now-public value $\tilde{z}$:

> *Step 3: Tag Checking.* If no accusations have been produced in Step 2, then players check the tags of $\langle z \rangle = ([z], [\gamma(z)])$; this is done running a subroutine `ZeroTest` on $[\gamma(z)] - \tilde{z}[\alpha]$, which outputs $\top$ if it is a sharing of 0, and $\bot$ if it is not (except with small probability).
>
> `BlockCheck` outputs the message "Success" if the tag check succeeds, and "Fail with Agreement" if it fails.

Note that in step 3 above, the players cannot just do a public reconstruction of the sharing $[\gamma(z)] - \tilde{z}[\alpha]$ to check whether it is a sharing of zero, because in case it is not, the value $\gamma(z) - \tilde{z}\alpha$ reveals information on α. That is why a slightly more involved subroutine `ZeroTest` is invoked, which publicly reconstructs a *random multiple* of $[\gamma(z)] - \tilde{z}[\alpha]$.

If the tag check in step 3 above fails, then this means that a dishonest player P_i must have broadcast a false share z_i during step 2, *or* (as we will see) he has broadcast some false share as part of the execution of `ZeroTest`; in either case, he has broadcast a linear combination (with coefficients that may depend on the $\tilde{z}^{(i)}$) of values he is committed to, by means of the commitments from the preprocessing phase and by the linearity of all computations. P_i can and will now be *publicly identified* as cheater by means of a protocol `CommitCheck`, which simply asks the players to open the commitments to the claimed and broadcast values. We note that CommitCheck causes a significant overhead to the efficiency of the protocol because the players need to perform computations on a large number of commitments, proportional to the size of the circuit; in return, however, it publicly identifies a cheating player.

Note that due to space contstraints, the details of the subroutines Rand, CommitCheck and ZeroTest are given in the appendix, but they are pretty much as expected (except for the issue mentioned above regarding ZeroTest).

3.3   Security of Our Protocol

In this section we argue security of our protocol. We focus on the actual computation phase; similar techniques allow us to secure the input-sharing and output-reconstruction phases as well.

The security of the protocol clearly relies on the secrecy of the global key α, which we measure as follows. Let v denote the adversary's *view* at a given point in the online protocol.[5] Then, the adversary's *(average) guessing probability* of the global key α is given by

$$p_{\mathsf{guess}}(\alpha|v) := \sum_{\hat{v}} p(v = \hat{v}) \cdot \max_{\hat{\alpha}} p(\alpha = \hat{\alpha}|v = \hat{v}).$$

In Appendix A we will prove the following security properties for the checking protocol BlockCheck. Recall, the purpose of BlockCheck is to verify the correctness and consistency[6] of $\tilde{z}^{(1)}, \cdots, \tilde{z}^{(t)}$, which is the collection of values that P_k announces as the reconstructed values for $\langle \epsilon \rangle$ and $\langle \delta \rangle$ for each invocation of the multiplication subprotocol in the checked block.

Proposition 1. *BlockCheck satisfies the following:*

- Correctness of BlockCheck: *if all players behave honestly and hence all $\tilde{z}^{(h)}$ are correct and consistently announced by P_k, then BlockCheck outputs "Success" with probability 1.*
- Soundness of BlockCheck: *if at least one of the $\tilde{z}^{(h)}$ is incorrect, i.e. $\neq z^{(h)}$, or inconsistently announced by P_k, then the following holds except with probability at most*

$$\delta = (2|C|/n + 1)/q + p_{guess}(\alpha|v),$$

where v is the adversary's view before the execution of BlockCheck. BlockCheck outputs a "Fail"; furthermore, if it outputs "Fail with Conflict",

---

[5] Here and below, when we make information-theoretic statements, we understand v to *not* include the encryptions/commitments of the honest parties shares etc. that were produced during the preprocessing phase. Adding these elements to the adverary's view of course renders the information-theoretic statements invalid, but has a negligible effect with respect to a computationally bounded adversary.

[6] Recall that dishonest P_k may send different values for $\tilde{z}^{(i)}$ to different players.

then either the king player P_k or all of the accusing players are dishonest (or both), and if it outputs "Fail with Agreement", then all $\tilde{z}^{(h)}$ have been consistently announced by P_k, and a dishonest player has broadcast as part of BlockCheck an incorrect version of a value to which he is committed by means of a linear combination (depending on the $\tilde{z}^{(h)}$'s) of the commitments produced in the preprocessing phase.

Notice that for the above soundness error to be small, we need to bound $p_{\textsf{guess}}(\alpha|v)$. Clearly, at the beginning of the online phase it is $1/q$, but it may increase during the course of the protocol. We have the following upper bound, which will be proved in Appendix A:

Proposition 2. *Throughout the entire protocol, the adversary's guessing probability of α is bounded by*

$$p_{guess}(\alpha|v) \leq \frac{1}{q - 2n} + \frac{2n}{q}.$$

Finally, for completeness, we state here that CommitCheck, which will be invoked if BlockCheck results in "Fail with Agreement", does the job and identifies a dishonest player. Crucial for CommitCheck to work properly is that the $\tilde{z}^{(h)}$ have been consistently announced by P_k (so that there is agreement on the linear combination to be computed on the commitments), but this is ensured by the soundness of BlockCheck.

Proposition 3. *Under the binding property of the underlying commitment scheme, if a dishonest player has broadcast as part of BlockCheck an incorrect value, then this player will be publicly identified by CommitCheck. Furthermore, no honest player will incorrectly be identified as being dishonest.*

The security of the protocol is now straightforward: as a worst-case scenario, we will assume that the adversary controls all but one of the players. First notice that if the adversary decides to behave (semi)-honestly, then by the correctness of BlockCheck the protocol will reach the end of the circuit and CommitCheck will not be executed.

On the other hand, if the adversary misbehaves in (at least) one of the invocations of the multiplication subprotocol in one of the blocks, either by sending an incorrect share of $\langle \varepsilon \rangle$ or $\langle \delta \rangle$ to P_k, or by having dishonest P_k announce inconsistent values (or both), then this will be detected by BlockCheck that will announce "Fail with Conflict" or "Fail with Agreement", depending on the adversary's precise behavior.

In the case of a "Fail with Conflict", the incorrect data is dismissed and the block is rebooted with a fresh king player that is not in the list $\mathcal{L}_{\textsf{suspects}}$ of suspect players. Since every re-boot adds a new player to $\mathcal{L}_{\textsf{suspects}}$, namely the previous king player, we can have at most n such reboots in total before the protocol produces the correct output or before $\mathcal{L}_{\textsf{suspects}}$ is "full", and in that case the protocol stops and every honest player has correctly identified at least one dishonest player (because an honest player ends up in $\mathcal{L}_{\textsf{suspects}}$ only by accusing a dishonest player). Notice that the commitment check is not executed in this case. On the other hand, if `BlockCheck` ends with a "Fail with Agreement", then `CommitCheck` is invoked and will publicly identify a dishonest player.

As for the overall error probability, by combining the soundness error of `BlockCheck` with the bound on p_{guess}, and observing that `BlockCheck` is invoked at most $2n$ times — as we have n blocks plus at most n reboots — we obtain an overall error probability of at most

$$\varepsilon = 2n \cdot \left(\frac{1}{q - 2n} + \frac{2|C|/n + 2n + 1}{q} \right)$$

To sum up, and using a similar checking mechanism for ensuring correctness of the input-sharing and the output-reconstruction phases, our new multiparty computation protocol satisfies the following.

Theorem 1. *For any computationally bounded adversary that cannot break the encryptions/commitments used in the preprocessing phase, except with negligible probability, an execution of our protocol results in one of the following cases (depending on the adversary's strategy):*

I. Success: *the protocol reaches the end of the circuit and outputs the correct result to all players. In this case,* `CommitCheck` *is not executed.*
II. Identification without agreement: *the protocol aborts, but each honest player has identified at least one dishonest player. Also in this case,* `CommitCheck` *is not executed.*
III. Identification with agreement: *the protocol aborts, and the honest players have in-agreement identified at least one dishonest player.*

Furthermore, in all cases, the adversary learns no information on the honest players' inputs, beyond the result of evaluating the circuit C on the inputs.

3.4   The Complexity of Our Protocol

We discuss in this section the complexity of our protocol; as with the previous sections, we focus on the multiplication check, which is the most expensive part of our protocol. The input sharing and the output reconstruction, moreover, can be analyzed in a similar fashion (i.e., in the general case they yield a complexity of the same order of magnitude as the original SPDZ, and exceed it only to unanimously identify a dishonest player).

We thus focus on the multiplication check. We first study the complexity of processing and checking a single block:

– First, the gates of the block are evaluated as in standard SPDZ; this yields a complexity of $|C|/n \cdot O(n) = O(|C|)$ field operations (in total over all players) and the same number of field elements for point-to-point communication, and no broadcasts.

– At the end of the block, the subprotocol `BlockCheck` is executed. Its computation complexity is dominated by computing the linear combination of $t = 2 \cdot |C|/n$ sharings on n shares in step 1; in total, as we will see in Appendix A.2, `BlockCheck` has a computation complexity of $O(|C| + n^2)$ field operations, plus preparing $4n$ commitments. Its communication complexity consists of no point-to-point communication, and $3n$ broadcasts of field elements and $4n$ of commitments and openings.

Now as we have seen, `BlockCheck` can lead an execution of `CommitCheck`, to a re-boot of the current block, or simply to the processing of the following block. The exact cost of `CommitCheck` depends on how the commitments were implemented, but it certainly causes a significant overhead given that it involves a number of cryptographic operations that grows with the size of the circuit; however, `CommitCheck` leads to the public exposure of a dishonest player, so there is little incentive for the adversary to enforce this. As argued in Sect. 3.3, we can have at most n reboots in total before the protocol aborts; as such, the overhead of the reboots causes at most a factor 2 overhead to the ordinary computation of the n blocks.

We thus get the following result summarizing the complexity of our protocol:

Proposition 4. *Except in the case where* `CommitCheck` *is enforced by the adversary, which would lead to an identification-with-agreement of at least a dishonest player, our protocol has the following complexity:*

– *Computation:* $O(n|C| + n^3)$ *field operations, plus preparing* $8n^2$ *commitments (as part of* `Rand` *and of* `ZeroTest`*);*
– *Communication:* $O(n|C|)$ *field elements for point-to-point communication plus* $O(n^2)$ *broadcasts.*[7]

In case `CommitCheck` *is executed, the communication complexity remains the same, while players need to execute* $O(n^2|C|)$ *cryptographic operations on top of the original computational complexity.*[8]

Compared to the original SPDZ protocol, in case all players behave honestly, our protocol is as efficient as the original protocol, up to an additive overhead caused by an increased number of commitments and broadcasts[9], but this overhead is independent of the circuit size and thus negligible except for small circuits. In case of active cheating — unless a dishonest player cheats so bluntly that

---

[7] Note that we treat broadcast as a given primitive here; implementing it using the point-to-point communication and, say, digital signatures, causes some (communication and computation) overhead, but this overhead is independent of the circuit size.

[8] The actual cost of these cryptographic operations depends on how the commitment scheme is implemented.

[9] Plus that we have to do *real* broadcasts, whereas in the original SPDZ protocol without cheater detection it is good enough to do a simple consistency check and abort as soon as there is an inconsistency.

CommitCheck is invoked and he will be publicly identified as being a cheater — the (computation and communication) complexity of our protocol is larger by a factor 2 only, plus the same kind of additive overhead that does not depend on the circuit size.

4   Conclusion

We presented an alternative to the original SPDZ multiparty computation protocol. In contrast to the original protocol, our version allows for *cheater detection*. As such, our protocol is much less vulnerable to a "denial of service" attack: if a dishonest player enforces the protocol to abort, he will be identified and measures can be taken. Furthermore, in our protocol, this feature comes essentially *for free*: as long as everything works as supposed, our protocol is *as efficient* as the original SPDZ (up to an additive overhead that is negligible except for small circuits); but as soon as a fault is detected, instead of simply aborting and being clueless about who cheated, we can proceed and — depending on the adversary's behavior — still *complete the computation* or *identify cheaters without agreement* with a factor 2 overhead, or *identify cheaters with agreement* but with a significant overhead.

As such, we think that our multiparty computation protocol is an attractive alternative to the original SPDZ protocol when considering real life scenarios where dishonest parties may have various incentives for sabotaging an execution.

An obvious open problem is to have agreement on the cheater(s) *in all cases*, and/or without a significant overhead; however, this seems hard to achive without increasing the complexity of the honest execution.

A   The Protocol BlockCheck in Detail

We shall now begin the study of the sub-protocol Block Check; we first establish some notation rules that will be used in the whole section: t will denote a positive integer; we assume that t multiplication opening values $\langle z^{(1)} \rangle, \cdots, \langle z^{(t)} \rangle$ have been publicly opened via a king player P_k, and we will use the following notation: for each shared value $\langle z^{(h)} \rangle$,

- each player P_j has sent $z_j^{(h)}$ to P_k;
- $\tilde{z}_j^{(h)}$ denotes the value received by P_k from P_j (so if P_j is honest, $\tilde{z}_j^{(h)} = z_j^{(h)}$);
- P_k has computed and sent to each P_j the value $z^{(h)}$;
- $\tilde{z}^{(h)}(j)$ denotes the value received by each P_j from P_k (so if P_k is honest, $\tilde{z}^{(h)}(j) = z^{(h)}$).

The goal of BlockCheck is to detect errors in this process; as we have seen, the first step of the check consists in computing a (quasi-) random linear combination of the values to be checked. This is performed by generating a seed via the subroutine Rand, and then using the powers of the seed as coefficients of the linear combination. We first define Rand, which assumes that players have access to a commitment scheme (as in standard SPDZ):

Rand:

The protocol is used to generate a random seed $e \in \mathbb{F}_q$.

(i) Each player P_j selects random $e_j \leftarrow \mathbb{F}_q$ and broadcasts a commitment $\texttt{Commit}(e_j)$ to it;

(ii) all the commitments are then opened, so that all players get $e_1, \cdots, e_n$;

(iii) the output of $\texttt{Rand}$ is the value $e := \sum_{j=1}^{n} e_j$.

We now show that any error that occurred during the opening of the values $\langle z^{(1)} \rangle, \cdots, \langle z^{(t)} \rangle$ will affect their linear combination as well (with high probability); the proof is a standard argument, and is omitted here. We refer to the full version of the paper for the details.

Lemma 1. *Let e be a seed generated by $\texttt{Rand}$; consider the following linear combination with coefficients given by the powers of e:*

$$\langle z \rangle := \sum_{h=1}^{t} e^h \cdot \langle z^{(h)} \rangle, \quad \tilde{z}(j) := \sum_{h=1}^{t} e^h \cdot \tilde{z}^{(h)}(j) \text{ for any } j = 1, \cdots, n.$$

Assume that for a given index $h \in \{1, \cdots, t\}$ the value received by a given player P_j is incorrect, i.e. $\tilde{z}^{(h)}(j) \neq z^{(h)}$; then $\tilde{z}(j) \neq z$ except with probability t/q.

Similarly, if the values received by two players P_j and P_i for an index h are different (i.e. $\tilde{z}^{(h)}(j) \neq \tilde{z}^{(h)}(i)$), then the same will hold for the corresponding linear combinations, i.e. $\tilde{z}(j) \neq \tilde{z}(i)$ except with probability t/q.

The next step of $\texttt{BlockCheck}$ is the "public opening and conflict" phase; it has already been defined in previous sections, but we will re-write it here in order to make this chapter as self-contained as possible:

PublicOpening:

The protocol takes as input a shared value $[z]$ and the index k of the king player P_k; initialize the boolean value $\mathbf{b}$ to $\top$ and the list L to the empty set $\emptyset$.

(i) For each $j = 1, \cdots, n$, player P_j broadcast z_j and P_k broadcast $\tilde{z}_j$; if the two values do not coincide, set $\mathbf{b} = \bot$ and $L \leftarrow L \cup \{P_j\}$.

(ii) If $\mathbf{b} = \bot$, the protocol stops and output $(\bot, L)$.

(iii) Players set $\tilde{z} := \sum_j z_j$; for each $j = 1, \cdots, n$, player P_j broadcasts $\tilde{z}(j)$. If this value is different from $\tilde{z}$, set $\mathbf{b} = \bot$ and $L \leftarrow L \cup \{P_j\}$.

(iv) The protocol outputs $(\mathbf{b}, L, \tilde{z})$.

The following lemma is a direct consequence of the definition of the algorithm, and states that the public opening routine is correct and sound:

Lemma 2. *Let* $(\mathbf{b}, L, \tilde{z})$ *be the output of* $PublicOpening$ $([z])$ *with king player* P_k; *we then have the following properties:*

- (correctness) *if* $\langle z \rangle$ *has been correctly reconstructed and players follow the instructions of the protocol, then* $\mathbf{b} = \top$ *and* $L = \emptyset$.
- (soundness) *if* $\tilde{z}(j) \neq \tilde{z}(i)$ *for some honest players* P_j *and* P_i, *then* $\mathbf{b} = \bot$ *and* $L \neq \emptyset$.
Furthermore, in this case either P_k *or all players in* L *are dishonest.*

The last step consists in checking the tags of the value $\langle z \rangle = ([z], [\gamma(z)])$; as we have previously discussed, this is performed by using the subroutine ZeroTest to check that the value $[\gamma(z)] - \tilde{z}[\alpha]$ opens to 0.

As hinted in Sect. 3.2, we need to be careful when checking the tags via ZeroTest, as this can increase the adversary's guessing probability of α. We introduce the following definition to model the information on α possessed by the adversary:

Definition 1. *Given a distribution* $p(x, v)$, *we say that the distribution of* x *given* v *is a list of size* m *if there exists a (conditional) distribution* $p(\ell|v)$, *where the range of* ℓ *consists of lists of* m *elements in the range of* x, *such that the following two properties hold for the joint distribution* $p(x, v, \ell) := p(x, v) \cdot p(\ell|v)$:

(I) $p(x \in \ell) \leq \max_{\hat{\ell} \in Im(\ell)} p(x \in \hat{\ell})$;
(II) $p(x|v = \hat{v}, \ell = \hat{\ell}, x \notin \hat{\ell}) = p(x|x \notin \hat{\ell})$ *for every* $\hat{v}, \hat{\ell}$ *such that the formula is well-defined.*

In a nutshell, we use the above definition to formalize the following situation: let v denote the adversary's view and $x := \alpha$; assume that the distribution of α given v is a list of size m. This means that the adversary has tried to guess the value of α for m consecutive times, and he has learned whether his guess was correct or not after each guess.

We now state the basic properties of ZeroTest, which will in turn imply the desired properties of the tag check; we assume that ZeroTest outputs a boolean value $\mathbf{b} \in \{\top, \bot\}$, marking whether the input opens to zero or not, and some extra data that will be omitted in the following lemma.

Lemma 3. *Let* $\mathbf{b}$ *be the output of* $ZeroTest$ $([x])$; *we then have the following properties:*

- (correctness): *if* $x = 0$ *and players follow the instructions of the protocol, then* $\mathbf{b} = \top$ *with probability 1.*
- (soundness): *consider the joint distribution* $p(x, v_0)$, *where* v_0 *denotes the adversary's view before the execution of* $ZeroTest$. *Then*

$$p(\mathbf{b} = \top) \leq 1/q + p_{guess}(x|v_0).$$

Furthermore, if $x = 0$ *but* $\mathbf{b} = \bot$, *then a dishonest player has broadcast an incorrect version of a value to which he is committed by means of a linear combination of the commitments produced in the preprocessing phase.*

– (privacy): *Assume that x is uniformly distributed and that the distribution of x given v_0 is a list of size m_0. Then after the execution of* ZeroTest$([x])$*, the distribution of x given v is a list of guesses of size at most $m := m_0 + 1$, where v denotes the adversary's view after the execution of* ZeroTest.

Now that we have fixed the notation for the subroutines, we can state the definition of BlockCheck in a more formal way:

BlockCheck:

The protocol takes as input a block and the index k of the king player P_k; denote by $\langle z^{(1)} \rangle, \cdots, \langle z^{(t)} \rangle$ the multiplication opening values of the block.

(i) Players execute Rand to get a random seed $e \in \mathbb{F}_q$, then compute the linear combination $\langle z \rangle := \sum_{h=1}^{t} e^h \langle z^{(h)} \rangle$.

(ii) Run $(\mathbf{b}, L, \tilde{z}) \leftarrow$ PublicOpening$([z])$; if $\mathbf{b} = \bot$, BlockCheck stops and outputs the message "Fail with Conflict" together with the list L.

(iii) Run $(\mathbf{b}, (\langle a \rangle, \langle b \rangle, \langle c \rangle), \langle r \rangle) \leftarrow$ ZeroTest$([\gamma(z)] - \tilde{z}[\alpha])$.

(iv) If $\mathbf{b} = \top$, output the message "Success";
if $\mathbf{b} = \bot$, output the message "Fail with Agreeement" together with the elements $((\langle a \rangle, \langle b \rangle, \langle c \rangle), \langle r \rangle)$.

We can now prove the properties of BlockCheck claimed in Sect. 3.3; we omit the proof here, as it can be easily derived from the definition of BlockCheck.

Proposition 5. *BlockCheck satisfies the following:*

Correctness of BlockCheck: *if all players behave honestly and hence all $\tilde{z}^{(j)}$ are correct and consistently announced by P_k, then BlockCheck outputs "Success" with probability 1.*

Soundness of BlockCheck: *if at least one of the $\tilde{z}^{(j)}$ is incorrect, i.e. $\neq z^{(j)}$, or inconsistently announced by P_k, then the following holds except with probability at most*

$$\delta = (2|C|/n + 1)/q + p_{guess}(\alpha|v),$$

where v is the adversary's view before the execution of BlockCheck. BlockCheck outputs "Fail"; furthermore, if it outputs "Fail with Conflict", then either the king player P_k or all of the accusing players are dishonest (or both), and if it outputs "Fail with Agreement", then all $\tilde{z}^{(j)}$ have been consistently announced by P_k, and a dishonest player has broadcast as part of BlockCheck an incorrect version of a value to which he is committed by means of a linear combination (depending on the $\tilde{z}^{(j)}$'s) of the commitments produced in the preprocessing phase.

Finally, we can now prove the bound on the adversary's guessing probability of the global key α:

Proposition 6. *Throughout the entire protocol, the adversary's guessing probability of α is bounded by*

$$p_{guess}(\alpha|v) \leq \frac{1}{q - 2n} + \frac{2n}{q}.$$

Proof. Clearly, the adversary can increase his guessing probability only during the execution of `ZeroTest`; this, by definition of `BlockCheck`, is executed only when the value $\tilde{z}$ is consistent among players, so that its input is equal to $[x] := [\gamma(z)] - \tilde{z}[\alpha] = (z - \tilde{z})[\alpha]$. Hence we can assume as a worst-case scenario that $z \neq \tilde{z}$, so that the adversary's guessing probabilities of α and of x coincide.

Notice that at the beginning of the computation, the distribution of α given the adversary's view is a list of guesses of size 0; hence we can inductively apply Lemma 3, so that during the execution of the protocol the distribution of α given the adversary's view is a list of guesses of size at most $2n$ (recall that `BlockCheck`, and hence `ZeroTest`, is executed at most $2n$ times). Hence according to Definition 1, and given that α is uniformly distributed, there exists a distribution $p(\ell|v)$ with the following properties:

(I) $p(\alpha \in \ell) \leq 2n/q$;
(II) $\max_{\hat{\alpha},\hat{\ell}} p(\alpha = \hat{\alpha}|v = \hat{v}, \ell = \hat{\ell}, \alpha \notin \hat{\ell}) = 1/(q - m)$.

Now from this we can deduce the claimed upper bound on the guessing probability: indeed, by using the law of total probability with the events $(\alpha \in \ell)$ and $(\alpha \notin \ell)$, we obtain

$$p_{\text{guess}}(\alpha|v) = \sum_{\hat{v}} p(v = \hat{v}) \cdot \max_{\hat{\alpha}} p(\alpha = \hat{\alpha}|v = \hat{v}) \leq \frac{1}{q - 2n} + \frac{2n}{q}.$$

$\square$

A.1   The Tag Checking in Detail

We discuss in this section the sub-routine `ZeroTest`, meant to check whether some shared value $[x]$ is equal to zero or not. The key point is that we cannot simply open $[x]$: indeed, in the actual scenario this value will be equal to $[\gamma(z)] - \tilde{z}[\alpha]$ for some shared value $\langle z \rangle$; now the adversary could select any value Δz and let $\tilde{z} = z + \Delta z$, so opening $[\gamma(z)] - \tilde{z}[\alpha] = \Delta z \cdot [\alpha]$ will actually let the adversary learn the global key α. This is not a problem in the original SPDZ protocol, since it will abort if the value does not open to 0, but it is a problem for our protocol, which carries on even if the result is not zero. To avoid this, we will perform a multiplication of $[x]$ with a random shared value:

`ZeroTest`:
The protocol takes as input a shared value $[x]$.

(i) Players select a random shared value $\langle r \rangle$ and a fresh multiplication triplet $(\langle a \rangle, \langle b \rangle, \langle c \rangle)$.
(ii) Players compute $[rx]$ with multiplication triplet $(\langle a \rangle, \langle b \rangle, \langle c \rangle)$ as described in Section 2, but with a different communication model: instead of sending their data to a king player that acts as a relay, they will broadcast a commitment to it, then open all the commitments before moving to the next round.

(iii) Each player P_j broadcasts a commitment $\texttt{Commit}((rx)_j)$ to his share of $[rx]$, then all commitments are opened, so that players obtain rx.
(iv) Set $\mathbf{b} = \top$ if $rx = 0$, $\mathbf{b} = \bot$ otherwise; output $(\mathbf{b}, (\langle a \rangle, \langle b \rangle, \langle c \rangle), \langle r \rangle)$.

From now on, we will adopt a slight abuse of notation by writing formulae such as $\texttt{ZeroTest}([x]) = \mathbf{b}$, i.e. considering only the boolean value among the outputs of the protocol. We first prove that the subprotocol is correct and sound:

Lemma 4. *ZeroTest satisfies the following properties:*

- Correctness: *if players follow the instructions of the protocol, $\texttt{ZeroTest}([0]) = \top$ with probability 1.*
- Soundness: *consider the joint distribution $p(x, v_0)$, where v_0 denotes the adversary's view before the execution of ZeroTest; then*

$$p(\mathit{ZeroTest}([x]) = \top) \leq 1/q + p_{\mathit{guess}}(x|v_0).$$

Furthermore, if $x = 0$ but $\mathbf{b} = \bot$, then a dishonest player has broadcast an incorrect version of a value to which he is committed by means of a linear combination of the commitments produced in the preprocessing phase.

Proof

- Correctness: trivially, $\texttt{ZeroTest}$ will open $[r \cdot 0] = [0]$.
- Soundness: by definition of the protocol, the output of $\texttt{ZeroTest}([x])$ is equal to $\top$ if and only if $\mathbf{b} = 0$, where

$$\mathbf{b} := (r - \tilde{r})(x - \tilde{x}) - \tilde{y}$$

where r is a variable uniformly distributed and independent of $x, \tilde{x}, \tilde{r}$ and $\tilde{y}$, and the variables $\tilde{r}, \tilde{x}$ and $\tilde{y}$ are chosen by the adversary, and are thus determined by his current view (since we can assume without loss of generality that the adversary is deterministic).

Now notice that for any $\hat{v}_0$ we have the following inequality:

$$p((r - \tilde{r}(\hat{v}_0))(x - \tilde{x}(\hat{v}_0)) = 0 | v_0 = \hat{v}_0) \leq 1/q + \max_{\hat{v}} p(x = \hat{x} | v_0 = \hat{v}_0)$$

In turn, by applying the law of total probability to $p((r - \tilde{r})(x - \tilde{x}) - \tilde{y} = 0)$ with the events $(v_0 = \hat{v}_0)$, we obtain the following inequality:

$$p((r - \tilde{r})(x - \tilde{x}) - \tilde{y} = 0) \leq 1/q + p_{\texttt{guess}}(x|v_0).$$

Finally, if $x = 0$ but $\mathbf{b} = \bot$, then necessarily a player has communicated some incorrect values during $\texttt{ZeroTest}$; hence since all communications are performed by broadcast, he is committed to the incorrect value, so that the claim is proved. $\qquad\square$

Finally, we need to discuss the privacy of `ZeroTest`; we first remark that Definition 1, formalizing our privacy notion, yields the following consequences:

Remark 1. Assume that the *uniform* distribution x is a list of size m given v; we then have the following properties:

(i) $p(x \in \ell) \leq m/q$ (immediate consequence of (I));
(ii) $p(x = y | x \notin \ell) \leq 1/(q - m)$ for any $y = y(v)$ (consequence of (II) via the law of total probability).

Furthermore, let r be a random variable independent of both v and x, and set $v' := (v, r)$. Then it trivially holds that if $p(x, v)$ satisfies the above definition, then so does $p(x, v')$.

Lemma 5. *Given a distribution $p(x, v_0)$, where v_0 denotes the adversary's view, assume that the* uniform *distribution of x given v_0 is a list of size m_0. Then after the execution of `ZeroTest([x])`, the distribution of x given v is a list of guesses of size at most $m := m_0 + 1$, where v denotes the adversary's view after the execution of `ZeroTest`.*

Proof. By looking at the instructions to compute and open $[xr]$ to P_i, we see that what the adversary can learn the following values (plus random sharings of them): $\gamma := x - a$, $\delta := r - b$ and $\pi := (r - \tilde{r})(x - \tilde{x})$, where a, b and r are jointly uniformly distributed and independent of each other and of $v, x, \tilde{x}, \tilde{r}$.

$\tilde{x}$ and $\tilde{r}$ are chosen by the adversary, and are thus determined by his view (since we assume without loss of generality that the adversary is deterministic).

Now given the adversary's view v_0 before the execution of `ZeroTest`, the adversary's *current* view is equal to $(v_0, \gamma, \delta, \pi)$; notice that a and b are (jointly) random and independent of x, r, v_0 and π, and thus so are $\gamma = x - a$ and $\delta = r - b$, so that we may restrict the view to $v := (v_0, \pi)$ (cf. Remark 1)[10].

Now by inductive hypothesis, there exists a conditional distribution $p(\ell_0 | v_0)$ such that properties I and II hold for $p(x, v_0, \ell_0) := p(x, v_0) \cdot p(\ell_0 | v_0)$; in a natural way, we define the new distribution to be

$$p(\ell = (x_1, \cdots, x_{m_0}, x_m) | v) := p(\ell_0 = (x_1, \cdots, x_{m_0}) | v_0) \cdot p(\tilde{x}(v_0) = x_m | v_0).$$

We now prove that properties I and II hold for $p(x, v, \ell)$: first of all, notice that $p(x \in \ell) = p(x \in \ell_0) + p(x = \tilde{x}(v_0) | x \notin \ell_0) \cdot p(x \notin \ell_0)$. Hence thanks to Remark 1 we have that

$$p(x \in \ell) \leq m_0/q + (1/(q - m_0)) \cdot ((q - m_0)/q) = m/q.$$

Hence property I holds; we can thus focus on property II. As a first step, notice that

$$p(x | v = (\hat{v}_0, \hat{\pi}), \ell = \hat{\ell}, x \notin \hat{\ell}) = p(x | v_0 = \hat{v}_0, \ell_0 = \hat{\ell}_0, x \notin \hat{\ell}_0, x \neq \tilde{x}(\hat{v}_0))$$

---

[10] For the same reason, we omit here the fact that the view also contain random sharings of $x - a$, $r - b$ and π.

since if $x \notin \hat{\ell}$, then in particular $x \neq \tilde{x}(\hat{v}_0)$; hence we can re-write $\pi = \hat{\pi}$ as $r = \tilde{r}(v_0) + \hat{\pi}/(x - \tilde{x}(\hat{v}_0))$, and can be removed because r is independent of x, v_0 and ℓ_0. We thus get the following equality:

$$p(x|(v_0, \pi) = (\hat{v}_0, \hat{\pi}), \ell = \hat{\ell}, x \notin \hat{\ell}) = p(x|x \notin \hat{\ell}_0, x \neq \tilde{x}(\hat{v}_0))$$

which means that property II holds.   □

A.2   The Complexity of the Block Check

We briefly discuss in this section the complexity of BlockCheck, which was presented in Sect. 3.4. First notice that since each block contains at most $|C|/n$ gates, there are at most $2|C|/n$ multiplication opening values to be checked in each block; we thus get the following complexity:

- $4n$ commitments need to be prepared, broadcast and opened (n to produce a random seed via Rand, and $3n$ during ZeroTest);
- the computational complexity of a block check is in $O\left(|C| + n^2\right)$ field operations (excluding computation on commitments), essentially given by the cost of computing the linear combination of the values to be checked;
- finally, the block check requires broadcasting $3n$ field elements for the dispute phase of PublicOpening. Notice that we do not use point-to-point communication.

B   The Commitment Check

We now discuss how to authenticate shares of a value; as remarked in Sect. 2, for every shared value z that is $[\cdot]$-shared in the pre-processing phase each player P_i holds randomness ρ_{z_i} and the value $e_{z_i} := \text{Enc}(z_i, \rho_{z_i})$ has been broadcast. We give here the details on how to use these encryptions as a commitment scheme:

EncryptionCheck:
the protocol takes as input the index i of a player P_i and his share $z_i = \sum_{h=1}^{M} \lambda^{(h)} z_i^{(h)}$, where all $\left[z^{(h)}\right]$ are computed in the preprocessing phase;
let $e_i^{(h)} := \text{Enc}\left(z_i^{(h)}, \rho_i^{(h)}\right)$ (these values are public, cf. Section 2).

(i)   Players set $e_i := \sum_{h=1}^{M} \lambda^{(h)} e_i^{(h)}$;
(ii) P_i computes and broadcasts $\rho_i := \sum_{h=1}^{M} \lambda^{(h)} \rho_i^{(h)}$;
(iii) players set $e_i \leftarrow \text{Enc}(z_i, \rho_i)$.

If $e_i = \text{Enc}(z_i, \rho_i)$, the protocol outputs $\top$; otherwise, it outputs $\bot$.

Trivially, if P_i behaves honestly, EncryptionCheck will output $\top$; on the other hand, if the share $\tilde{z}_i$ he submitted is not correct, then the output will be $\bot$ since $\text{Enc}(z_i, \rho_i) \neq \text{Enc}(\tilde{z}_i, \tilde{\rho}_i)$ for any possible randomness $\tilde{\rho}_i$.

We are now ready to define the protocol CommitCheck, that simply applies EncryptionCheck to all shares submitted during the multiplication of two values:

CommitCheck:

The protocol takes as input the index i of a player P_i, a shared value $\langle z \rangle$ and the values $(\langle a \rangle, \langle b \rangle, \langle c \rangle), \langle r \rangle$ used to check its tag.

 (i) Run EncryptionCheck(z_i) for P_i, denote by $\mathbf{b}_1$ its output;

 (ii) run EncryptionCheck($\gamma(z)_i - \tilde{z}\alpha_i - a_i$) for P_i, denote by $\mathbf{b}_2$ its output;

(iii) run EncryptionCheck($r_i - b_i$) for P_i, denote by $\mathbf{b}_3$ its output;

(iv) run EncryptionCheck($c_i + (\gamma(z) - \tilde{z}\alpha - a)\, b_i + (r - b)a_i + (\gamma(z) - \tilde{z}\alpha - a)(r - b)$) for P_i, denote by $\mathbf{b}_4$ its output.

Output $\mathbf{b}_1 \wedge \mathbf{b}_2 \wedge \mathbf{b}_3 \wedge \mathbf{b}_4$.

The following proposition summarizes the security property of CommitCheck; we omit the proof, as it can be easily deduced from the definition of the protocol.

Proposition 7. *Under the binding property of the underlying commitment scheme, if a dishonest player has broadcast as part of BlockCheck an incorrect value, then this player will be publicly identified by CommitCheck. Furthermore, no honest player will incorrectly be identified as being dishonest.*

C   Checking the Input and Output of the Computation

We show in this section how to secure the input-sharing and output-reconstruction phases; we use the main ideas and techniques of the multiplication check.

We first describe in more detail how the input sharing is performed in the original SPDZ protocol: each shared value $\langle r \rangle$ produce in the preprocessing phase comes with another type of sharing, denoted by

$$\llbracket r \rrbracket := \left([r], \left(\beta_i, \gamma(r)_1^i, \cdots, \gamma(r)_n^i \right)_{i=1,\cdots,n} \right),$$

where each player P_i holds $r_i, \beta_i, \gamma(r)_1^i, \cdots, \gamma(r)_n^i$ and $r\beta_i = \sum_j \gamma(r)_i^j$ for any i. Now in classical SPDZ, whenever a player P_i holds input x, a random shared value $\llbracket r \rrbracket$ is selected; then each player P_j communicates r_j and $\gamma(r)_i^j$ to P_i, who computes r and checks that $r\beta_i = \sum_j \gamma(r)_i^j$; P_i can then broadcast either an error message or the value $\varepsilon := x - r$. The input is then shared as $\langle r \rangle + \varepsilon$.

We add to this protocol our system of accusations and, as a last resort, the commitment checks:

InputShare:

The protocol is used to share an input x held by player P_i; a fresh king player P_k and a shared value $\langle r \rangle, [\![r]\!]$ are selected.

(i) for each $j \neq i$, player P_j sends $(r_j, \gamma(r)_i^j)$ to P_k, who in turn communicates these elements to P_i.

(ii) P_i computes $y := r\beta_i - \sum_j \gamma(r)_i^j$. If $y = 0$, he broadcasts $(\top, \varepsilon := x - r)$; players share x as $\langle r \rangle + \varepsilon$ and the protocol stops.

(iii) If $y \neq 0$, P_i broadcasts $\bot$. Then for each $j \neq i$, player P_j broadcasts $(r_j, \gamma(r)_i^j)$.

(iv) The king player P_k broadcast a list L of players that he accuses of inconsistent behaviour; if $L \neq \emptyset$, then P_k and all the players in L are added to the list of suspect players. InputShare is then rebooted; if all player are suspect, then the overall protocol aborts.

(v) If $L = \emptyset$, then P_i can accuse P_k of inconsistent behaviour; if that is the case, P_i and P_k are added to the list of suspect players, and the protocol is rebooted. If all player are suspect, then the overall protocol aborts.

(vi) Given that all values are now public, players run EncryptionCheck(r_j) and EncryptionCheck$\left(\gamma(r)_i^j\right)$. If all players pass the encryption check, P_i is deemed dishonest and the protocol aborts

---

The following proposition follows from the definition of InputShare and proves that the protocol is secure:

Proposition 8. *Let x be an input held by player P_i; InputShare satisfies the following properties:*

- Correctness: *if players behave honestly, InputShare(x) produces no accusations and players obtain a $\langle \cdot \rangle$-sharing of x.*
- Soundness: *if a player different from P_i behaves dishonestly during the execution of InputShare, then except with probability $1/q$ he will be deemed suspect or dishonest.*
- Privacy: *if P_i is honest, the adversary's guessing probability of x is equal to $\max_{\hat{x}} p(x = \hat{x})$.*

We now introduce an output-checking phase which makes use of the protocols introduced in the previous sections: it simply reconstructs the output, then checks its tag with ZeroTest and, if an error is detected, requires player to authenticate their shares via CommitCheck.

OutputCheck:

The protocol takes as input the shared value $\langle z \rangle$, output of the circuit.

(i) Each player P_i broadcasts his share z_i of $[z]$;

(ii) players set $\tilde{z} \leftarrow \sum_i z_i$; they then run ZeroTest $([\gamma(z)] - \tilde{z}[\alpha])$. Denote by $(\mathbf{b}, (\langle a \rangle, \langle b \rangle, \langle c \rangle), \langle r \rangle)$ its output;

(iii) if $\mathbf{b} = \top$, the protocol stops and output outputs $\tilde{z}$;

(iv) if $\mathbf{b} = \bot$, then player run $\mathbf{b}(i) \leftarrow \text{CommitCheck}(\langle z \rangle)$ with values $(\langle a \rangle, \langle b \rangle, \langle c \rangle), \langle r \rangle$ for each player P_i; if $\mathbf{b}(i) = \bot$, the protocols outputs the message "P_i dishonest" and stops.

The following proposition proves that the protocol is correct and sound; we omit the proof here, as it can be easily obtained from the definition of OutputCheck, and refer to the full version of the paper for the details.

Proposition 9. *OutputCheck satisfies the following properties:*

– Correctness: *if players submit the correct shares of $[z]$ and behave honestly during ZeroTest, then OutputCheck will output the correct value z;*

– Security: *assume that $\tilde{z} \neq z$ or that the adversary behaved dishonestly in the ZeroTest phase; then OutputCheck will produce an accusation to a dishonest player except with probability $1/q + p_v$, where p_v is the adversary's guessing probability of α given his view v.*

In the concrete setting, this error probability will be equal to $1/q + 1/(q - 2n)$.

References

1. Baum, C., Orsini, E., Scholl, P.: Efficient secure multiparty computation with identifiable abort. IACR Cryptology ePrint Archive 2016:187 (2016)

2. Ben-Or, M., Goldwasser, S., Wigderson, A.: Completeness theorems for non-cryptographic fault-tolerant distributed computation. In: STOC 1988, pp. 1–10. ACM (1988)

3. Bendlin, R., Damgård, I., Orlandi, C., Zakarias, S.: Semi-homomorphic encryption and multiparty computation. In: Paterson, K.G. (ed.) EUROCRYPT 2011. LNCS, vol. 6632, pp. 169–188. Springer, Heidelberg (2011). doi:10.1007/978-3-642-20465-4_11

4. Canetti, R.: Universally composable security: a new paradigm for cryptographic protocols. In: FOCS 2001, pp. 136–145. IEEE Computer Society (2001)

5. Chaum, D., Crépeau, C., Damgard, I.: Multiparty unconditionally secure protocols. In: STOC 1988, pp. 11–19. ACM (1988)

6. Damgård, I., Keller, M., Larraia, E., Pastro, V., Scholl, P., Smart, N.P.: Practical covertly secure MPC for dishonest majority – or: breaking the SPDZ limits. In: Crampton, J., Jajodia, S., Mayes, K. (eds.) ESORICS 2013. LNCS, vol. 8134, pp. 1–18. Springer, Heidelberg (2013). doi:10.1007/978-3-642-40203-6_1

7. Damgård, I., Pastro, V., Smart, N., Zakarias, S.: Multiparty computation from somewhat homomorphic encryption. In: Safavi-Naini, R., Canetti, R. (eds.) CRYPTO 2012. LNCS, vol. 7417, pp. 643–662. Springer, Heidelberg (2012). doi:10.1007/978-3-642-32009-5_38

8. Goldreich, O., Micali, S., Wigderson, A.: How to play any mental game or a completeness theorem for protocols with honest majority. In: STOC 1987, pp. 218–229. ACM (1987)

9. Ishai, Y., Ostrovsky, R., Zikas, V.: Secure multi-party computation with identifiable abort. In: Garay, J.A., Gennaro, R. (eds.) CRYPTO 2014. LNCS, vol. 8617, pp. 369–386. Springer, Heidelberg (2014). doi:10.1007/978-3-662-44381-1_21

10. Yao, A.C.: Protocols for secure computations. In: FOCS, pp. 160–164. IEEE Computer Society (1982)

Error-Correcting Codes Against Chosen-Codeword Attacks

Kenji Yasunaga[✉]

Kanazawa University, Kakuma-machi, Kanazawa, Japan
yasunaga@se.kanazawa-u.ac.jp

Abstract. We study the problem of error correction for computationally bounded channels under chosen-codeword attacks (CCA). In the CCA setting, the channel can introduce a p-fraction of errors by accessing to the encoding and the decoding oracles. Since the unique decoding is not possible for $p \geq 1/4$, we consider list-decodable codes. We present an optimal-rate coding scheme by assuming the existence of one-way functions. The construction is based on the list-decodable code of Guruswami and Smith [5] for computationally bounded channels.

1 Introduction

The problem of error correction for computationally bounded channels was first studied by Lipton [9]. He reduced the problem of error correction in the secret-key (or shared randomness) setting to the problem of error correction in binary symmetric channels (BSC). In his scheme, a message m is encoded into $c = \pi^{-1}(C(m)) \oplus \mu$, where C is an error correcting code for BSC, and π and μ are a random bit permutation and a random mask, respectively, which are privately shared between the sender and the receiver. When an error e was introduced, on input $y = c \oplus e$, the decoder sends $\pi(y \oplus \mu) = C(m) \oplus \pi(e)$ to the decoder of C. Since $\pi(e)$ is like a random error in BSC, C can correct it. The scheme can achieve an optimal rate in the secret-key setting since there are several optimal-rate (capacity-achieving) schemes for BSC [1,2]. Lipton showed that, by assuming a pseudorandom generator exists, the length of the secret key can be reduced to n^{-d} for any constant $d > 0$, where n is the length of c.

Lipton's scheme beautifully reduced the error correction in the secret-key setting to that in BSC. However, the scheme only achieves *one-time* security. Thus, in order to send k messages reliably, we need to generate k secret keys. The situation is very similar to that of the one-time pad for secret-key encryption.

In modern cryptography, more powerful attacks are considered for encryption schemes, for which the one-time pad is not secure. In a chosen-plaintext attack (CPA), an adversary is allowed to access to the encryption oracle. In addition, the adversary can access to the decryption oracle in a chosen-ciphertext attack (CCA). The CCA security is widely accepted as the standard security notion for encryption schemes.

In this work, we introduce an analogous notion to chosen-ciphertext attack security, called *chosen-codeword attack (CCA)* security, for the problem of

© Springer International Publishing AG 2016
A.C.A. Nascimento and P. Barreto (Eds.): ICITS 2016, LNCS 10015, pp. 177–189, 2016.
DOI: 10.1007/978-3-319-49175-2_9

error correction. Intuitively, a coding scheme is said to be CCA secure if for any probabilistic polynomial-time (PPT) adversarial channel, the scheme can correct any error introduced by the channel even if it can access to both the encoding and the decoding oracles. We assume that adversarial channels can introduce at most p-fraction errors, where $p \in (0, 1/2)$ is called the error rate. The CCA security of the coding scheme captures strong attack scenarios, in which adversarial channels can introduce errors by using various information obtained via the encoding and decoding functions.

We present an optimal-rate coding scheme that is CCA secure in the secret-key setting. The construction is based on the framework of Guruswami and Smith [6], which provides a one-time secure coding scheme for computationally bounded channels.

It is first observed that, in order to tolerate attacks using the encoding oracle, it is necessary to relax the goal of decoding to *list decoding*, where the decoder outputs a polynomial-size list containing an original message. As discussed in [10], if an adversarial channel can obtain polynomially-many valid codewords, the channel can cause a non-negligible error for unique decoding when the error rate $p > 1/4$. Thus, we aim to construct a list-decodable code with optimal rate $1 - H(p) - \varepsilon$ for any constant ε, where p is the error rate and $H(\cdot)$ is the binary entropy function.

Guruswami and Smith [6] showed an optimal-rate list-decodable code for computationally bounded channels. Their scheme does not assume the existence of a shared secret key. However, they only presented a probabilistic construction that is not fully explicit. To implement their scheme, the sender and the receiver need to share the random coins privately to the channel. The only probabilistic part of [6] is a primitive called a *pseudorandom code*, which is a list-decodable code whose codewords themselves are pseudorandom. We would like to construct an explicit scheme that is secure against polynomial-time channels. Since the scheme of [6] can been seen as an explicit scheme in the secret-key setting. We aim to construct an explicit secret-key code that is CCA secure for polynomial-time adversaries.

Our scheme is built with several cryptographic primitive including pseudorandom generators, pseudorandom functions, and secure message authentication codes. All the three primitives can be constructed by assuming the existence of one-way functions [3,4,7].

1.1 Ideas of the Construction

Our approach is to enhance the error correctability of the scheme of [6] to have CCA security. In order to prove CCA security, we need to show that the responses of the encoding/decoding oracles are useless for an adversarial channel. It is sufficient to show that the oracle responses can be *simulated* without using the secret key.

We observe that the codewords of the scheme [5] are pseudorandom. Thus, simulation of the encoding oracle can be done by preparing a random string for every oracle query. When an adversarial channel makes the i-th query m_i to the encoding oracle, the simulator responds with a random string c_i. By pseudorandomness of codewords, the simulation can be done successfully.

To achieve CCA security, we need to simulate the decoding oracle. As in achieving CCA security for encryption schemes, we employ a message authentication code (MAC). To encode a message m, we first generate a MAC tag τ of m, and feed (m, τ) to the encoder. By this modification, the adversarial channel cannot generate a valid codeword without querying the encoding oracle. Otherwise, such a channel can be used for breaking the security of MAC. As in simulating the encoding oracle, we use a list of pairs (m_i, c_i) for every oracle query m_i to the encoding oracle, where c_i is a random string. On querying y to the decoding oracle, the simulator responds with the list of all m_i for which the corresponding codeword c_i is within a distance $\lceil pn \rceil$ from y. Since the encoding of [6] is inherently probabilistic, it seems necessary to check exponentially-many possible codewords of m_i for each i. However, this problem can be resolved by making the encoding *deterministic*, which can be done by using a pseudorandom function F. In encoding a message m, the value $F_{sk}(m)$ is used as random coins for the encoder, where sk is the secret key of F shared between the sender and the receiver. As long as sk is secret, $F_{sk}(m)$ looks random. Since there is a unique codeword for each message m_i, the responses of the decoding oracle can be simulated in the above way.

We employ several cryptographic primitives, and hence our construction is relatively simple compared to the original construction of [6]. We could avoid using a randomness-efficient sampler, a generator of t-wise independent permutations, a generator of t-wise independent strings, and a code correcting t-wise independent errors. Instead, we use standard cryptographic primitives, a pseudorandom generator, a pseudorandom function, and a message authentication code.

1.2   Related Work

Lipton [9] introduced the notion of computationally bounded channels, and proposed an optimal-rate scheme that has one-time security in the secret-key setting.

Langberg [8] studied secret-key coding schemes for computationally *unbounded* channels, and showed the existence of an optimal-rate coding scheme with optimal secret-key size.

Micali et al. [10,11] proposed a coding scheme in the public-key setting in which the encoder has a secret key of digital signature and the decoder has the corresponding verification key. They considered an attack scenario in which an adversarial channel can observe several valid codewords. However, their security model is essentially different from the model in which the channel can access to the encoding oracle. In the model of [10,11], the sender can use the *time stamp* to encode messages. Since the channel is not allowed to access to the signing oracle, it cannot obtain multiple codewords with the same time stamp. Indeed, the use of time stamps allows to circumvent the impossibility of unique decoding.

Guruswami and Smith [6] studied coding schemes for computationally bounded channels where the time complexity is a prior bounded polynomial. They presented a probabilistic construction of an optimal-rate coding scheme in which neither a secret key nor a public key is used.

2   Preliminaries

2.1   Notations

For $n \in \mathbb{N}$, we write $[n] = \{1, 2, \ldots, n\}$. For a finite set Σ and an integer $n \in \mathbb{N}$, $x \in \Sigma^n$ is called a vector or string over the alphabet Σ. A function $f : \mathbb{N} \to \mathbb{N}$ is called *negligible* in n if for every positive polynomial $p(\cdot)$, there exists $n_0 \in \mathbb{N}$ such that for every integer $n > n_0$, $f(n) < 1/p(n)$. We write $\mathsf{negl}(\cdot)$ as a negligible function. The uniform distribution over $\{0, 1\}^n$ is denoted by U_n.

2.2   Error-Correcting Codes

The Hamming distance between two vectors $x, y \in \Sigma^n$ is defined to be $\Delta(x, y) = |\{i \in [n] : x_i \neq y_i\}|$, where $x = (x_1, \ldots, x_n)$ and $y = (y_1, \ldots, y_n)$. The Hamming weight of $x \in \Sigma^n$ is $\mathsf{wt}(x) = |\{i \in [n] : x_i \neq 0\}|$. For a finite set Σ and $R \in (0, 1]$, a *code* over an alphabet Σ with an *information rate* R is a mapping $C : \Sigma^k \to \Sigma^n$, where $k/n = R$. We refer to k and n as the *message length* and the *code length*, respectively. An encoded message $C(x)$ is called a *codeword*. We also refer to C as the set $\{C(x) : x \in \Sigma^k\}$ of the codewords.

A code C over Σ is called (δ, L)-*list decodable* if for any $y \in \Sigma^n$, there is at most $\ell \leq L$ codewords $c_1, \ldots, c_\ell \in C$ such that $\Delta(y, c_i) \leq \delta n$ for all $i \in [\ell]$.

3   Formal Model

We define a coding scheme that is parameterized by a security parameter n, which is equal to the code length.

Definition 1 (Secret-Key Coding Scheme). *A secret-key coding scheme Π consists of three polynomial-time algorithms* Setup, Enc, Dec, *a finite alphabet Σ, and an information rate R. For every sufficiently large $k \in \mathbb{N}$, let $n = \lfloor k/R \rfloor$. On input 1^n,* Setup *outputs the secret key sk. On input 1^n, sk, and a message $m \in \Sigma^k$,* Enc *outputs a codeword $c \in \Sigma^n$. On input 1^n, pk, and a string $y \in \Sigma^n$,* Dec *outputs a message $m \in \Sigma^k$ or $\perp$. The input of the parameter 1^n to* Enc *and* Dec *may be omitted for simplicity. It is required that for every k and key sk generated by* Setup(1^n), *it holds that* $\Pr[\mathsf{Dec}_{sk}(\mathsf{Enc}_{sk}(m)) = m] = 1$ *for any $m \in \{0, 1\}^k$.*

An adversarial channel W consists of two algorithms W_1 and W_2. To define the error correctability, we define the following game for a coding scheme over Σ of rate R. First, the setup algorithm generates the secret key. Then, W_1 chooses a challenge message $m^* \in \Sigma^k$. After that, on input the codeword c^* of the chosen message, W_2 outputs $y \in \Sigma^n$, where $n = \lfloor k/R \rfloor$. A channel is called *p-error* if W_2, on input c^*, always outputs y satisfying $\Delta(c^*, y) \leq \lceil pn \rceil$. We say that W is *probabilistic polynomial-time (PPT)* if both W_1 and W_2 run in time polynomial in n.

We define the security against chosen-codeword attack (CCA security). In this security, the encoding oracle $\mathsf{Enc}_{sk}(\cdot)$ and the decoding oracle $\mathsf{Dec}_{sk}(\cdot)$ are available to an adversarial channel. Since the unique decoding is not possible if the channel can access to the encoding oracle and the error rate $p > 1/4$, we say that a coding scheme is CCA secure if the scheme can output a polynomial-size list that contains the challenge message.

Definition 2 (CCA Security). *Let $\Pi = (\mathsf{Setup}, \mathsf{Enc}, \mathsf{Dec}, \Sigma, R)$ be a secret-key coding scheme of rate R, and $W = (W_1, W_2)$ an adversarial channel. For $k \in \mathbb{N}$, we define the advantages of W as*

$$\mathsf{Adv}_{W,\Pi}^{CCA}(k)$$
$$= \Pr \left[m^* \notin L : \begin{array}{l} sk \leftarrow \mathsf{Setup}(1^n), (m^*, st) \leftarrow W_1^{\mathsf{Enc}_{sk}(\cdot), \mathsf{Dec}_{sk}(\cdot)}(1^n), \\ c^* \leftarrow \mathsf{Enc}_{sk}(m^*), y^* \leftarrow W_2^{\mathsf{Enc}_{sk}(\cdot), \mathsf{Dec}_{sk}(\cdot)}(st, c^*), \\ L \leftarrow \mathsf{Dec}_{sk}(y^*) \end{array} \right],$$

where $n = \lfloor k/R \rfloor$. We say Π is (p, T, ε)-CCA secure if $\mathsf{Adv}_{W,\Pi}^{CCA}(k) \leq \varepsilon(n)$ for every p-error probabilistic $T(n)$-time channel W.

4   Our Construction

4.1   Overview

Our construction is based on the framework of Guruswami and Smith [6].

A message m is encoded as $\pi^{-1}(C(m)) \oplus \mu$, where C is a random-error correcting code, π is a random bit permutation, and μ is a random mask. This part is called a *payload* codeword, and is divided into $\ell - \kappa$ blocks $C_1, \ldots, C_{\ell-\kappa}$. The seeds s_π and s_μ for π and μ should be shared between the sender and the receiver. We will not include s_π and s_μ in the secret key. Instead, we will send them privately by jamming them into the payload codeword. The control information s is encoded by a Reed-Solomon code, so that it will be recovered by a (generalized) list decoding. Let $(f(\alpha_1), \ldots, f(\alpha_\kappa))$ be the encoded information, where each α_i is an element of a finite field, and f is the polynomial corresponding to the control information s. Then, each pair of element $(\alpha_i, f(\alpha_i))$ is encoded into a block D_i by a *pseudorandom code (PRC)*. The resulting blocks $D_1, \ldots, D_\kappa$ are randomly mixed into the payload blocks $(C_1, \ldots, C_{\ell-\kappa})$. The information V of the positions of the control-information blocks is also included into the control information s. By the property of PRC, each block C_i is pseudorandom. Since the payload codeword is masked by a random string μ, the resulting codeword is also pseudorandom.

In decoding, first, the list decoding of the pseudorandom code is applied to each block. Then, a list of pairs $(\alpha_j, \beta_{jh})_h$ is recovered for each j. By applying the (generalized) list decoding of the Reed-Solomon code to the list $\{(\alpha_j, \beta_{jh})_h\}_j$, we can recover a list of control information. For each candidate control information s, by recovering π, μ, V from s, the payload part is decoded with the decoder of the random-error correcting code.

As described in Sect. 1.1, we use pseudorandom functions (PRF) to make the encoding deterministic. The first PRF is used for generating the control information from a message m. The second PRF is for sampling random coins for the pseudorandom code. Also, as explained in Sect. 1.1, we add a MAC tag to the message m. The secret key consists of the two keys of PRFs and the secret keys of MAC and PRC.

4.2   Ingredients

We use the following tools in our construction:

- A random p-error correcting code REC : $\{0,1\}^{R'n} \to \{0,1\}^n$ of rate $R' = 1 - H(p) - \varepsilon'$ for any positive constant ε'. It is required that for every message $m \in \{0,1\}^{R'n}$ and error vector $e \in \{0,1\}^n$ of Hamming weight at most $\lceil pn \rceil$, the decoder of REC, on input $\mathsf{REC}(m) \oplus \pi(e)$, outputs m with probability at least $1 - \mathsf{negl}(n)$, where π is a random bit permutation. Any capacity-achieving code in binary symmetric channels with cross-over probability p satisfies the property.
- A Reed-Solomon code RS : $\mathbb{F}^{k+1} \to \mathbb{F}^n$ of rate $R_1 = O(\varepsilon)$ that enables a generalized list decoding. For n distinct elements $\{\alpha_1, \ldots, \alpha_n\}$ from a finite field $\mathbb{F}$, the codeword of $m = (m_0, \ldots, m_k) \in \mathbb{F}^{k+1}$ is $\mathsf{RS}(m) = (f(\alpha_1), \ldots, f(\alpha_n))$, where $f(X) = m_0 + m_1 X + \cdots + m_k X^k$. The list decoding property guarantees that, given n distinct pairs $(\alpha_i, \beta_i) \in \mathbb{F}^2$ for $i \in [n]$, one can find a list P of all polynomials f of degree at most k that satisfy $f(\alpha_i) = \beta_i$ for at least t values of $i \in [n]$. Sudan's algorithm [12] is sufficient for our purpose. It runs in time polynomial in n and $\log |\mathbb{F}|$, and works as long as the agreement parameter $t > \sqrt{2kn}$. The size of the list P is at most $\sqrt{2n/k}$.
- A pseudorandom code family PRC = $\{\mathsf{PRC}_s : \{0,1\}^{R_2 b} \times \{0,1\}^b \to \{0,1\}^b\}$ of rate R_2 indexed by a key $s \in \{0,1\}^b$ with the following properties: (1) For any constant $\varepsilon < 1/2$, PRC_s is $(1/2 - \varepsilon, L)$-list decodable with high probability, where L and R_2 only depend on ε, independent of b, and the probability is taken over $s \in \{0,1\}^b$; (2) For any $m \in \{0,1\}^{R_2 b}$, $\mathsf{PRC}_s(m, U_b)$ is pseudorandom. Specifically, it is required that for any n^c-time adversary and a sequence of $q = n^d$ messages $(m_1, \ldots, m_q) \in (\{0,1\}^{R_2 b})^q$, it is difficult to distinguish $(\mathsf{PRC}(m_1, r_1), \ldots, \mathsf{PRC}(m_\ell, r_q))$ from U_{qb} with probability more than $1/n^c$, where $c, d > 0$ are constants, and each r_i is chosen uniformly at random from $\{0,1\}^b$.

A probabilistic construction with parameters $R_2 \geq \varepsilon^{O(1)}$ and $L \leq (1/\varepsilon)^{O(1)}$ is presented in [6]. Their construction can be seen as an explicit construction in the secret-key setting, where a shared key s is used for choosing a pseudorandom generator for n^c-time adversaries. By setting $b = O(\log n)$, the list-decoding algorithm can be performed in time polynomial in n. We use this explicit construction in our scheme.

- A pseudorandom generator (PRG) $G : \{0,1\}^n \rightarrow \{0,1\}^{p(n)}$, where $p(\cdot)$ is any polynomial. It is required that for any PPT algorithm, it is difficult to distinguish $G(U_n)$ from the uniform distribution $U_{p(n)}$. Such G exists assuming one-way functions exist [7].
- A pseudorandom function (PRF) family $\mathcal{F} = \{F^n\}_{n \in \mathbb{N}}$, where $F^n = \{F_s : \{0,1\}^n \rightarrow \{0,1\}^n\}_{s \in \{0,1\}^n}$ is a collection of functions indexed by a key $s \in \{0,1\}^n$. For any PPT algorithm, it is difficult to distinguish whether it has oracle access to F_s or a random function. Such $\mathcal{F}$ can be constructed assuming the existence of one-way functions [4,7].
- A message authentication code (MAC) (Tag, Vrfy), where the key is chosen uniformly at random from $\{0,1\}^n$. It guarantees that for any PPT adversary, given access to Tag and Vrfy oracles, it is difficult to forge a pair (m,t) of a message and a tag that passes the verification of Vrfy. We use a code with short tag. Namely, on input a key $s \in \{0,1\}^n$ and a message $m \in \{0,1\}^n$, Tag outputs a tag $t \in \{0,1\}^{n^\gamma}$ for some constant $\gamma \in (0,1)$. Such a code exists assuming the existence of one-way functions [3,4,7].
- A generator P for permutations $\pi : [n] \rightarrow [n]$ of the set $[n]$ that uses $O(n \log n)$ bits to specify a permutation. We use a straightforward construction in which a permutation is chosen from the set of the possible $n!$ permutations of $[n]$. For a vector $x = (x_1, \ldots, x_n) \in \{0,1\}^n$, we write $\pi(x) = (y_1, \ldots, y_n)$, where $y_{\pi(i)} = x_i$ for $i \in [n]$.

4.3   The Construction

For any positive real $p < 1/2$ and ε, we construct a code of rate $R = 1 - H(p) - \varepsilon$ that is p-CCA secure. We assume that $2\varepsilon < 1/2 - p$. For a message length $k \in \mathbb{N}$, the code length is $n = \lfloor k/R \rfloor$. For any message $m \in \{0,1\}^k$, the encoded codeword $c \in \{0,1\}^n$ consists of ℓ blocks $(B_1, \ldots, B_\ell)$, where each block B_i is of length $b = c \log n$ for some constant $c > 0$, and thus $\ell = n/(c \log n)$. We set the following parameters: $\lambda = n^\gamma$ for a constant $\gamma \in (0,1)$, $n' = \lfloor (k+\lambda)/R' \rfloor = (\ell - \kappa)b$, $\kappa = \lceil 6\lambda/(R_1 R_2 b) \rceil$, where R' is the rate of REC, $R_1 = O(\varepsilon^2/L^2)$ is the rate of RS over $\mathbb{F}$ with $|\mathbb{F}| = 2^{R_2 b/2}$, and $R_2 = \varepsilon^{O(1)}$ is the rate of PRC.

Setup Algorithm. On input a parameter 1^n, the setup algorithm chooses four random keys $s_1, s_2, s_3, s_4 \in \{0,1\}^n$ for two PRF families $\mathcal{F}_1$ and $\mathcal{F}_2$, a MAC (Tag, Vrfy), and a PRC family PRC, respectively. The first PRF $\mathcal{F}_1$ consists of $\{F_s^1 : \{0,1\}^k \rightarrow \{0,1\}^{3\lambda}\}_{s \in \{0,1\}^n}$. The second PRF $\mathcal{F}_2$ consists of $\{F_s^2 : \{0,1\}^k \times [\ell] \rightarrow \{0,1\}^b\}_{s \in \{0,1\}^n}$. The tagging algorithm Tag, on input a secret key s_3 and a message $m \in \{0,1\}^k$, outputs a tag of length λ. The secret key SK is (s_1, s_2, s_3, s_4).

Encoding Algorithm. The encoding consists of the payload encoding and the control-information encoding. On input a message $m \in \{0,1\}^k$, the control information $s = (s_\pi, s_\mu, s_V) \in \{0,1\}^{3\lambda}$ is generated as $F_{s_1}^1(m)$, where $|s_\pi| = |s_\mu| = |s_V| = \lambda$.

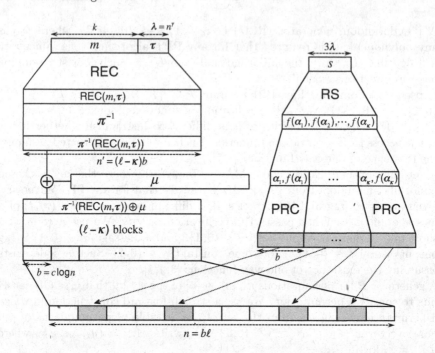

Fig. 1. Construction of the code

The payload codeword is generated as follows: first, the tag $\tau = \mathsf{Tag}_{s_3}(m)$ is generated, and a PRG $G_\pi : \{0,1\}^\lambda \rightarrow \{0,1\}^{O(n \log n)}$ is used to produce $r = G_\pi(s_\pi)$. We use r and P (the generator of permutation of the set $[n']$) to generate a permutation $\pi = P(r)$. A PRG $G_\mu : \{0,1\}^\lambda \rightarrow \{0,1\}^{n'}$ is used to generate $\mu = G_\mu(s_\mu)$. Finally, we take π and $\mathsf{REC} : \{0,1\}^{k+\lambda} \rightarrow \{0,1\}^{n'}$ to produce the payload codeword $c_p = \pi^{-1}(\mathsf{REC}(m,\tau)) \oplus \mu$.

In the control-information encoding, first, s is encoded to a codeword $(f(\alpha_1), \ldots, f(\alpha_\kappa))$ by Reed-Solomon code RS of rate R_1 over a finite field $\mathbb{F}$. A PRG $G_V : \{0,1\}^\lambda \rightarrow [\ell]^\kappa$ is used to generate $r' = G_V(s_V)$. We use r' to produce a set $V = \{v_1, \ldots, v_\kappa\}$ of distinct κ random samples in $[\ell]$. Let $\mathsf{PRC} : \mathbb{F}^2 \times \{0,1\}^b \rightarrow \{0,1\}^b$ be a pseudorandom code of rate R_2 that is $(p + \varepsilon, L)$-list decodable, where $p + \varepsilon < 1/2 - \varepsilon$, $R_2 = \varepsilon^{O(1)}$, and $L = (1/\varepsilon)^{O(1)}$. For $i \in [\kappa]$, each pair of elements $(\alpha_i, f(\alpha_i))$ is encoded to the v_i-th block $B_{v_i} = \mathsf{PRC}((\alpha_i, f(\alpha_i)), F_{s_2}^2(m, i))$, where the output of PRF is used for random coins. The control-information codeword is $(B_{v_1}, B_{v_2}, \ldots, B_{v_\kappa})$.

The payload codeword c_p is divided into $\ell - \kappa$ blocks $(B_{i_1}, B_{i_2}, \ldots, B_{i_{\ell-\kappa}})$, where i_j is the j-th smallest element in $[\ell] \setminus V$, and each block $B_i \in \{0,1\}^b$ and $n' = (\ell - \kappa)b$. The final codeword is $(B_1, B_2, \ldots, B_\ell) \in (\{0,1\}^b)^\ell = \{0,1\}^n$.

The construction is summarized in Fig. 1.

Decoding Algorithm. On input $y \in \{0,1\}^n$, divide y into ℓ blocks $(Y_1, Y_2, \ldots, Y_\ell) \in (\{0,1\}^b)^\ell$.

For $i \in [\ell]$, decode block Y_i by the list-decoding algorithm of PRC. By combining the output lists for all $i \in [\ell]$, a list L_1 of pairs $\{(\alpha_j, \beta_{jh})_h\}_j$ for $j \in [\kappa]$ is obtained. The size of L_1 is at most ℓL. Then, apply the list-decoding algorithm of RS to L_1 with an agreement parameter $t = \varepsilon\kappa/2$ to generate a list L_2 of control information $\tilde{s} = (\tilde{s}_\pi, \tilde{s}_\mu, \tilde{s}_V)$. The size of L_2 is at most $\sqrt{2/R_1} = O(L/\varepsilon)$.

Let L_3 be the empty list. For each $\tilde{s} = (\tilde{s}_\pi, \tilde{s}_\mu, \tilde{s}_V) \in L_2$, do the following. Recover $\tilde{\pi} = P(G_\pi(\tilde{s}_\pi))$, $\tilde{\mu} = G(\tilde{s}_\mu)$, and $\tilde{V} = \{v_1, \ldots, v_\kappa\}$, where $G_V(\tilde{s}_V)$ is used to produce $\tilde{V}$. Let $\tilde{y}$ be the concatenation of blocks $(Y_{i_1}, Y_{i_2}, \ldots, Y_{i_{\ell-\kappa}}) \in \{0,1\}^{n'}$, where i_j is the j-th smallest element in $[\ell] \setminus \tilde{V}$. Decode $\tilde{z} = \pi(\tilde{y} \oplus \tilde{\mu})$ with the decoding algorithm of REC. Let $(\tilde{m}, \tilde{\tau})$ be the output. If $\mathsf{Vrfy}(\tilde{m}, \tilde{\tau})$ outputs false, go back and choose next $\tilde{s}$ from L_2. Otherwise, recover $\tilde{s}'$ as $F_{s_1}(\tilde{m})$. If $\tilde{s}' \neq \tilde{s}$, go back and choose next $\tilde{s}$ from L_2. Else, recover the encoded message $\tilde{c}$ for a message $\tilde{m}$ and a control information $\tilde{s}$ by following the encoding algorithm. Check if the Hamming distance between $\tilde{c}$ and y is at most $\lceil pn \rceil$. If so, add $\tilde{m}$ to L_3; and otherwise do nothing. Then, go back and choose next $\tilde{s}$ from L_2.

After choosing all elements in L_2, output L_3 if $L_3 \neq \emptyset$, and $\perp$ otherwise.

The Rate of the Code. For any positive constant $p < 1/2$ and ε, we choose a random p-error correcting code of rate $R' = 1 - H(p) - \varepsilon'$ such that $0 < \varepsilon' < \varepsilon$. It holds that $R' = (k + \lambda)/n'$. The length of the control-information blocks is $\kappa b \leq c_0 b$ for sufficiently large constant c_0. Thus, the rate of the code is

$$R = \frac{k}{n' + \kappa b} \geq \frac{R'n' - \lambda}{n' + c_0 b} = R' - \frac{R'c_0 b/\lambda + 1}{(n' + c_0 b)/\lambda}.$$

Note that $b = c \log n$ and $\lambda = n^\gamma$ for $\gamma \in (0,1)$. Since $R'c_0 b/\lambda = o(1)$ and $(n' + c_0 b)/\lambda = \Omega(n^{1-\gamma})$, we have that $R = 1 - H(p) - \varepsilon' - O(n^{-(1-\gamma)}) \geq 1 - H(p) - \varepsilon$ for sufficiently large n.

5   Security Proof

We prove the following theorem.

Theorem 1. *Assume that there exist one-way functions. For any positive constants $p < 1/2, \varepsilon, c$, the coding scheme of rate $R \geq 1 - H(p) - \varepsilon$ described in Sect. 4.3 is (p, n^c, n^{-c})-CCA secure.*

Proof. We prove the security with a sequence of hybrid games where the first game corresponds to the original CCA security game.

- Game$_0$: The original CCA security game between the challenger and the channel.
  1. The secret key $SK = (s_1, s_2, s_3, s_4) \in \{0,1\}^{4n}$ is chosen uniformly at random.
  2. The channel makes queries for $m \in \{0,1\}^k$ to the encoding oracle and for $y \in \{0,1\}^n$ to the decoding oracle, and outputs $m^* \in \{0,1\}^k$. The responses of the oracles are made according to the encoding and the decoding algorithms.

3. Let $s = (s_\pi, s_\mu, s_V) = F_{s_1}^1(m^*)$. The payload codeword is generated as $\pi^{-1}(\mathsf{REC}(m, \tau)) \oplus \mu$, where $\pi = P(G_\pi(s_\pi))$, $\tau = \mathsf{Tag}_{s_3}(m^*)$, $\mu = G_\mu(s_\mu)$. Then, s is encoded as $(f(\alpha_1), \ldots, f(\alpha_\kappa))$ by RS. Let $V^* = \{v_1, \ldots, v_\kappa\}$ be the set generated from the seed $r' = G_V(s_V)$. The v_i-th block B_{v_i} is generated as $\mathsf{PRC}_{s_4}((\alpha_i, f(\alpha_i)), F_{s_2}^2(m, i))$. The payload codeword is divided into $\ell - \kappa$ blocks $(B_{i_1}, \ldots, B_{i_{\ell-\kappa}})$, where i_j is the j-th smallest element in $[\ell] \setminus V^*$. The challenge codeword $c^* = (B_1, B_2, \ldots, B_\ell)$ is given to the channel.

4. The channel makes queries to the encoding and the decoding oracles, and outputs $y^* \in \{0, 1\}^n$ such that $\Delta(y, c^*) \leq \lceil pn \rceil$.

5. Let L be the output of the decoding algorithm on input y^*. If $m^* \notin L$, the channel wins. Otherwise, the channel loses.

- Game_1: The same as Game_0 except that all the outputs of PRFs are replaced with uniformly random strings. Specifically, s is chosen uniformly at random, and the uniformly random bits are used as random coins for PRC.

- Game_2: The same as Game_1 except that all the outputs of PRGs are replaced with uniformly random strings. Specifically, the input to the permutation generator P and $(v_1, \ldots, v_\kappa)$ are chosen uniformly at random.

- Game_3: The same as Game_2 except that for every query m to the encoding oracle and the challenge message m^*, the corresponding codeword is generated by choosing a uniformly random string from $\{0, 1\}^n$.

- Game_4: The same as Game_3 except that for every query m to the encoding oracle, prepare an entry (m, c) in a list L_Q, where c is the codeword of m. The pair of the challenge message and codeword (m^*, c^*) is also included in L_Q. For every query m to the encoding oracle, responds with c such that $(m, c) \in L_Q$; for every query y to the decoding oracle, respond with a list $\{m \in \{0, 1\}^k : (m, c) \in L_Q \text{ and } \Delta(y, c) \leq \lceil pn \rceil\}$.

- Game_5: The same as Game_4 except that the channel is not allowed to query the oracles at Steps 2 and 4.

The probability that a channel wins is called an advantage of the channel.

First, it can be shown that the advantage of any PPT channel in Game_1 is negligibly close to that in Game_0. This is because the keys s_1 and s_2 for PRFs are not disclosed to the channel, and thus the security of PRF guarantees it.

It follows from the security of PRG that the advantage of any PPT channel in Game_2 is negligibly close to that in Game_1.

In Game_3, all the codewords are chosen uniformly at random. The change is not detected by n^c-time channels with advantage more than n^{-c} for any $c > 0$ because for each codeword, the payload part is masked by a random string μ, and the control-information part is pseudorandom due to the property of PRC. Thus, the advantage of any PPT channel in Game_3 is close to that in Game_2 within n^{-c}.

Lemma 1. *Let $c > 0$ be any constant. For any n^c-time channel, the advantage in Game_4 is close to that in Game_3 within n^{-c}.*

Proof. It is necessary to prove that the response to the oracle queries can be replaced with the responses using the list L_Q.

Assume that there exists an n^c-time channel W for which the advantage in Game_4 is greater than that in Game_3 by n^{-c}. By fixing the random coins of W, there is a deterministic channel W_0 that achieves the same advantages as W.

Since W_0 is deterministic, we can prepare a list L_Q for answering the oracle queries by W_0. The list L_Q is constructed as follows. Let m_i be the i-th query to the encoding oracle, and y_i the i-th query to the decoding one. For each m_i, choose $c_i \in \{0,1\}^n$ uniformly at random, and add (m_i, c_i) to L_Q. The pair (m^*, c^*) of the challenge message and ciphertext is also added to L_Q. Then, for each y_i, we sample the number $\ell_i \in \mathbb{N}$, which represents the number of valid codewords within a distance $\lceil pn \rceil$ from y_i. The number ℓ_i is chosen according to the distribution D such that $\Pr[D = j] = p_j$ for $j \in [2^{Rn}]$, where p_j is the probability that a fixed Hamming ball of radius pn contains j codewords when all codewords are chosen uniformly at random. For chosen ℓ_i, if the number of codewords c_j in L_Q satisfying $\Delta(y_i, c_j) \leq \lceil pn \rceil$ is less than ℓ_i, add pairs (m_j, c_j) of random message and codeword to L_Q so that $\ell_i = |\{(m_j, c_j) \in L_Q | \Delta(y_i, c_j) \leq \lceil pn \rceil\}|$. Since each ℓ_j is bounded above by a polynomial in n, the size of L_Q is also bounded by a polynomial in n.

Note that, since it is necessary to generate MAC tags to generate valid codewords, W_0 cannot generate valid codewords by himself. Since each message has the unique codeword, W_0 cannot generate a valid codeword c' of a message m from the codeword $c(\neq c')$ of m obtained by querying to the encoding oracle. Thus, all valid codewords appeared in the game are included in the list L_Q.

Since every response to the encoding query looks random for W_0, the encoding oracle can be simulated by using L_Q. For each decoding query y_i, the response by using L_Q is equivalent to that of the decoding oracle of random codes. Therefore, both the encoding and the decoding oracles can be simulated successfully.

Next, we show that the channel cannot generate query y for which there is some $(m, c) \in L_Q$ satisfying $\Delta(y, c) \leq \lceil pn \rceil$, but the decoding algorithm outputs a list in which m is not included. It means that, on input y, the decoder fails to recover m. We show that the decoding algorithm can recover m for such y with high probability.

For $(m, c) \in L_Q$, let $e = y \oplus c$. For an error vector $e \in \{0,1\}^n$ and a set $V \subseteq [n]$, which specifies the positions of the control blocks, we say that V is *good* for e if there are at least $\varepsilon\kappa/2$ control blocks in which the fraction of errors is at most $p + \varepsilon$.

Let π and V be the permutation and the set that are generated in encoding m to c. Then, V is independent of e. This is because the payload part of c is pseudorandom by the random mask μ, and the control-information part of c is also pseudorandom by the property of PRC. Thus, the information on V is not revealed from c, and hence V is independent of e. Since V is chosen uniformly at random independently from e, V is good for e except with negligible probability. The analysis can be done in a similar way to the proof of [6, Lemma 7.11]. When V is good for e, due to the list-decoding property of PRC, the decoding algorithm can generate a list L_1 that contains correct symbols $f(\alpha_i)$ for at least $\varepsilon\kappa/2$ control blocks. Since the PRC decoding outputs a list at most L, the size of L_1 is at most ℓL. On input L_1, the list decoding of RS outputs a list L_2 of size $O(L/\varepsilon)$ that contains the correct control information $s = (s_\pi, s_\mu, s_V)$, which is equal to the value of PRF $F_{s_1}^1$ on input m. Given the correct value s, the correct values of π, μ, V can be recovered. By the same reason as for V, π is chosen uniformly at random independently from e. Thus, it follows from the p-error correctability of REC that the decoder of REC outputs the correct m with probability at least $1 - \mathsf{negl}(n)$.

We have proved that for any query y to the decoding oracle, (1) if there is no $(m, c) \in L_Q$ satisfying $\Delta(y, c) \leq \lceil pn \rceil$, the decoder output $\perp$; (2) if there is $(m, c) \in L_Q$ satisfying $\Delta(y, c) \leq \lceil pn \rceil$, the decoder outputs a list containing m. Therefore, the response of the decoding oracle in Game_2 can be replaced with the response using L_Q as in Game_3. The statement follows.   □

Next, we show that for any PPT channel W that has the advantage ε in Game_4, there is a PPT channel W' that has the same advantage in Game_5. It is sufficient to show that W' can simulate the encoding and decoding oracles for W in Game_4. As described in the proof of Lemma 1, by preparing the list L_Q, W' can simulate the encoding and the decoding oracles for W in Game_4.

Finally, we argue that the advantage of any n^c-time channel W in Game_5 is at most n^{-c}. Note that the only valid codeword W obtains in Game_5 is the challenge codeword c^* of the challenge message m^*. As discussed in the proof of Lemma 1, it is difficult for W to generate y for which $\Delta(y, c^*) \leq \lceil pn \rceil$ and the decoder outputs $\perp$ or a list in which m^* is not included. Therefore, the advantage of any n^c-time channel in Game_5 is at most n^{-c}.

We have proved that, for any n^c-time channel, the advantages in Game_i are close each other within n^{-c} for $i \in \{0, 1, 2, 3, 4, 5\}$, and the advantage in Game_5 is at most n^{-c}. By taking a constant c sufficiently large enough, we can conclude that, for any n^c-time channel, the advantage in Game_0 is at most n^{-c}, which implies that the coding scheme is (p, n^c, n^{-c})-CCA secure.   □

Acknowledgment. This research was supported in part by JSPS/MEXT Grant-in-Aid for Scientific Research Numbers 15H00851 and 16H01705.

References

1. Arikan, E.: Channel polarization: a method for constructing capacity-achieving codes for symmetric binary-input memoryless channels. IEEE Trans. Inf. Theory **55**(7), 3051–3073 (2009)
2. Forney, G.D.: Concatenated Codes. MIT Press, Cambridge (1966). MIT research monograph, no. 37
3. Goldreich, O., Goldwasser, S., Micali, S.: On the cryptographic applications of random functions (extended abstract). In: Blakley, G.R., Chaum, D. (eds.) CRYPTO 1984. LNCS, vol. 196, pp. 276–288. Springer, Heidelberg (1985). doi:10.1007/3-540-39568-7_22

4. Goldreich, O., Goldwasser, S., Micali, S.: How to construct random functions. J. ACM **33**(4), 792–807 (1986)
5. Guruswami, V., Smith, A.: Codes for computationally simple channels: explicit constructions with optimal rate. In: FOCS, pp. 723–732. IEEE Computer Society (2010)
6. Guruswami, V., Smith, A.: Optimal-rate code constructions for computationally simple channels. CoRR abs/1004.4017 (2013). This is an extended version of [5]
7. Håstad, J., Impagliazzo, R., Levin, L.A., Luby, M.: A pseudorandom generator from any one-way function. SIAM J. Comput. **28**(4), 1364–1396 (1999)
8. Langberg, M.: Private codes or succinct random codes that are (almost) perfect. In: Proceedings 45th Symposium on Foundations of Computer Science (FOCS 2004), Rome, Italy, 17–19 October 2004, pp. 325–334. IEEE Computer Society (2004)
9. Lipton, R.J.: A new approach to information theory. In: Enjalbert, P., Mayr, E.W., Wagner, K.W. (eds.) STACS 1994. LNCS, vol. 775, pp. 699–708. Springer, Heidelberg (1994). doi:10.1007/3-540-57785-8_183
10. Micali, S., Peikert, C., Sudan, M., Wilson, D.A.: Optimal error correction against computationally bounded noise. In: Kushilevitz, E., Malkin, T. (eds.) TCC 2016. LNCS, vol. 9563, pp. 1–16. Springer, Heidelberg (2005). doi:10.1007/978-3-540-30576-7_1
11. Micali, S., Peikert, C., Sudan, M., Wilson, D.A.: Optimal error correction for computationally bounded noise. IEEE Trans. Inf. Theory **56**(11), 5673–5680 (2010)
12. Sudan, M.: Decoding of reed solomon codes beyond the error-correction bound. J. Complex. **13**(1), 180–193 (1997)

Efficient Generic Zero-Knowledge Proofs from Commitments (Extended Abstract)

Samuel Ranellucci[1(✉)], Alain Tapp[2], and Rasmus Zakarias[1]

[1] Department of Computer Science, Aarhus University, Aarhus, Denmark
{samuel,rwl}@cs.au.dk
[2] DIRO, Université de Montréal, Montreal, Canada
tappa@iro.umontreal.ca

Abstract. Even though zero-knowledge has existed for more than 30 years, few generic and efficient constructions for zero-knowledge exist. In this paper, we present a new kind of commitment scheme on which we can build a novel and efficient zero-knowledge protocol for circuit satisfiability. Our commitment scheme can be constructed in a black-box manner from any commitment scheme. We can prove knowledge of the AES-key which map a particular plaintext to a particular ciphertext in less than 300 milliseconds with a soundness-error of 2^{-40}. The communication complexity of our protocol is less then $5 \cdot k \cdot |C|$ where k is the statistical security parameter and $|C|$ is the circuit size.

1 Introduction

Zero-knowledge was introduced in 1985 by Goldwasser et al. in their seminal paper [16] introducing interactive proof system and the concept of knowledge complexity.

Informally, a zero-knowledge proof is an interactive protocol that allows a prover to persuade a verifier of the validity of some NP statement where the prover is given as input a witness that the statement is true. Essentially, the verifier should learn nothing more than the fact that the prover knows a witness that satisfies the statement.

One motivating example is that of graph isomorphism: the NP statement here is that two graphs are isomorphic. The witness is an isomorphism held by the prover mapping one graph into the other. One obvious way for the prover to convince the verifier would be to send the isomorphism. However, this reveals much more information than the one bit of information to be conveyed, namely

S. Ranellucci and R. Zakarias—The authors acknowledge support from the Danish National Research Foundation and The National Science Foundation of China (under the grant 61061130540) for the Sino-Danish Center for the Theory of Interactive Computation, within part of this work was performed; and from the CFEM research center, supported by the Danish Strategic Research Council.

S. Ranellucci and R. Zakarias—Supported by the European Research Council Stating Grant 279447.

A.C.A. Nascimento and P. Barreto (Eds.): ICITS 2016, LNCS 10015, pp. 190–212, 2016.
DOI: 10.1007/978-3-319-49175-2_10

whether the graphs are isomorphic or not. Zero-knowledge proofs are interactive proof systems that allows a prover to convince a verifier of the validity of a statement without providing him any additional information. In particular, the verifier cannot use his view in a zero-knowledge proof for a given statement, to prove the validity of the same statement to another party.

Following this groundbreaking work, [1] showed that for any relation that can be proven by an interactive proof system, it can also be proven in zero-knowledge. Thus, the potential for applications of zero-knowledge is expansive. A large body of work has shown that specialized efficient constructions for specific NP relations are possible. However, even though zero-knowledge has existed for more than 30 years, there are still very few generic constructions for zero-knowledge. Moreover, the generic constructions that do exist, use the relatively impractical Karp reductions [19] to NP-complete languages [15].

Generic constructions for zero-knowledge are starting to emerge. The recent line of work starting with [18] focus on the novel idea of using garbled circuits for zero-knowledge proofs of generic statements. This line of work was continued by Frederiksen et al. in [12] where they build specialized garbling schemes tailored for zero-knowledge proofs. The garbling approach communicates at least one symmetric encryption per And-gate in the circuit. Similarly, for security parameter κ and circuit size n our protocol exhibits worst-case communicated complexity $O(n\kappa)$. In contrast to the garbling approach, our protocol only requires a small constant of bits per and-triple (roughly five). On the other hand, we have [17] with worst-case complexity $O(n)$ when the prover uses the scalable multiparty computation technique from [11]. However, this construction is quite involved and even nine years after its publication no implementation is provided yet[1]. Naturally for large enough circuits [17] should be faster. We conjecture that our scheme, given its smaller constants, outperforms their (in terms of execution time) construction for practical application-sized circuits like AES ($\sim 40K$ gates).

In parallel with our work, the work of [13] also construct an efficient zero-knowledge protocol based on commitment schemes. In their work, they first study the concrete efficiency of [17]. They then construct a more efficient protocol by first generating a sigma protocol with constant soundness error and then run this protocol many times in parallel. Their idea to construct such a protocol by extending [17], they construct a secure computation protocol with three parties such that the view of any two parties reveal no information.

Another main selling point for our construction is that it is conceptually simple: only an understanding of the notion for commitments and xor-sharing are necessary to master it. Also, we demonstrate that our construction is practical by presenting an implementation which exhibits small running times. In particular we present an example application where the prover proofs knowledge of an AES-encryption-key encrypting a particular public plaintext to a particular public ciphertext. To sum up, our protocol is no novelty in terms of asymptotic complexity, however, we emphasize that the concrete constants are small, its

---

[1] Though the authors say an implementation is under way.

construction is conceptually simple (an advantage when selling it to non-crypto experts) and it takes only a moderate effort to implement.

1.1 Contribution

In this paper, we present a novel approach for achieving generic zero-knowledge proofs. Similar to the line of work using garbled circuits, our construction uses the idea of proving knowledge of a satisfying assignment for a circuit. However, our construction differs from the garbling approach in several ways. Our construction is very simple, using only one primitive, a commitment scheme. Our construction is similar to [21] which over a finite field $\mathbb{F}$ has complexity $O(|\mathbb{F}| \cdot n)$ for a field of size $|\mathbb{F}| > \kappa$. Their approach operates on a gate-by-gate basis. As our field is small, namely $\mathbb{F}_2$, we bundle the entire circuit together obtaining a string of size $O(n)$ and prove all gates in one go with soundness one-quarter and then we repeat 2.5κ rounded up times.

In contrast to the garbling approach, our scheme is public-coin zero-knowledge. More precisely, the challenge from the verifier is sampled uniformly at random. This means that the Fiat-Shamir heuristic could be applied to our protocol to make it non-interactive.

Our protocol for zero-knowledge is universally composable (UC). The protocol relies on a commitment that we construct that has a special property. Namely, that it possible for the committer to prove linear relationships among committed bits by using a zero-knowledge proof. Our scheme is also information-theoretic. It can be constructed in a black-box manner from any commitment scheme.

Our scheme can be efficiently instantiated in the random oracle model. However, this introduces the extra assumption. Recent work on commitments in the standard model prove to be even more efficient and add no additional assumptions, see the PKC 2015 paper in [7] (improving on [10]). By using their scheme, it makes our construction extremely efficient. This is because their scheme only relies on encoding for a linear code like Reed-Solomon, which can be done efficiently using the FFT-transform.

In a bit more detail, we take a similar approach to the one used in [3,9,20]. In these works, they also use commitments which allows proofs of linear relationships to prove statements in zero-knowledge. Their commitments, however, only commit to individual bits. To commit to a bit b, the sender selects at random s pairs of bits b_i^0, b_i^1 such that $b_i^0 \oplus b_i^1 = b$ and commits to each of these bits individually. This is known as Rudich's trick. Unfortunately, each commitment has an overhead of s commitments. By virtue of [22], the overhead of their protocol in the information-theoretic setting with correlated randomness is quadratic in the security parameter. In contrast, the overhead of our protocol in that setting is linear in the security parameter.

We employ strings in our construction, using a novel way of committing to bit-strings that enables zero-knowledge proofs of linear relations. In particular, we present efficient protocols for proving equality and inequality of bits in a string given two regular commitments to the xor-sharing of that string. From this proof, we can also show by using auxiliary bits that for a committed string m and for indices i, j, k, we have that $m_i \wedge m_j = m_k$.

From this, we build protocols for circuit satisfiability where a prover proves to a verifier that he has knowledge of a witness w that satisfies the circuit. The prover does this by committing to a truth assignment of all gates in the circuit along with some additional information. Then he proves relationships (corresponding to the gates of the circuit) between bits in the committed string. We leave out the details of the UC construction to the full version of this paper.

By the hiding property of the commitment scheme, the verifier learns nothing about the inputs to the circuit. In the end, the prover essentially opens the output bit of the circuit by proving that the output bit of the circuit committed to is one and this is essentially the only new information that the verifier learns.

For a circuit of size n with ι input gates, α and-gates and β linear gates our construction communicates $4\alpha + \beta$ bits of data with soundness one-quarter. To form a secure protocol with security $2^{-\kappa}$, we repeat our construction 2.5κ times realizing a protocol with communication complexity $O(\kappa n)$. We emphasize once again that the constants involved are small.

We first present our xor-commitment scheme. This is followed by honest-verifier zero-knowledge proofs about committed values for xor-commitments. We then proceed to describe an honest-verifier zero-knowledge protocol for circuit satisfiability. Finally, we describe a benchmark implementation with AES.

2   Definitions and Notation

2.1   Universal Composability

The UC framework was introduced by Canetti in [4] to analyse the security of cryptographic protocols and primitives under arbitrary composition. It follows the real world–ideal world paradigm. We use the simplified formulation of UC from [8], which is similar in spirit to the simplified universal composability framework [5]. See [4,8] for further details. In this work we consider security against static adversaries.

For the rest of the paper, we assume that both players have access to an ideal commitment scheme. This can be realized from a setup assumption such as a common reference string. We show how to realize the zero-knowledge functionality in the $\mathcal{F}_{\mathsf{COM}}$-hybrid model. To simplify the description of our protocol, we interpret the operation $\mathsf{com}(m)$ as the sender sending the commit command to the ideal functionality. We also do the same for the open command. In Appendix A, we include the ideal functionalities for commitment and zero-knowledge.

Definition 1. *An interactive proof system (P, V) for a language L is honest-verifier zero-knowledge, if there exists a PPT algorithm S, called the simulator, such that for any $(x, w) \in R$ where R is the witness relation of L, the view produced by the simulator on input x is indistinguishable from the view produced by the interaction of an honest prover P given (x, w) with an honest verifier v with input x.*

Formally, for every $(x, w) \in R$, for every $e \in \{0, 1\}^t$, it holds that

$$\{S(x, e)\} \overset{perf}{\equiv} \{\langle P(x, w), V(x, e)\rangle\}$$

where $S(x)$ denotes the output of S on input (x, e) and $\langle P(x, w), V(x, e)\rangle$ denotes the output transcript between P and V where P has input x, w, V has input x and V's random tape is e.

2.2 Notation

In our protocols, the verifier never provides input. We use $\Phi_p(a; b)$ to denote a protocol between a prover and a verifier with name p where a is the private input of the prover and b is the public input to the protocol. A commitment is considered public input. In these protocols, the notation Output $(a; b)$ denotes the sender having private output a and the public output as b. We use $\perp$ to denote no inputs or output. We of course use accept or reject to denote that a verifier accepts or rejects a proof. For a simulator, the notation $S_V^p(d; e)$ denotes the simulator for a protocol that is called p with verifier V where d is the public input of the protocol and e is the random tape of the verifier.

3   Commitments with Linear Proofs

In this section, we define a commitment scheme which allows a prover to prove linear relationships between different bits of the committed string. These relationships include equality and inequality. From the (in)equality proofs, we build a protocol for proving that a set of bits sum up to a particular value. The proofs are complete and honest-verifier zero-knowledge. The soundness-error of this protocol is one-half. We use the notation $\text{xom}(m)$ to say that a prover commits to a message m allowing him to conduct proofs of linear relationships between individual bits in m.

The proofs are sigma protocols: Three messages are communicated, where the verifier's challenge consists of a single bit. Proofs within a single string can be combined as sigma protocols can be combined. If a commitment takes part in two tests with distinct challenges, then the committed value is revealed. This implies that the soundness-error of these proofs cannot be reduced below one-half. We work with strings. Therefore, we define some notation. The xor-commitment scheme is defined after the notation.

Notation. For an ℓ-bit string m, we denote the i-th bit of m as m_i. When a message m is xor-shared, we denote the xor-shares of $m = m^0 \oplus m^1$ as m^0 and m^1. We sometimes combine these notations and take m_i^0 to mean the i-th bit of the share m^0 and similarly for m_i^1.

Commitment scheme supporting linear proofs. We now give the details of our commitment scheme supporting linear proofs. Our scheme relies on the ideal functionality for commitment schemes. We denote it as com(). In the following, we describe how we *commit* to messages and *open* our commitments.

$$\Phi_{\texttt{commit}}(m; \perp)$$

prover   verifier

$r \in_R \{0,1\}^l$

$m^0 = r, m^1 = m \oplus r$

$$\xleftarrow{\qquad\qquad M = (M^0, M^1) = \texttt{com}(m^0), \texttt{com}(m^1) \qquad\qquad}$$

Output $(m^0, m^1; M)$

Fig. 1. The sender wants to commit to a message m. The output of the prover are two shares m^0, m^1 of m. The public output consists of two commitments, one for each share. The commitments are respectively M^0, M^1.

To commit to a string $m \in \{0,1\}^\ell$, we first choose a string $r \in \{0,1\}^\ell$ uniformly at random and set $m^0 = r$ and $m^1 = m \oplus r$. Then we commit to both strings using the commitment functionality to form $\texttt{xom}(m) = (M^0, M^1) = (\texttt{com}(m^0), \texttt{com}(m^1))$. To open an $\texttt{xom}(m)$ entirely we open both commitments and reveal m. The commitment protocol is depicted in Fig. 1.

Partial Opening. The linear proofs require the partial opening of the xor-commitment. This means that we only open one of the commitments associated to $\texttt{xom}(m)$. We denote the action of a prover opening the value of the standard commitment $\texttt{com}(m^t)$ as $\mathsf{Reveal}(M, t)$. When we have a simulator, the notation $\mathsf{Reveal}(M, c) = m'$ means that a simulator sends the message (reveal, m') for the commitment M^c (he opens M^c to m').

Properties with $\texttt{xom}(\cdot)$. We give here observations stipulating important but straightforward facts regarding xor-shared strings. We use the observations from this section to generate proofs for linear relationships between different positions of the committed string m.

Observation 1. $\forall m \in \{0,1\}^\ell, c \in \{0,1\}$, *the following two distributions are indistinguishable*

$$\{(c, m^c) \mid m^0 \in_R \{0,1\}^\ell, m^1 = m^0 \oplus m\}$$
$$\{(c, r) \mid r \in_R \{0,1\}^\ell\}$$

Observation 2. *Let* $m = m^0 \oplus m^1$, *if* $m_i = m_j$ *then there exists* δ *such that* $\delta = m_i^0 \oplus m_j^0 = m_i^1 \oplus m_j^1$.

Observation 3. *Let* $m = m^0 \oplus m^1$, *if* $m_i \neq m_j$ *then there exists* ϵ *such that* $\epsilon = m_i^0 \oplus m_j^0 = 1 \oplus m_i^1 \oplus m_j^1$.

Observation 4. $\forall c \in \{0,1\}, m \in \{0,1\}^\ell, i, j \in \{1,\ldots,\ell\}, i \neq j, m_i = m_j$, the following two distributions are indistinguishable.

$$\{(c,\delta,m^c) \mid m^0 \in_R \{0,1\}^\ell, m^1 = m^0 \oplus m, \delta = m_i^0 \oplus m_j^0\}$$
$$\{(c,\delta,r) \mid \delta \in_R \{0,1\}, r \in_R \{\bar{r} \in \{0,1\}^\ell \mid r_i \oplus r_j = \delta\}\}$$

Observation 5. $\forall c \in \{0,1\}, m \in \{0,1\}^\ell, i, j \in \{1,\ldots,\ell\}, i \neq j, m_i \neq m_j$, the following two distributions are indistinguishable

$$\{(c,\epsilon,m^c) \mid m^0 \in_R \{0,1\}^\ell, m^1 = m^0 \oplus m, \epsilon = m_i^0 \oplus m_j^0\}$$
$$\{(c,\epsilon,r) \mid \epsilon \in_R \{0,1\}, r \in_R \{\bar{r} \in \{0,1\}^\ell \mid r_i \oplus r_j = \epsilon \oplus c\}\}$$

4 Zero-Knowledge with Soundness-Error One-Half

In our first result, we show how to do an honest-verifier zero-knowledge proof of equality between two bits in the string m from $\texttt{xom}(m)$. The basic idea is as follows: we exploit Observation 2 that states that if the bits m_i and m_j are equal, then there exists a δ such that $m_i^0 \oplus m_j^0 = m_i^1 \oplus m_j^1 = \delta$. On the other hand, if $m_i \neq m_j$, then by Observation 3, no such δ exists. The protocol is depicted in Fig. 2.

To show *completeness*, we observe that if the statement is true e.g. $m_i = m_j$ then $\delta = m_i^b \oplus m_j^b, b \in \{0,1\}$ and the verifier accepts. For *soundness* consider the first step of the protocol: the prover reveals δ. This forces a cheating prover to prepare to answer a b' such that $m_i^{b'} \oplus m_j^{b'} = \delta$. Then the verifier selects a b at random for which the prover can only reply correctly if $b = b'$. This ensures that a cheating prover gets caught with probability one-half.

4.1 Protocol for Equality

In this section we formally prove that the protocol in Fig. 2 is an honest-verifier zero-knowledge with soundness-error one-half. For a string $m \in \{0,1\}^l$, let $M = \texttt{xom}(m) = (\texttt{com}(m^0), \texttt{com}(m^1))$, we show how to prove for a given i,j that $m_i = m_j$.

Theorem 1. *The protocol in Fig. 2 is an honest-verifier zero-knowledge interactive proof system with soundness-error one-half.*

Proof. **Completeness:** To show completeness, we show that an honest verifier is convinced by an honest prover. These cases are exhaustive assuming that $m_i = m_j$. Assuming $m_i = m_j$, we consider two cases:

$m_i^0 = m_j^0$: In this case, $m_i^1 = m_j^1$. This implies that $\delta = 0 = m_i^0 \oplus m_j^0 = m_i^1 \oplus m_j^1$ and thus the check the verifier makes is true for both choices of ϵ and thus he accepts.

$m_i^0 \neq m_j^0$: In this case, $m_i^1 \neq m_j^1$. This implies that $\delta = 1 = m_i^0 \oplus m_j^0 = m_i^1 \oplus m_j^1$ and the verifier accepts.

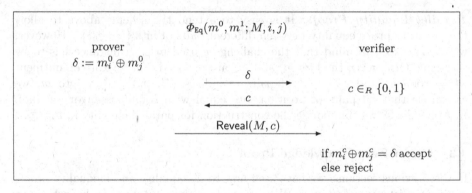

Fig. 2. Protocol for proof of equality. The prover is committed to m with shares m^0, m^1 which results in commitments $\texttt{xom}(m) = (M^0, M^1)$ and wants to prove equality between m_i and m_j for a public input i, j.

Soundness: To show that soundness holds with probability one-half, we consider a cheating prover and show that the verifier accepts with probability at most one-half. That is, let us assume that $m_i \neq m_j$ and consider a dishonest prover that tries to convince the verifier that they equal. If $m_i^0 \neq m_j^0$ then $m_i^0 \oplus m_j^0 \neq m_i^1 \oplus m_j^1$. Therefore, by Observation 3 there exists a challenge $c \in \{0,1\}$ that results in the verifier rejecting the proof. Therefore, a cheating prover is detected with probability one-half.

Honest-Verifier Zero-knowledge: To prove zero-knowledge, we give a simulator that generates the view $(\delta, c, \textsf{Reveal}(M, c) = m^c)$ which is indistinguishable from the view generated by an honest prover and verifier.

Simulator $S_V^{\textsf{Eq}}(M, i, j; c)$

1 Sample $\delta \in_R \{0,1\}$
2 Sample $r \in_R \{0,1\}^\ell$ s.t. $r_i \oplus r_j = \delta$
3 Output $(\delta, c, \textsf{Reveal}(M, c) = m^c)$

Fig. 3. Simulator for equality.

Consider the simulator in Fig. 3. We argue that the view generated by the simulator is indistinguishable from a real execution by noticing that the distribution of values revealed in the simulation is indistinguishable from the distribution of values revealed in the real protocol. This follows from Observations 1 and 4.

$\square$

4.2 Parallel Equality Proofs and Proofs of Inequality

Proofs of Inequality: The proof of inequality is very similar to the equality proof. The main difference is that there exists an ϵ such that for any $c \in \{0, 1\}$, $\epsilon = m_i^c \oplus m_j^c \oplus c$ instead of $\delta = m_i^0 \oplus m_j^0$ as before. We put the protocol and its proof in Appendix B.

Parallel Equality Proofs: It is easy to extend the scheme above to allow the prover to prove equality between different pairs of bits $\{(i_k, j_k)\}_k$. However, we need to keep in mind that the challenge c used in each instance has to be the same. Otherwise, the bits m_i and m_j are revealed. For an xor-commitment $M = \mathsf{xom}(m)$ and for a set of pairs of indices $\{(i_v, j_v)\}_{v=1,\ldots,t}$ into m, we can prove that all pairs of positions are equal with soundness-error one-half. In Appendix C, we summarize the construction for parallel equality in Fig. 9.

4.3   Linear Zero-Knowledge Proof

In the previous sections, we have seen how to do equality and inequality proofs of bits in a committed message. We can combine these two in a single protocol to convince a verifier that for a set of positions, the bits associated to the set sum up to a particular value. This covers equality and inequality as special cases.

We now describe a protocol for convincing a verifier that for a set of bit-position, the bits sum up to a particular value. As before, the prover commits to a message m producing commitment $M = (\mathsf{com}(m^0), \mathsf{com}(m^1))$ associated with shares m^0, m^1. Additionally, the public input of the protocol is two things. The first thing is a set of indices, I, and the second is the expected value b, that the bits associated to the set $m_i, i \in I$ are supposed to sum up to. More precisely, our protocol proves:

$$\left(\bigoplus_{i \in I} m_i \right) = b$$

This captures our previous protocols for (in)equality. E.g. we see that equality is covered by putting two elements in the set and setting the expected value to 0. If instead, we set the expected value to one, we have an inequality proof instead. In addition, by only putting a single index in the set, it is a proof that m_i equals the expected value without revealing anything else. Essentially, we can open a single bit position in this way. Figure 4 shown below depicts our protocol for proving the xor-relation between different bits. We note that there is also a parallel version of this proof system which follows the same basic idea as the parallel equality proof. A description of the parallel version can be found in Appendix D.

Theorem 2. *The Linear zero-knowledge protocol in Fig. 4 is an honest-verifier zero-knowledge proof system with soundness-error one-half.*

Proof. **Completeness:** Assuming honest parties, the prover sends δ created as stipulated. We consider four cases based on whether we are proving even ($b = 0$ is analogous to equality) or odd ($b = 1$ is analogous to inequality) parity with challenge $c \in \{0, 1\}$. In more detail we consider ($b = 0, c = 0$), ($b = 0, c = 1$), ($b = 1, c = 0$) and ($b = 1, c = 1$). We collapse the two first cases to one case $b = 0$.

$$0 = \left(\bigoplus_{i \in I} m_i \right) = \bigoplus_{i \in I} (m_i^0 \oplus m_i^1) \Rightarrow \bigoplus_{i \in I} m_i^0 = \bigoplus_{i \in I} m_i^1 = \delta$$

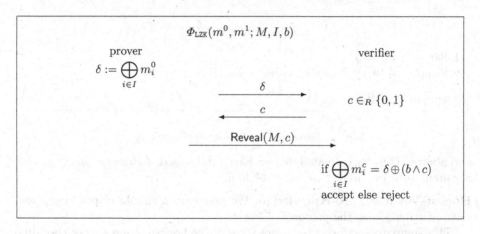

Fig. 4. Linear zero-knowledge. The prover has private input m^0, m^1 which are xor-shares of m. M^0, M^1 denote the commitments to shares m^0, m^1 respectively. The public input is M^0, M^1 and a set of indices I. The prover wants to prove to the verifier that $\bigoplus_{i \in I}(m_i) = b$.

Because $b = 0$ our verifier checks that

$$\delta = \bigoplus_{i \in I} m_i^c = \bigoplus_{i \in I} m_i^0 = \bigoplus_{i \in I} m_i^1$$

Thus the verifier accepts.

$b = 1$: In this case, we are proving odd parity. That is for the bits $m_i, i \in I$ have an odd number of bits set to one. Thus, there is no common δ between the xor of m_i^0 and $m_i^1, i \in I$. Similarly for inequality, we have:

$$1 = \bigoplus_{i \in I} m_i = \bigoplus_{i \in I}(m_i^0 \oplus m_i^1) \Rightarrow \bigoplus_{i \in I} m_i^0 = 1 \oplus \bigoplus_{i \in I} m_i^1 = \delta$$

That is whether $\delta = 1 \oplus \bigoplus_{i \in I} m_i^c$ is now dependent on c and the fact that we are proving odd parity, $b = 1$. Hence the verifier checks and accepts that:

$$\delta = \left(\bigoplus_{i \in I} m_i^c\right) \oplus (b \wedge c)$$

Soundness: Assuming the claim is false, $\bigoplus_{i \in I} m_i \neq b$, the cheating prover attempts to convince the verifier otherwise.

Sending $\delta = \bigoplus_{i \in I} m_i^0 \oplus c'$ to the verifier, the prover can reply correctly only for one $c' \in \{0, 1\}$, namely if

$$\delta = (b \wedge c') \oplus \bigoplus_{i \in I} m_i^{c'}.$$

Thus with probability one-half, the verifier sends $c \neq c'$ in which case sending m^c (to satisfy the commitment in M) the verifier sees an inconsistency with δ

Simulator $S_V^{\text{LZK}}(M, I, b; c)$

1 Sample $\delta \in_R \{0, 1\}$.

2 Sample $r \in \{0, 1\}^\ell$ such that $\bigoplus_{i \in I} m_i^c = \delta \oplus (c \wedge b)$

3 Output $(\delta, c, \text{Reveal}(M, c) = r)$

Fig. 5. Simulator for Linear zero-knowledge

and aborts. Thus by case analysis, we have established that the cheating prover is caught with probability at least one-half.

Honest-Verifier Zero-Knowledge: We give here a simulator producing the same distribution as the protocol of Fig. 4.

This simulator performs the exact steps of the honest prover except choosing the underlying message at random. By the *hiding* property of the underlying commitment scheme, the view $(\delta, c, \text{Reveal}(M, c) = m^c)$ is indistinguishable from the view generated between an honest prover and an honest verifier (Fig. 5). $\square$

5   And-Proof with Soundness-Error Three-Quarter

In this section, we show how a prover can show that for an $\texttt{xom}(m)$ to a string m and for three indices (i, j, k) of the string, it holds that $m_i \wedge m_j = m_k$. This is done by using a helper triple of values that are made explicitly for this purpose. To construct such a proof, we exploit the following relationship:

$$x \wedge y = z \iff z = \textsf{Maj}(x, y, 0).$$

The use of majority gates in zero-knowledge protocols was first used in [2]. We add an additional three bits per and-triple. The three bits are chosen to be a random permutation of the two input values and an additional value of zero. The protocol for this proof is depicted in Fig. 6 and proceeds as follows: the verifier for each and-triple, randomly asks the prover to either show that the three committed bits are a permutation of the two inputs and an extra value of zero, or asks the prover to show that the majority of the three additional bits is equal to the output bit (i.e. an and-triple of the relationship above). We refer to the first test as the permutation test and the second test as the majority test. If the bits do not form a valid triple, then for one of the two tests, the prover has probability one-half of failing that test. Thus overall, a cheating prover gets caught with probability one-quarter. Thus the soundness-error is three-quarter.

Theorem 3. *The protocol $\Phi_{\texttt{Mult}}|$ in Fig. 6 is an honest-verifier zero-knowledge interactive proof system with soundness-error three-quarter.*

Completeness: If for a given triple of indices i, j, k, $m_i \wedge m_j = m_k$ and a disjoint triplet i', j', k' has the property that there exists $\{d, e, f\} = \{i', j', k'\}$ such that $m_d = m_i, m_e = m_j, m_f = 0$ then there also exists a triple $\{u, v, w\} = \{i', j', k'\}$ such that $m_u = m_v = m_k$. Since there is a permutation for both tests, the completeness of the protocol follows from Theorem 2.

$$\Phi_{\texttt{Mult}}(m_0, m_1; M, i, j, k, i', j', k')$$

$prover$ $\qquad\qquad\qquad\qquad\qquad\qquad\qquad\qquad\qquad$ $verifier$

$$\xleftarrow{\hspace{3cm} b \hspace{3cm}} \qquad b \in_R \{0,1\}$$

If b = 0:

$\Phi_{\texttt{Triplet}}$

$\pi \in_R S_3$ s.t.
$\quad (e,f,g) = \pi(i',j',k') \implies (m_e, m_f, m_g) = (m_i, m_j, 0)$

$(e,f,g) \leftarrow \pi(i',j',k') \xrightarrow{\hspace{3cm} \pi \hspace{3cm}} (e,f,g) \leftarrow \pi(i',j',k')$

$S \leftarrow \{(\{i,e\},0),(\{j,f\},0),(\{g\},0)\}$

$$\Phi_{\texttt{PLZK}}(m^0, m^1; M, S)$$

If b = 1:

$\Phi_{\texttt{Majority}}$

$\mu \in_R S_3$ s.t.
$\quad (e,f,g) = \mu(i',j',k') \implies (m_e, m_f, m_g) = (z,z,\cdot)^a$

$(e,f,g) \leftarrow \mu(i',j',k') \xrightarrow{\hspace{3cm} \mu \hspace{3cm}} (e,f,g) \leftarrow \mu(i',j',k')$

$S \leftarrow \{(\{k,e\},0),(\{k,f\},0)\}$

$$\Phi_{\texttt{PLZK}}(m^0, m^1; M, S)$$

---

[a] μ is assigned a permutation that takes the majority of zeros or ones z in the triplet $(m_i, m_j, m_{k'})$ and places that value in the first two entries of the triplet $\mu(m_i, m_j, m_{k'}) = (z, z, \cdot)$. The last entry can be any value ensuring there is always a choice to be made here.

Fig. 6. Multiplication proof.

Soundness: For a cheating prover, we show that he convinces the verifier with probability at most three-quarters. Since $m_i \wedge m_j \neq m_k$, there cannot exists a disjoint set of indices $\{i', j', k'\}$ such that the following conditions can hold.

1. $\exists e, f, g : \{e, f, g\} = \{i', j', k'\}$ and $m_d = m_i, m_e = m_j, m_f = 0$
2. $\exists u, v, w : \{u, v, w\} = \{i', j', k'\}$ and $m_k = m_u = m_v$.

As such, for one of the two tests, the adversary has to cheat on an equality test. Thus, since the test is randomly chosen, from Theorem 2 we can see that the soundness-error is three-quarter.

Zero-Knowledge. We differ to Appendix E the description of the simulator and the proof of indistinguishability. The basic intuition though is that since we use auxiliary bits for the and-triple, the permutation looks random, then if we can simulate the equality proofs then we can simulate this proof. Since the equality proofs are zero-knowledge, we can use the simulator for the equality proofs to construct a simulator for this proof. We end up with the following theorem.

6   Honest-Verifier Zero-Knowledge Proof for Circuit Satisfiability

In this section, we give an honest-verifier zero-knowledge proof protocol for circuit satisfiability. We assume that the public circuit is known to both the verifier and the prover and that the prover knows a witness w. Without loss of generality we also assume the circuit consists of and-gates and xor-gates. Once we have the protocols for linear zero-knowledge (Sect. 4.3) and and-proofs (Sect. 5), it is relatively easy to construct a protocol for satisfiability. The prover commits to an evaluation of the circuit and uses the appropriate protocol for each gate. The complete protocol is summarized in Fig. 7.

The protocol requires a constant number of rounds and essentially goes as follows. We have labelled the six main steps of the protocol. First, the prover use the witness to perform an evaluation of the circuit and notes the output value for each gate. The following two steps are required for the prover to prepare himself to prove the consistency of the and-gates. As explained in Sect. 5, he has to prepare the data for the *helper triples and the* majority permutation. Then in the first challenge, the verifier asks for the information to validate one of the two tests. Now that the verifier has all the information needed for the verification, the last challenge will verify that all of the required linear relations hold. These relations come from the xor-gates of the circuit and from the challenge used to verify the and-gates.

6.1   Generating the Set S

This subsection describes how the set S of linear relations in the last step of protocol Φ_{CS} is carried out given that the previous steps have taken place, see Fig. 7. The set S depends only on the structure of public circuit C and the choice of the challenge bit b. Each party generates the set S. For each gate in C indexed by $u \in [\ell]$, we let i_u, j_u, k_u be the indices into the string m (and w as it is a prefix of m) corresponding to the two input bits and output bit respectively. Also, if the gate is an and-gate there exists an r (think the r-th and-gate) for the helper triple such that $(\ell + 3r, \ell + 3r + 1, \ell + 3r + 2)$ denote the indices in m for the helper triple corresponding to r. Also, we do an abuse of notation and take $(e_r, f_r, g_r) = \mu_r(m_{\ell+3r}, m_{\ell+3r+1}, m_{\ell+3r+2})$ to be the concrete bit values (not indices) for the majority permutation. S is generated as follows based on the type of gate it is.

$$\Phi_{CS}$$

Initialize The prover and the verifier takes as input a circuit C of size $|C| = \alpha + \beta$ with α and-gates and β linear gates. The circuit will have exactly one output bit. The prover takes additionally a *witness* w.

prover [**evaluation**] The circuit C has an ordering of its wires such that for each index $i \in I$, the bit m_i uniquely defines a particular wire. Thus using his witness w the prover generates a satisfying assignment for the circuit $x = x_0 \ldots x_{\ell-1}$ and sets x a prefix of m. That is $m_i = x_i$ for each $i \in [\ell]$.

prover [**helper triples**] For each and-gate with index $r = 0, ..., a - 1$, the bits $(x_{i_r}, x_{j_r}, X_{k_r})$ are such that $x_{i_r} \wedge x_{j_r} = x_{k_r}$. The prover selects a random permutation $\pi_r \in S_3$ and creates a helper triple $(m_{\ell+3r}, m_{\ell+3r+1}, m_{\ell+3r+2}) = \pi_r(m_{i_r}, m_{j_r}, 0)$. The prover sets Π as the set of permutations $\Pi = \{\pi_r\}_{r=0,...,a-1}$.

prover [**majority permutation**] The prover finds a *Majority* permutation μ_r such that if you set $(e_r, f_r, g_r) = \mu_r(m_{\ell+3r}, m_{\ell+3r+1}, m_{\ell+3r+2})$ then $m_{k_r} = e_r$ and $m_{k_r} = f_r$. Let $\mathcal{M}$ denote this set of majority permutations $\mathcal{M} = \{\mu_r\}_{r=0,...,a-1}$.

prover [**commitments**] When prover has formed m of length L he selects a string $r \in \{0,1\}^L$ uniformly at random and create $m^0 = r$, $m^1 = m^0 \oplus r$. Then he invokes the ideal functionality $\mathcal{F}_{COM}$ twice, sending an xor-commitment $(M^0, M^1) = (\text{com}(m^0), \text{com}(m^1))$ to the verifier.

verifier [**first challenge**] He samples a random $b \in \{0,1\}$ and sends it to the prover.

prover If $b = 0$ he sends Π to the verifier, if $b = 1$ he sends $\mathcal{M}$.

prover — verifier [**second challenge**] Both run the protocol of parallel linear relations with M, M^0, M^1 and a set $S = \{(I_r, b_r)\}_{r=0,...,\ell}$ described in section (6.1).

Fig. 7. Zero-knowledge with soundness-error three-quarter.

Xor-gate: The gate at u is an xor-gate thus we add $(\{i_u, j_u, k_u\}, 0)$ to S proving that the three bit positions xor to zero.

And-gate: The gate at u is an and-gate.

- If $b = 0$: add $(\{i_u, \ell + 3r\}, 0), (\{j_u, \ell + 3r + 1\}, 0), (\{k_u\}, 0)$ to S.
- If $b = 1$: add $(\{k_u, a_r\}, 0), (\{k_u, b_r\}, 0)$ to S.

7 Implementation

The protocol has been implemented in C for fine-grained control over the Big-O constants. The implementation is available at https://github.com/AarhusCrypto/EmpiricalZeroKnowledge.

Our test setup is two machines acting as Prover and Verifier connected on a GigaBit ethernet network of our department. Our machines has 8 GigaBytes of memory and Intel(R) Core(TM) i7-3770K CPU @ 3.50GHz with 8 cores. Our primary benchmark application is that of AES. We have an optimized AES-circuit with 6800 and-gates and 26816 linear gates taking 3 ms with soundness one-quarter. Communication complexity is 4 bits per And-gate and 1 bit per linear gate for soundness one quarter. A description of how to run our implementation can be found in Appendix F.

8 Conclusion

We can take the protocols described above and use them to construct a universally-composable zero-knowledge proof. We leave the description of the protocol to the full version of this paper. This is accomplished by using parallel repetition and applying transformations that take honest-verifier zero-knowledge proofs and converts them to UC zero-knowledge proofs. We have instantiated the UC secure protocol. We have implemented it and have shown that we can prove knowledge of an AES-key encrypting a particular plaintext to a specific ciphertext in less than 300 milliseconds with soundness-error 2^{-40}.

In addition to what have been presented in this extended abstract, the following two theorems can be proven formally. The protocol is secure in the $\mathcal{F}_{COM}$-hybrid model.

Theorem 4. *Our protocol is public-coin and securely realizes $\mathcal{F}_{ZK}$ in the $\mathcal{F}_{COM}$-hybrid model with soundness error 2^{-k} using $5k$ calls to $\mathcal{F}_{COM}$.*

In the random oracle model we can instantiate commitments via hash functions. This improves the efficiency of the protocol.

Theorem 5. *Our protocol can be securely realized in the random-oracle model with communication complexity $O(5 \cdot k \cdot |C| + 5k^2)$.*

Since the protocol is public-coin, the Fiat-Shamir heuristic can also be applied to make it non-interactive.

A Universal Composability Framework

The Universal Composability framework was introduced by Canetti in [4] In this framework, protocol security is analysed by comparing an ideal world execution and a real world execution under the supervision of an *environment* $\mathcal{Z}$, which is represented by a *PPT* machine and has access to all communication between individual parties. In the ideal world execution, dummy parties (possibly controlled by a *PPT simulator*) interact directly with the ideal functionality $\mathcal{F}$, which works as a fully secure third party that computes the desired function or primitive. In the real world execution, several *PPT* parties (possibly corrupted by a real world adversary $\mathcal{A}$) interact with each other by means of a protocol π that realizes the ideal functionality. The real world execution is represented by the ensemble $\text{EXEC}_{\pi,\mathcal{A},\mathcal{Z}}$, while the ideal execution is represented by the $\text{IDEAL}_{\mathcal{F},\mathcal{S},\mathcal{Z}}$. The rationale behind this framework lies in showing that the environment $\mathcal{Z}$ is not able to efficiently distinguish between $\text{EXEC}_{\pi,\mathcal{A},\mathcal{Z}}$ and $\text{IDEAL}_{\mathcal{F},\mathcal{S},\mathcal{Z}}$, thus implying that the real world protocol is as secure as the ideal functionality. It is known that a setup assumption is needed for UC realizing oblivious transfer as well as most "interesting" ideal functionalities [6].

A.1 Ideal Functionalities

Functionality $\mathcal{F}_{\text{COM}}$

$\mathcal{F}_{\text{COM}}$ runs with two parties: the sender and the receiver.

- On input $(\text{commit}, \text{sid}, m)$ from the sender, if the pair $(\text{sid}, \cdot)$ has not been recorded, record the pair (sid, m) and send $(\text{committed}, \text{sid})$ to the receiver. Otherwise, do nothing.
- On input $(\text{open}, \text{sid}, m)$ from the sender, if a pair (sid, m) has been recorded, send (reveal, m) to the receiver. Otherwise, do nothing.

Functionality $\mathcal{F}_{\text{ZK}}$

$\mathcal{F}_{\text{ZK}}$ runs with two parties: a prover P and a verifier V and is parametrized with a relationship R.

- On input $(\text{Prove}, \text{sid}, x, w)$ from P, if no message of the form $(\cdot, \text{sid}, \cdot, \cdot)$ and if $(x, w) \in R$, send the message $(\text{proven}, \text{sid}, x)$ to V. Otherwise, ignore the command.

B Inequality Protocol

The inequality proof only differs with the equality proof in which tests the verifier does. In the equality protocol, the verifier tests if $m_i^c \oplus m_j^c = \delta$. In the inequality proof, the verifier tests if $m_i^c \oplus m_j^c \oplus c = \delta$. We can see that this protocol is sound and complete by Observation 3. We can show that it is zero-knowledge from Observation 5 and by applying the same reasoning used to prove the zero-knowledge property of the equality proof (Fig. 8).

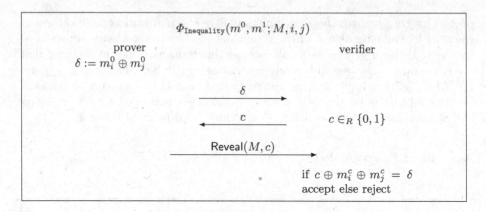

Fig. 8. Inequality

C Parallel Equality Proofs

As before, we take $M = (\mathsf{com}(m^0), \mathsf{com}(m^1))$ as input to mean that an XOR commitment already happened beforehand. For the set of pairs of indices $I = \{(i_r, j_r)\}_{r=1,\dots,t}$, we generate the δ_r and send a string $\Delta = \delta_1, \dots, \delta_t$ rather than one bit, to the verifier. Also, the verifier now checks t positions, one for each bit in Δ.

By applying the same reasoning used in the equality protocol, we can see that our protocol for parallel equality in Fig. 9 is also an Honest-verifier Zero-Knowledge proof system with soundness-error one-half.

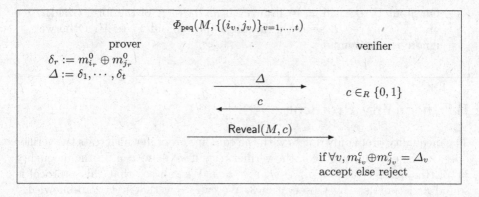

Fig. 9. Parallel Equality proof

D   Parallel Linear Proof

In Fig. 10, we include a protocol for parallel linear zero-knowledge.

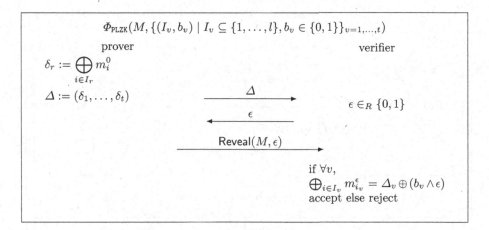

$$\Phi_{\text{PLZK}}(M, \{(I_v, b_v) \mid I_v \subseteq \{1, \ldots, l\}, b_v \in \{0,1\}\}_{v=1,\ldots,t})$$

prover   verifier

$$\delta_r := \bigoplus_{i \in I_r} m_i^0$$

$$\Delta := (\delta_1, \ldots, \delta_t)$$

$$\xrightarrow{\quad \Delta \quad}$$

$$\epsilon \in_R \{0,1\}$$

$$\xleftarrow{\quad \epsilon \quad}$$

$$\xrightarrow{\text{Reveal}(M, \epsilon)}$$

if $\forall v$,
$\bigoplus_{i \in I_v} m_{i_v}^\epsilon = \Delta_v \oplus (b_v \wedge \epsilon)$
accept else reject

Fig. 10. Parallel linear Zero-knowledge

E   Simulation of Mult

The simulation of the and-proof is fairly simple. Basically, the simulation will see which test the verifier would ask for based on the given random tape. The simulator then selects a random permutation, it selects that permutation that the prover would send. The simulator then see's which equality test would be run based on the choice of test. The simulator uses the random tape and the simulator for the parallel equality to generate a view for each of the equality tests. He then outputs the combined view for all of these things put together. By the zero-knowledge property of the parallel equality test, we can see that the generated view is indistinguishable from the view generated by the transcript of an interaction between an honest prover and an honest verifier (Fig. 11).

F   Reproducing Our Empirical Studies

We have implemented our protocol. The implementation can be found at http://tinyurl.com/om6vvh6

Software Structure: The software project is written from scratch using only few dependencies on the system like some libstdc functionality. We do this in order to have fine grained control of the performance of our program. The structure is as follows:

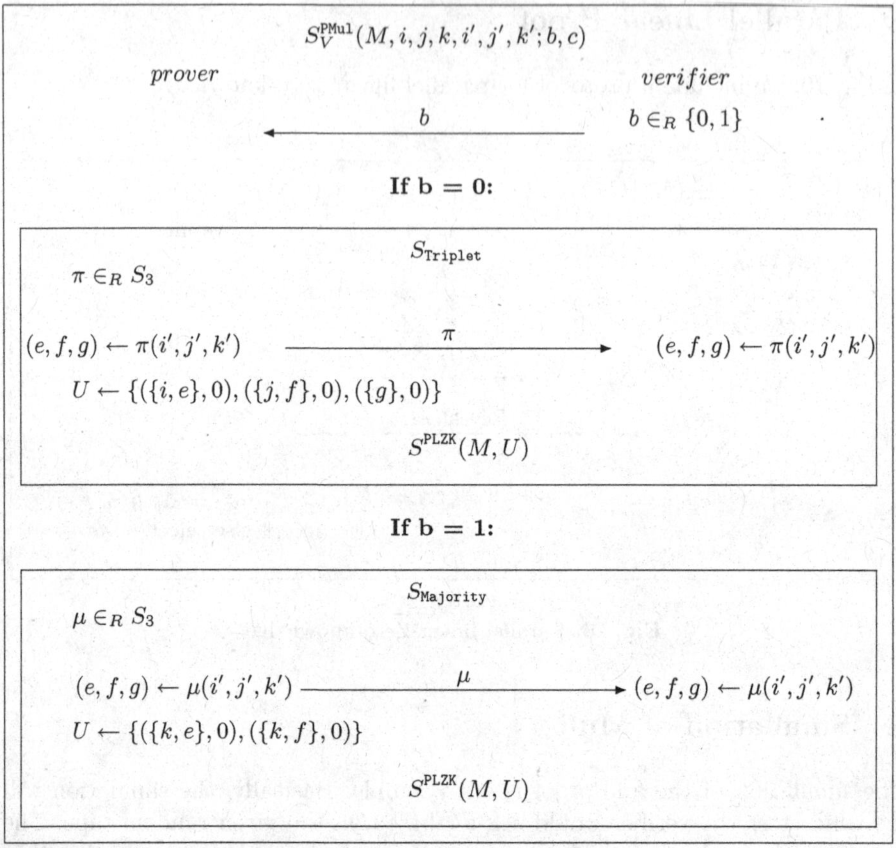

$$S_V^{\text{PMul}}(M, i, j, k, i', j', k'; b, c)$$

prover		verifier
	$\xleftarrow{\quad\quad b \quad\quad}$	$b \in_R \{0,1\}$

If b = 0:

S_{Triplet}

$\pi \in_R S_3$

$(e, f, g) \leftarrow \pi(i', j', k') \xrightarrow{\quad\quad \pi \quad\quad} (e, f, g) \leftarrow \pi(i', j', k')$

$U \leftarrow \{(\{i, e\}, 0), (\{j, f\}, 0), (\{g\}, 0)\}$

$S^{\text{PLZK}}(M, U)$

If b = 1:

S_{Majority}

$\mu \in_R S_3$

$(e, f, g) \leftarrow \mu(i', j', k') \xrightarrow{\quad\quad \mu \quad\quad} (e, f, g) \leftarrow \mu(i', j', k')$

$U \leftarrow \{(\{k, e\}, 0), (\{k, f\}, 0)\}$

$S^{\text{PLZK}}(M, U)$

Fig. 11. Multiplication simulator

platform Inside the platform directory we have all the OS/HW dependent code

common Inside common we have library code needed to implement the protocol, including network management in **CArena** and data-structures in project **ds**.

empiricalZK holds two projects: **RTZ14** which is the code for protocol described in this paper. **IKOS** will later be populated with an efficient implementation of the MPC in the HEAD idea which is in its infant stage right now. We wish to publish a comparison between IKOS and RTZ14 (this protocol) in a follow up paper.

All projects are GNU Auto-Make/Conf projects producing a static library and some also an executable. Each project defines a configuration item with version control for maintenance.

Dependencies: The code is written with in C for speed and portability. It includes work by Nayuki Minase published at http://www.nayuki.io/page/fast-sha2-hashes-in-x86-assembly.

The build system on FreeBSD 10, OSX and GNU Linux requires:

GNU Bash 4.3.11(2)
Automake 1.14
Autoconf 2.69

Or on Windows 8/10 a working Community version of Visual Studio Express 2013 or later is required.

Getting the Source: Install git on your system and do

```
git clone http://tinyurl.com/om6vvh6
(you may need to replace this by the actual url).
```

Building from Source Code, FreeBSD, Linux and OSX: On these systems building the source is done by changing directory to where you have checked out the source and locating the `build.sh` script.

```
user@host \$ ./build.sh release
```

Will build the prover executable in empiricalZK/rtz14/linux/src/prover.

Building from Source Code, Windows 8/10: On Windows we have a test solution that as a bi-product of running the test programs also produces the prover.exe in empiricalZK/rtz14/win64/rtz14/Release/prover.exe.

You can run this executable from a Command Prompt invoking it with no argument to see your options and for running it providing arguments to do a Zero-knowledge proof.

Reproducing Our Results: Our benchmark application is proving knowledge of a particular AES key given a public plaintext and ciphertext. The structure of the circuit we prove to satisfy is depicted in Fig. 12. The circuit includes public constant assignments for the plaintext and the Prover convinces the Verifier that he has knowledge of an Aes-Key encrypting this particular plaintext to a ciphertext built into the circuit. That is, our binary AES is extended with the top-triangle on Fig. 12 which is a small comparison circuit with public constants stipulating the expected ciphertext and comparing with the output of the AES circuit (the larger triangle below it). In the end all the Verifier learns is that the prover has a witness w making the (public) circuit true, thus encrypting the given plaintext to the expected ciphertext.

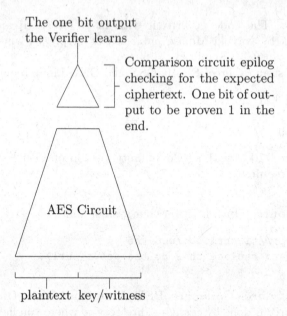

Fig. 12. A modified binary AES circuit for proving knowledge of a key encrypting a particular plaintext to a particular ciphertext.

Our lab computers has the following specifications:

```
CPU: i7-3770K CPU @ 3.50GHz with 8 cores Mem: 8Gb of Ram Net:
Gigabit LAN OS:  3.13.0-59-generic #98-Ubuntu SMP Fri Jul 24
21:05:26 UTC 2015 x86_64 x86_64 x86_64 GNU/Linux
```

for both Verifier and Prover. On the machine intended for the Prover do

```
./rtz14 -circuit ../test/AES -witness 00000000000000000000000000000000
        -port 2020
```

This will start a prover process listening for a Verifier to connect. The circuit in ../test/AES is the following and we prove in this case that we have knowledge of a key (this witness above which is the zero key) encrypting the all zero plaintext (that is 16 zero bytes) to the AES ciphertext under the zero key, namely:

```
0 1 1 0 0 1 1 0 1 0 0 1 0 1 1 1
1 1 0 1 0 0 1 0 0 0 1 0 1 0 1 1
1 1 1 1 0 1 1 1 0 1 0 1 0 0 0 1
0 0 1 1 0 1 0 0 1 1 0 1 1 1 0 0
0 0 0 1 0 0 0 1 0 0 1 1 0 0 1 0
0 1 0 1 1 1 1 1 1 0 0 1 1 0 1 0
0 1 0 1 0 0 1 1 0 0 1 0 1 1 0 0
1 1 0 1 0 1 0 0 0 1 1 1 0 1 0 0
```

To start the Verifier you need the ip address of the Prover, assuming it is xxx.yyy.zzz.www execute the following on the Verifier Machine:

```
./rtz14 -circuit ../test/AES -port 2020 -ip xxx.yyy.zzz.www
```

The process uses the -witness argument to distinguish whether to run as Prover or Verifier. This proves with error probability $3/4$ that the prover knows such a witness. Because of completeness this will always succeed if the Prover inputs the correct witness, otherwise the Verifier only accepts with a 75 % probability. In a real word application with statistical security parameter s the protocol will be repeated $3s$ times to reduce the probability that a cheating Prover wins to 2^{-s}. Our experiment above runs in $3ms$ on our test machines thus for security parameter $\kappa = 128$ we expect a real world running time of $9\kappa ms \approx 2.5$ seconds.

References

1. Ben-Or, M., Goldreich, O., Goldwasser, S., Håstad, J., Kilian, J., Micali, S., Rogaway, P.: Everything provable is provable in zero-knowledge. In: Goldwasser, S. (ed.) CRYPTO 1988. LNCS, vol. 403, pp. 37–56. Springer, Heidelberg (1990). doi:10.1007/0-387-34799-2_4
2. Boyar, J., Peralta, R.: On the concrete complexity of zero-knowledge proofs. In: Brassard, G. (ed.) CRYPTO 1989. LNCS, vol. 435, pp. 507–525. Springer, Heidelberg (1990). doi:10.1007/0-387-34805-0_45
3. Brassard, G., Chaum, D., Crépeau, C.: Minimum disclosure proofs of knowledge. J. Comput. Syst. Sci. **37**, 156–189 (1988)
4. Canetti, R.: Universally composable security: a new paradigm for cryptographic protocols. Cryptology ePrint Archive, Report 2000/067
5. Canetti, R., Cohen, A., Lindell, Y.: A simpler variant of universally composable security for standard multiparty computation. In: Gennaro, R., Robshaw, M. (eds.) CRYPTO 2015. LNCS, vol. 9216, pp. 3–22. Springer, Heidelberg (2015). doi:10.1007/978-3-662-48000-7_1
6. Canetti, R., Fischlin, M.: Universally composable commitments. In: Kilian, J. (ed.) CRYPTO 2001. LNCS, vol. 2139, pp. 19–40. Springer, Heidelberg (2001). doi:10.1007/3-540-44647-8_2
7. Cascudo, I., Damgård, I., David, B., Giacomelli, I., Nielsen, J.B., Trifiletti, R.: Additively homomorphic UC commitments with optimal amortized overhead. In: Katz, J. (ed.) PKC 2015. LNCS, vol. 9020, pp. 495–515. Springer, Heidelberg (2015). doi:10.1007/978-3-662-46447-2_22
8. Cramer, R., Damgård, I., Nielsen, J.: Secure Multiparty Computation and Secret Sharing, 1st edn. Cambridge University Press, Cambridge (2015)
9. Crépeau, C., van de Graaf, J., Tapp, A.: Committed oblivious transfer and private multi-party computation. In: Coppersmith, D. (ed.) CRYPTO 1995. LNCS, vol. 963, pp. 110–123. Springer, Heidelberg (1995). doi:10.1007/3-540-44750-4_9
10. Damgård, I., David, B., Giacomelli, I., Nielsen, J.B.: Compact VSS and efficient homomorphic UC commitments. In: Sarkar, P., Iwata, T. (eds.) ASIACRYPT 2014. LNCS, vol. 8874, pp. 213–232. Springer, Heidelberg (2014). doi:10.1007/978-3-662-45608-8_12
11. Damgrd, I., Ishai, Y.: Scalable secure multiparty computation. In: Dwork, C. (ed.) Advances in Cryptology - CRYPTO 2006. Lecture Notes in Computer Science, vol. 4117, pp. 501–520. Springer, Heidelberg (2006)

12. Frederiksen, T.K., Nielsen, J.B., Orlandi, C.: Privacy-free garbled circuits with applications to efficient zero-knowledge. In: Proceedings Advances in Cryptology - EUROCRYPT 2015–34th Annual International Conference on the Theory and Applications of Cryptographic Techniques, Sofia, Bulgaria, 26–30 April 2015, Part II, pp. 191–219 (2015)
13. Giacomelli, I., Madsen, J., Orlandi, C.: Zkboo: Faster zero-knowledge for Boolean circuits. IACR Cryptology ePrint Archive 2016/163 (2016)
14. Goldreich, O., Micali, S., Wigderson, A.: How to play any mental game. In: Proceedings of the Nineteenth Annual ACM Symposium on Theory of Computing, STOC 1987, New York, NY, USA, ACM (1987)
15. Goldreich, O., Micali, S., Wigderson, A.: Proofs that yield nothing but their validity or all languages in np have zero-knowledge proof systems. J. ACM (JACM) **38**(3), 690–728 (1991)
16. Goldwasser, S., Micali, S., Rackoff, C.: The knowledge complexity of interactive proof systems. SIAM J. Comput. **18**, 186–208 (1989)
17. Ishai, Y., Kushilevitz, E., Ostrovsky, R., Sahai, A.: Zero-knowledge from secure multiparty computation. In: Proceedings of the Thirty-Ninth Annual ACM Symposium on Theory of Computing, pp. 21–30. ACM (2007)
18. Jawurek, M., Kerschbaum, F., Orlandi, C.: Zero-knowledge using garbled circuits: how to prove non-algebraic statements efficiently. In: 2013 ACM SIGSAC Conference on Computer and Communications Security, CCS 2013 (2013)
19. Richard, M.K.: Reducibility among combinatorial problems. In: Miller, R.E., Thatcher, J.W., Bohlinger, J.D. (eds.) Complexity of Computer Computations. The IBM Research Symposia Series, pp. 85–103. Springer, New York (1972)
20. Kilian, J.: A note on efficient zero-knowledge proofs and arguments. In: Proceedings of the Twenty-Fourth Annual ACM Symposium on Theory of Computing, pp. 723–732. ACM (1992)
21. Rabin, M.O., Mansour, Y., Muthukrishnan, S., Yung, M.: Strictly-black-box zero-knowledge and efficient validation of financial transactions. In: Czumaj, A., Mehlhorn, K., Pitts, A., Wattenhofer, R. (eds.) ICALP 2012. LNCS, vol. 7391, pp. 738–749. Springer, Heidelberg (2012). doi:10.1007/978-3-642-31594-7_62
22. Ranellucci, S., Tapp, A., Winkler, S., Wullschleger, J.: On the efficiency of bit commitment reductions. In: Proceedings of Advances in Cryptology - ASIACRYPT 2011–17th International Conference on the Theory and Application of Cryptology and Information Security, Seoul, South Korea, 4–8 December 2011, pp. 520–537 (2011)

Unconditionally Secure Revocable Storage: Tight Bounds, Optimal Construction, and Robustness

Yohei Watanabe[1,2(✉)], Goichiro Hanaoka[2], and Junji Shikata[3,4]

[1] Graduate School of Informatics and Engineering,
The University of Electro-Communications, Chofu, Japan
watanabe@uec.ac.jp
[2] Information Technology Research Institute, AIST, Tokyo, Japan
hanaoka-goichiro@aist.go.jp
[3] Graduate School of Environment and Information Sciences,
Yokohama National University, Yokohama, Japan
shikata@ynu.ac.jp
[4] Institute of Advanced Sciences, Yokohama National University, Yokohama, Japan

Abstract. Data stored in cloud storage sometimes requires long-term security due to its sensitivity (e.g., genome data), and therefore, it also requires flexible access control for handling entities who can use the data. *Broadcast encryption* can partially provide such flexibility by specifying privileged receivers so that only they can decrypt a ciphertext. However, once privileged receivers are specified, they can be no longer dynamically added and/or removed. In this paper, we propose a new type of broadcast encryption which provides long-term security and appropriate access control, which we call unconditionally secure *revocable-storage broadcast encryption* (RS-BE). In RS-BE, privileged receivers of a ciphertext can be dynamically updated without revealing any information on the underlying plaintext. Specifically, we define a model and security of RS-BE, and derive tight lower bounds on sizes of secret keys required for a one-time secure RS-BE scheme when the ciphertext size is equal to the plaintext size. Our lower bounds can be applied to traditional broadcast encryption. We then construct a one-time secure RS-BE scheme with a trade-off between sizes of ciphertexts and secret keys, and our construction for the smallest ciphertext size meets all bounds with equalities. Furthermore, to detect an improper update, we consider security against modification attacks to a ciphertext, and present a concrete construction secure against this type of attacks.

Keywords: Broadcast encryption · Information-theoretic security · Revocable storage · Unconditional security

1 Introduction

1.1 Background

In recent years, the progress of cloud technologies has been remarkable, and cloud-based applications are becoming widespread. One area in which cloud

© Springer International Publishing AG 2016
A.C.A. Nascimento and P. Barreto (Eds.): ICITS 2016, LNCS 10015, pp. 213–237, 2016.
DOI: 10.1007/978-3-319-49175-2_11

technology has the potential to provide significant impact, is advanced medical treatment, and applications of cloud technology in this area is currently being investigated intensively [5,44]. To provide such advanced medical services, it is required to store the data of individual patients using cloud storage. However, this data is generally very sensitive and should be protected carefully. Especially, when storing genome data using cloud storage, computationally secure encryption is considered to provide insufficient protection since genetic properties will be inherited by descendants of the genome owner, and thus, significantly long-term security is required [5,6]. For example, even if we encrypt genome data using a 2048-bit RSA cryptosystem, which is considered sufficiently secure in most applications, security will only be guaranteed until 2030 [7], which is not sufficient for protecting genome privacy (which must take into account the privacy of our descendants).

A promising approach for obtaining sufficiently strong security for medical data is to utilize information-theoretically secure encryption, e.g. the one-time pad. However, the one-time pad is only a (standard) symmetric encryption scheme, and thus, not suitable for effective use in a cloud environment. Namely, in a cloud storage system, there are potentially many users who will be given permission to access the stored data, and these privileged users are furthermore dynamically determined. It is obvious that such a scenario cannot be easily handled by using only (standard) symmetric encryption. *Broadcast encryption* (BE) [21] which allows multiple receivers to decrypt a logically single ciphertext seems to partially yield the required functionality. However, when the sender encrypts a plaintext in BE, he is forced to fix the set of privileged users and cannot dynamically add and/or remove receivers. For handling dynamic changes to the set of privileged receivers (in the context of attribute-based encryption [37]), Sahai, Seyalioglu, and Waters proposed *revocable-storage attribute-based encryption* [36] in which a ciphertext in a cloud storage system can be periodically updated according to a changing set of privileged users. However, their scheme is computationally secure and does not guarantee security against future powerful adversaries.

Therefore, it is important to investigate suitable cryptographic primitives which simultaneously provide a high level of security for sensitive data and sufficient flexibility to implement appropriate access control.

1.2 Our Contributions

In this paper, we propose the notion of unconditionally secure *revocable-storage BE* (RS-BE) which yields information-theoretic security and the above required functionality for cloud storage. In an RS-BE scheme, similarly to BE, the sender chooses a set of (initial) privileged users and encrypts a plaintext so that only these users can decrypt the ciphertext. Moreover, the *storage manager* can update the ciphertext to reflect changes in the set of privileged users. Here, the update procedure is carried out without revealing the plaintext, and thus, the storage manager cannot learn anything about the encrypted plaintext. We furthermore show tight lower bounds on the sizes of ciphertexts and secret keys in the unconditionally secure setting, and present an optimal construction which achieves these bounds as well as a robust construction which is resilient to a maliciously behaving storage manager.

More specifically, our contributions are as follows. Firstly, in Sect. 2, we give a formal model and security definitions of unconditionally secure RS-BE. As in the previous BE schemes [8,11,21,46], we consider an RS-BE scheme for one-time use for simplicity. Then, in Sect. 3, we clarify that it is possible to construct an unconditionally secure RS-BE scheme in which the ciphertext length is the same as the plaintext length. We note that this is an important and desired property since ciphertexts are stored in the cloud permanently or for a long time, and therefore, compactness of ciphertexts is one of the most important aspects to consider in the design of an RS-BE scheme. We then investigate lower bounds on the sizes of decryption keys, encryption keys, and the storage manager's keys under the condition that the ciphertext size is the same as the plaintext size. These bounds can also be seen as a generalization of the bounds for (traditional) BE, and furthermore imply a tight bound on the size of encryption keys in BE which, to the best of our knowledge, has not been clarified before our work. In Sect. 4, we show an unconditionally secure RS-BE scheme with an efficient trade-off between the ciphertext and secret-key sizes. More precisely, for arbitrary $\delta \in \{1, 2, \ldots, n\}$ we present an unconditionally secure RS-BE scheme with efficient secret-key sizes when the ciphertext size is at most δ times as large as the plaintext size. In particular, our construction meets all of these bounds with equalities when $\delta = 1$ (i.e., a scheme where the ciphertext size is always equal to the plaintext size). This means that these bounds are *tight* and the proposed construction is *optimal* for $\delta = 1$. In Sect. 5, we furthermore consider a scenario in which a maliciously behaving storage manager can try to modify the encrypted plaintext. This is related to *non-malleability* in the context of ordinary encryption. In an RS-BE scheme, malleability may cause a serious problem since the ciphertext is periodically updated, but an improper update carried out by a malicious storage manager may not be immediately detectable by the users. We define robustness, which is a security notion against such a malicious update, and derive a lower bound on the ciphertext size for a robust RS-BE scheme. Then, we present a concrete robust construction based on an ordinary RS-BE scheme presented in Sect. 4 and *an algebraic manipulation detection code* (AMD-code for short) [18]. We show one of instantiations of the robust scheme is *almost optimal* in the sense of the ciphertext size. Therefore, the above lower bound on the ciphertext size is almost tight.

1.3 Related Work

Berkovits [8] first considered the concept of BE, and Fiat and Naor [21] developed a formal and systematic approach to the construction of BE schemes. Since then, BE schemes have been improved both in the computationally secure setting [14,20,22,31,35] and in the unconditionally secure setting [8,11,12,16,21, 26,29,33,34,42,46], and used in various situations such as copyright protection in the real world. In particular, lower bounds on secret keys for unconditionally secure BE (USBE) schemes have previously been investigated [11, 12, 26]. However, some problems nonetheless remain. Blundo and Cresti [11] derived lower bounds on USBE in the context of key predistribution schemes (KPSs) [9, 30]. However, these bounds are specific to the application to KPS, and are not true lower bounds for USBE in general. Also, Blundo et al. [12] derived lower bounds for USBE, but these bounds are not tight. Furthermore, Kurosawa et al. [26] showed tight lower bounds on the size of decryption keys for USBE through equivalence between USBE and KPS, however, they did not mention lower bounds on encryption keys in their paper. In contrast, we derive tight lower bounds on both of the sizes of encryption keys and decryption keys for USBE without using such equivalence, and it turns out that the tight lower bound on the size of decryption keys in [26] is a special case of ours.

Recently, many researchers have investigated how we can *securely* use cloud data storage for various purposes [1, 23, 25, 27, 28, 36, 39, 41, 47]. Sahai, Seyalioglu, and Waters [36] first dealt with the concept of a revocable storage, and proposed revocable-storage attribute-based encryption (RS-ABE). They assume ciphertexts are stored in external storage, such as cloud data storage, and considered revocable attribute-based encryption [4, 13] with ciphertext updatable functionality (to be precise, [13] in the context of identity-based encryption). However, RS-ABE is only computationally secure, and hence cannot guarantee long-term security.

In the unconditionally secure setting, proactive secret sharing schemes [15, 24, 32, 43] and fully dynamic secret sharing schemes [10] also provide functionality for updating shares. However, such updating functionality and its aim in these schemes are different from those in our RS-BE scheme. To provide flexible access control, key assignment schemes [2, 3, 38] are considered. In key assignment schemes, a trusted entity defines several security classes, and assigns secret keys corresponding to the security classes. We can get an encryption scheme which supports the same access control by the one-time pad with the assigned key. However, these classes cannot be dynamically changed after distributing the keys.

Thus, we cannot directly apply these techniques, and we need to define and to construct RS-BE schemes from scratch.

2   Revocable-Storage Broadcast Encryption

2.1   Model

In RS-BE, there are $n + 2$ entities, a sender E, n users $U_1, \ldots, U_n$, and a storage manager SM. Let $\mathcal{U} := \{U_1, \ldots, U_n\}$ be a set of all users. First, E generates an encryption key ek, n decryption keys $dk_1, dk_2, \ldots, dk_n$, and a maintenance key mk. E then distributes $dk_1, dk_2, \ldots, dk_n$, and mk to $U_1, U_2, \ldots, U_n$, and SM via secure channels, respectively. E can specify a subset $\mathcal{S}$ (called a *privileged set*) of $\mathcal{U}$ such that $\mathcal{S} \neq \emptyset$, and encrypt a plaintext by using his encryption key ek so that only users in the privileged set can decrypt the resulting ciphertext. The ciphertext is stored in an external storage such as cloud storage. A user U_i in the privileged set S takes the ciphertext from the storage himself, then he decrypts the ciphertext by using his decryption key dk_i. The storage manager SM can change *any* privileged set S of the ciphertext into *any* privileged set S' (even if *not* $S' \subset S$) by using his maintenance key mk without decryption (i.e., without revealing the underlying plaintext). At sender's request or by some kind of rule, the storage manager SM changes the privileged set of the ciphertext, and then SM replaces the old one with the new one.

Formally, RS-BE is executed as follows. Let $\mathcal{M}$ be a set of possible plaintexts. For any subset $\mathcal{J} := \{U_{i_1}, \ldots, U_{i_j}\} \subset \mathcal{U}$, let $\mathcal{C}_{\mathcal{J}}$ be a set of all possible ciphertexts for the privileged set $\mathcal{J}$, and let $\mathcal{C} := \bigcup_{\mathcal{J} \subset \mathcal{U}} \mathcal{C}_{\mathcal{J}}$. Let $\mathcal{EK}$ be a set of possible encryption keys, and let $\mathcal{MK}$ be a set of maintenance keys. Let $\mathcal{DK}_i$ be a set of possible decryption keys for U_i, and let $\mathcal{DK} := \bigcup_{i=1}^{n} \mathcal{DK}_i$.

Definition 1 (RS-BE). *A revocable-storage broadcast encryption (RS-BE for short) scheme Π involves $n+2$ entities, $E, U_1, U_2, \ldots, U_n$ and SM, and consists of the following four-tuple of algorithms (Setup, Enc, Dec, Upd) with five spaces, $\mathcal{M}, \mathcal{C}, \mathcal{EK}, \mathcal{DK},$ and $\mathcal{MK}$, where all of the above algorithms except Setup are deterministic and all of the above spaces are finite.*

1. *$(ek, mk, dk_1, \ldots, dk_n) \leftarrow Setup()$: It outputs an encryption key $ek \in \mathcal{EK}$, n decryption keys $(dk_1, \ldots, dk_n) \in \prod_{i=1}^{n} \mathcal{DK}_i$, and a maintenance key $mk \in \mathcal{MK}$.*
2. *$c_S \leftarrow Enc(ek, m, S)$: It takes an encryption key ek, a plaintext $m \in \mathcal{M}$, and an initial privileged set $S \subset \mathcal{U}$ as input, and outputs a ciphertext c_S.[1]*
3. *m or $\perp \leftarrow Dec(dk_i, c_S, S, U_i)$: It takes a decryption key dk_i of a user U_i, the ciphertext c_S, the privileged set S, and the identity U_i as input, and outputs m or $\perp$.*
4. *$c_{S'}$ or $\perp \leftarrow Upd(mk, c_S, S, S')$: It takes a maintenance key mk, the ciphertext c_S, its privileged set S, and a new privileged set S' as input, and outputs a ciphertext $c_{S'}$ for S' or $\perp$.*

In RS-BE Π, we require the following correctness holds:

(a) For all $n \in \mathbb{N}$, all $(ek, mk, dk_1, \ldots, dk_n) \leftarrow Setup(n)$, all $m \in \mathcal{M}$, all $S \subset \mathcal{U}$, and all $U_i \in S$, $m \leftarrow Dec(dk_i, Enc(ek, m, S), S, U_i)$
(b) For all $n \in \mathbb{N}$, all $(ek, mk, dk_1, \ldots, dk_n) \leftarrow Setup(n)$, all $m \in \mathcal{M}$, all $S, S' \subset \mathcal{U}$, $Upd(mk, Enc(ek, m, S), S') = Enc(ek, m, S')$

(a) means the *decryption correctness* and (b) means the *updating correctness*.

In RS-BE, for simplicity we assume the one-time model where it is allowed for the sender to encrypt a plaintext and store a ciphertext only once. Note that it is unrestricted for the storage manager to execute the algorithm *Upd* (i.e. the ciphertext can be updated unboundedly).

---

[1] More precisely, a description of S is needed to decrypt and update the ciphertext. For simplicity, we assume that all entities share the information of S since there are various ways of sharing the information (e.g., it can be sent to users using the broadcast channel, or stored on a publicly accessible authenticated bulletin board).

2.2   Security Definition

We consider perfect secrecy against at most ω colluders and the storage manager. Here, we note that in principle, it is impossible to guarantee security against collusion of them since the storage manager can change any privileged set of a ciphertext into any privileged set. Therefore, we consider security in the case that at most ω colluders and the storage manager try to attack separately.[2] Namely, we consider the following two kinds of security notions: (1) At most ω colluders who are not included in the privileged set cannot get any information on the underlying plaintext from the ciphertext (a traditional security notion for BE). (2) The storage manager cannot get any information on the underlying plaintext from the ciphertext. The reason why we consider the second one is that if the storage manager can obtain the underlying plaintext or some information on it, it is only necessary to encrypt the same plaintext with a new privileged set and replace an old ciphertext with the new one by a sender to change privileged sets. Hence, we require the storage manager can update the ciphertext without decryption (without leaking any information on the underlying plaintext). For any $\mathcal{J} := \{U_{i_1}, \ldots, U_{i_j}\} \subset \mathcal{U}$, let $\mathcal{DK}_{\mathcal{J}} := \mathcal{DK}_{i_1} \times \cdots \times \mathcal{DK}_{i_j}$ be a set of possible secret keys of $\mathcal{J}$. Let M, $C_{\mathcal{S}}$, EK, DK_i $(1 \leq i \leq n)$, $DK_{\mathcal{J}}$ $(\mathcal{J} \subset \mathcal{U})$, and MK be random variables which takes values on $\mathcal{M}$, $\mathcal{C}_{\mathcal{S}}$, $\mathcal{EK}$, $\mathcal{DK}_i$ $(1 \leq i \leq n)$, $\mathcal{DK}_{\mathcal{J}}$ $(\mathcal{J} \subset \mathcal{U})$, and $\mathcal{MK}$, respectively. Formally, security of RS-BE is defined by Shannon entropy as follows. If readers are not familiar with Shannon entropy, see Appendix A.

Definition 2 (Security of RS-BE). *Let Π be an RS-BE scheme. Π is said to be $(\leq n, \leq \omega)$-one-time secure if the following conditions are satisfied:*

(1) For any privileged set $\mathcal{S} \subset \mathcal{U}$, and any set of colluders $\mathcal{W} \subset \mathcal{U}$ such that $\mathcal{S} \cap \mathcal{W} = \emptyset$ and $|\mathcal{W}| \leq \omega$, it holds that $H(M \mid C_{\mathcal{S}}, DK_{\mathcal{W}}) = H(M)$.
(2) For any privileged set $\mathcal{S} \subset \mathcal{U}$, it holds that $H(M \mid C_{\mathcal{S}}, MK) = H(M)$.

Remark 1. In the model of RS-BE (Definition 1), if SM does not exist (i.e., mk is empty string and we do not consider the algorithm Upd), and we therefore do not consider the condition (2) in Definition 2, then Definitions 1 and 2 are the same as those of $((\leq n, \leq \omega)$-one-time secure) traditional BE schemes [11,21,26,42]. Hence, we can say our scheme is natural extension of the BE schemes.

Remark 2. The condition (1) in Definition 2 implies that the number of ciphertexts taken by $\mathcal{W}$ from the storage is at most one. However, it is natural to think that $\mathcal{W}$ can access the storage multiple time and take ciphertexts for various privileged sets. Namely, for more realistic definition, we should consider the following security condition (1') instead of (1):

---

[2] We also discuss an RS-BE scheme secure against collusion of at most ω colluders and the storage manager under a restricted transformation rule of the storage manager's key in Appendix B.

(1') For any privileged sets $\mathcal{S}_1, \ldots, \mathcal{S}_k \subset \mathcal{U}$ $(1 \leq k \leq 2^n)$, and any set of colluders $\mathcal{W} \subset \mathcal{U}$ such that $\left(\bigcup_{i=1}^{k} \mathcal{S}_i \right) \cap \mathcal{W} = \emptyset$ and $|\mathcal{W}| \leq \omega$, it holds that $H(M \mid C_{\mathcal{S}_1}, \ldots, C_{\mathcal{S}_k}, DK_{\mathcal{W}}) = H(M)$.

For convenience, we call Π a strongly secure RS-BE scheme if it satisfies the conditions (1') and (2), and just call Π a secure RS-BE scheme if it satisfies Definition 2 (the conditions (1) and (2)). Actually, tight lower bounds on secret keys required for such a strongly secure RS-BE scheme are the same as those required for the secure RS-BE scheme (the bounds will appear in Theorem 1). Therefore, we can obtain the same optimal construction, in the sense that the construction meets equality in every lower bound, which will be proposed in Sect. 4. In addition to this, to deal with RS-BE as natural extension of traditional BE, we consider the above weaker security definition (Definition 2).

3   Tight Lower Bounds on Sizes of Ciphertexts and Secret Keys

In this section, we show lower bounds on the sizes of ciphertexts and secret keys required for a $(\leq n, \leq \omega)$-one-time secure RS-BE scheme. As mentioned in [12,29,33,34], in traditional BE schemes, there is a trade-off between the ciphertext size and the secret key size. RS-BE schemes also have such a trade-off. Although our construction which will be presented in Sect. 4 covers any ciphertext length, we here consider lower bounds on secret-key sizes required for an $(\leq n, \leq \omega)$-one-time secure RS-BE scheme where the ciphertext length is as small as possible. The reason for this is when we consider applying RS-BE to cloud storage, compactness of a ciphertext is one of the most important factors to be taken into account, since in such a scenario, a ciphertext is stored in cloud permanently or for a long-time.

For the above reason, we first investigate the *tight* lower bound on the size of ciphertexts, and then, derive lower bounds on sizes of secret keys under the condition that the ciphertext length is optimal. A lower bound which can be immediately obtained is $H(C_{\mathcal{S}}) \geq H(M)$, and actually, by a simple observation, this bound is proven to be tight. We formally state this as follows.

Proposition 1. *Let Π be an $(\leq n, \leq \omega)$-one-time secure RS-BE scheme. Then, for any $\mathcal{S} \subset \mathcal{U}$, $H(C_{\mathcal{S}}) \geq H(M)$ and there exists a concrete construction which meets this bound with equality.*

Proof. For any $\mathcal{S} \subset \mathcal{U}$ and $U_i \in \mathcal{S}$, we have

$$H(C_{\mathcal{S}}) \geq H(C_{\mathcal{S}} \mid DK_i) \tag{1}$$

$$\geq H(C_{\mathcal{S}} \mid DK_i) - H(C_{\mathcal{S}} \mid DK_i, M) \tag{2}$$

$$= I(C_{\mathcal{S}}; M \mid DK_i) = H(M \mid DK_i) - H(M \mid DK_i, C_{\mathcal{S}}) = H(M),$$

where the last equality follows from independence of M and DK_i and the decryption correctness.

Then, we show a construction which meets this bound with equality. A secret key of the one-time pad is assigned for every possible $\mathcal{S} \subset \mathcal{U}$. Namely, $ek := (\{k_\mathcal{S} \mid \mathcal{S} \subset \mathcal{U}\})$, $dk_i := (k_\emptyset, \{k_\mathcal{S} \mid \mathcal{S} \subset \mathcal{U} \wedge U_i \in \mathcal{S}\})$ $(1 \leq i \leq n)$, and $mk := \{k_\mathcal{S} \mid \mathcal{S} \subset \mathcal{U} \wedge \mathcal{S} \neq \emptyset\}$, where each $k_\mathcal{S}$ is chosen from a finite field uniformly at random. In Enc, for any $\mathcal{S}$, it outputs $c_\mathcal{S} := m + k_\emptyset + k_\mathcal{S}$. In Dec, if $U_i \in \mathcal{S}$, it can output $m = c_\mathcal{S} - k_\emptyset - k_\mathcal{S}$. In Upd, for any $\mathcal{S}$ and $\mathcal{S}'$, it outputs $c_{\mathcal{S}'} := c_\mathcal{S} - k_\mathcal{S} + k_{\mathcal{S}'}$. This construction is $(\leq n, \leq \omega)$-one-time secure since any $\mathcal{W}$ such that $\mathcal{S} \cap \mathcal{W} = \emptyset$ does not have $k_\mathcal{S}$ and SM does not have $k_\emptyset$. □

Next, we derive lower bounds on sizes of secret keys when the ciphertext size is optimal (i.e. the ciphertext length is equal to the plaintext length).

Theorem 1. *Let Π be an $(\leq n, \leq \omega)$-one-time secure RS-BE scheme. Then, the following lower bounds hold under the condition $H(C_\mathcal{S}) = H(M)$ for any $\mathcal{S} \subset \mathcal{U}$:*

$$(i) \ H(EK) \geq \sum_{j=0}^{\omega} \binom{n}{j} H(M),$$

$$(ii) \ H(DK_i) \geq \sum_{j=0}^{\omega} \binom{n-1}{j} H(M) \ \text{for any } i \in \{1, 2, \ldots, n\},$$

$$(iii) \ H(MK) \geq \left(\sum_{j=0}^{\omega} \binom{n}{j} - 1 \right) H(M).$$

Proof. The proof follows from the following lemmas.

Lemma 1. *For any $\mathcal{S} \subset \mathcal{U}$ and any $\mathcal{W} \subset \mathcal{U}$ such that $\mathcal{W} \cap \mathcal{S} = \emptyset$ and $|\mathcal{W}| \leq \omega$, let Y_i $(1 \leq i \leq k)$ be a privileged set such that $Y_i \cap \mathcal{W} \neq \emptyset$. Then, we have $H(C_\mathcal{S} \mid M, C_{Y_1}, \ldots, C_{Y_k}, DK_\mathcal{W}) \geq H(M)$ under the condition $H(C_\mathcal{S}) = H(M)$ for any $\mathcal{S} \subset \mathcal{U}$.*

Proof. From Eqs. (1) and (2) in Theorem 1, and the condition $H(C_\mathcal{S}) = H(M)$, we have $H(C_\mathcal{S} \mid DK_i) = H(C_\mathcal{S} \mid DK_i) - H(C_\mathcal{S} \mid DK_i, M)$ for any $\mathcal{S} \subset \mathcal{U}$ and $U_i \in \mathcal{S}$. Therefore, we have

$$H(C_\mathcal{S} \mid DK_i, M) = 0. \tag{3}$$

For $H(M, C_\mathcal{S}, C_{Y_1}, \ldots, C_{Y_k} \mid DK_\mathcal{W})$, we have

$$
\begin{aligned}
H(M, &C_\mathcal{S}, C_{Y_1}, \ldots, C_{Y_k} \mid DK_\mathcal{W}) \\
&= H(C_\mathcal{S} \mid DK_\mathcal{W}) + H(M \mid DK_\mathcal{W}, C_\mathcal{S}) + H(C_{Y_1}, \ldots, C_{Y_k} \mid DK_\mathcal{W}, C_\mathcal{S}, M) \\
&= H(C_\mathcal{S} \mid DK_\mathcal{W}) + H(M) + H(C_{Y_1}, \ldots, C_{Y_k} \mid DK_\mathcal{W}, C_\mathcal{S}, M) \tag{4} \\
&= H(C_\mathcal{S} \mid DK_\mathcal{W}) + H(M), \tag{5}
\end{aligned}
$$

where Eq. (4) follows from the condition (1) of Definition 2, and Eq. (5) follows from Eq. (3) (i.e. $H(C_{Y_j} \mid DK_\mathcal{W}, M) = 0$) since $Y_j \cap \mathcal{W} \neq \emptyset$ for any Y_j $(1 \leq j \leq k)$.

On the other hand, for $H(M, C_\mathcal{S}, C_{Y_1}, \ldots, C_{Y_k} \mid DK_W)$, we have

$$
\begin{aligned}
H(M, &C_\mathcal{S}, C_{Y_1}, \ldots, C_{Y_k} \mid DK_W) \\
&= H(M \mid DK_W) + H(C_{Y_1}, \ldots, C_{Y_k} \mid DK_W, M) \\
&\qquad\qquad\qquad + H(C_\mathcal{S} \mid DK_W, M, C_{Y_1}, \ldots, C_{Y_k}) \\
&= H(M) + H(C_\mathcal{S} \mid DK_W, M, C_{Y_1}, \ldots, C_{Y_k}), \qquad\qquad (6)
\end{aligned}
$$

where Eq. (6) follows from independence of M and DK_W and the same reason for Eq. (5).

Hence, from Eqs. (5) and (6), we have

$$
H(C_\mathcal{S} \mid DK_W, M, C_{Y_1}, \ldots, C_{Y_k}) = H(C_\mathcal{S} \mid DK_W). \qquad (7)
$$

In the following, we show $H(C_\mathcal{S} \mid DK_W) \geq H(M)$.
For $H(M, C_\mathcal{S} \mid DK_\mathcal{S}, DK_W, EK)$, we have

$$
\begin{aligned}
H(M, &C_\mathcal{S} \mid DK_\mathcal{S}, DK_W, EK) \\
&= H(C_\mathcal{S} \mid DK_\mathcal{S}, DK_W, EK) + H(M \mid DK_\mathcal{S}, DK_W, EK, C_\mathcal{S}) \\
&= H(C_\mathcal{S} \mid DK_\mathcal{S}, DK_W, EK), \qquad\qquad\qquad\qquad\qquad (8)
\end{aligned}
$$

where Eq. (8) follows from the decryption correctness (i.e. $H(M \mid DK_\mathcal{S}, C_\mathcal{S}) = 0$).
On the other hand, for $H(M, C_\mathcal{S} \mid DK_\mathcal{S}, DK_W, EK)$, we have

$$
\begin{aligned}
H(M, &C_\mathcal{S} \mid DK_\mathcal{S}, DK_W, EK) \\
&= H(M \mid DK_\mathcal{S}, DK_W, EK) + H(C_\mathcal{S} \mid DK_\mathcal{S}, DK_W, EK, M) \\
&= H(M \mid DK_\mathcal{S}, DK_W, EK), \qquad\qquad\qquad\qquad\qquad (9)
\end{aligned}
$$

where Eq. (9) follows from the algorithm Enc (i.e. $H(C_\mathcal{S} \mid EK, M) = 0$).
Hence, we have

$$
\begin{aligned}
H(C_\mathcal{S} \mid DK_W) &\geq H(C_\mathcal{S} \mid DK_\mathcal{S}, DK_W, EK) \\
&= H(M \mid DK_\mathcal{S}, DK_W, EK) \qquad\qquad (10) \\
&= H(M), \qquad\qquad\qquad\qquad\qquad\quad (11)
\end{aligned}
$$

where Eq. (10) follows from Eqs. (8) and (9), and Eq. (11) follows from independence of M and $(EK, DK_1, \ldots, DK_n)$.

From Eqs. (7) and (11), we have $H(C_\mathcal{S} \mid M, C_{Y_1}, \ldots, C_{Y_k}, DK_W) \geq H(M)$.
$\qquad\qquad\qquad\qquad\qquad\qquad\qquad\qquad\qquad\qquad\qquad\qquad\qquad\qquad\square$

Lemma 2. *We have $H(EK) \geq \sum_{j=0}^{\omega} \binom{n}{j} H(M)$ under the condition $H(C_\mathcal{S}) = H(M)$ for any $\mathcal{S} \subset \mathcal{U}$.*

Proof. Let $\mathscr{W} := \{W \subset \mathcal{U} \mid |W| \leq \omega\} = \{W_1, \ldots, W_t\}$ be the family of all possible sets of colluders, where $t = \sum_{j=0}^{\omega} \binom{n}{j}$. Moreover, let $\mathscr{S}(\mathscr{W}) := \{\mathcal{S}_1, \ldots, \mathcal{S}_t\}$, where $\mathcal{S}_i = \mathcal{U} \setminus \mathcal{W}_i$ such that $\mathcal{W}_i \in \mathscr{W}$ $(1 \leq i \leq t)$. Without loss of generality, $|\mathcal{S}_1| \geq \cdots \geq |\mathcal{S}_t|$. Then, we have

$$H(EK) = H(EK \mid M) \tag{12}$$
$$\geq I(EK; C_{\mathcal{S}_1}, \ldots, C_{\mathcal{S}_t} \mid M)$$
$$= H(C_{\mathcal{S}_1}, \ldots, C_{\mathcal{S}_t} \mid M) - H(C_{\mathcal{S}_1}, \ldots, C_{\mathcal{S}_t} \mid M, EK)$$
$$= H(C_{\mathcal{S}_1}, \ldots, C_{\mathcal{S}_t} \mid M) \tag{13}$$
$$= \sum_{j=1}^{t} H(C_{\mathcal{S}_j} \mid M, C_{\mathcal{S}_1}, \ldots, C_{\mathcal{S}_{j-1}})$$
$$\geq \sum_{j=1}^{t} H(C_{\mathcal{S}_j} \mid M, C_{\mathcal{S}_1}, \ldots, C_{\mathcal{S}_{j-1}}, DK_{\mathcal{W}_j})$$
$$\geq \sum_{j=0}^{\omega} \binom{n}{j} H(M), \tag{14}$$

where Eq. (12) follows from independence of M and EK, Eq. (13) follows from the algorithm Enc (i.e. $H(C_{\mathcal{S}_i} \mid EK, M) = 0$ $(1 \leq i \leq t)$), and Eq. (14) follows from Lemma 1. $\square$

Lemma 3. *For any* $i \in \{1, \ldots, n\}$, *we have* $H(DK_i) \geq \sum_{j=0}^{\omega} \binom{n-1}{j} H(M)$ *under the condition* $H(C_{\mathcal{S}}) = H(M)$ *for any* $\mathcal{S} \subset \mathcal{U}$.

Proof. Let $\mathscr{W}^{(i)} := \{\mathcal{W} \subset \mathcal{U} \setminus \{U_i\} \mid |\mathcal{W}| \leq \omega\} = \{\mathcal{W}_1, \ldots, \mathcal{W}_\ell\}$ be the family of all possible sets of colluders except for sets of colluders containing U_i, where $\ell = \sum_{j=0}^{\omega} \binom{n-1}{j}$. Moreover, let $\mathscr{S}(\mathscr{W}^{(i)}) := \{\mathcal{S}_1, \ldots, \mathcal{S}_\ell\}$, where $\mathcal{S}_i = \mathcal{U} \setminus \mathcal{W}_i$ such that $\mathcal{W}_i \in \mathscr{W}^{(i)}$ $(1 \leq i \leq \ell)$. Without loss of generality, $|\mathcal{S}_1| \geq \cdots \geq |\mathcal{S}_\ell|$. We note $U_i \in \mathcal{S}$ for any $\mathcal{S} \in \mathscr{S}(\mathscr{W}^{(i)})$. Then, we have

$$H(DK_i) = H(DK_i \mid M) \tag{15}$$
$$\geq I(DK_i; C_{\mathcal{S}_1}, \ldots, C_{\mathcal{S}_\ell} \mid M)$$
$$= H(C_{\mathcal{S}_1}, \ldots, C_{\mathcal{S}_\ell} \mid M) - H(C_{\mathcal{S}_1}, \ldots, C_{\mathcal{S}_\ell} \mid M, DK_i)$$
$$= H(C_{\mathcal{S}_1}, \ldots, C_{\mathcal{S}_\ell} \mid M) \tag{16}$$
$$= \sum_{j=1}^{\ell} H(C_{\mathcal{S}_j} \mid M, C_{\mathcal{S}_1}, \ldots, C_{\mathcal{S}_{j-1}})$$
$$\geq \sum_{j=1}^{\ell} H(C_{\mathcal{S}_j} \mid M, C_{\mathcal{S}_1}, \ldots, C_{\mathcal{S}_{j-1}}, DK_{\mathcal{W}_j})$$
$$\geq \sum_{j=0}^{\omega} \binom{n-1}{j} H(M), \tag{17}$$

where Eq. (15) follows from independence of M and DK_i, Eq. (16) follows from Eq. (3) in Lemma 1 (i.e. $H(C_{\mathcal{S}_j} \mid DK_i, M) = 0$ $(1 \leq j \leq \ell)$), and Eq. (17) follows from Lemma 1. $\square$

Lemma 4. *We have* $H(MK) \geq \left(\sum_{j=0}^{\omega} \binom{n}{j} - 1\right) H(M)$ *under the condition* $H(C_{\mathcal{S}}) = H(M)$ *for any* $\mathcal{S} \subset \mathcal{U}$.

Proof. Let $\mathscr{W}$ and $\mathscr{S}(\mathscr{W})$ be the same as those in Lemma 2. Then, we have

$$
\begin{aligned}
H(MK) &\geq H(MK \mid C_{\mathcal{S}_1}) \geq I(MK; C_{\mathcal{S}_2}, \ldots, C_{\mathcal{S}_t} \mid C_{\mathcal{S}_1}) \\
&= H(C_{\mathcal{S}_2}, \ldots, C_{\mathcal{S}_t} \mid C_{\mathcal{S}_1}) - H(C_{\mathcal{S}_2}, \ldots, C_{\mathcal{S}_t} \mid C_{\mathcal{S}_1}, MK) \\
&= H(C_{\mathcal{S}_2}, \ldots, C_{\mathcal{S}_t} \mid C_{\mathcal{S}_1}) \qquad\qquad\qquad\qquad\qquad (18) \\
&= \sum_{j=2}^{t} H(C_{\mathcal{S}_j} \mid C_{\mathcal{S}_1}, \ldots, C_{\mathcal{S}_{j-1}}) \\
&\geq \sum_{j=2}^{t} H(C_{\mathcal{S}_j} \mid M, C_{\mathcal{S}_1}, \ldots, C_{\mathcal{S}_{j-1}}, DK_{\mathcal{W}_j}) \\
&\geq \left(\sum_{j=0}^{\omega} \binom{n}{j} - 1\right) H(M), \qquad\qquad\qquad\qquad (19)
\end{aligned}
$$

where Eq. (18) follows from the algorithm *Upd* (i.e. $H(C_{\mathcal{S}_i} \mid C_{\mathcal{S}_1}, MK) = 0$ ($2 \leq i \leq t$)), and Eq. (19) follows from Lemma 1. $\qquad\square$

Now, the proof of Theorem 1 is completed. $\qquad\square$

As we will see in the next section, the above lower bounds are tight since our construction will meet all the above bounds with equalities. Therefore, we define optimality of constructions of RS-BE as follows.

Definition 3 (Optimality). *A construction of an* $(\leq n, \leq \omega)$-*one-time secure RS-BE scheme is said to be* optimal *if it meets equality in every bound of (i)–(iii) in Theorem 1.*

In a similar way, we can also derive tight lower bounds on secret keys required for another class of RS-BE schemes, called $(t, \leq \omega)$-one-time secure RS-BE schemes [16,26,29,33], in which the number of privileged users is constant in all time periods, and show an optimal construction under this condition (see the full version of this paper [45] for details).

4   Construction

In this section, we propose a construction of an $(\leq n, \leq \omega)$-one-time secure RS-BE scheme with a trade-off between ciphertext sizes and secret-key sizes. Namely, we construct an $(\leq n, \leq \omega)$-one-time secure RS-BE scheme with efficient secret-key sizes by allowing a ciphertext to become larger, though we considered lower bounds on the secret-key sizes only when the ciphertext size is equal to the plaintext size in the previous section. Specifically, we focus on an $(\leq n, \leq \omega)$-one-time secure RS-BE scheme where the ciphertext size is equal to integer multiple of the plaintext size. More precisely, we assume that the maximum ciphertext size is δ times as large as the plaintext size, and we parameterize such $\delta \in \{1, 2, \ldots, n\}$ as follows.

Definition 4. *For an* $(\leq n, \leq \omega)$-*one-time secure (RS-)BE scheme* Π, *we define*

$$\delta := \frac{\max_{\mathcal{S} \subset \mathcal{U}} \log |\mathcal{C}_{\mathcal{S}}|}{\log |\mathcal{M}|}.$$

Then, Π *is said to be* $(\leq n, \leq \omega; \delta)$-*one-time secure.*

To the best of our knowledge, there are only two ways of efficient constructing unconditionally secure BE schemes with such a trade-off: One is *the block-design approach* for $(t, \leq \omega; \delta)$-one-time secure BE schemes, which was proposed by Blundo et al. [12]; and the other is *the multi-KPSs approach* for $(\leq n, \leq \omega; \delta)$-one-time secure BE schemes, which was recently proposed by Watanabe and Shikata [46]. The block design approach in [12] can be applied to $(t, \leq \omega; \delta)$-one-time secure BE schemes since the cardinality of $\mathcal{S}$ is always exactly t, and therefore, it seems difficult to apply the former technique for constructing $(\leq n, \leq \omega; \delta)$-one-time secure BE schemes. Therefore, we utilize the latter technique, but improve it by using polynomials over a finite field. Before explaining their original construction, we briefly explain a key predistribution system (KPS), which is a crucial primitive to their construction.

KPS [9,30]. Suppose that there are a trusted authority (TA) and n users $\mathcal{U} := \{U_1, U_2, \ldots, U_n\}$. TA generates initial secret keys for each user, and distributes them securely. *Any subset* $\mathcal{S}$ *of* $\mathcal{U}$ *can share a session key by using their own secret keys in a non-interactive way.* A KPS is said to be an $(\leq n, \leq \omega)$-KPS if *any at most* ω *users not in the subset cannot get any information on the session key.*

The idea of their construction is as follows. For $(\leq n, \leq \omega; \delta)$-one-time secure BE schemes where the maximum ciphertext size is δ times as large as the plaintext size, the user set $\mathcal{U}$ is split into δ subsets $\mathcal{U}_1, \mathcal{U}_2, \ldots, \mathcal{U}_{\delta}$ such that $|\mathcal{U}_1| \geq |\mathcal{U}_2| \geq \cdots \geq |\mathcal{U}_{\delta}|$. Then, we apply an $(\leq |\mathcal{U}_j|, \leq \omega_j)$-KPS to each subset $\mathcal{U}_j$, where $\omega_j := \min\{|\mathcal{U}_j| - 1, \omega\}$. The encryption procedures are just generating session keys for each privileged subset $\mathcal{S}_j := \mathcal{U}_j \cap \mathcal{S}$ and computing at most δ one-time pads of a plaintext by using each session key. They showed the optimal condition of $(|\mathcal{U}_1|, |\mathcal{U}_2|, \ldots, |\mathcal{U}_{\delta}|)$ for minimizing secret-key sizes as follows:

Proposition 2 (Theorem 2 and Corollary 2 in [46]). *Let* $a := \lfloor n/\delta \rfloor$, $\delta_2 := n \bmod \delta$, *and* $\delta_1 := \delta - \delta_2$. *When we apply an optimal construction of each underlying KPS (e.g., the Fiat–Naor KPS [21]) to the above* $(\leq n, \leq \omega; \delta)$-*one-time secure BE scheme, then sizes of the secret keys are minimized when* $|\mathcal{U}_1| = |\mathcal{U}_2| = \cdots = |\mathcal{U}_{\delta_1}| = a$ *and* $|\mathcal{U}_{\delta_1+1}| = |\mathcal{U}_{\delta_1+2}| = \cdots = |\mathcal{U}_{\delta}| = a + 1$. *Namely, we have*

$$\text{(i) } \log |\mathcal{EK}| = \left(\delta_1 \sum_{j=0}^{\tilde{\omega}} \binom{a}{j} + \delta_2 \sum_{j=0}^{\hat{\omega}} \binom{a+1}{j} \right) \log |\mathcal{M}|,$$

$$\text{(ii) } \sum_{i=1}^{n} \log |\mathcal{DK}_i| = \left(\delta_1 a \sum_{j=0}^{\tilde{\omega}} \binom{a-1}{j} + \delta_2 (a+1) \sum_{j=0}^{\hat{\omega}} \binom{a}{j} \right) \log |\mathcal{M}|,$$

where $\tilde{\omega} := \min\{a - 1, \omega\}$ *and* $\hat{\omega} := \min\{a, \omega\}$.

We construct an $(\leq n, \leq \omega; \delta)$-one-time secure RS-BE scheme based on the above construction with a certain improvement, and give the idea as follows. We here assume the case that $a := n/\delta \in \mathbb{N}$ for simplicity. Each user subset can be expressed as $\mathcal{U}_j := \{U_1^{(j)}, U_2^{(j)}, \ldots, U_a^{(j)}\} = \{U_{(j-1)a+1}, \ldots, U_{ja}\}$ $(1 \leq j \leq \delta)$, where $U_i^{(j)} := U_{(j-1)a+i}$, and we define a set $\widetilde{\mathcal{U}} := \{V_1, V_2, \ldots, V_a\}$. For setup, an $(\leq a, \leq \tilde{\omega})$-KPS for $\widetilde{\mathcal{U}}$ is invoked δ times, where $\tilde{\omega} := \min\{a-1, \omega\}$, and we write $(dk_1^{(j)}, dk_2^{(j)}, \ldots, dk_a^{(j)})$ as j-th output of the KPS. Namely, for each $i \in \{1, 2, \ldots, a\}$, $dk_i^{(1)}, dk_i^{(2)}, \ldots,$ and $dk_i^{(\delta)}$ are secret keys for V_i but completely independent of each other. Therefore, we correlate these keys $(dk_i^{(1)}, dk_i^{(2)}, \ldots, dk_i^{(\delta)})$ with each other by using polynomials over a finite field, and each $dk_i^{(j)}$ is assigned to a secret key for $U_i^{(j)}$. This is an improved point as mentioned earlier, and this leads to the success of reducing sizes of an encryption key (and maintenance key).

The detailed construction of an $(\leq n, \leq \omega; \delta)$-one-time secure RS-BE scheme $\Pi = (Setup, Enc, Dec, Upd)$ is as follows.

1. $(ek, mk, dk_1, \ldots, dk_n) \leftarrow Setup()$: Let q be a prime power such that $q > n$, and $\mathbb{F}_q$ be a finite field with q elements. Let $a := \lfloor n/\delta \rfloor$, $\delta_2 := n \bmod \delta$, and $\delta_1 := \delta - \delta_2$. Without loss of generality, let $\mathcal{U}_j := \{U_1^{(j)}, U_2^{(j)}, \ldots, U_a^{(j)}\} = \{U_{(j-1)a+1}, \ldots, U_{ja}\}$ for $j \in \{1, 2, \ldots, \delta_1\}$, where $U_i^{(j)} := U_{(j-1)a+i}$, and $\mathcal{U}_j := \{U_1^{(j)}, U_2^{(j)}, \ldots, U_{a+1}^{(j)}\} = \{U_{\delta_1 a + (j-\delta_1-1)(a+1)+1}, \ldots, U_{\delta_1 a + (j-\delta_1)(a+1)}\}$ for $j \in \{\delta_1 + 1, \delta_1 + 2, \ldots, \delta\}$, where $U_i^{(j)} := U_{\delta_1 a + (j-\delta_1-1)(a+1)+i}$, respectively.[3] Consider user sets $\widetilde{\mathcal{U}} := \{V_1, V_2, \ldots, V_a\}$ and $\widehat{\mathcal{U}} := \widetilde{\mathcal{U}} \cup \{V_{a+1}\}$, and define the following families of subsets:

$$\widetilde{\mathscr{W}} := \{W \subset \widetilde{\mathcal{U}} \mid |W| \leq \tilde{\omega}\},$$
$$\widetilde{\mathscr{W}}^{(i)} := \{W \subset \widetilde{\mathcal{U}} \mid W \in \widetilde{\mathscr{W}} \wedge V_i \notin W\},$$
$$\widetilde{\mathscr{W}}(\mathcal{S} \subset \widetilde{\mathcal{U}}) := \{W \in \widetilde{\mathscr{W}} \mid |W| = \min\{\tilde{\omega}, a - |\mathcal{S}|\}\},$$
$$\widehat{\mathscr{W}} := \{W \subset \widehat{\mathcal{U}} \mid |W| \leq \hat{\omega}\},$$
$$\widehat{\mathscr{W}}^{(i)} := \{W \subset \widehat{\mathcal{U}} \mid W \in \widehat{\mathscr{W}} \wedge V_i \notin W\},$$
$$\widehat{\mathscr{W}}(\mathcal{S} \subset \widehat{\mathcal{U}}) := \{W \in \widehat{\mathscr{W}} \mid |W| = \min\{\hat{\omega}, a + 1 - |\mathcal{S}|\}\},$$

where $\tilde{\omega} := \min\{a-1, \omega\}$ and $\hat{\omega} := \min\{a, \omega\}$. Let $\tilde{k} := \min\{\omega, \delta - 1\}$ and $\hat{k} := \{\omega, \delta_2 - 1\}$. Choose two kinds of polynomials over $\mathbb{F}_q$ uniformly at random as follows:

$$f_W(x) := r_W^{(0)} + r_W^{(1)} x + \cdots + r_W^{(\tilde{k})} x^{\tilde{k}} \text{ for every } W \in \widetilde{\mathscr{W}},$$
$$f_W(x) := r_W^{(0)} + r_W^{(1)} x + \cdots + r_W^{(\hat{k})} x^{\hat{k}} \text{ for every } W \in \widehat{\mathscr{W}} \setminus \widetilde{\mathscr{W}}.$$

---

[3] For example, when $n = 8$ and $\delta = 3$, then $\mathcal{U}_1 := \{U_1^{(1)}, U_2^{(1)}\} = \{U_1, U_2\}$, $\mathcal{U}_2 := \{U_1^{(2)}, U_2^{(2)}, U_3^{(2)}\} = \{U_3, U_4, U_5\}$, and $\mathcal{U}_3 := \{U_1^{(3)}, U_2^{(3)}, U_3^{(3)}\} = \{U_6, U_7, U_8\}$.

Furthermore, also compute $f'_\emptyset(x) := f_\emptyset(x) - r_\emptyset^{(0)}$. Set $ek := \{f_W(x) \mid W \in \widehat{\mathscr{W}}\}$, $mk := \{f_W(x) \mid W \in \widehat{\mathscr{W}} \setminus \{\emptyset\}\} \cup \{f'_\emptyset(x)\}$. For every $U_h = U_i^{(j)}$, set $dk_h = dk_i^{(j)} := \{f_W(j) \mid W \in \widehat{\mathscr{W}}^{(i)}\}$ if $1 \leq h \leq \delta_1 a$, or $dk_h = dk_i^{(j)} := \{f_W(j) \mid W \in \widehat{\mathscr{W}}^{(i)}\}$ if $\delta_1 a + 1 \leq h \leq n$.[4] Output $(ek, mk, dk_1, \ldots, dk_n)$.

2. $c_{\mathcal{S}} \leftarrow Enc(ek, m, \mathcal{S})$: For a plaintext $m \in \mathbb{F}_q$, compute as follows. For every j such that $1 \leq j \leq \delta_1$, let $\mathcal{S}_j := \{V_i \in \widetilde{\mathcal{U}} \mid U_i^{(j)} \in \mathcal{S} \cap \mathcal{U}_j\}$. For every $\mathcal{S}_j$ such that $\mathcal{S}_j \neq \emptyset$, compute

$$c_j := m + f_\emptyset(j) + \sum_{W \in \widehat{\mathscr{W}}(\mathcal{S}_j)} f_W(j).$$

Similarly, for every j such that $\delta_1 + 1 \leq j \leq \delta$, let $\mathcal{S}_j := \{V_i \in \widehat{\mathcal{U}} \mid U_i^{(j)} \in \mathcal{S} \cap \mathcal{U}_j\}$. For every $\mathcal{S}_j$ such that $\mathcal{S}_j \neq \emptyset$, compute

$$c_j := m + f_\emptyset(j) + \sum_{W \in \widehat{\mathscr{W}}(\mathcal{S}_j)} f_W(j).$$

Output $c_{\mathcal{S}} := \{c_j\}_{\mathcal{S}_j \neq \emptyset}$.

3. m or $\perp \leftarrow Dec(dk_h, c_{\mathcal{S}}, \mathcal{S}, U_h)$: If $U_h \notin \mathcal{S}$, output $\perp$. Otherwise, suppose that $U_h = U_i^{(j)} \in \mathcal{U}_j$. If $j \leq \delta_1$, let $\mathcal{S}_j := \{V_i \in \widetilde{\mathcal{U}} \mid U_i^{(j)} \in \mathcal{U}_j \cap \mathcal{S}\}$, and output $m = c_j - f_\emptyset(j) - \sum_{W \in \widehat{\mathscr{W}}(\mathcal{S}_j)} f_W(j)$. Otherwise, let $\mathcal{S}_j := \{V_i \in \widehat{\mathcal{U}} \mid U_i^{(j)} \in \mathcal{U}_j \cap \mathcal{S}\}$, and output $m = c_j - f_\emptyset(j) - \sum_{W \in \widehat{\mathscr{W}}(\mathcal{S}_j)} f_W(j)$.

4. $c_{\mathcal{S}'}$ or $\perp \leftarrow Upd(mk, c_{\mathcal{S}}, \mathcal{S}, \mathcal{S}')$: Without loss of generality, choose some $c_j \in c_{\mathcal{S}}$ such that $|\mathcal{U}_j| = a$. Compute $c_\emptyset := c_j - f'_\emptyset(j) - \sum_{W \in \widehat{\mathscr{W}}(\mathcal{S}_j)} f_W(j) = m + r_\emptyset^{(0)}$, where $\mathcal{S}_j := \{V_i \in \widetilde{\mathcal{U}} \mid U_i^{(j)} \in \mathcal{S} \cap \mathcal{U}_j\}$. Note that $c_\emptyset$ can be computed by choosing c_j such that $|\mathcal{U}_j| = a + 1$. for every j such that $1 \leq j \leq \delta_1$, let $\mathcal{S}'_j := \{V_i \in \widetilde{\mathcal{U}} \mid U_i^{(j)} \in \mathcal{S}' \cap \mathcal{U}_j\}$. If $\mathcal{S}'_j \neq \emptyset$, compute $c_j := c_\emptyset + f'_\emptyset(j) + \sum_{W \in \widehat{\mathscr{W}}(\mathcal{S}'_j)} f_W(j)$. For every j such that $\delta_1 + 1 \leq j \leq \delta$, let $\mathcal{S}'_j := \{V_i \in \widehat{\mathcal{U}} \mid U_i^{(j)} \in \mathcal{S}' \cap \mathcal{U}_j\}$. If $\mathcal{S}'_j \neq \emptyset$, compute $c_j := c_\emptyset + f'_\emptyset(j) + \sum_{W \in \widehat{\mathscr{W}}(\mathcal{S}'_j)} f_W(j)$. Output $c_{\mathcal{S}} := \{c_j\}_{\mathcal{S}'_j \neq \emptyset}$.

We can easily see that the above construction satisfies the correctness. We show the following theorem.

Theorem 2. *The resulting RS-BE scheme Π is $(\leq n, \leq \omega; \delta)$-one-time secure. In particular, Π is optimal when $\delta = 1$.*

Proof. First, we show the above construction meets the condition (1) in Definition 2. Without loss of generality, we consider $|\mathcal{S}| = n - \omega$ and $|\mathcal{W}| = \omega$. Let $\mathcal{S}_j := \mathcal{U}_j \cap \mathcal{S}$ and $\mathcal{W}_j := \mathcal{U}_j \setminus \mathcal{S}_j$. As in the Fiat–Naor KPS [21], we can easily prove that in each subset $\mathcal{U}_j$, $\mathcal{W}_j$ cannot obtain any information

---

[4] For readability, we consider $1, 2, \ldots, \delta$ denote elements of $\mathbb{F}_q$.

on m from c_j since they do not have at least one randomness $f_\mathcal{W}(j)$, where $\mathcal{W} := \{V_i \in \tilde{\mathcal{U}} \mid U_i^{(j)} \in \mathcal{W}_j\}$, used for the ciphertext c_j. Next, we prove that $\mathcal{W}_j$ cannot compute such $f_\mathcal{W}(j)$ with decryption keys of other colluders (i.e., $\mathcal{W}_1, \ldots, \mathcal{W}_{j-1}, \mathcal{W}_{j+1}, \ldots, \mathcal{W}_\delta$). There are the following three cases: (i) $\omega < \delta_2 < \delta$; (ii) $\delta_2 \le \omega < \delta$; and (iii) $\delta_2 < \delta \le \omega$. We here consider the cases (i) and (iii). (i) For every $\mathcal{W} \in \widetilde{\mathcal{W}}$, the colluders can get at most ω values of the polynomial $f_\mathcal{W}(x)$. However, they cannot guess at least one coefficient of $f_\mathcal{W}(x)$ with probability larger than $1/q$ since the degree of $f_\mathcal{W}(x)$ is ω. Furthermore, for every $\mathcal{W} \in \widehat{\mathcal{W}} \setminus \widetilde{\mathcal{W}}$, the colluders can also get at most ω values of the polynomial $f_\mathcal{W}(x)$, and hence they cannot guess at least one coefficient of $f_\mathcal{W}(x)$ with probability larger than $1/q$ for the same reason. (iii) The colluders may get δ values of the polynomial $f_\mathcal{W}(x)$ for some $\mathcal{W} \in \widetilde{\mathcal{W}}$, and then they can guess the polynomial. However, they cannot get any new information from this since they already have all useful information (i.e., $f_\mathcal{W}(1), f_\mathcal{W}(2), \ldots, f_\mathcal{W}(\delta)$). If the colluders can also get at most $\delta - 1$ values of the polynomial $f_\mathcal{W}(x)$ for some $\mathcal{W} \in \widetilde{\mathcal{W}}$, they cannot guess at least one coefficient of $f_\mathcal{W}(x)$ with probability larger than $1/q$ the degree of $f_\mathcal{W}(x)$ is $\delta - 1$. The same holds for every $\mathcal{W} \in \widehat{\mathcal{W}} \setminus \widetilde{\mathcal{W}}$. We can prove the case (ii) in a way similar to the above cases. Hence, for any $\mathcal{S} \subset \mathcal{U}$, and any $\mathcal{W} \subset \mathcal{U}$ such that $\mathcal{S} \cap \mathcal{W} = \emptyset$ and $|\mathcal{W}| \le \omega$, $H(M \mid C_\mathcal{S}, DK_\mathcal{W}) = H(M)$.

Next, we show the above construction meets the condition (2) in Definition 2. $r_\emptyset^{(0)}$ is always used for computing c_j for any $\mathcal{S} \subset \mathcal{U}$ and any $j \in \{1, 2, \ldots, \delta\}$, whereas SM does not have $r_\emptyset^{(0)}$. Hence, he can only guess m randomly as in the one-time pad. Thus, for any $\mathcal{S} \subset \mathcal{U}$, $H(M \mid C_\mathcal{S}, MK) = H(M)$.

Moreover, it is straightforward to see that the above construction is optimal when $\delta = 1$. $\square$

Corollary 1. *The sizes of secret keys in the above construction are as follows:*

$$(i) \ \log |\mathcal{EK}| = \left((\tilde{k} - \hat{k}) \sum_{j=0}^{\tilde{\omega}} \binom{a}{j} + (\hat{k} + 1) \sum_{j=0}^{\hat{\omega}} \binom{a+1}{j} \right) \log |\mathcal{M}|,$$

$$(ii) \ \sum_{i=1}^{n} \log |\mathcal{DK}_i| = \left(\delta_1 a \sum_{j=0}^{\tilde{\omega}} \binom{a-1}{j} + \delta_2 (a+1) \sum_{j=0}^{\hat{\omega}} \binom{a}{j} \right) \log |\mathcal{M}|,$$

$$(iii) \ \log |\mathcal{MK}| = \left((\tilde{k} - \hat{k}) \sum_{j=0}^{\tilde{\omega}} \binom{a}{j} + (\hat{k} + 1) \sum_{j=0}^{\hat{\omega}} \binom{a+1}{j} - 1 \right) \log |\mathcal{M}|.$$

Note that $\tilde{k} := \min\{\omega, \delta - 1\}$, $\hat{k} := \min\{\omega, \delta_2 - 1\}$, $\tilde{\omega} := \min\{a - 1, \omega\}$, *and* $\hat{\omega} := \min\{a, \omega\}$.

This corollary means that the larger the ciphertext size (i.e., δ) is, the smaller sizes of the encryption and maintenance keys are. More precisely, our construction is more efficient than the original construction in [46] when $\delta > \omega$. On the other hand, the decryption-key size is the same as that in [46] (i.e., a construction from δ_1 ($\le a, \le \tilde{\omega}$)-KPS and δ_2 ($\le a + 1, \le \hat{\omega}$)-KPS). Therefore, in our construction we have to assume $\delta_1\tilde{\omega} + \delta_2\hat{\omega}$ colluders in total, though there are actually only ω colluders at most. Therefore, δ must satisfy $\omega \geq \delta_1\tilde{\omega} + \delta_2\hat{\omega}$ for a non-redundant construction in the sense of the number of colluders. Since it holds $\omega \geq \delta_1(a-1) + \delta_2 a = \delta a - \delta_1 = \delta(\frac{n-(n \bmod \delta)}{\delta}) - \delta_1 = n - \delta$, such a non-redundant RS-BE scheme can be achieved when $\delta = 1$ or $\delta \geq n - \omega$. Hence, in terms of the encryption and maintenance key sizes, our construction is more efficient than a construction based on [46] if $n \geq 2\omega+1$ especially when $\delta \geq n-\omega$. Note that by setting mk to an empty string, the above construction is also the most efficient $(\leq n, \leq \omega; \delta)$-one-time secure BE scheme ever.

Remark 3. Our construction might be inappropriate for a scenario where the plaintext size is small but there are a huge number of users, since $|\mathcal{M}| = \mathbb{F}_q$, where q is $q > n$. We can then avoid such restriction by combining the combinatorial construction technique by Fiat and Naor [21], the multi-KPSs-construction technique by Watanabe and Shiakta [46], and the above construction. Specifically, we instantiate each underlying KPS of the BE scheme in [46] by the KPS construction by Fiat and Naor [21] over $\mathbb{F}_q$, and then propose the *Upd* algorithm based on the above construction. We would like to stress that although this construction is applicable for arbitrary $|\mathcal{M}|$ and n, the sizes of secret keys (in particular, encryption and maintenance keys) of this construction are larger than those of the proposed construction in this section when $\delta > \omega$. For the detailed construction, see Appendix C.

5   Robust Construction

We now consider a scenario in which a maliciously behaving storage manager can try to modify the encrypted plaintext. This is related to *non-malleability* in the context of ordinary encryption. In an RS-BE scheme, malleability may cause a serious problem since the ciphertext is periodically updated, but an improper update carried out by a malicious storage manager may not be immediately detectable by the users. More specifically, we consider security against a storage manager who tries to modify a ciphertext so that a user in the privileged set obtains a modified plaintext which differs from an original plaintext encrypted by the sender. In addition to this, since ciphertexts of RS-BE schemes are stored in external storage such as cloud storage (in other words, the ciphertexts are accessible at any time), we should also consider security against such a modification attack by colluders. Formally, we consider two types of adversaries as in Definition 2, and define the robustness of RS-BE as follows.

Definition 5 (Robust RS-BE). *Let Π be an $(\leq n, \leq \omega)$-one-time secure RS-BE scheme. Π is said to be γ-robust if $\max\{P_1, P_2\} \leq \gamma$, where P_1 and P_2 are defined as follows:*

(1) For any $\mathcal{S}_1, \ldots, \mathcal{S}_k \subset \mathcal{U}$ $(1 \leq k \leq 2^n)$, any $U_i \in \mathcal{S}_k$, and any $\mathcal{W} \subset \mathcal{U}$ such that $\left(\bigcup_{i=1}^k \mathcal{S}_i\right) \cap \mathcal{W} = \emptyset$ and $|\mathcal{W}| \leq \omega$, we define $P_1(\mathcal{S}_1, \ldots, \mathcal{S}_k, U_i, \mathcal{W})$ as:

$$P_1(\mathcal{S}_1, \ldots, \mathcal{S}_k, U_i, \mathcal{W}) :=$$

$$\max_{c'_{\mathcal{S}_k}} \max_{c_{\mathcal{S}_1}, \ldots, c_{\mathcal{S}_k}} \max_{dk_{\mathcal{W}}} \Pr(Dec(dk_i, c'_{\mathcal{S}_k}, \mathcal{S}_k, U_i) \notin \{m, \bot\} \mid c_{\mathcal{S}_1}, \ldots, c_{\mathcal{S}_k}, dk_{\mathcal{W}}),$$

where $c_{\mathcal{S}_j} = Enc(ek, m, \mathcal{S}_j)$ $(1 \leq j \leq k)$. *Note that* $Enc(ek, m, \mathcal{S}_{j+1}) = Upd(mk, Enc(ek, m, \mathcal{S}_j), \mathcal{S}_j, \mathcal{S}_{j+1})$ *for any* $\mathcal{S}_j, \mathcal{S}_{j+1}$ $(1 \leq j \leq k-1)$ *(the updating correctness).* P_1 *is defined as* $P_1 := \max\limits_{\mathcal{S}_1, \ldots, \mathcal{S}_k, U_i, \mathcal{W}} P_1(\mathcal{S}_1, \ldots, \mathcal{S}_k, U_i, \mathcal{W})$.

(2) *For any* $\mathcal{S}, \mathcal{S}' \subset \mathcal{U}$ *and any* $U_i \in \mathcal{S}'$, *we define* $P_2(\mathcal{S}, \mathcal{S}', U_i)$ *as:*

$$P_2(\mathcal{S}, \mathcal{S}', U_i) := \max_{c'_{\mathcal{S}'}} \max_{c_{\mathcal{S}}} \max_{mk} \Pr(Dec(dk_i, c'_{\mathcal{S}'}, \mathcal{S}', U_i) \notin \{m, \bot\} \mid c_{\mathcal{S}}, mk),$$

where $c_{\mathcal{S}} = Enc(ek, m, \mathcal{S})$. *Then,* P_2 *is defined as* $P_2 := \max\limits_{\mathcal{S}, \mathcal{S}', U_i} P_2(\mathcal{S}, \mathcal{S}', U_i)$.

We can derive a lower bound on the ciphertext-size as follows.

Proposition 3. *Let* Π *be a* γ-*robust and* $(\leq n, \leq \omega)$-*one-time secure RS-BE scheme. Then, for any* $\mathcal{S} \subset \mathcal{U}$ *it holds that* $|\mathcal{C}_{\mathcal{S}}| \geq \frac{|\mathcal{M}|-1}{\gamma^2} + 1$.

Proof. First, let $\mathcal{C}_i(m, \mathcal{S}) := \{c_{\mathcal{S}} \in \mathcal{C}_{\mathcal{S}} \mid Dec(dk_i, c_{\mathcal{S}}, \mathcal{S}, U_i) = m$ for some $dk_i \in \mathcal{DK}_i\}$. We fix arbitrary $m \in \mathcal{M}$, $U_i \in \mathcal{U}$, and $\mathcal{S} \subset \mathcal{U}$ such that $U_i \in \mathcal{S}$. Then, we have

$$\gamma \geq \max_{c'_{\mathcal{S}}} \max_{c_{\mathcal{S}}} \Pr(Dec(dk_i, c'_{\mathcal{S}}, \mathcal{S}, U_i) \notin \{m, \bot\} \mid c_{\mathcal{S}})$$

$$\geq \max_{m'} \max_{c'_{\mathcal{S}}} \max_{c_{\mathcal{S}}} \Pr(Dec(dk_i, c'_{\mathcal{S}}, \mathcal{S}, U_i) = m' \mid c_{\mathcal{S}}) \tag{20}$$

$$\geq \max_{m'} \frac{1}{|\mathcal{C}_i(m', \mathcal{S})|} \sum_{c'_{\mathcal{S}} \in \mathcal{C}_i(m', \mathcal{S})} \max_{c_{\mathcal{S}}} \Pr(Dec(dk_i, c'_{\mathcal{S}}, \mathcal{S}, U_i) = m' \mid c_{\mathcal{S}})$$

$$\geq \frac{1}{|\mathcal{C}_i(m', \mathcal{S})|}, \tag{21}$$

where Eq. (20) follows from

$$P_2(\mathcal{S}, \mathcal{S}, U_i) \geq P_1(\mathcal{S}, U_i, \mathcal{W} = \emptyset) = \max_{c'_{\mathcal{S}}} \max_{c_{\mathcal{S}}} \Pr(Dec(dk_i, c'_{\mathcal{S}}, \mathcal{S}, U_i) \notin \{m, \bot\} \mid c_{\mathcal{S}}),$$

and Eq. (21) follows from the following simple fact: For n real numbers $x_1, x_2, \ldots, x_n \in \mathbb{R}$, it holds that $\max\{x_i\}_{i=1}^n \geq \frac{1}{n} \sum_{i=1}^n x_i$. Therefore, we have $|\mathcal{C}_i(m', \mathcal{S})| \geq 1/\gamma$.

On the other hand, we have

$$\gamma \geq \max_{c'_{\mathcal{S}}} \max_{c_{\mathcal{S}}} \Pr(Dec(dk_i, c'_{\mathcal{S}}, \mathcal{S}, U_i) \notin \{m, \bot\} \mid c_{\mathcal{S}})$$

$$\geq \frac{|\bigcup_{m' \neq m} \mathcal{C}_i(m', \mathcal{S})|}{|\mathcal{C}_{\mathcal{S}}| - 1} \tag{22}$$

$$= \frac{\sum_{m' \neq m} |\mathcal{C}_i(m', \mathcal{S})|}{|\mathcal{C}_\mathcal{S}| - 1} \tag{23}$$

$$\geq \frac{|\mathcal{M}| - 1}{(|\mathcal{C}_\mathcal{S}| - 1)\gamma}, \tag{24}$$

where Eq. (22) follows from probability of random guessing of $c'_\mathcal{S}$ such that $Dec(dk_i, c'_\mathcal{S}, \mathcal{S}, U_i) \notin \{m, \perp\}$, Eq. (23) follows from the fact that the Dec algorithm is deterministic, and Eq. (24) follows from $|\mathcal{C}_i(m', \mathcal{S})| \geq 1/\gamma$. Hence, we have $|\mathcal{C}_\mathcal{S}| \geq (|\mathcal{M}| - 1)/\gamma^2 + 1$.   □

We can construct a robust scheme by using an *algebraic manipulation detection code* (AMD-code), which is defined as follows.

Definition 6 (AMD-code [18]). *Let $\mathcal{M}_{\mathrm{AMD}}$ be a set of messages such that $|\mathcal{M}_{\mathrm{AMD}}| = \eta$, and $\mathbb{G}$ be a commutative group of order λ. An algebraic manipulation detection code (AMD-code) Φ consists of the following two-tuple algorithms (Encode, Decode), where Encode is a probabilistic encoding map Encode : $\mathcal{M}_{\mathrm{AMD}} \to \mathbb{G}$ and a deterministic decoding map Decode : $\mathbb{G} \to \mathcal{M}_{\mathrm{AMD}} \cup \{\perp\}$ such that $\mathsf{Decode}(\mathsf{Encode}(m)) = m$ with probability one for every $m \in \mathcal{M}_{\mathrm{AMD}}$. Φ is an $(\eta, \lambda, \varepsilon)$-AMD-code if for every $m \in \mathcal{M}_{\mathrm{AMD}}$ and for every $\Delta \in \mathbb{G}$, the probability that $\mathsf{Decode}(\mathsf{Encode}(m) + \Delta) \notin \{m, \perp\}$ is at most ε.*

A robust RS-BE scheme is constructed by modifying the proposed $(\leq n, \leq \omega; \delta)$-one-time secure RS-BE scheme in Sect. 4 as follows: Before encrypting a plaintext $m \in \mathbb{F}_q$, the Enc algorithm runs $\hat{m} \leftarrow \mathsf{Encode}(m)$; and after decrypting a ciphertext, then the Dec algorithm runs $m \leftarrow \mathsf{Decode}(\tilde{m})$, where $\tilde{m}$ is the decryption result. We assume outputs of Encode and Decode are properly encoded into (a sequence of) elements of $\mathbb{F}_q$. Note that most of this construction is realized by using algebraic structure (i.e., over $\mathbb{F}_q$).

Theorem 3. *If Φ is an (q, q^ξ, ε)-AMD-code, then the resulting RS-BE scheme Π by the above construction is $(\leq n, \leq \omega; \xi\delta)$-one-time secure and ε-robust.*

Proof (Sketch). It is easy to see the above construction is $(\leq n, \leq \omega; \xi\delta)$-one-time secure. Let $k_\mathcal{S}$ be a part of a key in the ciphertext $c_\mathcal{S}$ (i.e., $c_\mathcal{S} = \mathsf{Encode}(m) + k_\mathcal{S}$). If an adversary, SM or colluders, applies any algebraic operation F to the ciphertext, then it holds $F(c_\mathcal{S}) = F(\mathsf{Encode}(m) + k_\mathcal{S}) = \mathsf{Encode}(m) + \Delta + k_\mathcal{S}$. Since $\Pr(\mathsf{Decode}(\mathsf{Encode}(m) + \Delta) \notin \{m, \perp\}) \leq \varepsilon$, it holds $\max\{P_1, P_2\} \leq \varepsilon$.   □

Remark 4. If we want to construct an $(\leq n, \leq \omega; \hat{\delta})$-one-time secure and γ-robust RS-BE scheme over $\mathbb{F}_q$, we have $|\mathcal{C}_\mathcal{S}| \geq (|\mathcal{M}| - 1)/\gamma^2 + 1 = (q^2(q - 1))/c^2 + 1 = q^3/c^2 - o(q^3)$, where we assume $\mathcal{M} = \mathbb{F}_q$ and $\gamma = c/q$ for some constant c. This means that we cannot realize a robust RS-BE scheme where a ciphertext consists of only one or two elements of $\mathbb{F}_q$.

Actually, for example, one of the most efficient construction of an (q, q^ξ, ε)-AMD-code, where $\xi = 3$ and $\varepsilon = 1/q$, is as follows. Encode: For $m \in \mathbb{F}_q$, choose $r \in \mathbb{F}_q$ and output $(m, r, mr) \in \mathbb{F}_q^3$. Decode: For (m', r', π), output m' if it holds

$m'r' = \pi$. Otherwise, output $\bot$. If we apply the above specific $(q, q^3, 1/q)$-AMD-code to our robust construction based on $(\leq n, \leq \omega; \delta)$-one-time secure (but non-robust) RS-BE scheme, then we have $|\mathcal{M}| = q$, $|\mathcal{C_S}| = q^{3\delta}$, and $\gamma = 1/q$. Now, it holds $|\mathcal{C_S}| \geq (|\mathcal{M}| - 1)/\gamma^2 + 1 = q^2(q-1) + 1 = q^3 - o(q^2)$. Therefore, the proposed robust construction is *almost optimal* in the sense of the ciphertext size if $\delta = 1$ (i.e., when the underlying $(\leq n, \leq \omega; \delta)$-one-time secure RS-BE scheme in the previous section is also optimal in the sense of the ciphertext size).

Furthermore, the above specific construction requires triple sizes of each parameter in the normal (i.e., non-robust) construction. Then, the proposed robust construction seems to achieve optimal parameter sizes if the underlying RS-BE scheme is optimal (i.e., if $\delta = 1$).

Acknowledgments. We would like to thank the anonymous reviewers for fruitful comments, and in particular, for pointing out that an AMD-code is useful for robust constructions. We would also like to thank "Shin-Akarui-Angou-Benkyou-Kai" for their valuable comments. Yohei Watanabe is supported by JSPS Research Fellowships for Young Scientists. This work (Yohei Watanabe) was supported by Grant-in-Aid for JSPS Fellows Grant Number 25·3998 and 16J10532. This work (Junji Shikata) was supported by JSPS KAKENHI Grant Number 15H02710, and it was in part conducted under the auspices of the MEXT Program for Promoting the Reform of National Universities.

Appendix

A   Shannon Entropy

We briefly describe Shannon entropy. For details, see [17,19] for the excellent instruction. Let X and Y be random variables which take values in sets $\mathcal{X}$ and $\mathcal{Y}$, respectively.

Definition 7 (Shannon Entropy [40]). *Shannon entropy $H(X)$ is defined by*

$$H(X) := -\sum_{x \in \mathcal{X}} \Pr(X = x) \log \Pr(X = x).$$

Furthermore, the joint entropy $H(X, Y)$ and conditional entropy $H(X|Y)$ of a pair of random variables (X, Y) with a joint probability distribution P_{XY} are defined by

$$H(X, Y) := -\sum_{x \in \mathcal{X}} \sum_{y \in \mathcal{Y}} \Pr(X = x, Y = y) \log \Pr(X = x, Y = y),$$

$$H(X|Y) := \sum_{y \in \mathcal{Y}} \Pr(Y = y) H(X|Y = y),$$

respectively. Moreover, mutual information is also defined by

$$I(X; Y) := H(X) - H(X|Y) = H(Y) - H(Y|X).$$

The following properties of Shannon entropy are used in this paper (for details, see [17,19]):

- For a random variable X, it holds that $\log |\mathcal{X}| \geq H(X) \geq 0$, where the first equality holds if and only if a probability distribution of $\mathcal{X}$ is uniform, and the second equality holds if and only if there exists some $x \in \mathcal{X}$ such that $\Pr(X = x) = 1$.
- It holds that $H(X, Y) = H(X) + H(Y|X) = H(Y) + H(X|Y)$. More generally, it holds that $H(X_1, X_2, \ldots, X_n) = \sum_{i=1}^{n} H(X_i|X_1, \ldots, X_{i-1})$.
- For two random variables X and Y, it hold that $H(X) \geq H(X|Y)$, where equality holds if and only if X and Y are independent.
- It holds that $I(X; Y) \geq 0$, where the equality holds if and only if X and Y are independent of each other.

B   Collusion-Resistant RS-BE Scheme

We consider security against collusion of at most ω colluders and a storage manager. Intuitively, if a storage manager can change any privileged set of a ciphertext into any privileged set by using his maintenance key mk, we cannot achieve RS-BE secure against collusion of a set of colluders and the storage manager. Therefore, here we simply set the following transformation rule for mk: For any $\mathcal{S}, \mathcal{S}' \subset \mathcal{U}$, $Upd(mk, c_{\mathcal{S}}, \mathcal{S}, \mathcal{S}')$ outputs an updated ciphertext $c_{\mathcal{S}'}$ if $\mathcal{S}' \subset \mathcal{S}$ holds, otherwise it outputs $\perp$. Namely, we only consider dynamic revocation of users.

We define collusion-resistant security as follows.

Definition 8 (Collusion-Resistant RS-BE). *Let Π be an RS-BE scheme. Π is said to be collusion-resistantly $(\leq n, \leq \omega)$-one-time secure if the following conditions are satisfied: For any privileged set $\mathcal{S} \subset \mathcal{U}$, and any set of colluders $\mathcal{W} \subset \mathcal{U}$ such that $\mathcal{S} \cap \mathcal{W} = \emptyset$ and $|\mathcal{W}| \leq \omega$, it holds that*

$$H(M \mid C_{\mathcal{S}}, DK_{\mathcal{W}}, MK) = H(M).$$

A construction which satisfies Definition 8 is as follows.

1. $(ek, mk, dk_1, \ldots, dk_n) \leftarrow Setup()$: Let q be a prime power such that $q > n$, and $\mathbb{F}_q$ be a finite field with q elements. It chooses n polynomials $f^{(h)}(x) := \sum_{i=0}^{\omega} a_i x^i$ $(h = 1, \ldots, n)$ over $\mathbb{F}_q$ uniformly at random, and computes $n - 1$ polynomials $g^{(\ell)}(x) := f^{(\ell)}(x) - f^{(\ell-1)}(x)$ $(2 \leq \ell \leq n)$. Then, it outputs $ek := f^{(1)}(x)$, $dk_i := (f^{(1)}(i), \ldots, f^{(n)}(i))$ $(1 \leq i \leq n)$, and $mk := (g^{(2)}(x), \ldots, g^{(n)}(x))$.
2. $c_{\mathcal{S}} \leftarrow Enc(ek, m, \mathcal{S})$: Let $\mathcal{S} = \{U_{i_1}, \ldots, U_{i_k}\}$ $(1 \leq k \leq n)$ be a privileged set. For every U_{i_j}, it computes $c_{i_j}^{(1)} := m + f^{(1)}(i_j)$, and sets a counter $t := 1$. Finally, it outputs $c_{\mathcal{S}} := (t, c_{i_1}^{(t)}, \ldots, c_{i_k}^{(t)})$.
3. m or $\perp \leftarrow Dec(dk_i, c_{\mathcal{S}}, \mathcal{S}, U_i)$: If $U_i \in \mathcal{S}$, it computes $m = c_i^{(t)} - f^{(t)}(i)$ and outputs it. Otherwise, it outputs $\perp$.

4. $c_{\mathcal{S}'}$ or $\perp \leftarrow Upd(mk, c_{\mathcal{S}}, \mathcal{S}, \mathcal{S}')$: Let $\mathcal{S}' = \{U_{i_1}, \ldots, U_{i_k}\}$. If $\mathcal{S}' \subset \mathcal{S}$ does not hold, it outputs $\perp$. Otherwise, for every $U_{i_j} \in \mathcal{S}' \subset \mathcal{S}$, it computes $c_i^{(t+1)} := c_{i_j}^{(t)} + g^{(t+1)}(i_j)$ $(1 \leq j \leq k)$. Finally, it sets $t := t + 1$ and outputs $c_{\mathcal{S}'} := (t, c_{i_1}^{(t)}, \ldots, c_{i_k}^{(t)})$.

Proposition 4. *The resulting RS-BE scheme Π by the above construction is collusion-resistantly $(\leq n, \leq \omega)$-one-time secure.*

Proof. It is not so difficult to prove this proposition. Without loss of generality, we consider that $\mathcal{W} := \{U_1, \ldots, U_\omega\}$ is a set of colluders and $\mathcal{S} := \{U_{\omega+1} \ldots, U_n\}$ is a privileged set. Consider the case that the set of colluders $\mathcal{W}$ and the storage manager will guess $k_{\mathcal{S}}$ to obtain the plaintext m by the using their secret keys. Since each degree of x of $f^{(h)}(x)$ $(1 \leq h \leq n)$ is at most ω, at most ω colluders cannot obtain $f^{(h)}(x)$ from $f_i^{(h)}(1), \ldots, f^{(h)}(\omega)$ $(1 \leq h \leq n)$. Hence, they cannot obtain any information on $f^{(h)}(x)$ $(1 \leq h \leq n)$ even if they have $g^{(\ell)}(x)$ $(2 \leq \ell \leq n)$. Hence, for any $\mathcal{S} \subset \mathcal{U}$, and any $\mathcal{W} \subset \mathcal{U}$ such that $\mathcal{S} \cap \mathcal{W} = \emptyset$ and $|\mathcal{W}| \leq \omega$, $H(M \mid C_{\mathcal{S}}, DK_{\mathcal{W}}, MK) = H(M)$. $\qquad\square$

C Construction for Arbitrary Plaintext Sizes and Number of Users

We show how we construct an $(\leq n, \leq \omega; \delta)$-one-time secure RS-BE scheme for arbitrary $|\mathcal{M}|$ and n, even when $|\mathcal{M}| \leq n$, where n is the number of users. We first consider an instantiation of an $(\leq n, \leq \omega; \delta)$-one-time secure BE scheme by the Fiat–Naor KPS [21]. Since the Fiat–Naor KPS was combinatorially designed by not using polynomials, the construction works even when $q \leq n$. We can then propose the Upd algorithm by modifying the construction. Note that the sizes of secret keys (in particular, encryption and maintenance keys) of this construction are larger than those of our construction in Sect. 4 when $\delta > \omega$.

The detailed construction of an $(\leq n, \leq \omega)$-one-time secure RS-BE scheme $\Pi = (Setup, Enc, Dec, Upd)$ is as follows.

1. $(ek, mk, dk_1, \ldots, dk_n) \leftarrow Setup()$: Let $\mathbb{F}_q$ be a finite field with q elements, where q is a prime power. Let $a := \lfloor n/\delta \rfloor$, $\delta_2 := n \bmod \delta$, and $\delta_1 := \delta - \delta_2$. Without loss of generality, let $\mathcal{U}_j := \{U_1^{(j)}, \ldots, U_a^{(j)}\} = \{U_{(j-1)a+1}, \ldots, U_{ja}\}$ for $j \in \{1, 2, \ldots, \delta_1\}$ and $\mathcal{U}_j := \{U_1^{(j)}, \ldots, U_{a+1}^{(j)}\} = \{U_{\delta_1 a + (j-\delta_1-1)(a+1)+1}, \ldots, U_{\delta_1 a + (j-\delta_1)(a+1)}\}$ for $j \in \{\delta_1 + 1, \delta_1 + 2, \ldots, \delta\}$. Define the following families of subsets:

$$\mathscr{W}_j := \{\mathcal{W} \subset \mathcal{U}_j \mid |\mathcal{W}| \leq \omega_j\},$$

$$\mathscr{W}_j^{(i)} := \{\mathcal{W} \subset \mathcal{U}_j \mid \mathcal{W} \in \mathscr{W}_j \wedge U_i \notin \mathcal{W}\},$$

$$\mathscr{W}_j(\mathcal{S} \subset \mathcal{U}_j) := \{\mathcal{W} \in \mathscr{W}_j \mid |\mathcal{W}| = \min\{\tilde{\omega}, |\mathcal{U}_j| - |\mathcal{S}|\}\},$$

where $\omega_j := \min\{a-1, \omega\}$ for $1 \leq j \leq \delta_1$ and $\omega_j := \min\{a, \omega\}$ for $\delta_1 + 1 \leq j \leq \delta$. Choose $R \in \mathbb{F}_q$ uniformly at random. Then, for each $\mathcal{U}_j$ $(1 \leq j \leq \delta)$, compute as follows. For $\emptyset_j := \emptyset \in \mathcal{W}_j$, choose $r'_{\emptyset_j} \in \mathbb{F}_q$ uniformly at random, and compute $r_{\emptyset_j} := R + r'_{\emptyset_j}$. For every $\mathcal{W} \in \mathcal{W}_j \setminus \{\emptyset\}$, choose $r_\mathcal{W} \in \mathbb{F}_q$ uniformly at random. Set $ek := \{r_\mathcal{W} \mid \mathcal{W} \in \mathcal{W}_j\}_{j=1}^\delta$, $mk := \{r'_{\emptyset_1}, r'_{\emptyset_2}, \ldots, r'_{\emptyset_\delta}\} \cup \{r_\mathcal{W} \mid \mathcal{W} \in \mathcal{W}_j \setminus \{\emptyset\}\}_{j=1}^\delta$. For every $U_h = U_i^{(j)}$, set $dk_h = dk_i^{(j)} := \{r_\mathcal{W} \mid \mathcal{W} \in \mathcal{W}_j^{(i)}\}$. Output $(ek, mk, dk_1, \ldots, dk_n)$.

2. $c_\mathcal{S} \leftarrow Enc(ek, m, \mathcal{S})$: Let $\mathcal{S}_j := \mathcal{S} \cup \mathcal{U}_j$. For every $\mathcal{S}_j$, compute

$$c_j := m + r_{\emptyset_j} + \sum_{\mathcal{W} \in \mathcal{W}_j(\mathcal{S}_j)} r_\mathcal{W},$$

unless $\mathcal{S}_j = \emptyset$. Output $c_\mathcal{S} := \{c_j\}_{\mathcal{S}_j \neq \emptyset}$.

3. m or $\perp \leftarrow Dec(dk_h, c_\mathcal{S}, \mathcal{S}, U_h)$: If $U_h \notin \mathcal{S}$, output $\perp$. Otherwise, suppose that $U_h = U_i^{(j)} \in \mathcal{U}_j$. Output $m = c_j - r_{\emptyset_j} - \sum_{\mathcal{W} \in \mathcal{W}_j(\mathcal{S}_j)} r_\mathcal{W}$.

4. $c_{\mathcal{S}'}$ or $\perp \leftarrow Upd(mk, c_\mathcal{S}, \mathcal{S}, \mathcal{S}')$: Let $\mathcal{S}_i := \mathcal{S} \cup \mathcal{U}_i$ and $\mathcal{S}'_j := \mathcal{S}' \cup \mathcal{U}_j$. Without loss of generality, choose some $c_i \in c_\mathcal{S}$. Compute $c_\emptyset := c_i - r'_{\emptyset_i} - \sum_{\mathcal{W} \in \mathcal{W}_i(\mathcal{S}_i)} r_\mathcal{W} = m + R$, where $\emptyset_i := \emptyset \in \mathcal{W}_i$. For every $\mathcal{S}'_j$, compute

$$c'_j := c_\emptyset + r'_{\emptyset_j} + \sum_{\mathcal{W} \in \mathcal{W}_j(\mathcal{S}'_j)} r_\mathcal{W},$$

unless $\mathcal{S}'_j = \emptyset$, , where $\emptyset_j \in \mathcal{W}_j$. Output $c_{\mathcal{S}'} := \{c'_j\}_{\mathcal{S}'_j \neq \emptyset}$.

Proposition 5. *The resulting RS-BE scheme Π is $(\leq n, \leq \omega; \delta)$-one-time secure. In particular, Π is optimal when $\delta = 1$.*

Proof (Sketch). We here give a sketch since it is not so difficult to prove. Without loss of generality, we consider $\mathcal{S} := \{U_1, U_2, \ldots, U_{n-\omega}\}$ and $\mathcal{W} := \{U_{n-\omega+1}, U_{n-\omega+2}, \ldots, U_n\}$. Let $\mathcal{S}_j := \mathcal{S} \cap \mathcal{U}_j$ and $\mathcal{W}_j := \mathcal{U}_j \setminus \mathcal{S}_j$. As in [21], it is obvious that each $\mathcal{W}_j$ does not have at least one randomness $r_{\mathcal{W}_j}$. Therefore, $\mathcal{W}$ cannot obtain any information on m. Furthermore, SM cannot also get any information on m since he does not know R.   □

References

1. Ateniese, G., Burns, R., Curtmola, R., Herring, J., Khan, O., Kissner, L., Peterson, Z., Song, D.: Remote data checking using provable data possession. ACM Trans. Inf. Syst. Secur. **14**(1), 12:1–12:34 (2011)
2. Ateniese, G., De Santis, A., Ferrara, A.L., Masucci, B.: Provably-secure time-bound hierarchical key assignment schemes. In: The 13th ACM Conference on Computer and Communications Security, CCS 2006, pp. 288–297. ACM, New York (2006)
3. Ateniese, G., De Santis, A., Ferrara, A.L., Masucci, B.: Provably-secure time-bound hierarchical key assignment schemes. J. Cryptol. **25**(2), 243–270 (2012)
4. Attrapadung, N., Imai, H.: Attribute-based encryption supporting direct/indirect revocation modes. In: Parker, M.G. (ed.) IMACC 2009. LNCS, vol. 5921, pp. 278–300. Springer, Heidelberg (2009). doi:10.1007/978-3-642-10868-6_17

5. Ayday, E., De Cristofaro, E., Hubaux, J., Tsudik, G.: The chills and thrills of whole genome sequencing. Computer **PP**(99), 1 (2013)
6. Ayday, E., De Cristofaro, E., Hubaux, J.P., Tsudik, G.: Whole genome sequencing: revolutionary medicine or privacy nightmare? Computer **48**(2), 58–66 (2015)
7. Barker, E., Barker, W., Burr, W., Polk, W., Smid, M.: Recommendation for key management - part 1: General (revision 3). NIST Special Publication 800-57, July 2012
8. Berkovits, S.: How to broadcast a secret. In: Davies, D.W. (ed.) EUROCRYPT 1991. LNCS, vol. 547, pp. 535–541. Springer, Heidelberg (1991). doi:10.1007/3-540-46416-6_50
9. Blom, R.: An optimal class of symmetric key generation systems. In: Beth, T., Cot, N., Ingemarsson, I. (eds.) EUROCRYPT 1984. LNCS, vol. 209, pp. 335–338. Springer, Heidelberg (1985). doi:10.1007/3-540-39757-4_22
10. Blundo, C., Cresti, A., Santis, A., Vaccaro, U.: Fully dynamic secret sharing schemes. In: Stinson, D.R. (ed.) CRYPTO 1993. LNCS, vol. 773, pp. 110–125. Springer, Heidelberg (1994). doi:10.1007/3-540-48329-2_10
11. Blundo, C., Cresti, A.: Space requirements for broadcast encryption. In: Santis, A. (ed.) EUROCRYPT 1994. LNCS, vol. 950, pp. 287–298. Springer, Heidelberg (1995). doi:10.1007/BFb0053444
12. Blundo, C., Mattos, L.A.F., Stinson, D.R.: Trade-offs between communication and storage in unconditionally secure schemes for broadcast encryption and interactive key distribution. In: Koblitz, N. (ed.) CRYPTO 1996. LNCS, vol. 1109, pp. 387–400. Springer, Heidelberg (1996). doi:10.1007/3-540-68697-5_29
13. Boldyreva, A., Goyal, V., Kumar, V.: Identity-based encryption with efficient revocation. In: Proceedings of the 15th ACM Conference on Computer and Communications Security, CCS 2008, pp. 417–426. ACM, New York (2008)
14. Boneh, D., Gentry, C., Waters, B.: Collusion resistant broadcast encryption with short ciphertexts and private keys. In: Shoup, V. (ed.) CRYPTO 2005. LNCS, vol. 3621, pp. 258–275. Springer, Heidelberg (2005). doi:10.1007/11535218_16
15. Canetti, R., Gennaro, R., Herzberg, A.: Proactive security: long-term protection against break-ins. CryptoBytes **3**, 1–8 (1997)
16. Chen, H., Ling, S., Padró, C., Wang, H., Xing, C.: Key predistribution schemes and one-time broadcast encryption schemes from algebraic geometry codes. In: Parker, M.G. (ed.) IMACC 2009. LNCS, vol. 5921, pp. 263–277. Springer, Heidelberg (2009). doi:10.1007/978-3-642-10868-6_16
17. Cover, T.M., Thomas, J.A.: Elements of Information Theory, 2nd edn. Wiley-Interscience, Hoboken (2006)
18. Cramer, R., Dodis, Y., Fehr, S., Padró, C., Wichs, D.: Detection of algebraic manipulation with applications to robust secret sharing and fuzzy extractors. In: Smart, N. (ed.) EUROCRYPT 2008. LNCS, vol. 4965, pp. 471–488. Springer, Heidelberg (2008). doi:10.1007/978-3-540-78967-3_27
19. Csiszár, I., Koerner, J.: Information Theory: Coding Theorems for Discrete Memoryless Systems, 2nd edn. Cambridge University Press, Cambridge (2011)
20. Dodis, Y., Fazio, N.: Public key broadcast encryption for stateless receivers. In: Feigenbaum, J. (ed.) DRM 2002. LNCS, vol. 2696, pp. 61–80. Springer, Heidelberg (2003). doi:10.1007/978-3-540-44993-5_5
21. Fiat, A., Naor, M.: Broadcast encryption. In: Stinson, D.R. (ed.) CRYPTO 1993. LNCS, vol. 773, pp. 480–491. Springer, Heidelberg (1994). doi:10.1007/3-540-48329-2_40

22. Gentry, C., Waters, B.: Adaptive security in broadcast encryption systems (with Short Ciphertexts). In: Joux, A. (ed.) EUROCRYPT 2009. LNCS, vol. 5479, pp. 171–188. Springer, Heidelberg (2009). doi:10.1007/978-3-642-01001-9_10

23. Halevi, S., Harnik, D., Pinkas, B., Shulman-Peleg, A.: Proofs of ownership in remote storage systems. In: Proceedings of the 18th ACM Conference on Computer and Communications Security, CCS 2011, pp. 491–500. ACM, New York (2011)

24. Herzberg, A., Jarecki, S., Krawczyk, H., Yung, M.: Proactive secret sharing or: how to cope with perpetual leakage. In: Coppersmith, D. (ed.) CRYPTO 1995. LNCS, vol. 963, pp. 339–352. Springer, Heidelberg (1995). doi:10.1007/3-540-44750-4_27

25. Kamara, S., Lauter, K.: Cryptographic cloud storage. In: Sion, R., Curtmola, R., Dietrich, S., Kiayias, A., Miret, J.M., Sako, K., Sebé, F. (eds.) FC 2010. LNCS, vol. 6054, pp. 136–149. Springer, Heidelberg (2010). doi:10.1007/978-3-642-14992-4_13

26. Kurosawa, K., Yoshida, T., Desmedt, Y., Burmester, M.: Some bounds and a construction for secure broadcast encryption. In: Ohta, K., Pei, D. (eds.) ASIACRYPT 1998. LNCS, vol. 1514, pp. 420–433. Springer, Heidelberg (1998). doi:10.1007/3-540-49649-1_33

27. Liu, J., Wang, H., Xian, M., Huang, K.: A secure and efficient scheme for cloud storage against eavesdropper. In: Qing, S., Zhou, J., Liu, D. (eds.) ICICS 2013. LNCS, vol. 8233, pp. 75–89. Springer, Heidelberg (2013). doi:10.1007/978-3-319-02726-5_6

28. Liu, Z., Li, J., Chen, X., Yang, J., Jia, C.: TMDS: thin-model data sharing scheme supporting keyword search in cloud storage. In: Susilo, W., Mu, Y. (eds.) ACISP 2014. LNCS, vol. 8544, pp. 115–130. Springer, Heidelberg (2014). doi:10.1007/978-3-319-08344-5_8

29. Luby, M., Staddon, J.: Combinatorial bounds for broadcast encryption. In: Nyberg, K. (ed.) EUROCRYPT 1998. LNCS, vol. 1403, pp. 512–526. Springer, Heidelberg (1998). doi:10.1007/BFb0054150

30. Matsumoto, T., Imai, H.: On the key predistribution system: a practical solution to the key distribution problem. In: Pomerance, C. (ed.) CRYPTO 1987. LNCS, vol. 293, pp. 185–193. Springer, Heidelberg (1988). doi:10.1007/3-540-48184-2_14

31. Naor, D., Naor, M., Lotspiech, J.: Revocation and tracing schemes for stateless receivers. In: Kilian, J. (ed.) CRYPTO 2001. LNCS, vol. 2139, pp. 41–62. Springer, Heidelberg (2001). doi:10.1007/3-540-44647-8_3

32. Nikov, V., Nikova, S.: On proactive secret sharing schemes. In: Handschuh, H., Hasan, M.A. (eds.) SAC 2004. LNCS, vol. 3357, pp. 308–325. Springer, Heidelberg (2004). doi:10.1007/978-3-540-30564-4_22

33. Padró, C., Gracia, I., Martín, S.: Improving the trade-off between storage and communication in broadcast encryption schemes. Discret. Appl. Math. 143(1–3), 213–220 (2004)

34. Padró, C., Gracia, I., Martín, S., Morillo, P.: Linear broadcast encryption schemes. Discret. Appl. Math. 128(1), 223–238 (2003)

35. Phan, D.H., Pointcheval, D., Strefler, M.: Security notions for broadcast encryption. In: Lopez, J., Tsudik, G. (eds.) ACNS 2011. LNCS, vol. 6715, pp. 377–394. Springer, Heidelberg (2011). doi:10.1007/978-3-642-21554-4_22

36. Sahai, A., Seyalioglu, H., Waters, B.: Dynamic credentials and ciphertext delegation for attribute-based encryption. In: Safavi-Naini, R., Canetti, R. (eds.) CRYPTO 2012. LNCS, vol. 7417, pp. 199–217. Springer, Heidelberg (2012). doi:10.1007/978-3-642-32009-5_13

37. Sahai, A., Waters, B.: Fuzzy identity-based encryption. In: Cramer, R. (ed.) EUROCRYPT 2005. LNCS, vol. 3494, pp. 457–473. Springer, Heidelberg (2005). doi:10.1007/11426639_27

38. Santis, A.D., Ferrara, A.L., Masucci, B.: Unconditionally secure key assignment schemes. Discret. Appl. Math. **154**(2), 234–252 (2006)
39. Shacham, H., Waters, B.: Compact proofs of retrievability. J. Cryptol. **26**(3), 442–483 (2013)
40. Shannon, C.E.: A mathematical theory of communication. Bell Syst. Tech. J. **27**, 379–423, 623–656 (1948). http://cm.bell-labs.com/cm/ms/what/shannonday/shannon1948.pdf
41. Stanek, J., Sorniotti, A., Androulaki, E., Kencl, L.: A secure data deduplication scheme for cloud storage. In: Christin, N., Safavi-Naini, R. (eds.) FC 2014. LNCS, vol. 8437, pp. 99–118. Springer, Heidelberg (2014). doi:10.1007/978-3-662-45472-5_8
42. Stinson, D.: On some methods for unconditionally secure key distribution and broadcast encryption. Des. Codes Crypt. **12**(3), 215–243 (1997)
43. Stinson, D.R., Wei, R.: Unconditionally secure proactive secret sharing scheme with combinatorial structures. In: Heys, H., Adams, C. (eds.) SAC 1999. LNCS, vol. 1758, pp. 200–214. Springer, Heidelberg (2000). doi:10.1007/3-540-46513-8_15
44. The Presidential Commission for the Study of Bioethical Issues: Privacy and progress in whole genome sequencing. President's Bioethics Commission Releases Report on Genomics and Privacy, October 2012
45. Watanabe, Y., Hanaoka, G., Shikata, J.: Unconditionally secure revocable storage: tight bounds, optimal construction, and robustness. Cryptology ePrint Archive, Report 2016/064 (2016). http://eprint.iacr.org/
46. Watanabe, Y., Shikata, J.: Constructions of unconditionally secure broadcast encryption from key predistribution systems with trade-offs between communication and storage. In: Au, M.-H., Miyaji, A. (eds.) ProvSec 2015. LNCS, vol. 9451, pp. 489–502. Springer, Heidelberg (2015). doi:10.1007/978-3-319-26059-4_27
47. Yang, K., Jia, X., Ren, K.: Attribute-based fine-grained access control with efficient revocation in cloud storage systems. In: Proceedings of the 8th ACM SIGSAC Symposium on Information, Computer and Communications Security, ASIA CCS 2013, pp. 523–528. ACM, New York (2013)

Entropy, Extractors and Privacy

A Practical Fuzzy Extractor for Continuous Features

Vladimir P. Parente[1]([✉]) and Jeroen van de Graaf[2]

[1] Graduate Program in Electrical Engineering,
Universidade Federal de Minas Gerais, Av. Antônio Carlos 6627,
31270-901 Belo Horizonte, MG, Brazil
vladimir@dcc.ufmg.br
[2] Computer Science Department, Universidade Federal de Minas Gerais,
Av. Antônio Carlos 6627, 31270-010 Belo Horizonte, MG, Brazil

Abstract. Many fuzzy extractors have been presented for *discrete* data; here we present a fuzzy extractor for *continuous* data. Our approach uses the code-offset method extended to $\mathbb{R}^n$ by using lattice codes and Euclidean distance. This is accomplished in the Unconstrained Power Channel, a theoretical artifact especially developed for lattice codes used in scenarios other than telecommunication, in which the noise is assumed to be white Gaussian. To prove security we give a lower bound on the min-entropy of the common secret that an adversary necessarily faces; we also provide an upper bound. In addition we present a construction using Low-Density Lattice Codes. Our construction is more practical than existing proposals since it can be used with a feature of *any* dimension n and with some noise distributions that are not white Gaussian inherent to that feature.

Keywords: Fuzzy extractor · Code-offset method · Low-Density Lattice Codes · Key reconciliation · Continuous source

1 Introduction

1.1 Information Reconciliation for Discrete Data

Correlated data shared between two parties can be used as a starting point for establishing a secret key. A well-known example is the BB84 quantum key distribution protocol [BB84], in which the correlation between some quantum states prepared by one party and measured by the other is used as a starting point to extract a common key. An important substep in this process is *key reconciliation* or *information reconciliation*: Alice and Bob each have a string x and y which are similar but not identical, and they would like to compute a shorter random string s which is identical.

This work has been supported by the Brazilian agency CAPES.

A.C.A. Nascimento and P. Barreto (Eds.): ICITS 2016, LNCS 10015, pp. 241–258, 2016.
DOI: 10.1007/978-3-319-49175-2_12

The first approach proposed in the BB84 context used error-correcting codes [BB84, Cré97]: Alice chooses a suitable linear code, calculates the syndrome of x, and sends it to Bob. The latter, using this syndrome together with y, can recover Alice's information exactly, provided that their strings are similar enough. This method is also known as the code offset method. Later, interactive information reconciliation protocols were proposed [BS94]. We do not consider these techniques in this study.

1.2 Fuzzy Extractors for Discrete Data

More recently, information reconciliation is also being used in the context of authentication based on biometric data. A *fuzzy extractor* takes some fuzzy information x (such as a biometric reading) as input and, combined with helper information, is able to extract a uniform random string s. Moreover, this process is repeatable, in the sense that a new, slightly different reading y, combined with the same helper information, will lead to the same string s. So this setting is somewhat different from key establishment: instead of two parties comparing correlated information, there are now two different moments in time: enrollment, and authentication. The readings x and y at these two moments need to be reconciled, i.e. it needs to be decided if they are sufficiently similar.

Biometric features are not uniformly distributed and not perfectly reproducible. However, as discussed in [DRS08], it is possible to derive a secret key almost uniformly distributed given that the legitimate parties have some correlated common feature, even in the presence of an adversary who eavesdrops on the communication channel. Some results, like [JW99] and [JS02] can be interpreted as fuzzy extractors. Observe that these papers quantize the data, i.e. convert them to bits, and apply one of the known information reconciliation techniques mentioned in the previous subsection.

But the features used in these reconciliation schemes (biometric, audio or acceleration features) are inherently continuous, which causes problems. For example, when using the syndrome decoding approach with an error-correcting code on binary strings derived from the quantized feature, then, as discussed in [ŠT09], the following problems often arise: (1) the errors are not uniformly random, (2) the error probabilities depend on the value of the feature vector itself, (3) the quantization used causes unequal error probabilities, and (4) when several components of the feature vector are combined into a n-dimensional space, the quantization leads to asymmetries in the bit representation of equally likely errors. Therefore, in order to avoid these problems, it is interesting to postpone the quantization step and, instead, apply reconciliation directly on the features still in continuous format.

1.3 Information Reconciliation for Continuous Data

The underlying motivation for this research is the following realistic scenario: in order to obtain correlated data, the two parties use the sensors of their smartphones (or similar devices). For instance they hold the two devices together and shake them for some seconds, or they hold them close to one another, switch on the microphone and make an audio recording. The signal processing performed locally by each device results in two features, X and Y vectors in $\mathbb{R}^n$, which are similar but not identical. We assume that the parties now use some wireless communication channel (like Bluetooth) to reconcile their features to obtain a common secret S.

Observe that, unlike the BB84 setting, the correlated data is of continuous (or analogue) nature. The natural strategy, to quantize the data, i.e. convert it to bits, and apply one of the known information reconciliation techniques mentioned above, leads to problems, as explained in the previous Section. So we take a different approach: we postpone the quantization step and, instead, perform reconciliation directly on the continuous data (the features).

Low-Density Lattice Codes (LDLC) play an important role in this approach. This is a novel class of codes that perform error correction not over $\{0,1\}^n$ but over $\mathbb{R}^n$. So the distance notion used is not the Hamming distance, but the Euclidean distance. In the context of telecommunication engineering, the advantage of LDLC is that they stay closer to the physical characteristics of a real communication channel; after all, a binary symmetric channel is merely an abstraction of some underlying physical communication channel. For this reason, LDLC are able to approach the channel capacity, while today's processors are sufficiently fast to deal with the increased complexity caused by the fact that computations have to be performed on real numbers (or rather, their approximations, floating-point numbers) instead of bits.

So the basic novelty of this paper is to perform non-interactive information reconciliation based on coding theory over $\mathbb{R}^n$ using lattice codes, instead of some conventional code over $\{0,1\}^n$. But this is not as simple as it may sound, because the geometry of lattices and lattice codes is quite complex. Another complication is that the scenario in which we use lattice codes is different from the one for which they have been originally designed. In the context of using lattice codes for telecommunication, the power of the channel is a natural constraint on the capacity. But we are applying lattice codes for reconciliation, and in this scenario there exists no limit on the channel's capacity nor a meaningful definition of Signal-to-Noise Ratio. In order to rectify this situation, Poltyrev [Pol94] proposed the notion of an Unconstrained Power Channel, a theoretical artifact in which the channel capacity becomes meaningful again and for which a Generalized Signal-to-Noise Ratio can be defined. See Sect. 2.2 for more details.

1.4   Related Work: Fuzzy Extractors for Continuous Data

All schemes for information reconciliation for continuous data that we are aware of have been presented in the context of fuzzy extractors, and our reconciliation scheme can also be interpreted in this context, thus allowing a meaningful comparison. In [BDHV07b], the definitions from [DRS08] are extended to continuous features and some schemes are analyzed that can be seen as continuous source fuzzy extractors (cs-fuzzy extractor) such as [TAKSBV05, CZC04, LT03]. Another important scheme that works on continuous features is [BDHV07a], which can be seen as a generalization of the scheme proposed in [LT03] regarding the number of quantizers. In [VTOSŠ10] some properties of the cs-fuzzy extractors are added and is mentioned that no universal optimal fuzzy extractors exists for continuous distributions; also a new construction based on the Euclidean distance is shown. [ZLZ06] also created a scheme based on the Euclidean distance of the features.

A major disadvantage of these results is that most of them use explicitly the Euclidean distance as metric; however, no efficient method is specified to find the point (a lattice point for example) that minimizes this distance for a certain chosen point of $\mathbb{R}^n$ for arbitrary dimension n. So, in practice these schemes do not scale in the size of the feature, n. In addition, most proposals apply error correction of a feature vector $X = (x_1, ..., x_n)$ by applying correction on the individual components $x_1, ..., x_n$. Instead, by using lattice codes we are interpreting X as a vector in R^n and use the Euclidean distance. This measure is much more appropriate for quantifying the distance between two features X and Y. Since the whole vector X is used in the error correction process this leads to improved error correction performance.

1.5   Contributions of This Paper

The main objective of this research is to develop a fuzzy extractor for *continuous* data such as features, as opposed to reconciliation of *discrete* data (bit strings). The contributions of this research can be summarized as follows:

- Our scheme is the first fuzzy extractor that uses lattice codes. These codes work over a continuous space in $\mathbb{R}^n$, rather than over a discrete space in $\{0, 1\}^n$. In particular, we use lattice codes in the Unconstrained Power Channel [Pol94]. This model is necessary in order to obtain a meaningful definition of the channel capacity.
- We obtain an upper bound on the min-entropy that a passive adversary may obtain about the key. This bound does not depend on the particular lattice code chosen.
- We show how to instantiate our scheme using Low-Density Lattice Codes, an efficient subclass of lattice codes whose complexity in time and memory requirements is linearly proportional to the feature size n.
- Our scheme can be used to work with features of *any* dimension n (discussed in Sect. 6) and with *any* type of noise distribution inherent to that feature (discussed in Sect. 4), provided that the noise is at least white. Alternative proposals for continuous source fuzzy extractors do not have this property. Therefore, with the proper adjustments, the scheme can work with any kind of features, such as correlated acceleration data, correlated audio data etc.

2   Preliminaries

2.1   Lattice

Following [CS98], we briefly summarize the basic definitions of a lattice. A lattice Λ is defined by its basis vectors $(v_1, v_2, \cdots, v_n)$ with $v_i \in \mathbb{R}^m$. The generator matrix $M_{m \times n}$ (with $m \geq n$) of the lattice Λ is composed by its basis vectors. Lattice points are defined to be $x = Mb$ where b is an n-dimensional integer vector. Therefore, every lattice point is in R^m. The Gram matrix A of the lattice Λ is defined to be $A = MM^t$. The determinant of the lattice is det Λ = det A, so if M is square, then det $\Lambda = (\det M)^2$. Given a set of points $\mathcal{P} = \{P_1, P_2, \cdots\} \in \mathbb{R}^n$, a Voronoi cell $V(P_i)$ consists of those points of $\mathbb{R}^n$ that are at least as close to P_i as to any other P_j. In other words $V(P_i) = \{x \in \mathbb{R}^n : d(x, P_i) \leq d(x, P_j) \ \forall j\}$. The volume of each Voronoi cell (volume of the lattice) $Vol(\Lambda) = \sqrt{|\det \Lambda|}$. So if M is square, then $Vol(\Lambda) = |\det M|$.

2.2 Lattice Codes and the Unconstrained Power Channel

In [KDL09] an introduction about lattice codes is presented, which is going to be the guide to this Section. A lattice defines an infinite number of constellation points, and without some restriction the definition of its capacity to decode becomes meaningless. Therefore, a lattice code is defined as the intersection of a finite chosen region, usually called shaping region, B and a infinite coding lattice Λ. Information is encoded to one of M levels for each of the n dimensions. Therefore, the number of codepoints is M^n.

More formally, an n-dimensional lattice code is defined by its $n \times n$ lattice generator matrix G and a shaping region B. Every codeword is of the form $x = Gb$, where $b \in \mathbb{Z}^n$. Therefore, $G^{-1}x \in \mathbb{Z}^n$ for all x. The parity check matrix is defined to be $H = G^{-1}$. Given a noisy codeword $y = x + w$, where w is a noise with distribution $N(0, \sigma^2)$, the syndrome is defined as $s = frac\{Hy\}$, where $frac\{x\} = x - \lfloor x \rceil$. Note that y is a lattice point iff $frac\{Hy\} = 0$. Hence if $s = frac\{Hy\}$, then $s = frac\{H(x + w)\} = frac\{H(w)\}$.

If communication happens through a real channel, the energy used to transmit has to be finite. In this case we can calculate the average power needed to send a chosen word of this code.

$$P_{av} = \frac{1}{M^n} \sum_{x \in \Lambda \cap B} ||x||^2 \tag{1}$$

and the Signal-to-Noise Ratio (SNR) is P_{av}/σ^2.

However, if lattices codes are used in scenarios other than communication (such as ours) then this power constraint is absent. To be able to give a meaningful interpretation of capacity for such cases, there exists a theoretical tool, the *unconstrained power channel* (UPC), see [Pol94]. A chosen point of Λ is transmitted by n uses of the AWGN channel with noise variance σ^2 with no power restriction; a constrained is imposed by including $Vol(\Lambda)$, the density of the lattice (or the volume of the Voronoi cell). The *Generalized Signal to Noise Ratio* ($GSNR$) for a lattice Λ and noise power σ^2 is now defined as:

$$GSNR = \frac{Vol(\Lambda)^{\frac{2}{n}}}{2 \pi e \sigma^2} \tag{2}$$

In a UPC, error correction with a small probability of error is possible only if $GSNR \geq 1$, whereas error correction is impractical if $GSNR < 1$. Therefore the maximum noise power which still corrects errors given a lattice Λ can be calculated setting $GSNR = 1$.

$$\sigma_{max}^2 = \frac{Vol(\Lambda)^{\frac{2}{n}}}{2\pi e}. \tag{3}$$

2.3 Discrete and Continuous Fuzzy Extractors

A *fuzzy extractor* takes some fuzzy information x (such as a biometriç reading) as input and, combined with helper information Q, is able to extract a uniform random string s of length l. Discrete fuzzy extractors are defined in [DRS08]. In [BDHV07b] this definition is extended to continuous fuzzy extractors for biometric data. Our definitions and proofs are strongly based on [BDHV07b] and its sequel, [VTOSŠ10], and readers who want more details than provided in this brief summary are encouraged to consult these two papers.

The formal definition of fuzzy extractors specifies two random procedures, "generate" and "regenerate", together with a security and a correctness property. Loosely speaking, the *security* property says that an outside (passive) observer gains negligible information about s. The definition and proof we present in Sect. 5 are inspired on [VTOSŠ10], definition 2.5. Our proof, which uses the UPC, does not depend on the particular lattice codes chosen, but the security level achieved does.

The *correctness* property states that if the two features are sufficiently close, then Gen almost always succeeds. In the context of biometrics this means that the False Rejection Rate (FRR) should be small. In our scheme the FRR depends on the correction capacity of the code chosen and is very difficult to approximate analytically. Practical experiments have shown a FRR of a few percent; details are beyond the scope of this paper.

In this paper we define the statistical distance between two probability distributions A and B as $SD(A, B) = sup_v |Pr(A = v) - Pr(B = v)|$. This somewhat unusual definition simplifies the proofs. The min-entropy of a discrete random variable X is defined as $H_\infty(X) = -\log(max_x p_X(x))$. Finally, l denotes the length of the string s, and U_l the uniform distribution over $\{0, 1\}^l$.

Definition 1 [BDHV07b]. *A $(\mathcal{M}_g, m, l, \epsilon)$ discrete fuzzy extractor is a pair of randomized procedures* Gen *and* Reg *where:*

Gen *is a (necessarily randomized) generation function which, on input $w \in \mathcal{M}$, extracts a private string $s \in \{0, 1\}^l$ and a public string Q, such that for all random variables W over $\mathcal{M}$ such that $H_\infty[W] \geq m$ and independent variables $\langle s, Q \rangle \leftarrow$ Gen$[w]$ it holds that $SD[\langle s, Q \rangle, \langle U_l, Q \rangle] \leq \epsilon$.*

Reg *is a regeneration function which, given a word $w' \in \mathcal{M}$ and a public string Q, outputs a string $s \in \{0, 1\}^l$ such that for any words $w, w' \in \mathcal{M}$ satisfying $d(w, w') \leq t$ and any possible pair $\langle s, Q \rangle \leftarrow$ Gen$[w]$, it holds that $s =$ Reg$[w', Q]$.*

We proceed to define a fuzzy extractor for continuous features (distributions). Let $\mathcal{X}_a$ be the probability distribution that describes a user (a stands for authentic), while $\mathcal{X}_g$ represents the distribution of the whole population (g means global). Also let D_g be the quantization of $\mathcal{X}_g$ and define $m = H_\infty(D_g)$. This quantization is necessary because we need to have a meaningful value for the min-entropy of $\mathcal{X}_g$. Also, at some point the algorithm will have to do a quantization in order to output the discrete secret s. Therefore, it is natural to analyze $\mathcal{X}_g$ by some quantization.

In Sect. 3.4 of [BDHV07b] it is shown that ϵ, the distance to the uniform distribution, can be bounded as a function of the min-entropy m and the length l:

$$\epsilon(m,l) = \begin{cases} 0, & \text{if } m = l \\ 2^{-l}, & \text{if } l-1 < m < l \\ 2^{-m} - 2^{-l}, & \text{if } m \leq l-1 \end{cases}$$

Also, recall that, intuitively, Reg should only work if the two features are sufficiently similar. In the next definition this condition is substituted by stipulating that the regeneration procedure should succeed with probability $P_{suc} = 1 - FRR$.

Definition 2 [BDHV07b]. *An $(\mathcal{X}_g, m, l, FRR)$ continuous-source fuzzy extractor for the user distribution $\mathcal{X}_a$ is a pair of randomized procedures* Gen *and* Reg *where:*

Gen *is a (necessarily randomized) generation function which, on input $\mathcal{X}_a$, extracts a private string $s \in \{0,1\}^l$ and a public string Q, such that for any user distribution $\mathcal{X}_a$ the following holds: if $\langle s, Q \rangle \leftarrow$ Gen$[\mathcal{X}_a]$ then $SD[\langle s, Q \rangle, \langle U_l, Q \rangle] \leq \epsilon(m, l)$.*

Reg *is a regeneration function which, given a measurement u' sampled from $\mathcal{X}_a$ and a public string Q, outputs a string $s =$ Reg$[u', Q] \in \{0,1\}^l$ where $\langle s, Q \rangle \leftarrow$ Gen$[\mathcal{X}_a]$, with probability equal to the detection probability $1 - FRR$.*

3   A CS-Fuzzy Extractor Assuming White Gaussian Noise

We are now ready to present our continuous-source fuzzy extractor based on lattice codes, instantiating Definition 2 by specifying the two procedures Gen and Reg.

Definition 3 *(Instantiation of Definition 2). Let $\mathcal{X}_g$ be the global distribution of the feature and X_d its domain, the distribution of the feature of a user be $\mathcal{X}_a$, a lattice Λ with generator matrix G and D_g the distribution $\mathcal{X}_g$ quantized by Λ with $H_\infty(D_g) = m$. This means that we quantize $\mathcal{X}_g$ by the decoding its realization to the nearest lattice point. We define the functions* Gen: $X_d \rightarrow \mathbb{R}^n \times \{0,1\}^l$ *and* Reg: $X_d \times \mathbb{R}^n \rightarrow \{0,1\}^l$ *as follows:*

Gen *receives as input $\mathcal{X}_a$ and outputs a secret information $s \in \{0,1\}^l$ that is equal to a random point $b \in \mathcal{B}^n$ where $\mathcal{B} = \{-2^{\frac{l}{2n}}, \cdots, 2^{\frac{l}{2n}} - 1\}$ and a* *public vector $Q \in \mathbb{R}^n$ such as $Q = S + X_a$, where S is found by taking $S = Gb$. Also $SD((s, Q), (U_l, Q)) \leq \epsilon(m, l)$.*

Reg *receives as inputs the points $Y, Q \in \mathbb{R}^n$, where Y is a measurement of X_a, and outputs a string $s \in \{0,1\}^l$ with probability $1 - FRR$. Using the UPC, the string s is found after calculating the nearest lattice point of $Q - Y$, taking its index, converting to a string of a bits regenerating finally s.*

Recall that the FRR, i.e. the probability that error correction fails, depends on the choice of Λ, as shown by Eq. (3) on page 6. The difference $Q - Y$ equals $S + X_a - Y$, so in our model this implies that S is the original information with noise $X_a - Y$.

Our cs-fuzzy extractor can be viewed as the code-offset method applied in $\mathbb{R}^n$. With minor modifications it can be used as a key reconciliation scheme, as depicted in Fig. 1.

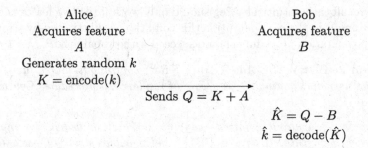

Fig. 1. Code-offset method in $\mathbb{R}^n$

4 Dealing with Different Types of Noise

4.1 Gaussian Approximation Using the Central Limit Theorem

The UPC has the supported maximum noise (i.e. allowing error correction) described by Eq. (3). However, this equation only holds if the noise has Gaussian distribution, which in practice is not always true. So, if the correction needs to be maximized to achieve the theoretical limit, then the features need to be adjusted.

Analyzing the scheme, the vector $S + X - Y$ is decoded to the nearest lattice point. Therefore, $X - Y$ can be seen merely as a noise e. As X and Y are two n-dimensional vectors then the position i of the noise e is:

$$e[i] = X[i] - Y[i] \tag{4}$$

Assuming that each position of the vectors X and Y are respectively i.i.d (independent and identically distributed) random variables, then we can conclude that e is a white noise. So, the central limit theorem can be used to adjust the noise to have a distribution closer to the Gaussian.

This theorem (as described in [Was04, p. 77]) states that if there are n i.i.d random variables $(X_1, X_2, \cdots, X_n)$, with mean μ and variance σ^2, and $\overline{X} = \frac{1}{n}\sum_{i=1}^{n} X_i$, then:

$$\overline{X} \approx N\left(\mu, \frac{\sigma^2}{n}\right) \tag{5}$$

as $n \to \infty$. Hence, if a moving average filter without the constant for division is used in X and Y before the difference is calculated, then the result will be:

$$e_{smooth}[i] = \sum_{t=-t_2}^{t_1} X[t+i] - Y[t+i] \quad t_1, t_2 \in \mathbb{Z}^+, \tag{6}$$

By Eq. (4):

$$e_{smooth}[i] = \sum_{t=-t_2}^{t_1} e[t+i] \tag{7}$$

As the size of the window increases, $e_{smooth}[i]$ will be closer to a Gaussian random variable with mean $(t_1 + t_2 + 1)\mu_e$ and variance $(t_1 + t_2 + 1)\sigma_e^2$ making the correction easier in the UPC.

The cost of this operation is that the entropy of the feature will be decreased. For example the original distribution could be uniform, but after this process it will be closer to a Gaussian.

Also, this will work only if the noise is already white (X and Y are white). If it is not, then the feature extraction as to be changed or some whitening method has to be used on the features to at least make correction possible. However, there is an important point. X and Y need to be white processes but, at the same time, $X[i]$ and $Y[i]$ need to have high correlation $\forall i$ and, for an adversary that tries to impersonate a legitimate part with a degraded feature, the correlation has to be low.

In [YRB98] a Singular Value Decomposition (SVD) of the correlation matrix between X and Y that works exactly in this desired way has been shown. Therefore, we have a way to make to the correlation 0 between samples. This may not make them independent, but it may be enough for the Gaussian approximation. Only a good estimation of the correlation matrix is needed.

4.2 Variance Normalization to Stay Within the Correction Capacity

Still, the noise power can assume values larger than the theoretical limits. To avoid this, only a simple change of the lattice needs to be performed. However, depending on the correction scheme used, this may not possible. Because $Vol(\Lambda)$ is a constant, the maximum noise power supported is also a constant. Therefore, the remaining option is to process the feature.

So, by Eq. (6), if X and Y are multiplied by c, then the error will be also multiplied by this constant.

$$e_{smooth}[i] = c\sum_{t=-t2}^{t1} X[t+i] - Y[t+i] \tag{8}$$

So, the noise power $\sigma^2 = \text{var}(X - Y)$ is multiplied by c^2. The $GSNR$ as described by Eq. (2) will be:

$$GSNR = \frac{Vol(\Lambda)^{\frac{2}{n}}}{2\pi e\sigma^2 c^2}$$

$$= \frac{\sqrt[n]{|det\,G|^2}}{2\pi e\sigma^2 c^2}$$

$$= \frac{\sqrt[n]{(\frac{1}{c^n}|det\,G|)^2}}{2\pi e\sigma^2} \qquad (9)$$

$$= \frac{\sqrt[n]{(|det\,\frac{G}{c}|)^2}}{2\pi e\sigma^2}$$

The maximum noise is:

$$\sigma^2_{max} = \frac{\sqrt[n]{(\frac{1}{c^n}|det\,G|)^2}}{2\pi e\sigma^2} \qquad (10)$$

We summarize this as follows.

Fact 1. *A feature vector X normalized by some constant c is equivalent to multiplying the $Vol(\Lambda)$ by the n-th power of the inverse of the same constant.*

Fact 2. *The supported maximum noise when the feature vector X is normalized by some constant c is the same of the sublattice Λ_S of Λ with $G_s = \frac{1}{c}G$ and $Vol(\Lambda_S) = \frac{1}{c^n}Vol(\Lambda)$.*

5   Proof of Security of Our Fuzzy Extractor

We will now analyze the cs-fuzzy extractor of Definition 3. We will prove not only the security of the cs-fuzzy extractor proposed with a lower bound but also the maximum min-entropy of the secret with an upper bound. Both limits give us a more precise idea of the security of the scheme.

Assuming that the adversary is passive and that he has knowledge of Q, $\mathcal{X}_g$ and the lattice Λ used, he can simply estimate the region in which S can occur. Figure 2 shows one instance of our scheme pointing out the global distribution $\mathcal{X}_g$ and the region that the adversary knows. Note that, depending on the realization of Q, the possible values of S change. The distribution $\mathcal{X}_g$ has been translated and reflected in order to correctly analyze the probability distribution function of S.

Property S_3 of [VTOSŠ10] for a worst-case $\tilde{m}$-secure fuzzy extractor dictates a lower bound for the min-entropy of the secret information given the helper data. Before we prove that our fuzzy extractor has this property, we will prove an upper bound of the min-entropy of the secret. It will give us a natural bound and also the idea to how to prove the lower bound.

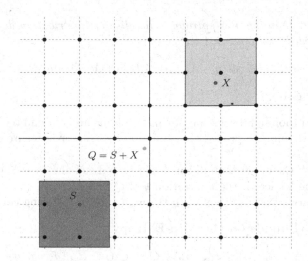

Fig. 2. Security Analysis of the Code-Offset Method

Theorem 1 (Upper Bound for the Adversary on the Min-Entropy).

For an adversary, the min-entropy of the secret information S given that he has knowledge of the lattice Λ used, of the global distribution $\mathcal{X}_g$ and of the realization q of the transmitted information Q, is less or equal than the min-entropy of the discrete distribution defined as $q - \mathcal{X}_g$ decoded to the nearest lattice point.

$$H_\infty(S|\mathcal{X}_g, Q = q, \Lambda) \le H_\infty(decode(q - \mathcal{X}_g)) \tag{11}$$

The proof of this theorem is in Appendix A.

The value $H_\infty(decode(q-\mathcal{X}_g))$ depends of the lattice chosen, the realization q of Q and the global distribution of the feature and can be calculated empirically.

Using the idea presented for the upper bound, we are ready to present the lower bound of the min-entropy.

Theorem 2 (Lower Bound for the Adversary on the Min-Entropy).

Define the random variable $\mathcal{X}_{tf} = [f_1(X_1), f_2(X_2), \cdots, f_n(X_n)]$ with the function f returning a random variable as

$$f_i(X_i) = \begin{cases} X_i & \text{if } b_i - a_i > ||c_{max}|| \\ p(\frac{a_i+b_i}{2}) = 1 \text{ and } 0 \text{ otherwise,} & \text{otherwise.} \end{cases}$$

Let $||c_{max}||$ stand for the length of the biggest vector of the generator matrix G of Λ and $[a_i, b_i]$ stands for the interval of occurrence of X_i. Let the matrix C be an n-dimensional diagonal matrix with non-zero elements as $c_1, c_2, \cdots, c_n$ with $c_i = \frac{b_i-a_i-||c_{max}||}{b_i-a_i}$ if X_i is not a constant, otherwise $c_i = 1$ for $1 \le i \le n$.

For an adversary, the min-entropy of the secret information S given that he has knowledge of the lattice Λ used, of the global distribution $\mathcal{X}_g = [X_1, X_2, \cdots, X_n]$ and of the realization q of the transmitted information Q is *greater or equal than the min-entropy of the discrete distribution defined as been* $q - \mathcal{X}_{min}$ *decoded to the nearest lattice point.*

$$H_\infty(decode(q - \mathcal{X}_{min})) \leq H_\infty(S|\mathcal{X}_g, Q = q, \Lambda) \tag{12}$$

where $\mathcal{X}_{min} = C\mathcal{X}_{tf}$.

The complete proof and discussion of this theorem can be found on Appendix B.

With this bound, we proved that our fuzzy extractor is secure according to property S_3.

Just as with the upper bound, this lower bound can also be calculated empirically using the lattice Λ, the realization q of Q and X_g.

We summarize the results of both theorems in the following corollary.

Corollary 1 (Bounds on the Min-Entropy)

$$H_\infty(decode(q - \mathcal{X}_{min})) \leq H_\infty(S|\mathcal{X}_g, Q = q, \Lambda) \leq H_\infty(decode(q - \mathcal{X}_g)) \tag{13}$$

One important fact is that the parameter $Vol(\Lambda)$ determines the density of lattice points and, therefore, the min-entropy. By Eq. (3), the same parameter $Vol(\Lambda)$ also determines the maximum supported noise. So, there is a trade-off between correction capacity and security.

As discussed in Sect. 4.2, the normalization can be done to lower down the noise power. However, given a lattice Λ, it may be used to decrease its volume and, at the same time, increase the min-entropy. By Fact 1, the $Vol(\Lambda)$ can be changed and, consequently, the security level and correction capacity of the fuzzy extractor can be adjusted without changing the lattice Λ. Furthermore, the lower bound provided by Theorem 2 also uses this normalization to analyze the multiplication by C as the shrinking of X_g or the increasing of $Vol(\Lambda)$.

6   Practical Construction with Low-Density Lattice Codes

Low-Density Lattice Codes (defined in [SFS08]) are capacity achieving codes with efficient coding and decoding algorithms. They use an n-dimensional lattice with a square non-singular generator matrix G, with $G^{-1} = H$, where H is the parity check matrix which is always sparse and with $|\det H| = |\det G| = 1$.

The uncoded message b is an n-dimensional vector of integers. The encoded message S is a point of the lattice with $S = Gb$, $(S \in \mathbb{R}^n)$. According to [SFS08] the complexity of encoding has linear time and memory requirements if the Jacobi method is used. For decoding, because of the sparse structure of H, it is possible to use a belief-propagation algorithm similar to those used for Low-Density Parity Check Codes [Gal62]. Its execution time and memory usage have linear complexity too.

Because LDLC work in the UPC with $|\det G| = 1$, by Eq. (3) the maximum supported noise power (i.e. still allowing error correction) is:

$$\sigma^2_{max\_LDLC} = \frac{1}{2\pi e} \tag{14}$$

For the generation of G and H, [SFS08] gives an efficient, non-deterministic algorithm which creates a random parity matrix needing as inputs only the desired dimension n and the sparsity level d of the matrix (numbers of nonzero elements in each column or in each line).

If we use LDLC in the code-offset method of Fig. 1, then we can easily create the generator matrix G for any size of the feature. Also we will have the advantages of linear complexity in execution time and memory for the encoding and decoding steps. Observe that the noise may not have Gaussian distribution or power below the acceptable limit as shown by Eq. (14). However, as discussed in Sect. 4, both problems can be solved with a modified moving average filter and the normalization of the data, respectively. Therefore, LDLC are a practical, suitable choice for the code-offset method in $\mathbb{R}^n$.

We can add the functionalities of the LDLC to the construction of Sect. 3. The decoder of LDLC finds the nearest lattice point and the lattices used are randomly generated with volume equal to 1.

7   Conclusion

The question of reconciliating continuous features (as opposed to bits) is both interesting and important. In this paper we presented a novel approach using lattice codes. In particular, we proposed a new practical cs-fuzzy extractor using LDLC in the UPC with the code-offset method. The advantages are its linear complexity in execution time and memory requirements, and the generalization to any dimension.

In Sect. 4 two more phases to the cs-fuzzy extractor were introduced in order to make any feature suitable to be used. The first phase shows how to adjust the feature to be close to a Gaussian and the second shows a normalization that bounds the noise power to make correction possible.

We derived in Sect. 5 an upper bound and a lower bound for the entropy of the key given a passive adversary, proving that the proposed fuzzy extractor is secure. This bounds are not attached to a specific code, but with the UPC.

8   Open Questions and Possible Future Work

First, it is desirable to prove a tighter bound on $H_\infty(S|\mathcal{X}_g, Q = q, \Lambda)$, the min-entropy that an adversary can obtain about the secret. Another possibility is to substitute the Low-Density Lattice Codes with some other lattice codes, such as LDA [PBZB12]. We suspect this leads to a better performance.

More general theoretical questions concern the possibility of using these techniques for Continuous-Variable Quantum Key Distribution (see for instance [LHHPZ15]). Also, it is well-known that a noisy channel can be used as a starting point for Oblivious Transfer between two parties [CK88]. So one obvious approach is to prove a *lower* bound on the noise between Alice and Bob and present a practical OT protocol based on correlated features.

The fuzzy extractor presented here has been applied to a pairing protocol for smartphones based on audio. The signal processing performed on the audio is quite complex, and will be discussed in another paper.

Appendix

A   Proof of Theorem 1

Proof In order to know which realization of the secret information was chosen, the adversary takes the realization of the public transmitted information q and decreases from the distribution $\mathcal{X}_g$. This results in a translation of $\mathcal{X}_g$. The consequence is that this translation changes the configuration of lattice points inside the domain of the distribution. Therefore, it is necessary to analyze the security for each realization of Q.

Given q, the used lattice Λ and because $S = Q - \mathcal{X}_a$, the adversary knows the possible realizations of S. The probability of each realization S_i of S is that the value is inside its Voronoi cell. Therefore

$$P[S_i] = \int \cdots \int_{V_q(S_i)} p_X(-v_1 + q_1, \cdots, -v_n + q_n)dv_1 \cdots dv_n, \ S_i \in \mathcal{S} \quad (15)$$

where $V_q(S_i)$ stands for the Voronoi cell of the point S_i regarding the set with the same domain of $q - \mathcal{X}_g$ and $\mathcal{S} = \{S_1, S_2, \cdots, S_m\}$ with $\mathcal{S} \subseteq \Lambda$.

However, the division of the space using the domain of $p - \mathcal{X}_g$ and the lattice Λ can be different. Some regions that belong to some Voronoi cell of a point of $\mathcal{S}$ could be closer to an outside point. The set of points $\mathcal{M} = \{M_1, M_2, \cdots, M_k\}$ is defined with the following property

$$V'(M_j) = \mathcal{S} \cap V(M_j), M_j \in \Lambda, j \in \mathbb{Z}^+ \quad (16)$$

with $V'(M_j) \neq \emptyset$ and $V(M_j)$ is its Voronoi cell regarding the lattice Λ.

If S could be mapped to those points, then their probabilities are

$$P[M_j] = \int \cdots \int_{V'(M_j)} p_X(-v_1 + q_1, \cdots, -v_n + q_n)dv_1 \cdots dv_n, V'(M_j) \neq \emptyset \quad (17)$$

The maximum value possible for $P[M_j]$ is $V'(M_j) = \min(V(M_j), \max(V_q(S_i)))$. In other words, when $V(M_j) \subseteq \mathcal{P}$. Because $\mathcal{S} \subseteq \mathcal{M}$, then

$$\max(P[S_i]) \geq \max(P[M_j]) \quad (18)$$

This implies that

$$H_\infty(\mathcal{S}) \leq H_\infty(\mathcal{M}) \quad (19)$$

The set $\mathcal{M}$ is exactly the decoding of the points of $q - \mathcal{X}_g$ without any restriction, therefore

$$H_\infty(\mathcal{M}) = H_\infty(\text{decode}(q - \mathcal{X}_g)) \quad (20)$$

The probability of the points of $\mathcal{S}$ for an adversary can be seen as

$$P[\mathcal{S}] = P[S|\mathcal{X}_g, Q = q, \Lambda] \tag{21}$$

By Eqs. (19), (20) and (21) we conclude that

$$H_\infty(S|\mathcal{X}_g, Q = q, \Lambda) \le H_\infty(\text{decode}(q - \mathcal{X}_g)) \tag{22}$$

B   Proof of Theorem 2

This proof will use the same idea of the proof for the upper bound. The difference is that we will create a distribution $\mathcal{X}_{min}$ that is just the adjustment of the distribution $\mathcal{X}_g$ in a way that $q - \mathcal{X}_{min}$ will always decode to a lattice point covered by the domain X_d of $\mathcal{X}_g$. This adjustment can be seen as the decrease of the region determined by X_d or the increase of the volume of the lattice Λ.

Proof. In order to know which realization of the secret information was chosen, the adversary takes the realization of the public transmitted information q and decreases from the distribution $\mathcal{X}_g$. This results in a translation of $\mathcal{X}_g$. The consequence is that this translation changes the configuration of lattice points inside the domain of the distribution. Therefore, it is necessary to analyze the security for each realization of Q.

Given q, the used lattice Λ and because $S = Q - \mathcal{X}_a$, the adversary knows the possible realizations of S. The probability of each realization S_i of S is that the value is inside its Voronoi cell. Therefore

$$P[S_i] = \int \cdots \int_{V_q(S_i)} p_X(-v_1 + q_1, \cdots, -v_n + q_n) dv_1 \cdots dv_n, \ S_i \in \mathcal{S} \tag{23}$$

where $V_q(S_i)$ stands for the Voronoi cell of the point S_i regarding the set with the same domain of $q - \mathcal{X}_g$ and $\mathcal{S} = \{S_1, S_2, \cdots, S_m\}$ with $\mathcal{S} \subseteq \Lambda$.

However, the division of the space using the domain of $q - \mathcal{X}_g$ and the lattice Λ can be different. Some regions that belong to some Voronoi cell of a point of $\mathcal{S}$ could be closer to an outside point. Because of this, we will shrink the domain of $q - \mathcal{X}_g$ in a way that the decoding will find only lattice points inside this region.

Finding the exactly configuration of lattice points is hard, but we know that lattice points are a linear combination of vectors of the generator matrix G and that the maximum distance between lattice point is the length $||c_{max}||$ of the biggest vector of G. Therefore, if we decrease $||c_{max}||$ from a lattice point, we will pass by another lattice point.

Now, assuming that $\mathcal{X}_g = [X_1, X_2, \cdots, X_n]$ and that the domain of each X_i is $[a_i, b_i]$ with $b_i - a_i > ||c_{max}||$, then we can transform each X_i in a way that if we choose a point inside X_d then it will decoded also to a point inside X_d. If we use the interval $\left[a_i + \frac{||c_{max}||}{2}, b_i - \frac{||c_{max}||}{2}\right]$ with $1 \le i \le n$, all points in this region will be decoded to a lattice point that belongs to $q - \mathcal{X}_g$. However, the fact that $b_i - a_i \le ||c_{max}||$ may occur. In this case, we will treat X_i as a constant with $p(\frac{a_i+b_i}{2}) = 1$ and 0 otherwise. The value $\frac{a_i+b_i}{2}$ is chosen in order to force the decoding function to find a point inside $q - \mathcal{X}_g$. The consequence of this approach is that the variable X_i does not contribute to the overall min-entropy.

First we define a function f that transforms the random variables that have a interval of occurrence less than $||c_{max}||$:

$$f_i(X_i) = \begin{cases} X_i & \text{if } b_i - a_i > ||c_{max}|| \\ p(\frac{a_i+b_i}{2}) = 1 \text{ and } 0 \text{ otherwise}, & \text{otherwise} \end{cases}$$

With this function, we have only the random variables that we can surely map to lattice points inside the domain of $q - \mathcal{X}_g$.

It is important to notice that the decrease in the interval is just a multiplication of the random variable X_i by the constant $c_i = \frac{b_i-a_i-||c_{max}||}{b_i-a_i}$. The resulting probability density function is $p_{Y_i}(y_i) = p_{X_i}(\frac{y_i}{c_i})\frac{1}{c_i}$. We can conclude that $c < 1$ and $\lim\limits_{b_i-a_i \to \infty} c_i = 1$, or in other words, if the interval is large enough the approximation will be close.

We define $X_{tf} = [f_1(X_1), \cdots, f_n(X_n)]$ and the diagonal matrix C with elements as

$$c_i = \begin{cases} \frac{b_i-a_i-||c_{max}||}{b_i-a_i} & \text{if } b_i - a_i > ||c_{max}|| \\ 1, & \text{otherwise} \end{cases}$$

Taking $\mathcal{X}_{min} = CX_{tf}$ will give a smaller region where all points will be decoded to points of $q - \mathcal{X}_d$. The set $\mathcal{M} = \{M_1, \cdots, M_k\}$ is defined as the one with the elements that will be the outcome of $\text{decode}(q - \mathcal{X}_{min})$. Assuming that the domain of $q - \mathcal{X}_g$ will be a convex area, their probabilities are

$$P[M_j] = \int \cdots \int_{V'(M_j)} p_{\mathcal{X}_{min}}(-v_1 + q_1, \cdots, -v_o + q_o)dv_1 \cdots dv_o$$

$$= \prod_{i=1}^{n} \frac{1}{c_i} \int \cdots \int_{V'(M_j)} p_X\left(-v_1 + q_1, \cdots, -v_o + q_o | X_{o+1} = \right. \tag{24}$$

$$q_{o+1} - \frac{a_{o+1} + b_{o+1}}{2}, \cdots X_n = q_n - \frac{a_n + b_n}{2}\right)dv_1 \cdots dv_o$$

with $0 \le o \le n$ and $V'(M_j)$ is the Voronoi cell regarding $q - \mathcal{X}_{min}$.

Because $\mathcal{M} \subseteq \mathcal{S}$, then

$$\max(P[M_j]) \ge \max(P[S_i]) \tag{25}$$

This implies that

$$H_\infty(\mathcal{M}) \le H_\infty(\mathcal{S}) \tag{26}$$

The set $\mathcal{M}$ is the decoding of the points of $q - \mathcal{X}_{min}$ without any restriction, therefore

$$H_\infty(\mathcal{M}) = H_\infty(\text{decode}(q - \mathcal{X}_{min})) \tag{27}$$

The probability of the points of $\mathcal{S}$ for an adversary can be seen to be

$$P[\mathcal{S}] = P[S|\mathcal{X}_g, Q = q, \Lambda] \tag{28}$$

By Eqs. (26), (27) and (28) we conclude that

$$H_\infty(\text{decode}(q - \mathcal{X}_{min})) \leq H_\infty(S|\mathcal{X}_g, Q = q, \Lambda) \tag{29}$$

References

[BB84]   Bennett, C.H., Brassard, G.: Quantum cryptography: public key distribution and coin tossing. In: Proceedings of the IEEE International Conference on Computers, Systems, and Signal Processing, Bangalore, India, pp. 175–179 (1984)

[BB84]   Bennett, C.H., Brassard, G., Crépeau, C., Skubiszewska, M.-H.: Practical quantum oblivious transfer. In: Feigenbaum, J. (ed.) CRYPTO 1991. LNCS, vol. 576, pp. 351–366. Springer, Heidelberg (1992). doi:10.1007/3-540-46766-1_29

[BDHV07a] Buhan, I.R., Doumen, J.M., Hartel, P.H., Veldhuis, R.N.J.: Constructing practical fuzzy extractors using QIM. Technical report TR-CTIT-07-52, Centre for Telematics and Information Technology University of Twente (2007)

[BDHV07b] Buhan, I.R., Doumen, J.M., Hartel, P.H., Veldhuis, R.N.J., Fuzzy Extractors for Continuous Distributions. In: Proceedings of the 2nd ACM Symposium on Information, Computer and Communications Security, pp. 353–355. ACM (2007)

[BS94]   Brassard, G., Salvail, L.: Secret-key reconciliation by public discussion. In: Helleseth, T. (ed.) EUROCRYPT 1993. LNCS, vol. 765, pp. 410–423. Springer, Heidelberg (1994). doi:10.1007/3-540-48285-7_35

[CK88]   Crépeau, C., Kilian, J.: Achieving oblivious transfer using weakened security assumptions (extended abstract). In: FOCS 1988–29th Annual Symposium on Foundations of Computer Science, pp. 42–52 (1988)

[Cré97] Crépeau, C.: Efficient cryptographic protocols based on noisy channels. In: Fumy, W. (ed.) EUROCRYPT 1997. LNCS, vol. 1233, pp. 306–317. Springer, Heidelberg (1997). doi:10.1007/3-540-69053-0_21

[CS98]   Conway, J.H., Sloane, N.J.A.: Sphere Packings, Lattices Groups. Springer, Heidelberg (1998). ISBN: 0387985859

[CZC04] Chang, Y.J., Zhang, W., Chen, T.: Biometrics-based cryptographic key generation. In: IEEE International Conference on Multimedia and Expo, vol. 3, pp. 2203–2206 (2004)

[DRS08] Dodis, Y., Reyzin, M., Smith, A.: Fuzzy extractors: how to generate strong keys from biometrics and other noisy data. SIAM J. Comput. 38(1), 97–139 (2008)

[Gal62] Gallager, R.G.: Low-density parity-check codes. IRE Trans. Inf. Theory 8(1), 21–28 (1962)

[JS02]   Juels, A., Sudan, M.: A fuzzy vault scheme. In: Proceedings of IEEE International Symposium on Information Theory, p. 408. IEEE (2002)

[JW99]   Juels, A., Wattenberg, M.: A fuzzy commitment scheme. In: Proceedings of the 6th ACM Conference on Computer and Communications Security, pp. 28–36. ACM (1999)

[KDL09]   Kurkoski, B.M., Dauwels, J., Loeliger, H.-A.: Power-constrained communications using LDLC lattices. In: IEEE International Symposium on Information Theory ISIT, pp. 739–743. IEEE (2009)

[LHHPZ15] Lin, D., Huang, D., Huang, P., Peng, J., Zeng, G.: High performance reconciliation for continuous-variable quantum key distribution with LDPC code. Int. J. Quantum Inf. **13**(02), 1550010 (2015)

[LT03]   Linnartz, J.-P., Tuyls, P.: New shielding functions to enhance privacy and prevent misuse of biometric templates. In: Kittler, J., Nixon, M.S. (eds.) AVBPA 2003. LNCS, vol. 2688, pp. 393–402. Springer, Heidelberg (2003). doi:10.1007/3-540-44887-X_47

[PBZB12] di Pietro, N., Boutros, J.J., Zémor, G., Brunel, L.: Integer low-density lattices based on construction A. IEEE Inf. Theory Workshop (ITW) **2012**, 422–426 (2012)

[Pol94]   Poltyrev, G.: On coding without restrictions for the AWGN channel. IEEE Trans. Inf. Theory **40**(2), 409–417 (1994)

[SFS08]   Sommer, N., Feder, M., Shalvi, O.: Low-density lattice codes. IEEE Trans. Inf. Theory **54**(4), 1561–1585 (2008)

[TAKSBV05] Tuyls, P., Akkermans, A.H.M., Kevenaar, T.A.M., Schrijen, G.-J., Bazen, A.M., Veldhuis, R.N.J.: Practical biometric authentication with template protection. In: Kanade, T., Jain, A., Ratha, N.K. (eds.) AVBPA 2005. LNCS, vol. 3546, pp. 436–446. Springer, Heidelberg (2005). doi:10. 1007/11527923_45

[VTOSŠ10] Verbitskiy, E.A., Tuyls, P., Obi, C., Schoenmakers, B., Škoric, B.: Key extraction from general non-discrete signals. IEEE Trans. Inf. Forensics Secur. **5**(2), 269–279 (2010)

[Was04]   Wasserman, L.: All of Statistics: A Concise Course in Statistical Inference. Springer, Heidelberg (2004). ISBN: 0387402721

[YRB98]   Yehia, H., Rubin, P., Bateson, E.V.: Quantitative association of vocal-tract and facial behavior. Speech Commun. **26**(1), 23–43 (1998)

[ZLZ06]   Zheng, G., Li, W., Zhan, C.: Cryptographic key generation from biometric data using lattice mapping. In: IEEE 18th International Conference on Pattern Recognition, vol. 4, pp. 513–516 (2006)

[ŠT09]   Škoric, B., Tuyls, P.: An efficient fuzzy extractor for limited noise. In: Symposium on Information Theory in the Benelux, pp. 193–200 (2009)

Almost Perfect Privacy for Additive Gaussian Privacy Filters

Shahab Asoodeh[✉], Fady Alajaji, and Tamás Linder

Department of Mathematics and Statistics, Queen's University,
Jeffery Hall, 48 University Ave., Kingston, ON, Canada
{asoodehshahab,fady,linder}@mast.queensu.ca

Abstract. We study the maximal mutual information about a random variable Y (representing non-private information) displayed through an additive Gaussian channel when guaranteeing that only ε bits of information is leaked about a random variable X (representing private information) that is correlated with Y. Denoting this quantity by $g_\varepsilon(X,Y)$, we show that for perfect privacy, i.e., $\varepsilon = 0$, one has $g_0(X,Y) = 0$ for any pair of absolutely continuous random variables (X,Y) and then derive a second-order approximation for $g_\varepsilon(X,Y)$ for small ε. This approximation is shown to be related to the strong data processing inequality for mutual information under suitable conditions on the joint distribution P_{XY}. Next, motivated by an operational interpretation of data privacy, we formulate the privacy-utility tradeoff in the same setup using estimation-theoretic quantities and obtain explicit bounds for this tradeoff when ε is sufficiently small using the approximation formula derived for $g_\varepsilon(X,Y)$.

Keywords: Data privacy · Rate-privacy function · Estimation noise-to-signal ratio · MMSE · Additive Gaussian channel · Mutual information · Maximal correlation

1 Introduction

The ever increasing growth of social networks has brought major challenges in terms of data privacy. This paper focuses on a privacy problem which is relevant for users or designers of social networks: the trade-off between data privacy and customized services performance. On the one hand, users want their private data to remain secret, and on the other hand, they also desire to benefit from customized services that require personal information in order to function properly. In this context, it is reasonable to assume that the user has two kinds of data: private data such as passport numbers, credit cards numbers, etc.; and non-private data such as gender, age, etc. In general, private and non-private data are correlated. Thus, it is possible that enough non-private data discloses a non-negligible amount of private data. Therefore, it is necessary to develop techniques

---

S. Asoodeh—This work was supported in part by NSERC of Canada.

A.C.A. Nascimento and P. Barreto (Eds.): ICITS 2016, LNCS 10015, pp. 259–278, 2016.
DOI: 10.1007/978-3-319-49175-2_13

to provide/store personal data (user's point of view/designer's point of view) that yield the best customized services performance without compromising privacy. The goal of these techniques is to provide displayed data that will be used by customized services which contains as much non-private data as possible while revealing as little private data as possible. Also, for security reasons, the displayed data has to be produced using only non-private data. In general, this implies that the displayed data should be a randomized version of the non-private data.

To formulate this problem, we need to specify a privacy function and a utility function that respectively measure the amount of private and non-private data *leaked* into the displayed data. The authors of this paper recently suggested in [1] to use mutual information as the measure of both utility and privacy. Let X and Y denote the private and non-private data, respectively. The *rate-privacy function* $g_\varepsilon^{\mathsf{dis}}(X, Y)$ for discrete random variables X and Y having finite alphabets $\mathcal{X}$ and $\mathcal{Y}$, respectively is defined for any $\varepsilon \geq 0$ as the privacy-utility tradeoff

$$g_\varepsilon^{\mathsf{dis}}(X, Y) := \max_{\substack{P_{Z|Y} : X \,\multimap\, Y \,\multimap\, Z, \\ I(X;Z) \leq \varepsilon}} I(Y; Z), \tag{1}$$

where the auxiliary random variable Z is the privacy-constrained displayed data and $X \multimap Y \multimap Z$ denotes that X, Y, and Z form a Markov chain in this order. The channel $P_{Z|Y}$ is called the *privacy filter*. It is shown in [2] that $g_\varepsilon^{\mathsf{dis}}(X, Y)$ is in fact a corner point of an outer bound on the achievable region of the "dependence dilution" coding problem which provides an information-theoretic operational interpretation. It is also shown that if the channel from Y to X displays certain symmetry properties, then $g_\varepsilon^{\mathsf{dis}}(X, Y)$ can be calculated in closed form. For instance, if $P_{X|Y}$ is a binary symmetric channel (BSC) and $Y \sim \mathsf{Bernoulli}(0.5)$, then $g_\varepsilon^{\mathsf{dis}}(X, Y) = \frac{\varepsilon}{I(X;Y)}$.

As a more practical and operational notion of privacy, estimation-theoretic formulations of privacy are introduced in [3,4]. In particular, Calmon et al. [3] studied the case where $X = Y$ and defined the utility by $\Pr(\hat{Y}(Z) = Y)$ where $\hat{Y} : \mathcal{Z} \to \mathcal{Y}$ is the Bayes decoding map satisfying $I(Y; Z) \leq \varepsilon$ for discrete Y. Motivated by [5], which suggested the use of maximal correlation $\rho_m^2(X, Z)$ to measure the privacy level between X and Z, the authors in [4] recently generalized this model to arbitrary discrete X and Y, with the same utility function except that Z is required to satisfy $\rho_m^2(X, Z) \leq \varepsilon$. It was shown independently in [1,6] that if *perfect privacy* is required, i.e., Z must be statistically independent of X, then Z is also independent of Y unless the probability vectors $\{P_{Y|X}(\cdot|x) : x \in \mathcal{X}\}$ are linearly dependent (in which case Y is called *weakly independent* of X, see [7, Appendix II]). Hence, if Y is not weakly independent of X, then $g_0^{\mathsf{dis}}(X, Y) = 0$. Other formulations for privacy have appeared in [8–13].

The setting where (X, Y) is a pair of absolutely continuous random variables with $\mathcal{X} = \mathcal{Y} = \mathbb{R}$ is studied in [2] with both utility and privacy being measured by mutual information, and in [4], where both utility and privacy are measured in terms of the minimum mean-squared error (MMSE). In both cases, it is assumed that the privacy filter is an additive Gaussian channel with signal-to-noise ratio (SNR) $\gamma \geq 0$, i.e.,

$$Z = Z_\gamma := \sqrt{\gamma} Y + N_G, \tag{2}$$

where $N_G \sim \mathcal{N}(0,1)$ is independent of (X, Y). In particular, the rate-privacy function [2] is defined as

$$g_\varepsilon(X, Y) := \max_{\substack{\gamma \geq 0, \\ I(X;Z_\gamma) \leq \varepsilon}} I(Y; Z_\gamma). \tag{3}$$

Letting $\mathsf{mmse}(U|V)$ denote the MMSE of estimating U by observing V and letting var denote the variance, the estimation-theoretic privacy-utility tradeoff is defined in [4] by the *estimation noise-to-signal ratio* (ENSR):

$$\mathsf{sENSR}_\varepsilon(X, Y) := \min \frac{\mathsf{mmse}(Y|Z_\gamma)}{\mathsf{var}(Y)}, \tag{4}$$

where the minimum is taken over all $\gamma \geq 0$ such that $\mathsf{mmse}(f(X)|Z_\gamma) \geq (1-\varepsilon)\mathsf{var}(f(X))$ for any non-constant measurable function $f : \mathcal{X} \to \mathbb{R}$. Unlike $g_\varepsilon(X, Y)$, $\mathsf{sENSR}_\varepsilon(X, Y)$ has a clear operational interpretation; it is the smallest MMSE associated with estimating Y given Z from which no non-degenerate function f of X can be estimated efficiently. This notion is related to *semantic security* [14] in cryptography. An encryption mechanism is said to be semantically secure if the adversary's advantage for correctly guessing any function of the private data given an observation of the mechanism's output (i.e., the ciphertext) is required to be negligible. As opposed to the discrete case, perfect privacy is achieved if and only if $\gamma = 0$, which gives rise to $g_0(X, Y) = 0$ (or equivalently $\mathsf{sENSR}_0(X, Y) = 1$) for any absolutely continuous (X, Y).

1.1 Contributions

In this work, we investigate the "almost" perfect privacy regime, that is, when $\varepsilon > 0$ is close to zero and derive a second-order approximation for $g_\varepsilon(X, Y)$ (Corollary 2). We also obtain the first and second derivatives of the mapping $\varepsilon \mapsto g_\varepsilon(X, Y)$ for $\varepsilon \in [0, I(X; Y))$ (Theorem 1). For a pair of Gaussian random variables (X, Y), an expression for $g_\varepsilon(X, Y)$ is derived (Example 1) and it is shown that the optimal filter has SNR equal to $\frac{2^{2\varepsilon}-1}{1-2^{-2(I(X;Y)-\varepsilon)}}$ for all $\varepsilon < I(X; Y)$ and the SNR is infinity if $\varepsilon \geq I(X; Y)$. Functional properties of the map $\varepsilon \mapsto g_\varepsilon(X, Y)$ are obtained (Proposition 1); in particular, it is shown than although the map $\varepsilon \mapsto g_\varepsilon^{\mathsf{dis}}(X, Y)$ is concave [2], the map $\varepsilon \mapsto g_\varepsilon(X, Y)$ is neither convex nor concave, and is infinitely differentiable (Corollary 1). Using a recent result on the strong data processing inequality by Anantharam et al. [15], a lower bound is obtained for $g_\varepsilon(X, Y)$. Assuming $P_{Y|X}$ is a convolution with a Gaussian distribution, i.e., $Y = aX + M_G$, where $a \neq 0$ and $M_G \sim \mathcal{N}(0, \sigma_M^2)$ is independent of X, we obtain an inequality relating $\mathsf{mmse}(Y|Z_\gamma, X)$ to $\mathsf{mmse}(Y|Z_\gamma)$ from which a stronger version of Anantharam's data processing inequality is derived for our setup (Theorem 2).

One main result of this paper is to connect $g_\varepsilon(X,Y)$ with $\mathsf{sENSR}_\varepsilon(X,Y)$ in the almost perfect privacy regime when X is Gaussian (Theorem 4). This connection allows us to translate the approximation obtained for $g_\varepsilon(X,Y)$ to a lower bound for $\mathsf{sENSR}_\varepsilon(X,Y)$.

1.2 Preliminaries

For a given pair of absolutely continuous random variables (U,V), we interchangeably use P_{UV} to denote the joint probability distribution and also the joint probability density function (pdf). The MMSE of estimating U given V is given by

$$\mathsf{mmse}(U|V) := \mathbb{E}[(U - \mathbb{E}[U|V])^2] = \mathbb{E}[\mathsf{var}(U|V)],$$

where $\mathsf{var}(U|V) = \mathbb{E}[(U - \mathbb{E}[U|V])^2|V]$. Guo et al. [16] proved the following so-called I-MMSE formula relating the input-output mutual information of the additive Gaussian channel $Z_\gamma = \sqrt{\gamma}Y + N_\mathsf{G}$, where $N_\mathsf{G} \sim \mathcal{N}(0,1)$ is independent of X, with the MMSE of the input given the output:

$$\frac{\mathrm{d}}{\mathrm{d}\gamma}I(Y;Z_\gamma) = \frac{1}{2}\mathsf{mmse}(Y|Z_\gamma). \tag{5}$$

Since X, Y and Z_γ form the Markov chain $X \multimap Y \multimap Z_\gamma$, it follows that $I(X;Z_\gamma) = I(Y;Z_\gamma) - I(Y;Z_\gamma|X)$ and hence two applications of (5) yields [16, Theorem 10]

$$\frac{\mathrm{d}}{\mathrm{d}\gamma}I(X;Z_\gamma) = \frac{1}{2}\left[\mathsf{mmse}(Y|Z_\gamma) - \mathsf{mmse}(Y|Z_\gamma,X)\right]. \tag{6}$$

The second derivative of $I(Y;Z_\gamma)$ and $I(X;Z_\gamma)$ are also known via the formula [17]

$$\frac{\mathrm{d}}{\mathrm{d}\gamma}\mathsf{mmse}(Y|Z_\gamma,X) = -\mathbb{E}[\mathsf{var}^2(Y|Z_\gamma,X)]. \tag{7}$$

Rényi [18] defined the *one-sided maximal correlation between U and V* (see also [13, Definition 7.4]) as

$$\eta_V^2(U) := \sup_g \rho^2(U,g(V)) = \frac{\mathsf{var}(\mathbb{E}[U|V])}{\mathsf{var}(U)}, \tag{8}$$

where $\rho(\cdot,\cdot)$ is the (Pearson) correlation coefficient, the supremum is taken over all measurable functions g, and the equality follows from the Cauchy-Schwarz inequality. The law of total variance implies that

$$\mathsf{mmse}(U|V) = \mathsf{var}(U)(1 - \eta_V^2(U)). \tag{9}$$

In an attempt of symmetrizing $\eta_V^2(U)$, Rényi [18] (see also [19,20]) defined the *maximal correlation* as

$$\rho_m^2(U,V) = \sup_{f,g} \rho^2(f(U),g(V)). \tag{10}$$

Comparing (8) with (10) reveals that

$$\rho^2(X,Y) \le \eta_X^2(Y) \le \rho_m^2(X,Y). \tag{11}$$

Clearly, unlike maximal correlation, $\eta_X(Y)$ is asymmetric, i.e., in general $\eta_X(Y) \ne \eta_Y(X)$, and hence according to Rényi's postulates [18], it is not a "proper" measure of dependence. However, it turns out to be an appropriate measure of separability between private and non-private information in the almost perfect privacy regime (see Corollary 2). On the other hand, maximal correlation satisfies all the Rényi's postulates [18]. In particular, it is symmetric and for jointly Gaussian random variables U and V with correlation coefficient ρ, we have $\rho_m^2(U,V) = \rho^2$.

2 Rate-Privacy Function for Additive Privacy Filters

Consider a pair of absolutely continuous random variables (X,Y) distributed according to P_{XY}. Let X and Y represent the *private data* and the *non-private data*, respectively. We think of X as having fixed distribution P_X and Y being generated by the channel $P_{Y|X}$, predefined by nature. Now consider the setting where Alice observes Y and wishes to describe it as accurately as possible to Bob in order to get a utility from him. Due to the correlation between Y and the private data X, Alice needs to provide Bob a noisy version Z of Y, such that Z cannot reveal more than ε bits of information about X. In fact, we assume that Z is obtained via the privacy filter, $Z = Z_\gamma$ defined in (2). The aim is to pick $\gamma \ge 0$ such that Z_γ preserves the maximum amount of the information about Y while satisfying the privacy constraint. The rate-privacy function $g_\varepsilon(X,Y)$, defined in (3), quantifies the tradeoff between these conflicting goals [2]. Note that since $I(Y;Z_\gamma) = I(Y;Y + \frac{1}{\sqrt{\gamma}}N_G)$, we can interpret $\frac{1}{\gamma}$ as the noise variance. Due to the data processing inequality, one can restrict ε to the interval $[0, I(X;Y))$ in the definition of $g_\varepsilon(X,Y)$ and consequently for any $\varepsilon \ge I(X;Y)$ the optimal noise variance must be zero and hence $g_\varepsilon(X,Y) = \infty$. The case where the displayed data is required to carry no information at all about X, i.e., where $\varepsilon = 0$, is often called *perfect privacy*.

The maps $\gamma \mapsto I(Y;Z_\gamma)$ and $\gamma \mapsto I(X;Z_\gamma)$ are strictly increasing over $[0,\infty)$ [2, Lemmas 16, 17] and hence there exists a unique $\gamma_\varepsilon \in [0,\infty)$ such that $I(X;Z_{\gamma_\varepsilon}) = \varepsilon$ and $g_\varepsilon(X,Y) = I(Y;Z_{\gamma_\varepsilon})$. This observation yields the following proposition.

Proposition 1. *For absolutely continuous random variables (X,Y), we have*

1. *The map $\varepsilon \mapsto \gamma_\varepsilon$ is strictly increasing and continuous, and it satisfies $\gamma_0 = 0$ and $\gamma_{I(X;Y)} = \infty$.*
2. *The map $\varepsilon \mapsto g_\varepsilon(X,Y)$ is non-negative, increasing and, continuous on $[0, I(X;Y))$, and it satisfies $g_0(X,Y) = 0$ and $g_{I(X;Y)}(X,Y) = \infty$.*

3. Let $D(Y)$ denote the "non-Gaussianness" of Y, defined as $D(Y) := D$ $(P_Y||P_{Y_G})$ (here $D(\cdot||\cdot)$ is the Kullback-Leibler divergence) with Y_G being a Gaussian random variable having the same mean and variance as Y. Then we have

$$\frac{1}{2}\log\left(1 + \gamma_\varepsilon 2^{-2D(Y)}\mathrm{var}(Y)\right) \le g_\varepsilon(X, Y) \le \frac{1}{2}\log(1 + \gamma_\varepsilon \mathrm{var}(Y)).$$

Proof. Parts 1 and 2 can be proved directly from continuity and strict monotonicity of the maps $\gamma \mapsto I(Y; Z_\gamma)$ and $\gamma \mapsto I(X; Z_\gamma)$. The upper bound in part 3 is a direct consequence of the fact that a Gaussian input maximizes the mutual information between input and output of an additive Gaussian channel. The lower bound follows from the entropy power inequality [21, Theorem 17.7.3] which states that $2^{2h(Z_\gamma)} \ge \gamma 2^{2h(Y)} + 2\pi e$ and hence

$$g_\varepsilon(X, Y) = I(Y; Z_{\gamma_\varepsilon}) \le \frac{1}{2}\log\left(\gamma_\varepsilon 2^{2h(Y)} + 2\pi e\right) - \frac{1}{2}\log(2\pi e),$$

from which and the fact that $D(Y) = h(Y_G) - h(Y)$, the lower bound immediately follows.   □

In light of Proposition 1, it is clear that, unless X and Y are independent, Z_γ is independent of X if and only if $\gamma = 0$, which implies $g_0(X, Y) = 0$. As mentioned in the introduction, this is in contrast with the discrete rate-privacy function (1), where $g_0^{\mathrm{dis}}(X, Y)$ may be positive (for example, when Y is an erased version of X, see [2, Lemma 12]).

Example 1. Let (X_G, Y_G) be a pair of Gaussian random variables with zero mean and correlation coefficient ρ. Then Z_γ is also a Gaussian random variable with variance $\gamma \mathrm{var}(Y_G) + 1$. Without loss of generality assume that Y_G has unit variance. Then

$$I(X_G; Z_\gamma) = \frac{1}{2}\log\left(\frac{\gamma + 1}{\gamma - \gamma\rho^2 + 1}\right),$$

and hence for any $\varepsilon \in [0, I(X_G; Y_G))$ the equation $I(X_G; Z_\gamma) = \varepsilon$ has the unique solution

$$\gamma_\varepsilon = \frac{1 - 2^{-2\varepsilon}}{2^{-2\varepsilon} + \rho^2 - 1}.$$

Thus, we obtain

$$g_\varepsilon(X_G, Y_G) = \frac{1}{2}\log(1 + \gamma_\varepsilon) = \frac{1}{2}\log\left(\frac{\rho^2}{2^{-2\varepsilon} + \rho^2 - 1}\right)$$

$$= \frac{1}{2}\log\left(1 + \frac{2^{2\varepsilon} - 1}{1 - 2^{-2(I(X_G;Y_G)-\varepsilon)}}\right). \tag{12}$$

The graph of $g_\varepsilon(X_G, Y_G)$ is depicted in Fig. 1 for $\rho = 0.5$ and $\rho = 0.8$. It is worth noting that $g_\varepsilon(X_G, Y_G)$ is related to the Gaussian rate-distortion function $R_G(D)$ [21]. In fact, $g_\varepsilon(X_G, Y_G) = R_G(D_\varepsilon)$ for $\varepsilon \le I(X_G; Y_G)$ where

$$D_\varepsilon = \frac{2^{-2\varepsilon} - 2^{-2I(X_G;Y_G)}}{\rho^2},$$

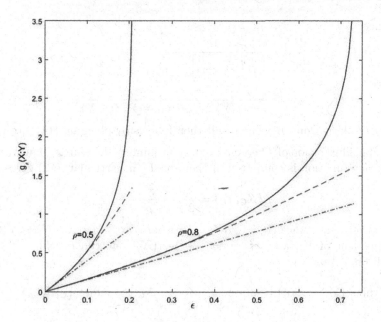

Fig. 1. The rate-privacy function for a pair of Gaussian (X_G, Y_G), given by (12), for $\rho = 0.5$ and $\rho = 0.8$. The first and second-order approximations are also shown in red and green, respectively. (Color figure online)

is the mean squared distortion incurred in reconstructing Y given the displayed data Z_γ.

The next result provides the first derivative $g'_\varepsilon(X, Y)$ of the function $\varepsilon \mapsto g_\varepsilon(X, Y)$ at any $\varepsilon < I(X; Y)$.

Theorem 1. *For any absolutely continuous random variables (X, Y), we have*

$$g'_\varepsilon(X, Y) = \frac{\mathsf{mmse}(Y | Z_{\gamma_\varepsilon})}{\mathsf{mmse}(Y | Z_{\gamma_\varepsilon}) - \mathsf{mmse}(Y | Z_{\gamma_\varepsilon}, X)}.$$

Proof. Since $g_\varepsilon(X, Y) = I(Y; Z_{\gamma_\varepsilon})$, we have

$$\frac{\mathrm{d}}{\mathrm{d}\varepsilon} g_\varepsilon(X, Y) = \left[\frac{\mathrm{d}}{\mathrm{d}\gamma} I(Y; Z_\gamma) \right]_{\gamma = \gamma_\varepsilon} \frac{\mathrm{d}}{\mathrm{d}\varepsilon} \gamma_\varepsilon$$

$$\overset{(a)}{=} \frac{1}{2} \mathsf{mmse}(Y | Z_{\gamma_\varepsilon}) \frac{\mathrm{d}}{\mathrm{d}\varepsilon} \gamma_\varepsilon, \qquad (13)$$

where (a) follows from (5). In order to calculate $\frac{\mathrm{d}}{\mathrm{d}\varepsilon} \gamma_\varepsilon$, notice that $\varepsilon = I(X; Z_{\gamma_\varepsilon})$ and hence taking the derivative of both sides of this equation with respect to ε yields

$$1 = \left[\frac{\mathrm{d}}{\mathrm{d}\gamma} I(X; Z_\gamma) \right]_{\gamma = \gamma_\varepsilon} \frac{\mathrm{d}}{\mathrm{d}\varepsilon} \gamma_\varepsilon,$$

and hence

$$\frac{\mathrm{d}}{\mathrm{d}\varepsilon}\gamma_\varepsilon = \frac{1}{\left[\frac{\mathrm{d}}{\mathrm{d}\gamma}I(X;Z_\gamma)\right]_{\gamma=\gamma_\varepsilon}}$$

$$\overset{(a)}{=} \frac{2}{\mathsf{mmse}(Y|Z_{\gamma_\varepsilon}) - \mathsf{mmse}(Y|Z_{\gamma_\varepsilon},X)}, \qquad (14)$$

where (a) follows from (6). The result then follows by plugging (14) into (13). $\square$

As a simple illustration of Theorem 1, consider jointly Gaussian X_G and Y_G whose rate-privacy function is computed in Example 1. In particular, (12) gives

$$g'_\varepsilon(X_\mathsf{G}, Y_\mathsf{G}) = \frac{2^{-2\varepsilon}}{2^{-2\varepsilon} + \rho^2 - 1}. \qquad (15)$$

On the other hand, since $X_\mathsf{G} = \sqrt{\alpha}Y_\mathsf{G} + N_1$ where $\alpha = \rho^2\mathsf{var}(X)$, $N_1 \sim \mathcal{N}(0, \sigma_N^2)$ is independent of Y_G, and $\sigma_N^2 = (1 - \rho^2)\mathsf{var}(X)$, one can conclude from [16, Proposition 3] that

$$\mathsf{mmse}(Y_\mathsf{G}|Z_\gamma, X_\mathsf{G}) = \mathsf{mmse}\left(Y_\mathsf{G}|Z_\gamma, \frac{1}{\sigma_N^2}X_\mathsf{G}\right) = \mathsf{mmse}(Y_\mathsf{G}|Z_{\gamma+a}),$$

where $a = \frac{\rho^2}{1-\rho^2}$. Recalling that $\mathsf{mmse}(Y_\mathsf{G}|Z_\gamma) = \frac{1}{1+\gamma}$, we obtain

$$\frac{\mathsf{mmse}(Y_\mathsf{G}|Z_\gamma)}{\mathsf{mmse}(Y_\mathsf{G}|Z_\gamma) - \mathsf{mmse}(Y_\mathsf{G}|Z_{\gamma+a})} = \frac{1 + (1 - \rho^2)\gamma_\varepsilon}{\rho^2}$$

$$= \frac{2^{-2\varepsilon}}{2^{-2\varepsilon} + \rho^2 - 1},$$

which equals (15).

In light of Theorem 1, we can now show that the map $\varepsilon \mapsto g_\varepsilon(X, Y)$ is in fact infinitely differentiable over $(0, I(X;Y))$.

Corollary 1. *For a pair of absolutely continuous (X, Y), the map $\varepsilon \mapsto g_\varepsilon(X, Y)$ is infinitely differentiable at any $\varepsilon \in (0, I(X;Y))$. Moreover, if all the moments of Y is finite, then $\varepsilon \mapsto g_\varepsilon(X, Y)$ is infinitely right differentiable at $\varepsilon = 0$.*

Proof. It is shown in [17, Proposition 7] that $\gamma \mapsto \mathsf{mmse}(Y|Z_\gamma)$ is infinitely differentiable at any $\gamma > 0$ and infinitely right differentiable at $\gamma = 0$ if all the moments of Y are finite. Thus the corollary follows from Theorem 1 noting that since $\mathbb{E}[Y^k] < \infty$ for all k, we also have $\mathbb{E}[Y^k|X = x] < \infty$ for almost all x (except for x in a set of zero P_X-measure). It therefore follows that $\gamma \mapsto \mathsf{mmse}(Y|Z_\gamma, X)$ is also infinitely right differentiable at $\gamma = 0$. $\square$

We remark that using (7) and Theorem 1, one can easily calculate the second derivative as

$$g''_\varepsilon(X, Y) = \frac{\mathrm{d}^2}{\mathrm{d}\varepsilon^2}g_\varepsilon(X, Y)$$

$$= \frac{2\left(\mathsf{mmse}(Y|Z_{\gamma_\varepsilon}, X)\mathbb{E}[\mathsf{var}^2(Y|Z_{\gamma_\varepsilon})] - \mathsf{mmse}(Y|Z_{\gamma_\varepsilon})\mathbb{E}[\mathsf{var}^2(Y|Z_{\gamma_\varepsilon}, X)]\right)}{[\mathsf{mmse}(Y|Z_{\gamma_\varepsilon}) - \mathsf{mmse}(Y|Z_{\gamma_\varepsilon}, X)]^3}.$$

$$(16)$$

The following corollary, which is an immediate consequence of Theorem 1, provides a second-order approximation for $g_\varepsilon(X, Y)$ as $\varepsilon \downarrow 0$ and thus an approximation to the the rate-privacy function in the almost perfect privacy regime.

Corollary 2. *For a given pair of absolutely continuous random variables* (X, Y), *we have as* $\varepsilon \downarrow 0$,

$$g_\varepsilon(X, Y) = \frac{\varepsilon}{\eta_X^2(Y)} + \Delta(X, Y)\varepsilon^2 + o(\varepsilon^2),$$

where

$$\Delta(X, Y) = \frac{1}{\eta_X^4(Y)} \left(\frac{\operatorname{var}^2(Y) - \mathbb{E}[\operatorname{var}^2(Y|X)]}{\operatorname{var}^2(Y)\eta_X^2(Y)} - 1 \right), \tag{17}$$

and $\eta_X^2(Y)$ *is the one-sided maximal correlation between* X *and* Y *defined in* (8).

Proof. According to Corollary 1, we can use the second-order Taylor expansion to approximate $g_\varepsilon(X, Y)$ around $\varepsilon = 0$, resulting in

$$g_\varepsilon(X, Y) = \varepsilon g_0'(X, Y) + \frac{\varepsilon^2}{2} g_0''(X, Y) + o(\varepsilon^2).$$

From Theorem 1 and (16) we have $g_0'(X, Y) = \frac{1}{\eta_X^2(Y)}$ and $g_0''(X, Y) = 2\Delta(X, Y)$, respectively, from which the corollary follows. $\qquad\square$

Since $\rho_m^2(X_\mathsf{G}, Y_\mathsf{G}) = \rho^2$ for jointly Gaussian X_G and Y_G with correlation coefficient ρ, (11) implies that $\eta_{X_\mathsf{G}}^2(Y_\mathsf{G}) = \rho^2$ and $\Delta(X_\mathsf{G}, Y_\mathsf{G}) = \frac{1-\rho^2}{\rho^4}$, and therefore Corollary 2 implies that for small $\varepsilon > 0$,

$$g_\varepsilon(X_\mathsf{G}, Y_\mathsf{G}) = \frac{1}{\rho^2}\varepsilon + \frac{1-\rho^2}{\rho^4}\varepsilon^2 + o(\varepsilon^2).$$

This second-order approximation as well as the first-order approximation are illustrated in Fig. 1 for $\rho = 0.5$ and $\rho = 0.8$.

Polyanskiy and Wu [22] have recently generalized the strong data processing inequality of Anantharam et al. [15] for the case of continuous random variables X and Y with joint distribution P_{XY}. Their result states that

$$\sup_{\substack{X \multimap Y \multimap U, \\ 0 < I(U;Y) < \infty}} \frac{I(X; U)}{I(Y; U)} = S^*(Y, X), \tag{18}$$

where

$$S^*(Y, X) := \sup_{\substack{Q_Y, \\ 0 < D(Q_Y \| P_Y) < \infty}} \frac{D(Q_X \| P_X)}{D(Q_Y \| P_Y)},$$

where P_X and P_Y are the marginals of P_{XY} and $Q_X(\cdot) = \int P_{X|Y}(\cdot|y)Q_Y(\mathrm{d}y)$. In addition, it is shown in [22] that the supremum in (18) is achieved by a binary U. Replacing U with Z_γ, we can conclude from (18) that

$$\frac{I(X; Z_\gamma)}{I(Y; Z_\gamma)} \le S^*(Y, X),$$

for any $\gamma \geq 0$. Letting $\gamma = \gamma_\varepsilon$, the above yields that

$$g_\varepsilon(X, Y) \geq \frac{\varepsilon}{S^*(Y, X)}. \tag{19}$$

Clearly, this bound may be expected to be tight only for small $\varepsilon > 0$ since $g_\varepsilon(X, Y) \to \infty$ as $\varepsilon \to I(X; Y)$, as shown in Proposition 1. Note that Theorem 1 implies $\lim_{\varepsilon \downarrow 0} \frac{g_\varepsilon(X,Y)}{\varepsilon} = \frac{1}{\eta_X^2(Y)}$. On the other hand, it can be easily shown that $\eta_X^2(Y) \leq S^*(Y, X)$, with equality when X and Y are jointly Gaussian and hence the inequality (19) becomes tight for small ε and jointly Gaussian X and Y.

The bound in (19) would be significantly improved if we could show that $g_\varepsilon(X, Y) \geq g_\varepsilon(X_\mathsf{G}, Y_\mathsf{G})$, where X_G and Y_G are jointly Gaussian having the same means, variances, and correlation coefficient as (X, Y). This is because in that case we could write

$$g_\varepsilon(X, Y) \geq g_\varepsilon(X_\mathsf{G}, Y_\mathsf{G}) \overset{(a)}{\geq} \frac{\varepsilon}{\eta_{X_\mathsf{G}}^2(Y_\mathsf{G})} = \frac{\varepsilon}{\rho^2(X_\mathsf{G}, Y_\mathsf{G})} = \frac{\varepsilon}{\rho^2(X, Y)} \overset{(b)}{\geq} \frac{\varepsilon}{\eta_X^2(Y)}, \tag{20}$$

where (a) and (b) follow from (12) and (11), respectively. However, as shown in Appendix A, the inequality $g_\varepsilon(X, Y) \geq g_\varepsilon(X_\mathsf{G}, Y_\mathsf{G})$ does not in general hold[1]. It is therefore possible to have $g_\varepsilon(X, Y) < \frac{\varepsilon}{\eta_X^2(Y)}$ for some $0 < \varepsilon < I(X; Y)$. To construct an example, it suffices to construct P_{XY} for which $\varepsilon \mapsto g_\varepsilon(X, Y)$ is locally concave at zero (i.e., $g_0''(X, Y) < 0$) and hence its graph lies below the tangent line $\frac{\varepsilon}{\eta_X^2(Y)}$ for some $\varepsilon > 0$. Let $Y \sim \mathcal{N}(0, 1)$ and $X = Y \cdot 1_{\{Y \in [-1,1]\}}$. Then it can be readily shown that $\mathbb{E}[\mathrm{var}(Y|X)] < \mathbb{E}[\mathrm{var}^2(Y|X)]$, which implies that $\Delta(X, Y) < 0$. Hence, since $g_0''(X, Y) = 2\Delta(X, Y)$, we have that $g''(X, Y) < 0$. This observation is illustrated in Fig. 2.

As remarked earlier, the map $\varepsilon \mapsto g_\varepsilon(X, Y)$ is in general not convex and thus one cannot conclude that $g_\varepsilon'(X, Y) \geq g_0'(X, Y) = \frac{1}{\eta_X^2(Y)}$. However, it can be shown that this implication holds if P_{XY} has more structure. In the next theorem, we assume that Y is a noisy version of X through an additive Gaussian channel.

Theorem 2. *For a given $X \sim P_X$ with variance σ_X^2, and $Y = aX + M_\mathsf{G}$ with $M_\mathsf{G} \sim \mathcal{N}(0, \sigma_M^2)$ independent of X, we have:*

1. *If $a^2 \sigma_X^2 \geq \sigma_M^2$, then $\varepsilon \mapsto g_\varepsilon(X, Y)$ is convex.*
2. *For any $a > 0$ and $\varepsilon \in [0, I(X; Y))$, we have*

$$g_\varepsilon(X, Y) \geq \frac{\varepsilon}{\eta_X^2(Y)}. \tag{21}$$

Furthermore, we have

$$\inf_{\gamma \geq 0} \frac{\mathsf{mmse}(Y|Z_\gamma, X)}{\mathsf{mmse}(Y|Z_\gamma)} = 1 - \eta_X^2(Y), \tag{22}$$

---

[1] We will see in the next section that this holds in the estimation-theoretic formulation of privacy, i.e., the Gaussian case is the *worst* case when the privacy filter is an additive Gaussian channel and the utility and privacy are measured as $\mathsf{mmse}(Y|Z_\gamma)$ and $\mathsf{mmse}(X|Z_\gamma)$, respectively.

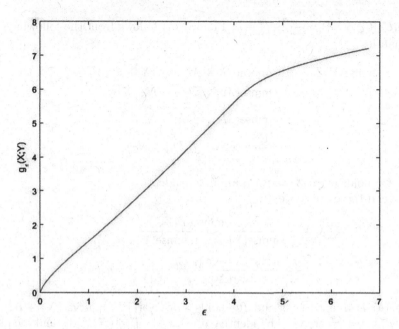

Fig. 2. The rate-privacy function for $Y \sim \mathcal{N}(0,1)$ and $X = Y \cdot 1_{\{Y \in [-1,1]\}}$. The map $\varepsilon \mapsto g_\varepsilon(X,Y)$ is clearly locally concave at zero. Note that here $I(X;Y) = \infty$ and hence ε is unbounded.

and

$$\sup_{\gamma > 0} \frac{I(X;Z_\gamma)}{I(Y;Z_\gamma)} = \eta_X^2(Y). \tag{23}$$

Proof. The first part follows from a straightforward computation showing that if $a^2 \text{var}(X) \geq \sigma_M^2$, then $\Delta(X,Y) \geq 0$.

To prove the second part, note that for any $\gamma \geq 0$ we have

$$\begin{aligned}
\text{mmse}(Y|Z_\gamma) &= \text{mmse}(aX + M_G | a\sqrt{\gamma}X + \sqrt{\gamma}M_G + N_G) \\
&\overset{(a)}{=} \frac{1}{\gamma}\text{mmse}\left(N_G | a\sqrt{\gamma}X + \sqrt{\gamma}M_G + N_G\right) \\
&\overset{(b)}{\leq} \frac{a^2\text{var}(X) + \sigma_M^2}{1 + \gamma(a^2\text{var}(X) + \sigma_M^2)} < \frac{a^2\text{var}(X) + \sigma_M^2}{1 + \gamma\sigma_M^2} \\
&\overset{(c)}{=} \frac{1}{\gamma}\left(\frac{a^2\text{var}(X) + \sigma_M^2}{\sigma_M^2}\right)\text{mmse}\left(N_G | \sqrt{\gamma}M_G + N_G\right) \\
&\overset{(d)}{=} \left(\frac{a^2\text{var}(X) + \sigma_M^2}{\sigma_M^2}\right)\text{mmse}(Y|Z_\gamma, X), \tag{24}
\end{aligned}$$

where (a) follows from the fact that $\text{mmse}(U|\alpha U + V) = \frac{1}{\alpha^2}\text{mmse}(V|\alpha U + V)$ for $\alpha \neq 0$, (b) and (c) hold by [23, Theorem 12] which states that $\text{mmse}(U|U + V_G) \leq$

$\mathsf{mmse}(U_{\mathsf{G}}|U_{\mathsf{G}} + V_{\mathsf{G}}) = \frac{\mathsf{var}(U)\mathsf{var}(V)}{\mathsf{var}(U)+\mathsf{var}(V)}$. Finally, (d) follows from the following chain of equalities

$$
\begin{aligned}
\mathsf{mmse}(Y|Z_\gamma, X) &= \mathsf{mmse}(aX + M_{\mathsf{G}}|a\sqrt{\gamma}X + \sqrt{\gamma}M_{\mathsf{G}} + N_{\mathsf{G}}, X) \\
&= \mathsf{mmse}(M_{\mathsf{G}}|\sqrt{\gamma}M_{\mathsf{G}} + N_{\mathsf{G}}, X) \\
&\overset{(e)}{=} \mathsf{mmse}(M_{\mathsf{G}}|\sqrt{\gamma}M_{\mathsf{G}} + N_{\mathsf{G}}) \\
&= \frac{1}{\gamma}\mathsf{mmse}(N_{\mathsf{G}}|\sqrt{\gamma}M_{\mathsf{G}} + N_{\mathsf{G}})
\end{aligned}
$$

where (e) holds since X and M_{G} are independent.

We can therefore write

$$
\begin{aligned}
g'_\varepsilon(X, Y) &= \frac{\mathsf{mmse}(Y|Z_{\gamma_\varepsilon})}{\mathsf{mmse}(Y|Z_{\gamma_\varepsilon}) - \mathsf{mmse}(Y|Z_{\gamma_\varepsilon}, X)} \\
&\overset{(a)}{\geq} \frac{a^2\mathsf{var}(X) + \sigma_M^2}{a^2\mathsf{var}(X)} \overset{(b)}{=} \frac{1}{\eta_X^2(Y)} = g'_0(X, Y),
\end{aligned}
\tag{25}
$$

where (a) is due to (24) and (b) holds since $\mathsf{var}(Y) = a^2\mathsf{var}(X) + \sigma_M^2$ and $\mathsf{var}(\mathbb{E}[Y|X]) = a^2\mathsf{var}(X)$. The identity $g_\varepsilon(X,Y) = \int_0^\varepsilon g'_t(X,Y)\mathrm{d}t$, and inequality (25) together imply that $g_\varepsilon(X,Y) \geq \frac{\varepsilon}{\eta_X^2(Y)}$ for $\varepsilon \leq I(X;Y)$.

Furthermore, according to Theorem 1, the inequality (25) yields (22). Using the integral representation of mutual information in (5) and (6), we can write for any $\gamma \geq 0$

$$
\begin{aligned}
I(X;Z_\gamma) &= \frac{1}{2}\int_0^\gamma [\mathsf{mmse}(Y|Z_t) - \mathsf{mmse}(Y|Z_t, X)]\,\mathrm{d}t \\
&\leq \frac{\eta_X^2(Y)}{2}\int_0^\gamma \mathsf{mmse}(Y|Z_t)\mathrm{d}t = \eta_X^2(Y)I(Y;Z_\gamma),
\end{aligned}
\tag{26}
$$

where the inequality is due to (22). The equality (23) then follows from (26). $\square$

It should be noted that both MMSE and mutual information satisfy the data processing inequality, see, [15,23], that is, $\mathsf{mmse}(U|V) \leq \mathsf{mmse}(U|W)$, and $I(U;W) \leq I(U;V)$ for $U \multimap V \multimap W$. Therefore, (22) can be thought of as a strong version of the data processing inequality for MMSE for the trivial Markov chain $Y \multimap (Z_\gamma, X) \multimap Z_\gamma$. Also, (23) can be viewed as a strong data processing inequality for the mutual information for the Markov chain $X \multimap Y \multimap Z_\gamma$ which is slightly stronger than (18) in the special case of an additive Gaussian channel as $\eta_X^2(Y) \leq S^*(Y, X)$.

3   Estimation-Theoretic Formulation

Consider the same scenario as in the previous section: Alice observes Y, which is correlated with the private data X according to a given joint distribution P_{XY}, and wishes to transmit a random variable Z to Bob to receive a utility from him. An *operational* measure of privacy is proposed in [4] where Alice generates the displayed data Z via a privacy filter $P_{Z|Y}$ such that Bob cannot efficiently estimate any non-trivial function of X given Z. As before, her goal is to maximize the utility (or equivalently minimize the cost) between Y and the displayed data Z. The next definition formalizes this privacy guarantee. We call a function f of random variable X *non-degenerate* if $f(X)$ is not almost everywhere constant with respect to the probability measure P_X. Also, we assume throughout this section that X and Y have finite second moments.

Definition 1. *Given a pair of jointly absolutely continuous random variables (X, Y) with joint distribution P_{XY} and $0 \leq \varepsilon \leq 1$, we say Z satisfies ε-strong estimation privacy, if there exists a channel $P_{Z|Y}$ that induces a joint distribution $P_X \times P_{Z|X}$, via the Markov condition $X \multimap Y \multimap Z$, satisfying*

$$\mathsf{mmse}(f(X)|Z) \geq (1 - \varepsilon)\mathsf{var}(f(X)), \quad \text{or equivalently,} \quad \eta_Z^2(f(X)) \leq \varepsilon, \quad (27)$$

for any non-degenerate Borel function f. Similarly, Z is said to satisfy ε-weak estimation privacy, if (27) is satisfied only for the identity function $f(x) = x$.

It is shown in [4] that ε-strong estimation privacy is equivalently characterized by the requirement $\rho_m^2(X, Z) \leq \varepsilon$. In other words, $\mathsf{mmse}(f(X)|Z) \geq (1 - \varepsilon)\mathsf{var}(f(X))$ for any non-degenerate Borel function f if and only if $\rho_m^2(X, Z) \leq \varepsilon$. Let the utility that Alice receives from Bob be measured by $\frac{\mathsf{var}(Y)}{\mathsf{mmse}(Y|Z)}$, which she aims to maximize. For mathematical convenience, we define the *cost* that Alice suffers by describing Z in lieu of Y as the estimation noise-to-signal ratio (ENSR), $\frac{\mathsf{mmse}(Y|Z)}{\mathsf{var}(Y)}$, and hence Alice equivalently aims to minimize the ENSR. Focusing on additive Gaussian privacy filter $Z = Z_\gamma$, we can formalize the privacy-utility tradeoff as

$$\mathsf{sENSR}_\varepsilon(X, Y) := \inf_{\gamma \in \mathcal{C}_\varepsilon(P_{XY})} \frac{\mathsf{mmse}(Y|Z_\gamma)}{\mathsf{var}(Y)} = 1 - \sup_{\gamma \in \mathcal{C}_\varepsilon(P_{XY})} \eta_{Z_\gamma}^2(Y),$$

where $\mathcal{C}_\varepsilon(P_{XY})$ is the set of parameters γ corresponding to ε-strong privacy, i.e.,

$$\mathcal{C}_\varepsilon(P_{XY}) := \{\gamma \geq 0 : \rho_m^2(X, Z_\gamma) \leq \varepsilon\}.$$

Similarly,

$$\mathsf{wENSR}_\varepsilon(X, Y) := 1 - \sup_{\gamma \in \partial \mathcal{C}_\varepsilon(P_{XY})} \eta_{Z_\gamma}^2(Y),$$

where

$$\partial \mathcal{C}_\varepsilon(P_{XY}) := \{\gamma \geq 0 : \eta_{Z_\gamma}^2(X) \leq \varepsilon\}.$$

Note that both the maximal correlation and the one-sided maximal correlation satisfy the data processing inequality, that is, $\rho_m^2(X, Z_\gamma) \leq \rho_m^2(Y, Z_\gamma)$ and $\eta_{Z_\gamma}^2(X) \leq \eta_Y(X)$. Therefore, in the definition of $\mathsf{sENSR}_\varepsilon(X, Y)$ and $\mathsf{wENSR}_\varepsilon(X, Y)$, we can restrict ε as $0 \leq \varepsilon \leq \rho_m^2(X, Y)$ and $0 \leq \varepsilon \leq \eta_Y^2(X)$, respectively.

Example 2. Let X_G and Y_G be jointly Gaussian with correlation coefficient ρ. Without loss of generality assume that $\mathbb{E}[X_G] = \mathbb{E}[Y_G] = 0$. Since $\rho_m^2(X_G, Z_\gamma) = \rho^2(X_G, Z_\gamma)$, we have

$$\rho_m^2(X_G, Z_\gamma) = \rho^2 \frac{\gamma \mathsf{var}(Y_G)}{1 + \gamma \mathsf{var}(Y_G)},$$

which implies that the mapping $\gamma \mapsto \rho_m^2(X_G, Z_\gamma)$ is strictly increasing. Also, the equation $\rho_m^2(X_G, Z_\gamma) = \varepsilon$ for $0 \le \varepsilon \le \rho_m^2(X_G, Y_G) = \rho^2$ has a unique solution

$$\gamma_\varepsilon := \frac{\varepsilon}{\mathsf{var}(Y_G)(\rho^2 - \varepsilon)},$$

and $\rho_m^2(X, Z_\gamma) \le \varepsilon$ for any $\gamma \le \gamma_\varepsilon$. On the other hand, $\mathsf{mmse}(Y_G|Z_\gamma) = \frac{\mathsf{var}(Y_G)}{1+\gamma \mathsf{var}(Y_G)}$, which shows that the map $\gamma \mapsto \mathsf{mmse}(Y_G|Z_\gamma)$ is strictly decreasing. Hence,

$$\mathsf{sENSR}_\varepsilon(X_G, Y_G) = \frac{\mathsf{mmse}(Y_G|Z_{\gamma_\varepsilon})}{\mathsf{var}(Y_G)} = 1 - \frac{\varepsilon}{\rho^2}. \tag{28}$$

Clearly for jointly Gaussian X_G and Y_G we have $\eta_{Z_\gamma}^2(X_G) = \rho_m^2(X_G, Z_\gamma) = \varepsilon$, for any $\gamma \ge 0$ and consequently $\mathcal{C}_\varepsilon(P_{X_G Y_G}) = \partial \mathcal{C}_\varepsilon(P_{X_G Y_G})$, that is, for $0 \le \varepsilon \le \rho^2$,

$$\mathsf{sENSR}_\varepsilon(X_G, Y_G) = \mathsf{wENSR}_\varepsilon(X_G, Y_G) = 1 - \frac{\varepsilon}{\rho^2}. \tag{29}$$

Unlike $g_\varepsilon(X, Y)$, the quantity $\mathsf{sENSR}_\varepsilon(X, Y)$ is maximized among all pairs of random variables (X, Y) with identical means, variances and correlation coefficient when X and Y are jointly Gaussian. Thus, Example 2 yields a sharp upper-bound for $\mathsf{sENSR}_\varepsilon(X, Y)$. This is stated in the following theorem.

Theorem 3 [4]. *For any given jointly absolutely continuous (X, Y), we have for $0 \le \varepsilon \le \rho_m^2(X, Y)$,*

$$\mathsf{wENSR}_\varepsilon(X, Y) \le \mathsf{sENSR}_\varepsilon(X, Y) \le \mathsf{sENSR}_\varepsilon(X_G, Y_G) = 1 - \frac{\varepsilon}{\rho_m^2(X, Y)},$$

where (X_G, Y_G) is a pair of Gaussian random variables with the same means, variances, and correlation coefficient as (X, Y).

Next, we turn our attention to the approximation of $\mathsf{sENSR}_\varepsilon(X, Y)$ in the almost perfect privacy regime. Unfortunately, there is no known approximation for $\rho_m^2(X, Z_\gamma)$ and $\mathsf{mmse}(X|Z_\gamma)$ around $\gamma = 0$. Nevertheless, we can use the first-order approximation of $g_\varepsilon(X, Y)$ to derive an approximation for $\mathsf{sENSR}_\varepsilon(X, Y)$ around $\varepsilon = 0$. The next theorem shows this approximation for the special case where $P_{Y|X}$ is an additive noise channel.

Theorem 4. *If $X \sim \mathcal{N}(b, \sigma_X^2)$ and $Y = aX + M$, where $a, b \in \mathbb{R}^+$, and M is a noise random variable having a density, then for sufficiently small ε*

$$\mathsf{sENSR}_\varepsilon(X_G, Y) \ge 2^{-D(Y)} 2^{-2g_{\varepsilon+o(\varepsilon)}(X_G, Y)}. \tag{30}$$

Proof. We start by deriving an inequality relating $\mathsf{mmse}(Y|Z_\gamma)$ and $I(Y;Z_\gamma)$ which originates from the Shannon lower bound for the rate-distortion function. Since the Gaussian distribution maximizes the differential entropy [21, Theorem 8.6.5], we have $h(Y|Z = z) \leq \frac{1}{2}\log(2\pi e \mathrm{var}(Y|Z = z))$ for any random variable Z. It immediately follows from Jensen's inequality that

$$h(Y|Z_\gamma) \leq \frac{1}{2}\log(2\pi e \, \mathsf{mmse}(Y|Z_\gamma)),$$

and hence

$$\mathsf{mmse}(Y|Z_\gamma) \geq \frac{1}{2\pi e}2^{2h(Y|Z_\gamma)} = \mathrm{var}(Y)2^{2(h(Y)-h(Y_\mathsf{G}))}2^{-2I(Y;Z_\gamma)}, \qquad (31)$$

from which we obtain

$$\inf_{\substack{\gamma \geq 0, \\ I(X;Z_\gamma)\leq\varepsilon}} \frac{\mathsf{mmse}(Y|Z_\gamma)}{\mathrm{var}(Y)} \geq 2^{-D(Y)}2^{-2g_\varepsilon(X,Y)}, \qquad (32)$$

where $D(Y)$ is the non-Gaussianness of Y defined in Proposition 1. We note that a similar inequality is proved in [2, Lemma 13] for arbitrary noise distribution provided that Y is Gaussian. Although, inequality (32) provides an operational interpretation of $g_\varepsilon(X,Y)$, it does not relate $g_\varepsilon(X,Y)$ to $\mathsf{sENSR}_\varepsilon(X,Y)$. Such a relationship would follow if $\rho_m^2(X,Z_\gamma) \leq \varepsilon$ implied $I(X;Z_\gamma) \leq \varepsilon$ for a given (X,Y), because then according to (32), one could conclude that $\mathsf{sENSR}_\varepsilon \geq 2^{-D(Y)}2^{-2g_\varepsilon(X,Y)}$. However, this implication does not hold in general. Nevertheless, we show in the sequel that this implication holds for Gaussian X in the almost perfect privacy regime when $P_{Y|X}$ is an additive noise channel. First we notice that for jointly Gaussian X_G and Y_G, we have $I(X_\mathsf{G}; \sqrt{\gamma}Y_\mathsf{G} + N_\mathsf{G}) = -\frac{1}{2}\log(1 - \rho^2(X_\mathsf{G}, \sqrt{\gamma}Y_\mathsf{G} + N_\mathsf{G}))$. Hence, since $\rho_m^2(X_\mathsf{G}, \sqrt{\gamma}Y_\mathsf{G} + N_\mathsf{G}) = \rho^2(X_\mathsf{G}, \sqrt{\gamma}Y_\mathsf{G} + N_\mathsf{G})$, the above implication clearly holds, i.e., $\rho_m^2(X_\mathsf{G}, \sqrt{\gamma}Y_\mathsf{G} + N_\mathsf{G}) \leq \varepsilon$ implies $I(X_\mathsf{G}; \sqrt{\gamma}Y_\mathsf{G} + N_\mathsf{G}) \leq \varepsilon$. On the other hand, specializing the decomposition (37) proved in Appendix A for $U = X_\mathsf{G}$ and $V = Z_\gamma$, we can write

$$I(X_\mathsf{G}; Z_\gamma) = I(X_\mathsf{G}; \sqrt{\gamma}Y_\mathsf{G} + N_\mathsf{G}) + D(Z_\gamma|X_\mathsf{G}) - D(Z_\gamma), \qquad (33)$$

where $D(V|U)$ for a pair of absolutely continuous random variables (U,V) is defined as

$$D(V|U) := D(P_{V|U}||P_{V_\mathsf{G}|U_\mathsf{G}}|P_U) = \mathbb{E}_{UV}\left[\log\frac{P_{V|U}}{P_{V_\mathsf{G}|U_\mathsf{G}}}\right], \qquad (34)$$

where $(U_\mathsf{G}, V_\mathsf{G})$ is a pair of Gaussian random variables having the same means, variances and correlation coefficient as (U,V), and $P_{V_\mathsf{G}|U_\mathsf{G}}(\cdot|u)$ and $P_{V|U}(\cdot|u)$ are the conditional densities of V_G and V given $U_\mathsf{G} = u$ and $U = u$, respectively.

As shown in [16, Appendix II] if $\mathrm{var}(Y) < \infty$, then as $\gamma \to 0$

$$D(Z_\gamma) = o(\gamma). \qquad (35)$$

Lemma 1 in Appendix B shows that $D(Z_\gamma|X_G)$ also behaves like $o(\gamma)$ if $\text{mmse}(Y|X_G) = \text{mmse}(Y_G|X_G)$. In light of this lemma, (33) and (35), we can conclude that

$$I(X_G; Z_\gamma) \leq I(X_G; \sqrt{\gamma}Y_G + N_G) + \frac{\gamma}{2}[\text{mmse}(Y_G|X_G) - \text{mmse}(Y|X_G)] + o(\gamma).$$

Thus if P_{XY} satisfies $\text{mmse}(Y|X_G) = \text{mmse}(Y_G|X_G)$, or equivalently $\mathbb{E}[\text{var}(Y|X_G)] = 1 - \rho^2(X,Y)$, we have

$$I(X_G; Z_\gamma) \leq I(X_G; \sqrt{\gamma}Y_G + N_G) + o(\gamma). \tag{36}$$

Since $\rho_m^2(X_G, Z_\gamma) \geq \rho_m^2(X_G, \sqrt{\gamma}Y_G + N_G)$, we can conclude from (36) that, $\rho_m^2(X_G, Z_\gamma) \leq \varepsilon$ implies $I(X_G; Z_\gamma) \leq \varepsilon + o(\gamma)$ for sufficiently small γ (or equivalently ε). Note that it is straightforward to show that $\rho_m^2(X_G, Z_\gamma) \leq \varepsilon$ implies $\gamma \leq \frac{\varepsilon}{\rho^2(X_G,Y) - \varepsilon}$ (see Example 2). Hence, in the almost perfect privacy regime, $\rho_m^2(X_G, Z_\gamma) \leq \varepsilon$ is satisfied with γ which is at most linear in ε. Therefore, (36) allows us to conclude that $\rho_m^2(X_G, Z_\gamma) \leq \varepsilon$ implies that $I(X_G; Z_\gamma) \leq \varepsilon + o(\varepsilon)$.

The condition $\mathbb{E}[\text{var}(Y|X_G)] = 1 - \rho^2(X,Y)$ is satisfied if the channel from X_G to Y is additive, that is, $Y = aX_G + M$, where $a \in \mathbb{R}^+$ and M is a noise random variable with a density having variance $1 - \rho^2(X_G, Y)$. However, since $\mathbb{E}[\text{var}(Y|X_G)] = \mathbb{E}[\text{var}(Y|rX_G)]$ for any $r \neq 0$, the variance condition can be removed.   □

The lower-bound (30) can be further simplified by invoking Corollary 2, which results in

$$\text{sENSR}_\varepsilon(X_G, Y) \geq 2^{-D(Y)}\left(1 - \frac{2\varepsilon}{\eta_{X_G}^2(Y)}\right) + o(\varepsilon).$$

One the other hand, as proved in [4], when Y is Gaussian, Y_G, then

$$1 - \frac{\varepsilon}{\rho^2(X,Y_G)} \leq \text{sENSR}_\varepsilon(X, Y_G) \leq 1 - \frac{\varepsilon}{\rho_m^2(X,Y_G)},$$

for any $\varepsilon \leq \rho_m^2(X,Y)$. We have therefore tight lower bounds for $\text{sENSR}_\varepsilon(X,Y)$ when either X or Y is Gaussian.

4   Conclusion

In this paper, we studied the problem of approximating the maximal amount of information one can transmit about a random variable Y over an additive Gaussian channel without revealing more than a certain (small) amount of information about another random variable X that represents sensitive or private data. Specifically, letting $g_\varepsilon(X,Y)$ denote the maximum of $I(Y; Z_\gamma)$ over $\gamma \geq 0$, where $Z_\gamma := \sqrt{\gamma}Y + N_G$ and $N_G \sim \mathcal{N}(0,1)$ is independent of (X,Y), subject to $I(X; Z_\gamma) \leq \varepsilon$, we showed that $g_\varepsilon(X,Y) = \frac{\varepsilon}{\eta_X^2(Y)} + \Delta(X,Y)\varepsilon^2 + o(\varepsilon)$ where

$\eta_X^2(Y)$ and $\Delta(X,Y)$ are two asymmetric measures of correlation between X and Y. For the special case of jointly Gaussian X and Y, the approximation was compared with the exact value of $g_\varepsilon(X,Y)$. As a side result, we also showed that this approximation leads to a slightly improved version of the strong data processing inequality under some suitable conditions on $P_{Y|X}$.

We also studied an estimation-theoretic formulation of the privacy-utility tradeoff for the same setup. Let $\mathsf{sENSR}_\varepsilon(X,Y)$ be the smallest achievable MMSE in estimating Y given Z_γ such that MMSE in estimating any function f of X given Z_γ is lower bound by $(1-\varepsilon)\mathsf{var}(f(X))$. We then showed that when X is Gaussian and Y is the output of an additive noise channel then $\mathsf{sENSR}_\varepsilon(X,Y) \geq 2^{-D(Y)}2^{-2g_\varepsilon(X,Y)}$ for sufficiently small ε, where $D(Y)$ is the non-Gaussianness of Y. The significance of this bound is that it gives an operational interpretation for $g_\varepsilon(X,Y)$ in terms of MMSE. Using the approximation obtained for $g_\varepsilon(X,Y)$, we derived a lower bound for $\mathsf{sENSR}_\varepsilon(X,Y)$ for small ε which is linear in ε.

A   Connection Between Mutual Information and Non-Gaussianness

For any pair of random variables (U,V) with $I(U;V)< \infty$, let $P_{V|U}(\cdot|u)$ be the conditional density of V given $U=u$. Then, we have

$$I(U;V) = \mathbb{E}_{UV}\left[\log \frac{P_{V|U}(V|U)}{P_V(V)}\right]$$

$$= \mathbb{E}_{UV}\left[\log \frac{P_{V|U}(V|U)}{P_{V_\mathsf{G}|U_\mathsf{G}}(V|U)}\right] + \mathbb{E}_{UV}\left[\log \frac{P_{V_\mathsf{G}|U_\mathsf{G}}(V|U)}{P_{V_\mathsf{G}}(V)}\right] - \mathbb{E}_{UV}\left[\log \frac{P_V(V)}{P_{V_\mathsf{G}}(V)}\right]$$

$$= I(U_\mathsf{G};V_\mathsf{G}) + D(V|U) - D(V), \tag{37}$$

where $(U_\mathsf{G},V_\mathsf{G})$ is a pair of Gaussian random variable having the same means, variances and correlation coefficient as (U,V), and $P_{V_\mathsf{G}|U_\mathsf{G}}(\cdot|u)$ is the conditional density of V_G given $U_\mathsf{G}=u$, and the quantity $D(V|U)$ is defined in (34). Replacing U and V with X and Z_γ, respectively, the decomposition (37) allows us to conclude that

$$I(X;Z_\gamma) = I(X_\mathsf{G};\sqrt{\gamma}Y_\mathsf{G} + N_\mathsf{G}) + D(Z_\gamma|X) - D(Z_\gamma),$$

and therefore, if $Y = Y_\mathsf{G}$ is Gaussian, we have

$$I(X;Z_\gamma) = I(X_\mathsf{G};Z_\gamma) + D(Z_\gamma|X) \geq I(X_\mathsf{G};Z_\gamma),$$

from which we conclude that when Y is Gaussian then $I(X;Z_\gamma) \leq \varepsilon$ implies that $I(X_\mathsf{G};Z_\gamma) \leq \varepsilon$ and hence $g_\varepsilon(X,Y_\mathsf{G}) \leq g_\varepsilon(X_\mathsf{G},Y_\mathsf{G})$.

B   Completion of the Proof of Theorem 4

Lemma 1. *For Gaussian X_G and absolutely continuous Y with unit variance, we have*

$$D(Z_\gamma|X_\mathsf{G}) \leq \frac{\gamma}{2}\left[\mathsf{mmse}(Y_\mathsf{G}|X_\mathsf{G}) - \mathsf{mmse}(Y|X_\mathsf{G})\right] + o(\gamma).$$

Proof. Let E be an auxiliary random variable defined as

$$E = \begin{cases} 1, & |Y| \leq L \\ 0, & \text{otherwise,} \end{cases}$$

for some real number $M > 0$. Note that

$$
\begin{aligned}
D(Z_\gamma | X_G = x) &= h(\sqrt{\gamma} Y_G + N_G | X_G = x) - h(Z_\gamma | X_G = x) \\
&\leq h(\sqrt{\gamma} Y_G + N_G | X_G = x) - h(Z_\gamma | X_G = x, E) \\
&= \frac{1}{2} \log(2\pi e(1 + \gamma \text{var}(Y_G | X_G = x))) \\
&\quad - \Pr(E = 1) h(Z_\gamma | X_G = x, E = 1) - \Pr(E = 0) h(Z_\gamma | X_G = x, E = 0) \\
&\overset{(a)}{\leq} \frac{1}{2} \log(2\pi e(1 + \gamma \text{var}(Y_G | X_G = x))) - \Pr(E = 0) h(N_G) \\
&\quad - \Pr(E = 1) h(Z_\gamma | X_G = x, E = 1)
\end{aligned}
\tag{38}
$$

where (a) follows from the fact that $h(Z_\gamma | X_G = x, E = 0) \geq h(N_G)$.

Prelov [24] showed that for any random variable Y such that

$$\mathbb{E}[|Y|^{2+\alpha}] \leq K < \infty, \tag{39}$$

for some $\alpha > 0$, then

$$h(\sqrt{\gamma} Y + N_G) = \frac{1}{2} \log(2\pi e) + \frac{\text{var}(Y)}{2}(\gamma + o(\gamma)), \tag{40}$$

where $o(\gamma)$ term depends only on K. Since $Y|\{E = 1\}$ satisfies (39), we can use (40) to evaluate $h(Z_\gamma | X_G = x, E = 1)$ in (38) which yields

$$
\begin{aligned}
D(Z_\gamma | X_G = x) &\leq \frac{1}{2} \log(2\pi e(1 + \gamma \text{var}(Y_G | X_G = x))) - \Pr(E = 0)\frac{1}{2} \log(2\pi e) \\
&\quad - \Pr(E = 1)\left[\frac{1}{2} \log(2\pi e) + \frac{\text{var}(Y | X_G = x, E = 1)}{2}(\gamma + o(\gamma)) \right] \\
&= \frac{1}{2} \log(1 + \gamma \text{var}(Y_G | X_G = x)) \\
&\quad - \frac{\text{var}(Y | X_G = x, E = 1)}{2}(\gamma + o(\gamma)) \Pr(E = 1).
\end{aligned}
\tag{41}
$$

Note that since $\text{var}(Y) < \infty$ and X_G has a positive density, $\text{var}(Y | X_G = x) < \infty$ for almost all x (except for x in a set of zero Lebesgue measure). Hence, we can choose L sufficiently large such that for any given $\delta > 0$,

$$\Pr(E = 1) \geq 1 - \delta,$$

and

$$\text{var}(Y | X_G = x, E = 1) \geq \text{var}(Y | X_G = x) - \delta.$$

Therefore, invoking the inequality $\log(1 + u) \leq u$ for $u > 0$, we can write

$$D(Z_\gamma | X_G = x) \leq \frac{\gamma}{2} [\text{var}(Y_G | X_G = x) - (\text{var}(Y | X_G = x) - \delta)(1 - \delta)] + o(\gamma),$$

from which and the fact the δ is arbitrarily small the result follows.   □

References

1. Asoodeh, S., Alajaji, F., Linder, T.: Notes on information-theoretic privacy. In: Proceedings of the 52nd Annual Allerton Conference on Communication, Control, and Computing, pp. 1272–1278, September 2014
2. Asoodeh, S., Diaz, M., Alajaji, F., Linder, T.: Information extraction under privacy constraints. Information 7(1) (2016). http://www.mdpi.com/2078-2489/7/1/15
3. Calmon, F.P., Varia, M., Médard, M., Christiansen, M.M., Duffy, K.R., Tessaro, S.: Bounds on inference. In: Proceedings of the 51st Annual Allerton Conference on Communication, Control, and Computing, pp. 567–574, October 2013
4. Asoodeh, S., Alajaji, F., Linder, T.: Privacy-aware MMSE estimation. In: Proceedings of the IEEE International Symposium on Information (ISIT), July 2016. arXiv:1511.02381v3
5. Makhdoumi, A., Fawaz, N.: Privacy-utility tradeoff under statistical uncertainty. In: Proceedings of the 51st Allerton Conference on Communication, Control, and Computing, pp. 1627–1634, October 2013
6. Calmon, F.P., Makhdoumi, A., Médard, M.: Fundamental limits of perfect privacy. In: Proceedings of the IEEE International Symposium on Information Theory (ISIT), pp. 1796–1800 (2015)
7. Berger, T., Yeung, R.: Multiterminal source encoding with encoder breakdown. IEEE Trans. Inf. Theor. 35(2), 237–244 (1989)
8. Reed, I.S.: Information theory and privacy in data banks. In: Proceedings of the National Computer Conference and Exposition, ser. AFIPS 1973, pp. 581–587. ACM, New York (1973)
9. Yamamoto, H.: A source coding problem for sources with additional outputs to keep secret from the receiver or wiretappers. IEEE Trans. Inf. Theor. 29(6), 918–923 (1983)
10. Sankar, L., Rajagopalan, S., Poor, H.: Utility-privacy tradeoffs in databases: an information-theoretic approach. IEEE Trans. Inf. Forensics Secur. 8(6), 838–852 (2013)
11. Asoodeh, S., Alajaji, F., Linder, T.: On maximal correlation, mutual information and data privacy. In: Proceedings of the IEEE 14th Canadian Workshop on Information Theory (CWIT), pp. 27–31, June 2015
12. Rebollo-Monedero, D., Forne, J., Domingo-Ferrer, J.: From t-closeness-like privacy to postrandomization via information theory. IEEE Trans. Knowl. Data Eng. 22(11), 1623–1636 (2010)
13. Calmon, F.P.: Information-theoretic metrics for security and privacy. Ph.D. dissertation, MIT, September 2015
14. Goldwasser, S., Micali, S.: Probabilistic encryption. J. Comput. Syst. Sci. 28(2), 270–299 (1984)
15. Anantharam, V., Gohari, A., Kamath, S., Nair, C.: On maximal correlation, hypercontractivity, the data processing inequality studied by Erkip, Cover. Preprint, arXiv:1304.6133v1 (2014)
16. Guo, D., Shamai, S., Verdú, S.: Mutual information and minimum mean-square error in Gaussian channels. IEEE Trans. Inf. Theor. 51(4), 1261–1282 (2005)
17. Guo, D., Wu, Y., Shamai, S., Verdú, S.: Estimation in Gaussian noise: properties of the minimum mean-square error. IEEE Trans. Inf. Theor. 57(4), 2371–2385 (2011)
18. Rényi, A.: On measures of dependence. Acta Mathe. Acad. Scient. Hung. 10(3), 441–451 (1959)

19. Gebelein, H.: Das statistische problem der korrelation als variations- und eigenwert-problem und sein zusammenhang mit der ausgleichungsrechnung. Zeitschrift f ur angew. Math. und Mech. **21**, 364–379 (1941)
20. Sarmanov, O.: The maximum correlation coefficient (nonsymmetric case). Dokl. Akad. Nauk SSSR **120**(4), 715–718 (1958)
21. Cover, T.M., Thomas, J.A.: Elements of Information Theory. Wiley-Interscience, Hoboken (2006)
22. Polyanskiy, Y., Wu, Y.: Dissipation of information in channels with input constraints. IEEE Trans. Inf. Theor. **62**(1), 35–55 (2016)
23. Wu, Y., Verdú, S.: Functional properties of minimum mean-square error and mutual information. IEEE Trans. Inf. Theor. **58**(3), 1289–1301 (2012)
24. Prelov, V.V.: Capacity of communication channels with almost Gaussian noise. Teor. Veroyatnost. i Primenen. **33**(3), 433–452 (1988)

A Better Chain Rule for HILL Pseudoentropy - Beyond Bounded Leakage

Maciej Skórski[(✉)]

University of Warsaw, Warsaw, Poland
maciej.skorski@mimuw.edu.pl

Abstract. Chain rules are inequalities used to estimate by how much entropy decreases when conditioning on some extra knowledge. Their popular application is to argue about security, by proving that the entropy of a secret remains sufficiently high even in the presence of leakage. We provide a chain rule for HILL/Metric conditional pseudoentropy (applicable for leakage-resilient cryptography), with the following new features:

(a) Better quality loss - when conditioning on already conditioned distribution, the loss due to the "internal" conditional part is *additive*, not multiplicative as conjectured in folklore,

(b) Better quantity loss - the leakage length is replaced by the *effective leakage length* which equals the "pseudoentropy gap" of the leakage conditioned on the secret,

(c) Flexible quality loss - the loss can be *continuously traded* between both computational resources: time and advantage.

The relevance of these results is as follows: (a) is a result complementary to recent negative results (TCC'13) on the chain rule for HILL pseudoentropy - it explains that an efficient chain rule for HILL pseudoentropy is possible under certain conditions. With (b) we can extend some leakage resilient constructions, beyond the bounded leakage model, to capture noisy leakages (studied extensively in recent EUROCRYPT papers); interestingly, we show that the new chain rule can handle specific noisy leakages better than the noisy-leakage framework. Finally using (c) we can unify all previous results and techniques about pseudoentropy chain rules.

1 Introduction

1.1 Entropy Notions and Chain Rules

In information theory the most fundamental quantity is Shannon entropy, which measures the uncompressibility of a distribution. In cryptography one extensively uses a more conservative measure called *min-entropy*, which bounds the unpredictability of a random variable (very important for randomness extraction [22] or key derivation [4]). In both cases, the most important tools used to argue about entropy are chain rules, which bounds the amount of entropy in a

A.C.A. Nascimento and P. Barreto (Eds.): ICITS 2016, LNCS 10015, pp. 279–299, 2016.
DOI: 10.1007/978-3-319-49175-2_14

random variable conditioned on another distribution (leakage in cryptographic applications). For Shannon entropy $\mathbf{H}(\cdot)$ the simple chain rule is

$$\mathbf{H}(X|Z_1, Z_2) = \mathbf{H}(X|Z_1) - \mathbf{H}(Z_2)$$

which states that the information loss equals the entropy of extra knowledge. For the notion of min-entropy $\widetilde{\mathbf{H}}_\infty ()$, which is defined precisely in Sect. 2, we have the following analogue

Theorem 1 (Chain rule for min-entropy [3]). *For any random variables* X, Z_1, Z_2 *we have*

$$\widetilde{\mathbf{H}}_\infty(X|Z_1, Z_2) \geqslant \widetilde{\mathbf{H}}_\infty (X|Z_1) - \mathbf{H}_0(Z_2)$$

where $\mathbf{H}_0(Z_2)$ *is the negative binary logarithm of the support sze of* Z_2 *(defined in Sect. 2).*

This result captures the following intuition: with ℓ bits of extra information, one can increase the chances of guessing the secret by at most a factor of 2^ℓ. Putting in other words: security, measured in the logarithmic unpredictability scale, goes down by at most the length of leakage string. Let us now state a concrete question which shows how chain rules are important for cryptographic applications

> Suppose that a pseudorandom generator $\mathsf{PRG} : \{0,1\}^{64} \to \{0,1\}^{256}$ leaks 10 bits of information about its seed. Can we still exploit remaining $246 = 256 - 10$ bits in the output?

Note that leakage of only 1 bit of the seed can make PRG completely insecure[1]. However, we can intuitively expect that remaining security bits are still "somewhere inside", thought not necessarily directly accessible. To answer questions of this sort, the concept of min-entropy was extended to computational settings, where we require the given random variable not to have certain entropy itself, but rather to be close to a distribution with high min-entropy (perhaps conditioned on some auxiliary/leakage information). This leads to the popular notion of HILL Entropy $\widetilde{\mathbf{H}}_{s,\epsilon}^{\mathrm{HILL}} ()$, which extends the notion of pseudorandomness, and its weaker technical variant Metric Entropy $\mathbf{H}_{s,\epsilon}^{\mathrm{Metric}} ()$ defined precisely in Sect. 2.2. Note that these notions are parametrized by the pair (s, ϵ) which stands for the size (time)/advantage pair, that is for computational resources. This captures the fact that, in the computational world, the amount of entropy observed in a random variable depends on attacker's resources. The following result gives a chain rule for pseudoentropy.

---

[1] Theoretically, this could be also a bit of the output and then it can be distinguished from random with advantage close to $\frac{1}{2}$.

Theorem, informal 1 (Chain Rule for pseudoentropy). *For any random variables X, Z we have*

$$\widetilde{\mathbf{H}}^{\mathrm{HILL}}_{s',\epsilon'}(X|Z) \geqslant \mathbf{H}^{\mathrm{HILL}}_{s,\epsilon}(X) - \mathbf{H}_0(Z_2)$$

where s'/ϵ' degrades with respect to s/ϵ at most exponentially in $m = \mathbf{H}_0(Z_2)$ and polynomially in ϵ^{-1}.

It is important to keep in mind that not only the entropy amount goes down (referred to as the *quantity loss*), but also the security level measured in (s, ϵ) decreases (refereed to as *quality loss*). This is different than the information-theoretic case, when computational resources doesn't matter.

Pseudoentropy chain rules appeared for the first time as a tool giving a solution for the question about pseudorandom generators stated above and found further applications in leakage resilient cryptography [2,9–11,15,18]. Interestingly, they were discovered independently as *dense model theorems* in computational complexity [21].

For cryptographic applications we want the ratio s/ϵ to be as high as possible; this ratio is a simple and useful measure of security, called[2] *time-advantage ratio* [17]. Exponential degradation in m still allows for meaningful applications, if we assume *logarithmically bounded leakage*. Even then, there are some inherent limitations that will be discussed in more detail in the next subsection.

1.2 Motivation: Limitations of Pseudoentropy Chain Rules

The aim of this work is to improve pseudoentropy chain rules, with the focus on the following issues

(a) Known bounds apply only to bounded leakage (more generally: leakage which consumes only few bits of security - but we don't know a good characterization of this class)
(b) Pseudoentropy chain rules do not generalize easily to the conditional case (a counterexample found in [16])
(c) Known bounds lose mostly in advantage (except bounds for unconditional chain rules in [15,19] or sometimes in size [19] - there is no flexibility which is desired for some applications (see [15,19])

1.3 Our Results

We revisit the chain rule problem for the conditional case, and prove a new optimized variant trying to address the issues mentioned above. Our chain rule has the following form:

$$\mathbf{H}^{\mathrm{Metric}}(X|Z_1, Z_2) \geqslant \mathbf{H}^{\mathrm{Metric}}(X|Z_1) - \Delta$$

---

[2] Our setting is non-uniform so here we think of circuit size as "time".

where

$$\Delta = \mathbf{H}_0\left(Z_2\right) - \mathbf{H}^{\text{Metric}}\left(Z_2 | X, Z_1\right),$$

is the improved amount loss (the quantity refereed to as *unpredictability deficiency*), and the loss in quality that can be continuously moved from time to advantage and improves previous bounds (only additive exponential loss in the length of Z_1 and a multiplicative exponential loss in Δ). While we will not give here explicit parameters for the sake of clarity, referring to Theorems 3 and 4 for precise statements and proofs, we discuss advantages of our result over prior works below. We state our result in terms of metric entropy because it is more convenient to work with, but it can be converted to HILL entropy (considered a standard pseudorandomness measure) using general transformations (see Sect. 2.2). In subsequent subsections we informally discuss our work and related results.

1.3.1   Quality Bounds Much Better Than Folklore

Since the counterexample given in [16] it has been folklore that chain rules lose an exponential factor in the leakage already captured, modeled as Z_1. This essentially means that *captured leakages leak again* and looks counterintuitive, but the explanation is that the definition of conditional pseudoentropy averages different advantage contributions so that one may cancel another; a naive way is to assume that $\mathbf{H}^{\text{Metric}}\left(X|Z\right) \geqslant k$ implies something about $\mathbf{H}^{\text{Metric}}\left(X|Z = z\right)$ for individual values of z, but this is not the case. More precisely, this feature is called *decomposable entropy* [12] and can be shown at the price of a (heavy) complexity loss (by a factor exponential in $|Z|$, see [23]).

In general, for $Z_1 \in \{0,1\}^{m_1}, Z_2 \in \{0,1\}^{m_2}$ we can prove

$$\mathbf{H}^{\text{Metric}}_{s',\epsilon'}\left(X|Z_1, Z_2\right) \geqslant \mathbf{H}^{\text{Metric}}_{s,\epsilon}\left(X|Z_1\right) - m_2$$

with the loss in the time-success ratio depending on the *leakage already captured*

$$\frac{s'}{\epsilon'} = \Omega(1) \cdot 2^{-m_1 - m_2} \cdot \frac{s}{\epsilon}$$

The issue with this loss in quality appears for example in memory delegation [2], where the authors impose other restrictions to eliminate the dependency on already captured leakage to make the conditional chain rule efficient.

In Remark 6 we show that the loss due to Z_1 is actually *additive* not multiplicative. This difference is important. In particular, we can prove that as long as circuits are at least exponential in the conditional part length, we lose only a factor due to new leakage - as expected! This observation is complementary to the negative result of [16], as we prove that under certain conditions (namely for $s > 2^{m_1}$)

$$\frac{s'}{\epsilon'} = \Omega(1) \cdot 2^{-m_2} \cdot \frac{s}{\epsilon}.$$

We summarize this discussion in Table 1.

Table 1. Different results for conditional chain rule

Reference	Loss	Condition
[16]	$\frac{s'}{\epsilon'} = \text{superpoly}(m_1 + m_2) \cdot \frac{s}{\epsilon}$	Upper bounds, only for specific distributions
[2]	$\frac{s'}{\epsilon'} = \Omega(1) \cdot 2^{-m_2} \cdot \frac{s}{\epsilon}$	Samplability assumptions
[12]	$\frac{s'}{\epsilon'} = \Omega(1) \cdot 2^{-m_2} \cdot \frac{s}{\epsilon}$	Decomposability assumptions
This paper	$\frac{s'}{\epsilon'} = \Omega(1) \cdot 2^{-m_2} \cdot \frac{s}{\epsilon}$	s exponential in m_1

Remark 1 (Our bounds vs counterexample [16]). *The bounds we get do not contradict the negative result in [16], as the counterexample is a different parameter regime, namely s being polynomial in m_1. Then $s \ll 2^{m_1}$ and our bounds don't apply.*

1.3.2 Flexibility - Distributing Loss Between Size and Advantage

Our chain rule allows moving the loss from advantage to circuit size continuously. At first glance may be not obvious why to do so, as it is tempting to think of security as interchanging multiplicative losses between s and ϵ, so that the ratio s/ϵ remains constant. However, while may be the case of weak pseudorandom-functions (where k-bit keys are believed to offer security given by any time-advantage pair (s, ϵ) such that $s/\epsilon = 2^k$), this is not true for example for the RSA encryption (where the advantage dramatically goes down after achieving a certain amount of time, enough to apply factoring by number theoretic sieves). Also, certain results from key derivation [5] yield relatively big losses in advantage and in some parameter regimes are beaten by alternative techniques based on chain rules, as discussed in [19]. We believe that such a continuous transformation may be of interest also because it establishes an elegant connection between two "extreme" cases for which chain rules were known before (proved using different techniques).

More concretely, special cases of our bounds match [11,19], best chain rules so far in terms of quality loss, as shown in [19]. Thus we retrieve all known results from a single, comprehensive formula. For more details see Sect. 5.1.

1.3.3 Relaxing Bounded Leakage

In the bounded leakage model we assume that the adversary can learn a function f of a secret state S such that the output of f is at most λ-bit long (where λ is logarithmically small in security parameters s, ϵ). Recently, there has been a lot of interests in the so called noisy-leakage model [6,8,20]. This approach measures the "noise" in a secret S given a leakage function f by comparing the distance of distributions $f(S)$ and $f(S')$ given S, where S' is a fresh copy of S. This model in particular can handle unbounded leakages and is considered a good alternative for bounded leakages, also practically motivated. On the other hand, it is known [18] that for leakage-resilient constructions the bounded leakage assumption can be relaxed to the following condition imposed on leakage functions f (which is trivially satisfied by bounded leakages, when the output of f is λ-bit long)

Given $f(S)$, the pseudoentropy of a secret state S goes down at most by λ bits.

The only thing is that it's hard to give a characterization of this class. In this paper we present a partial progress. Namely, our chain rule in Theorem 4 and Corollary 4 show that this is possible, whenever

$$\mathbf{H}_0(f(S)) - \mathbf{H}^{\mathrm{Metric}}(f(S)|S) \leqslant \lambda,$$

or under a weaker but more intuitive condition (studied also [12]).

$$\mathbf{H}_0(f(S)) - \mathbf{H}_\infty(f(S)|S) \leqslant \lambda,$$

the quantity being referred to as *unpredictability deficiency* or *unpredictability gap*. These conditions essentially mean that $f(S)$ has almost full possible entropy (up to λ bits with respect to its length), and can be intuitively explained by two reasons: either $f(S)$ is simply short, or it is unpredictable because of "noise". The gap can be considered the *effective leakage length*, as we essentially substract the randomness from the full string. While a similar result for information-theoretic entropy is trivial (see Lemma 1), proving it in our psuedoentropy setting it requires some work and tools.

See Theorem 4 and Corollary 4 for the precise statements and Sect. 5.2 for an illustrative application - we show that in some situations our chain rule handles noisy leakages better than the original noisy leakage framework! While this relaxation of the bounded leakage model and the noisy leakage model are incomparable in general, this points out that the bounded leakage tools can be adapted and applied much beyond their original scope (Tables 2 and 3).

Table 2. A comparison of different leakage models

Reference	Model	Condition
[9, 18]	Bounded leakage	$\mathbf{H}_0(f(S)) \leqslant \lambda$
[12]	Bounded unpredictability gap (information-theoretic)	$\mathbf{H}_0(f(S)) - \mathbf{H}_\infty(f(S)|S) \leqslant \lambda$
This paper	Bounded unpredictability gap (computational)	$\mathbf{H}_0(f(S)) - \mathbf{H}^{\mathrm{Metric}} f(S)|S \leqslant \lambda$
[20]	Noisy leakage	$f(S)|S \approx^\epsilon f(S)|S'$

Table 3. Best known chain rules for unconditional HILL pseudoentropy

Author	Loss in s'	ϵ'	Comments
[11]	s	$2^\lambda \epsilon$	
[19]	$2^{-\lambda} s$	ϵ	
This paper	$\ell^{-1} s$	$\ell^{-1} 2^\lambda \epsilon$	$1 \leqslant \ell \leqslant 2^\lambda$

Remark 2 (Our noisy chain rule vs [12]). *Our result is stronger than [12] in two ways*

(a) *We calculate the unpredictability gap in terms of computational entropy. This way we capture also computational noise, while the condition in [12] is information-theoretic*

(b) *Our result holds also in a conditional setup, where $f(S)$ is already conditioned on something else. For simplicity we don't present this improvement here, and refer to Theorem 4 for more details.*

1.4 Our Techniques

Our proof is based on techniques from convex optimization, successfully used in recent works on chain rules [19]. Roughly speaking, we use KKT optimality conditions to characterize the structure of this adversarial function, which gives the best possible advantage. Based on this we apply a threshold cut (typical for chain rule/dense model theorems proofs) which transform the distinguisher we start with into a very regular function, which makes the remaining technical calculations easy.

1.5 Paper Organization

In Sect. 2 we explain basic concepts and notions. Auxiliary lemmas are provided in Sects. 3, and 4 we present our main results. Some applications are discussed in detail in Sect. 5.

2 Preliminaries

2.1 Basic Definitions

Definition 1 (Support). The support of a discrete random variable X, denoted by $\mathrm{supp}(X)$, is the set of its outcomes which appear with non-zero probability.

Definition 2 (Computational and statistical distances). For any random variables X_1, X_2 taking values in a finite set $\mathcal{X}$, and a real function D on $\mathcal{X}$ we define the advantage of D as

$$\delta^D(X_1, X_2) = |\,\mathbb{E}\,\mathsf{D}(X_1) - \mathbb{E}\,\mathsf{D}(X_2)|.$$

If $\mathcal{D}$ is a class of real functions then we define

$$\delta^{\mathcal{D}}(X_1, X_2) = \max_{D \in \mathcal{D}} |\,\mathbb{E}\,\mathsf{D}(X_1) - \mathbb{E}\,\mathsf{D}(X_2)|$$

and call this quantity the computational distance of X_1 and X_2 against the class $\mathcal{D}$ (in computational settings $\mathcal{D}$ typically consists of functions computable by small circuits). Letting D run over all $[0,1]$-valued functions we recover the notion of the statistical distance

$$\mathrm{SD}(X_1, X_2) = \max_D |\,\mathbb{E}\,\mathsf{D}(X_1) - \mathbb{E}\,\mathsf{D}(X_2)| = \frac{1}{2}\sum_x |\Pr[X_1 = x] - \Pr[X = x_2]|.$$

Definition 3 (Hartley Entropy). The Hartley entropy of a random variable X equals

$$\mathbf{H}_0(X) = -\log|\mathrm{supp}(X)|$$

Definition 4 (Min-Entropy). The *min-entropy* of a random variable X is defined as

$$\mathbf{H}_\infty(X) = \min_x \log(1/\Pr[X = x]).$$

Definition 5 (Average conditional min-Entropy [3]). For a pair (X, Z) of random variables, the *average min-entropy* of X conditioned on Z is

$$\widetilde{\mathbf{H}}_\infty(X|Z) = -\log \mathbb{E}_{z \leftarrow Z}[\max_x \Pr[X = x|Z = z]] = -\log \mathbb{E}_{z \leftarrow Z}[2^{-\mathbf{H}_\infty(X|Z=z)}].$$

2.2 Pseudoentropy

Definition 6 (HILL pseudoentropy [13,14]). A variable X has *HILL entropy*

$$\widetilde{\mathbf{H}}^{\mathrm{HILL}}_{s,\epsilon}(X|Z) \geqslant k \iff \exists Y \, \mathbf{H}_\infty(Y) = k \, \forall D \text{ of size } s: \, \delta^D(X, Y) \leqslant \epsilon$$

For a joint distribution (X, Z), we say that X has k bits *conditional Hill entropy* (conditioned on Z) if

$$\widetilde{\mathbf{H}}^{\mathrm{HILL}}_{s,\epsilon}(X|Z) \geqslant k$$

$$\iff \exists (Y, Z), \widetilde{\mathbf{H}}_\infty(Y|Z) = k \, \forall D \text{ of size } s: \delta^D((X, Z), (Y, Z)) \leqslant \epsilon$$

Remark 3 (Probabilistic vs deterministic distinguishers). *In the definition above it doesn't matter whether distinguishers are deterministic or probabilistic (the reduction goes by fixing coins [11]). Metric Entropy defined below is, however, different.*

Definition 7 (Metric pseudoentropy [1]). A variable X has *Metric entropy* at least k if

$$\mathbf{H}^{\mathrm{Metric}}_{s,\epsilon}(X|Z) \geqslant k \iff \forall D \text{ [0,1]-valued of size } s \, \exists Y_D, \, \mathbf{H}_\infty(Y_D) = k \, : \, \delta^D(X, Y_D) \leqslant \epsilon$$

For a joint distribution (X, Z), we say that X has k bits *conditional metric entropy* (conditioned on Z) if

$$\widetilde{\mathbf{H}}^{\mathrm{HILL}}_{s,\epsilon}(X|Z) \geqslant k$$

$$\iff \forall D \text{ [0,1]-valued of size } s \, \exists (Y, Z), \widetilde{\mathbf{H}}_\infty(Y|Z) = k : \delta^D((X, Z), (Y, Z)) \leqslant \epsilon$$

Metric entropy is weaker than HILL by definition (the subtle difference is in the order of quantifiers), however more convenient to work with. Fortunately, it's possible to do a conversion with some loss in circuit size.

Theorem 2 (Metric-HILL transformation [1]). *If $\mathbf{H}^{\mathrm{Metric}}_{s,\epsilon}(X|Z) \geqslant k$ then $\widetilde{\mathbf{H}}^{\mathrm{HILL}}_{s',\epsilon'}(X|Z) \geqslant k$ where $\epsilon' = O(\epsilon)$ and $s' = \Omega\left(s\epsilon^2/(\mathbf{H}_0(X) + \mathbf{H}_0(Z))\right)$.*

3   Auxiliary Facts

It may be instructive to extend the chain rule for min-entropy beyond bounded leakages, as it motivates the similar question for pseudoentropy. Below we give a short proof.

Lemma 1. *For any random variables $X \in \{0,1\}^n, Z \in \{0,1\}^m$ we have*

$$\widetilde{\mathbf{H}}_\infty(X|Z) \geqslant \mathbf{H}_\infty(X) - (\mathbf{H}_0(Z) - \mathbf{H}_\infty(Z|X))$$

Proof. Suppose $X \in \{0,1\}^n, Z \in \{0,1\}^m, \mathbf{H}_\infty(X) \geqslant k$ and $\mathbf{H}_\infty(Z|X) \geqslant m - \Delta$. Then

$$\sum_z P_Z(z) \max_x P_{X|Z=z}(x) = \sum_z{}' \max_x \left(P_X(x) P_{Z|X=x}(z) \right)$$

$$\leqslant \sum_z 2^{-k} \cdot 2^{-m+\Delta} = 2^{-(k-\Delta)}. \tag{1}$$

□

The remaining lemmas are technical facts used to manipulate distinguishers, obtained by convex optimization techniques. Due to space constraints we don't explain these techniques in detail. However, we elaborate more on intuitions in the remarks below and refer to papers [24,25] where these tools are discussed in more detail. In short, these lemmas study the shape of the distribution maximizing the advantage under entropy constraints.

Lemma 2 (Maximimal expectation given min-entropy constraints). *Let* $\mathsf{D} : \{0,1\}^n \times \{0,1\}^m \to \mathbb{R}$ *be an arbitrary function, and* $0 < k < n$ *be a fixed number. Then the optimal solution* Y^* *to the program*

$$\underset{Y}{\text{maximize}} \qquad \mathbb{E}\mathsf{D}(Y, Z) \tag{2}$$

$$\text{s.t.} \qquad \widetilde{\mathbf{H}}_\infty(Y|Z) \geqslant k \tag{3}$$

where Y runs over all random variables jointly distributed with Z, can be characterized as follows: there exists non-negative numbers $t(0)$ and $t(z), z \in \{0,1\}^m$ such that the following two conditions are satisfied

(i) For every z, the sum $\sum_x \max(\mathsf{D}(x,z) - t(z), 0) = t_0$
(ii) For every z, the distribution $\mathbf{P}_{Y^*|Z=z}()$ puts its biggest weight uniformly on the set $\{x : \mathsf{D}(x,z) > t(z)\}$ and zero on the set $\{x : \mathsf{D}(x,z) < t(z)\}$

Remark 4 (Motivation and Intuition). *Below we highlight two key points*

(a) Maximizing the distinguisher expectation over constrained distributions arise naturally when we use Metric pseudoentropy. To see this, note that when $\mathbf{H}^{\mathrm{Metric}}(X) < k$ then there is a disnguisher D for X and all Y of min-entropy k. The advantage can be written as $\mathbb{E}\mathsf{D}(x) - \mathbb{E}\mathsf{D}(Y)$ and is minimized, precisely when $\mathbb{E}\mathsf{D}(Y)$ is maximized. We can ask what is the worst possible choice of Y. It turns out, that we conclude from this more about the shape of the distinguisher.

(b) Threshold transformations *arises naturally as* KKT multipliers, *when we study the shape of the worst possible distinguisher. They come up quite often in proofs, for example [11, 21, 26], though authors do not give them a rigorous treatment. In short, we use these transformations to make the distinguisher fit the distribution support which is more convenient for technical reasons. Note that (i) means precisely that the total "mass" of* D *above the threshold is the same for every z and (ii) means that the distinguisher above the threshold fits the support of* $\mathbf{P}_{Y^*|Z=z}()$.

The following corollary is an easy consequence of Lemma 2.

Corollary 1 (Cutting distinguishers supports). *Let function* D, *distribution* Y^* *and numbers* t_0, $t(z)$ *be as in Lemma 2. Then in particular, for every x and z*

$$(\mathsf{D}(x,z) - t(z)) \cdot \mathbf{P}_{Y^*,Z}(x,z) \geqslant 0. \tag{4}$$

Moreover, Lemma 2 also holds for D *replaced by* $\mathsf{D}'(x,z) = (\mathsf{D}(x,z) - t(z))^+$, *the same optimal distribution* Y^*. *and numbers* $t(z)$ *replaced by* 0.

Corollary 2 (Regular distinguisher). *Suppose that* D *separates* X *and all distributions* Y *of min-entropy* k *given* Z, *that is*

$$\mathbb{E}\,\mathsf{D}(X,Z) \geqslant \mathbb{E}\,\mathsf{D}(Y,Z) + \epsilon, \quad \text{for every } Y \text{ s.t. } \widetilde{\mathbf{H}}_\infty(Y|Z) \geqslant k. \tag{5}$$

Then, D′ *defined as in Lemma 2 satisfies*

$$\mathbb{E}\,\mathsf{D}'(X,Z) \geqslant \mathbb{E}\,\mathsf{D}'(Y,Z) + \epsilon, \quad \text{for every } Y \text{ s.t. } \widetilde{\mathbf{H}}_\infty(Y|Z) \geqslant k, \tag{6}$$

moreover, D′ *is regular in the following sense: for some fixed number* t_0

$$\sum_x \mathsf{D}'(x,z) = t_0 \quad \text{for every } z. \tag{7}$$

Remark 5 (How we use regular distinguishers). *Note that* D *as above satisfies* $\mathbb{E}\,\mathsf{D}(Y,Z) \leqslant 2^{-k} t_0$ *for every* Y *of min-entropy* k *given* Z. *The threshold transformation is extremely useful in proofs, because it reduces the dependency of the advantage on the shape of distinguishers and distributions.*

Hence, we conclude that D′ is a new "universal" distinguisher between X and all distributions Y with entropy k, given Z. The proof of Corollary 2 appears in Appendix A.

4   Results

4.1   Flexible Chain Rule for Conditional Pseudoentropy

Theorem 3. *For any finitely supported random variables* $X \in \{0,1\}^n, Z_1 \in \{0,1\}^{m_1}, Z_2 \in \{0,1\}^{m_2}$ *and every* s, ϵ *we have*

$$\mathbf{H}^{\text{Metric}}_{s',\epsilon'}(X|Z_1,Z_2) \geqslant \mathbf{H}^{\text{Metric}}_{s,\epsilon}(X|Z_1) - \mathbf{H}_0(Z_2) \tag{8}$$

where the degradation in security parameters is given by

$$s' = s/\ell - 2^{m_1} - 2 \qquad (9)$$

$$\epsilon' = 2^{m_2}\epsilon/\ell \qquad (10)$$

and ℓ is an arbitrary integer between 1 and $|\mathrm{supp}(Z_2)|$.

Remark 6 (The loss due to already conditioned part is additive). *Interestingly, the loss due to Z_1 is additive - this is different than in folklore where the loss of the form $s' = s/2^{m_1}$ and $\epsilon' = 2^{m_2}\epsilon$, so that the ratio s'/ϵ' loses, with respect to s/ϵ, a factor exponential in $m_1 + m_2$.*

Corollary 3 (No loss from already captured leakages for big circuits). *Suppose that $s > 2 \cdot 2^{m_1}$. Then the chain rule holds true with $s' > s$ and $\epsilon' = 2^{m_2}\epsilon$, that is there is no loss due to Z_1.*

The proof of Theorem 3 appears in Appendix B.

4.2 A Conditional Chain Rule for Noisy Leakage

Theorem 4. *For any finitely supported random variables X, Z_1, Z_2 and every s, ϵ we have*

$$\mathbf{H}^{\mathrm{Metric}}_{s',\epsilon'}(X|Z_1, Z_2) \geqslant \mathbf{H}^{\mathrm{Metric}}_{s,\epsilon}(X|Z_1) - \Delta \qquad (11)$$

where

$$s' = s/\ell - 2^{m_1} - 2 \qquad (12)$$

$$\Delta = \mathbf{H}_0(Z_2) - \mathbf{H}^{\mathrm{Metric}}_{s',\epsilon''}(Z_2|X, Z_1) \qquad (13)$$

$$\epsilon' = 2^{\Delta}\epsilon + \frac{2^{m_2}\epsilon''}{\ell} \qquad (14)$$

and the choice of ϵ'' is free.

In particular, for $\epsilon'' = 0$ and empty Z_1 we obtain

Corollary 4 (A condition for capturing noisy leakage). *Suppose that f is an arbitrary leakage function, then for any S we have*

$$\mathbf{H}^{\mathrm{Metric}}_{s,2^{\lambda}\epsilon}(S|f(S)) \geqslant \mathbf{H}^{\mathrm{Metric}}_{s,\epsilon}(S) - \lambda$$

where

$$\lambda = \mathbf{H}_0(f(S)) - \widetilde{\mathbf{H}}_{\infty}(f(S)|S)$$

Remark 7. *Note that this result is a very easy exercise for min-entropy - but it seems to be much harder for pseudoentropy, similarly to the case of the standard chain rule. Interestingly, the condition is very similar to the noisy leakage condition. Here we require entropies of $f(S')|S$ and $f(S)|S$ to be close (note that $\mathbf{H}_0(f(S')|S) = \mathbf{H}_0(f(S')) = \mathbf{H}_0(f(S))$, whereas for the latter case we want distributions $f(S)|S$ and $f(S')|S$ to be close.*

Remark 8. *Note that if output of f is long, then it cannot be deterministic - in fact, needs to be "noisy".*

The proof of Theorem 4 appears in Appendix C.

5   Applications

5.1   Known Chain Rules for Unconditional Pseudoentropy

Our chain rule Theorem 3 is flexible in the sense that we can trade the quality loss between s and ϵ. In particular, setting Z_1 to be a point mass we derive an unconditional chain rule of the following form

$$\mathbf{H}_{s',\epsilon'}^{\mathrm{Metric}}(X|Z) \geqslant \mathbf{H}_{s,\epsilon}^{\mathrm{Metric}}(X) - \lambda$$

where $\lambda = \mathbf{H}_0(Z)$. We cover two extreme cases: the chain rule which loses only in ϵ [11] and the chain rule which loses only in s [19]. A brief summary is given in the table below. Chain rules with worse parameters are omitted (a survey is given in [19]).

5.2   Stream Ciphers Resilient Against Noisy Leakages

5.2.1   Stream Ciphers Basics

We start with the definition of weak pseudorandom functions, which are *computationally indistinguishable* from random functions, when queried on random inputs and fed with uniform secret key.

Definition 8 (Weak pseudorandom functions). A function $\mathsf{F} : \{0,1\}^k \times \{0,1\}^n \to \{0,1\}^m$ is an (ϵ, s, q)-secure weak PRF if its outputs on q random inputs are indistinguishable from random by any distinguisher of size s, that is

$$\left| \Pr\left[\mathsf{D}\left((X_i)_{i=1}^q, \mathsf{F}((K, X_i)_{i=1}^q) \right) = 1 \right] - \Pr\left[\mathsf{D}\left((X_i)_{i=1}^q, (R_i)_{i=1}^q \right) = 1 \right] \right| \leqslant \epsilon$$

where the probability is over the choice of the random $X_i \leftarrow \{0,1\}^n$, the choice of a random key $K \leftarrow \{0,1\}^k$ and $R_i \leftarrow \{0,1\}^m$ conditioned on $R_i = R_j$ if $X_i = X_j$ for some $j < i$.

Stream ciphers generate keystreams in a recursive manner. The security requires the output stream should be indistinguishable from uniform[3].

Definition 9 (Stream ciphers). A *stream-cipher* $\mathsf{SC} : \{0,1\}^k \to \{0,1\}^k \times \{0,1\}^n$ is a function that need to be initialized with a secret state $S_0 \in \{0,1\}^k$ and produces a sequence of output blocks $X_1, X_2, \ldots$ computed as

$$(S_i, X_i) := \mathsf{SC}(S_{i-1}).$$

A stream cipher SC is (ϵ, s, q)-secure if for all $1 \leqslant i \leqslant q$, the random variable X_i is (s, ϵ)-pseudorandom given $X_1, \ldots, X_{i-1}$ (the probability is also over the choice of the initial random key S_0).

---

[3] We note that in a more standard notion the entire stream $X_1, \ldots, X_q$ is indistinguishable from random. This is implied by the notion above by a standard hybrid argument, with a loss of a multiplicative factor of q in the distinguishing advantage.

Now we define the security of leakage resilient stream ciphers, which follows the "only computation leaks" assumption.

Definition 10 (Leakage-resilient stream ciphers [15]). *A leakage-resilient stream-cipher is $(\epsilon, s, q, \lambda)$-secure if it is (ϵ, s, q)-secure as defined above, but where the distinguisher in the j-th round gets λ bits of arbitrary adaptively chosen leakage about the secret state accessed during this round. More precisely, before $(S_j, X_j) := \mathsf{SC}(S_{j-1})$ is computed, the distinguisher can choose any leakage function f_j with range $\{0,1\}^\lambda$, and then not only get X_j, but also $\Lambda_j := f_j(\hat{S}_{j-1})$, where $\hat{S}_{j-1}$ denotes the part of the secret state that was modified (i.e., read and/or overwritten) in the computation $\mathsf{SC}(S_{j-1})$.*

5.2.2 Constructions and Provable Security

The first construction of a leakage-resilient stream cipher was proposed by Dziembowski and Pietrzak in [9]. On Fig. 1 below we present a simplified construction of this cipher [18], based on a weak pseudorandom function (wPRF), which follows the description in Sect. 5.2.1. The security of leakage-resilient stream ciphers is defined in Sect. 5.2.1. The key technical difficulty is to prove that a wPRF remains secure when seeded with a high-entropy key (instead uniform). This is where one applies chain rules. Below we state the security for this construction, and refer to [15,18] for more details.

Theorem 5 (Proving Security of Stream Ciphers [15,18]). *If F is a $(\epsilon_F, s_F, 2)$-secure weak PRF then SC^F (defined in Sect. 5.2.1) is a $(\epsilon', s', q, \lambda)$-secure leakage resilient stream cipher where*

$$\epsilon' = q \cdot \left(\epsilon_F 2^\lambda\right)^{\Omega(1)}, \quad s' = s_F \cdot \left(\epsilon_F 2^\lambda\right)^{O(1)}$$

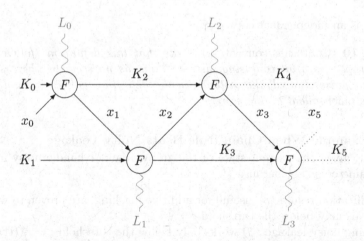

Fig. 1. The EUROCRYPT'09 stream cipher (adaptive leakage). F denotes a weak pseudorandom function. By K_i and x_i we denote, respectively, values of the secret state and keystream bits. Leakages are denoted in gray with L_i

Here we skip the exact constants for the sake of clarity, as they there are more similar results [10, 27] and the provable security is anyway not very impressive for practical settings of parameters. Incorporating our chain rule into the existing proof, we can extend the class of admissible leakage functions as follows

Definition 11 (Leakages with unpredictability deficiency). For any λ we say that a leakage function f has unpredictability deficiency λ on a secret S if

$$\mathbf{H}_0(f(S)) - \tilde{\mathbf{H}}_\infty \left(f(S) | S \right) \leqslant \lambda$$

(can be also formulated for HILL entropy)

To summarize, from Theorem 4 we obtain the following result

Corollary 5 (Capturing noisy leakages). *Theorem 5 holds true with bounded leakages replaced by Definition 11.*

Remark 9 (Sketch of proof). *This follows by replacing the assumption of bounded leakage in one of the proof using chain rules [9, 18] by our assumption on the (pseudo)entropy gap. The security after this step is captured by the chain rule, therefore the remaining parts of the proofs remain unchanged.*

5.3   Better Handling (some) Noisy Leakages

5.4   Noisy Leakage Basics

Definition 12 ([20], generalized). Leakge Z of a secret X is called ϵ-noisy w.r.t X if

$$\mathrm{SD}((X, Z), (X, Z')) \leqslant \epsilon$$

where Z' is an independent copy of Z.

Remark 10 (Confusing convention). *Note that this definition (following the original paper) is a bit confusing, as $\epsilon = 1$ means no security whereas $\epsilon = 0$ means full noise. Indeed, the distance in the definition is 0 if and only if the leakage is independent on the secret.*

5.4.1   Example When Chain Rule Beats Noisy Leakage

Note that, given the current state of the art, we cannot handle noisy leakages with parameters $\epsilon > \frac{1}{2}$ because

(a) amplification results [8], usefull for additive masking, are proven to work (in general) only below the threshold $\epsilon = \frac{1}{2}$
(b) chaining noisy leakages [7] works only below the threshold $\epsilon = \frac{1}{2}$ (the parameters sum up).

Below we provide a more concrete example, when meaningful bounds are possible due to our pseudoentropy chain rule, but nothing is guaranteed by the noisy leakage model.

There exists a secret $X \in \{0,1\}^{256}$ and two independent leakages $Z_1, Z_2 \in \{0,1\}^{256}$ such that for X given Z_1, Z_2

(a) The noisy leakage model provides no security for X given Z_1, Z_2
(b) The chain rule in Theorem 4 provides 188 pseudoentropy bits of quality $(s, \epsilon) = (\infty, 2^{-63})$

Proof. Let X be a uniform 256-bit secret and Z_1, Z_2 be arbitrary independent 256-bit leakages such that $\widetilde{\mathbf{H}}_\infty (Z_i|X) \geqslant 254$ for $i = 1, 2$. It is easy to see that these leakages are $\frac{3}{4}$-noisy, in the sense of Definition 12. We would like to know how much security remains in X, given Z_1 and Z_2. Note first, that general rules for noisy leakage [7] give a meaningless noise level $\epsilon = \frac{3}{4} + \frac{3}{4} > 1$, which doesn't guarantee security. Consider now security measured by HILL entropy. Clearly we have $\mathbf{H}_\infty (Z_1, Z_2|X = x) \geqslant \mathbf{H}_\infty (Z_1|X = x) + \mathbf{H}_\infty (Z_2|X = x)$ for every x. By the Markov inequality, we conclude that

$$\mathbf{H}_\infty (Z_1, Z_2|X = x) \geqslant 254 + 254 - 64$$

with probability $1 - 2^{-64}$ over $x \leftarrow X$. If X is statistically indistinguishable (with $\epsilon = 2^{-64}$) uniform then by Theorem 4, where Z_2 is empty and Z_1 is replaced by our tuple (Z_1, Z_2)), we see that

$$\widetilde{\mathbf{H}}_{s,\epsilon}^{\mathrm{HILL}} (X|Z_1, Z_2) \geqslant 188 \quad \text{where } s = \infty, \epsilon = 2^{-63}$$

that is, X given Z_1, Z_2 is statistically indistinguishable from having 188 bits of entropy (the quantity loss is therefore 68 bits). This is enough to reuse X for unpredictability applications (which tolerate relatively small entropy deficiencies) or to extract 60 bits of almost uniform (within distance $\epsilon = 2^{-64}$) bits by randomness extractors. $\qquad\square$

6   Open Problems

Strengthening the result about relaxing bounded leakage model in Corollary 4, for example by replacing information-theoretic unpredictability gap with computational entropy gap, may be an interesting problem - we leave it for future research.

A   Proof of Corollary 2

Proof. Let Y^* be the distribution maximizing the expectation of D as in Eq. (2) D' be defined as in Lemma 2. Since D'

$$\mathbb{E}\, \mathsf{D}'(X, Z) = \mathbb{E}_{(x,z)\sim(X,Z)} \max(\mathsf{D}(x, z) - t(z), 0)$$
$$\geqslant \mathbb{E}_{(x,z)\sim(X,Z)} \mathsf{D}(x, z) - \mathbb{E}_{(x,z)\sim(X,Z)} t(z) \tag{15}$$
$$= \mathbb{E}\, \mathsf{D}(X, Z) - \mathbb{E}\, t(Z) \tag{16}$$

Denote $\mathbf{H}_\infty (Y^*|Z = z) = k(z)$. We have $\mathbb{E}_{z \sim Z}\, 2^{-k(z)} = 2^{-k}$. In the other hand, from Eq. (4) we have

$$\mathbb{E}\,D'(Y^*, Z) = \sum_{x,z} \max\left(D(x, z) - t(z), 0\right) \cdot \mathbf{P}_{Y^*, Z}(x, z)$$

$$= \sum_{x,z} \left(D(x, z) - t(z)\right) \cdot \mathbf{P}_{Y^*, Z}(x, z)$$

$$= \mathbb{E}\,D(Y^*, Z) - \mathbb{E}\,t(Z) \qquad (17)$$

Given Eqs. (16) and (17) we have

$$\mathbb{E}\,D'(X, Z) \geqslant \mathbb{E}\,D'(Y^*, Z) + \epsilon$$

but in view of Corollary 1 this proves much more, namely

$$\mathbb{E}\,D'(X, Z) \geqslant \mathbb{E}\,D'(Y, Z) + \epsilon \quad \text{for every } Y \text{ such that } \widetilde{\mathbf{H}}_\infty (Y|Z) \geqslant k. \qquad (18)$$

□

B   Proof of Theorem 3

Proof. Threshold transformation Assuming contrarily, for the sake of a contradiction, we have

$$\mathbb{E}\,D(X, Z_1, Z_2) \geqslant \mathbb{E}\,D(Y, Z_1, Z_2) + \epsilon' \qquad (19)$$

Then, according to Eq. (6) we have

$$\mathbb{E}\,D'(X, Z_1, Z_2) - \mathbb{E}\,D'(Y, Z_1, Z_2) \geqslant \epsilon' \qquad (20)$$

for every Y such that $\widetilde{\mathbf{H}}_\infty (Y|Z_1, Z_2) \geqslant k$ and some D of size s'. and moreover, by Eq. (7), that for some t_0

$$\forall z_1, z_2 : \sum_{x, z_1, z_2} D'(x, z_1, z_2) = t_0. \qquad (21)$$

Distinguisher for conditional part removed Let $Y = Y^*$ be the distribution maximizing $\mathbb{E}\,D'(Y, Z_1, Z_2)$ over the constraint $\widetilde{\mathbf{H}}_\infty (Y|Z_1, Z_2) \geqslant k'$. For the maximizing distribution we can assume $\widetilde{\mathbf{H}}_\infty (Y^*|Z_1, Z_2) = k'$. According to Eqs. (20) and (21) we have

$$\mathbb{E}_{z \sim Z_2}\left[\mathbb{E}\,D'((X, Z_1)|_{Z_2 = z_2}, z_2)\right] = \mathbb{E}\,D'(X, Z_1, Z_2)$$

$$\geqslant \mathbb{E}\,D'(Y^*, Z_1, Z_2) + \epsilon'.$$

$$= 2^{-k'} t_0 + \epsilon'$$

Thus, for every ℓ there exists a subset S of $|S| = \ell$ elements z_2 (more precisely: the set of values z corresponding to the biggest values of $\mathbb{E}\, \mathsf{D}'((X, Z_1)|_{Z_2=z_2}, z_2)$ such that

$$\sum_{z_2 \in S} \mathbf{P}_{Z_2}(z_2)\, \mathbb{E}\, \mathsf{D}'((X, Z_1)|_{Z_2=z_2}, z_2) \geqslant \frac{\ell}{2^{m_2}}\left(2^{-k'} t_0 + \epsilon'\right) \qquad (22)$$

Note that

$$\mathbb{E}_{(x,z) \sim (X, Z_1)} \max_{z_2 \in S} \mathsf{D}'(x, z, z_2) \geqslant \sum_{x, z_1} \mathbf{P}_{X, Z_1}(x, z_1) \sum_{z_2 \in S} \mathbf{P}_{Z_2 | X=x, Z_1=z_1}(z)\mathsf{D}'(x, z_1, z_2)$$

$$= \sum_{z_2 \in S} \mathbf{P}_{Z_2}(z_2)\, \mathbb{E}\, \mathsf{D}'((X, Z_1)|_{Z_2=z_2}, z_2) \qquad (23)$$

In turn, for every fixed value z_1 by Eq. (21) we obtain

$$\frac{\ell}{2^{m_2}} \cdot 2^{-k'} t_0 = 2^{-k'-m_2} \cdot \sum_x \sum_{z_2 \in S} \mathsf{D}'(x, z_1, z_2)$$

$$\geqslant 2^{-k'-m_2} \cdot \sum_x \max_{z_2 \in S} \mathsf{D}'(x, z_1, z_2) \qquad (24)$$

Define

$$\mathsf{D}''(x, z_1) = \max_{z_2 \in S} \mathsf{D}'(x, z_1, z_2). \qquad (25)$$

Combining Eqs. (22) to (24) we obtain

$$\forall z_1: \quad \mathbb{E}_{(x,z) \sim (X, Z_1)} \mathsf{D}''(x, z) \geqslant 2^{-k'-m_2} \cdot \sum_x \mathsf{D}''(x, z_1) + \frac{\ell\epsilon'}{2^{m_2}} \qquad (26)$$

(note that only the right-hand side depends on z_1). Let Y be any distribution such that $\widetilde{\mathbf{H}}_\infty(Y|Z_1) \geqslant k = k' + m_2$, and let $\mathbf{H}_\infty(Y|_{Z_1=z}) = k(z)$. Note that we have

$$\max_{z_1}\left(2^{-k'-m_2} \cdot \sum_x \mathsf{D}''(x, z_1)\right) = 2^{-k} \cdot \max_{z_1}\left(\sum_x \mathsf{D}''(x, z_1)\right)$$

$$\geqslant \sum_{z_1} \mathbf{P}_{Z_1}(z_1) \sum_x \mathsf{D}''(x, z_1) \cdot 2^{-k(z_1)}$$

$$\geqslant \sum_{z_1} \mathbf{P}_{Z_1}(z_1) \sum_x \mathsf{D}''(x, z_1) \cdot \mathbf{P}_{Y|_{Z_1=z_1}}(z_1)$$

$$= \mathbb{E}_{(x,z) \sim (Y, Z_1)} \mathsf{D}''(Y, Z_1) \qquad (27)$$

Since Eq. (26) holds for every z_1, Eq. (27) implies

$$\mathbb{E}_{(x,z) \sim (X, Z_1)} \mathsf{D}''(x, z) \geqslant \mathbb{E}_{(x,z) \sim (Y, Z_1)} \mathsf{D}''(Y, Z_1) + \frac{\ell\epsilon'}{2^{m_2}}, \qquad (28)$$

for every Y such that $\widetilde{\mathbf{H}}_\infty(Y|Z) \geqslant k$.

<u>Complexity</u> To complete the proof it remains to observe that D'' can be computed by a cicuit of size $s = \ell s' + 2^{m_1}\ell + \ell$. Indeed, computing $D'(x, z_1, z_2) = \max(D(x, z_1, z_2) - t(z_1, z_2), 0)$ for all possible values $z_2 \in S$ requires size $\ell s' + 2^{m_1}\ell + \ell$, and then computing $D'' = \max_{z_2 \in S} D'(x, z_1, z_2)$ from D' requires an additive overhead ℓ (maximum over ℓ outputs). $\square$

C   Proof of Theorem 4

Proof. The proof is based on the proof of Theorem 3 and starts exactly in the same way as the proof of Theorem 3, repating its first step. The difference is in the second step, where we define the distinguisher. Similarly, we start with the inequality

$$\mathbb{E}_{z \sim Z_2}\left[\mathbb{E}\, D'((X, Z_1)|_{Z_2=z_2}, z_2)\right] = \mathbb{E}\, D'(X, Z_1, Z_2)$$
$$\geqslant \mathbb{E}\, D'(Y^*, Z_1, Z_2) + \epsilon'.$$
$$= 2^{-k'}t_0 + \epsilon'.$$

Similarly to Eq. (22), for any ℓ there is a set S of cardinality ℓ (whose elements correspond to ℓ biggest values being averaged on the left-hand side) such that

$$\sum_{z_2 \in S} \mathbf{P}_{Z_2}(z_2)\, \mathbb{E}\, D'((X, Z_1)|_{Z_2=z_2}, z_2) \geqslant \frac{\ell}{2^{m_2}}\left(2^{-k'}t_0 + \epsilon'\right) \qquad (29)$$

The left-hand side can be alternatively written as

$$\mathbb{E}\, D''(X, Z_1, Z_2) = \sum_{z_2 \in S} \mathbf{P}_{Z_2}(z_2)\, \mathbb{E}\, D'((X, Z_1)|_{Z_2=z_2}, z_2)$$

where $D''(x, z_1, z_2) = D'(x, z_1, z_2) \cdot \mathbf{1}_S(z_2)$, (here $\mathbf{1}_S$ is the characteristic function of S). Suppose that $\mathbf{H}^{\mathrm{Metric}}_{s'', \epsilon''}(Z_2|Z_1, X) \geqslant m_2 - \Delta$ where s'' is bigger than the complexity of D''. Then there is Z_2' such that $\widetilde{\mathbf{H}}_\infty(Z_2'|Z_1, X) = m_2 - \Delta$ and $\mathbb{E}\, D''(X, Z_1, Z_2) \leqslant \mathbb{E}\, D''(X, Z_1, Z_2') + \epsilon''$. Therefore, we have

$$\mathbb{E}\, D''(X, Z_1, Z_2) - \epsilon'' \leqslant \mathbb{E}\, D''(X, Z_1, Z_2')$$
$$= \sum_{x, z_1} \mathbf{P}_{X, Z_1}(x, z_1) \sum_{z_2} \mathbf{P}_{Z_2'|Z_1=z_1, X=x}(z_2) D''(x, z_1, z_2)$$
$$= \sum_{x, z_1} \mathbf{P}_{X, Z_1}(x, z_1) \sum_{z_2 \in S} \mathbf{P}_{Z_2'|Z_1=z_1, X=x}(z_2) D'(x, z_1, z_2)$$
$$\leqslant 2^{\Delta - m_2}t_0,$$

where in the last line we used Eq. (21) and $\widetilde{\mathbf{H}}_\infty(Z_2'|Z_1, X) = m_2 - \Delta$. This can be rewritten as

$$\epsilon'' + \sum_{x, z_1} \mathbf{P}_{X, Z_1}(x, z_1) \frac{\sum_{z_2 \in S} D'(x, z_1, z_2)}{2^{m_2 - \Delta}} \geqslant \sum_{z_2 \in S} \mathbf{P}_{Z_2}(z_2)\, \mathbb{E}\, D'((X, Z_1)|_{Z_2=z_2}, z_2)$$
$$(30)$$

From Eqs. (29) and (30) we conclude that

$$\epsilon'' + 2^\Delta\, \mathbb{E}_{(x,z)\sim(X,Z_1)} \left[\frac{\sum_{z_2\in S} \mathsf{D}'(x,z,z_2)}{2^{m_2}} \right] \geq \frac{\ell}{2^{m_2}} \left(2^{-k'} t_0 + \epsilon' \right)$$

or equivalently

$$\frac{2^{m_2}\epsilon''}{\ell} + 2^\Delta\, \mathbb{E}_{(x,z)\sim(X,Z_1)} \left[\frac{\sum_{z_2\in S} \mathsf{D}'(x,z,z_2)}{\ell} \right] \geq \left(2^{-k'} t_0 + \epsilon' \right) \qquad (31)$$

In turn, for every fixed value z_1 by Eq. (21) we obtain

$$2^{-k'} t_0 = 2^{-k'}\ell^{-1} \cdot \sum_x \sum_{z_2\in S} \mathsf{D}'(x,z_1,z_2)$$

$$= 2^{-k'} \cdot \sum_x \frac{\sum_{z_2\in S} \mathsf{D}'(x,z_1,z_2)}{\ell} \qquad (32)$$

Defining a new distinguisher D'' as the average over S from D' (note that it outputs numbers between 0 and 1)

$$\mathsf{D}''(x,z_1) = \frac{\sum_{z_2\in S} \mathsf{D}'(x,z_1,z_2)}{\ell} \qquad (33)$$

we can combine Eqs. (31) and (32) with Eq. (21) as

$$\forall z_1: \quad \frac{2^m \epsilon''}{2^\Delta \ell} + \mathbb{E}_{(x,z)\sim(X,Z_1)}\, \mathsf{D}''(x,z) \geq 2^{-k'-\Delta} \cdot \sum_x \mathsf{D}''(x,z_1) + \frac{\epsilon'}{2^\Delta} \qquad (34)$$

Let Y be any distribution such that $\widetilde{\mathbf{H}}_\infty (Y|Z_1) \geq k = k' + \Delta$, and let $\mathbf{H}_\infty \left(Y|_{Z_1=z} \right) = k(z)$. Note that we have

$$\max_{z_1} \left(2^{-k'-\Delta} \cdot \sum_x \mathsf{D}''(x,z_1) \right) = 2^{-k} \cdot \max_{z_1} \left(\sum_x \mathsf{D}''(x,z_1) \right)$$

$$\geq \sum_{z_1} \mathbf{P}_{Z_1}(z_1) \sum_x \mathsf{D}''(x,z_1) \cdot 2^{-k(z_1)}$$

$$\geq \sum_{z_1} \mathbf{P}_{Z_1}(z_1) \sum_x \mathsf{D}''(x,z_1) \cdot \mathbf{P}_{Y|_{Z_1=z_1}}(z_1)$$

$$= \mathbb{E}_{(x,z)\sim(Y,Z_1)}\, \mathsf{D}''(Y,Z_1) \qquad (35)$$

Since Eq. (35) holds for every z_1, Eq. (34) implies

$$\mathbb{E}_{(x,z)\sim(X,Z_1)}\, \mathsf{D}''(x,z) \geq \mathbb{E}_{(x,z)\sim(Y,Z_1)}\, \mathsf{D}''(Y,Z_1) + \frac{\epsilon' - 2^m \ell^{-1}\epsilon''}{2^\Delta}, \qquad (36)$$

for every Y such that $\widetilde{\mathbf{H}}_\infty (Y|Z) \geq k$.

Step 3: Complexity To complete the proof it remains to observe that D'' can be computed by a cicuit of size $s = \ell s' + 2^{m_1}\ell + \ell$. Indeed, computing $\mathsf{D}'(x,z_1,z_2) = \max(\mathsf{D}(x,z_1,z_2) - t(z_1,z_2), 0)$ for all possible values $z_2 \in S$ requires size $\ell s' + 2^{m_1}\ell + \ell$, and then computing $\mathsf{D}'' = \ell^{-1}\sum_{z_2} \mathsf{D}'(x,z_1,z_2)$ from D' requires an additive overhead ℓ (average over ℓ outputs). $\qquad \square$

References

1. Barak, B., Shaltiel, R., Wigderson, A.: Computational analogues of entropy. In: Arora, S., Jansen, K., Rolim, J.D.P., Sahai, A. (eds.) APPROX/RANDOM 2003. LNCS, vol. 2764, pp. 200–215. Springer, Heidelberg (2003)
2. Chung, K.-M., Kalai, Y.T., Liu, F.-H., Raz, R.: Memory delegation. In: Rogaway, P. (ed.) CRYPTO 2011. LNCS, vol. 6841, pp. 151–168. Springer, Heidelberg (2011)
3. Dodis, Y., Ostrovsky, R., Reyzin, L., Smith, A.: Fuzzy extractors: how to generate strong keys from biometrics and other noisy data. SIAM J. Comput. **38**(1), 97–139 (2008)
4. Dodis, Y., Pietrzak, K., Wichs, D.: Key derivation without entropy waste. In: Nguyen, P.Q., Oswald, E. (eds.) EUROCRYPT 2014. LNCS, vol. 8441, pp. 93–110. Springer, Heidelberg (2014)
5. Dodis, Y., Yu, Y.: Overcoming weak expectations. In: Sahai, A. (ed.) TCC 2013. LNCS, vol. 7785, pp. 1–22. Springer, Heidelberg (2013)
6. Duc, A., Dziembowski, S., Faust, S.: Unifying leakage models: from probing attacks to noisy leakage. In: Nguyen, P.Q., Oswald, E. (eds.) EUROCRYPT 2014. LNCS, vol. 8441, pp. 423–440. Springer, Heidelberg (2014). doi:10.1007/978-3-642-55220-5_24
7. Dziembowski, S., Faust, S., Skorski, M.: Noisy leakage revisited. In: Oswald, E., Fischlin, M. (eds.) EUROCRYPT 2015. LNCS, vol. 9057, pp. 159–188. Springer, Heidelberg (2015). doi:10.1007/978-3-662-46803-6_6
8. Dziembowski, S., Faust, S., Skórski, M.: Optimal amplification of noisy leakages. In: Kushilevitz, E., Malkin, T. (eds.) TCC 2016. LNCS, vol. 9563, pp. 291–318. Springer, Heidelberg (2016). doi:10.1007/978-3-662-49099-0_11
9. Dziembowski, S., Pietrzak, K.: Leakage-resilient cryptography. In: Proceedings of the 2008 49th Annual IEEE Symposium on Foundations of Computer Science, FOCS 2008, pp. 293–302. IEEE Computer Society, Washington, DC, USA (2008)
10. Faust, S., Pietrzak, K., Schipper, J.: Practical leakage-resilient symmetric cryptography. In: Prouff, E., Schaumont, P. (eds.) CHES 2012. LNCS, vol. 7428, pp. 213–232. Springer, Heidelberg (2012). doi:10.1007/978-3-642-33027-8_13
11. Fuller, B., O'Neill, A., Reyzin, L.: A unified approach to deterministic encryption: new constructions and a connection to computational entropy. In: Cramer, R. (ed.) TCC 2012. LNCS, vol. 7194, pp. 582–599. Springer, Heidelberg (2012). doi:10.1007/978-3-642-28914-9_33
12. Fuller, B., Reyzin, L.: Computational entropy and information leakage. Cryptology ePrint Archive, Report 2012/466 (2012). http://eprint.iacr.org/
13. Hastad, J., Impagliazzo, R., Levin, L.A., Luby, M.: A pseudorandom generator from any one-way function. SIAM J. Comput. **28**(4), 1364–1396 (1999)
14. Hsiao, C.-Y., Lu, C.-J., Reyzin, L.: Conditional computational entropy, or toward separating pseudoentropy from compressibility. In: Naor, M. (ed.) EUROCRYPT 2007. LNCS, vol. 4515, pp. 169–186. Springer, Heidelberg (2007). doi:10.1007/978-3-540-72540-4_10
15. Jetchev, D., Pietrzak, K.: How to fake auxiliary input. In: Sahai, A. (ed.) TCC 2014. LNCS, vol. 8349, pp. 566–590. Springer, Heidelberg (2014)
16. Krenn, S., Pietrzak, K., Wadia, A.: A counterexample to the chain rule for conditional HILL entropy. In: Sahai, A. (ed.) TCC 2013. LNCS, vol. 7785, pp. 23–39. Springer, Heidelberg (2013)
17. George, M., Michael, L.: Pseudorandomness and Cryptographic Applications. Princeton University Press, Princeton (1994)

18. Pietrzak, K.: A leakage-resilient mode of operation. In: Joux, A. (ed.) EURO-CRYPT 2009. LNCS, vol. 5479, pp. 462–482. Springer, Heidelberg (2009)
19. Pietrzak, K., Skórski, M.: The chain rule for HILL pseudoentropy, revisited. In: Lauter, K., Rodríguez-Henríquez, F. (eds.) LATINCRYPT 2015. LNCS, vol. 9230, pp. 81–98. Springer, Heidelberg (2015). doi:10.1007/978-3-319-22174-8_5
20. Prouff, E., Rivain, M.: Masking against side-channel attacks: a formal security proof. In: Johansson, T., Nguyen, P.Q. (eds.) EUROCRYPT 2013. LNCS, vol. 7881, pp. 142–159. Springer, Heidelberg (2013). doi:10.1007/978-3-642-38348-9_9
21. Reingold, O., Trevisan, L., Tulsiani, M., Vadhan, S.: Dense subsets of pseudorandom sets. In: Proceedings of the 2008 49th Annual IEEE Symposium on Foundations of Computer Science, FOCS 2008, pp. 76–85. IEEE Computer Society, Washington (2008)
22. Shaltiel, R.: An introduction to randomness extractors. In: Loeckx, J. (ed.) ICALP 2011. LNCS, vol. 14, pp. 21–41. Springer, Heidelberg (2011). doi:10.1007/978-3-642-22012-8_2
23. Skórski, M.: Modulus computational entropy. In: Lehmann, A., Wolf, S. (eds.) ICITS 2013. LNCS, vol. 9063, pp. 179–199. Springer, Heidelberg (2014)
24. Skorski, M.: Metric pseudoentropy: characterizations, transformations and applications. In: Lehmann, A., Wolf, S. (eds.) ICITS 2015. LNCS, vol. 9063, pp. 105–122. Springer, Heidelberg (2015). doi:10.1007/978-3-319-17470-9_7
25. Skórski, M., Golovnev, A., Pietrzak, K.: Condensed unpredictability. In: Halldórsson, M.M., Iwama, K., Kobayashi, N., Speckmann, B. (eds.) ICALP 2015. LNCS, vol. 9134, pp. 1046–1057. Springer, Heidelberg (2015). doi:10.1007/978-3-662-47672-7_85
26. Vadhan, S., Zheng, C.J.: A uniform min-max theorem with applications in cryptography. In: Canetti, R., Garay, J.A. (eds.) CRYPTO 2013. LNCS, vol. 8042, pp. 93–110. Springer, Heidelberg (2013)
27. Yu, Y., Standaert, F.-X.: Practical leakage-resilient pseudorandom objects with minimum public randomness. In: Dawson, E. (ed.) CT-RSA 2013. LNCS, vol. 7779, pp. 223–238. Springer, Heidelberg (2013). doi:10.1007/978-3-642-36095-4_15

Author Index

Printed in the United States
By Bookmasters